Decision Support Systems, Advances in

Edited by

Ger Devlin

Decision Support Systems, Advances in

Edited by S. M. Muyeen

Republished by InTech

Janeza Trdine 9, 51000 Rijeka, Croatia

Technical Editor Teodora Smiljanic

Cover Designer Dino Smrekar

Additional hard copies can be obtained from orders@intechopen.com

Decision Support Systems, Advances in, Edited by Ger Devlin
p. cm.
ISBN 978-953-307-069-8

For EU product safety concerns:
IN TECH d.o.o., Prolaz Marije Krucifikse Kozulić 3, 51000 Rijeka, Croatia,
info@intechopen.com or visit our website at intechopen.com.

Meet the editor

Dr Ger Devlin obtained his primary degree in BSc. Applied Physics from Dublin City University in 2001. He joined Analog Devices B.V. during his degree where he worked as a fabrication engineer in the research and development department. On returning to academia in 2003, Dr. Devlin was awarded his PhD degree in Engineering from the Department of Biosystems Engineering, UCD in 2007. His PhD focused on the use of Geographical Information Systems (GIS) and GPS technology in conjunction with developing Spatial Decision Support Systems for biomass and bioenergy supply chain optimisation and the concept of carbon friendly transportation networks. He is Ireland¿s representative on COST Action FP0902 - Development and Harmonization of new operational research and assessment procedures for sustainable forest biomass supply. For this action he was also appointed the Short Term Scientific Mission (STSM) manager which oversees the application and awarding of research grants for researchers to conduct short study missions in Universities and research institutes through Europe as well as Canada, USA, New Zealand, Japan, Russia, Australia and South Africa. He is also Ireland's representative on the International Energy Association (IEA) Task 43 - BioEnergy from biomass feedstocks. Dr Devlin currently has in excess of 40 publications that include peer review papers, 1 book and book chapters in the areas of biomass supply chains and logistics, biomass for energy markets, LCA, pyrolysis of biomass for liquid fuels and supply chain optimisation. He is reviewer for several peer review journals including Fuel Processing Technology, Transportation Research Part D, Journal of Transport Geogrpahy, International Journal of Forest Engineering, Journal of Forest Energy, Canadian Journal of Forest Research and ASABE to name a few.

Preface

"Be willing to make decisions. That's the most important quality in a good leader. Don't fall victim to what I call the 'ready-aim-aim-aim-aim syndrome'. You must be willing to fire."

T. Boone Pickens

As the quote above states, be willing to make decisions. This book by In-Tech publishing helps the reader understand the power of informed decision making by covering a broad range of DSS (Decision Support Systems) applications in the fields of medical, environmental, transport and business. The expertise of the chapter writers spans an equally extensive spectrum of researchers from around the globe including universities in Canada, Mexico, Brazil and the United States, to institutes and universities in Italy, Germany, Poland, France, United Kingdom, Romania, Turkey and Ireland to as far east as Malaysia and Singapore and as far north as Finland.

Decision Support Systems are not a new technology but they have evolved and developed with the ever demanding necessity to analyse a large number of options for decision makers (DM) for specific situations, where there is an increasing level of uncertainty about the problem at hand and where there is a high impact relative to the correct decisions to be made. DSS's offer decision makers a more stable solution to solving the semi-structured and unstructured problem. This is exactly what the reader will see in this book.

As I read through the chapters it is soon evident that this book provides a wide resource of applications as to how one can design, develop and implement a DSS in the areas such as environmental science and engineering looking at such applications from determining spatial risk zones of the Popocatepetl volcano in Mexico, to developing a web based DSS to manage the growing of wheat crops for a less intensive and more sustainable method of farming in Italy. Other chapters include an ecohydrological and morphological DSS used in the North Rhine Westphalia (NRW) in Germany to help adhere to the EU Water Framework Directive. An online DSS to look and predict the hydrodynamic and water quality in Lake Constance in the Bodensee region in Germany is also presented.

A medical DSS developed in Poland and the USA describes the advances in computer based medical systems to improve the initial patient diagnosis and subsequent therapy to eliminate potential human error. A similar application in Germany looks at the tools of artificial intelligence (A.I.) in medicine to again, assist in the decision making of symptoms, tests disease and eventual treatment options. Chapters 8 and 10 discuss other medical DSS's.

The transport sector is also addressed in Turkey by looking into the vehicle routing problem (VRP) concerning the pick-up and distribution of goods through a mathematical and algorithimic programming approach - Vehicle Routing Problems with Pick-Up and Delivery (VRPPD). A similar typed application was developed in Ireland for optimally determining articulated trucking routes based on distance and cost per kilometre. Decision support for truck route modelling (D-TRM). Chapter 12 looks at the ever popular location selection problem, but this time using a fuzzy logic function deployment method developed in both Iran and Canada.

Tools for the business sector include developing a virtual collaborative decision environment (VCDE) in chapter 14 to simulate decision making regarding a virtual company. In Malaysia, a new era of Active or Intelligent DSS (iDSS) assists managers with intelligent techniques for the operations of HR management.

"In any moment of decision the best thing you can do is the right thing, the next best thing is the wrong thing, and the worst thing you can do is nothing."

Theodore Roosevelt

Editor

Ger Devlin
Biosystems Engineering, University College Dublin
Belfield, Dublin 4,
Ireland

Contents

A Web-based Decision Support System for Managing Durum Wheat Crops

Vittorio Rossi, Pierluigi Meriggi, Tito Caffi,
Simona Giosué and Tiziano Bettati
*Università Cattolica del Sacro Cuore, Piacenza, Horta Srl, Piacenza,
CRPA, Reggio Emilia,
Italy*

1. Introduction

One important goal in agricultural crop production is to develop less intensive and integrated farming systems with lower inputs of fertilizers and pesticides, and with restricted use of the natural resources (water, soil, energy, etc.). The main objectives of these systems are to maintain crop production in both quantitative and qualitative terms, maintain or preferably improve farm income, and at the same time reduce negative environmental impacts as much as possible. Achieving all of these objectives is a prerequisite for sustainable agriculture (Geng et al., 1990; Jordan & Hutcheon, 1996). Integrated Production (IP) (Boller et al., 2004) and Integrated Farming (IF) (EISA, 2001) have been developed as holistic concepts that involve all crop and farming activities and that shape these activities according to the individual site and farm.

The Thematic Strategy on the Sustainable Use of Pesticides adopted in 2006 by the European Commission aims to establish minimum rules for the use of pesticides in the Community so as to reduce risks to human health and the environment from the use of pesticides. A key component of this Strategy is implementation of Integrated Pest Management (IPM), which will become mandatory as of 2014. In the context of IPM, the EU will develop crop-specific standards, the implementation of which would be voluntary. According to ENDURE (2009), IPM creates synergies by integrating complementary methods drawing from a diverse array of approaches that include biocontrol agents, plant genetics, cultural and mechanical methods, biotechnologies, and information technologies, together with some pesticides that are still needed to control the most problematic pests and to manage critical situations.

Concepts of IPM, IP, and IF are based on dynamic processes and require careful and detailed organisation and management of farm activities at both strategic and tactical levels. This means that time must be invested in management, business planning, data collection and detailed record keeping, and identification of required skills and provision for appropriate training to ensure safe farm operation. In IPM, IP, and IF, farm managers must also know where to obtain expert advice, and they must be willing to accept scientific and technical advances that benefit the environment, food quality, and economic performance, and that therefore can be integrated into the crop management as soon as they are reliable (EISA, 2001).

Decision Support Systems (DSSs) collect, organize, and integrate all types of information required for producing a crop; DSSs then analyse and interpret the information and finally use the analysis to recommend the most appropriate action or action choices (Agrios, 2005). Expert knowledge, management models, and timely data are key elements of DSS and are used to assist producers with both daily operational and long-range strategic decisions (Sonka et al., 1997). Computer-based DSSs have gained increasing importance since the 1980s, and a large number of DSSs have been developed to assist extension agents, consultants, growers, and other agricultural actors in crop management. Despite their promise, DSSs have contributed little to practical IP in field because of a series of problems (Parker et al., 1997). For example, many simple DSS tools are not widely used because they address only specific problems, whereas agricultural producers must manage a wide range of problems generated by the entire production system. Other obstacles to the practical use of DSSs have been discussed by Magarey et al. (2002).

In this work, a web-based, interactive DSS for holistic crop management of high-quality durum wheat in the Po Valley (North Italy) is described. This interactive DSS incorporates solutions for overcoming possible obstacles for its practical use.

Durum wheat is a case study of particular interest. This crop traditionally accounts for 8% of total EU wheat production; the major producers of durum wheat in the EU are Italy, Spain, France, and Greece, which typically produce about 48, 22, 18, and 10%, respectively, of total EU durum output. Italy and Canada are the main producers worldwide. Durum wheat is traditionally grown in central and southern Italy, but the hectares cropped with durum wheat have recently increased in North Italy. In Emilia-Romagna, for instance, the area has increased by 45% in 2008 (about 67,000 hectares, with a production of about 400,000 tons) compared with 2007 (46,000 hectares) and by more than 100% compared with 2006 (32,000 hectares). This increase is mainly caused by positive trends in the national and international pasta markets; in 2008, the internal consumption of pasta was greater than 1.5 million tons (more than 2.8×10^9 euros), and the export was about 1.6 million tons (about 1.9×10^9 euros) (UNIPI, 2008). Another important factor has been the willingness of the Italian pasta industries to reduce the import of durum wheat. To increase the supply of domestic durum wheat, an important project involving industries, grower associations, and local governments was started for producing high-quality durum wheat in North Italy (Rabboni, 2009). Quality of durum wheat, particularly the protein content and gluten quality, is strictly dependent on cropping choices and cultivation practices, from soil preparation to harvest.

2. Structure of the DSS

The DSS described in this work was designed to overcome most of the obstacles that usually limit DSS use in practical crop management. Magarey et al. (2002) depicted a twenty-first century DSS as a tool that incorporates total management solutions for growers, and they referred to this DSS as the "super consultant". For durum wheat, the management solutions to be addressed are shown in Figure 1; they include the pre-cultivation strategic choices, the tactical decisions made during the cultivation phase (including harvest), and several post-harvest decisions. Many parts of this "super consultant" have already been developed, but these components need to be integrated to produce a holistic system.

Pre-cultivation and cultivation decisions are important because they cannot be postponed, are often irreversible, represent a substantial allocation of resources, and have a wide range of consequences that impact the farm business for years to come; all of these possible consequences must be considered by using economic and environmental indicators. These decisions are also difficult because they are complex (they involve many interacting factors and have trade-offs between risk and reward) and/or involve uncertainty (mainly due to the erratic climate) (Clemen, 1990).

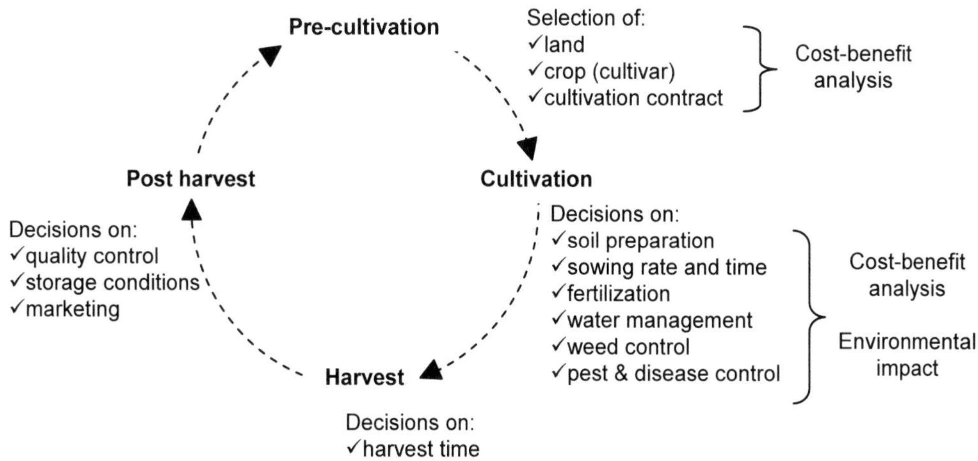

Fig. 1. Main decisions to be made in the production of durum wheat.

The super consultant must be delivered through the World Wide Web (Magarey et al., 2002). A web site eliminates the need for software at the user level and provides a mechanism for a merging of push and pull approaches. Furthermore, it allows the DSS to be updated easily and continuously, so that new knowledge can be provided to farmers even before it is published in research journals (Reddy & Pachepsky, 1997). The super consultant should also have greater automation of interpretation than the current DSS (Magarey et al., 2002). This requires that decision supports are based on static-site profiles and site-specific information; the static-site profile information includes factors about the site that do not change substantially during the growing season (such as previous crop, soil characteristics, cultivar, etc.), while site-specific information may change continuously and must be transmitted directly to the DSS as measurements (such as weather data) or scouting reports (such as the current crop status). Therefore, the DSS for durum wheat was designed to be used in an interactive manner via the Internet.

Lack of clarity about the role of DSSs in decision making, as well as organisational problems related to user support, are among the causes of failure of several DSSs (Rossing & Leeuwis, 1999). DSSs should not be designed or used to replace the decision maker but to help the user make choices by providing additional information; the user remains responsible for the choice and the implementation of actions (Harsh et al., 1989).

Based on the previous considerations, the DSS for durum wheat production was designed following the conceptual diagram of Figure 2. As indicated in this figure, both static-site profiles and site-specific information (data) are viewed as flowing from the environment via instrumented sensors or human activities (scouting, analyses, etc.) to a database. The information is manipulated, analyzed, and interpreted though comparison with available expert knowledge as part of the decision process. The information is processed for producing a decision support. As noted earlier, the decision itself is the responsibility of the user, and the DSS is not designed to replace the decision maker but to help in making choices by providing additional information. A decision results in an action to be executed within the crop environment. After the action is carried out, the environment is again monitored to begin a new cycle of information flow. Thus, information flows to and from the environment in an endless loop that begins with sensing and ends with action (Sonka et al., 1997).

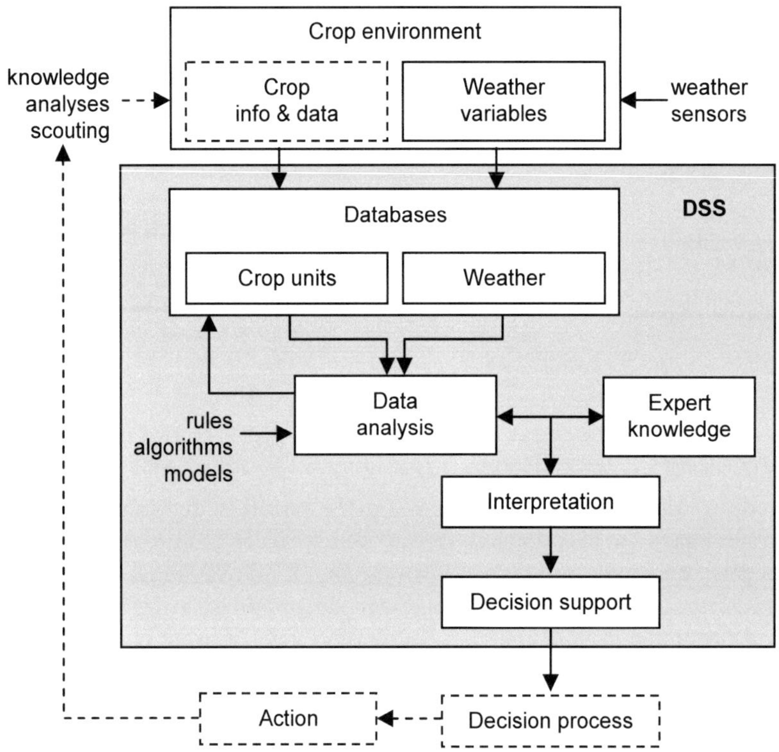

Fig. 2. Conceptual diagram of the DSS for durum wheat cultivation.

2.1 Actors and infrastructures of the DSS

The actors of the DSS and the main infrastructures that they use are shown in Figure 3. The DSS provider is a spin-off company of the University of Piacenza (North Italy), Horta Srl, that manages the process through the web-portal http://www.horta-srl.com. The technological infrastructure is managed by CRPA, a company specialized in the use of new information and communication technologies in agriculture. The DSS provider also manages the network of weather stations and of control crops, which provide input data for the DSS. The users of the DSS are the client enterprises (i.e., a single farm, or an organisation that represents many farms, that stipulates an agreement with the provider for accessing the DSS) and the crop manager(s). The crop manager is a person (usually a technician or an advisor) who makes decisions about crop management or suggests the proper actions to the grower. The crop manager directly interacts with the DSS for creating one or more crop units (i.e., a field sown on a uniform piece of land, with the same wheat variety, and cropped in an uniform manner all season long), inputting the crop specific data, and viewing the DSS output. She/he can also interact with the provider for help in interpreting the DSS output.

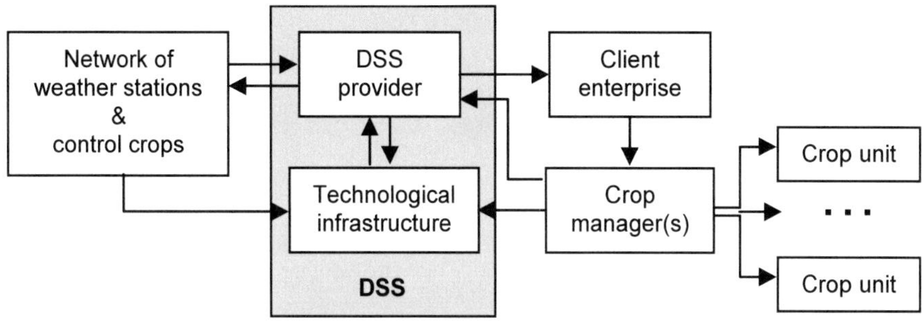

Fig. 3. Actors and infrastructures involved in the DSS for cropping high-quality durum wheat.

2.2 Monitoring the crop environment

A network of weather stations has been created that covers the four climatic areas of the Po Valley (Nanni & Prodi, 2008): i) the Western Po Valley, which includes the flat territory of Turin and Cuneo, characterized by a high rainfall rate and the lowest temperature regime in the Valley ; ii) the Oltrepò Pavese and the district of Alessandria, with similar rainfall as the Western Po Valley but higher temperatures; iii) the Central and Eastern Po Valley, characterized by low winter and high summer rainfall, with the coastal area having higher winter temperatures than the internal territories; and iv) the Friuli plains, which has the highest rainfall in the Valley. Nineteen agro-meteorological stations were installed in selected "representative knots" of each area, based on the surface cropped with durum wheat, as shown in Table 1 and Fig. 4. Additional knots can be included in this network by using agro-meteorological stations belonging to external providers.

Durum wheat–growing areas in North Italy	Hectares cropped with durum wheat (in 2009)	Number of agro-meteorological stations installed
Western Po Valley	1,500	2
Oltrepò Pavese and the district of Alessandria	1,200	1
Central and Eastern Po Valley	87,000	15
Friuli plains	300	1

Table 1. Distribution of the agro-meteorological stations in durum wheat-growing areas of the Po Valley (North Italy).

The agro-meteorological stations (Davis Instruments Corp., Hayward, California) measure air temperature (°C), relative humidity (%), leaf wetness (yes/no), and rainfall (mm) at 1.5 m above the soil. Each station is equipped with an autonomous power source, i.e., a 20-W solar panel and a 60-Ah electric battery.

A network of "reference crops" is created near the agro-meteorological stations. These crops are periodically monitored during the wheat-growing season by the DSS provider in order to collect field data on the crop status. This information is used by the DSS provider for ongoing evaluation and for improved interpretation of the DSS output.

Both static-site and site-specific information are needed for running the DSS in commercial crops. Static-site information depicts the profile of each crop unit, the soil characteristics

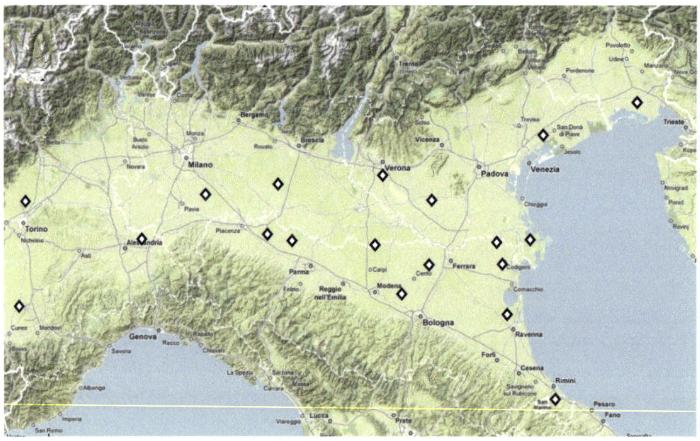

Fig. 4. Geographical distribution of the agro-meteorological stations (diamonds) in the durum wheat-growing areas of the Po Valley (North Italy).

(texture, fertility, organic matter content, etc.) and the contribution of organic fertilization (Tab. 2). Site-specific information is collected during the wheat-growing season by scouting or field observation. This information represents easily collected data describing plant growth, structure of the weed population, and health of the crop.

Identification of the user	Profile of the cropping system
Name of the authorized user	Previous crop
Identification of the crop unit	Soil cultivation methods
Plot surface (ha)	Date of sowing
Geographical coordinates	Yield destination (grains and straw)
Complete address	Variety
Soil texture and fertility	Expected yield (t/ha)
Sand (%)	Organic fertilization
Lime (%)	Regular or occasional
Clay (%)	Frequency of distribution
Organic matter (%)	Concentration of nitrogen (%)
Total (‰) and soluble (ppm) nitrogen	Quantity (t/ha)

Table 2. Main information concerning the static-site profile of each durum wheat crop unit.

2.3 Management of data fluxes

Both weather and crop data are automatically stored in specific databases of the DSS. Each weather station is equipped with a TCP-IP gateway (Netsens Srl, Sesto Fiorentino, Firenze) that sends the data via GPRS/EDGE every 3 to 15 minutes, depending on the weather variable. When weather data are supplied by external providers, an internet-based procedure makes it possible to download the data automatically at fixed time intervals (see section 3.1.1 for further details). As previously mentioned (section 2.2), the crop data are inputted via the Internet into the specific database by the crop manager through an easy-to-use interface of the DSS (see section 3.1.2).

2.4 Data analysis

The weather and crop data are analyzed to produce decision supports for the key aspects of durum wheat cultivation. A step-by-step problem-solving procedure based on important factors relating to the specific process is used for producing decision supports for sowing, nitrogen fertilization, and weed control; decision supports concerning crop growth, pests, and diseases are produced through mathematical models.

The problem-solving process consists of a sequence of sections that fit together; these are: problem definition, problem analysis, generation of possible solutions, analysis of the solutions, and selection of the best solution(s). The process initially involves formally defining the problem to be solved. This first step not only involves formalizing the problem but also ensuring that the correct problem has been identified. The next step in the process is to determine the current situation and what components of the situation have created the problem; a set of criteria by which to evaluate any new solutions are also defined. The next step in problem solving is to generate a number of possible solutions. At this stage, the process generates many solutions but does not evaluate them. In the analysing section of the problem-solving process, the various factors associated with each of the potential solutions are investigated; good and bad points and other factors relevant to each solution are noted but solutions are still not evaluated. In the last step, the various influencing factors for each possible solution are examined and decisions are made about which solutions to keep and which to discard. This selection procedure is frequently iterative; a shortlist of potential solutions is prepared first and then further refined by increasing the depth in the analysis of each solution. Usually the process yields one or a few viable solutions. A good example of this process-solving procedure is provided by Atri et al. (2005) for post-emergence weed management in winter wheat.

Mathematical models are simplified representations of reality (De Wit, 1993). A plant disease model is a simplification of the relationships between a pathogen, a host plant, and the environment that cause an epidemic to develop over time and / or space. Most models used in the DSS for durum wheat have been published (Rossi et al., 1996; Rossi et al., 1997; Rossi & Giosuè, 2003; Rossi et al., 2003a and b; Rossi et al., 2007), and some are extensively used in Italian warning systems for decision making in crop protection at the territorial scale (Bugiani et al., 1993). The disease and plant models used in the DSS were developed following a fundamental approach, where 'fundamental' is the alternative to 'empirical' (Madden & Ellis, 1988). Empirical models describe behaviour of the system on the basis of observations alone and explain nothing of the underlying processes. Fundamental models (also referred to as explanatory, theoretical, or mechanistic models) explain the same behaviour on the basis of what is known about how the system works in relation to the influencing variables (Wainwright & Mulligan, 2004). Fundamental models are also dynamic in that they analyse components of the epidemic and their changes over time due to the external variables influencing them. Dynamic modelling is based on the assumption that the state of the pathosystem in every moment can be quantitatively characterised and that changes in the system can be described with mathematical equations (Rabbinge & De Wit, 1989). The models are also weather-driven, because the weather variables are the main inputs of the model.

The models used in the DSS are tools for simulation and prediction, i.e., they represent a category of models used for extrapolation beyond measured times and spaces (Anderson, 1974; Wainwright & Mulligan, 2004). In this context, prediction is the process of estimation in unknown past or current situations, which is different from forecasting, the latter term being reserved for extrapolations at future times. Nevertheless, these predictive models can be used as forecasters by using weather forecasts as input factors, or by linking past or current conditions of the epidemic to the future conditions (Campbell & Madden, 1990). For instance, appearance of new disease lesions on the plant depends on infection that occurred some time before and on plant tissue colonisation during the incubation period; infection depends, in turn, on the availability of viable propagules, which have been produced on sporulating lesions, released into the air, and deposited on the plant surface. Therefore, forecasting significant stages of epidemics, like outbreak or increase in intensity, consists of identifying previous significant events and the relationship between past and future events based on the factors influencing both the occurrence of events and their dimension (De Vallavieille-Pope et al., 2000)

2.5 Decision supports

The DSS produces several kinds of output, at different scales of complexity. The DSS provider can access the results with the highest level of detail because the provider must have a complete understanding of the biological process that underlie the production of the decision support. The provider constantly compares this output with the real situation observed in the reference crops (see section 2.2). This kind of output is not shown herein.

The crop manager accesses the output concerning the crop unit(s) she/he has created. Two kinds of output are available for each crop unit. The first output is a "dashboard" with images that summarize current weather conditions, crop growth, and disease risk for a selected station (Fig. 5); in this dashboard, the other functionalities (fertilisation, weed control, etc.) are displayed by icons (not shown). The manager can also click on the image of any disease and observe the level of risk of the selected station in comparison with that of the other stations (Fig. 6).

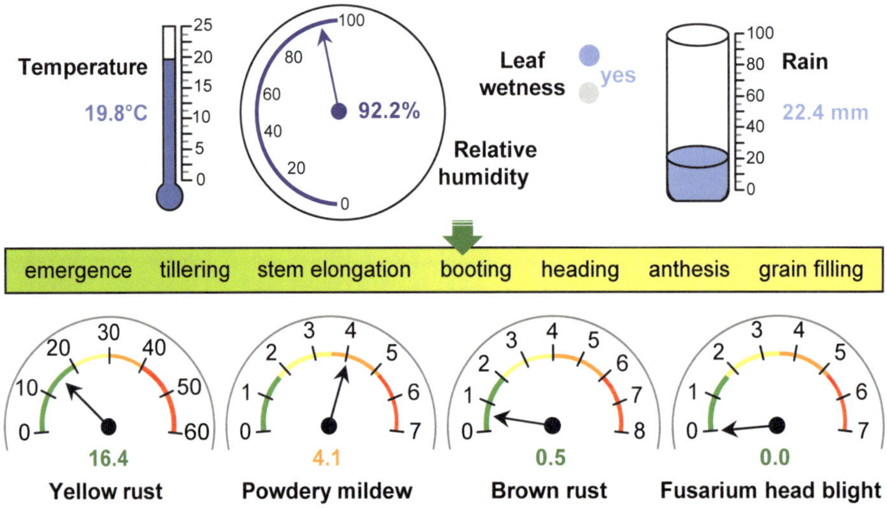

Fig. 5. Example of the dashboard showing current temperature, relative humidity, leaf wetness, and rain; the calculated crop growth stage (green arrow); and level of disease risk (from low in green to very high in red) for yellow rust, powdery mildew, brown rust, and *Fusarium* head blight.

Fig. 6. Example of the map that makes it possible to compare the level of disease risk of a selected agro-meteorological station with that of other stations. The risk ranges from low (green, not present in this figure) to very high (red); the white marker indicates an agro-meteorological station that has not send the data necessary for running the disease models and calculating the level of risk.

The second, more detailed output is accessible by clicking on either images or icons of the dashboard. Some examples of these decision supports are shown in section 4. This approach is similar to the lite- and full-expert system depicted by Magarey et al. (2002): when the lite-expert system detects a potential problem or risk, the user may choose to run the full-expert system to receive more information and a larger choice of recommendations.

3. Technological infrastructure

3.1 DSS design

The technological infrastructure of the DSS comprises the four interrelated components shown in Fig. 7: Weather, Crop, Analyze, and Access.

3.1.1 The "Weather" component

The "Weather" component manages the collection and storage of the weather data as well as the procedures for the quality control of these data. This component consists of the five sub-components shown in Fig. 8.

The "Weather Sensors" subcomponent manages the network of agro-meteorological stations. Each station is equipped with the 2G/2.5G TCP-IP Gateways module produced by Netsens, a module that permits a permanent connection to a server via GPRS/EDGE with a TCP-IP protocol. The "Data Receiver" subcomponent is the infrastructure that receives the data from the agro-meteorological stations in real time (every 3 to 10 min, depending on the weather variable) through the Gateways module, stores these data in a temporary database, computes the hourly values for the variables of interest, and finally stores them in the "Weather DB". This software is provided by Netsens. The "Data Loader" subcomponent imports the weather data from external providers to the "Weather DB". This software, written in Java, periodically accesses via FTP the content of one or more shared folders,

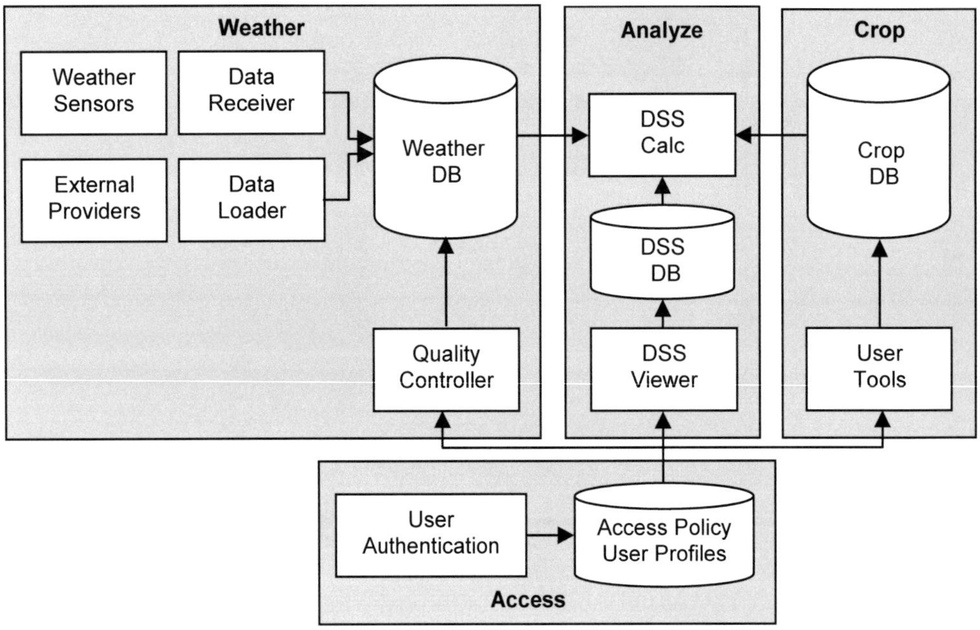

Fig. 7. The four components of the DSS: Weather, Crop, Analyze, and Access.

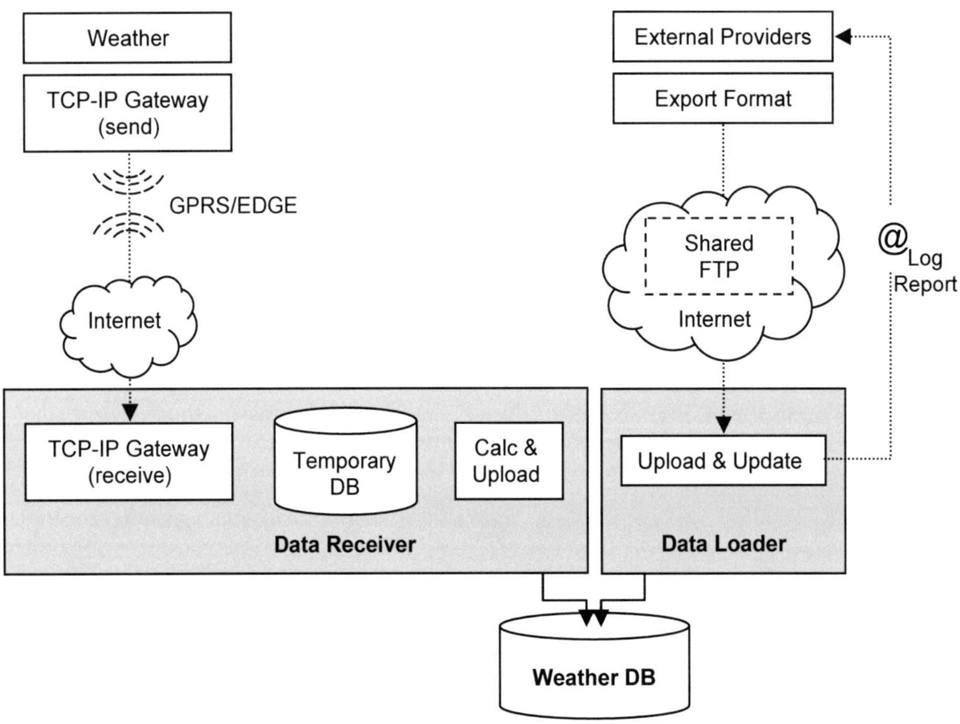

Fig. 8. Procedures concerning management of weather data coming from the network of agro-meteorological stations (on the left) and/or from external data providers (on the right), until the data storage in the Weather database.

scans them for the presence of data, and performs the download on the database. Afterward, the Data Loader produces a file (Log file) with the information concerning the download made, drawing particular attention to possible problems; the Log file is automatically sent by e-mail to the data provider. The "Weather DB" stores the weather data of each knot of the network with both hourly and daily steps; updating occurs asynchronously from the two subcomponents "Data Receiving" and "Data Loader". The "Quality Controller" subcomponent performs the quality control of the weather data. It consists of some internet services, written in Java, that produce HTML/JavaScript pages that can be accessed by the DSS provider only using an internet browser. The following quality criteria are considered: i) data accuracy (control on data format, comparison with historical ranges, comparison with data from the neighbouring weather stations); ii) completeness of the hourly and daily data series; and iii) working status of the weather stations (Fig. 9).

Fig. 9. Example of the DSS tool showing the real-time working status of the agro-meteorological stations. Green markers indicate a regular flux of data, yellow markers signal a short delay of the station in sending data, while red markers indicate that no data are coming from the station. When the user clicks on the proper marker, the table shows the current data measured by any station selected.

3.1.2 The "Crop" component

The "Crop" component manages administration and storage of the data from the crop units. It has two subcomponents: "User Tools" and "Crop DB". User Tools are procedures written in Java that, through a series of HTML/JavaScript pages, make it possible to: i) define the user; ii) create crop units; iii) define the agro-meteorological station(s) that represents a crop unit; and iv) insert the specific crop information/data (Fig. 10). The "Crop DB" stores in a database all of the crop unit data mentioned above.

3.1.3 The "Analyze" component

The "Analyze" component contains the procedures for calculating the decision supports (i.e., the main output of the DSS) and for storing them in a database that can be accessed by the users through the "Access" component. The "Analyze" component includes three subcomponents: i) "DSS Calc", which contains the algorithms that use the inputs for producing the output; ii) "DSS DB", which stores the results of the calculation procedures (i.e., the output); and iii) "DSS Viewer", which makes it possible to view the output stored in the "DSS DB" (for those modules that are batch calculated) or to start a new, on-demand calculation of output. The batch-calculated modules are "Crop Growth" and "Diseases";

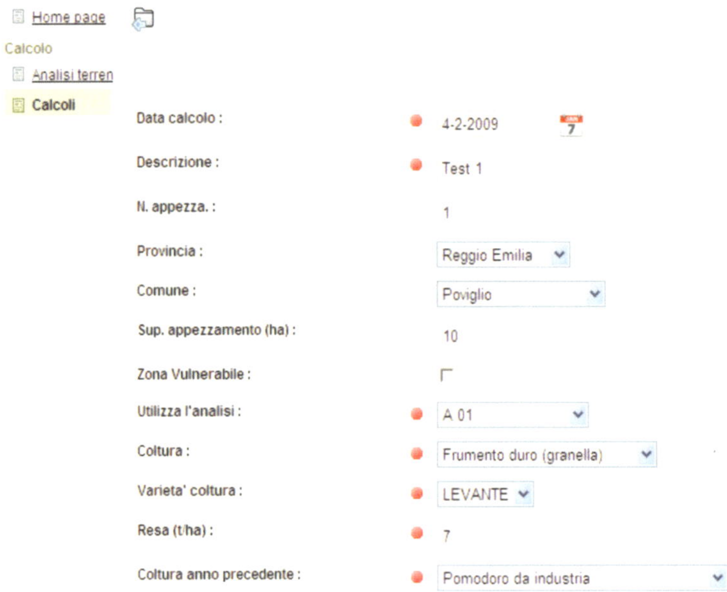

Fig. 10. Part of the interface of the DSS that the crop manager uses (via the Internet) to insert the specific crop information/data required for producing the decision supports.

they are implemented in Java and, every night, the software reads the input data from the Weather DB and the Crop DB, calculates the output for each crop unit, and stores this output in the DSS DB. The on-demand calculated modules are "Sowing", "Fertilization", "Weeds", and "Fungicides"; they are implemented with query-and-stored procedures that use the data from the Weather DB and the Crop DB. "DSS Viewer" shows in a simple way the key elements that support decision making (see section 2.5).

3.1.4 The "Access" component

The "Access" component includes folders and procedures required for managing the users, connecting to the different modules, and accessing the DSS. This component is supplied by the infrastructure of the web-portal http://www.agrishare.com, which makes it possible to manage the different users, including: i) the provider of the DSS, who can access all the information and interact with the whole system; ii) the client enterprise; iii) the crop manager(s); and the crop unit(s) created by each crop manager.

3.2 Hardware and operating systems

The technological infrastructure used for developing the DSS is hosted on three servers, as shown in Table 3 and Figure 11.

4. DSS output

This section discusses examples of the decision supports provided by the DSS for choosing crop rotation, determining the optimum rate of sowing, checking crop growth and development, defining nitrogen fertilization in terms of fertilizer dose and application schedule, defining weed management actions, and making decisions about disease control.

Server	Operating System and DSS components
Oracle Application Server HP ProLiant DL360 G5 (n. 1 CPU)	Linux SUSE SLES 9 SP3 Oracle Application Server 9.0.4.3.0 Enterprise Edition Oracle Internet Directory • agrishare.com infrastructure
Oracle DBMS Server HP Proliant DL380 G5 (n. 1 CPU)	• Linux SuSE SLES10 SP1 • Oracle DBMS 10.2.0.3.0 Standard Edition
DSS Server Umbrabded hardware (n. 4 six core CPU) Intel Xeon 7400	• Linux SUSE SLES 10 SP2 x86_64 • JBoss 4.2.3 Application Server • PostgreSQL 8.3 DBMS • NetSens TCP-IP Gateway infrastructure • - MySQL and Custon procedures

Table 3. Technological infrastructure of the DDS.

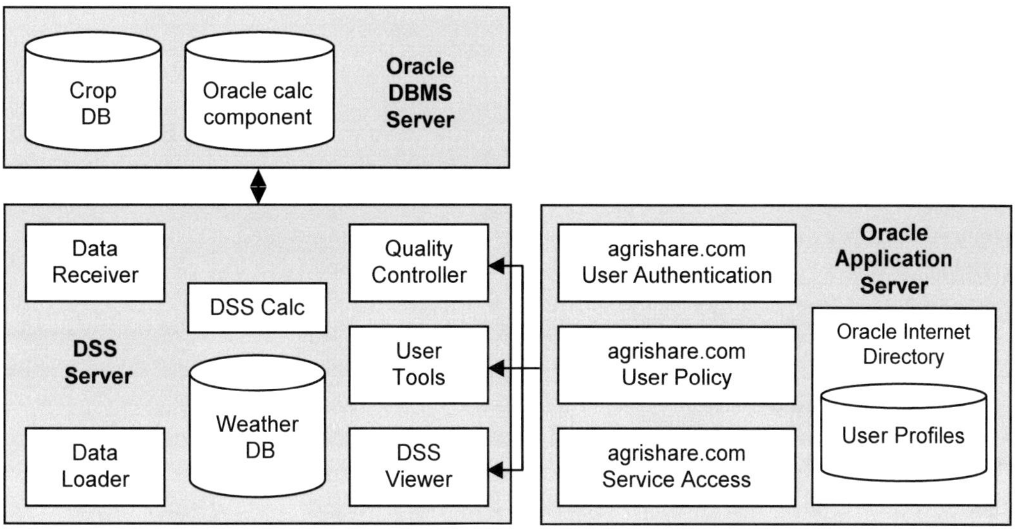

Fig. 11. Server, databases, and software used in the DSS.

4.1 Crop rotation

Crop rotation is a key agronomic practice for the cultivation of durum wheat; rotations of 3 or 4 years are strongly recommended, with at least two to three different crops per rotation. Monoculture or succession with other cereals is discouraged, especially if pathogen inoculum is present in the crop residue.

To help farmers correctly chose crops to be included in rotation with durum wheat, the DSS provides a series of possible crops with indexes of suitability, including economics; the grower can select both crops and indexes of interest, and then look for the crop scores (Fig. 12).

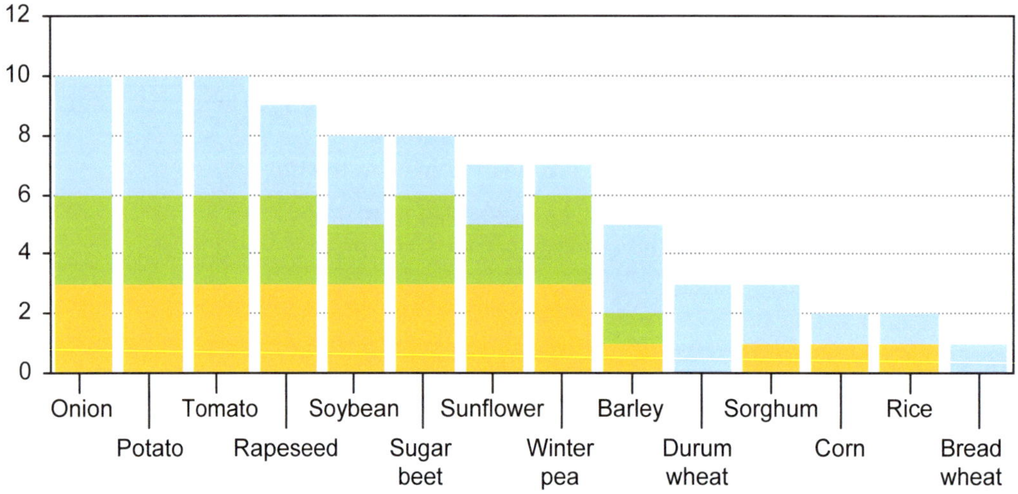

Fig. 12. Example of decision support for selecting crops that precede durum wheat in the rotation, based on residual disease pressure for durum wheat (orange), residual fertility (green), and expected income for the selected crop (blue).

4.2 Sowing

Density of sowing affects the capture of available resources by the crop and strongly influences crop yield and quality. Growth rate is greater when wheat crops are drilled with low plant density than with high plant density, and the same yield is attained because the reduced number of spikes on the low density plant is compensated for by an increased number of kernels per spike (Whaley et al., 2000). Plants grown with low plant density also have greater leaf area, longer leaf area duration, increased radiation use efficiency (because of better distribution of solar radiation through the canopy), and increased canopy nitrogen ratio. As a consequence, kernel size and protein content are greater with low plant density than with high plant density.

Currently, the density of seeds used for durum wheat in northern Italy ranges from 450 to 550 viable seeds per m^2. In several conditions, these densities are excessive, and there is a risk of reducing the yield quality because of lodging. Optimum seed density depends on cultivar tillering capacity and growth habit, depth and time of sowing, soil aggregation (structure) as a result of soil tillage, and soil moisture (Spink and Blake, 2004).

The DSS takes into account the previously cited variables to determine the ideal population of plants to maximize yield quantity and quality, with particular regard to protein content and kernel size (Fig. 13). The data for calculating the theoretical number of seeds to be sown are: tillering capability of the cultivar, type of soil (in relation to the probable presence of soil aggregates), date of sowing (in relation to seedling emergence and production of tillers), and predicted temperatures after sowing (which affect tillering and which are used as thermal summations, base 5°C, from October to March). Predicted losses of seedlings during emergence are estimated based on seedbed quality, sowing depth, and risk of flooding. All of these data are taken from the Crop and Weather DBs. The DSS provides suggestion on the optimum amount of seed to be used, in kg per hectare.

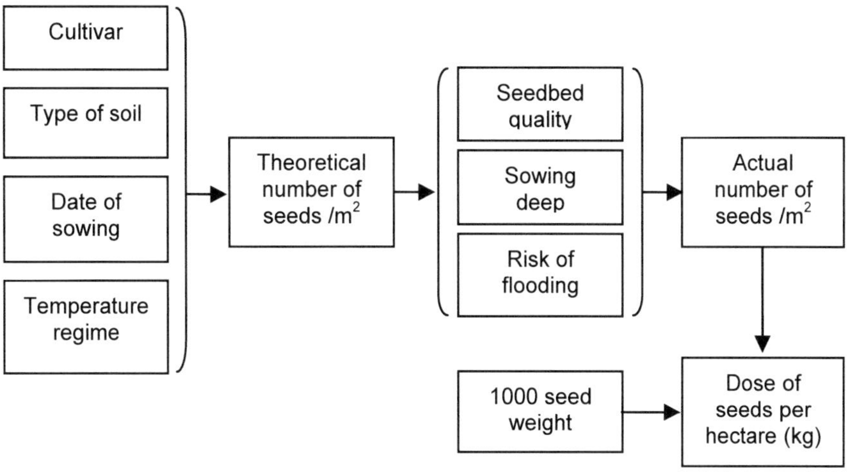

Fig. 13. Flow chart of the step-by-step problem-solving procedure used by the DSS for calculating the optimum seeding rate per hectare.

4.3 Crop growth and development

Crop growth and development is an important variable in decision making because it is relevant to fertilization, weed management, and disease control. Weather and crop-specific data are used as inputs for running a dynamic model that predicts the timing of all key growth stages, leaf-by-leaf development, and tillering.

The basic concepts of the crop model are reported in Rossi et al. (1997). Dynamics of total and green area of each leaf, of spikes, and of stems are calculated from the time of their appearance until complete senescence based on date of sowing, wheat cultivar, and weather variables. An example of the DSS output is provided in Fig. 14.

4.4 Fertilization

Nitrogen fertilization is more complicated and the results are more variable with wheat than with many other field crops. Nitrogen (N) fertilizer is also a significant cost in durum wheat production and can adversely impact both crop and environment when the mineral N leaches out of the crop field and into aquifers. N influences grain yield, grain protein, and grain protein concentration (Toderi & D'Antuono, 2000). Because N is obtained from the soil, plant-available soil N directly influences grain protein yield. The ratio of grain protein yield to total grain yield determines grain protein concentration (percentage of protein); consequently, the influence of N fertilizer on this ratio determines its influence on percentage of grain protein. In general, the higher the yield goal, the more important N management becomes; timing is as important as the amount of N applied (Lòpez-Bellido et al., 2006; Meriggi & Bucci, 2007). For instance, N added too early can result in significant losses of N, and when extra N is added as insurance, the potential for lodging and disease increases.

The decision supports provided by the DSS are aimed at fostering economically and environmentally sustainable practices, practices that enable farmers to balance production and environmental goals. The decision supports help the farmer manage N fertilisation so that the N is available when the crop requires the mineral nutrient, and so that the crop takes up all of the N input to prevent the N from leaching into the ground water.

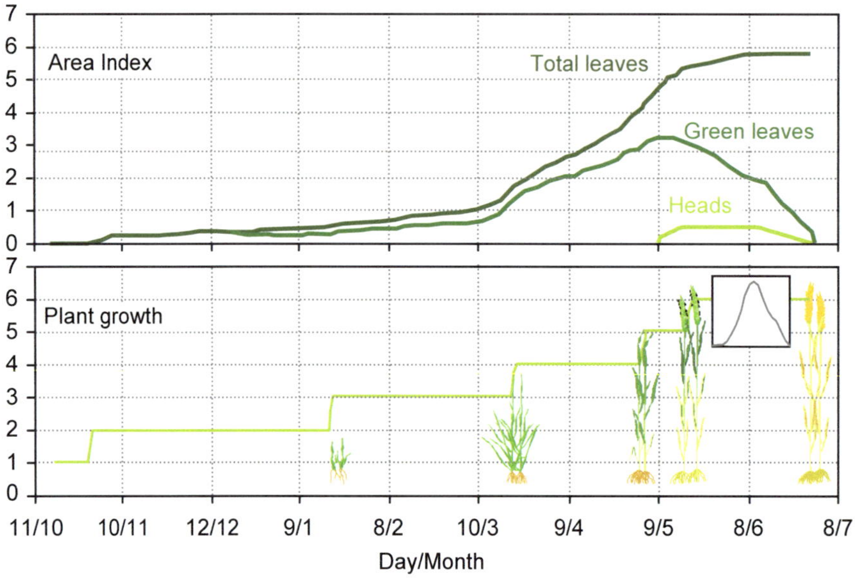

Fig. 14. Dynamics of both green and total LAI (Leaf Area Index), and of HAI (Head Area Index) from sowing to the current day, and relevant growth stages (tillering, stem elongation, booting, anthesis, full ripening). The progress course of anthesis is also shown (small graph) as an important factor influencing decision making for controlling Fusarium head blight. Phases of plant growth are grouped as: 1, sowing to emergence; 2, emergence to tillering; 3, tillering to stem elongation; 4, stem elongation to booting; 5, booting to anthesis; and 6, anthesis to ripening.

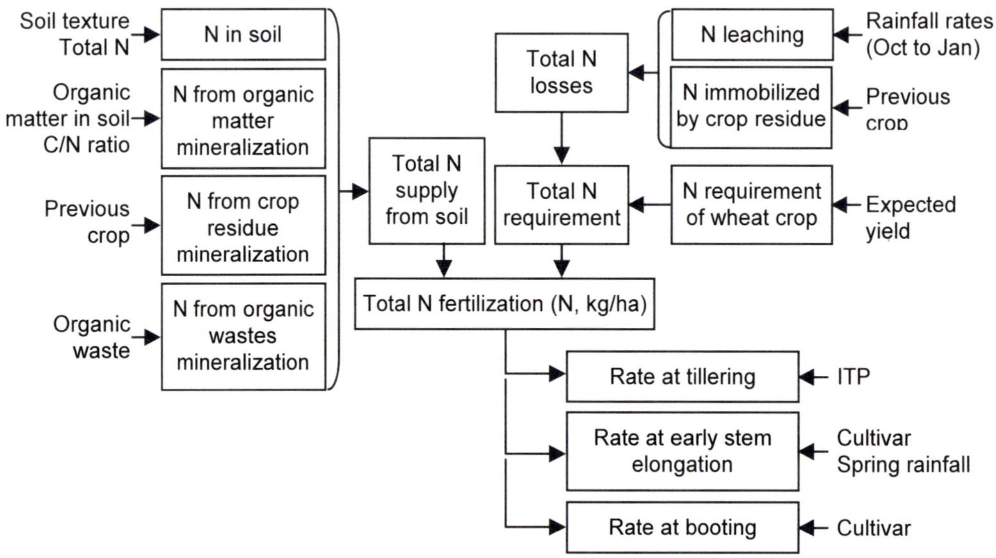

Fig. 15. Flow chart of the procedure used by the DSS for calculating the required level of nitrogen (N) inputs and N application rates in durum wheat; ITP is a specific thermo-pluviometric ratio.

The fertilization tool provides information on the total amount of N fertilizer to be applied for individual crops, as well as options for determining application times and split rates. This tool uses a Nitrogen Simplified Balance Sheet initially developed and calibrated by the Emilia-Romagna Region (www.ermesagricoltura.it) (Fig. 15). All data necessary for calculating the DSS output are stored in the Crop Unit and Weather databases. Quantities of fertiliser inputs (in kg of N per hectare) to be applied depends on N supply and N demand. N supply depends on the natural stock of nitrogen in soil and on the mineralization rate of soil organic matter, previous crop residues, and organic wastes or manures that have been eventually incorporated in soil. N demand depends on the wheat crop demand (which in turn depends on the expected crop yield) and on the N losses due to rainfall in autumn and winter, and on immobilization of N by residue of the previous crop. Splitting of the total N input in different rates depends on crop growth stages (as an estimate of the crop N demand) and weather conditions, i.e., spring rainfall and a specific thermo-pluviometric ratio that accounts for the combined effect of temperature and rain.

4.5 Weed management

Making weed management decisions is often a challenging process. The broad spectrum of weeds present in wheat fields combined with the many herbicides available on the market can make choosing a herbicide or a tank-mixture for a specific field difficult. Selection of a suitable herbicide involves biological traits such as crop characteristics, qualitative and quantitative composition of weed flora, time of weed emergence, relative herbicide efficacy, and weed competitiveness before and after control. The selection also involves economic factors such as grain and herbicide costs, economic damage caused by the weeds, and environmental considerations (Berti et al., 2003).

The DSS aims to achieve economical, environmentally safe, and sustainable weed management. The task is to control weeds with only one herbicide treatment in such a way as to control all the weeds (broadleaves and grasses) at the same time, preferably when they are in earliest growth stages so that herbicide dose is low and competition between weed and crop is minimized.

Variables influencing the decision making process are shown in Fig. 16. Characteristics of the weed population must be defined at the specific-plot level by the crop manager by scouting or on the basis of the previous experience. In the case of scouting, the DSS provides guidelines for identifying weeds and estimating their relative abundance. Soil type and crop growth stage at the current date are available in the specific databases; growth stage of the wheat plant is important for estimating potential yield losses due to weed competition and for selecting selective herbicides. Weather data come from the Weather DB. Some weather variables influence activity and efficacy of both soil-acting and contact-acting herbicides (Bouma, 2008).

The DSS provides advice on the basis of interactions of weeds and wheat and selects the best herbicides with optimum dosage, optimum application time (day and hour of the day, i.e., morning, afternoon, or sunset), and optimum application method. Herbicides are ranked based on both economical and environmental performances. For the economical analysis, herbicides are ranked based on cost, reflecting a balance that includes estimated yield losses due to the weeds, wheat price, expected yield, and herbicide and distribution costs. For the environmental analysis, herbicides are ranked based on dose/treatment index and risk of drift and leaching. Advice is also provided about limitations of the suggested herbicides compared with those of other chemicals.

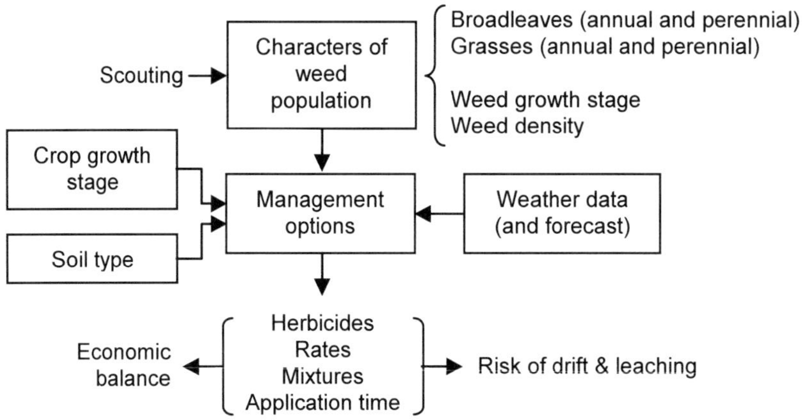

Fig. 16. Flow chart of the procedure used by the DSS for suggesting the best weed management options for each particular field condition.

4.6 Pest and disease control

The following leaf and head diseases are considered in the DSS: powdery mildew, yellow and brown rusts, *Septoria*-disease complex, and Fusarium head blight. No insect pests are currently included in the DSS because currently there are no important insect pests of durum wheat in North Italy and generally no insecticides are applied to the crop.

As previously stated, decision supports for managing the indicated fungal diseases were drawn from previously published models. An example is given for Fusarium head blight (FHB) and related mycotoxins.

FHB is caused by several *Fusarium* species and is a serious disease of durum wheat in North Italy and in many other areas around the world (Parry et al., 1995); accumulation of mycotoxins in kernels produced by the infected heads is of great concern, and maximum mycotoxin limits have been imposed by EU Commission Regulation (EC) No 856, 6 June 2005. The relational diagram of the FHB-wheat model is shown in Fig. 17 (Rossi et al., 2003a).

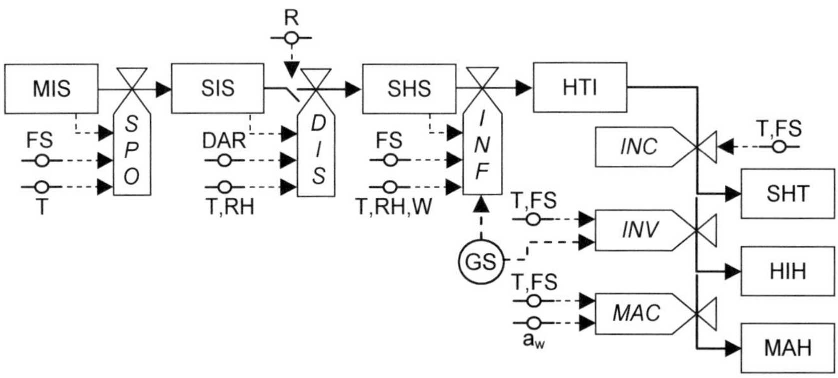

Fig. 17. Diagram of the model for Fusarium head blight of wheat and related mycotoxins.

The inoculum source is the fungal mycelium in basal wheat organs or in cereal straw (MIS, Mycelium in Inoculum Sources); the model assumes that MIS is always present for all *Fusarium* species (FS), in equal dose. Inoculum produced on sources (SIS, Spores on Inoculum Sources) depends on a sporulation rate (SPO), while the amount of spores reaching the head tissues (SHS, Spores on Head Surface) is regulated by a dispersal rate (DIS). An infection rate (INF) accounts for the proportion of the head tissue affected (HTI, Head Tissue Infected). At the end of incubation (INC), FHB symptoms appear on spikes (SHT, Scab on Head Tissue); fungal invasion of head tissues (HIH, Hyphae Invading Head tissue) and mycotoxin production (MAH, Mycotoxin Accumulation on Heads) are regulated by invasion (INV) and mycotoxin accumulation (MAC) rates, respectively. Rates are influenced by air temperature (T), relative humidity (RH), rainfall (R), the number of consecutive days with rain (DAR), wetness duration (W), and free water in the host tissue (a_W). Rates are also influenced by FS and host growth stage (GS). An index for mycotoxin production in affected kernels, named FHB-tox, is calculated daily for two *Fusarium* species, *F. graminearum* and *F. culmorum*, which are the main producers of deoxynivalenol (DON) and zearalenone (ZEN); this index is accumulated over the growing season until harvest. Variables for calculating FHB-tox are SPO, DIS, INF, GS, and INV.

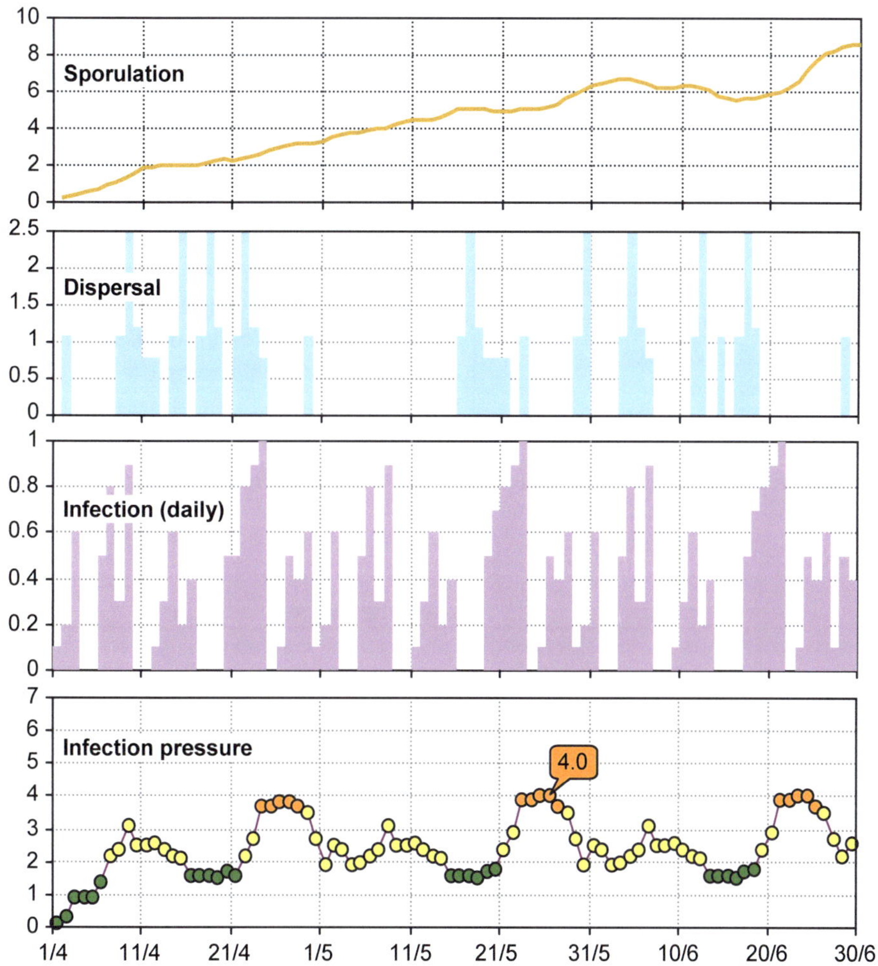

Fig. 18. Example of the decision supports provided by the DSS for managing Fusarium head blight on durum wheat.

The DSS provides four different decision supports (Fig. 18): i) dynamics of pathogen sporulation as a measure of potential pressure of the pathogen; ii) index of spore dispersal as a measure of the inoculum that reaches the heads; iii) daily index of infection as a measure of the proportion of the inoculum able to cause infection of the head tissue; and iv) infection pressure, i.e., the index of infection accumulated over the incubation period of the disease, as a measure of the disease symptoms that will appear in the next days. Four classes of disease risk are defined based on the level of the infection pressure, and specific recommendations are provided for each class (Table 4).

Risk classes	Comments	Recommendations
Low	Environmental conditions are not suitable for disease development.	No specific control actions are necessary to date.
Moderate	Environmental conditions support disease onset in some healthy crops or disease development in the affected crops.	Scout the crop; presence of disease signs requires a thorough evaluation of a possible fungicide application.
High	The disease is likely established in several crops. Environmental conditions are suitable for further disease development.	Probability of disease development is high. If these conditions remain for $\geq$ 3 consecutive days, scout the crop and, if the disease is present, a fungicide application is recommended. Look up the DSS for risk of other diseases for choosing the best fungicide*.
Very high	The disease is likely established in many crops. Environmental conditions are very suitable for further disease development.	Probability of disease development is very high. Scout the crop and, if the disease is present, a fungicide application is strongly recommended as soon as possible. Look up the DSS for risk of other diseases for choosing the best fungicide*.
* If the crop is subjected to a production disciplinary that regulates the use of fungicides, consult the disciplinary for any constraints on fungicides and maximum number of applications.		

Table 4. Classes of risk for the durum wheat diseases, corresponding comments, and recommendations provided by the DSS.

The DSS also produces a risk index for the contamination of grains by mycotoxins (Rossi et al., 2007). This index is calculated using specific crop information (from the Crop DB) that significantly accounts for the presence of mycotoxins in kernels: weather conditions (X1), cereal growing-area (X2), cereal species (X3), resistance level of the wheat cultivar (X4), previous crop (X5), and kind of soil tillage (X6). Each of these factors has different levels of increasing proneness to FHB (Y1 to Y5). For instance, weather ranges from unfavourable to FHB to very conducive through five increasing levels of proneness defined based on the

FHB-tox calculated by the previously described model (FHB-tox ≤10 to FHB-tox >25). The risk level is calculated by the equation of Table 5. In this equation, X1Yn to X6Yn are the values present in the corresponding cells of Table 5. R ranges between -3.86 and 4.43. The DSS finally defines four levels of increasing risk: low (R≤-2), intermediate (-2<R≤-0.44), high (-0.44<R≤1.2), and very high (R>1.2). For instance, when R=-2.0, the probability of mycotoxin-free grains is about 95%; when R=2.5, the probability of high contamination is greater than 85%.

Influencing variables		Groups of increasing proneness to FHB				
		Y1	Y2	Y3	Y4	Y5
Weather	X1	0.921	1.842	2.763	3.684	4.605
Growing area	X2	0.519	1.038	1.557	-	-
Cereal species	X3	0.655	1.310	1.965	-	-
Cultivar	X4	0.342	0.684	1.026	1.368	-
Previous crop	X5	0.272	0.544	0.816	-	-
Soil tillage	X6	0.343	0.686	1.029	-	-
Risk (R) = -6.915 + X1Yn + X2Yn+ X3Yn+ X4Yn+ X5Yn+ X6Yn						

Table 5. Coefficients (XnYn) for calculating the level of risk for mycotoxin accumulation in cereal kernels according to equation (R), based on the proneness to Fusarium head blight (FHB) as indicated by different influencing variables.

5. Conclusion

A holistic vision of crop cultivation problems. The DSS for cropping high-quality durum wheat embraces the concept of the integrated approach in designing multidisciplinary decision support systems. This DSS takes into account and provides decision supports for all the key elements of the production chain, from strategic choices to tactical operations. In this way, the DSS should overcome one of the main obstacles to widespread practical use of other DSSs, which is an inadequate consideration of all aspects of production (Parker et al., 1997; Rossing & Leeuwis, 1999; BCPC, 2000; Magarey et al., 2002).

Converting complex decision processes into simple decision supports. DSSs vary in complexity, with production guides at the simple end of the spectrum and a full-expert system at the complex end. Both simple and complex DSSs have disadvantages (Magarey et al., 2002), but farmers generally require clear and concise information. Farmers usually react unfavourably to the delivery of a large amount of redundant information: they need the information to be presented in an attractive, intelligent, and useful form (BCPC, 2000).

The DSS for durum wheat cultivation uses sophisticated technologies and methods for analysing data to produce simple and easy-to-understand decision supports. In that way, the DSS combines the advantages of both simple DSSs (low cost, ease of delivery in multiple ways, and limited time requirements for learning and use of the DSS) and more sophisticated ones (greater integration of knowledge, greater grower choice of management tools and consideration of associated risks). The DSS is then a simple tool that performs a complex task efficiently and effectively.

Furthermore, implementation of the DSS in the World Wide Web should increase its accessibility. A survey by the USDA's National Agricultural Statistics Service found that, in

1999, 40% of US farmers owned or leased computers, although only 29% had access to the Internet; by 2005, these numbers had increased to 55% and 51%, respectively (NASS, 2006). A similar trend is occurring in Europe (EITO, 2001). Today or in the very near future, users will not need to be in their office to access the super consultant: they will communicate with the DSS via personnel data assistants and web-active mobile phones.

Coupling information at territorial and crop scales. In Italy, regional or district scale information products are provided by extension services and, especially, by public services (Rossi et al., 2000). For instance, the PPO (Plant Protection Organisation) of the Emilia-Romagna Region provides public advice, usually on a weekly basis, on the current and forthcoming risks for pests and diseases, and suggestions about the use of pesticides according to the regional IPM guidelines. Growers can freely access this information, usually through the Internet or articles in local newspapers. The DSS for durum wheat does not conflict with this information but enlarges its efficacy by bringing information from the territorial scale to the crop scale. For this reason, several tools used in the DSS for producing decision supports are common to those used by the PPO.

Providing criteria for justifying actions. The trend in agriculture is toward more complex, technologically based crop management, with greater regulation and oversight by both government and processors on the use of chemicals (fertilizers, pesticides, etc.). For example, the Directive on Sustainable Use of Pesticides requires the use of IPM in all the EC Member States by 2014, and asks governments to establish and apply methods for determining whether farmers apply IPM principles in practical crop management. In this context, site-specific data, scouting reports, and recommendations from the DSS will serve as acceptable criteria for justifying (to regulatory authorities, wholesalers, or processors) the application of chemicals.

Perspectives. A preliminary survey showed that the potential users farm about 150,000 hectares. In 2008/09, the DSS was provided free-of-charge to about 30 selected crop managers for validation purposes; similarly, the service will be available with no fees to about 200 crop managers in 2009/10. Later, access to the DSS will be restricted by password to fee-paying users; subscribers will be billed on a per-hectare schedule.

As noted earlier, many DSSs have not been used by farmers. An example is Wheatman, a computerised DSS designed for winter cropping decisions in the northeastern Australian grain belt (Hayman & Easdown, 2002). Use of Wheatman for tactical decision making has been limited by farmer perceptions about the nature of farm management in general and about Wheatman in particular. In contrast to the grain farmers in northeastern Australia, the durum wheat farmers in northern Italy should appreciate the advantages offered by a DSS. Durum wheat farmers in North Italy are accustomed to following guidelines, and they periodically seek advice about crop protection because IPM has been emphasized in this region for about 30 years. In addition, a farm-to-fork project that involves grower associations, milling and pasta industries, and public entities has increased the hectareage cropped with durum wheat, and farmers involved in this project must apply cropping guidelines for producing high quality grains and must document their decisions. As previously mentioned, the Directive on Sustainable Use of Pesticides will stress this procedure starting in 2014. Given this context of farmer and public perceptions and concerns, the widespread use of the DSS seems likely.

6. Acknowledgements

The authors are grateful to CGS Sementi SpA (http://www.cgssementi.it/) and Società Produttori Sementi SpA (http://www.prosementi.com/index.php/ita/) for helping to fund the development of the "DSS for cropping high-quality durum wheat".

7. References

Agrios, G.N. (2005). *Plant pathology* (5° Ed), Academic Press, ISBN 0120445654, New York

Anderson, J.R. (1974). Simulation: methodology and application in agricultural economics. *Review of Marketing and Agricultural Economics*, Vol. 42, No. 1, (March 1974) pp. 3-55, ISSN 0034-6616

Atri, A.; Zand, E.; Baghestani, M.; Khalghani, J. & Partovi, M. (2005). A decision support system for post-emergence weed management in winter wheat, *Proccedings of the 5th conference of the European Federation for Information Technology in Agriculture, 3rd World Congress on Computer in Agriculture and Natural Resources*, pp. 63-66, Vila Real, Portugal, 25-28 July 2005

BCPC (2000). *The role of decision support systems in the farm business of the future, Discussion Forum*, 9 December 1999, IACR-Rothamsted, Harpenden, Hertfordshire, The British Crop Protection Council, Farnham, Surrey

Berti, A.; Bravin, F. & Zanin, G. (2003). Application of Decision-Support Software for Postemergence Weed Control. *Weed Science*, Vol. 51, No. 4, (Jul. - Aug. 2003) pp. 618-627, ISSN 0043-1745

Boller, E.F.; Avilla, J.; Joerg, E.; Malavolta, C.; Wijnands, F.G. & Esbjerg, P. (2004). Guidelines for Integrated Production - Principles and Technical Guidelines. 3rd edition. *IOBC/wprs Bulletin*, Vol. 27, No. 2 (3rd edition), 49 pp, ISBN 92-9067-163-5

Bouma, E. (2008). *Weather and crop protection*, Roodbont Publishers, ISBN 978-90-8740-002-6, Zutphen, The Netherlands

Bugiani, R.; Cavanni, P. & Ponti, I. (1993). An advisory service for the occurrence of *Phytophthora infestans* on tomato in Emilia-Romagna Region. *Bulletin OEPP/EPPO*, Vol. 23, No. 4, (December 1993) pp. 607-613, ISSN 0250-8052

Campbell, C.L. & Madden, L.V. (1990). *Introduction to Plant Disease Epidemiology*, Wiley, ISBN 0-471-83236-7, New York

Clemen, R.T. (1990). *Making Hard Decisions. An Introduction to Decision Analysis*, PWS-Kent Publishing Co., ISBN 0534260349, Boston, MA

De Vallavieille-Pope, C.; Giosuè, S.; Munk, L.; Newton, A.C.; Niks, R.E.; Østergårdf, H.; Pons-Kühnemanng, J.; Rossi, V. & Sache, I. (2000). Assessment of epidemiological parameters and their use in epidemiological and forecasting models of cereal airborne diseases. *Agronomie*, Vol. 20, pp. 715-727, ISSN 0249-5627

De Wit, C.T. (1993). Philosophy and terminology. In: *On system analysis and simulation of ecological processes*, Leffelaar P.A. (ed), Kluwer Academic Publishers, Dordrecht

EISA (2001). A Common Codex for Integrated Farming. European Initiative for Sustainable Development in Agriculture, http://www.fao.org/prods/PP17501/EISA.htm

EITO (2001). European Information Technology Observatory 2001, Frankfurt European Information Technology Observatory (EITO)

ENDURE (2009). ENDURE's definition of IPM. http://www.endure-network.eu/

Geng, S.; Hess, C.E. & Auburn, J. (1990). Sustainable agricultural systems: Concepts and definition. *Journal of Agronomy and Crop Science*, Vol. 165, No. 2, (March 1990) pp. 73-85, ISSN 0931-2250

Harsh, S.B.; Loyd, J.W. & Borton, L.R. (1989). Models as an aid to decision making. *Acta Horticulturae*, Vol. 248, (September 1989) pp. 27-48, ISSN 0567-7572

Hayman, P.T. & Easdown, W.J. (2002). An ecology of a DSS: reflections on managing wheat crops in the northeastern Australian grains region with WHEATMAN. *Agricultural Systems*, Vol. 74, No. 1, (October 2002) pp. 57–77, ISSN 0308-521X

Jordan, V.W.L., & Hutcheon, J.A. (1996). Multifunctional crop rotation: the contributions and interactions for integrated crop protection and nutrient management in sustainable cropping systems. *Aspects of Applied Biology*, Vol. 47, pp. 301-308, ISSN 0265-1491

Lòpez-Bellido, L.; Lòpez-Bellido, R.J. & Loòpez-Bellido, F.J. (2006). Fertilizer Nitrogen Efficiency in Durum Wheat under Rainfed Mediterranean Conditions: Effect of Split Application. *Agronomy Journal*, Vol. 98, pp. 55-62

Madden, L.V. & Ellis, M.A. (1988). How to develop plant disease forecasters, In: *Experimental Techniques in Plant Disease Epidemiology*, Kranz J., Rotem J. (Eds), pp. 191-208, Springer-Verlag, ISBN 3-540-18128-8, New York

Magarey, R.D.; Travis, J.W.; Russo, J.M.; Seem, R.C. & Magarey, P.A. (2002). Decision Support Systems: Quenching the Thirst. *Plant Disease*, Vol. 86, No. 1, (January 2002) pp. 4-14, ISSN 0191-2917

Meriggi, P. & Bucci, V. (2007). Campagna 2008: indicazioni per la concimazione azotata del grano tenero e duro. *Agronomica*, Vol. 6, pp. 4-6

Nanni, T. & Prodi, F. (2008). Cambiamenti climatici: la situazione in Italia. *Energia*, Vol. 29, No. 1, pp. 66-71

NASS (2006). Farm computer usage and ownership in 2005. National Agricultural Statistics Service, United States Department of Agriculture, www.nass.usda.gov/nh/2006 Farm Computer Use.pdf

Parker, C.G.; Campion, S. & Kure H. (1997). Improving the uptake of decision support systems in agriculture, In: Thysen I. & Kristensen A.R. (Eds.), *Proceedings of the First European Conference for Information Technology in Agriculture*, Copenhagen, Denmark, 15-18 June 1997, pp. 129-134, Copenhagen: EFITA, The Royal Veterinary and Agricultural University

Parry, D.W.; Jenkinson, P. & McLeod, L. (1995). *Fusarium* ear blight (scab) in small grain cereals - a review. *Plant Pathology*, Vol. 44, No. 2, pp. 207-238, ISSN 0032-0862

Rabbinge, R. & de Wit, C.T. (1989). Systems, models and simulation, In: *Simulation and systems management in crop protection*, Rabbinge R., Ward S.A., van Laar H.H. (Eds.), pp. 3-15, Pudoc, Wageningen, The Netherlands

Rabboni, T. (2009). Rinnovato l'Accordo di filiera Grano duro di alta qualità. *Filiera Grano Duro News*, Vol. 10, No. 1

Reddy, V.R. & Pachepsky, Y.A. (1997). Input Optimization and Crop Management Using Decision-support System GLYCIM/GUICS, In: *Proceedings of the International Congress on Modeling and Simulation,* A. David McDonald and Michael McAleer (Eds.), Vol. 3, pp. 1143-1147

Rossi, V.; Racca, P.; Pancaldi, D. & Alberti, I. (1996). Appearance of *Puccinia recondita* f sp *tritici* on winter wheat: a simulation model. *EPPO Bulletin,* Vol. 26, No. 3-4, (September 1996) pp. 555-566, ISSN 0250-8052

Rossi, V.; Racca, P.; Giosuè, S.; Pancaldi, D. & Alberti, I. (1997). A simulation model for the development of brown rust epidemics in winter wheat. *European Journal of Plant* Pathology, Vol. 103, No. 5, (July 1997) pp. 453-465, ISSN 0929-1873

Rossi, V.; Ponti, I. & Cravedi, P. (2000). The status of warning services for plant pests in Italy. *EPPO Bulletin*, Vol. 30, No. 1, (March 2000) pp. 19-29, ISSN 0250-8052

Rossi, V. & Giosuè, S. (2003). A dynamic simulation model for powdery mildew epidemics on winter wheat. *EPPO Bulletin*, Vol. 33, No. 3, (December 2003) pp. 389-396, ISSN 0250-8052

Rossi, V.; Giosuè, S. & Delogu, G. (2003a). A model estimating risk for Fusarium mycotoxins in wheat kernels. *Aspects of Applied Biology*, Vol. 68, pp. 229–234, ISSN 0265-1491

Rossi, V.; Giosuè, S.; Pattori, E.; Spanna, F. & Del Vecchio, A. (2003b). A model estimating the risk of Fusarium head blight on wheat. *EPPO Bulletin*, Vol. 33, No. 3, (December 2003) pp. 421-425, ISSN 0250-8052

Rossi, V.; Giosuè, S.; Terzi, V. & Scudellari, D. (2007). A decision support system for Fusarium head blight on small grain cereals. *EPPO Bulletin*, Vol.37, No. 2, (August 2007) pp. 359–367, ISSN 0250-8052

Rossing, W.H.A. & Leeuwis, C. (1999). Quality of modelling for Integrated Crop Management: Introduction to the workshop, *Proceedings of the 5th International Symposium on Computer Modelling in Fruit Research and Orchard Management*, Wageningen, The Netherlands, 28-31 July 1998, *IOBC/WPRS Bulletin*, Vol. 22, No. 6, *Acta Horticulturae*, pp. 147-150

Sonka, S.T.; Bauer, M.E. & Cherry, E.T. (1997). *Precision Agriculture in the 21st Century: Geospatial and Information Technologies in Crop Management*, National Academy Press, Washington, D.C.

Spink, J.H. & Blake, J.J. (2004). Can seed rate decisions be improved by improved prediction of establishment? HGCA conference 2004: Managing soil and roots for profitable production. 10.1 - 10.14

Toderi, G. & D'Antuono, L.F. (2000). Frumento. In: *Coltivazioni erbacee - Cereali e proteaginose,* Baldoni R. & Giardini L. (Eds.), pp. 33-108, Patron Editore, Bologna

UNIPI (2008). Andamento del settore delle paste alimentari. Unione Industriali Pastai Italiani, http://www.unipi-pasta.it/dati/andam.htm

Wainwright, J. & Mulligan, M. (2004). *Environmental modelling Finding simplicity in complexity*, John Wiley & Sons Ltd, ISBN 0-1-49618-9, Chichester

Whaley, J.M.; Sparkes, D.L.; Foulkes, M.J.; Spink, J.H.; Semere, T. & Scott, R.K. (2000). The physiological response of winter wheat to reductions in plant density. *Annals of Applied Biology*, Vol. 137, No. 2, (1 October 2000) pp.165-177, ISSN 0003-4746

2

Development of an Open Source GIS Based Decision Support System for Locating Wind Farms in Wallonia (Southern Belgium)

Philippe Lejeune[1], Thibaut Gheysen[2],
Quentin Ducenne[2] and Jacques Rondeux[1]
[1]Unit of Forest and Nature Management, Gembloux Agricultural University
[2]Global Forest Care
Belgium

1. Introduction

Energy policy is central to any country development. It covers not only economic but also social and environmental facets. Choices that have to be made in the scope of energy policy context require appropriate analytical tools and involve participatory processes (Stagl, 2006). Wind energy appears to be one of the most promising renewable resources with a total installed capacity of 120.8 GW at the end of 2008 (GWEC, 2008).

As a signatory of the Kyoto Protocol, Belgium is committed to reducing its GHG emissions by 7.5% between 1990 and 2010. The promotion of "renewable energy sources" is one of the measures for achieving such an objective, especially through the development of wind farms. Walloon authorities, in Southern Belgium, plan to produce 2,250 GWh with onshore wind turbines on the horizon 2020 (Econotec, 2009). This will represent 7.5 % of the region electricity consumption.

However, the development of this so-called "clean" energy has become an increasing source of conflicts. Most opponents complain about the negative visual impacts on landscapes (Gamboa & Munda, 2007; Rodman & Meentemeyer, 2006). Indeed, turbine blades can reach heights of up to 180 m above ground level and can be seen from distance over 20 km. Moreover, this kind of artificial structures is likely to cause significant noise nuisance, electromagnetic interference, disturbance of local wildlife, and others (Sparkes & Kidner, 1996).

The decision-making process regarding the location of wind energy plants is typically multi-faceted. Criteria related to economic, technical, environmental and social factors have to be combined in an appropriate manner (Cavallaro & Ciraolo, 2005). As often suggested, a participatory process involving stakeholders with a more or less important say is central to this decision-making scope (Rauschmayer & Wittmer, 2006). According to recent literature review, multi-criteria decision analysis (MCDA) techniques, and more specifically spatial multi-criteria decision analysis or SMCDA (Zucca et al., 2008), are most appropriate to help decision makers in such a context.

This study was ordered by Walloon authorities who are involved with the appraisal of numerous wind farm projects initiated by private investors. It is two-fold:

- it aims at mapping constraints relevant to wind farm project appraisal at regional level, and
- it aims at developing an approach meant to identify the most promising sites for wind power production in Wallonia.

In order to reach both objectives, an SDSS has been designed and developed. The methodology that has been adopted as well as some results obtained with this regional decision-making support tool are presented in this paper.

2. Study area

Wallonia is a relatively small region in the southern part of Belgium (figure 1), with an area of about 17.000 km² and a population of approximately 3,500,000 inhabitants; its northern part is densely populated. Under these conditions, any coherent approach to managing wind farm development policy must be supported by a system that can identify and map the potential constraints and suitability, since investments in these projects are mainly driven by individual private operators. These projects are numerous owing to their potential profitability.

Fig. 1. Wallonia is the southern region of Belgium.

3. Methodology

3.1 General methodology

The main steps relevant to the creation of an SMCDA are outlined hereafter.

- *Identification of Alternatives*

In the context of location of new wind farms, alternatives are defined as the different sites within the study area where wind energy can be developed.

- *Identification and Definition of Criteria*

The identification of criteria implies a systematic analysis of factors that may impact on the wind farms installation (Joerin et al., 2001). This task can be achieved through questionnaires (Baban & Parry, 2001), workshops organized with stakeholders (Stagl, 2006), or based on some expert knowledge or a combination of those (Rodman & Meetemeyer, 2006; Hansen, 2005).

Criteria can be divided in two broad categories (Eastman et al., 1993): constraints and factors. Constraints are generally expressed on a Boolean scale (true/false) and used to limit the next step of the analysis to some part of the study area where constraints are not met (Hansen, 2005). Factors give a continuous measurement of suitability related to certain aspects of the decision-making process. For aggregation purpose, those suitability factors are converted into suitability indexes and subsequently standardized on a continuous [0,1] scale through the use of membership functions (Zadeh, 1965; Chang et al., 2008).

- *Aggregation of Criteria*

Considering the aggregation of criteria, MSCDA can be divided in two groups, i.e. complete versus partial aggregation process. The Weighted Linear Combination method (WLC) is based on the concept of weighted average. It is a very popular method among complete aggregation techniques (Kangas et al., 2008). Methods using partial aggregation processes are called outranking methods among which ELECTRE (Roy, 1991) and PROMETHEE are widely known (Brans et al., 1986).

3.2 Specific methodology

Methodological choices made to develop our SDSS are presented below. They are summarized in the flowchart of the figure 2.

3.2.1 Criteria identification and definition

- *Constraint Criteria*

This main focus of the study is on identifying and defining constraint criteria. They are categorized as either environmental criteria or landscape criteria. Environmental criteria are mainly based on the regional government framework (Ministry for the Walloon Region, 2002), which includes a number of good practices pertaining to wind farm set up. Landscape criteria were defined by a team of researchers who are currently developing a landscape map of the Walloon Region (Feltz et al. 2003). The rationale behind the determination of criteria is given in Feltz et al. (2004). All the criteria were validated in meetings attended by the SDSS designers and the regional planning experts in charge of evaluating wind farm projects.

Twenty-five environmental criteria and fifteen landscape criteria were eventually selected. These 40 criteria are listed in Appendix 1. As explained below, the method proposed in this paper is not constrained by this list of specific criteria, i.e. the method can be easily adapted to different sets of criteria.

- *Suitability Criteria (factors)*

The system component devoted to suitability factors is adaptive and can be run without predefined criteria. All the functionalities have been included in order to create and manage a set of suitability criteria with a high degree of flexibility. Two criteria, the distance between wind farms and high voltage power lines and the distance between wind farms and housing areas have been used to exemplify how flexible the system is.

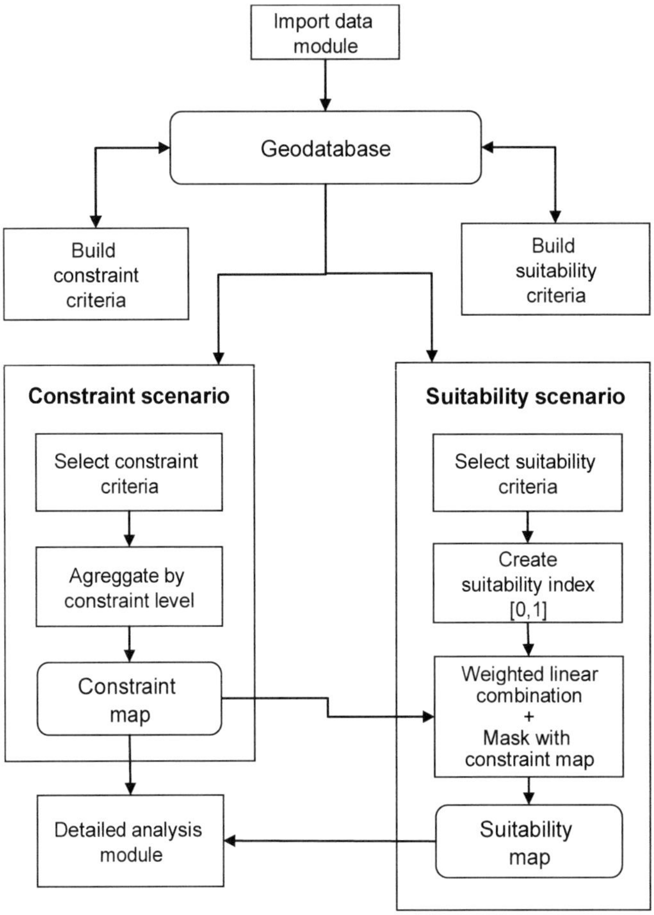

Fig. 2. Structured approach used in the decision-making aid system.

3.2.2 Translation of criteria into map format

- *Constraint Criteria*

The constraint criteria are converted into map format by using one of the following geoprocessing operations:

- The constraint zone is created by copying into a new layer the surface features in relation to the specific constraint identified beforehand;
- The constraint zone corresponds to a buffer zone drawn around the features in relation to which the constraint is identified. The use of this second representative mode reflects the fact that the nuisance or risk linked to any given constraint is present in the proximity of the feature and decreases as the feature's distance from the wind turbine increases.

Buffer zone distances are determined according to the likely impacts of the corresponding hazards and nuisances. Certain distances were based on objective technical considerations (e.g. distance from a railway track in relation to maximum height of turbine blades). Other distances were determined based on an educated guess, e.g. visual impact addressed by certain landscape criteria. In particular, the tools described below can be used to test the sensitivity of the final constraints map to some ranges of distances determining buffer zones addressed by certain criteria.

Basic thematic maps used to establish criteria are retrieved as vector layers, whereas layers including constraint criteria were produced in raster mode. This choice was governed by the large number of criteria used in producing the composite map.

Three constraint levels were identified, with each constraint criterion being linked to one of following levels:

- *Exclusion*: the set up of wind turbines should be prohibited;
- *Highly sensitive:* although wind turbines set up is theoretically prohibited, a derogation may be granted as long as an impact appraisal brings convincing evidences that the constraint does not exist at the specific location proposed for the wind turbine set up;
- Sensitive: authorization for building a wind turbine is conditional upon a detailed impact appraisal of the specific constraint.

- *Suitability Criteria*

The creation of factor maps showing suitability indexes can be based on two different approaches (figure 3): (i) a raster layer is built by computing the Euclidian distance from the features described in a vector layer, and the membership function is applied to the distance stored in each grid cells; (ii) the membership function is applied to a quantitative attribute associated to a polygon vector layer, and the this vector layer is then converted into a raster layer using the value of the newly created attribute. The membership functions are linear and defined by four control points a, b, c, d (figure 4).

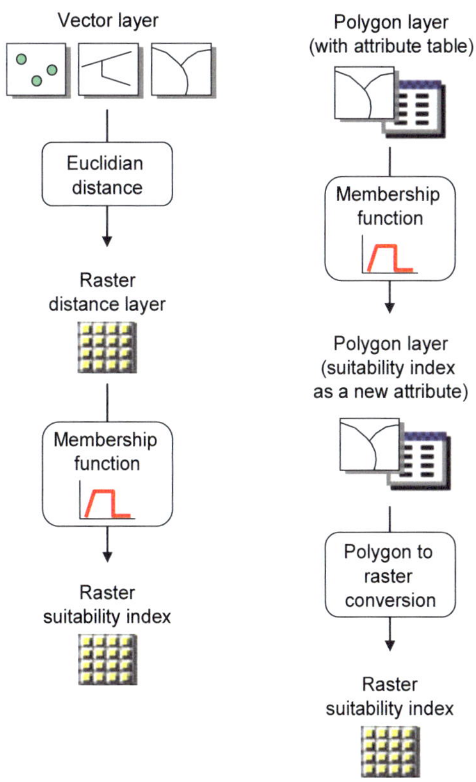

Fig. 3. Description of two approaches used to build suitability index maps.

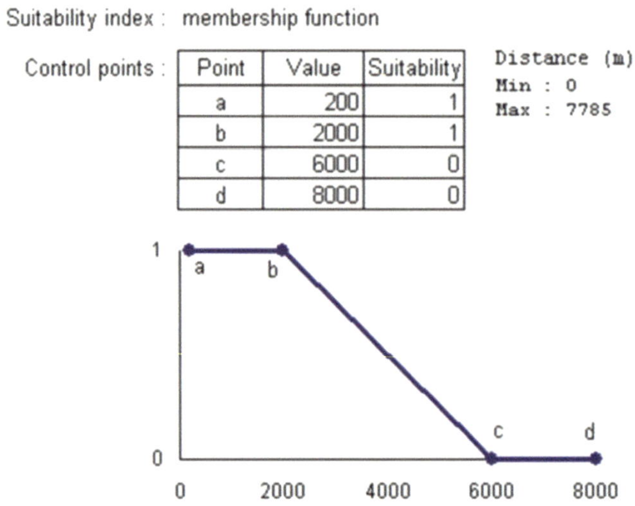

Fig. 4. Membership function used to convert a suitability criterion (in this example, the distance to the nearest high voltage power line is given in meters) into a suitability index.

3.2.3 Criteria aggregation

- *Constraint Criteria*

Composite constraint maps are produced in two stages. The first stage involves aggregating criteria by level of constraint, while the second stage involves applying the highest level of constraint to each pixel of the general map. The database also contains intermediate maps which show - for each pixel - the number of criteria per level of constraint, or the clustered pixel area for a given level of constraint.

On the one hand, the Boolean cluster model used in this study offers a low level of flexibility (Hansen, 2005; Hossain et al., 2003). On the other hand, this weakness is balanced by the existence of three levels of constraint. Moreover, an analysis module has been added to draw up a diagnosis for each wind turbine in a wind farm project in relation to all the constraint criteria (see next section).

- *Suitability Criteria*

The aggregation of suitability indexes uses weighted linear combination. In addition, an option is given to mask the suitability map using the exclusion criteria of a constraint scenario (eq 1).

$$S_k = \left(\sum_{j=1}^{n} w_j x_{j,k} \right) . \prod_{i=1}^{m} c_{i,k} \qquad (1)$$

where:

S_k : suitability index for pixel k,

n : number of suitability criteria,

m : number of constraint criteria,

w_j : weight for the j suitability criteria,

$x_{j,k}$: value of the suitability index j in the pixel k,

$c_{i,k}$: value (0-1) of the constraint criteria i (with exclusion level) in the pixel k.

3.3 SDSS development

Once the preliminary constraint map production tests had been finalised and discussed with the regional planning authority, it became clear that the management of such a large number of constraint criteria had to be based on specific GIS modelling tool if it was to be used and evolve efficiently. For instance, this tool had to be used to test the sensitivity of the results in relation to certain criteria, the definition of which was partly subjective. Indeed, such criteria are likely to be adjusted in the near future. This first phase of constraint definition was originally subject to an optional review of and an analysis on areas suitable for wind farms set up.

The tool concept lies on four pillars:

- A geodatabase where the bulk of cartographic data is stored and managed, including input layers, transformed data and output data, i.e. results;
- A relational database used to retrieve criteria features, constraints regarding carrying capacity as well as scenario parameters connecting criteria;
- A set of computing modules running data management and processing;
- A user-friendly interface.

The system functions on the basis of scenarios. A scenario is defined as a specific set of constraint criteria and/or suitability criteria over a given area used as a mask. Criteria are defined on the basis of a data source, i.e. input layer and a series of parameters, e.g. constraint levels, buffer distance, membership function, etc. It conveniently allows sensitivity analyses, i.e. assessing how results respond to a change in value of a specific criterion while other criteria remain unchanged.

In order to ease its access by various stakeholders involved in the decision-making process, the tool has been developed using an open source GIS platform. The software GRASS (Neteler & Mitasova, 2008) has been retained. GRASS features a solid library of management functionalities including spatial data analyses (Ramsey, 2007; Dunsford & Ames, 2008). Another open-source software, namely QGIS, has been used as the companion tool of GRASS, more particularly for its cartographic data display capability (Sherman, 2008).

Most often, original spatial data are available in ESRI shapefile format. A specific module enables those data to be imported as GRASS formatted data. Similarly, a data export module enables other GIS software to access resulting maps / output layers.

The relational database is retrieved as a Microsoft Access file. It is used to store criteria definitions, including the values of the related parameters, together with the main quantified results linked to the resulting composite maps produced, e.g. areas related to each constraint level, etc. Figure 5 illustrates the simplified structure of the geodatabase as well as its links with the relational database.

The various geoprocessing steps used to create criteria grids as well as the aggregation of these grids to produce some composite maps were based on a collection of Grass modules. The interface used to manage all those functionalities has been developed in VBA language and built up inside an Excel workbook (figure 6).

The software application is also featured with a module that allows a comprehensive diagnosis of either a current or a prospective wind turbine project regarding a constraint or suitability scenario. This diagnosis results in a map where a point layer with the accurate location of wind turbines overlay the composite map related to the scenario envisaged. This map also relates to a table where all criteria used in the specific scenario are characterized in regard of each single turbine. As far as constraint criteria are concerned, the distance to the nearest constraining feature is also is approximated.

4. Results

A map summarizing all possible constraints relevant to wind farm set up in Wallonia has been drawn taking into account 40 criteria categorised into three constraint levels.
As evidenced by a test made with a machine powered by a single core processor (Pentium 4-Prescott 3.0 GHz), it takes 63 minutes to run a scenario involving all the 40 criteria are. This time corresponds to the following operations: creation of criteria grids, aggregation of composite grids, calculation of results, i.e. areas and retrieving the results into the relational database.
The creation of a diagnosis report for a specific site with 10 wind turbines requires a computing time of about 9 minutes. Figure 7 presents the composite map based on the criteria selected by the group of experts empowered by the regional authority for supervising the study. Constraint-free areas represent 4.94% of the region, i.e. 836 km².
Figure 8 gives an example of a sensitivity analysis on the criterion addressing the distance between turbines and housing areas. It is noteworthy that this buffer distance is used as a noise nuisance criterion and is assigned an "exclusion" constraint level. A 350 m-distance was taken into account in the scenario presented in figure 7. Excluded areas, i.e. within a 350 m-distance from housing areas, increase from 53.9%, i.e.9,111 km² to 85.0%, i.e. 14,375 km² when the buffer to housing areas increased from 350 m to 1,000 m. As a distance of 1,000 m is used, the total constraint-free area falls below 2.8% of the total land area, i.e. 463 km².

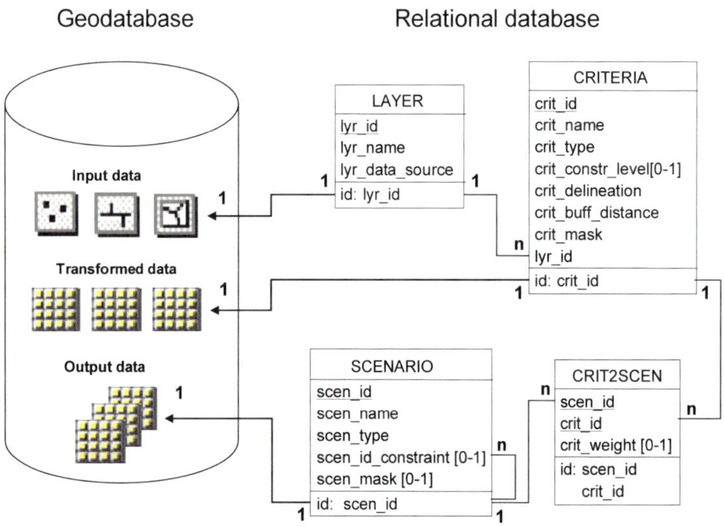

Fig. 5. Descriptive scheme of the relational database and its connection with the geodatabase. Input data are vector layers whereas transformed and output data are stored as raster grids. One grid corresponds to each criterion while a composite grid refers to each specific scenario.

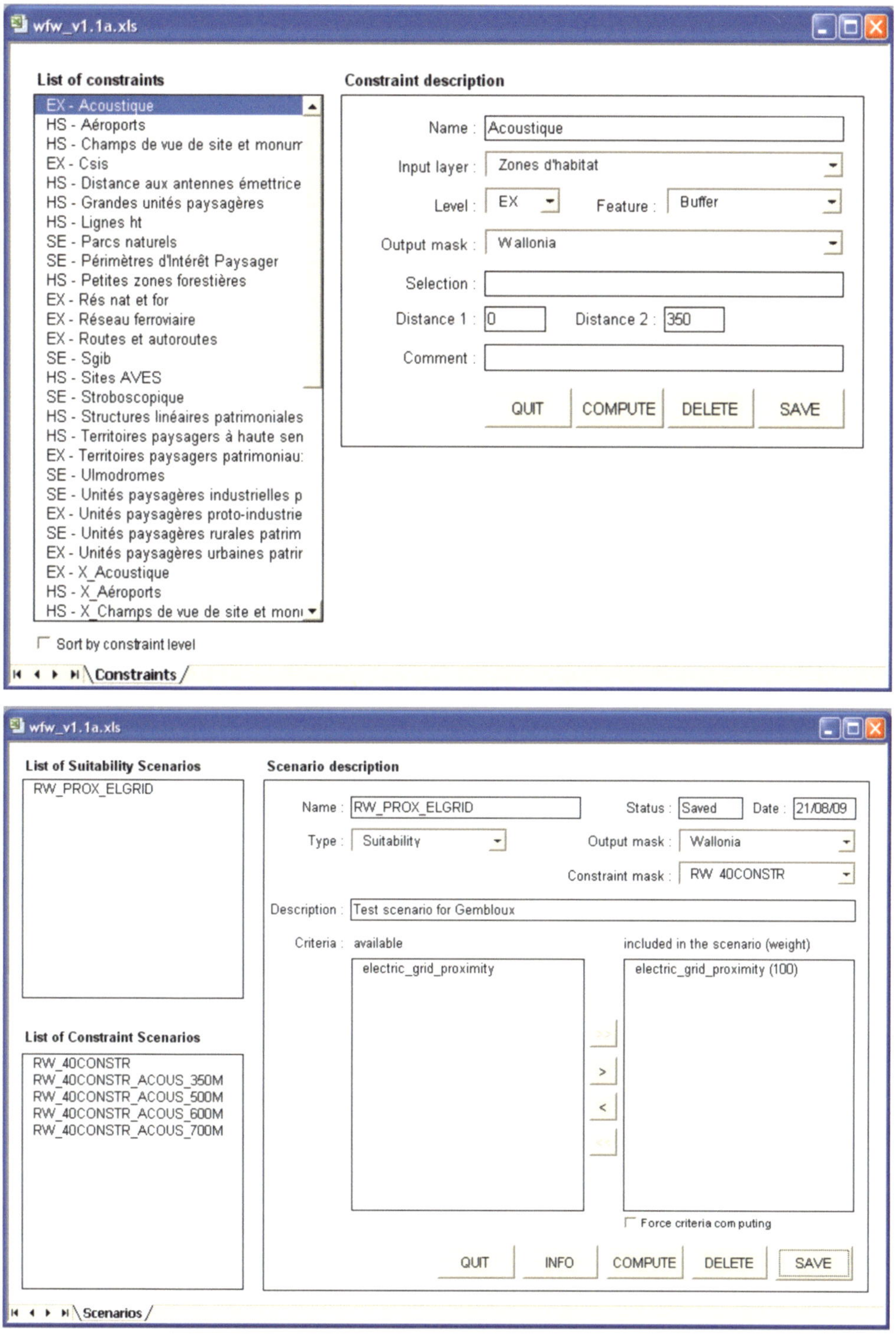

Fig. 6. Example of interfaces developed in Excel environment, which was found convenient to run the system functionalities.

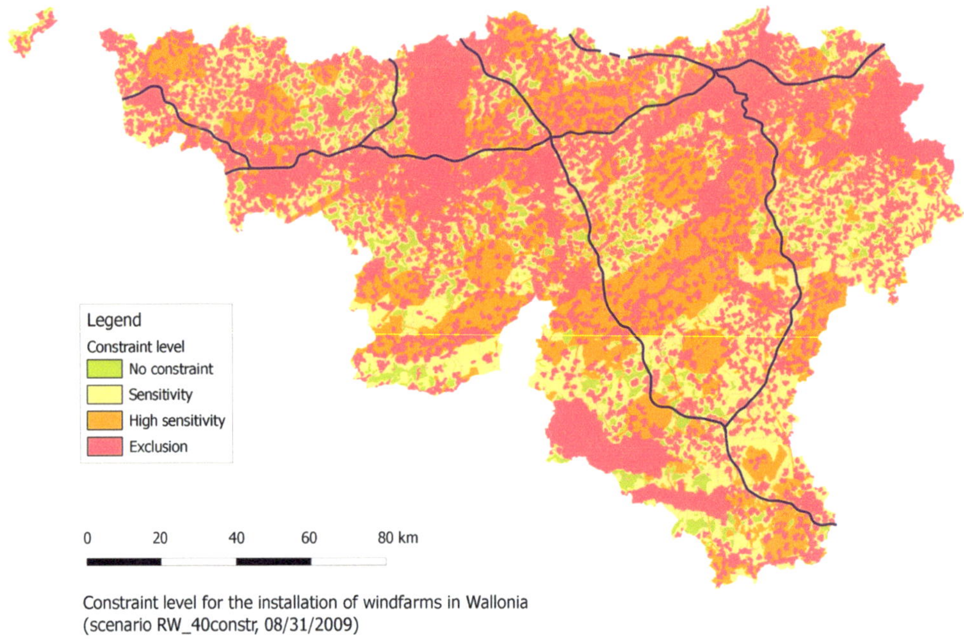

Fig. 7. Composite map for the Walloon region showing the constraint levels for the installation of wind farm projects (scenario based on the criteria definitions given in Appendix 1).

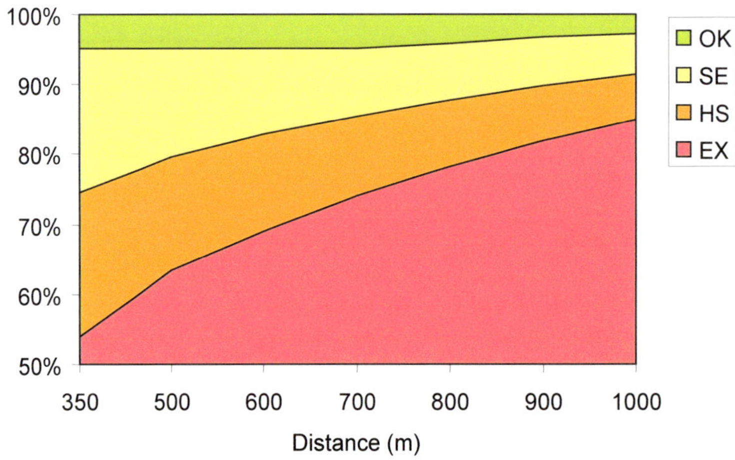

Fig. 8. Impact of an increase in the distance between turbines and housing areas in relation with the noise nuisance criterion on the area - expressed as a % of the region - devoted to each constraint level, i.e. EX: exclusion, HS: highly sensitive, SE: sensitive, OK: no constraint.

Figure 9 shows the results derived from a suitability scenario where two suitability indexes of even weights were combined. The first suitability index expresses a distance between the wind turbines and the power grid whereas the second index expresses the distance to housing areas. Excluded areas, i.e. areas conflicting with either each or both constraints, derived from the constraint map given in figure 6 have been masked.

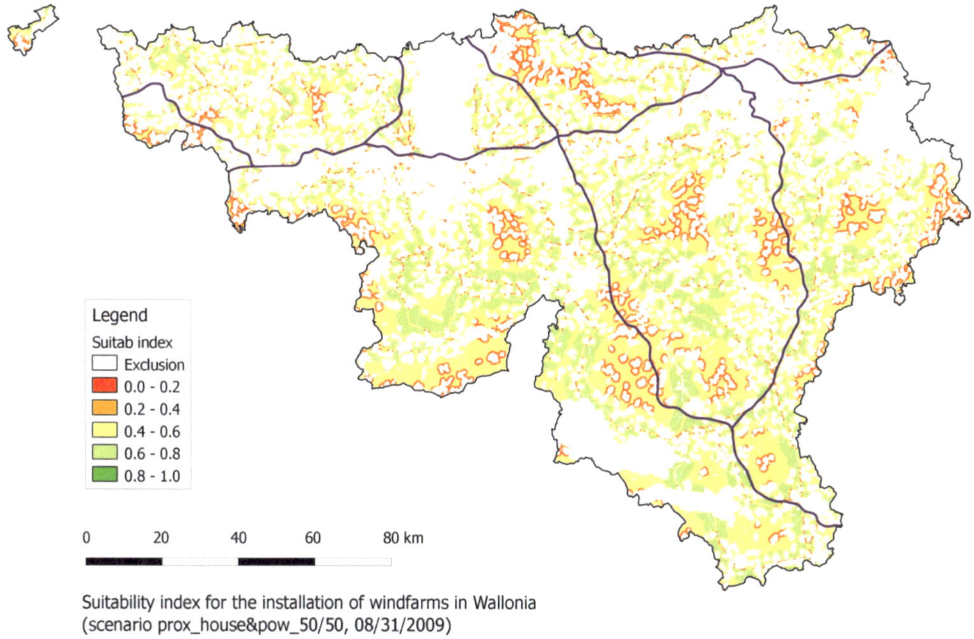

Fig. 9. Map describing a suitability scenario including a criterion relevant to the distance to high voltage power lines (weight = 50) and another criterion relevant to the distance to housing areas (weight = 50). This scenario also includes the mask corresponding to the exclusion constraint given in figure 7.

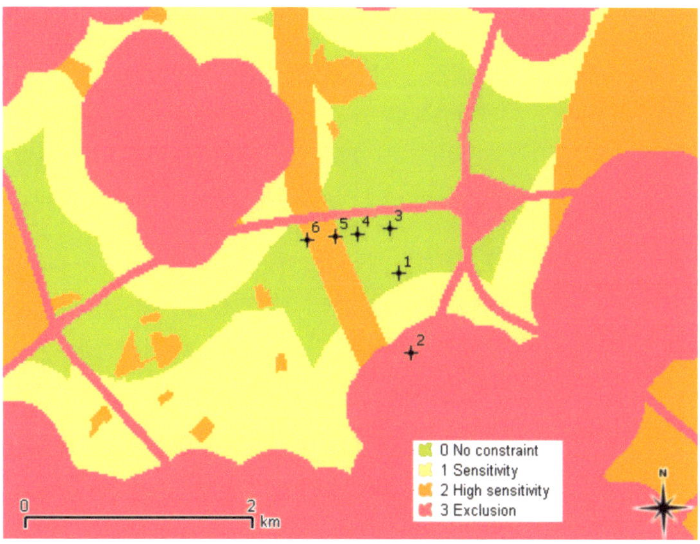

Fig. 10. Overlay of the location of a wind farm project and the composite constraints map.

Figure 10 shows the overlay of a wind farm project and the constraint map. Table 1 illustrates the section of the analysis report for this wind farm project that relates to environmental constraint criteria. This report accurately identifies which criteria is responsible for the determination of a constraint level with regard to each specific wind turbine. It also provides turbine specific information on the distances to the nearest features impacted by the various criteria.

		Turbine id											
		1		2		3		4		5		6	
Criteria		CL	DIST	CL	DIST	CL	DIST	CL	DIST	CL	DIST	CL	DIST
Environmental	SPA		> 10		> 10		> 10		> 10		> 10		> 10
	N2000		2.92		3.30		2.69		2.45		2.28		2.08
	BIRDS		6.53		6.24		6.74		6.98		7.16		7.38
	RES		> 10		> 10		> 10		> 10		> 10		> 10
	CSIS		9.48		8.94		9.79		9.64		9.55		9.43
	CZLPND		8.29		8.93		7.93		7.83		7.76		7.69
	ZHIB		> 10		> 10		> 10		> 10		> 10		> 10
	SHBV		2.01		1.74		2.25		2.48		2.45		2.22
	AIRP		> 10		> 10		> 10		> 10		> 10		> 10
	ALR		5.22		4.91		5.41		5.67		5.85		6.07
	MLR		> 10		> 10		> 10		> 10		> 10		> 10
	ACOU		0.79	**EX**	**0.00**		1.16		1.17		1.04		0.88
	FLICK		0.79		0.16		1.16		1.17		1.04		0.88
	HVL		0.49		0.32		0.57		0.29	**HS**	**0.10**	**HS**	**0.13**
	ROAD		0.47		0.20		0.15		0.17		0.18		0.18
	RAIL		4.93		4.52		5.18		4.98		4.85		4.69
	GREEN		0.61		0.89		0.48		0.76		0.96		1.20
	NAT		6.29		5.95		6.52		6.76		6.93		7.06
	PARC		3.10		2.64		3.39		3.21		3.10		2.97
	CPWPZ		6.65		6.20		6.93		7.14		7.16		6.95
	RPWPZ		2.96		3.63		2.58		2.59		2.59		2.59
	LSL		> 10		> 10		> 10		> 10		> 10		> 10
	IKR		> 10		> 10		> 10		> 10		> 10		> 10
	KR		> 10		> 10		> 10		> 10		> 10		> 10
	ANT		8.17		7.51		8.54		8.48		8.46		8.44

CL (Constraint level): EX = Exclusion, HS = Highly sensitive, SE = Sensitive
DIST: Distance (km) to the nearest constraint feature

Table 1. Extract from a detailed analysis report for a wind farm project

5. Conclusions and outlook for further development

The SDSS described in this chapter is designed to manage some cartographic layers relevant to analyzing constraints and potential of Walloon wind farm development in a straightforward and well-structured fashion.

The various computing interfaces above-mentioned allow laymen, i.e. operators who do not have expert knowledge of geoprocessing and database management systems, to generate and analyze scenarios under various constraints pertaining to areas conducive to wind farms set up either at the entire region level or in some specific study areas.

The functionalities that have been developed in the GIS open-source GRASS and QGIS environment contrast with a previous tool developed with a commercial GIS platform (Lejeune & Feltz, 2008). These functionalities have proven efficient enough and may substitute for other commercial and relatively expensive products.

Two features such as simplicity and accessibility make this project promising with a view of a greater involvement of stakeholders concerned with wind power development in Wallonia.

Bearing in mind that such analytical tools, both user-friendly and highly accessible, are today available and in line with the multi-criteria nature of the problem, it is anticipated that the next step in wind power policy planning shall imply the set up of genuine participatory process (Rauschmayer & Wittmer, 2006 ; Stagl, 2006 ; Gamboa & Munda, 2007). Many issues still need to be addressed at that level and there is much room for further improvement, e.g. who should the stakeholders' representatives be, when and how to initiate their involvement in the decision-making process, how should the decision-making process be structured, i.e. from regional planning to local project appraisal, etc. Many pending questions remain today unanswered.

6. References

Baban, S. M. J. & Parry, T. (2001). Developing and applying a GIS-assisted approach to locating wind farms in the UK. *Renewable Energy*, 24, 59-71

Brans, J.P.; Vincke, Ph. & Mareschal, B. (1986). How to select and how to rank projects: the PROMETHEE method. *European Journal of Operational Research* 24: 228–238.

Cavallaro, F. & Ciraolo, L. (2005). A multicriteria approach to evaluate wind energy plants on an Italian Island. *Energy Policy*, 33, 235-244

Chang, N.-B.; Parvathinathan, G. & Breeden, J. B. (2008). Combining GIS with fuzzy multicriteria decision-making for landfill siting in a fast-growing urban region, *Journal of Environmental Management*, 87, 139–153

Econotec Consultants. (2009). Projet d'actualisation du Pland pour la Maîtrise Durable de l'Energie (PMDE) en Wallonie à l'horizon 2020. *Service Public de Wallonie DG04 Département de l'Energie et du Bâtiment durable*. 307p.

Dunsford, H.A. & Ames D.P. (2008). An extensible, Interface-Based, Open Source GIS Paradigm: MapWindow 6.0 Developer Tools for the Microsoft Windows Platform. *Proceedings of the academic track of the 2008 free and Open Source Software for Geospatial (FOSS4G) conference*, incorporating the GISSA Conference, pp. 14-22, ISBN 978-0-620-42117-1, Cape Town, 29 September - 3 October, South Africa

Eastman, R.; Kyem, P. & Toledno, J. (1993). A procedure for multiple-objective decision making in GIS under conditions of conflicting objectives. In: J. Hents, H. Ottens and

H. Scholten (Eds). *4th European Conference on GIS (ESIG'93),* Estoril, Portugal, 10–12 November 1993, (EGIS foundation, Utrecht/Amsterdam), Vol. 1, pp. 439–447.

GWEC. (2008). *Global wind 2008 report.* Available at http://www.gwec.net/fileadmin /documents/Global_Wind_2008_Report.pdf

Feltz, C.; Droeven, E. & Kummert, M. (2003). Les territoires paysagers de Wallonie. Etude et documents, CPDT 4. *Division de l'Observatoire de l'Habitat* [D.O.H.], Namur

Feltz, C. ; Lejeune, P.; Cuvelier, M. & Schaar, C. (2004). Plan éolien wallon et Paysage. *Les Cahiers de l'Urbanisme,* 52, 15-23

Gamboa, G. & Munda, G. (2007). The problem of windfarm location: A social multi-criteria evaluation frameword. *Energy Policy,* 35, 1564-1583.

Hansen, H. (2005). GIS-based Multi-Criteria Analysis of Wind Farm Development. *Proceedings of the 10th Scandinavian Research Conference on Geographical Information Science (ScanGIS),* pp. 75-85, ISBN: 91-7323-126-6, Stockholm, Sweden, 13-15 June 2005, Department of Planning and Environment, Stockholm. Available at http://vbn.aau.dk/ws/fbspretrieve/1420302/Henning_ScanGIS_2005.pdf

Hossain, H.; Hood, A.; Sposito, V. & Cook, S. (2003). Strategic Regional Planning: mixing data, experts and GIS, *ESRI*

Joerin, F.; Thériault, M. & Musy., A. (2001). Using GIS and Outranking Multicriteria Analysis for Land-use Suitability Assessment. *International Journal of Geographical Information Sciences,* Vol. 15, No. 2, 153-174

Kangas, A.; Kangas, J. & Kurttila, M. (2008). *Decision Support for Forest Management.* Springer Science + Business Media B.V., ISBN 978-1-4020-6786-0, The Netherlands

Lejeune, P. & Feltz C. (2008). Development of a decision support system for setting up a wind energy policy across the Walloon Region (southern Belgium). *Renew Energy.* 33, pp. 2416 - 2422.

Ministry for the Walloon Region (2002). Cadre de référence pour l'implantation d'éoliennes en Région wallonne. *DGATLP,* Namur

Neteler, M. & Mitasova, H. (2008). *Open Source GIS A Grass GIS Approach.* Springer Science+Business Media, LLC, ISBN-13: 978-0-387-35767-6, New York, USA

Ramsey, P. (2007). The State of Open Source GIS. Refractions Research, 49p.

Rauschmayer, F. & Wittmer, H. (2006). Evaluating deliberative and analytical methods for the resolution of environmental conflicts. *Land Use Policy,* 23, 108-122

Rodman, L.C. & Meentemeyer R.K. (2006). A geographic analysis of wind turbine placement in Northern California. *Energy Policy,* 34, 2137-2149

Roy, B. (1991). The outranking approach and the foundations of Electre methods. *Theory and Decision* 31: 49–73.

Sherman, G. (2008). *Desktop GIS: Mapping the Planet with Open Source Tools.* The Pragmatic Programmers Ed., ISBN-13: 978-1-934356-06-7, USA

Sparkes, A. & Kindner, D. (1996). A GIS for the Environmental Impact Assessment of Wind Farms, *ESRI*

Stagl, S. (2006). Multicriteria evaluation and public participation: the case of UK energy policy. *Land Use Policy,* 23, 53-62

Zadeh, L.A. (1965). Fuzzy Sets. *Information and Control,* 8, 338–353

Zucca, A.; Sharifi, A.M. & Fabbri A. G. (2008). Application of spatial multi-criteria analysis to site selection for local park: A case study in the Bergamo Province, Italy. *Journal of Environmental Management,* 88, 752-769

Appendix 1a – list of the selected 'environmental' constraint criteria

Category	ID	Criteria	Alias	Reference features	Constraint level	Geo processing	Buffer zone (m)
Environmental	1	Special Protection Area	SPA	Polygon	EX	feature	
	2	Natura 2000 sites	N2000	Polygon	SE	feature	
	3	Site of ornithological value	BIRDS	Polygon	HS	buffer	150
	4	Nature Reserve	RES	Polygon	EX	feature	
	5	Underground cavity of scientific interest	CSIS	Point	EX	buffer	100
	6	Central zones of Local Plan for Nature Development	CZLPND	Polygon	EX	feature	
	7	zhib	ZHIB	Polygon	EX	feature	
	8	Site of high biological value	SHBV	Polygon	SE	feature	
	9	Airports	AIRP	Polygon	HS	buffer	5000
	10	Airplane landing runway	ALR	Point	HS	feature	
	11	Microlight landing runway	MLR	Point	SE	buffer	2000
	12	Acoustic effect	ACOU	Polygon	EX	buffer	350
	13	Zone of potential flicker effect	FLICK	Polygon	SE	buffer	700
	14	High voltage lines	HVL	Line	HS	buffer	150
	15	Proximity to roads	ROAD	Line	EX	buffer	40
	16	Proximity to railroad	RAIL	Line	EX	buffer	40
	17	"Green" parks	GREEN	Polygon	EX	feature	
	18	Area devoted to nature	NAT	Polygon	EX	buffer	200
	19	Parks	PARK	Polygon	EX	feature	
	20	Close protection of water producing zone	CPWPZ	Polygon	EX	feature	
	21	Remote protection of water producing zone	RPWPZ	Polygon	SE	feature	
	22	Landslide risk	LSL	Polygon	EX	feature	
	23	Area with important karstic risks	IKR	Polygon	EX	feature	
	24	Area with karstic risks	KR	Polygon	SE	feature	
	25	Risk of interference with radio antenna	ANT	Polygon	HS	buffer	600

Appendix 1b – list of the selected 'landscape' constraint criteria

Category	ID	Criteria	Alias	Reference features	Constraint level	Geo processing	Buffer zone (m)
Landscape	26	Heritage landscapes	PL	Polygon	EX	feature	
	27	Highly sensitive landscapes & territories	HSLT	Polygon	HS	feature	
	28	Small wood lots	SWL	Polygon	HS	feature	
	29	Hilly forests	HF	Polygon	HS	feature	
	30	Forest with recreational value	FRV	Polygon	HS	feature	
	31	Nature parks	NP	Polygon	SE	feature	
	32	Large common rural landscapes	LCRL	Polygon	HS	feature	
	33	Proto-industrial landscape units	PILU	Polygon	EX	feature	
	34	Industrial landscape units with heritage value	ILPV	Point	SE	buffer	2000
	35	Urban landscape units with heritage value	ULPV	Point	EX	feature	
	36	Rural landscape units with heritage value	RLPV	Polygon	SE	buffer	2000
	37	Linear features with heritage value	LFPV	Line	HS	buffer	1250
	38	Viewshed of classified monuments	VCM	Polygon	HS	feature	
	39	Zones of landscape value	ZLV	Polygon	SE	feature	
	40	Perimeter of landscape value	PLV	Polygon	SE	feature	

3

Forecasting Rubber Production using Intelligent Time Series Analysis to Support Decision Makers

Panida Subsorn, Dr. Jitian Xiao and Dr. Judy Clayden
Edith Cowan University
Australia

1. Introduction

Decision support system (DSS) have become a significant factor for many organisations as assistive tools for managers to deal with problems (Nakmuang, 2004). Although DSS are used globally in the agricultural, public, government and especially in business sectors, they have not been effectively utilised within the public agricultural rubber industry in Thailand. They assist decision makers to complete decision procedure activities, obtain data, documents, knowledge or models, increase the number of alternatives examined, achieve better understanding of the business, provide fast responses to unexpected situations, offer capability to carry out *ad hoc* analysis, obtain new insights and learning, facilitate improved communication, achieve cost savings, achieve better decisions, facilitate more effective teamwork, achieve time savings and better use of data resources (Keen, 1981; Olson & Courtney, 1992; Power, 2004; Royal Thai Army, 2007). DSS also present graphical information and may be integrated with expert systems (ES) and artificial intelligence (AI) and support both individual and group decision makers (Power, 2004, 2007). Intelligent DSS demonstrate a range of capabilities and have the capacity to deal with complex data or problems. Hence, the evolution of intelligent DSS has demonstrated increasing functionality, including data mining, geographical information systems (GIS), business intelligence (BI), group DSS (GDSS) and hybrid DSS (Intelligent Science Research Group, 2002; Power, 2007). These functionalities are applied in intelligent DSS in a wide range of sectors, especially tourism, agriculture, industry and commerce (Intelligent Science Research Group, 2002; Power, 2007).

Forecasting, as a significant capability of decision support systems, provides useful information and supports organizations by facilitating enhanced and desired performance or management in decision making. Moreover, forecasting is critical within industry because it enables prediction of future events and conditions by statistically analyzing and using data or information from the past (Markland & Sweigart, 1987; Tomita, 2007). Results from forecasting directly affect organizations in the areas of management, planning, production, sales and prices (Geurts, Lawrence, & Guerard, 1994; Markland & Sweigart, 1987; Olson & Courtney, 1992). Therefore forecasting requires a trustworthy tool to enhance accuracy before management decisions may be made.

This chapter examines the use of non-neural network training and neural network training in rubber production forecasting to create a feasible forecasting model for the Thai rubber industry. This chapter is organized as follows: the Thai rubber industry situation is described in Section 2. Section 3 presents the methods which will be used in this study. An experiment is developed by employing non-neural network training and neural network training Techniques in Section 4. Section 5 concludes the paper.

2. The public agricultural rubber industry in Thailand

The agricultural sector has been selected as it is a significant growth sector in Thailand; forecasting may assist in advancing this sector and thereby contribute to Thailand's economic development. Thailand is the world's largest rubber exporter to Japan, China and the United States of America with a 39% share of the world market (Office of Industrial Economics & Economic Research and Training Center, 1998; Rubber Research Institute of Thailand, 2007a; Subsorn, 2008). Thailand exports rubber sheet, rubber block, rubber latex and other primary rubber products, whereas only a small fraction of rubber production is reserved for manufacturing within Thailand (Office of Industrial Economics & Economic Research and Training Center, 1998; Rubber Research Institute of Thailand, 2007a; Subsorn, 2008).

Production in the public agricultural rubber industry in Thailand is increasing in order to satisfy market demand (Department of Agriculture, 2004). There are several factors related to production, namely seasonal changes, government policy and fluctuations in the global market (Tanguthai & Silpanuruk, 1995). Annual seasonal shifts directly affect rubber production nationally. Between February and September, rubber production decreases because of low levels of rubber latex during the rainy season. However, rubber production increases between October and January because of suitable climatic conditions such as cool climate and no rain (Tanguthai & Silpanuruk, 1995).

Government policy is another factor influencing rubber production in Thailand; this relates to supporting agriculturists to produce rubber in order to respond to market demand. The *National Economic and Social Development Plan (Issue 10)* for Thailand was developed to support agriculturists to respond to market demand, reduce costs and risks in production, gain more income and improve agricultural products and resource management (Office of the National Economic and Social Development Board, 2007).

Economic fluctuations directly relate to the global demand for rubber, the market trends and foreign currency exchange (Rubber Research Institute of Thailand, 2007b; Tanguthai & Silpanuruk, 1995). The global demand for rubber is increasing every year, which is the most important factor related to rubber production (Rubber Research Institute of Thailand, 2007b). This global market trend influences forward selling which is important for the marketing and sales of rubber in Thailand (Rubber Research Institute of Thailand, 2007b; Tanguthai & Silpanuruk, 1995). Hence, it is necessary to forecast rubber production in order to know the marketing future so that the industry can respond to the increased demand effectively. Foreign currency exchange directly affects rubber sales (Tanguthai & Silpanuruk, 1995). It influences profit and loss in rubber sales because products in the global market are traded in US dollars. Hence, fluctuations in the US dollar value will also directly affect the Thai Baht value which may positively or negatively affect the Thai economy.

In recent years, little attention has been paid to improving production forecasting models or enhancing accuracy in forecasts even though several studies in the Thai rubber industry have focused on management, control and forecasting and have illustrated the need for planned development (Leechawengwong, Prathummintra, & Thamsiri, 2002; Subsorn, 2008). However, a focus on improving forecasting is exceptional as this sector has been using the similar models for a long period of time. The existing models apply traditional statistical techniques and may not conduct sufficient tests of validity and reliability of forecasting results. Applying a modern forecasting technique may enhance forecasting results. Thus this chapter attempts to derive a feasible forecasting model for national rubber production in the Thai rubber industry by applying non-neural network training and neural network training techniques. The survival of the current models has created an excellent environment for this study, which aims to create a feasible forecasting model which may provide beneficial additional information for the Thai rubber industry. Results of this chapter may support policy makers in forecasting through its potential to enhance the accuracy of rubber production trends in a competitive environment and reduce losses and risks in development and policy plans.

3. Method

Many existing forecasting methods are differentiated by objectives and/or problems within organizations. Basically, they focus on improvement to gain better performance or to deal with current and future problems. However, some forecasting techniques may not manage particular situations or problems efficiently as they may not be entirely accurate. Hence, this study attempts to gain a feasible forecasting model based on a comparative method and to select a forecasting model which supplies less forecasting errors for this selected sector. In order to provide a better understanding, the following subsections provide a description of non-neural network and neural network Techniques, three main components and data analysis procedures for a feasible new forecasting model for the public agricultural rubber industry in Thailand.

3.1 Non-neural network training and neural network training techniques

i. Non-neural network training technique

Time series analysis is often applied in prediction for the component analysis of historical data sets to determine a forecasting model used to predict the future (Sangpong & Chaveesuk, 2007). There are several well-known time series forecasting techniques such as simple moving average (SMA), weight moving average (WMA), exponential smoothing (ES), seasonal autoregressive integrated moving average (SARIMA). This study deployed ES and SARIMA techniques for rubber production forecasting. The ES technique has the capability and efficiency to create trend and seasonal analysis for time series forecasting. The formula of the ES technique, particularly the simple seasonal exponential smoothing is as shown below.

$$\begin{aligned} L(t) &= \alpha(Y(t) - S(t-s)) + (1-\alpha)L(t-1) \\ S(t) &= \delta(Y(t)) + (1-\delta)S(t-s) \\ \hat{Y}_t(k) &= L(t) + S(t+k-s) \end{aligned} \tag{1}$$

where $\hat{Y}_t(k)$ is the model-estimated k-step ahead forecasting at time t for series Y, t is the trend, S is the seasonal length, α is the level smoothing weight and δ is the season smoothing weight (Statistical Package for the Social Sciences (SPSS), 2009c).

The SARIMA technique has the capability and efficiency to create seasonal time series forecasting based on a moving average (MA). Time series data from several consecutive periods of time are added and divided to obtain mean values to create the prediction (Sangpong & Chaveesuk, 2007). The formula of the SARIMA technique or equivalent to autoregressive integrated moving average (ARIMA) (0, 1, (1, s, +1)) (0, 1, 0) with restrictions among MA parameters is as follows:

$$\Phi(B)[\Delta y - \mu] = \Theta(B)a_t \qquad t = 1,\ldots,N \tag{2}$$

where

$$\begin{aligned} \Phi(B) &= \varphi_p(B)\Phi_P(B) \\ \Theta(B) &= \theta_q(B)\Theta_Q(B) \end{aligned} \tag{3}$$

where N is the total number of observations, $a_t(t = 1,2,\ldots,N)$ is the white noise series normally distributed with mean zero and variance σ_a^2, p is the order of the non-seasonal autoregressive part of the model, q is the order of the non-seasonal moving average part of the model, d is the order of the non-seasonal differencing, P is the order of the seasonal autoregressive part of the model, Q is the order of the seasonal moving average part of the model, s it the seasonality or period of the model, $\varphi_p(B)$ is the autoregressive (AR) polynomial of B of order p, $\theta_q(B)$ is the MA polynomial of B of order q, $\Phi_P(B)$ is the seasonal AR polynomial of BS of order P, $\Theta_Q(B)$ is the seasonal MA polynomial of BS of order Q, Δ is the differencing operator, B is the backward shift operator and μ is the optional model constant or the stationary series mean. Independent variables x_1, x_2,..., x_m may be included in the model as the formula is shown below.

$$\Phi(B)\left[\Delta\left(y_t - \sum_{i=1}^{m} c_i x_{it}\right) - \mu\right] = \Theta(B)a_t \tag{4}$$

where c_i, $i = 1,2,\ldots, m$ is the regression coefficients for the independent variables.

ii. Neural network (NN) training technique

NN is a well-known predictive technique which claims to provide more reliable results than other forecasting techniques (Sangpong & Chaveesuk, 2007; Statistical Package for the Social Sciences (SPSS), 2009a, 2009b). This technique creates the relationship between dependent and independent variables from several training data sets during the learning process. The results from this learning process are called neurons. Neurons arrange themselves in a level form and have connection lines to transfer or process data from input, hidden and output layers. Each connection line presents weights between each layer connection. Moreover, neurons adjust their weights via an activation function, which is the processing function to create the results, to calculate the desirable results (Fausett, 1994; Sangpong & Chaveesuk, 2007). The activation function deployed in this study is the sigmoid function, which is a non-linear function. Its formula is as shown below.

$$\gamma(c) = \frac{1}{1 + \exp(-c)} \tag{5}$$

Furthermore, this study employed a supervised learning technique and a feed-forward backpropagation neural network (BPN). Feed-forward BPN were considered to be suitable learning techniques for national rubber production forecasting because of their reliability and accuracy. The supervised learning technique is used to adjust weights for producing forecasting with fewer errors between an output from NN and a desirable output. A feed-forward architecture is the one way connection from input and hidden layers to output layers within the network in the model (Statistical Package for the Social Sciences (SPSS), 2009a). The input layer consists of independent variables or predictors. The hidden layer, consisting of unobservable nodes or units, presents a function to be utilized for independent variables or predictors. The output layer consists of dependent variable(s). Additionally, BPN has the capability to simulate the complicated relationship of the function correctly, which is called an universal approximator, without having knowledge previously of the function relationships (Funahashi, 1989; Hornik, Stinchcombe, & White, 1989; Sangpong & Chaveesuk, 2007).

However, overtraining of data sets may cause low efficiency of non-training data sets in the forecasting model. Thus data separation is introduced to solve this problem by dividing the same data set into two groups, namely a training data set and a test data set (Sangpong & Chaveesuk, 2007; Twomey & Smith, 1996). This study partitioned the data set at 70% for the training data set and 30 % for the testing data set.

The multilayer perceptron (MLP) was used in this study to facilitate the use of a supervised learning network and a feed-forward BPN. The MLP network is a function of one or many independent variables or predictors in the input layer which may reduce forecasting errors of one or many dependent variables in the output layer (Statistical Package for the Social Sciences (SPSS), 2009b). The MLP formulae are shown below.

Input layer: $J_0 = P$ units, $a_{0:1},\ldots, a_{0:J_0}$ with $a_{0:j} = x_j$

Hidden layer: J_i units, $a_{i:1},\ldots, a_{i:J_i}$ with $a_{i:k} = \gamma_j(c_{i:k})$ and

$$c_{i:k} = \sum_{j=0}^{J_{i-1}} w_{i:j,k} a_{i-1:j} \quad \text{where} \quad a_{i-1:0} = 1$$

Output layer: $J_\text{I} = R$ units, $a_{I:1},\ldots, a_{I:J_I}$ with $a_{I:k} = \gamma_I(c_{I:k})$ and

$$c_{I:k} = \sum_{j=0}^{J_1} w_{I:j,k} a_{i-1:j} \quad \text{where} \quad a_{i-1:0} = 1$$

Additionally, an error measurement in the forecasting model used in this study is the root mean square error (RMSE). The formula of this error measurement is shown below.

$$RMSE = \sqrt{\frac{\sum(Y(t) - \hat{Y}(t))^2}{n-k}} \tag{6}$$

where $RMSE$ is the root mean square error values of the forecasting model, Y is the original series of time (t), t is the time series, n is the number of non-missing residuals and k is the number of parameters in the model.

3.2 Components of the newly refined production forecasting model

This section presents a description of the three main components in the newly refined forecasting model for national rubber production in the public agricultural rubber industry in Thailand.

The input component consists of two main subcomponents, namely individual or group policy makers and input data for forecasting. Policy makers may retrieve or modify forecasting results via the existing database. Also, they may input new rubber data sets to create forecasts.

The processing component consists of three main subcomponents, namely time-series forecasting, artificial intelligence (AI) and error measurement. This study analyses rubber data sets into two main categories, namely non-neural network training and neural network training. Then each data set is separately processed using the Statistical Package for the Social Sciences (SPSS) to create forecasts. Lastly, forecasting errors for accuracy and reliability purposes are measured with each data set.

The output component consists of two main subcomponents, namely the forecasting results and the database. The results are produced during the processing component (above). Both forecasting data sets (non-neural network training and neural network training) are then compared to the actual corresonding data set. The forecast data is stored in the database for retrieval and modification for policy makers to make decisions.

3.3 Data analysis process

This chapter used a rubber production data set from the website of the Office of Agricultural Economics (OAE) in Thailand to examine a newly refined production forecasting model. The data set was collected on a monthly and yearly basis from the period January 2005 to December 2008. This chapter focused on national rubber production forecasting. The data analysis process involved six procedures, as shown in Fig. 1 and described below.

i. Data preparation

   Time series data from January 2005 to December 2008 was used to prepare a data set for four months, six months and one year for 2007 and 2008 forecasting. The reason for selecting forecasting for three different time periods is to enhance validity and reliability of the newly refined forecasting model.

ii. Sequence chart creation

   A sequence chart to consider national rubber production trends from January 2005 to December 2008 was plotted before the forecasts were created. This chart displayed national rubber production trends to examine a seasonality factor within the trends, so that suitable forecasting techniques were selected and utilized.

iii. Data processing

   Non-neural network training and neural network training were used with forecasting techniques provided in SPSS, namely ES and SARIMA. Analysis involved the use of these two time-series forecasting techniques for non-neural network training and neural network training.

iv. Error measurement

   Errors in the forecasts were examined while SPSS created the forecasts for non-neural network training and neural network training. Forecasting accuracy was thereby strengthened.

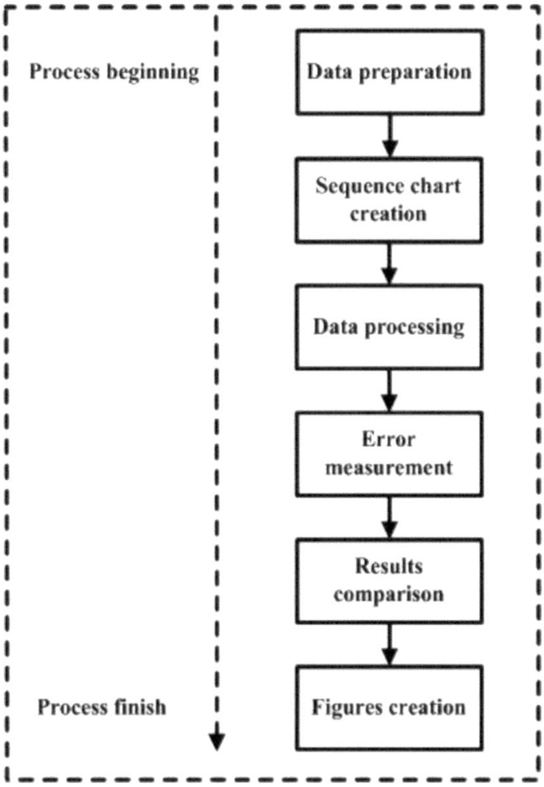

Fig. 1. Data analysis process

v. Comparison of results
Forecasting results from non-neural network training and neural network training were compared with the actual prodcution data set for national rubber production to determine the possibility of using this newly refined forecasting model for the public agricultural rubber industry in Thailand.

vi. Creation of figures
Figures were created to present forecasting results, comparisons and errors to policy makers and/or decision makers, so that they may have a better understanding or vision before planning and/or making decisions.

The following section presents experimental results, which were compared between non-neural network training and neural network training. Then, the results were classified and presented in four months, six months and one year subsets respectively.

4. Experimental results

This section presents rubber production trends and forecasting results. The trends are presented from January 2005 to December 2008 for rubber production. The forecasting results are presented for four months, six months and one year for 2007 and 2008. Fig. 2 illustrates rubber production trends from national rubber production. These show that rubber production usually decreases in the middle of the year. Rubber production increases at the end of the year. The rainy season usually occurs during June to October and the winter or mild season usually occurs during November to February. Hence, these results confirm that rubber production are related to time-series and seasonality factors.

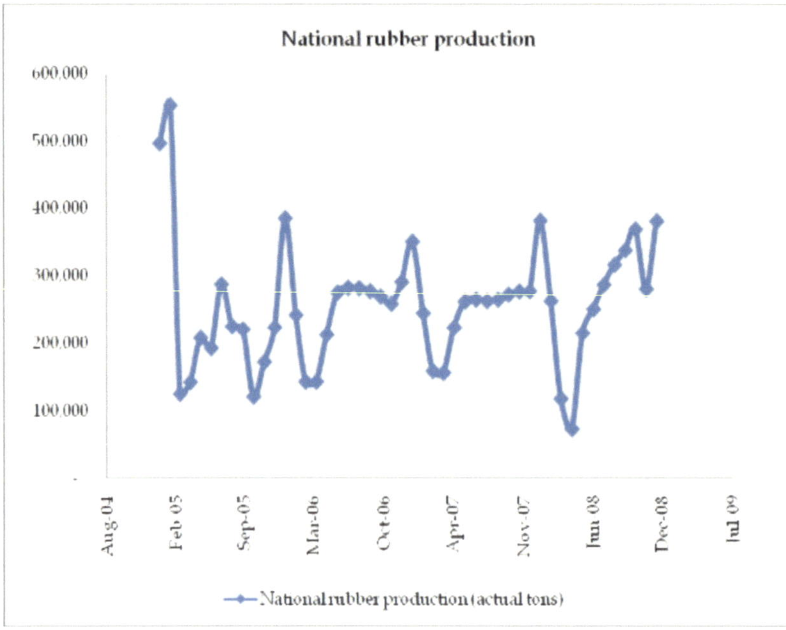

Fig. 2. National rubber production trend

Fig. 3 and Fig. 4 presents the comparison between the actual national rubber production with non-neural network training and neural network training to identify the best-fitting model in forecasting. Rubber production forecasting results were used with a hold-out sample method to deliver forecasting results validation and evaluation of forecasting accuracy. Rubber production data collected was based upon a hold-out sample method in this section.

The following subsections present forecasting results for national rubber production. They were divided into two main subsections as presented below.

4.1 National rubber production forecasts for 2007

The actual rubber production forecasts for 2007 are displayed in Fig. 3 and Tables 1-3, which compare non-neural network training and neural network training with the actual rubber production. It demonstrates that the one year prediction is more successful, for both non-neural network and neural network training techniques, than the four months and the six months predictions. The one year prediction has a root mean square error (RMSE) of 54591.4 for non-neural training and 54261.8 for neural network training. Moreover, the six months prediction is more accurate than the four months prediction. The six months prediction has a RMSE of 56657.4 for non-neural network training and 56141.8 for neural network training. The four months prediction has a RMSE of 57415.8 for non-neural network training and 56847.5 for neural network training.

Comparing the RMSE of each model, it is seen that the one year prediction provides the best-fitting forecasting model. Based on this analysis of national rubber production, this demonstrates that the use of neural network training, particularly for three different periods of time, was better than non-neural network training. Non-neural networks are used more appropriately when there is data fluctuation which may cause forecasting noise or errors. Moreover, it does not require independent variables in forecasts, unlike neural network forecasting. However, both non-neural network training and neural network training showed similar trends as displayed in the following Fig. 3.

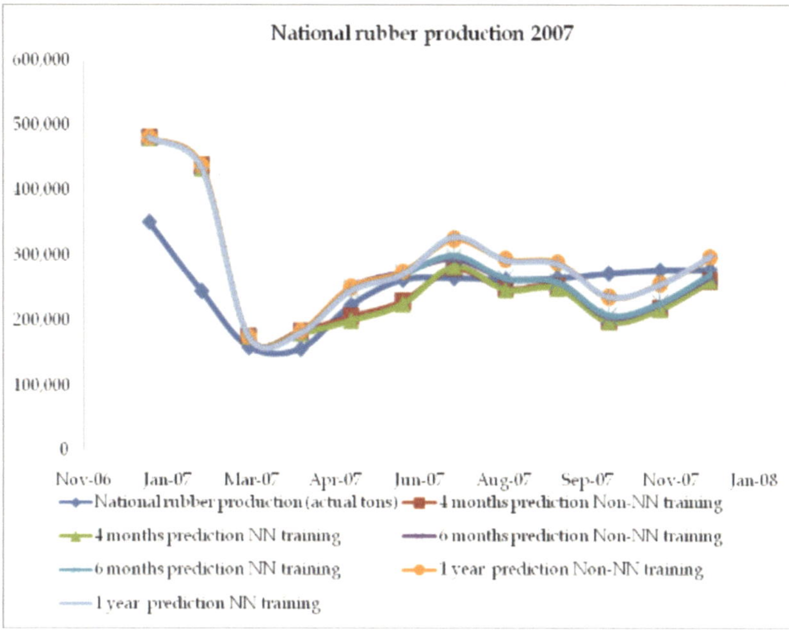

Fig. 3. National rubber production forecasts for 2007

Because it is difficult to show data clearly using graphs, actual figures have been included below in Tables 1-3. The tables include the actual production data and the corresponding predictions using non-neural network training and neural network training predictions respectively.

Date	National rubber production (actual tons)	Non-NN training prediction	NN training prediction
Jan-07	351,663	481,562	480,852
Feb-07	245,387	437,861	434,469
Mar-07	159,733	174,706	175,371
Apr-07	157,011	183,331	181,373
May-07	224,145	250,985	246,082
Jun-07	262,923	274,522	271,340
Jul-07	265,593	325,202	328,781
Aug-07	263,391	293,836	293,179
Sep-07	265,564	289,302	287,606
Oct-07	272,872	235,638	237,084
Nov-07	277,741	255,913	255,620
Dec-07	278,184	297,640	299,691

Table 1. One year national rubber prediction

Date	National rubber production (actual tons)	Non-NN training prediction	NN training prediction
Jan-07	351,663	481,562	480,852
Feb-07	245,387	437,861	434,469
Mar-07	159,733	174,706	175,371
Apr-07	157,011	183,331	181,373
May-07	224,145	250,985	246,082
Jun-07	262,923	274,522	271,340
Jul-07	265,593	295,649	300,577
Aug-07	263,391	264,282	264,975
Sep-07	265,564	259,748	259,402
Oct-07	272,872	206,085	208,880
Nov-07	277,741	226,360	227,416
Dec-07	278,184	268,088	271,488

Table 2. Six months national rubber prediction

Date	National rubber production (actual tons)	Non-NN training prediction	NN training prediction
Jan-07	351,663	481,562	480,852
Feb-07	245,387	437,861	434,469
Mar-07	159,733	174,706	175,371
Apr-07	157,011	183,331	181,373
May-07	224,145	205,852	200,660
Jun-07	262,923	229,389	225,918
Jul-07	265,593	280,069	283,359
Aug-07	263,391	248,703	247,758
Sep-07	265,564	251,902	249,828
Oct-07	272,872	198,238	199,306
Nov-07	277,741	218,513	217,842
Dec-07	278,184	260,240	261,913

Table 3. Four months national rubber prediction

4.2 National rubber production forecasts for 2008

The actual rubber production forecasts for 2007 are displayed in Fig. 4 and Tables 4-6, which compare non-neural network training and neural network training with the actual rubber production. It demonstrates that the four months prediction is more successful than the six months and the one year predictions. The four months prediction has a RMSE of 52807.5 for non-neural network training and 52020.3 for neural network training. Moreover, the six months prediction is more accurate than the one year prediction.The six months prediction has a root mean square error (RMSE) of 53031.7 for non-neural training and 52254.4 for neural network training. The one year prediction has a RMSE of 53936.8 for non-neural network training and 53398.2 for neural network training.

Comparing the RMSE of each model, it is seen that the four months prediction provides the best-fitting forecasting model. Based on this analysis of national rubber production, this demonstrates that the use of neural network training, particularly for three different periods of time, was better than non-neural network training. Non-neural networks are used more appropriately when there is data fluctuation which may cause forecasting noise or errors. Moreover, it does not require independent variables in forecasts, unlike neural network forecasting. However, both non-neural network training and neural network training showed similar trends as displayed in the following Fig. 4.

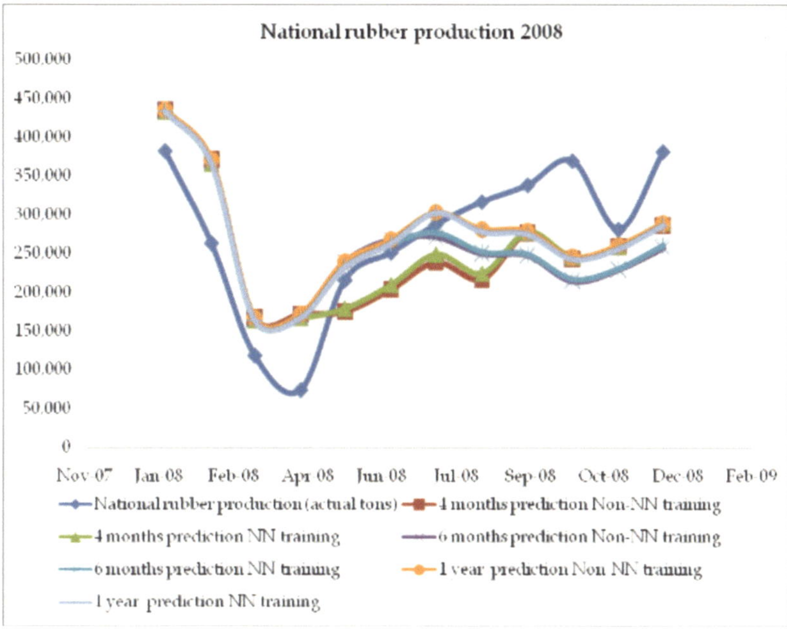

Fig. 4. National rubber production forecasts for 2008

Because it is difficult to show data clearly using graphs, actual figures have been included below in Tables 4-6.

Date	National rubber production (actual tons)	Non-NN training prediction	NN training prediction
Jan-08	382,784	436,014	433,865
Feb-08	263,678	371,455	366,969
Mar-08	118,678	167,467	164,537
Apr-08	74,203	172,310	167,664
May-08	215,961	239,791	232,806
Jun-08	251,524	268,409	263,379
Jul-08	287,558	303,085	302,535
Aug-08	317,122	281,440	278,140
Sep-08	338,903	279,142	275,063
Oct-08	369,928	245,802	243,100
Nov-08	281,325	260,942	256,651
Dec-08	381,908	288,908	286,743

Table 4. One year national rubber prediction

Date	National rubber production (actual tons)	Non-NN training prediction	NN training prediction
Jan-08	382,784	436,014	433,865
Feb-08	263,678	371,455	366,969
Mar-08	118,678	167,467	164,537
Apr-08	74,203	172,310	167,664
May-08	215,961	239,791	232,806
Jun-08	251,524	268,409	263,379
Jul-08	287,558	271,688	277,156
Aug-08	317,122	250,043	252,761
Sep-08	338,903	247,745	249,684
Oct-08	369,928	214,405	217,720
Nov-08	281,325	229,545	231,272
Dec-08	381,908	257,510	261,364

Table 5. Six months national rubber prediction

Date	National rubber production (actual tons)	Non-NN training prediction	NN training prediction
Jan-08	382,784	436,014	433,865
Feb-08	263,678	371,455	366,969
Mar-08	118,678	167,467	164,537
Apr-08	74,203	172,310	167,664
May-08	215,961	175,572	179,783
Jun-08	251,524	204,190	210,357
Jul-08	287,558	238,867	249,512
Aug-08	317,122	217,223	225,117
Sep-08	338,903	277,217	278,401
Oct-08	369,928	243,877	246,438
Nov-08	281,325	259,017	259,989
Dec-08	381,908	286,983	290,081

Table 6. Four months national rubber prediction

5. Conclusion

This chapter has investigated the best-fitting forecasting model for national rubber production forecasting for 2007 and 2008. The methods used in this study were based on non-neural network training and neural network training techniques to compare with the actual rubber production data for the best-fitting forecasting model. Hence, neural network training was presented to obtain more accurate forecasts for 2007 and 2008. To our knowledge, this is the preliminary study that brings a new perspective to policy makers in the public agricultural rubber industry in Thailand in creating forecasts with AI techniques. This proposed methodology may be considered as a successful decision support tool in national rubber production forecasting in Thailand. It appears that the prediction based on annual production figures is the most likely to be successfully implemented. However, further research over a longer period of time is need to judge more clearly how effectively this forecasting model may be applied to the public agricultural rubber industry in Thailand.

6. References

Department of Agriculture. (2004). *Academic Rubber Document*. Bangkok: Department of Agriculture.

Fausett, L. (1994). *Fundamentals of neurla networks: architectures, algorithms, and application*. USA: Prentice-Hall.

Funahashi, K. (1989). On the approximate realization of continous mappings by neural networks. *Neural networks, 2*, 183-192.

Geurts, M., Lawrence, K. D., & Guerard, J. (1994). *Forecasting Sales*. Greenwich, Connecticut: JAI PRESS INC.

Hornik, K., Stinchcombe, M., & White, H. (1989). Multilayer feedforward networks are universal apprixmators. *Neural networks, 2*, 359-366.

Intelligent Science Research Group. (2002). Intelligent Decision Support System. Retrieved 6 May 2007, from http://www.intsci.ac.cn/en/research/idss.html

Keen, P. G. W. (1981). Value Analysis: Justifying Decision Support Systems. *MIS Quarterly* 5(1), 1-16.

Leechawengwong, M., Prathummintra, S., & Thamsiri, Y. (2002). *The Development of Basic Rubber Database*. Bangkok: Rubber Research Institute of Thailand.

Markland, R. E., & Sweigart, J. R. (1987). *Quantitative methods: Applications to managerial decision making*. Canada: John Wiley & Sons Inc.

Markland, R. E., & Sweigart, J. R. (1987). *Quantitative Methods: Applications to Managerial Decision Making* Canada: John Wiley & Sons Inc.

Nakmuang, T. (2004). Decision Support Systems. Retrieved 18 March 2007, from http://www.sirikitdam.egat.com/WEB_MIS/107/index.html

Office of Industrial Economics, & Economic Research and Training Center. (1998). *Study of Industrial Structure for Enhancing Competitiveness of Rubber-Product Industries*. Bangkok: Ministry of Industry.

Office of the National Economic and Social Development Board. (2007). The National Economic and Social Development Plan Issue 10. Retrieved 29 May, 2007, from http://www.nesdb.go.th/Default.aspx?tabid=139

Olson, D. L., & Courtney, J. F. (1992). *Decision Support Models and Expert Systems*. New York: Macmillan Publishing Company.

Power, D. J. (2004). Types of Decision Support Systems (DSS). Retrieved 8 April 2007, from http://www.gdrc.org/decision/dss-types.html

Power, D. J. (2007). A Brief History of Decision Support Systems. Retrieved 1 April 2007, from http://dssresources.com/history/dsshistory.html

Royal Thai Army. (2007). Decision Support System. Retrieved 19 March 2007, from http://www.oac.rta.mi.th/.../%BA%B7%B7%D5%E8%2011.doc

Rubber Research Institute of Thailand. (2007a). *Academic Rubber Information 2007*. Bangkok: Rubber Research Institute of Thailand.

Rubber Research Institute of Thailand. (2007b). Rubber: Price Identifier Factor and Price Guarantee Plan in the Future. Retrieved 29 May, 2007, from http://www.rubberthai.com/newspaper/late_news/2550/May50/main.htm

Sangpong, S., & Chaveesuk, R. (2007). *Time series analysis techniques for forecasting pineapple yield in various sizes.* Paper presented at the การประชุมวิชาการด้านการวิจัยดำเนินงานแห่งชาติ ประจำปี ๒๕๕๐, Bangkok.

Statistical Package for the Social Sciences (SPSS). (2009a). Introduction to neural networks (Publication. Retrieved 9 June 2009, from Statistical Package for the Social Sciences (SPSS):

Statistical Package for the Social Sciences (SPSS). (2009b). MLP algorithms (Publication. Retrieved 9 June 2009, from Statistical Package for the Social Sciences (SPSS):

Statistical Package for the Social Sciences (SPSS). (2009c). TSMODEL algorithms (Publication. Retrieved 9 June 2009, from Statistical Package for the Social Sciences (SPSS):

Subsorn, P. (2008). *Enhancing rubber forecasting: The case of the Thai rubber industry.* Paper presented at the Ninth postgraduate electrical engineering & computing symposium (PEECS'2008), The University of Western Australia, Perth, Australia.

Tanguthai, S., & Silpanuruk, K. (1995). *Rubber Marketing Management*. Songkhla: The Thai Rubber Association.

Tomita, Y. (2007). Introduction to forecasting. Retrieved 8 April 2007, from www.math.jmu.edu/~tomitayx/math328/Ch1Slide.pdf

Twomey, J. M., & Smith, A. E. (1996). *Validation and verification. Artificial neural networks for civil engineers: Fundamentals and applications*. New York: ASCE Press.

4

Fuzzy Spatial Data Warehouse: A Multidimensional Model

Pérez David, Somodevilla María J. and Pineda Ivo H.
Facultad de Ciencias de la Computación, BUAP, Mexico

1. Introduction

A data warehouse is defined as an integration of a subject-oriented, a time-variant, and a non-volatile data. Based on the definition, we organize the data warehouse by domains (spatial areas) and in thematic categories (types of features) [1][2].

The loading and maintenance processes are one of the tasks that more effort and demand require. The ETL process needs a temporary storing place for the recovered data from its sources (transactional databases). In our study case, we have that the agency in charge of the study of Popocatepetl's behavior obtains the information from different sources as it's shown in Figure 1.

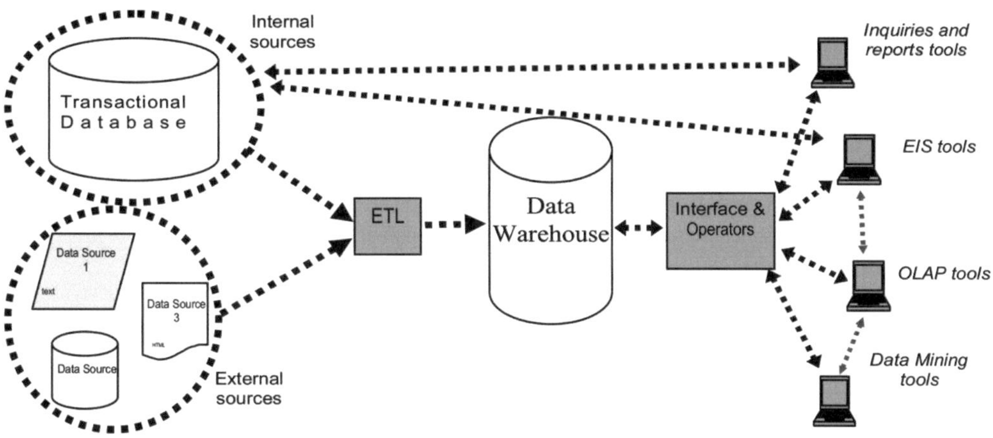

Fig. 1. Data Warehouse's Arquitecture

We present an object model for defining vague regions which rests on "traditional" (that is, exact) modeling techniques. This modeling strategy simultaneously expresses the authors' opinion that it is unnecessary to begin from scratch when modeling vague spatial objects. On the contrary, it is possible to extend, rather than to replace, the current theory of spatial database systems and GIS. Furthermore, moving from an exact to a vague domain does not necessarily invalidate conventional geometry; it is merely an extension. Consequently, the current exact object models that are restricted to determinate spatial objects can be

considered as simplified special cases of a richer class of models for general spatial objects. It turns out that this is exactly the case for the model to be presented.
The paper's structure is as follows, Section 2 presents modeling a fuzzy spatial datawarehouse considering the case when vague regions are included. Section 3 presents the construction of the fuzzy spatial data warehouse. Section 4 presents results and conclusion.

2. Related work

There are several representations and manipulation of vague regions, one of the most representatives is the Fuzzy Minimum Boundary Rectangle (FMBR) [4], that includes use of Fuzzy Logic to define degrees of memberships according to a membership function. In many geographical applications there is a need to model spatial phenomena not simply by sharp objects but rather through indeterminate or vague concepts. FMBR have been used to model such geographical data; it is considered an adequate tool to represent problems related with vague regions. FMBR is composed by two regions, the first region, called kernel, describes which part of the vague region belongs to it. The second region called boundary describes the fuzzy area of a vague region [4].
The Fuzzy Data Cube (FDC) [5] is a fuzzy multidimensional structure to query data in a darawarehouse using OLAP tools. It was initially defined for the sales problem, but in a different context, it is built by evaluating a membership function for each attributes stored in the data warehouse. The result is a degree of membership that is stored in the FDC. Part of this paper consists on to extend the definition of FDC considering a Spatial Database.
Working with the semantic of the attributes in a data cube is another approach that has not been widely considered. The representation of this model helps to draw conclusions with a higher degree of uncertainty [6], based on the classification performance in order to assist the decision support tasks, which has been an application of data cubes.

3. Modeling the fuzzy spatial data warehouse

Considering the previous work on section 2 and given that there is no a single existing model that integrates the concepts of Fuzzy Logic, spatial databases and data warehouses, our main goal is to develop a model considering such kind of integration.
The information under research requires a domain compressing the operational databases and other sources either internal or external [3], as it is shown in Figure 1. We assume that the data warehouse is represented as a multidimensional model [3], which represents the architecture of it. Figure 2 shows the proposed architecture of a Fuzzy Spatial Data Warehouse related with risk zones of Popocatepetl volcano.
In data warehousing context a *fact* represents the civil Protection Plan for natural disasters, and they are measured by demographic density and time to evacuate an area under threat. The information can be obtained by integration from each of the data warehouse's dimensions. Each dimension is organized by hierarchical levels; for instance de Space dimension is divided into state, region, county and town represented by their Fuzzy Minimum Boundary Rectangle (FMBR). As you can see this represents the levels of aggregation [3].
The treatment of spatial objects with indeterminate boundaries is especially problematic for the computer scientist who is confronted with the difficulties how to model such objects in a

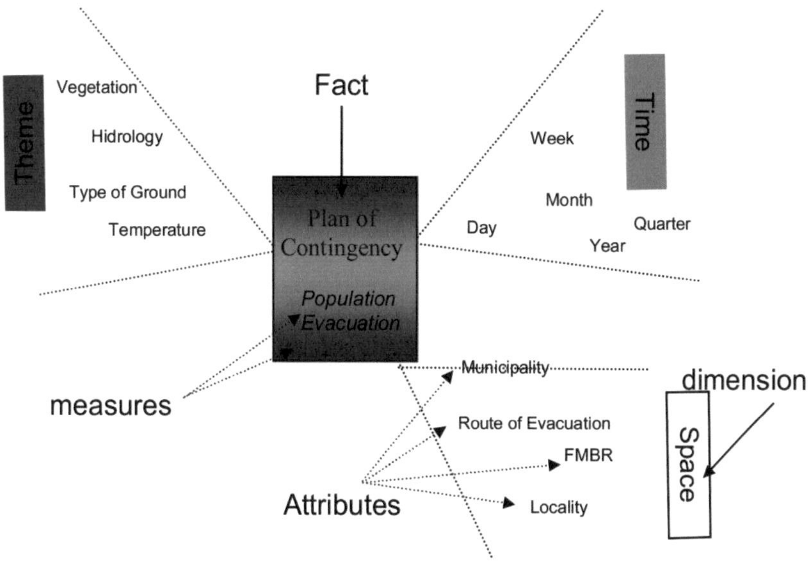

Fig. 2. Architecture proposed of a Fuzzy Spatial Data Warehouse

database system, so that they correspond to the user's intuition, how to finitely represent them in a computer format, how to develop spatial index structures for them, and how to draw them. Computer Scienctists are accustomed to the abstraction process of simplifying spatial phenomena of the real world through the concepts of conventional binary logic, reduction of dimension, and cartographic generalization to precisely defined, simply structured, and sharply bounded objects of Euclidean geometry like points, lines, and regions.

To define the Fuzzy Spatial Data Warehouse we begin with the dimensionality of the warehouse, based on the study case known, as risk areas nearby Popocatepetl volcano. To handle the information we use a Geographical Information System that contains georeferenced data from maps of the State of Puebla.

In Figure 4, it is shown the Snow Flake Schema [7] to be used in the Fuzzy Spatial Data Warehouse, as an extension of the multidimensional model shown in Figure 2. Notice how each of the dimensions are laid out. The main reason behind to select the Snow Flake Schema, is that the fact table is a table that uses the main table to relate with other fact sub tables. In such way, the datawarehouse has a tree like representation, where the root represents the principal fact table, and every node at the first level represents dimension and the remainder nodes with a level greater than 1 are called sub dimensional nodes.

Consider that a georeferenced data follows a recursive definition [11] of spatial concept, thus, it can be used to define a geographic concept. That is a geographic concept is either (i) a geographic data element, or it is (ii) a set of geographic concepts. Analogously, the physical manifestation of a geographic concept, namely a geographic object, is also expressible recursively as either a geographic element, or as a set of geographic objects, this definition is very important because that gives us the opportunity to work with star schema without ambiguity [7].

Thus far, working with the Snow Flake Schema it is possible to unfold each of the tables that each dimension describes, and adding the fuzzy spatial component to each table in order to be represented in the data warehouse.

3.1 Getting the spatial data from ArcGIS

The office in charge of natural disasters in México defined several risk zones in the Popocatepetl area, Figure 3 shows these areas including the county division in the State of Puebla. All the geographical information has to be stored in a vectorial format, where lines, points are stored as attributes of a spatial data base and each element represent a coordinate pair (x,y).

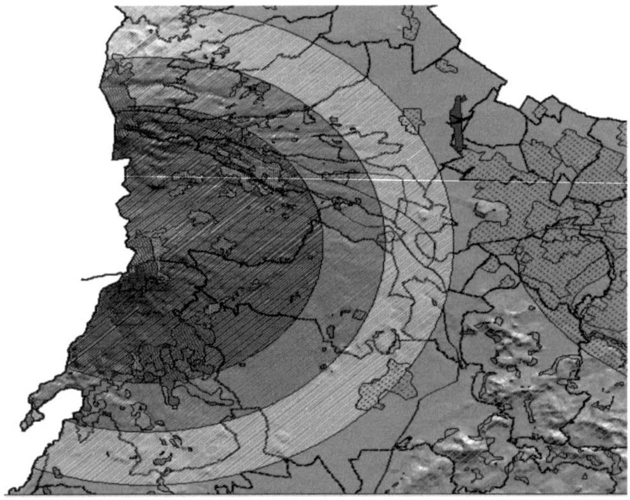

Fig. 3. Risk Zones in State of Puebla as they are shown with ArcGIS

Even though that the risk zones are well defined, they have a strong fuzzy component making that each object from a map (points, lines, polygons) to grow in volume, as it has been referenced, affecting the performance of the datawarehouse.

3.2 Fuzzy sets for the fuzzy spatial datawarehouse

Based on the nature of the geographic information, a fuzzy set is defined and related to each of the dimensions of the proposed schema (Figure 4). According to that schema for each dimension we have a set that represents certain degree of membership and based on that a label or a linguistic label is assigned. With that relationship, all the attributes get a semantic meaning in the warehouse (Figure 5).
Let see how that approach works; assume we have for each dimension or fact table a fuzzy set; and consider the fact table Plan of Contingency and we want to assign the degrees of membership to this set; notice that the available labels are MUCH, FEW or VERY FEW which represent the population where this variable belongs.

3.3 Spatial information in fuzzy spatial data warehouse

When researchers work with spatial data and data warehouses, they find that they know a few about implicit grouping hierarchy of such data, that is a problem because the preaggregation methods can not be applied to OLAP's operations [2][8][9]. Based on that, it is difficult to obtain different levels of grouping inside the data warehouse. In order to overcome this problem, three solutions are proposed in [2][8][9]:

1. Store the spatial pointers of each object without calculating the spatial measures from the spatial data cube.

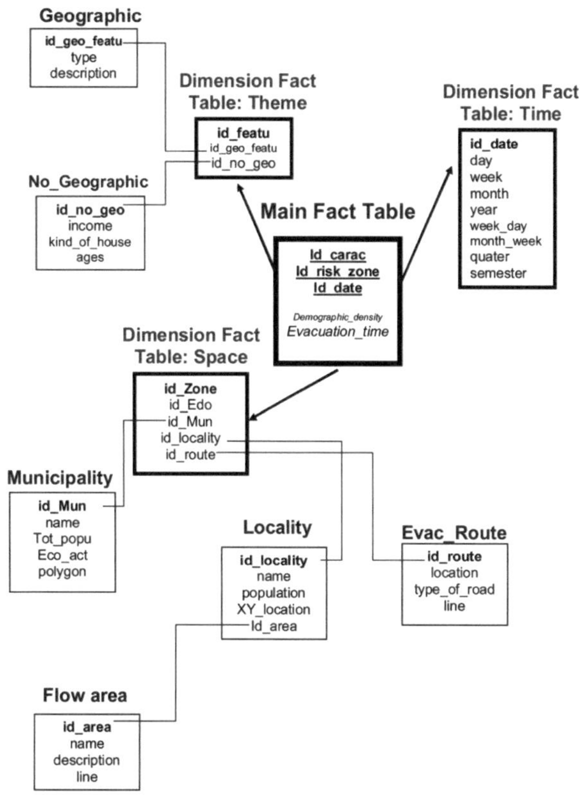

Fig. 4. Snow Flake Schema

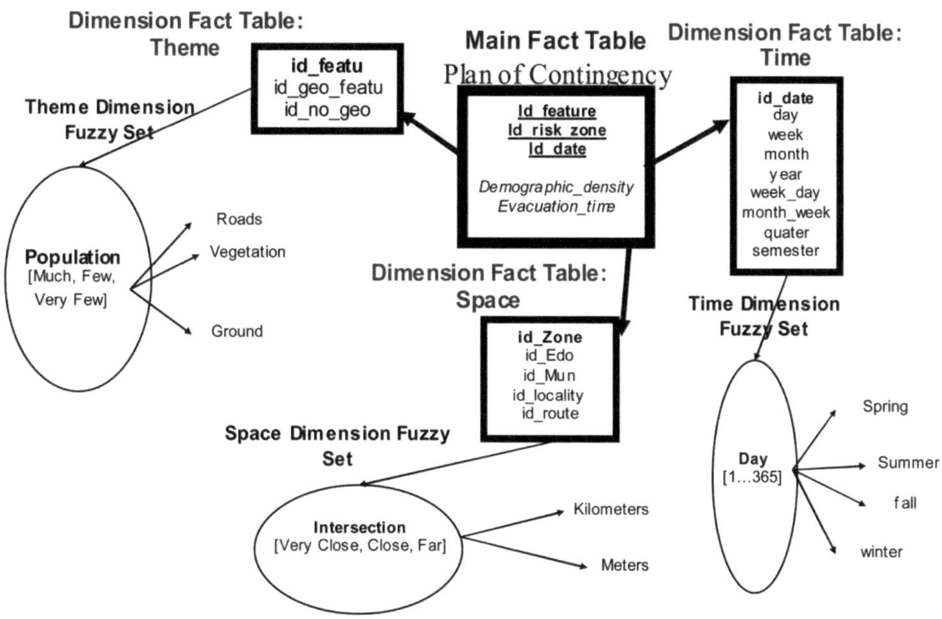

Fig. 5. Fuzzy Sets related to Data Warehouse Dimensions

2. Precompute and store some of the estimations about the spatial measures in the spatial data cube.
3. Perform selective operation measuring of some spatial measures the spatial data cube.

The way we obtain the spatial measures from the spatial data cube is by generating the information during the ETL process [10]. This process requires of spatial queries instead of query the data warehouse directly. We proposed to do this in three steps [10]:

1. Select the results that are close to the expected output from an SQL statement.
2. Load those results into the Data warehouse and create a new table for the spatial dimension.
3. Do the OLAP operations such as the generation of the data cube.

The first step is the most important, because it is possible to generate complex spatial queries [10]; together with the GIS, some of the operations that we perform are topological, intersection and distance operations among others. Figure 6 shows those operations involved.

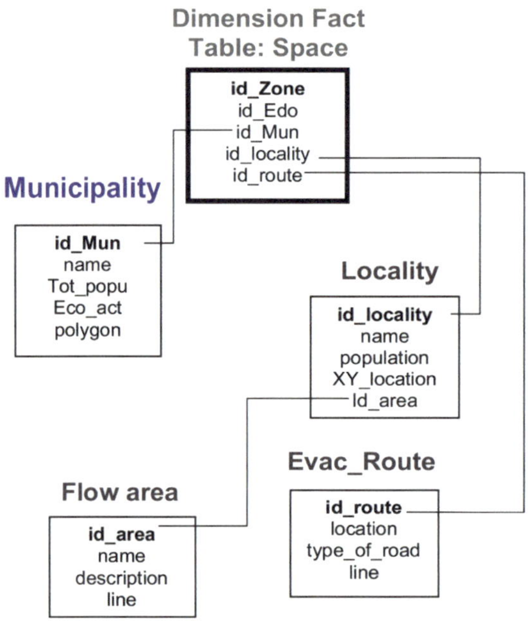

Fig. 6. Space Dimension from the Snow Flake Schema

For each table from Figure 6 is possible to create another spatial queries according to the information stored in the spatial database, and then, generate sort of aggregated data to be used in a future spatial query [2][10]. For instance, in County Table we have a polygon as spatial feature with its Cartesian coordinates.

As you can see in Figure 7, the attribute Polygon shows the coordinates for each county idenyified by ID_num, and working with this information inside the datawarehouse is not possible, because its representation is by levels of aggregation. If we want to answer a query like Q1: "Show all towns closer to an evacuation route", using the information stored in the ArcGIS's spatial database, what we can obtain is:

- The relationship between a distance value and the towns from the spatial fact table.
- Each distance value stored with a unique ID in order to distinguish them.

Id Mun	Name	Tot popu	Eco act	Polygon
1	ACAJETE	351	PLANT	(617350,2096890) ,(547660, 2135079),(651626, 2177004) ,(655233, 2177432),(617350,2096890) , (547660, 2135079)
2	ACATENO	423	FARMING	(675293, 2106590) ,(669084, 2706790),(679084, 2806293) ,(685233, 2101510), (675293, 2106590)
3	ACATLÁN	123	PLANT	(545869,2096890) ,(547660, 2135079),(595239, 2273004) ,(595999, 237732), (545869,2096890)

Fig. 7. County Table

- The attribute Polygon dropped in the County Table.
- A new table containing all the values.

Figure 8 shows such changes in the County Table.

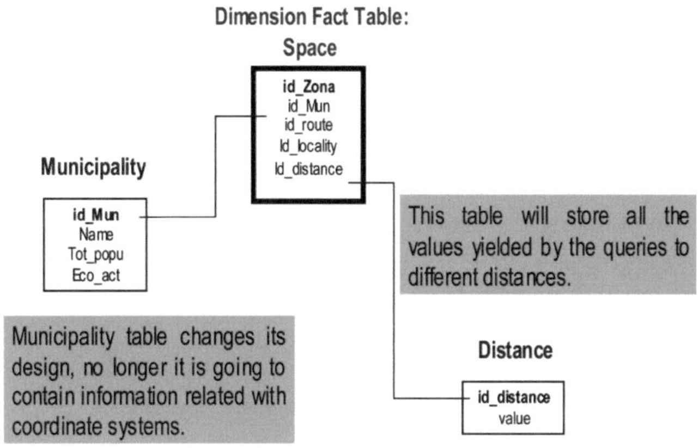

Fig. 8. Changes to the Schema of County and Distances

Our model let us to have several types of queries based on differents points of view. In our study case we proposed four different queries (considering distance) related to the spatial dimension.

Figure 9 shows how Distance, Within, Intersection, FMBR Asociated will be the new tables to Spatial Dimension. Intersection deals with the level of danger related to a town, Within shows the number of inhabitants close to an evacuation route and FMBR Asociated considers a potential area of lava flow close to town(s). Based on the schema of the figure 9, it is how the Spatial Information can be represented inside the data warehouse.

3.4 Fuzzy spatial data warehouse membership functions representation

Once all the spatial values have been assigned to the warehouse, one task has to be done; that is, the calculation of the degree of membership to each register that will be stored in the table. For example, let's see the table Within, that table is related with the number of inhabitants that live close to an evacuation route and its linguistic values are Very Few, Few and Many. These values depend on the amount of people who live in the surrounding area of an evacuation route.

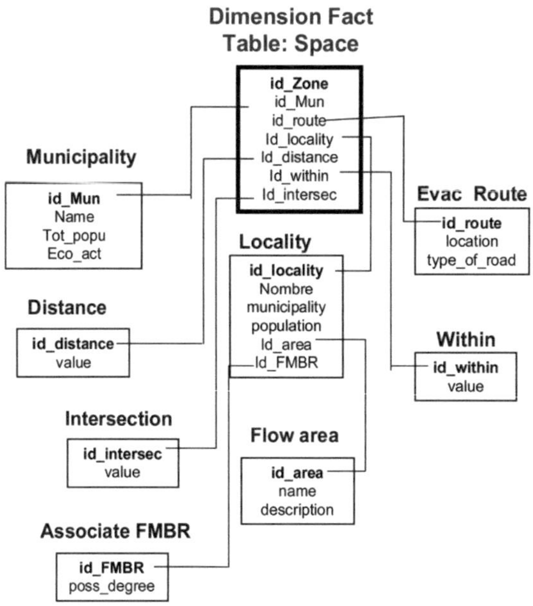

Fig. 9. Modified Schema for Spatial Dimension

As you can see in Figure 10 for an spatial value, a fuzzy value is matched, and its value comes as a result of evaluating the membership function.

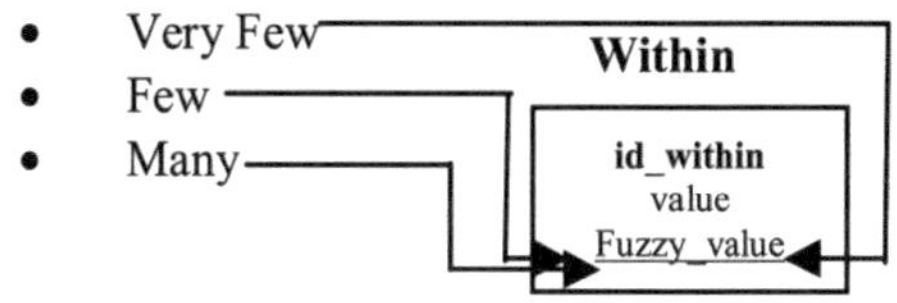

Fig. 10. Linguistic values associated to within function

In Figure 11 is shown the way an emprical value is calculated based on the Within Table, notice the relationship between the maximum speed limit in one road and the type of evacuation route and the number of passangers that certain bus can carry.

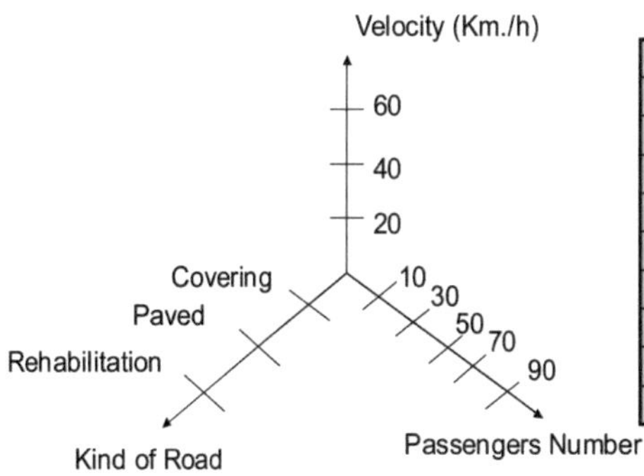

	10	30	50	70	90
Re-60	MP	MP	P	M	M
Re-40	MP	P	P	M	M
Re-20	P	P	M	M	M
Pa-60	MP	MP	MP	P	M
Pa-40	MP	P	P	M	M
Pa-20	MP	P	M	M	M
Rh-60	P	P	M	M	M
Rh-40	P	M	M	M	M
Rh-20	M	M	M	M	M

MP = Very Few, P = Few, M = Many

Fig. 11. Empirical Estimation of the Linguistic Variables

During the transition process the degrees of membership between speed, type of road and number of passangers are assigned according to the linguistic values, that variables have.
A new query needs to be done in order to determine if the statement could be fullfillment or not, such a query (statement) is ***"E1= Traveling in a paved road at high speed and carrying very few passangers"***. Table 1 shows the results of the evaluation of the command E1through the evaluation of the aggregated membership function (1). The result tells us that does not matter how well are the conditions, if the number of passangers is very low and the required time is not an issue.

$$\min(\max[\mu(\text{road}), \mu(\text{velocity}), \mu(\text{passengers})]) \tag{1}$$

	Road	Velocity	Passengers Num.
Pa-high-MP	1	1	0.2
Pa-half-MP	1	0.6	0.2
Pa-low-MP	1	[illegible]	0.2
Pa-high-P	1	1	0.5
Pa-half-P	1	0.6	0.5
Pa-low-P	1	0.3	0.5
Pa-high-M	1	1	1
Pa-half-M	1	0.6	1
Pa-low-M	1	0.3	1

$\min(\max[\mu(\text{road}), \mu(\text{velocity}), \mu(\text{passengers})]) = 0.3$

Table 1. Evaluation of the command E1

Kind of Road	**Paved**	**Covering**	**Rehabilitation**
μ(Road)	1	0.6	0.3
Passengers Number	**From 56 to 90**	**From 36 to 55**	**From 10 to 35**
μ(passengers)	1	0.5	0.2
Velocity (Km/h)	**60**	**40**	**20**
μ(velocity)	1	0.6	0.3

Table 2. Evaluation of the linguistic variables on (1)

Table 2 shows the empirical assignments of the membership degrees of the linguistic variables that are involved in the command E1. Based on the values assigned to the linguistic variables, the degree of fullfillment of E1 was found 0.3. This result means that is very few probable than few passengers be traveling in a paved road at high speed.

4. Conclusions

This work represents a part of the Intelligent Geographical Project, that will model a geographic area in the same way as in the real world appears, taking advantage of the

Information Technology. We have integrated ArcGIS technology with Fuzzy Theory, given the fact that linguistic variables get closer to coloquial language and they describe a geographic situation in a natural way.
The main contribution of this work is the integration of Fuzzy Logic with Spatial Databases in order to help during the decision support and OLAPs querying processes.
ArcGIS allows to obtain spatial features by the queries execution on maps. These spatial features are integrated into a multidimensional database allowing aggregation and disaggregation OLAP operations on it, avoiding the use of classic spatial access methods. In addition, spatial semantic is added to spatial and not spatial dimensions of the multidimensional model improving the decision making process. Finally, the Fuzzy Spatial Data Warehouse's design methodology proposed, simplify the use of the existing analysis tools for exploting the potential of Data Warehouses.

5. References

[1] Y. Wang, H. Shao. Data warehouse technology in process industry. in Intelligent Control and Automation. Proceedings of the 3rd World Congress. 2000.

[2] D. Papadias et. al. Efficient OLAP Operations in Spatial Data Warehouses. in Lecture Notes in Computer Science, vol. 2121. p. 443 - 459. 2001.

[3] J. Hernández, J. R. Quintana, C. Ferri. Introducción a la Minería de Datos. Capítulos 1, 2 y 9, Pearson Prentice Hall. 2005.

[4] M.J. Somodevilla, Fuzzy MBRs Modeling for Reasoning about Vague Regions, Doctoral Tesis, Tulane University, 2003.

[5] A. Reda, K. Mehmet, "Integrating Fuzziness into OLAP for Multidimensional Fuzzy Association Rules Mining", Third IEEE International Conference on Data Mining (ICDM'03) 2003 p. 469.

[6] L. Yubao, Y. Jian, "The Computation of Semantic Data Cube", GCC 2005, pp. 573-578.

[7] M. Levene, G. Loizou. Why is the Snowflake Schema a Good Data Warehouse Design? in Source, Information Systems Vol. 28 (Issue 3). pp. 225-240. ISSN 0306-4379. 2003.

[8] H. Ahn, N. Mamoulis, H. Wong. A Survey on Multidimensional Access Methods. UU-CS. 2001.

[9] N. Stefanovic, J. Han y K. Koperski. Object-Based Selective Materialization for Efficient Implementation of Spatial Data Cubes. in IEEE Transactions on Knowledge and Data Engineering, Vol. 12, No. 6. 2000 p. 938-958

[10] Y. Li, Y. Chen y F. Rao. The Approach for Data Warehouse to Answering Spatial OLAP Queries. In Intelligent Data Engineering and Automated Learning. p. 270-277. SpringerLink Date Tuesday, August 26, 2003. ISBN 978-3-540-40550-4.

[11] Aldridge, C.H., 1998, A Theory Of Empirical Spatial Knowledge Supporting Rough Set Based Knowledge Discovery in Geographic Databases. Ph.D. Thesis, University of Otago, Dunedin, New Zealand.

5

Rule-Based System for Morphological and Ecohydrological Decision Making

Hani Sewilam and Heribert Nacken
RWTH Aachen University
Germany

1. Introduction

"Fish habitat is defined as those parts of the environment that fish depend on, directly or indirectly, in order to carry out their life processes" (Alberta 2003). There are basic requirements that should be available so that fish can successfully carry out their life processes; fish must have food to be able to reproduce and need cover to protect themselves from predators. The biological, chemical and physical features of water streams must be suitable for the reproduction process. Changes in the morphology of water streams are significant factors that influence the habitat quality (Hauer et al. 2006). Geomorphic characteristics, such as channel size, slope, grain size distribution, the spatial configuration of bars and riparian vegetation, strongly influence the structure of fluvial habitats and, as a consequence, the biodiversity and ecosystem function (Zah et al. 2000). Scherer et al. (2006) analyse the correlation between the structural river quality and the existing fish fauna. The study points out that there is a significant correlation between the species composition and the aggregated hydromorphological indicators for the trout and grayling regions. Montgomery (2006) indicates that the historical effects of changes in river geomorphologic processes in the US led to disturbance regimes on salmon populations. This shows the significance of the morphological structure for the ecosystem of watercourses.

Over the past centuries, the ecological quality of watercourses in Europe and worldwide has been affected by human actions. Many physical alterations such as flood control measures, barrages, sluices as well as canalization and lining have significantly affected the Ecosystem mainly fish habitat. Improving the status of surface and ground water is a clear objective of the EU Water Framework Directive (EU WFD) to be achieved by 2015 (European Parliament 2000). The EU WFD committed the EU nations to carry out a characterisation of their water bodies by the end of 2004. This entailed a complete analysis of the characteristics of the surface and ground waters in each district, the review of the environmental impact of human activity (industry, farming, etc.) and an economic analysis of water use. The EU WFD also emphasizes the importance of preparing programmes of measures to achieve and maintain the good ecological status of watercourses.

The German Ministry of Environment and Conservation, Agriculture and Consumer Protection of the state of North Rhine-Westphalia (MUNLV) has achieved, over the past years, a significant improvement of the chemical status of the watercourses in North Rhine-Westphalia (NRW). The improvement of wastewater treatment and the decrease of industrial pollutants had a positive effect on the chemical quality already in 2001. Sixty

percent of the examined water courses reached a "good" or "very good" status. Thirty percent were rated as "moderate". The concentrations of nutrients and pollutants have notably decreased (North Rhine-Westphalia State Environment Agency (LUA NRW) 2002). On the other hand, the morphological structure of these watercourses has considerable deficits, particularly in urban areas. The results of a morphological quality assessment study indicate that 48.6% of the small and medium-sized watercourses in NRW are strongly affected by human activities. In urban areas this percentage increases to 73.6% (North Rhine-Westphalia State Environment Agency (LUA NRW) 2003).
To achieve the environmental objectives of the EU WFD, the MUNLV is in the course of preparing programmes of measures to improve the ecological status of the watercourses.
The programmes of measures have to be elaborated for each watercourse. The decision makers at ministerial and regional levels need supporting tools that enable them to plan the programmes of measures in NRW as well as identifying the suitability of water courses for fishes.
This chapter introduces a Decision Support System that partially contributes to the development of the programmes of measures. The tool considers only the morphological structure, since the improvement of morphological quality is the basis for a good ecological status. The developed system generates different scenarios for a morphological restoration measure, assesses their impacts and proposes a programme of morphological measures and preliminary cost estimation for all WFD-relevant watercourses in NRW. The DSS has been developed for use at both ministerial and regional levels. Decision makers at ministerial level need the tool for more strategic and resources allocation reasons. However, local or regional authorities need the tool to support the development of the morphological improvement programme of measures for their watercourses. In addition, this chapter introduces also the first results of further development of the DSS aiming to support the decision makers in identifying the impact of river restoration on the suitability of water streams for Salmon fish.

2. Characterization of watercourses

The characterization process is considered the first step toward implementation of the EU WFD. Characterization process is meant to assess environmental pressures on water bodies and the impact of human activity on watercourse status (Umwelt Bundes Amt 2005).
German Working Group of the Federal States (LAWA) (1998) has elaborated a characterization system that allows the assessment of the hydromorphological quality of water bodies. As listed in Table 1, the quality classification system considers 14 hydromorphological indicators which cover different morphological structure areas (longitudinal variation, bed configuration, bank structure, etc.). The classification system breaks down a water body into segments (100 m long). The segments should be assessed by allocating a value between 1 and 7 to each of its hydromorphological indicators, whereby class 1 stands for the natural state and class 7 for a completely changed state.

3. Rule-based modelling

Hydromorphologically related processes can be characterized as the most complex natural processes to be mathematically modelled. Normally, experts in the field of watercourse restoration do not communicate in the form of systems of differential equations or analytical

	Hydromorphological Indicators	Investigated Area
1 2	Curvature Mobility	Longitudinal Variation
3 4	Natural elements Anthropogenic migration barrier	Longitudinal Profile
5 6	Type and spreading of substrates Bed fixation	Bed Configuration
7 8 9	Cross-section form Cross-section depth Width variation	Cross Section
10 11 12	Vegetation Bank characteristics Natural Characteristics	Bank Structure
13 14	Foreland Bank Width	Stream Surroundings

Table 1. Hydromorphological Indicators and Related Investigated Areas

models, but they use natural languages and qualitative reasoning for the description of morphological relationships. Realistic and successful decisions to improve the morphological structure of watercourses are often based on expert knowledge. The main problems of the expert-based decision-making process are the scarcity of such experts and the enormous amount of data to be handled.

Artificial Intelligence (AI) techniques were meant to solve similar modelling problems.

The appearance of AI in environmental sciences publications began in the middle of the 1980s. In the 1990s there was a significant increase in the number of published papers in this field (Cortés et al. 2000). Knowledge-based modelling is among the AI techniques that are intensively used in modelling ecological processes. Knowledge can be represented in several ways, such as rules, frames and logical predicates. In most knowledge-based systems, knowledge is expressed in rules (Domanski 1989). The most powerful characteristic of rule-based modelling, making them different from traditional computer applications, is their capability to deal with qualitatively described situations. Different examples for rule-based ecological modelling can be found in literature (e.g. Bender et al. 1992, Vicente et al. 2004 and Schülter et al. 2006).

To deal with the enormous amount of data and to develop the targeted DSS, the rulebased modelling technique is used in this study. In NRW, there are about 120,000 watercourse segments (100 m) that should be investigated to answer questions such as: which segments should be rehabilitated and which combination of measures should be implemented? During an early stage of this research, the knowledge of experts was obtained through interviews and questionnaires. Based on the acquired knowledge, different 'if–then' rules have been formulated. Experts were asked again to interact together during workshops to assess the identified rules. In addition to the technical discussion, a classical voting procedure was followed in case of diverging opinions. The rules are devoted to solving two main modelling problems.

3.1 Identifying decision space

The first decision making step is to identify the decision space which is formulated through different restrictions. In this specific decision problem, the restrictions of implementing a morphological improvement measure are technical restrictions. The restoration measure which satisfies the predefined restrictions is considered a feasible decision scenario. The main idea is to identify the decision space using qualitative 'if-then' rules. The rules are included in Rule-Block 1. An example for considering technical restrictions using 'if-then' rules can be formulated as follows:

IF	Cross-Section Form	IS	Class 5, 6 or 7
AND	Cross-Section Depth	IS	Class 5, 6, or 7
AND	Width Variation	IS	Class 4, 5, 6, or 7
AND	Bank Characteristics	IS	Class 1, 2 or 3
THEN	Widening Cross Section	IS	Feasible Measure

It can be realized from this rule that widening the cross section is suitable for improving its form, depth and variation. On the other hand, enough bank width should be available to widen the cross section. The DSS offers 25 different measures to improve the morphological status of watercourses. For instance, removing the bed-fixing materials is a measure to rehabilitate the bed characteristics and placement of woody debris is proposed to improve the cross section. There is at least one rule for each measure to identify its feasibility.

3.2 Qualitative simulation

The second decision making step is to qualitatively predict the impact of implementing a feasible measure on the morphological structure of a watercourse segment over a predefined time duration. For this purpose, different restoration functions have been developed to describe the impact of each measure on one hydromorphological indicator. As a matter of fact, a measure could have impacts on more than one hydromorphological indicator. Therefore, the 25 measures included in the DSS have 95 restoration functions.

Figure 1 provides an example for a restoration function describing the impact of removing the bed-fixing materials on the type and spreading of substrates. To handle the different ecological effects due to diverse conditions and constraints in nature, the DSS offers three restoration scenarios for each measure (optimistic, medium and pessimistic).

Considering the optimistic scenario, the morphological status will improve tremendously after removing the bed-fixing materials (from class 7 to class 4). Assuming a time duration of 5 years, the morphological status will be improved from class 4 to class 3. Two other restoration functions are constructed for this measure because this measure also has a positive impact on the two indicators "bed fixation" and "anthropogenic migration barrier."

To summarize the impact of each measure on the investigated segment, another rule block which contains 'if-then' rules has been constructed. The rules capture the impact of the measures from the related restoration functions. This example illustrates the impact of removing bed fixation on different hydromorphological indicators after 5 years of implementation.

IF	Stream Bed Fixation	IS	Class 7
AND	Type and Spreading of Substrates	IS	Class 7
AND	Anthropogenic Migration Barrier	IS	Class 7
AND	Removing the Bed Fixation	IS	Implemented

AND	Development Time	IS	5 Years
THEN	Stream Bed Fixation	IS	Class 1
AND	Type and Spreading of Substrates	IS	Class 3
AND	Anthropogenic Migration Barrier	IS	Class 5

The 14 morphological indicators are used to assess the efficiency of the investigated scenario. After implementing the second rule base, each of the 14 indicators of the investigated segment gets a new morphological status. The new values of the morphological indicators are used to rank the scenarios. The DSS includes an algorithm that allows the user to select only low-cost measures. In this case, the number of investigated measures is reduced to include only low-cost ones. This means that the expensive measures will be excluded. At this stage, the DSS does not consider the connection between the segments. For example, the impact of implementing a certain measure in an upper reach on segments in lower reaches is not considered. However, this issue is considered for further development of the DSS by using data mining techniques.

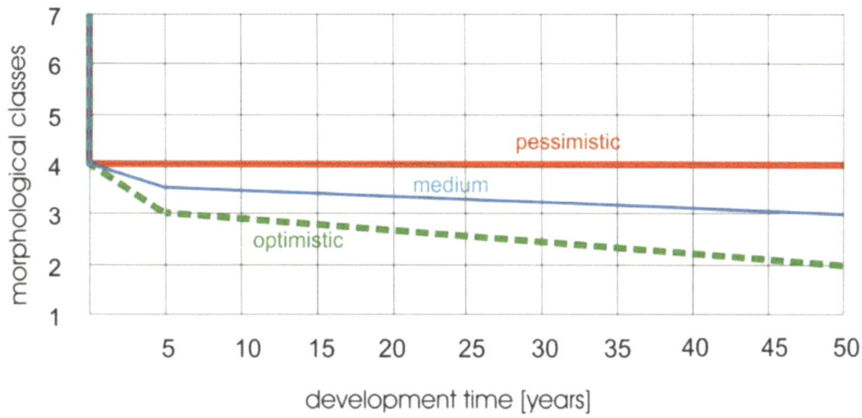

Fig. 1. Example of a restoration function for the measure "Removing the Bed Fixation" and its impact on the hydromorphological indicator "type and spreading of substrates"

4. Structure of the DSS

The overall structure of the DSS is shown in Fig. 2. It contains four major subsystems, namely, the graphical user interface (GUI) subsystem, the data management subsystem, the rule-inference subsystem and the assessment subsystem.

- The GUI subsystem serves to integrate the other three subsystems and to allow the decision maker or the user to interact with the DSS. The GUI coordinates all functions selected by the decision maker. It allows the user to have access to all data. The user can select the water body to be improved, identify the targeted morphological status (restoration objective) and time duration to reach this target. The user can also control the available restoration measures, add or remove rules in the database as well as the cost of the different scenarios. The proposed programme of measures for the selected water body is also delivered through the GUI.
- The data-management subsystem stores and organizes all data and rules necessary for the other subsystems to solve the decision problem. This subsystem contains all the

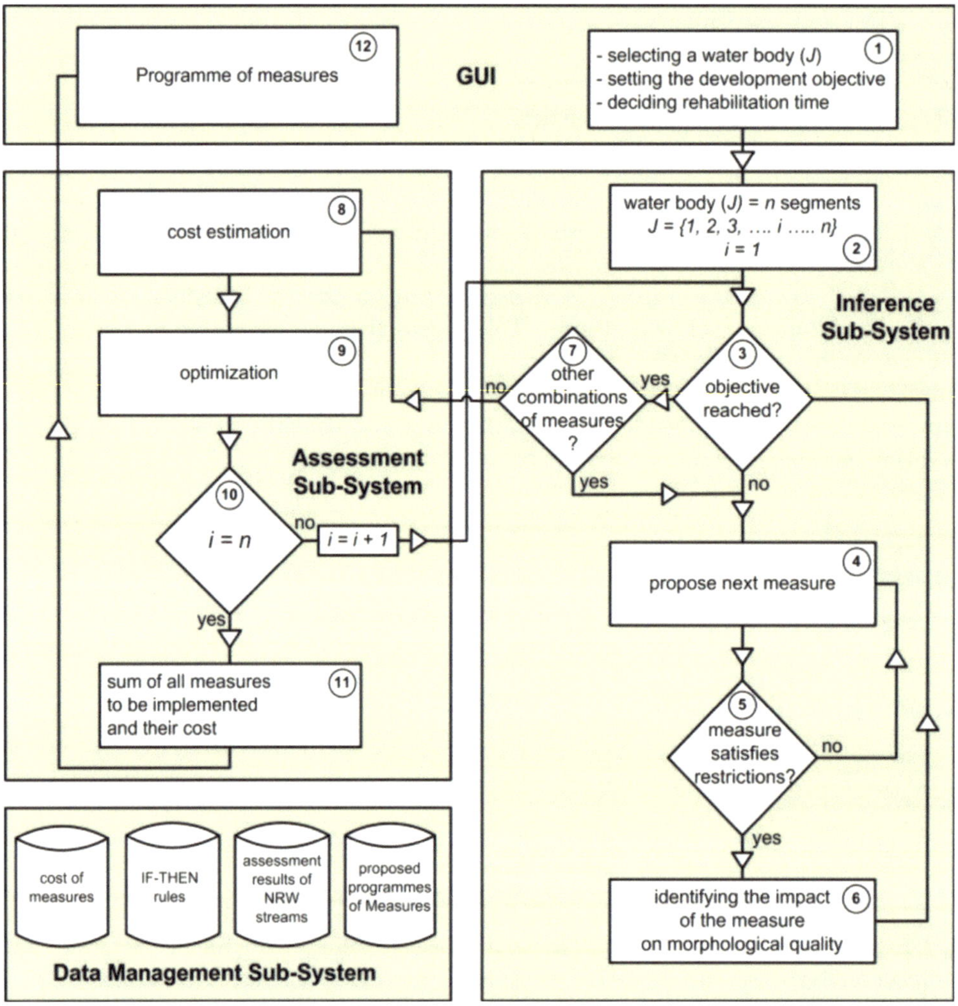

Fig. 2. The Architecture of the DSS and Decision Making Procedure

results of the morphological characterization in NRW (current status), rules for selecting the decision scenarios, rules for predicting the impact of implemented measures and cost of the measures.

- The rule-inference subsystem is the core component of the DSS which contains the two rule blocks. This subsystem is responsible for generating different restoration scenarios, checking their feasibility, implementing them and assessing their impact on the morphological structure of the investigated water body.
- The assessment subsystem is devoted to estimating the cost of the proposed measures. The DSS offers functions that estimate the cost of the measures. This subsystem contains also an optimization module that selects the best combination of measures for a certain water body based on the cost of the measures and their performance toward reaching the best possible morphological status. This subsystem also summarizes the measures selected for a certain water body as well as their cost to produce the expected programme of measures.

5. Development of morphological restoration measures

To improve the ecological status of watercourses, programmes of measures should be developed and implemented. Since this work targets only the morphological structure, the DSS has been developed to propose only morphological restoration measures as important components of the programmes of measures. Figure 2 illustrates the decision-making procedure toward developing an optimal combination of measures to improve the morphological status for a selected water body. The procedure can be summarized as follows:

1. The user selects a water body (J) and identifies the morphological development objectives that should be achieved by the DSS. For instance, the current status of the selected water body is class 6 and the restoration objective is to improve the structure to reach class 2. The user is also asked to identify the maximum duration to achieve the restoration objective (e.g. 4 years).
2. The system breaks down the selected water body to (n) number of segments (100 meters long).
3. If the current status of the investigated segment (i) is equal to or better than the targeted class, the system jumps to step 7. If not,
4. The system proposes a restoration measure.
5. The system implements the first rule block to check whether the selected measure satisfies the restrictions or not. If not, the system proposes another measure (back to step 3). If yes,
6. The system implements the second rule block to identify the impact of the selected measure on the morphological status of the investigated segment. Then the system moves again to step 3 to check whether the targeted objective has been achieved or not. If not, the same procedure will be followed to suggest additional measures to be implemented for the same segment (combination of several measures). If yes,
7. The system asks again whether there is any other combination of measures that can lead to the targeted morphological status. If the answer is yes, the system jumps to step 4. If not,
8. All the combinations of measures resulting from the previous steps that lead to the targeted status are sent to the cost estimation module. This module breaks down the measures into smaller sub-measures (site preparatory costs, planning costs, etc.) and picks up the cost of each sub-measure from the data-base subsystem. The costs depend on the size and the type of the river segment. The prices represent an average value of similar projects that have already been implemented and are the same for all rivers in NRW. The cost estimation aims mainly at comparing of different combinations of measures for one river. Since the costs are based on the same database, a comparison is possible.
9. Then, an optimization algorithm is started which aims to select the best "combination of measures" according to two selection criteria, (a) the combination of measures that leads to the best morphological quality, and (b) the cheapest combination of measures.
10. Then, the system asks whether all the segments of the selected water body have been investigated. If not, the system jumps to step 2. If yes,
11. The best combination of measures for each segment is aggregated to formulate a morphology-improving programme of measures for the selected water body. Then,
12. The GUI delivers the best three morphology-improving programmes of measures for the selected water body.

For any selected water body in NRW, the developed DSS produces a detailed report for the restoration programme of measures. The report includes the best three combinations of measures to be implemented and the estimated cost. The predicted results can be visualised using GIS.

6. Validation of the DSS

To demonstrate the applicability of the developed DSS, the data of the NRW restoration surveillance project "Erfolgskontrolle" have been used for comparison with the DSS results. This project aims to compare the status of watercourses before and after implementing morphological restoration measures (German Ministry of Environment and Conservation 2005). The majority of experts who participated in this project were not involved in formulating the rule base of the DSS. This is important for the reliability of the validation process. Data limitation was a problem that faced validating most of the river segments of the "Erfolgskontrolle" project. Therefore, validation tests were undertaken only for the segments with enough data to run the DSS.

To validate Rule Block 1, the DSS was run for the river segments of the "Erfolgskontrolle," which are spread all over NRW, with the same developing time and goal to be achieved. The proposed combinations of measures were compared with the ones implemented in the projects of the "Erfolgskontrolle." The results showed that the combinations of measures which were implemented in reality are included in the list of suggested combinations by the DSS.

To validate the restoration functions, the data of 16 different river segments analyzed in the "Erfolgskontrolle" project were used. With a special tool of the DSS ("Interaktive Prognose") the user can select specific measures proposed by Rule Block 1. This tool was used with the data of the "before" status and the developing time of the given data of the "Erfolgskontrolle." For each project an optimistic, a pessimistic and a normal scenario were run. The results of the "Interaktive Prognose" were compared with the real data of the "after" status. The results showed a good agreement between the predicted morphological status and the real world ones. In 14 projects the maximum recorded difference in the aggregated indicator using the medium restoration function is one morphology class.

7. Implementing the DSS in NRW

In order to allocate resources and develop general morphological programmes of measures in NRW, the MUNLV started implementing the DSS in different schemes. The MUNLV implemented the DSS for seven rivers in NRW: Stever, Berkel, Sieg, Niers, Issel, Wienbach and Ottersgraben. The experts involved described the DSS results as "reasonable" measures. For the Berkel, a lowland river with mainly agricultural landuse, the results are given here in more detail. The aggregated total morphological quality of the Berkel (mean quality of all segments) is currently class 6. The specified target for the morphological quality is class 3. The developing time is set at 18 years with minimal costs. The optimistic restoration scenario recommended mainly developing measures such as 'support for riverine vegetation', deadwood measures or 'broaden the bank width'. The DSS suggests that all anthropogenic migration barriers be removed to restore a continuous river. For some segments, no suitable measure is found or required for the overall goal of class 3. The suggested combinations of measures will improve the morphology to class 3 in 75% of the river segments as shown in Table 2. In total an aggregated morphological quality of class 3.47 is reached.

morphological quality class	1	2	3	4	5	6	7
distribution before the implementation [%]	0,0	0,0	0,6	9,0	18,5	61,7	10,1
proposed distribution after the implementation and the developing time [%]	0,0	3,6	75,8	0,8	2,7	11,6	5,6

Table 2. Distribution of the morphological quality classes before and after the measures of the Berkel

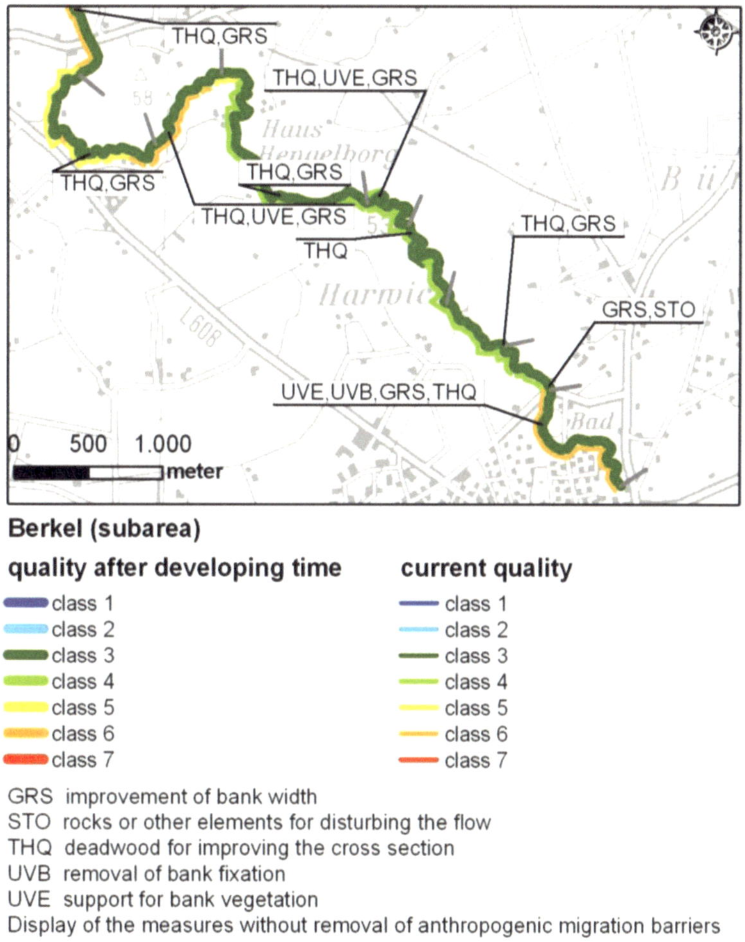

Fig. 4. Map with the results of the DSS for the Berkel (subarea)

Figure 3 shows the morphological quality for a certain reach of the River Berkel before and after implementing the proposed improvement measures. The given codes indicate the proposed improvement combination measure for the segments between the gray 'hatch'-bars. The thick line on the right (here completely green) shows the expected morphological quality class 18 years after the implementation of the proposed morphological measures. The thin line on the left side of the river (here orange, yellow and light green) expresses the current morphological quality, thus before the measures are implemented. The DSS is currently being implemented at several regional river authorities in NRW.

8. Fuzzy-Rule-Based habitat model for Salmon

In order to enable decision makers to investigate the impact of river restoration on its suitability for fish habitat, a separate Salmon habitat model has been developed. The model can be used to assess water river segments based on their morphological, biological and chemical characteristics. Fourteen indicators have been used as model inputs to estimate the suitability index for each segment. As listed in Table 3, eight morphological indicators as outputs of the DSS have been considered to be inputs for the fuzzy model. Other six bio-chemical indicators have been considered as model inputs. Selecting these indicators was based on interviews and questionnaires for fish experts to identify the most significant ones for Salmon habitat. The model aggregates and assesses the input indicators in four steps to reach the suitability index of river segment under investigation.

<table>
<tr><th>Input Indicators</th><th>Intermediate Indicators A</th><th>Intermediate Indicators B</th><th>Intermediate Indicators C</th><th>Model Output</th></tr>
<tr><td>Natural elements</td><td rowspan="2">Longitudinal Profile</td><td rowspan="4">Bed characteristics</td><td rowspan="8">Morphological Structure</td><td rowspan="14">Suitability Index</td></tr>
<tr><td>Anthropogenic migration barrier</td></tr>
<tr><td>Type and spreading of substrates</td><td rowspan="2">Bed Structure</td></tr>
<tr><td>Bed fixation</td></tr>
<tr><td>Cross-section form</td><td rowspan="2">Cross Section</td><td rowspan="4">Bank characteristics</td></tr>
<tr><td>Width variation</td></tr>
<tr><td>Natural characteristics</td><td rowspan="2">Bank structure</td></tr>
<tr><td>Bank characteristics</td></tr>
<tr><td colspan="3">Saprobic Index</td><td rowspan="6">Biological and chemical water quality</td></tr>
<tr><td>PH- Value</td><td rowspan="3">Water Quality A</td><td rowspan="5">Chemical and Physical parameters</td></tr>
<tr><td>Water Temperature</td></tr>
<tr><td>Ammonic Concentration</td></tr>
<tr><td>oxygen concentration in surface water</td><td rowspan="2">Water Quality B</td></tr>
<tr><td>oxygen concentration in interstitial water</td></tr>
</table>

Table 3. Input, Intermediate, and Output Indicators of the Salmon Habitat Model

The stepwise aggregation process has been carried out using fuzzy-rule-based approach. Figure 5 shows the structure of the model that has been developed using MATLAB Fuzzy-

Logic Toolbox in combination with Simulink. The gray boxes in the figure represent the model inputs. The coloured boxes are the rule-blocks that aggregate the input indicators to estimate the suitability index (blue block on the right side).

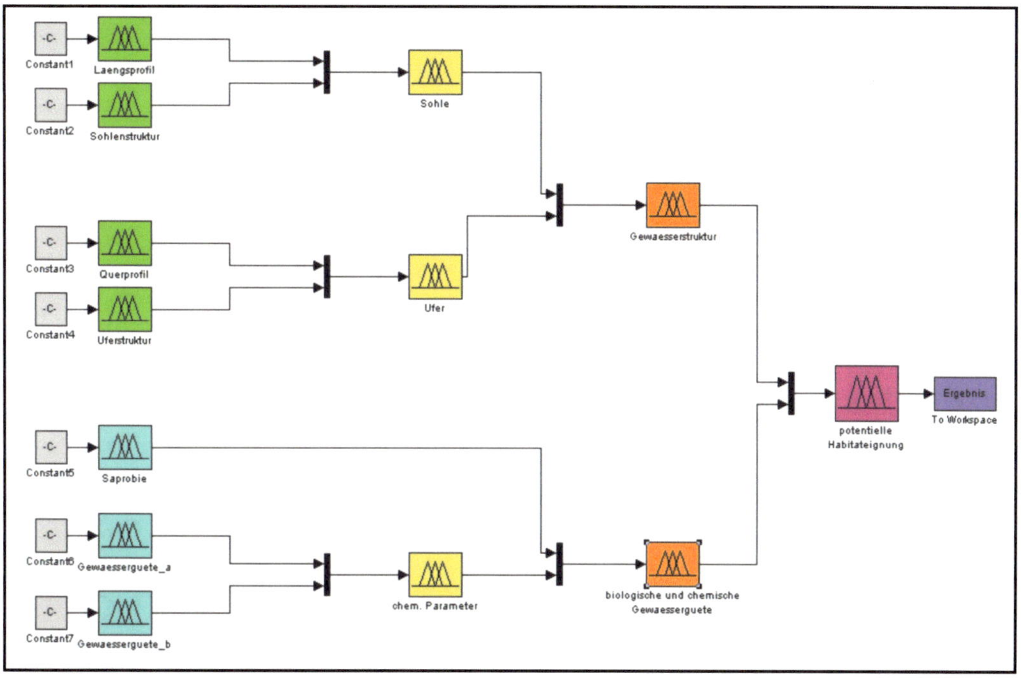

Fig. 5. Structure of the Fuzzy-Rule-Based Habitat Model

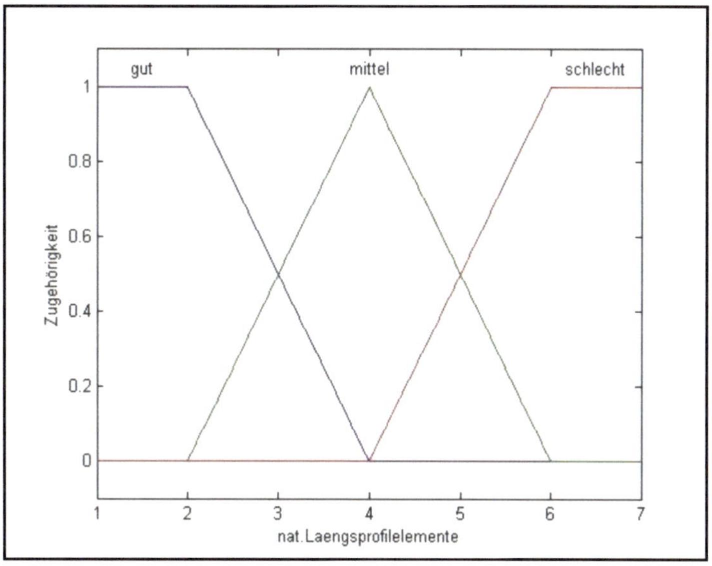

Fig. 6. Membership Functions of the Indicator Natural Elements

Each of the input and intermediate indicators are represented as linguistic variables with three terms. The output indicator "Habitat Suitability Index" has five terms. Each term is described either by triangular or trapezoidal membership function. The membership functions were initially spaced equally and then shifted and modified according to the opinion of fish experts and literature review. Figure (6) shows an example of the input linguistic variable "Natural elements" that is divided into three different membership functions. The membership function "good/gut" has a degree of one from 1 through 2. This membership value declines to zero when the value is 4. The same is followed to construct both membership functions middle/mittel and bad/schlecht. The same approach is followed for all indicators.

Selecting linguistic terms that are meaningful for users are considered while constructing the membership functions. For instance, the terms of the "temperature" are considered as follows: "cold, optimum, hot". Using such membership functions, the model inputs will be transformed to linguistic terms (fuzzified). For example, an input value of 6 means that the indicator "natural element" is classified as "good" with a membership degree of 1 (100%).

Fuzzy rules are then used to stepwise aggregate and assess the input terms in order to reach the overall goal (habitat suitability index). For instance, a rule that is used to assess and aggregate the indicators (Natural Elements and Anthropogenic migration barrier) into one intermediate indicator A (Longitudinal Profile) can be written as follows:

IF	Natural Elements	**IS**	good
AND	Anthropogenic migration barrier	IS	good
THEN	Longitudinal Profile	**IS**	good

In the rule-blocks, each rule has got a weight (from 0 to 1) that reflects its significance. Initially, all possible rules are generated and then assessed to get the suitable weight. This process is also carried out by fish experts and researchers. The centre of maximum method is then used to transform the linguistic terms of the fish habitat suitability index into crisp value (defuzzification process). The result of the model is a crisp suitability value of the assessed river segment that is between 0 and 1.

The first version of the habitat model was validated using field data for the water streams Menden, Eitorf and Weidenau. For the Menden and Eitrof the used data-sets are for the years 1992, 1994, 1997 and 2002. Input data for the period 1996 till 2002 have been used for the Weidenau. Annual average values for the chemical and biological indicators have been used to generate different scenarios for the input parameters. To validate the model output (habitat suitability index for salmon) the fish population in each water body in the same year has been used as reference for validating the model results. The model has resulted satisfactory correlation between habitat index and fish population.

9. Conclusion

The small and medium-sized watercourses in NRW are strongly affected by human activities. The developed DSS is a step towards the successful implementation of the EU WFD in NRW. It supports the planning of the morphological programme of measures in NRW. The system makes the knowledge of experts available for decision makers at ministerial and regional levels. This allows regional decision makers to plan restoration measures. Taking the cost factor into consideration allows decision makers at ministerial level to allocate morphological restoration resources and manpower within NRW.

The development of the salmon model is necessary to estimate the impact of restoration measures on fish habitat. The results of the first development phase have shown the

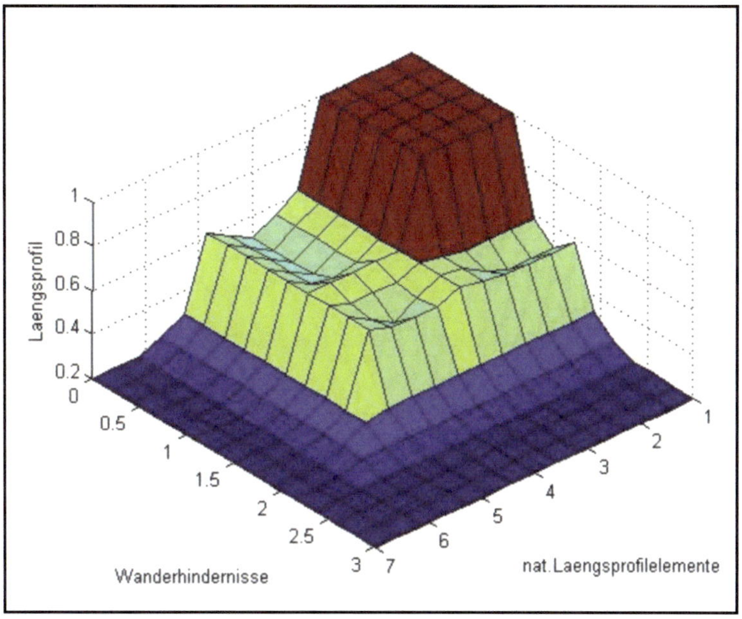

Fig. 7. Graphic Illustration of the Relation between the indicators "Natural Elements, Anthropogenic migration barrier and Longitudinal Profile.

Location	Year	Anthropogenic migration substrates	Anthropogenic	Art und Verteilung der Substrate	Bed Fixation	cross section form	width variation	bank natural cover	Bank Characterisitics	Saprobic Index	PH-Value	Temperature	Ammonic Concentration	Oxygen concentration in surface water	Oxygen concentration in intersitial water	Fish Population	**Habitat Suitability Index**
Menden	1992	4	0	3	3	4	45.9	4	4.5	2.1	7.8	12.9	0.02	10.8	9.81	75	**0.4321**
Menden	1994	4	0	3	3	4	60.1	4	4.5	2.3	8.48	12	0.02	9.59	8.59	66	**0.3721**
Menden	1997	4	0	3	3	4	32.3	4	4.5	2.71	8.17	12.2	0.02	12.5	11.5	10	**0.2632**
Menden	2002	4	0	3	3	4	68.2	4	4.5	2.12	7.33	14.1	0.03	12.1	11.1	5	**0.1921**
Eitorf	1992	1	0	1	1	2	24.8	3	3.5	2.2	7.4	21	0.04	7.6	6.6	53	**0.2632**
Eitorf	1994	1	0	1	1	2	34	3	3.5	2.2	8.1	24.8	0.04	6.9	5.9	47	**0.2632**
Eitorf	1997	1	0	1	1	2	18.2	3	3.5	1.85	8.3	22	0.03	9.2	8.2	7	**0.2122**
Eitorf	2002	1	0	1	1	2	39.6	3	3.5	1.87	8.3	19.1	0.03	9.05	8.05	3	**0.1889**
Weidenau	1996	5	1	5	5	6	1.29	4	7	2.5	7.7	14	0.03	10	9	13	**0.2305**
Weidenau	1997	5	1	5	5	6	1.1	4	7	2	7.9	14.9	0.08	10.3	9.3	2	**0.1831**
Weidenau	1998	5	1	5	5	6	2.94	4	7	2	8.4	20.4	0.03	9.1	8.1	2	**0.1831**
Weidenau	1999	5	1	5	5	6	2.21	4	7	2.5	8.7	19.3	0.05	12.7	11.7	2	**0.1831**
Weidenau	2000	5	1	5	5	6	2.06	4	7	2	8.2	14.6	0.05	10.3	9.3	3	**0.1831**
Weidenau	2001	5	1	5	5	6	2.22	4	7	2	8.1	11.3	0.05	10.3	9.3	1	**0.1831**
Weidenau	2002	5	1	5	5	6	2.99	4	7	2.5	7.9	11.3	0.05	10.1	9.1	1	**0.1831**

Table 4. Calculated Habitat Suitability Index for the Menden, Eitorf and Weidenau water streams

applicability of fuzzy logic to develop ecohydrological models that overcome the problem of associated uncertainty of indicators. The model enables mixing qualitative and quantitative data in a strict fuzzy mathematical framework. It was possible to integrate the qualitative knowledge of involved researchers and experts during constructing both membership functions and rule-bases.

Further development of the DSS should include coupling it with the fuzzy fish model and water quality model. It should also take into consideration bigger river sizes social aspects, collecting more restoration data for validating and improving the rule base as well as modelling the interaction between river segments.

10. References

Alberta Government (Transportation department) (2003): Fish Habitat Manual. http://www.trans.gov.ab.ca.

Bender, M., C. Katopodis, S. P. Simonovic 1992. A Prototype Expert System for Fishway Design. Environmental Monitoring and Assessment 23:115-127, 1992.

Cortés, U., M. Sànchez-Marrè, L Cecaronni, I. R.-Roda, and M. Poch, Environmental - Decision Support Systems, Applied Intelligence 13(1),77-91, 2000.

Domanski, B. 1989. A PROLOG-based Expert System for Tuning MVS/XA. Performance Evaluation Review Vol. 16 #2-4 February 1989.

European Parliament (2000) EU Water Framework Directive. Official Journal, L 327, 1-73

Fisher, S.G., Grimm, N.B., Marti, E., Holmes, R.M. and Jones, J.B., 1998. Material spiraling in stream corridors: A telescoping ecosystem model. Ecosystems, 1(1): 19-34.

German Working Group of the Federal States (LAWA) (1998): Gewässerstruktur-gütekartierung in der Bundesrepublik Deutschland, Verfahren für kleine und mittelgroße Fließgewässer.

German ministry of Environment and Conservation, Agriculture and Consumer Protection of the State of North Rhine-Westphalia (MUNLV NRW) (2005): Erfolgskontrolle von Maßnahmen zur Unterhaltung und zum naturnahen Ausbau von Fließgewässern. Köln.

Hauer, C., M. Liedermann and H. Habersack (2006) The Influence of Human Impact to River morphology and aquatic ecology at the Austrian Kamp River. Vol. 8, 07430, 2006. European Geosciences Union 2006. SRef-ID: 1607-7962/gra/EGU06-A-07430

Montgomery, D.R. 2006. Geomorphology and Restoration Ecology JoUrnal of Contemporary Water researCh & education issUe 134, pages 16-19, JUly 2006

North Rhine-Westphalia State Environment Agency (LUA NRW) (2002): Gewässergütebericht 2001 Nordrhein-Westfalen, Berichtszeitraum 1995 - 2000, Essen.

North Rhine-Westphalia State Environment Agency (LUA NRW) (2003): Strukturgütedaten NRW der kleinen und mittelgroßen Fließgewässer.

Scherer, V. R., R. Twelbeck and C. Linnenweber 2006. Gewässerstrukturgüte und Habitatqualität für Fischzönosen. Wasserwirtschaft, Vol. 96, 26-31.

Schülter, M., N. Rüger, A.G. Savitsky, N.M. Novikova, M. Matthies, H. Leith 2006. TUGAI: AN Integrated Simulation Tool for Ecological Assessment of Alternative Water Management Strategies in a Degraded River Delta. Springer Science - Environmental Management 38: 238-653 2006.

Umwelt Bundes Amt (2005) Water Framework Directive - Summary of River Basin District Analysis 2004 in Germany. Bonifatius, Paderborn.

Vicente, D., Vellido,A., Marti,E., Comas,J., Rodríguez-Roda,I. (2004). Exploration of the ecological status of Mediterranean rivers: clustering, visualizing and reconstructing streams data using Generative Topographic Mapping. Data Minig V, A,Zanasi,N.F.F. Ebecken & C.A. Brebbia (editors).

6

The Decision Support System BodenseeOnline for Hydrodynamics and Water Quality in Lake Constance

Ulrich Lang[1], Roland Schick[2] and Gerd Schröder[3]
[1]*Engineering Consultant Prof. Kobus and Associates, Wilhelmstr.11, 70182 Stuttgart*
[2]*Zweckverband Bodensee-Wasserversorgung, Süßenmühle 1, D-78354 Sipplingen*
[3]*Institute for Lake Research of LUBW, Argenweg 50/1, 88085 Langenargen*
Germany

1. Introduction

Lake Constance is a large prealpine lake. It is an unregulated natural body of water which is of very high cultural and ecological value, a unique tourist attraction, and an important drinking water resource. The Lake is an international water body, located between Germany, Switzerland, and Austria (Fig.1). It drains a total catchment area of 11 000 km^2 with an average annual total discharge of 12 km^3/a from a considerable number of tributaries, of which the Alpenrhein provides about 60%. The lake has a total volume of 48 km^3 and consists of two parts: the upper basin with a surface area of about 473 km^2, extending over a length of more than 60 km, and the lower basin with about 63 km^2, which is located downstream and connected by a short river reach (Seerhein) in Konstanz. The upper basin has an average depth of 90 m, with a maximum depth of 254 m and several extended shallow areas along the shoreline.

The Bodensee region was settled in prehistoric times and since then has played a prominent role in European history. In the last century, the area has experienced a fast economic growth, industry developments, and considerable population growth. At the same time, the natural lake at the rim of the Alps has become a unique tourist attraction. These developments have led to increasingly negative effects upon the lake water quality, which have triggered a combined effort of the riparian states. In 1959, the "Internationale Gewässerschutzkommission Bodensee (IGKB)" (International water protection commission for Lake Constance) was formed, and the riparian states have taken consequential steps for reducing the waste water inputs into the lake. Within several decades, these efforts have lead to a continuous improvement of the lake water quality, which by now has reached nearly its natural quality again, which meets drinking water standards.

1.1 Motivation

Lake Constance is the most important natural resource of drinking water in the southwest of Germany and in the Lake Constance region of Switzerland. Drinking water is abstracted in 16 locations around the lake (see Figure 1). More than five million people are supplied with drinking water from Lake Constance. The main water supplier of Lake Constance is the

Bodensee-Wasserversorgung (BWV). The BWV delivers drinking water into the region of Stuttgart, the capital of Baden-Württemberg. Half the population of Stuttgart obtains the drinking water from Lake Constance. The average delivery of drinking water is 4 m^3/s.

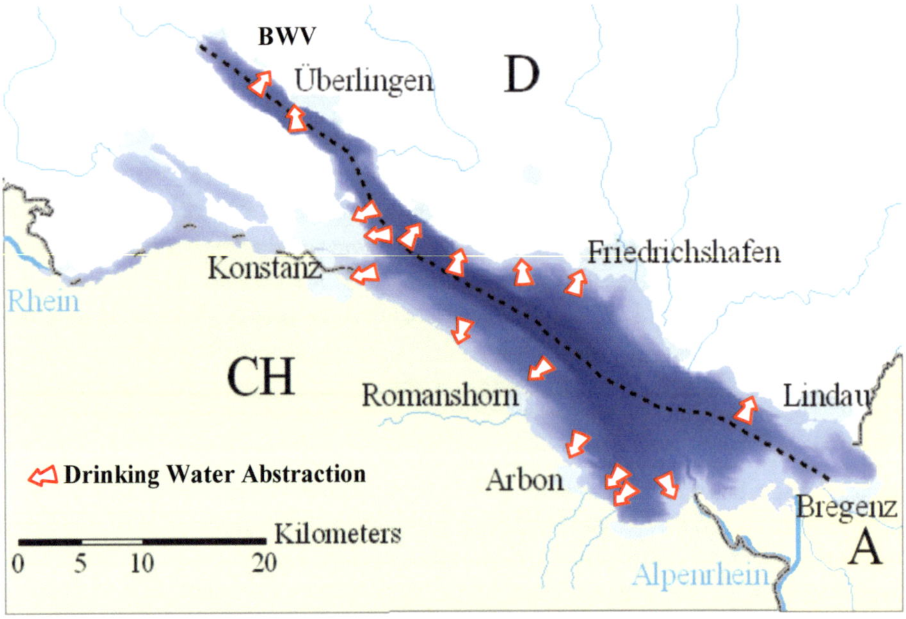

Fig. 1. Map of Lake Constance with drinking water abstractions

Lake Constance is under large pressure due to the intensive tourism and increase in population with an enlargement of industrial areas in the watershed and intensive agricultural uses as well. The main sources of hazards and risks for the water quality are accidents by transportation on the railways and roads around the lake and the air traffic to and from Zürich Kloten. Two terrible accidents with airplanes in the Lake Constance region demonstrate the vulnerability of the important drinking water resource. In 1994 a small aircraft fell into the lake near one of the main drinking water abstractions. It was supposed that nuclear material had been on board and the safety of the drinking water was questioned. In 2002 two airplanes crashed near Überlingen and it was incredibly lucky that the lake was neither affected nor partially contaminated by aircraft debris. The intensive use of Lake Constance by navigation and sailors is an additional source of hazards and risks for the water quality and the ecological system of Lake Constance. Initiated from the open questions around the two airplane crashes and based upon the potential risk of contaminations by hazardous material a decision support system for accident precaution is required for the lake.

Additionally, impacts due to extreme weather or hydrological conditions can affect the lake system temporarily. Extreme wind events or strong rainfall with flood conditions in the tributaries (e.g. August 2005) or high water levels in Lake Constance (Summer 1999) are examples that affect the lake temporarily. The flood event in August 2005 caused a high sediment inflow to the lake with resulting turbidity over more than half a year in the whole lake. Also, problems with driftwood occurred on the northern shore.

High water levels, such as in summer 1999, have tremendous impacts upon the shore. Buildings have to be protected and ecological damage on the reed areas are the consequences of high water levels in Lake Constance.

1.2 Objectives

A decision support system for Lake Constance has been developed in a multidisciplinary research project over a period of three years. This research project was financed by the German Research Foundation (Deutsche Forschungsgemeinschaft) and the Federal Ministry of Education and Research (Bundesministerium für Bildung und Forschung). The objective of the research project "BodenseeOnline, an Information System for Hydrodynamics and Water Quality" was to collect all relevant data and information for decision support, to develop numerical models for the prediction of hydrodynamic and water quality processes in the lake and to distribute the information to the stake holders. The decision support system BodenseeOnline has to deliver online or real time information about the up to date status of the lake. Three- dimensional numerical models calculate the interpretation of the lake status. These models must include all relevant processes affecting the lake hydrodynamics and major ecological components. The models calculate the transport of substances and simulate the nutrient cycle. They have to be validated with measured information and tested for a robust application in a continuous online model.

2. Hydrodynamic and ecological processes of Lake Constance

2.1 Hydrodynamics

The major driving forces of the flow and transport processes in the lake are shown in Fig.2. The energy transfer from the atmosphere leads to the typical seasonal heating of the water surface in spring and cooling in autumn, which in turn triggers the typical summer stratification and the turnover with complete mixing during winter.

Lake Constance is a monomictic lake with a stratification period between spring and late autumn. The surface temperature reaches values up to 20°C in summertime. The epilimnion thickness increases during the stratification period up to 20-30 m. The hypolimnion water temperature varies between 4 and 5 °C. The deep water is exchanged periodically after cold winters. The exchange of deep water takes place every 4 to 5 years dependent on the number of frost days, which are defined as days with air temperature below 0°C.

The major driving force of the lakewide circulation is the wind, which shows a highly variable distribution over the lake due to the local topography (Alps). The wind forces cause a complex flow field with internal waves in the stratified case. The Kelvin wave which travels counter clockwise around the lake has a period of 4 – 5 days depending on the stratification (thickness of epilimnion and temperature difference between epilimnion and hypolimnion). Due to the dimensions of the lake, these large-scale motions are modified by the Coriolis force.

The inflow and outflow conditions and all inputs of substances from tributaries or waste water treatment plants have to be considered to determine boundary conditions for the water quality and the transport characteristics of the lake. The main tributary is the river Alpenrhein, which flows into the eastern part of the lake. Because of the large load of suspended solids, dams have been built to lead the river plume with sediments to the deepest part of the lake. During flood events, density driven underflows with high sediment load can occur and can be observed mainly in the eastern part of the lake.

The lake geometry shows a number of specific features, in particular the "sill of Mainau", which separates the main upper Lake from the Überlinger See. Typical for prealpine lakes, the major inflow with floods and high water levels occurs during the snowmelt (late spring). In late summer to the winter season, often low flow situations are encountered.

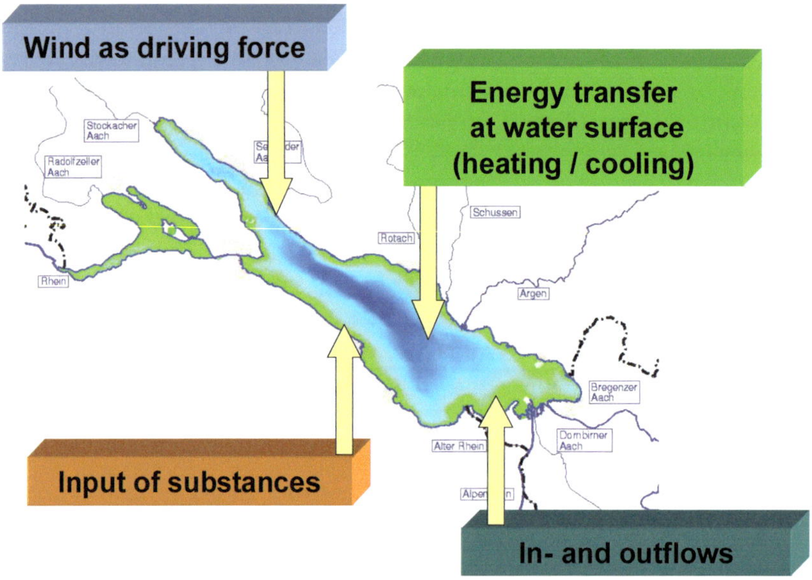

Fig. 2. Driving Forces and Inputs

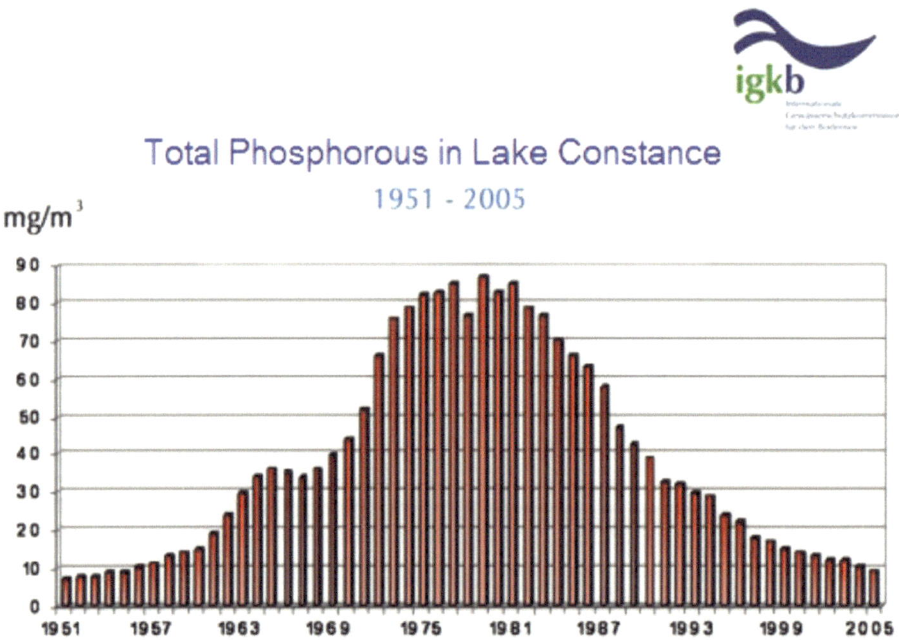

Fig. 3. Development of phosphorous concentrations between 1950 an 2005 (IGKB, 2004)

2.2 Ecological long term impacts

Before the industrialisation started after the Second World War, Lake Constance was an oligotrophic lake with low phosphorous concentrations, the limiting factor of the nutrient cycle. The lake became eutrophic during the sixties and seventies of the last century due to a high nutrient load from the tributaries and waste water (see Figure 3). The phosphorous concentrations reached levels of more than 80 mgP/m^3 around 1980. This led to large algae plumes during the summer period, which reduced the attractiveness of the lake for tourists. The bad water quality due to the algae plumes at the lake surface wasn't the only pollution risk for the lake. The large eutrophication threatened the deeper parts of the lake to become oxygen free. Several strong winters with cold air temperatures preserved the lake from an anaerobic hypolimnium before the efforts of enhanced waste water treatments have been effective. The phosphorous concentrations have now reached values of less than 10 mg/m^3, (as P) which were observed before the eutrophication started. The result is now a good water quality for the lake with rare algae plumes in summer which has to be preserved for the future.

3. BodenseeOnline model concept and database

A research team of five partner institutions has developed an Online Information System, which allows numerical simulation of the three-dimensional flow and transport processes of dissolved substances and sediments as well as the major biogeochemical cycle in Lake Constance. The components of the system "BodenseeOnline" are shown in Fig.4. The dynamic flow pattern in the lake can be simulated adequately and with high time resolution by coupling the wind model MassConsitentFlowmodel (MCF Scheuermann et al., 2008) for the regional wind distribution with the hydrodynamic model ELCOM (Hodges & Dallimore 2006). The coupled hydrodynamic-ecological model ELCOM-CAEDYM (Hipsey et al., 2007) is used to simulate the three-dimensional ecological processes in the lake.

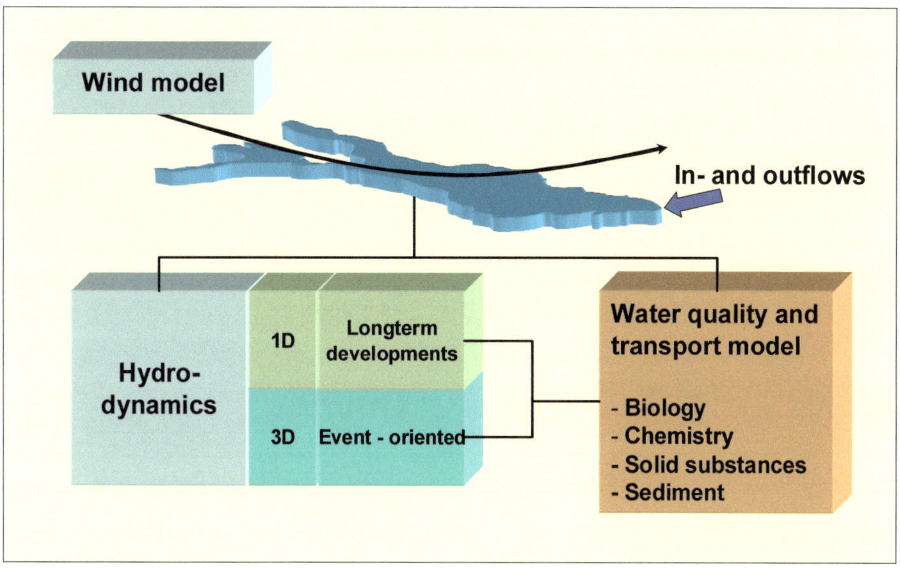

Fig. 4. The model system

For long-term considerations, the one dimensional model DYRESM (Hamilton & Schladow 1997) has been successfully applied in combination with the water quality model Computational Aquatic Ecosystem Dynamic Model (CAEDYM) (Hipsey et al., 2007) for the simulation of algal growth in spring, as well as for long-term shifts in the algal community composition attributable to the ongoing reoligotrophication of the lake.
The surface wave model Simulating WAves Nearshore (SWAN, Holthuijsen et al., 1989) is applied to estimate the two-dimensional wave structures on the lake surface introduced by wind.
The framework of BodenseeOnline is shown in Fig.5. The hydrological data for the entire catchment and all tributaries, as well as, all data taken by the state water authorities around the lake are provided daily by the three riparian countries. The national weather services provide the meteorological data and forecasts, and all water suppliers provide the data taken at their intake structures. The data is stored in the database, to which all users have access. The data base is split into two main parts: the data base of the measurements and the simulation results. Both parts can be visualized via a web interface. The access is restricted by user login with individualized views of the data.
In the decision support system BodenseeOnline, the various model components are directly linked to the BodenseeOnline database. The models are interactive: Estuary, Lake, and Coastal Ocean Model (ELCOM) for the flow and transport in the lake, MCF for the wind field above the lake as the dominant driving force for the flow and the internal waves, and CAEDYM for modelling the water quality. In order to provide the actual dynamic state of the lake, the model system contains a quarterly period of the lake dynamics, which is updated daily. This provides direct information about the actual dynamic state of the lake and a three day forecast of the lake dynamics. The actual predictions provide a unique pre-warning system in case of accidents or extreme events.

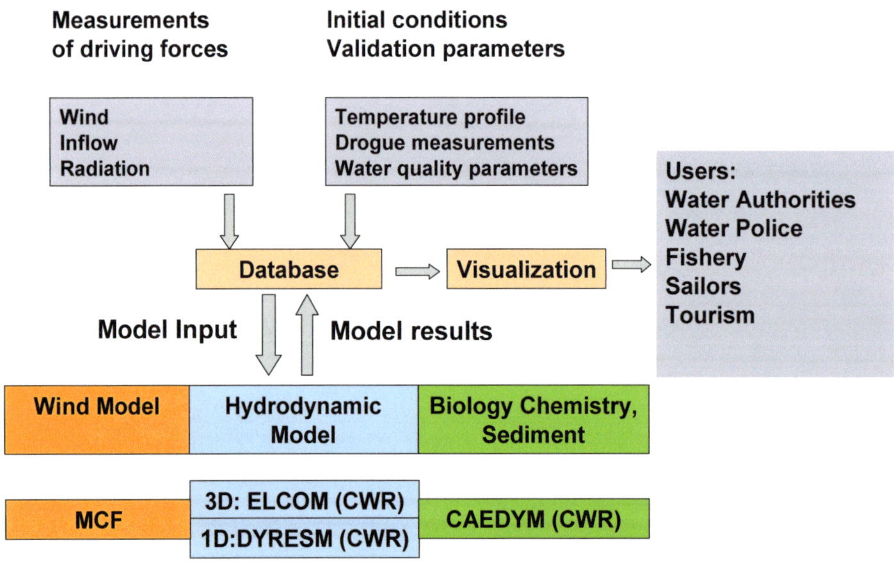

Fig. 5. Framework of the decision support system BodenseeOnline

3.1 Wind model

The wind model MCF covers an area of 70 x 40 km around the lake. The three-dimensional wind model simulates the wind distribution in the planetary boundary layer, which can be divided into the laminar boundary layer near ground surface, the Prandtl layer, and the Eckman layer as the boundary to the geostrophic wind. The orography defines the lower boundary, which includes the roughness of the surface with small roughness coefficients on the lake. The MCF model is a diagnostic, mass consistent, and free of divergence wind field which calculates hourly a steady state distribution of the wind. The model is driven by locally measured wind information or simulation results of a global wind model from the German weather survey which delivers the wind prognosis over the next three days.

3.2 Hydrodynamic model

The hydrodynamic lake ELCOM model is based on a finite difference approach. The numerical mesh consists of 52 layers in the vertical with a layer thickness of 2.5 m in the upper and 10 m in the lower part. The horizontal grid has a basic grid size of 400 m respectively, and 100 m at the river inflows and in the shallow areas.

The hydrodynamic model simulates the surface thermodynamic processes and mass fluxes at the lake surface. The surface exchanges include heating due to short wave radiation penetration into the lake and the fluxes at the surface due to evaporation, sensible heat (i.e. convection of heat from the water surface to the atmosphere) and long wave radiation. The short wave radiation is a direct input to the model from measurements. The incident long wave radiation (ILWR) is calculated by Iziomon et al. (2003) with data for vapour pressure e, air temperature T and cloud cover N.

$$ILWR = \sigma \cdot T^4 \left[1 - X_S \cdot \exp\left(\frac{-Y_s \cdot e}{T_a} \right) \right] \cdot \left(1 + Z_S \cdot N^2 \right) \tag{1}$$

Based on measurements from the black forest, the parameters Xs = 0.35, Ys = 10 and Zs = 0.0035 have been calibrated.

The heat energy budget of the lake implies a variable density of the lake water dependent upon the water temperature. Additionally, the density of the lake water varies due to salinity and load of suspended solids. The suspended solids are introduced by the river inflows. The major solid load takes place during flood events of the main rivers (e.g. Alpenrhein). The density of the Alpenrhein water increases significantly in cases of flooding. The sediment concentration of the Alpenrhein is only weekly measured. Thus continuous information of the sediment concentration is not available and must be deduced from the long term measurement relationship between discharge Q and sediment concentration C_s as:

$$C_s = 0{,}0004 \cdot Q^{2{,}2069} \tag{2}$$

The hydrodynamic online model simulates the development of the water temperature, salinity and sediment concentration. The river plumes are marked with a conservative tracer to determine the spatial distribution of the river water in case of accidents in the catchments.

3.3 Ecological model

An ecological model was integrated in the online model system BodenseeOnline running on Lake Constance simulating plankton succession and nutrient dynamics of this large lake. The ecological model (CAEDYM) is coupled with a hydrodynamic model. Input data for this

coupled hydrodynamic-ecological model system are meteorological variables and time-series for inflow volume and nutrient loads of the inflowing rivers stored in the common data base.
The core of the ecological model consists of a classical nutrient-phytoplankton-zooplankton (NPZ-) model, including the associated dynamics of phosphorus, nitrogen, and silica. For a proper representation of phytoplankton succession, four functional phytoplankton groups with specific physiological properties have been defined. By analysing the occurrences of these four functional groups in the field, distinguishable succession patterns emerged and model simulations were able to reproduce these patterns found within the observations.
The parameter set of the ecological model was defined by calibrating a three year period of phytoplankton development. The ecological model was coupled with the one-dimensional hydrodynamic model DYRESM to simulate the vertical mixing and thermal stratification dynamics of the lake.
For the online simulation, the ecological model has been coupled with the three-dimensional hydrodynamic model ELCOM on a regular coarse grid of 400 m cell size allowing spatially explicit simulations of the ecosystem.

3.4 Surface wave model

The wave model SWAN is used to simulate the spatial pattern of surface waves of the lake. The input for the wave model is the bathymetry and the two-dimensional wind field calculated by the wind model. The wind model provides information on the wave height, length, and period. The model runs in a predictive mode and delivers the users (e.g. sailors and navigation) of BodenseeOnline the expected wave data for the next three days.

3.5 Web based visualization

The user interface of BodenseeOnline is web-based access to the information. General information about the actual wind conditions, the flow field at the lake surface, the water temperatures, and the waves are available to the public. This data is presented in a map similar to the weather forecast. This map is updated daily and hourly, information for the next three days is presented. Further information needs a password to protect user access.
The specific users have the possibility to select time series of measured data stored in the database. The data can be displayed in graphs or downloaded for individual analysis. The update interval of the measurements is between 10 minutes and once the day depending upon the type of data and data owner.
The simulation results are stored in the database and can be visualized by the user in three different ways:

Vertical profiles:

The calculated parameters (e.g. temperature, algae concentration or concentration of river water) can be visualized at one location over depth (y-axis) in time (x-axis). Fig. 6 shows the concentration of calculated chlorophyll A and zooplankton concentration in the spring and summer of 2009. The algae started to grow in April after a stable stratification developed in Lake Constance. The maximum algae plumes were calculated to be in May before the zooplankton starts to proliferate.

Vertical cross sections:

All parameters can be visualized in given vertical profiles along the length axis of lake and perpendicular to the length axis. Because of the transient simulation, the time dependent development of the parameters can be presented in movies for individual time periods.

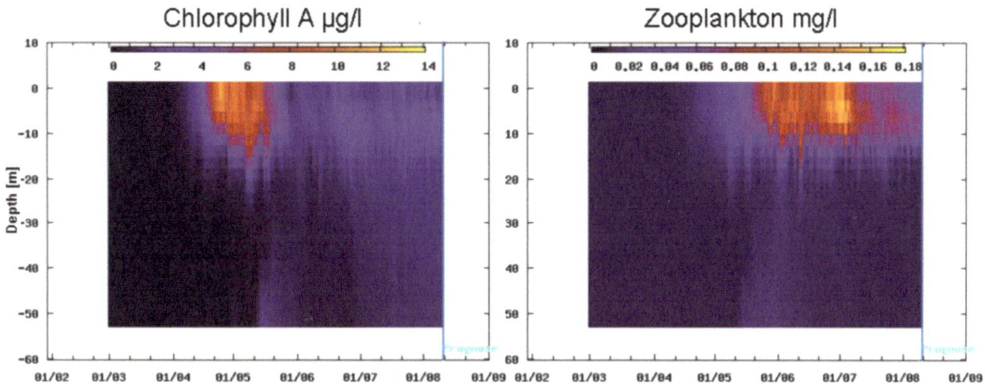

Fig. 6. Calculated profiles of chlorophyll A concentration and zooplankton concentration in BodenseeOnline in spring 2009

Horizontal cross sections:

The visualization of horizontal cross section is realized by using the Geographical Information System "GISTerm web" developed by the company disy. The GIS allows the selection of individual time steps at different vertical depths. The system reads the data from the database and prepares a shape-file for the selected parameter. This shape-file can be combined with topographic information and further simulation results.

One important feature of BodenseeOnline is the calculation of user-defined pathways in the calculated transient flow field. The flow path calculation is possible with the following options for several practical applications:

- Simulation of a single or multi particle movement: What is the expected arrival area of contaminants transported from a single release point?
- Simulation in the flow direction: Where does a contaminant move?
- Simulation against the flow direction: Where does a contaminant come from?
- Simulation of drift wood on the lake surface: Additionally to the lake current the drift by wind can be included in the flow path calculation by specifying the drag coefficients of a float

An example of calculated particle tracking movements in different depths of the lake is shown in Fig. 7. During the same time period particles can move in totally different directions from a common release point when these particles are placed in different depths.

4. Validation of the model system

The BodenseeOnline system provides an up-to-date overview of the present dynamic state of the lake and predictions for the short-term (3 days) developments of flow and water quality, based upon the meteorological forecasts. The prototype of BodenseeOnline has been validated for a variety of cases with measured data. The major validations are:

- Measurement campaign 2001 to evaluate the internal wave modelling
- Flood event August 2005 to evaluate the density driven inflow of suspended solids with lakewide transport
- Measurement campaign 2007 to evaluate the three-dimensional ecological modelling

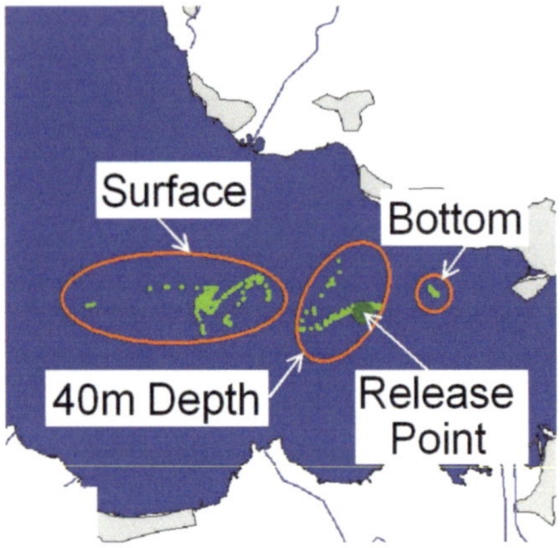

Fig. 7. The three-dimensional flow field: calculated simultaneous particle transport at various depths from a common release point

The validated BodenseeOnline system provides a suitable decision support tool for questions related to precautionary water resources protection, drinking water supply, and water resources management.

4.1 Measurement campaign 2001

In the model validation, a first field campaign has been conducted in 2001 (Appt and Stumpp, 2002). Nine thermistor chains have been installed in the lake to measure the temporal development of the vertical temperature profiles with the local internal wave structure (Appt et al., 2004). Each observation location has been additionally equipped with a wind sensor to observe the two-dimensional wind fields over the lake.

The lake was still stratified at the beginning of the field campaign. The epilimnion had a thickness of nearly 25 m. The meteorological conditions during the field campaign in autumn 2001 can be divided in two phases. The first phase was dominated by weak wind which introduced the typical Kelvin wave travelling counter clockwise in a three to four day period around the lake. A strong wind event started in the second period on 8th of November 2001. The wind came from a southwesterly direction with a maximum wind speed of 12 m/s. The duration of the wind event was nearly three days.

In Fig.8 it shows a longitudinal section through the lake, where the wind forces the surface water to move eastwards and in consequence leads to a counterflow in the hypolimnion. This is the interpretation of the hydrodynamic model. The locally measured temperature profiles can be compared directly to the calculated development of the temperatures (see bottom of Fig. 8).

Due to the strong wind event, a strong shift in the epilimnion water has been observed, with the consequence that at the observation point S2 hypolimnion water is upwelling to the surface. Observation point S2 is located near the sill of Mainau, which separates the main basin from the Überlinger See. The agreement between observation and model calculation is quite good. The internal wave movement before the wind event started as well as the upwelling caused by the wind event are simulated appropriate to the observations.

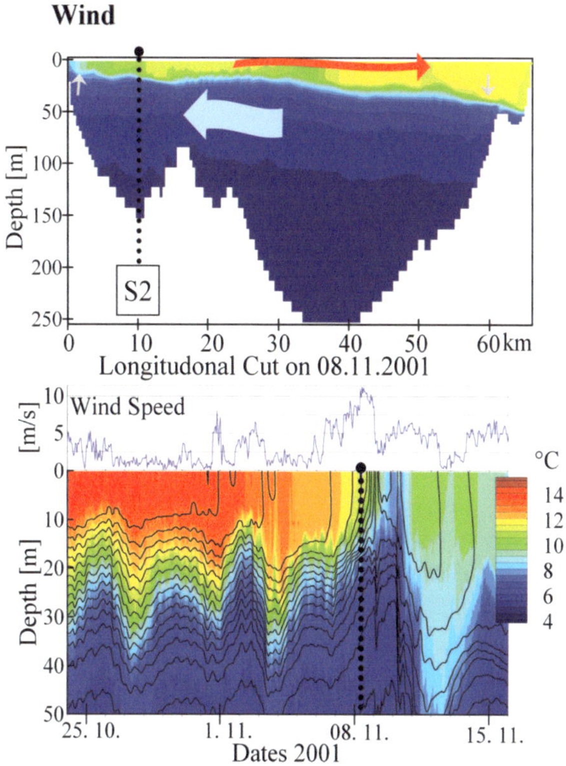

Fig. 8. Upper part: calculated temperature distribution along the longitudinal cut during a strong westerly wind: arrows show flow direction in the epilimnion- and hypolimnion. Lower part: measured (colours) and calculated (lines) temperature profile over time at point S2.

4.2 Flood event August 2005

Another set of data for validation of the model system was provided by an extreme flood event in summer 2005. The Alpenrhein entered the lake with a very high load of sediment and fairly warm temperatures. Due to the sediment load, the warm river water produced a downward density current, which reached the deepest part of the lake. The water temperatures at the lake bottom, which normally are around 4 to 5°C, temporarily reached values of up to 8°C. After the coarse sediment fractions had settled out, the warm water with the remaining fine sediments produced a buoyant plume rising to the thermocline, from where it was transported with the large-scale lake circulation. It finally reached the water supply intakes on the northern shore where it was observed as a strong increase in turbidity.

Observed values at two waterworks compared to model calculation results, which show fairly good agreement for this extremely complex process, are shown in Fig. 9. The first arrival time of sediment concentration and start of turbidity agrees between the observation and calculation, as well as the time lag between the two observation points because of the travel time between Immenstaad and BWV. While the maximum concentrations of turbidity and solid concentration can not directly be compared but the relation between the two observation points, which is very similar between the calculation and observation.

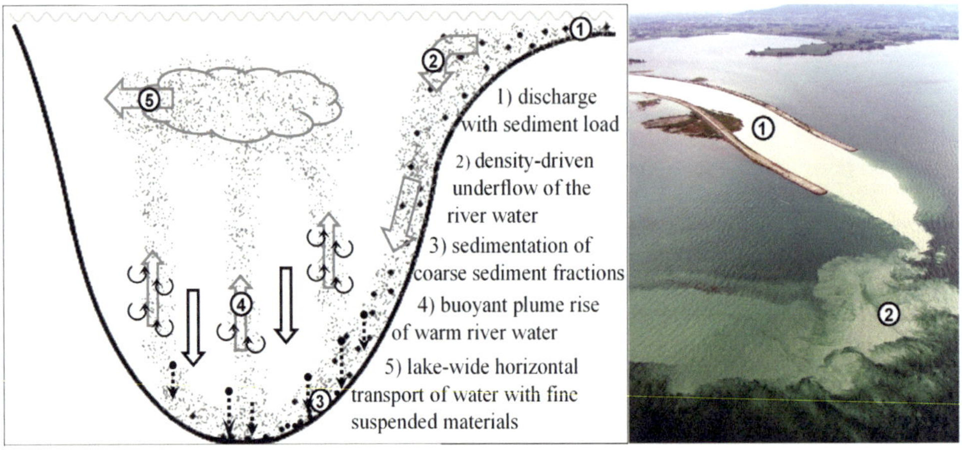

Fig. 9. Inflow of warm water during a flood event and density driven transport mechanism in the lake (photo: Peter Rey, HYDRA)

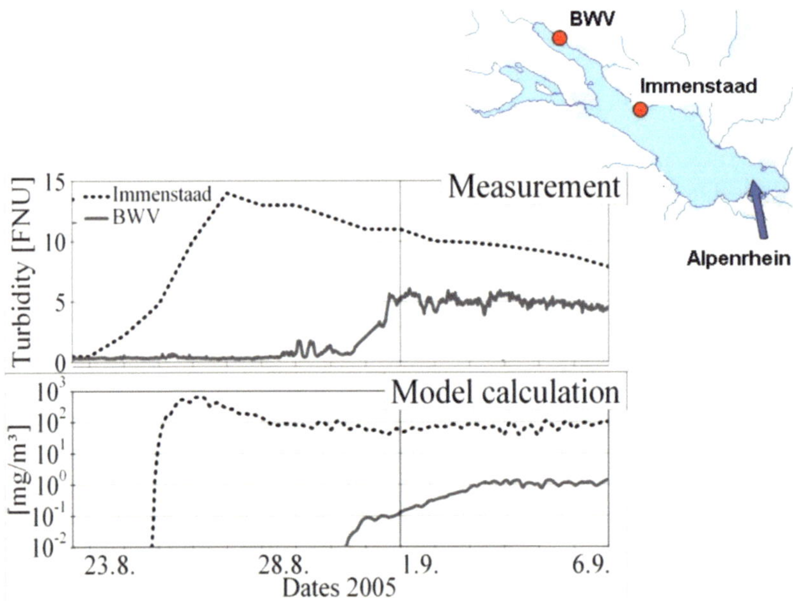

Fig. 10. Calculated suspended solid concentration and observed turbidity at two drinking water supply intakes after the extreme rain event in August 2005 with high discharge of warm water and sediment from the Alpenrhein

4.3 Field campaign 2007

During spring 2007, a lakewide field campaign was conducted in order to assess the three-dimensional distribution of temperature, phytoplankton, zooplankton, and fish (Eder et al. 2008). These biological parameters were measured in several cross sections at different dates to analyse their spatial distribution. The field campaign took place during a period of weak stratification with a strong wind event on the 8th of May 2007, which disturbed the stratification temporarily.

The three-dimensional online ecological-hydrodynamic model was used to simulate the processes during the field campaign. The model started at the beginning of algae growth in early spring. Fig. 11 shows the development of temperatures during the campaign calculated by the model as well as the temperatures observed at Überlinger See. The temporal development of the calculated temperatures agreed very well with the observations (see Fig. 11).

The observed distributions of plankton and temperatures were heavily affected by the strong westerly wind which forced the warm epilimnetic water into the Eastern part of the lake. Whereas, at the same time cold, hypolimnetic water depleted of plankton was upwelling to the surface in the western part.

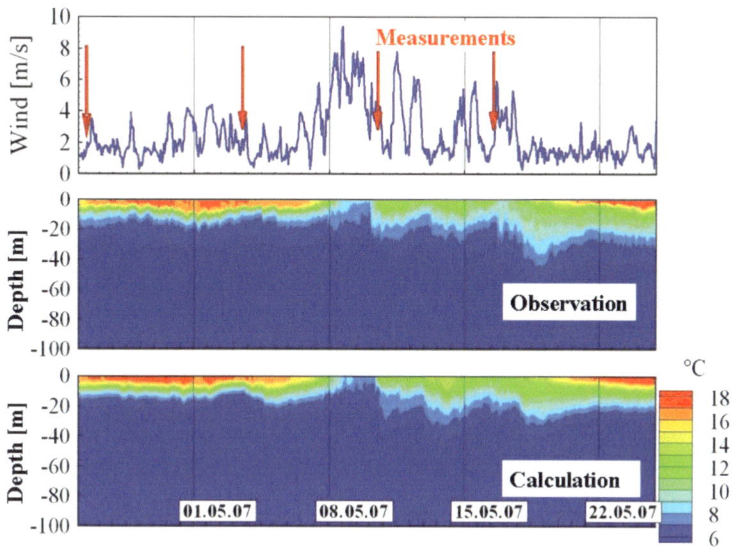

Fig. 11. Observed wind speed, observed and calculated temperature profile in Überlinger See during field campaign 2007

In Fig. 12, the distribution of chlorophyll A concentration in the lake was observed at two dates during the campaign. The comparison with the simulation results shows a good agreement. Direct after the wind event on the 10th of May, the algae had been transported to the Eastern part of the lake and to the Northern and Southern shores. At the second measurement (16th of May) the phytoplankton returns to Überlinger See with the same concentration as in the main basin.

The vertical cross section in Fig. 13 demonstrates that the vertical structure of the phytoplankton distribution is also simulated well in the numerical model. The main concentrations of phytoplankton can be found in this cross section near the Northern and Southern shores.

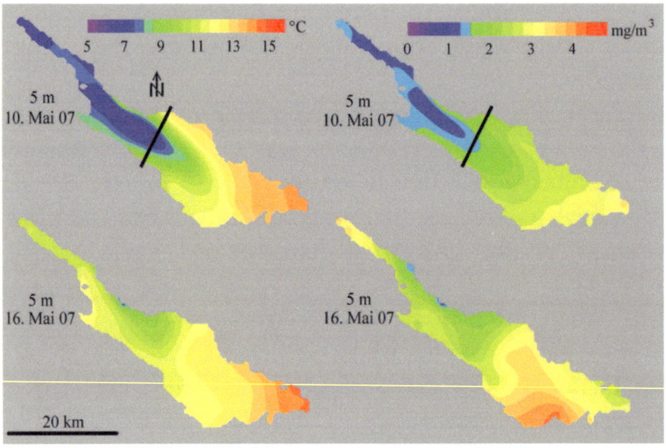

Fig. 12. Measured (left) and calculated (right) concentration of chlorophyll A at 5 m depth on two different days during field campaign 2007 (the black lines mark the location of the cross section in Fig. 13

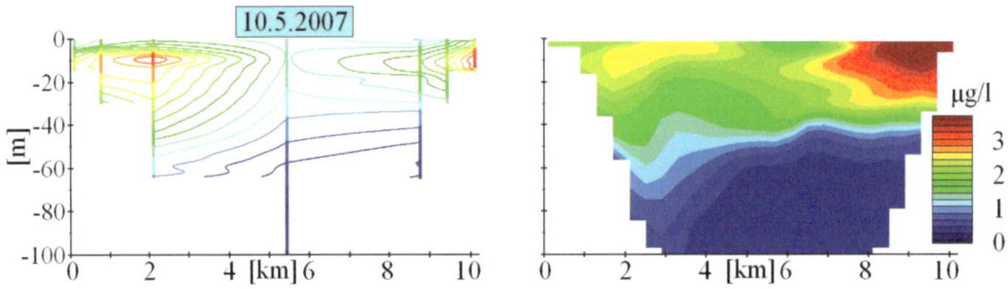

Fig. 13. Measured (left) and calculated (right) concentration of chlorophyll A in a vertical cross section (location see Fig. 12)

5. User needs and applications

The decision support system BodenseeOnline is of direct interest primarily for the water authorities of the riparian countries and for the water suppliers. Also, the system provides decision support for the design of protection measures and in cases of accidents. For catastrophic events or accidents, it is also of prime interest for the water police, fire brigades, and communities. Additionally, the databank is of direct interest for research institutions, for industries (cooling water, industrial water needs, energy), for organisations, for the environment, navigation, and tourism, as well as for the general public.

Regarding water resources management, it provides information for decisions with respect to the effects of hydraulic structures or events and activities leading to a change of inflow of substances. It allows prognoses for assessing the effect of measures for maintaining and improving the water quality and provides early warnings about the effects of floods on embankments and settlements.

Furthermore, the model system provides a framework for investigating local issues, based upon more refined local models with dynamic boundary conditions from the large scale model system. Examples are local inflow problems for tributaries (e.g. Schussen) or for the discharge of treated sewage water from water treatment plants, morphological changes or discharge of sediments in the lake, effects of changing the shoreline geometry, hydraulic structures, etc.

An important question that will be addressed with the model system relates to the possible effects of climate change on the lake and its ecology. First signals are the observation of several new species in the lake and the fact that during mild winters the lake does not show a complete turnover and mixing of the deep layers with a corresponding reoxygenation of the hypolimnion. Presently, the lake has good water quality and considerable oxygen concentrations in the deep layers, which have been maintained most recently even after two mild winters without turnover. However, if mild winters would occur more often, eventually the hypolimnion will exhibit anaerobic conditions with possibly dramatic effects for the water quality of the lake.

A prototype of the DSS BodenseeOnline for accidents, disturbances, pollution, or extreme events has been developed and validated with observed data. The prototype is running in a test phase, where the suitability of the system for practical uses has been demonstrated in several applications. One example is, an oil alert on the 28th of March 2009 when a large oil film was observed in the eastern part of the lake. The flow path tool was used to identify possible input locations of contamination (see Fig. 13). It demonstrated that the most likely source of contamination is near the Alpenrhein inflow. The calculated travel times indicated that the accident had happened only one or two days before the oil was detected.

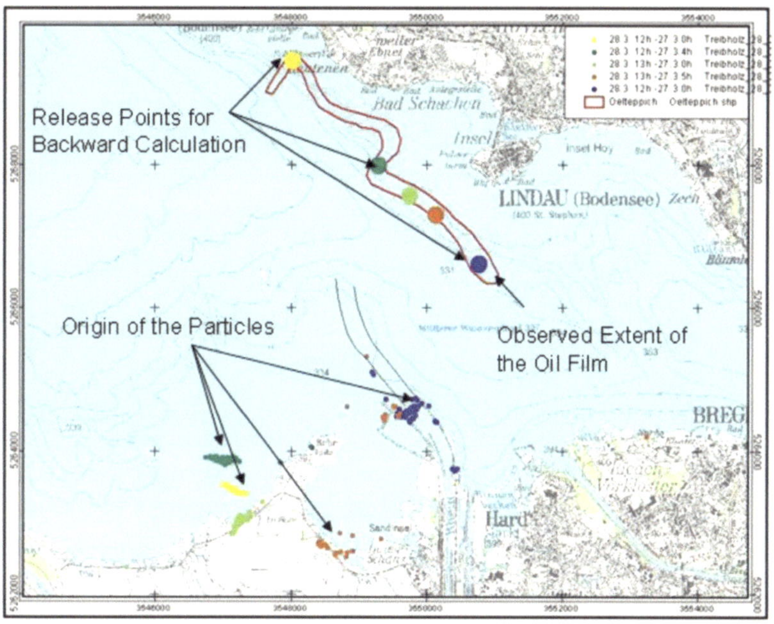

Fig. 14. Application of BodenseeOnline for an observed oil film with backward calculation of particles

Predictions of oil movement showed that the oil slick would be transported in a South-eastern direction in the hours after detection. But a medium wind event destroyed the oil film due to mixing by the surface waves.

6. Outlook: Decision support for drinking water treatment plants

It is planned to develop a further decision support system for the drinking water treatment plant of the main water supplier, Zweckverband Bodensee-Wasserversorgung (BWV). The BWV takes at an average 4 m^3/s lake water and pumps it to the water work at the hill of Sipplingen. The water is treated in a micro strainer system to remove the large particles. The next treatment step is the input of ozone for water disinfection and sand filters. Several basins are included in the treatment process for intermediate storage or as reactors. The aim of a further decision support system is to simulate the flow and transport through the treatment plant and to have estimations about realistic residence times in case of an accident with hazardous materials.

Fig. 15 shows a first calculation of the flow field in a drinking water basin with a volume of 12065 m^3 and a discharge of 2 m^3/s from left to right. Two tracers are applied to the simulations: tracer 1 entering the basin and tracer 2 being initially placed in the basin water. The outflow concentration of the inflow tracer decreases in several steps in a time period of 25000 s. The mean residence time of the basin is 6032 s. Thus the tracer 2 concentration is at the mean residence time still above 40 %, which means that only 60 % of the basin water has renewed after the mean residence time and the total mass of the tracers has exchanged after approximately 25000 s.

The pan is to set up a model for the complete drinking water treatment plant including all relevant substances for the treatment process and having an additional decision support system to control the treatment plant.

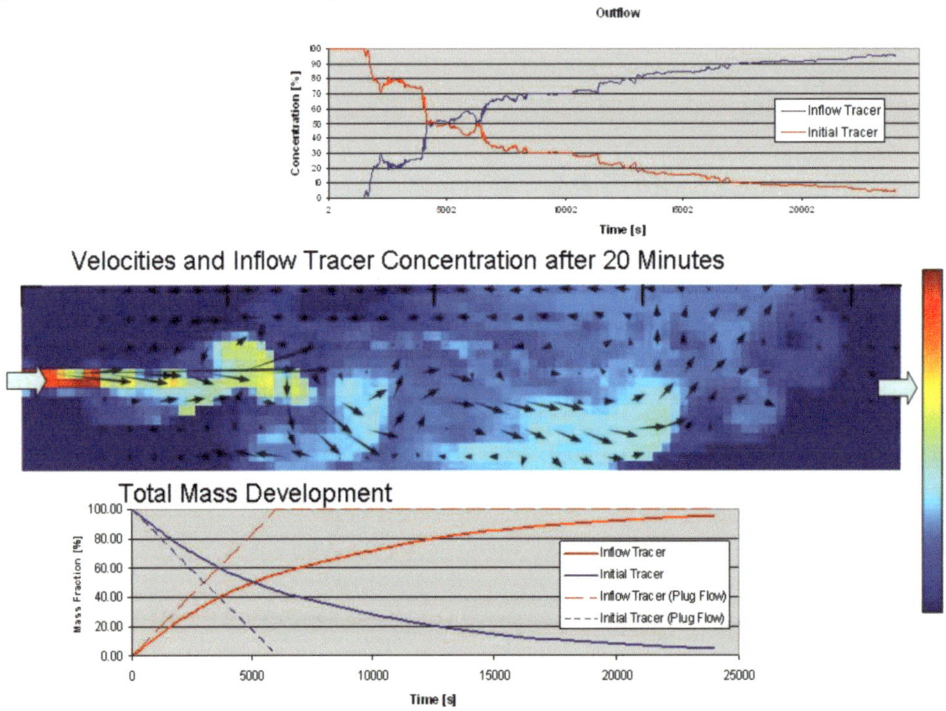

Fig. 15. Calculated tracer concentrations in a drinking water basin, top: Calculated outflow concentrations, middle: distribution of tracer concentration and velocities in a horizontal sheet, bottom: development of the total tracer mass

7. Conclusion

A decision support system for the management of Lake Constance was developed in an interdisciplinary research project over a period of 3 years. In collaboration with the riparian countries Germany, Switzerland and Austria, an online data base has been developed, in which relevant meteorological, hydrological and water quality data of Lake Constance are collected. The data base is coupled with a numerical online modelling system to simulate three dimensional hydrodynamic processes and ecosystem dynamics in the lake. The modelling system consists of a wind model forecasting the two dimensional wind fields over the lake, the hydrodynamic model ELCOM to calculate the flow process in the lake and the ecological model CAEDYM to simulate water quality. The hydrodynamic model is updated daily and a prediction over the next three days is included in the modelling system. The hydrodynamic model is validated on measuring campaigns of major hydrodynamic processes; e.g. wind induced lake wide internal waves during stratified conditions or inflow dynamics under extreme flood conditions with density dependent sediment transport. The water quality model is validated on long term data and lake-wide campaigns on chlorophyll a and zooplankton distributions in Lake Constance in May 2007.

The information system supports water management decisions under water protection aspects and in cases of accidents with hazardous substances. The user has access to the measured and calculated information via internet. Passwords protected areas give an individual view to the data and allow individual analysis of the hydrodynamic system with user initiated calculations for transport of dissolved substances or drifting objects on the lake surface.

The successful development and implementation of the decision support system BodenseeOnline provides a good example that interdisciplinary research is a prerequisite for solving complex water problems. It also shows that interaction among organisations, international cooperation, and data exchange are prerequisites for successful lake management. And finally, it demonstrates convincingly that appropriate hydraulic research can provide a direct approach to integrated and sustainable water management. Research results are implemented directly into daily water resource management.

8. References

Appt, J., Stumpp, S. (2002): "Die Bodensee-Messkampagne 2001, IWS/CWR Lake Constance Measurement Program 2001", *Mitteilungsheft 111*, Institut für Wasserbau, Universität Stuttgart

Appt, J., Imberger, J. und Kobus, H. (2004): Basin-scale motion in stratified Upper Lake Constance. *Limnol. Oceanogr.*, 49: 919-933.

Eder, M., Rinke, K., Kempke, S., Huber, A., Wolf, T.: "Seeweite Bodensee-Messkampagne 2007 als Test für BodenseeOnline", *Wasserwirtschaft* 10/2008, pp.34-38

Hamilton, D P. and Schladow, S.G. (1997): "Prediction of water quality in lakes and reservoirs: Part I - Model description", *Ecological Modelling*

Hipsey, M.R., Romero, J.R., Antenucci, J.P., Hamilton, D. (2007): Computational Aquatic Ecosystem Dynamic Model: CAEDYM, v3 *Science Manual. Centre for Water Research* (CWR), University of Western Australia, 2007

Hodges,B., Dallimore,C (2006).: Estuary , Lake and Coastal Ocean Model ELCOM, v.2.2 *Science Manual. Centre for Water Research* (CWR), University of Western Australia

Holthuijsen, L.H., Booij, N. and T.H.C. Herbers (1989): A prediction model for stationary, short-crested waves in shallow water with ambient currents, *Coastal Engineering*, 13, 23-54

IGKB (2004): Der Bodensee, Zustand - Fakten - Perspektiven, Internationale Gewässerschutzkommission für den Bodensee (IGKB), 1. Auflage 177 S..

Scheuermann, W., Schmidt, F., Krass, C. (2008): "Modellierung des Windfeldes als Antriebskraft für die interne Strömung im Bodensee", 10/2008, pp.22-25

7

Action Rules Approach to Solving Diagnostic Problems in Clinical Medicine

Hanna A. Wasyluk[1] and Zbigniew W. Raś[2,3]
[1]*The Medical Center of Postgraduate Education, Warszawa,*
[2]*University of North Carolina, Dept. of Comp. Science, Charlotte, N.C. 28223,*
[3]*Polish-Japanese Institute of Information Technology, Warszawa,*
[1,3]*Poland*
[2]*USA*

1. Introduction

The beginning of the twenty first century have brought considerable advances in the field of computer-based medical systems. It resulted from noticeable improvements in medical care, from ease of storage and access of digital imaging through gathering of computerized medical data to accessing on-line literature, patient monitoring, therapy planning and computer support for medical diagnosis. Similarly to other domains, decision-support systems have proven to be valuable tools that help practitioners in facing challenging medical problems, such as diagnosis and therapy. Given that stakes happen to be extremely high, support of decision-making plays a particularly important role in the field of medicine. As an example, in the domain of hepatology, inexperienced clinicians have been found to make a correct diagnosis in jaundiced patients in less than 45% of cases [1,2]. Incorrect diagnosis leads to suboptimal treatment that means waste of resources, time and sometimes of human life. Automating those processes that can be captured by focus on important signs and symptoms, eliminates human error and leads to overall improvements in the quality of medical care.

2. Liver disorders as particularly recommended area for computer-aided diagnostics

The domain of liver diseases is especially suited to application of computer-based methods and there are several reasons for high expectations from computer-aided diagnosis. Firstly, the number of cases of liver disorders is on the rise. In Poland, the number of new acute and chronic hepatitis cases is roughly half a million per year. Secondly, correct diagnosis, especially in early stages of disease, is difficult. There is variety of diseases that manifests with similar symptoms. Finally, early diagnosis is critical, as in some cases damage to the liver caused by an untreated disorder may by irreversible.
Typically, a patient suffering from symptoms suggesting of abdominal disorders seeks help of a family doctor. Primary care physicians face the daunting task of determining the source of discomfort based on patient-reported data and physical examination, possibly enhanced

with the results of basic medical tests. Correct diagnosis under these circumstances is difficult and accuracy can be low. Based on our observations, we estimate that at this stage only 40-60% of the cases are diagnosed correctly.
This rather low diagnostic performance is caused by several etiophysiological and organizational factors. These include the nature of the liver, e.g. its high productive reserves that often make the abnormalities noticeable only when the disease reaches an advanced stage. Growth of liver diseases is often slow and unspecific and the symptoms may by hardly noticeable. Liver disorders are influenced by environmental factors, such as alcohol intake, medications and dietary habits. There is still insufficient knowledge of immunological factors that cause certain pathologies of liver. Undiagnosed or misdiagnosed viral hepatitis often leads to irreversible defects of the liver that may have bearing on the manifestation of the possible later disorders. Reliable diagnosis of a liver disorder can be often established only based on the results of liver biopsy. However, biopsy is an examination that is performed only in specialized clinics and may not be available to primary care physician (1).

3. The HEPAR computer-aided diagnosis system

The HEPAR system was designed and built in collaboration between the Institute of Biocybernetics and Biomedical Engineering of the Polish Academy of Sciences and Medical Center of Postgraduate Education in Warsaw. The system, operating in the Gastroeterological Clinic of the Institute of Food and Feeding in Warsaw, allows for systematic collection and processing of clinical data of hepatological patients diagnosed and treated in the clinic. The system is equipped with a diagnostic module built around several statistical methods that have been found useful in diagnosis. An integral part of the HEPAR is database, created in 1990 and thoroughly maintained since then. The current database contains roughly 860 patients records - with the ultimate diagnosis verified by means of biopsy, laparoscopy and often longitudinal follow-up. Each hepatological case is described by over 150 different medical findings, such as patient self-reported data, results of physical examination, laboratory tests and finally a histopatologically verified diagnosis. The system includes the module supporting the physicians in making a diagnosis.
Computer-based systems accompanying a medical diagnosis can be based on variety of principles. Generally, diagnosis supporting rules used in such systems may reflect knowledge provided by medical doctors (experts), textbooks and regularities extracted from clinical databases. In accordance with this, we distinguish two kinds of systems: knowledge based systems and database systems (3).
HEPAR could be treated as a database system because decision rules used there relay mainly on information extracted from the hepatological database.
The patients from this database have been classified by clinicians into several adequate liver diseases. The support of diagnosis in HEPAR system is based on a comparison of a new patient case with similar cases from its database.
Graphical representation of the data on a plane in a form of *diagnostic* maps is particularly important in the HEPAR. The diagnostic maps represent the data on a plane in such a way that differences between selected diseases are enhanced. The diagnostic maps used in the system result form linear transformations of multivariate data sets into two dimensions. These transformations are obtained through minimization of the perceptron criterion functions, that have links to early research on neural networks [3].

Medical doctors willingly accept data mapping because it gives them an opportunity for a better understanding of a diagnostic problem.
The nearest neighbors techniques originated as one the pattern recognition methods. They have many practical applications related to a classification problem. Generally, the nearest neighbors classification or diagnostic rules are based on a comparison of a new object with the most similar objects that have been previously classified. The cases similar to presently diagnosing patients are found in the system either directly in the database or through their representation on *diagnostic map*.
This paper - presenting a new strategy of constructing action rules (called ARAS) and its application to the HEPAR database - is implying that such an approach might improve medical reasoning associated with the computer-aided diagnosis of patients with liver diseases.

4. Material and methods

Finding useful rules is an important task of a knowledge discovery process. Most researchers focus on techniques for generating patterns from a data set such as classification rules, association rules...etc. They assume that it is user's responsibility to analyze these patterns in order to infer solutions for specific problems within a given domain. The classical knowledge discovery algorithms have the potential to identify enormous number of significant patterns from data. Therefore, people are overwhelmed by a large number of uninteresting patterns and it is very difficult for a human being to analyze them in order to form timely solutions. Therefore, a significant need exists for a new generation of techniques and tools with the ability to assist users in analyzing a large number of rules for a useful knowledge [4].
Action rules can be seen as logical terms describing knowledge about possible actions associated with objects which is hidden in a database. Classical strategy for discovering action rules requires prior extraction of classification rules which next are evaluated pair by pair with a goal to build a strategy of action based on condition features in order to get a desired effect on a decision feature. An actionable strategy is represented as a term $r = [\omega \wedge (\alpha \to \beta)] \to (\phi \to \psi)]$, where ω, α, β, ϕ, and ψ are descriptions of objects, in our case seen as patients. The term r states that when a fixed condition ω is satisfied and the changeable behavior $(\alpha \to \beta)$ occurs in patients registered in a database so does the expectation $(\phi \to \psi)$.
This paper proposes a new strategy of agglomerative type, called ARAS, for constructing action rules directly from single classification rules.
The ARAS strategy has been implemented as one of the modules in HEPAR Clinical Decision Support System which consists of a clinical database and a set of tests and procedures, facilitating decision-making process for patients with liver disorders.

5. Constructing action rules

Action rules, introduced in [5] and investigated further in [6], [7], [8] are constructed from certain pairs of classification rules. Interventions, defined in [8], are conceptually very similar to action rules [10], [11].
The previous process of constructing action rules from pairs of classification rules is not only unnecessarily expensive but also gives too much freedom in constructing their classification parts. In [8] it was shown that action rules do not have to be built from pairs of classification

rules and that single classification rules are sufficient to achieve the same goal. However, this paper only proposed a theoretical lattice-theory type framework without giving any detailed algorithm for action rules construction. In this paper we propose a very simple LERS-type algorithm for constructing action rules from a single classification rule. LERS is a classical example of a bottom-up strategy which constructs rules with a conditional part of the length k+1 after all rules with a conditional part of the length k have been constructed. Relations representing rules produced by LERS are marked. System ARAS assumes that LERS is used to extract classification rules. This way system ARAS instead of verifying the validity of certain relations only has to check if these relations are marked by LERS. The same, if we use LERS as a pre-processing module for ARAS, then the overall complexity of the algorithm is decreased [12], [13].

System ARAS differs from the tree-based strategies for action rules discovery (for instance from DEAR [6]) because clusters generated by its second module are formed around target classification rules. An action rule can be constructed in ARAS from two classification rules only if both of them belong to the same cluster and one of them is a target classification rule. So, the complexity of the second module of ARAS is $0(k \cdot n)$, where n is the number of classification rules extracted by LERS and k is the number of clusters. The time complexity of the second module of DEAR is equal to $0(n \cdot n)$, where n is the same as in ARAS. The first module of ARAS is the same as the first module of DEAR, so their complexities are the same.

6. Application of action rules to HEPAR database

HEPAR database contains information about 758 patients described by 106 attributes (including 31 laboratory tests with values discretized to: below normal, normal, above normal). It has 14 stable attributes. Two laboratory tests are invasive: HBsAg [in tissue] and HBcAg [in tissue]. The decision attribute has 7 values: I (acute hepatitis), IIa (subacute hepatitis [types B and C]), IIb (subacute hepatitis [alcohol-abuse]), IIIa (chronic hepatitis [curable]), IIIb (chronic hepatitis [non-curable]), IV (cirrhosis-hepatitis), V (liver-cancer).

The diagnosis of liver disease depends on a combination of patient's history, physical examinations, laboratory tests, radiological tests, and frequently a liver biopsy. Blood tests play an important role in the diagnosis of liver diseases. However, their results should be analyzed along with the patient's history and physical examination. The most common radiological examinations used in the assessment of liver diseases are ultrasound and sonography. Ultrasound is a good test for the detection of liver masses, assessment of bile ducts, and detection of gallstones presence. However, it does not detect the degree of inflammation or fibrosis of the liver. Ultrasound is a noninvasive procedure and there are no risks associated with it. Liver biopsy enables the doctor to examine how much inflammation and how much scarring has occurred. Liver biopsy is an example of invasive procedure that carries certain risks to the patient. Therefore, despite of the importance of its results to the diagnosis, clinicians try to avoid biopsy as often as possible. However, liver biopsy is often the only way to establish correct diagnosis in patients with chronic liver disorders [14].

A medical treatment is naturally associated with reclassification of patients from one decision class into another one. In our research we are mainly interested in the reclassification of patients from the class IIb into class I and from the class IIIa into class I but without referring to any invasive tests results in action rules.

Database HEPAR has many missing values so we decided to remove all its attributes with more than 90% of null values under the assumption that these attributes are not related to

invasive tests. Also, subjective attributes (like history of alcohol abuse) and basic medical tests have been removed. Finally, we used classical null value imputation techniques to make the resulting database complete [15].
The next step of our strategy is to apply RSES software to find d-reducts [16].
The set R = {m, n, q, u, y, aa, ah, ai, am, an, aw, bb, bg, bm, by, cj, cm} is one of them and it does not contain invasive tests. The description of its values is given below:

m - Bleeding	an - Jaundice in pregnancy
n - Subjaundice symptoms	aw - Erythematous dermatitis
q - Eructation	bb - Cysts
u - Obstruction	bg - Sharp liver edge (stable)
y - Weight loss	bm - Blood cell plaque
aa - Smoking	by - Alkaline phosphatase
ah - History of viral hepatitis (stable)	cj - Prothrombin index
ai - Surgeries in the past (stable)	cm - Total cholesterol
am - History of hospitalization (stable)	dd -Decision attribute

7. Results and conclusion

Two action rules from among over eighty, discovered from the HEPAR database which was reduced to d-reduct R in this investigation, are given below:

I.

$$[(ah = 1) \wedge (ai = 2) \wedge (am = 2) \wedge (bg = 1)] \wedge [(cm = 1) \wedge (aw = 1) \wedge (u; \rightarrow 1) \wedge (bb = 1) \wedge (aa = 1) \wedge (q; \rightarrow 1) \wedge (m; \rightarrow 1) \wedge (n = 1) \wedge (bm; \rightarrow down) \wedge (y = 1) \wedge (by; norm \rightarrow up)] \Rightarrow (dd; IIIa \rightarrow I)$$

II.

$$[(ah = 1) \wedge (ai = 2) \wedge (am = 2) \wedge (bg = 1)] \wedge [(cm = 1) \wedge (aw = 1) \wedge (u; \rightarrow 1) \wedge (bb = 1) \wedge (aa = 1) \wedge (q; \rightarrow 1) \wedge (m; \rightarrow 1) \wedge (n = 1) \wedge (bm; \rightarrow down) \wedge (y = 1) \wedge (by; norm \rightarrow down)] \Rightarrow (dd; IIIa \rightarrow I)$$

Both presented above action rules are applicable to patients, who previously underwent surgery, but did not have viral hepatitis. By excluding certain symptoms, such as obstruction, bleeding etc., physicians might be able to re-classify the patient from class III A (advanced stadium of hepatopathy) to class I (initial phase of the disease). Under some circumstances, it might be considered as a substantial gain in problem-solving reasoning in the diagnostic/patients management process in liver diseases [17].

8. Perspectives for the future

In this chapter a new strategy of constructing action rules has been presented; it may help a medical doctor to state the final diagnosis easier using advice from the clinical decision support system. We tested this new strategy, called ARAS, on the medical database HEPAR and the results confirmed its clinical usefulness. What would be the next step in this promising strategy?

Generally speaking, action rules can be seen as logical expressions describing knowledge about actions associated with objects of interest. They are hidden in a database and a researcher's role is to discover them and use them to enhance a decision support system. Based on construction methods, action rules discovery can be divided into two types: rule-based and object-based approach.

In rule-based approach, actionable patterns [6], [7], [20], [21] are built on the foundations of pre-existing rules. It consists of two main steps: (1) in the first step, a standard learning method is used to detect interesting patterns in the form of classification rules, association rules, or clusters and (2) the second step is to use an automatic or semi-automatic strategy to inspect such results and derive possible action strategies. These strategies provide an insight of how values of some attributes need to be changed - so the desirable objects can be shifted to a desirable group. However, the standard data mining methods such as *LERS* [12] or *ERID* [10] (which is used for incomplete data sets) extract only the shortest or close to the shortest rules. Therefore, by following this approach, some meaningful action patterns can be easily missed.

In the object-based approach, action rules are discovered directly from a database [8], [18], [19] and the same their number is usually much larger than the number of rules discovered by following a rule-based approach. System ARAS is an exception - it follows rule-based approach, but because it does not require to construct pairs of rules in its discovery process, the number of action rules it discovers is comparable to numbers obtained when we follow object-based approaches.

Meta-actions [22] are defined as actions which trigger changes of flexible attributes either directly or indirectly because of correlations among certain attributes in the system. Links between meta-actions and changes they trigger within the values of flexible attributes can be defined by a mapping linking meta-actions with changes of attribute values used to describe objects in the decision system. In medical domain, taking a drug is a classical example of a meta-action. For instance, Lamivudine is used for treatment of chronic hepatitis B. It improves the seroconversion of e-antigen positive hepatitis B and also improves histology staging of the liver, but at the same time it can cause a number of other symptoms. This is why doctors have to order certain lab tests to check patient's response to that drug. We are planning to add the meta-actions module to HEPAR decision support system in the near future.

9. References

[1] Wasyluk H.: Second Evaluation of the Diagnostic Computer System HEPAR. Proceedings 6th World Multiconference of Systemics, Cybernetics and Informatics Orlando, USA, ed. N. Callaos, Vol. 2; 2002. p. 242-246.

[2] Wasyluk H., Oniśko A,, Drużdżel M.: Support of diagnosis of liver disorders based on a causal Bayesian network model. Med. Sci Monitor No 7, suppl. 1; 2001. p. 327- 332.

[3] Bobrowski L., Wasyluk H.: Diagnosis supporting rules of the HEPAR system, Proc. MEDINFO 2001, part 2, p. 1309-1313, IOS Press, Amsterdam.

[4] Pawlak Z.: Information systems - theoretical foundations. In: Information Systems Journal; 1991. Vol. 6. p. 205-218.

[5] Adomavicius G., Tuzhilin A.: Discovery of actionable patterns in databases: the action hierarchy approach. Proceedings of KDD097 Conference, Newport Beach, CA, AAAI Press; 1997.
[6] Tsay LS, Raś Z.W.: Action rules discovery system DEAR, method and experiments, in Journal of Experimental and Theoretical Artificial Intelligence, Taylor & Francis,Vol. 17, No. 1-2; 2005. p. 119-128.
[7] Tzacheva A., Raś Z.W.: Action rules mining, in: International Journal of Intelligent Systems, Wiley, Vol. 20, No. 7; 2005. p. 719-736.
[8] Raś Z.W., Dardzińska A.: Action rules discovery - a new simplified strategy. In: Foundations of Intelligent Systems, Esposito F. et al. (Eds.), LNAI, No. 4203, Springer; 2006. p. 445-453.
[9] Greco S., Matarazzo B., Pappalardo N., Słowiński R.: Measuring expected effects of interventions based on decision rules. In: Journal of Experimental and Theoretical Artficial Intelligence, Taylor Francis; 2005. Vol. 17. No. 1-2.
[10] Dardzińska A., Raś Z.W.: "Extracting Rules from Incomplete Decision Systems: System ERID". In: Foundations and Novel Approaches in Data Mining, (Eds. T.Y. Lin, S. Ohsuga, C.J. Liau, X. Hu), Advances in Soft Computing, Vol. 9, Springer; 2006. p. 143-154.
[11] Silberschatz A., Tuzhilin A.: On subjective measures of interestingness in knowledge discovery. Proceedings of KDD095 Conference, AAAI Press; 1995.
[12] Grzymała-Busse J.: A new version of the rule induction system LERS, in: Fundamenta Informaticae Journal., Vol. 31. No. 1; 1997. p. 27-39.
[13] Tsay LS., Raś Z.W.: Action rules discovery system DEAR3. In: Foundations of Intelligent Systems, LNAI, No. 4203, Springer; 2006. p. 483-492.
[14] Duniśko A., Drużdżel M., Wasyluk H.: Extension of the HEPAR II model to multiple-disorder diagnosis. In: Intelligent Information Systems, Advances in Soft Computing, Springer; 2000. p. 303-313.
[15] Raś Z.W., Wyrzykowska E., Wasyluk H.: ARAS: Action rules discovery based on agglomerative strategy, .in: Mining Complex Data, Post-Proceedings of the ECML/PKDD'07 Third International Workshop, MCD 2007, LNAI, Springer (in press
[16] RSES - http://logic.mimuw.edu.pl/rses/
[17] Wasyluk H., Raś Z.W., Wyrzykowska E,: Application of action rules to HEPAR clinical decision support system Exper&Clin. Hepatology 2008, 4(2), pp. 46-48.
[18] Im S., Ras Z.W., Wasyluk H.: Action Rule Discovery From Incomplete Data, in: Knowledge and Information Systems Journal, Springer, 2009, (will appear)
[19] Ras Z.W., Dardzinska A., Tsay L.S., Wasyluk H.: Association Action Rules, IEEE/ICDM Workshop on Mining Complex Data (MCD 2008), Pisa, Italy, ICDM Workshops Proceedings, IEEE Computer Society, 2008, 283-290.
[20] Yang Q., Chen H.,: Mining case for action recommendation, in Proceedings of ICDM 2002, IEEE Computer Society, 2002, 522-529.
[21] Yang Q., Yin J., Lin C.X., Chen T.: Postprocessing decision trees to extract actionable knowledge, in Proceedings of ICDM 2003, IEEE Computer Society, 2003, 685-688.

[22] Wang K., Jiang Y., Tuzhilin A.: Mining Actionable Patterns by Role Models, in Proceedings of the 22nd International Conference on Data Engineering, IEEE Computer Society, 2006, 16-25.

Assessing the Possibility of Identifying Precancerous Cervical Lesions using Aceto-White Temporal Patterns

Héctor-Gabriel Acosta-Mesa[1], Nicandro Cruz-Ramírez[1], Karina Gutiérrez-Fragoso[1], Rocío-Erandi Barrientos-Martínez[1] and Rodolfo Hernández-Jiménez[2]

[1]*School of Physics and Artificial Intelligence, Department of Artificial Intelligence, Universidad Veracruzana, Sebastián Camacho # 5, 91000, Xalapa,*
[2]*Obstetrician and Gynaecologist, Diego Leño # 22, C.P. 91000, Xalapa, Ver. México.*

1. Introduction

In 2005, according to projections by the World Health Organization (WHO, 2007), there are more than 500 000 new cases of cervical cancer worldwide, 90% of these occur in developing countries. It is estimated that over 1 000 000 women currently suffer from cervical cancer in the world. However, most of them has not been diagnosed or do not have access to necessary treatments. That same year, about 260 000 women died of this disease and about 95% of these deaths occurred in developing countries. Cervical cancer has remained one of the most serious threats to women's lives (WHO, 2007).

After Pap smear test, colposcopy is the most used technique to diagnose this disease because of its a higher sensitivity and specificity. One of the most important colposcopic findings is the level of white color intensity that the cervical tissue reaches after acetic acid application. The major problem with this technique is the intrinsic subjectivity of the test i.e. the amount and speed of color change perceived could be different for various observers; this fact may produce high variability on the diagnosis made by these experts. So the mechanisms to quantify near to absolute measurements of color and speed changes are needed to improve the test. It is difficult to find in the literature a general accepted score for the sensitivity and specificity reached by an expert colposcopist, but in average this test has high sensitivity (98%) but low specificity (48%) (Vlastos, 2002).

Some researchers have suggested the use of the temporal patterns intrinsic to the color changes (Balas, 2001; Stefanaki et al., 2001; Pogue Brian et al., 2001). Although some efforts have been made to characterize precancerous cervical lesion using aceto-white temporal patterns, to the best of our knowledge, there is not a complete understanding of how to use them to segment colposcopic images, and there is not an established methodology to automatically analyze colposcopic images using aceto-white temporal patterns for classification of cervical tissue.

In the present work, we compare the shape of the temporal patterns to establish relationships among similar shapes, and the correlation of those patterns with certain types of tissue. Our analysis not only shows results of those small areas from where the biopsies were acquired, but also considers the segmentation of the complete image, which is more realistic. This is particularly important since in a real computer aided system, the analysis of the complete image is needed, considering noisy data and outliers. We use a discretized version of the raw temporal pattern to develop a supervised Machine Learning (ML) processes, using one of the most effective probabilistic classifier Naïve Bayes (NB) (Friedman, 1997; Han, 2001; Duda, 2001).

The paper is structured in four sections: in the first section, the technical issues of subject preparation and data acquisition are explained, in the second part, data analysis methodology is explained, including image acquisition and preprocessing, time series extraction and discretization and machine learning implementation. In the third section results of the application of the methodology on real data of 38 patients are shown. Finally, in the fourth section some conclusions and future work are commented.

2. Materials and methods

2.1 Subject preparation

Thirty eight women with abnormal Papanicolaou, ages ranging from 22 to 35 years participated in the experiment. All of them gave informed written consent. Before colposcopy, the cervical mucus was cleaned using a cotton-wool swabs. The colposcopic tests were made spreading three milliliters of acetic acid (3%) over the cervix using a needle for fast application. A cotton-wool was put in the low part of the cervix to absorb the remaining acetic acid that drops after the application. A leg-holder structure was used to make the patient feels comfortable and to reduce movements. After colposcopy, a biopsy was taken for histological analysis and PCR test (Anderson, 1993).

2.2 Data acquisition

Images were acquired using a colposcope dfv Vasconsellos model CP-M7 with magnification 16 X without any optical filter. The viewing distance was 20 cm. and the field of view covers approximately a circle of 13 mm ratio. Images were acquired using a color camera Sony SSC-DC50A and a frame grabber Matrox Meteor-II/Standard driven by a HP workstation XW6000 running Matlab 7.0 image acquisition toolbox. During the first ten seconds of the image acquisition, 10 images (352x240) were taken as base line reference (1 frame/second), then after acetic acid application, three hundred images were taken in 5 minutes using the same sampling frequency. Control images taken at the beginning of each trial have a double purpose, the first one is to have a base reference to assess the signal percentage of change and the second one is to estimate the amount of signal noise. Each image was saved independently as a BMP file. Although we developed analysis over color images (results not shown in this article), in this publication we present results obtained processing the images in gray scale because results were similar.

3. Data analysis

The colposcopic image sequence can be represented as a sequence of t 2D images $I_t(x,y)$ with acquisition time t with $t < t+1$. The color variation over time of each pixel in the image provides a time series. The resulting image sequence can be viewed as a 3D image block $I(x,y,t)$ defined on the spatio-temporal domain. The methodology proposed in this paper to analyze the colposcopic sequences involves 3 main processes: image registration, time series extraction and supervised learning. Those processes are explained in detail in the following sections.

3.1 Data acquisition

The acquisition process of colposcopic images spans over 5 minutes. Even though the patient is fixed some, small random movements are unavoidable. They have often local character (patient's breathing, movements due to the muscle tonus, etc.). To be able to analyze the sequence of the images, the structures in the images should be brought into the same position by removing the differences due to the patient movements - the colposcopic images have to be registered. This step is essential in this application; the goal of the 2D image spatial alignment is to enable comparison between corresponding anatomical positions. There are various registration methods, a good overview can be found in (Brown, 1992). The appropriate method has to be chosen with respect to the expected geometric differences and the type of processed data.

Our previous experimental assessment suggests that the main source of the misalignments in colposcopic sequences can be modeled by simple translation (Acosta-Mesa et al., 2005). The method can transform the whole data using the same parameters, or can be local, depending on the local variations. It can be based directly on the image intensity values (area-based methods) or can be carried out using some features computed from the images (feature-based methods). Because colposcopic images do not contain many distinctive details, an area-based method was chosen. The classical representative of the area-based methods is the normalized cross-correlation (CC), this method exploits directly image intensities, this measure of similarity is computed for window pairs from the input and reference images and its maximum is searched (Zitova, 2003).

The input and the reference images are updated continuously starting with the first and second images of the sequence respectively, then the input and the reference images are redefined by the second and the third images and so on. The starting points to initialize the search are updated by the last position in which the pattern window was found. This registration strategy allows not only to contend with the fact that the searched pattern changes over time, but also, to reduce the spatial space over which to develop the search. Because cervical lesions are spread over the tissue as regions (forming areas with homogeneous tissue), a high spatial resolution is not needed. Then after registration the spatial resolution was reduced at 50% of the original size.

3.2 Time series extraction

The colposcopic set of images can be thought of as a spatiotemporal data matrix. Let ImageCube(m,n,t) represent a stack of t images of size (m,n). Thus there are (m x n) pixels, each of which is a time series of length t. Let p(i,j) represent the color of the pixel (i,j), i=1, ..., m, j=1, ..., n. The intensity value of each pixel over time is used to construct a time series, which we call, the **A**ceto-**w**hite **r**esponse **f**unction (Awrf). Figure 1 shows an example of aceto-white response function. In order increase the signal to noise ratio, the signal was smoothed using a polynomial approximation. As a way of standardization to permit comparison among different subjects, the values of each temporal pattern are divided by the mean value of its basal period (Acosta-Mesa et al., 2007). The resultant amplitude of the Awrf is then measured as a percentage of change with respect to the base line.

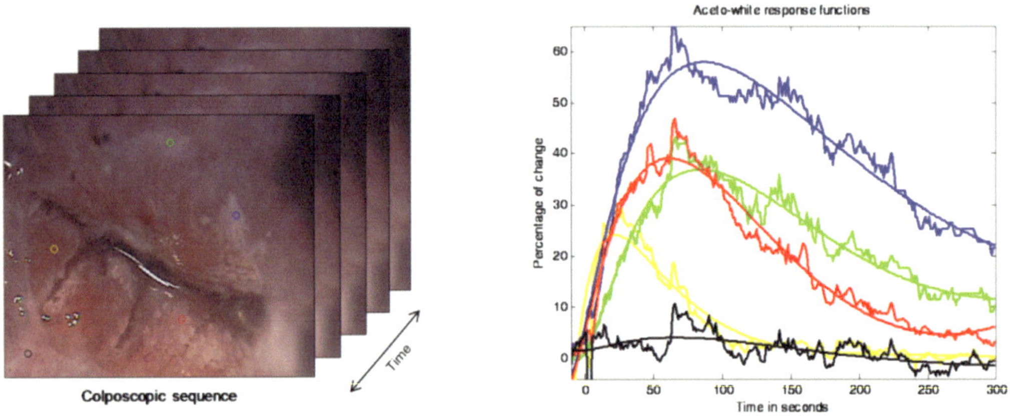

Fig. 1. Aceto-white response functions. At the right, temporal patterns observed on the pixels denoted by dots on the left image. As can be appreciated, different kinds of tissue produce Awrf with different percentage of change, speed of increase and decay. Next to each raw Awrf its polynomial fitted model is shown.

Time series databases are often extremely large. Due to the size of many databases of time series, methods have been developed to reduce the dimensionality. These methods produce approximations of time series through discretization schemes. The discretization process is focused on mapping variables with continuous values into discrete values. This mechanism has been widely used to compress data and facilitate their computational treatment. It is necessary to specify a set of parameters for the processing of data. The reduction of dimensionality in the x-axis is obtained by dividing the total length of the time series into fragments of a certain size (word size). It is also necessary to establish a number of intervals in the y-axis to compress the values of the time series (size of the alphabet) (Keogh & Pazzani, 2000). In this case, the parameters of word size and alphabet were selected experimentally. The time series were discretized with two criteria:

a. Piecewise Linear Approximation (PLA). The method involves setting the parameters of word size and alphabet for discretized time series and calculates the average of the signal in each segment (Allgower, 1988). In this case we used alphabet and word size of 10.
b. Piecewise Slope Approximation (PSA). This method is similar the one above, sets the parameters of word size and alphabet, but is based on calculating the values of slopes for each segment. In this case 7 possible values were used for the slopes describing the temporal pattern: 3 negative values, 0 representing no change and 3 positive values. Figure 2 illustrates an example of a temporal pattern that was discretized by these methods.

3.3 Supervised learning

Supervised learning is a machine learning area for constructing models from a set of observations presented as examples. The goal of these methods is to predict the class label of an unseen observation given the knowledge (model) extracted from the training data. Training data can be seen as a data base containing observations and their corresponding class label. When the class label value is categorical, supervised learning is called neighbors, decision trees, neural networks, naïve bayes, etc. The selection of the method

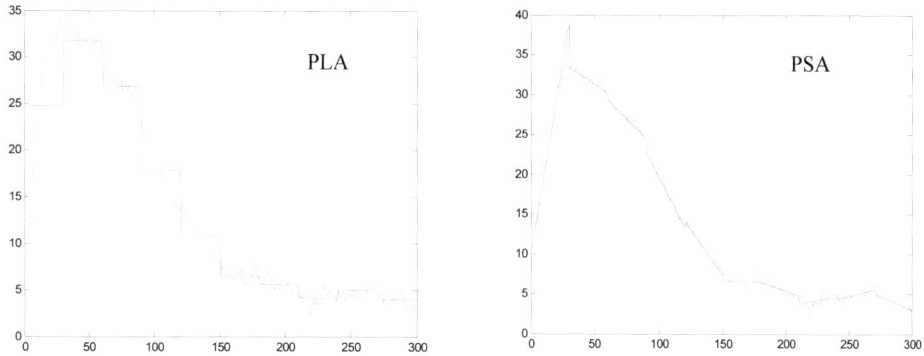

2 3 2 1 1 0 0 0 0 0   2 0 0 -1 0 0 0 0 0 0

Fig. 2. Example of a temporal pattern that was discretized. On the left the PLA method that calculates the average of each segment is shown and on the right the PSA method, based on the values of the slopes that describe the time series is shown.

depends on the kind of data and prior hypothesis, and most of the time has to be selected empirically (Mitchell, 1997; Pang-Ning et al., 2006; Hastie, 2001).

A colposcopic data set can be seen as a time series database, the classification (segmentation) task consists of finding similar temporal patterns with regular shapes belonging to the same type of tissue (class label). In this work we are interested in investigating the relationship between regular shapes and the class tissue. We propose to use the PLA representation of raw Awrf and the Naïve Bayes classifier. As will be explained this method is a direct way to explore the relationship between the shapes of temporal patterns and their corresponding type of tissue.

3.3.1 Naïve Bayes algorithm

The Naïve Bayes classifier (NB) is one of the most effective classifiers (Friedman, 1997; Duda, 2001) and against which state of the art classifiers have to be compared. Its main appeals are its simplicity and accuracy: although its structure is always fixed, i.e. the class variable has an arc pointing to every attribute (assumes linear independence among the attributes), it has been shown that this classifier has high classification accuracy and optimal Bayes' error (Han, 2001; Duda, 2001). In simple terms, the NB learns, from a training data sample, the conditional probability of each attribute given the class. Then, once a new case arrives, the NB uses Bayes' rule to compute the conditional probability of the class given the set of attributes selecting the value of the class with the highest posterior probability. This rule is shown in equation 1.

Bayes' Theorem

$$p(c_j|d) = \frac{p(d|c_j)p(c_j)}{p(d)} \tag{1}$$

Where:

$p(c_j \mid d)$ = probability of class c_j given instance d

$p(d \mid c_j)$ = probability of instance d given class c_j

$p(c_j)$ = probability of occurrence of class c_j
$p(d)$ = probability of occurrence of instance d

3.3.2 Classification accuracy

Performance of classification algorithms is evaluated using different metrics, the most common are accuracy, sensibility and specificity. All of them use a confusion matrix (see table 1) to evaluate the percentage of observation assigned to the correct class label during classification. In a training data set with binary class labels we have:

Real / Predicted	Positive	Negative
Positive	True Positive	False Negative
Negative	False Positive	True Negative

Table 1. Confusion matrix.

Where the accuracy on the classification process is computed as the rate of true positives plus true negatives against the total number of observations; the sensibility is the rate of true positive observations against the sum of true positive plus false negatives and the specificity is the rate of true negative observations against the sum of true negative plus false positives. All those metrics to estimate classification performance are computed repeatedly partitioning the data base in two sets, the first set is used to train the algorithm and the second one is used to validate the performance of the classifier, this process is called cross-validation (Mitchell, 1997). In the application described in the present paper, the training set is conformed by the observation of all patients minus one, the validation set is conformed by the observation of the patient that was excluded to the training set and so for all the cases. This particular case of cross validation is called leave-one-out cross- validation.

4. Methodology and results

Image registration was carried out using the cross-correlation technique explained above. The search window was defined selecting a region feature over which some anatomical features show high contrast boundaries, e.g. the cervical hole. In those cases in which the cervical hole was not a good reference a stain landmark was introduced using lugol solution (Anderson, 1993). Once the dataset was registered, we asked the expert colposcopist define points (pixels) on the colposcopic sequence of each patient to assign a class label on representative regions. To help the expert to do the class labeling, we develop a knowledge acquisition graphical interface where the expert can see the entire image of the colposcopic sequence. Also he was able to select the images at different times to look the aceto-white changes (see figure 3).

Based on the results reported by histology, the expert selected a pixel of the image in order to assign one of the following class labels: normal tissue, immature metaplasia, mature metaplasia, ectopy, low grade lesion, high grade lesion.

In the database each observation represents one temporal pattern. The number of observations is bigger than the number of patients because multiple pixels were selected from one region and in some patients more than one type of tissue were sampled. The cases were divided into two main classes or types of tissue: negative (normal) and positive (abnormal). The class negative includes: normal tissue (11,851) (patients and observations,

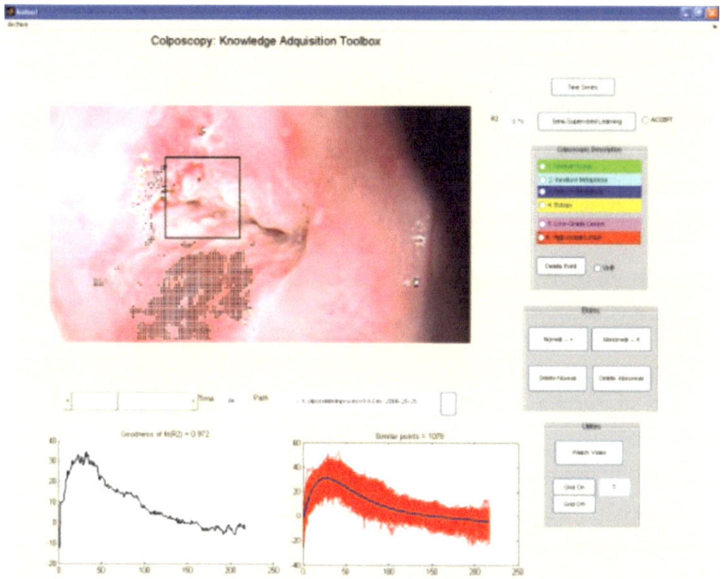

Fig. 3. Knowledge acquisition graphical interface. Using this tool, the user is able to assign a label to each representative region on tissue. The Awrf of each selected pixel of the image was displayed in a separate window. In a supervised fashion, for each selected pixel, a set of pixels with similar Awrf were suggested to the user in order to simplify the class labeling process.

respectively), immature metaplasia (7,156), mature metaplasia (5,189) and ectopia (2,91). On the positive class are considered: low grade lesion (26,1164) and high grade lesion (3,123). Once representative examples of tissue were labeled on each patient, a spatio-temporal data base was constructed containing, the patient identification, the observation's spatial position on the image, the class label and the temporal pattern extracted from the stereoscopic sequence relative to that position. The classification process was conducted in the WEKA software, in the Explorer module using the Naïve Bayes classifier. The classification performance was measured using leave-one-out cross-validation as explained above. Following the advice of the expert coposcopist, the class labels were binarized as follows: normal (normal tissue, immature metaplasia, mature metaplasia, ectopy), abnormal (low grade lesion, high grade lesion). Since the database contains more observations for the abnormal label, the occurrences were balanced using under sampling on the majority class (Pang-Ning et al., 2006; Han & Kamber, 2001). The classification results are shown in table 2.

Technique	Sensibility	Specificity	Accuracy
NB (PLA)	67	85	76
NB (Slopes)	61	80	70
k-NN	71	59	67
Colposcopists	98	48	73

Table 2. Classification performance. Performance values were computed as the mean values obtained on the classification over the 38 cases.

The values shown for k-NN were obtained from (Acosta-Mesa et al., 2008) and are presented for comparative purposes.
Supervised learning was also developed over the entire image, that is to say, not only on those positions (pixels) selected by the expert during class labeling. In this analysis the classification was developed in a similar way as before using leave-one-out. However, in this case all the temporal patterns belonging to the entire image were including in the validation set. As is obvious, under this approach it is not possible to validate performance on the classification process because the entire image was not labeled in the class labeling task. However, it was visually evaluated by the expert, concluding that segmentation results are coherent with those introduced in the training set. To the best of our knowledge, only one work has reported the segmentation of the entire image using the aceto-white effect, however, they did not use the complete aceto-white temporal pattern (Young, 2008). As an example, the image segmentation displayed by the graphical interface developed by us is shown in figure 4.

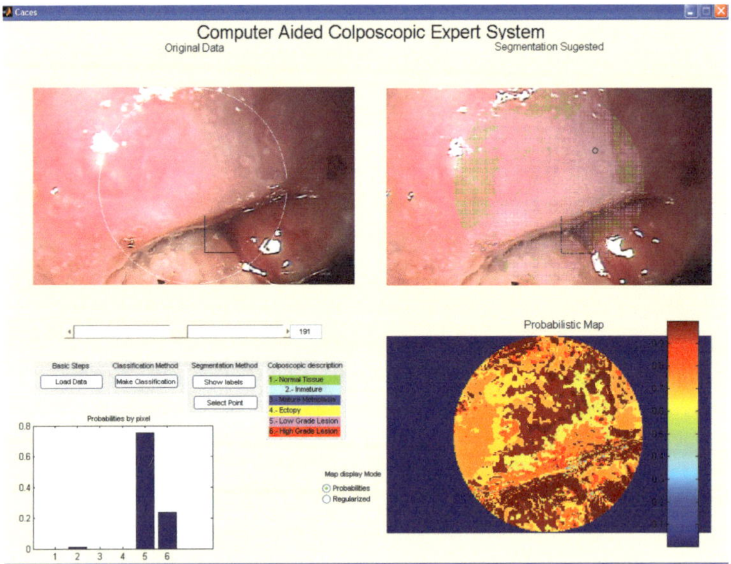

Fig. 4. Colposcopic image segmentation. The image at the left shows the original unknown colposcopic sequence given to the classifier. At the right, the image shows the labels suggested by the segmentation tool. Only the central part of the image, demarked by the circle, is analyzed to avoid artifacts introduced by illumination heterogeneities on the periphery. In the bottom left a histogram with the probability of a temporal pattern belonging to a tissue type (class) is shown. In the bottom right a geometric distribution of the likelihood of temporal patterns by type of tissue in them is also shown.

5. Conclusions and future work

In this pilot study our results show that normal and abnormal colposcopic findings can be discriminated using the temporal information intrinsic to the change of color occurred during aceto-whitening. The shape of the temporal patterns (Awrfs) can be used to segment a colposcopic image. Although some approaches have been proposed to analyze colposcopic images using temporal patterns, as far as we known, none of them has established a complete methodology to acquire and analyze colposcopic sequences in order to automatically segment the entire image. Our approach is one step toward it. However, more research in this field is needed in order to improve classification performance.

In this work, we present a way to automatically discriminate between normal and abnormal cervical tissue, using the machine learning supervised classification algorithm Naïve Bayes over the entire length of the aceto-white temporal pattern. Although this is one of the easiest machine learning classification techniques, it surpasses classification specificity reached by expert colposcopists, although the sensitivity reached by Naïve Bayes is lower than that reached by colposcopists. This behavior is presented in both the PLA method as PSA. These results can be explained because in the experiments discretization parameters were given in an arbitrary manner and this can affect the performance of classifiers.

As a continuation of this work we are using Time Series Data Mining (TSDM) techniques to explore compressed representations to facilitates classification (Last, Kandel, and Bunke 2004). Specifically, working with discrete representations of time series that can be treated using other approaches such as ID3, or its successor C4.5 algorithm, whereas the latter supports continuous values. Using these methods we want to explore the temporal pattern's feature that best separates the examples with the goal of achieving a better performance in the assessment of accuracy. We are also working on developing automatic mechanisms to determine the best scheme of discretization parameters. Finally, we continue growing the number of patients to be included in the training set in order to increase the space of cases.

6. Acknowledgement

The first author thanks the Mexican National Council for Science and Technology for the economic support of this project under the research grant: Fondo Sectorial de Investigación en Salud y Seguridad Social SSA/IMSS/ISSSTE-CONACYT (Salud-2003-C01-06).

7. References

Acosta-Mesa Héctor-Gabriel., Zitová Barbara., Ríos-Figueroa Homero., Cruz-Ramírez Nicandro., Marín-Hernández Antonio., Hernández-Jiménez Rodolfo., Cocotle-Ronzón Bertha-Elvia., and Hernández Galicia Efraín. (2005). Cervical Cancer Detection Using colposcopic Images: a Temporal Approach. *Proceeding of the Sixth International Conference on Computer Science* (IEEE Computer Society Press). 158-164.

Acosta-Mesa Héctor-Gabriel, Cruz-Ramírez Nicandro, Hernández-Jiménez Rodolfo, García-López Daniel-Alejandro. (2007). Modeling Aceto-White Temporal Patterns to Segment Colposcopic Images. *Advances in Artificial Intelligence* (LNCS. Springer-Verlag) 4478:548-555.

Acosta-Mesa Héctor-Gabriel, Cruz-Ramírez Nicandro, Hernández-Jiménez Rodolfo, Aceto-White Temporal Pattern Classification using k-NN to Identify Precancerous Cervical Lesion in Colposcopic Images. Computers in Biology and Medicine. Elsevier, 2009. 39: p. 778-784.

Acosta-Mesa Héctor-Gabriel, Cruz-Ramírez Nicandro, Hernández-Jiménez Rodolfo, Cocotle-Ronzón Bertha-Elvia. (2008). Aceto-White Temporal Patterns Classification using k-NN to Identify Precancerous Cervical Lesion in Colposcopic Images. Submitted for publication.

Allgower Eugen L. and Georg Kurt. (1988). Estimates for Piecewise Linear Approximations of Implicity Defined Manifolds. *SIAM Journal of Numerical Analysis.* 24:452-469

Anderson M., Jordan A. M, Sharp F. (1993). *A Text and Atlas of Integrated Colposcopy.* Mosby.
Balas, Costas. (2001). A Novel Optical Imaging Method for the Early Detection, Quantitative Grading, and Mapping of Cancerous and Precancerous Lesions of Cervix. *IEEE Transactions in Biomedical Engineering.* 48 (1):96-104.
Brown, Lisa Gottesfeld. (1992). A survey of Image Registration Techniques. *ACM Computing Surveys* (CSUR) 24 (4):325-376.
Burghardt Erich, Pickel Hellmuth, Girardi Frank. (2004). Primary care Colposcopy. *Textbook and Atlas. New Year: Thieme Medical Publisher Incorporated.*
Duda, R.O., Hart, Peter E., Stork, David G. (2001). *Pattern Classification.* John Wiley & Sons, INC.
Friedman, N., D. Geiger, and M. Goldszmidt.(1997). *Bayesian Network Classifiers.* Machine Learning. 29: p. 131-163.
Han, J. and Kamber, M. (2001). Data Mining: Concepts and Techniques. Morgan Kaufmann Publishers.
Hastie Trevor, Tibshirani Robert, Friedman Jerome. (2001). The Elements of Statistical Learning (Data mining, Inference and Prediction), *Springer series in statistics: Springer.*
Keogh, E. and Pazzani, M. (2000). A simple dimensionality reduction technique for fast similarity search in large time series databases. In *Proceedings of Pacific- Asia Conf. on Knowledge Discovery and Data Mining*, pp 122-133
Last Mark, Kandel Abraham, and Horst Bunke. (2004). *Data Mining in Time Series Databases.* World Scientific.
Mitchell, Tom M. (1997). Machine Learning. Edited by McGraw-Hill.
Pogue Brian, Zelenchuk Alex, Harper Gregory, and Burke Eschel. (2001). Analysis of Acetic Acid-induced Whitening of High-grade Squamous Intraepitelial Lesions. *Journal of Biomedical Optics.* 6 (4):397-403.
Schmid-Saugeon Phillipe , Kaufman Howard B. , Zelenchuk Alex , Harper Dian M. 2004. Time-Resolved Imaging of Cervical Acetowhitening. Draft paper (Available in Electronic Form on: http://www.schmid-saugeon.com/publications/ Philippe%20Schmid-Saugeon%202003%20Digital%20colposcope.pdf)
Stefanaki Irene., Androniki. Tosca, George. Themelis, and Costas. Balas. 2001. In Vivo Detection of Human Papilloma Virus-Induced Lesions of Anogenital Area after Application of Acetic Acid: a Novel and Accurate Approach to a Trivial Method. *Journal of Photochemistry and Photobiology.* 65:115-121.
Tan Pang-Ning, Steinbach Michael, and Kumar Vipin. (2006). Introduction to Data Mining. Edited by A.-W. P. Co.
Tapia Antonio, Garrido Francisco, Gómez Octavio. (2006). Salud:México 2001-2005. Información estratégica por entidad federativa, edited by S. d. I. y. C. Dirección General de Evaluación del Desempeño: Secretaría de Salud.
Vlastos Anne-Thérèse, Richards-Kortum Rebecca, Zuluaga Andres and Follen Michele. (2002). New approaches to cervivcal cancer screening. Contemporary Ob/Gyn:87-103.
World Health Organization (WHO). (2007). Control integral del cáncer cervicouterino. Guía de prácticas esenciales. 1st ed. Suiza:WHO.
Young Sun Park, Follen Michele, Rhodes Andrea Milbourne Helen. (2008). Automated image analysis of digital colposcopy for the detection of cervical neoplasia. *Journal of Biomedical Optics.* 13(1) (January/February 2008):014029-1 / 014029-10.
Zitova Barbara, F.J. (2003). Image Registration Methods: a Survey. *Image and vision computing* 21 (11):977-1000.

9

Clinical Decision Support with Guidelines and Bayesian Networks

Oliver Nee and Andreas Hein
OFFIS – Institute for Information Technology
Germany

1. Introduction

The field of medicine has been one of the favourite application areas for tools of artificial intelligence (AI) research for decades. One of the reasons for this focus may be the fact that decision making in medicine is hard and by all means a worthy challenge. This is not only due to the countless symptoms, tests, diseases and treatment options that make up the medical body of knowledge, but also because of the complexity of the human physiology and the resulting lack of absolutes in medicine. Traditional rule-based approaches try to employ first-order logic in order to model causal or diagnostic relationships between concepts do not work for complex medical reasoning because the connection between symptoms and conditions is just not a logical consequence in either direction of a rule. Given the impracticality of logically exhaustive rules and a certain measure of incomplete knowledge - be it theoretical due to incomplete science or practical due to a lack of data, an agent striving to make a decision can at best have a degree of belief in the truth of a statement. Bayesian networks can be used to model causal (or diagnostic) relationships using that degree of belief, allowing reasoning under uncertainty.

The difficulty of clinical decision making doesn't just affect computers. The diagnosis and treatment of complex diseases such as cardiovascular diseases require a series of decisions that are often based on incomplete data. Clinical Practice Guidelines (CPGs) help clinicians make these decisions by providing recommendations that are based on various levels of evidence. However, studies have shown that guideline compliance tends to be low unless the recommendations for a specific case are made when a decision needs to be made. In the clinical practice, this would be realized as a clinical decision support system (CDSS) that is integrated with other clinical information systems and that offers case-specific advice. Currently, all frameworks for computer-interpretable guidelines face the problem of having to deal with reasoning under uncertainty due to incomplete data or incomplete knowledge. Introducing a degree of belief in data items would increase the robustness of a CDSS.

This chapter discusses a CDSS built on Bayesian networks that is part of a system designed for cardiac tele-rehabilitation for patients after a myocardial infarction. The system replaces a rule-based variant that had been used to control the patients' exercise sessions, including the generation of alarms. The evaluation shows that the number of false alarms can be reduced by the introduction of Bayesian networks.

2. Decision support in medicine

2.1 Clinical practice guidelines

The Institute of Medicine defined clinical practice guidelines (CPGs) as "systematically developed statements to assist practitioner and patient decisions about appropriate health care for specific clinical circumstances" (Field & Lohr, 1992). For the sake of simplicity, clinical practice guidelines will simply be referred to as guidelines. Guidelines are created by scientifically working medical societies and exist to help doctors provide their patients with the best possible treatment. In Europe, for example, the European Society of Cardiology (ESC) provides over 30 guidelines covering various cardiological conditions and their treatment options. Guidelines are an application of evidence-based medicine (Elstein, 2004). Evidence-based medicine (EBM) makes use of tools such as meta-analysis of medical literature, risk-benefit analysis, and randomized controlled trials (RCTs) in order to qualify the level of evidence and subsequent recommendations. It should represent the current state of art in clinical medicine and aim to help the Doctors to provide the best medical care.

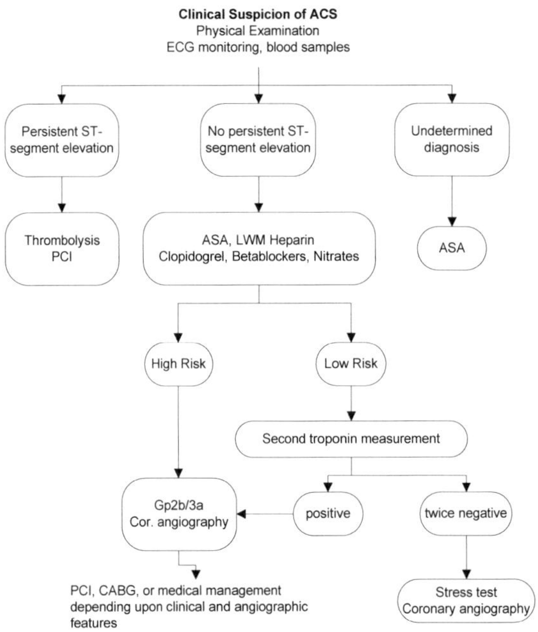

Fig. 1. Excerpt from a guideline

Fig. 1 shows an excerpt from a guideline (Bertand et al., 2002) that suggests a strategy for patients with a suspected acute coronary syndrome (ACS), a set of signs and symptoms related to the heart. Based on the results of the patient's electrocardiogram (ECG), the strategy discerns between various subtypes of the ACS and suggests suitable treatments. The simple flowchart representation of the strategy should not fool a reader into believing that a guideline is little more than that. The guideline that describes the strategy for the center branch (for patients who present without a persistent elevation of the ST-segment in their ECG) is 32 pages long and substantiates its findings with over 200 references.

Guidelines are not meant as ex cathedra statements telling Doctors how to treat their patients. Rather than that they should be understood as means of distributing knowledge, of making good clinical practice known to those who practice it. Guidelines are being endorsed because of their contents and the way these contents are being produced by expert groups. Simply gathering and condensing knowledge into guideline documents will not benefit the patients, putting that knowledge into action does. And in order to put the knowledge from guidelines into action, they need to be aware of it. Guidelines are published in medical journals and other media. However, this knowledge is rarely available to the physician at the point of care where decisions are made. It is not realistic to expect a cardiologist to remember the recommendations of more than 30 guidelines, and referring to them for each and every case would be too time-consuming. One way to aid this decision making process is the introduction of clinical decision support systems that should ideally be integrated into the IT systems that are being used in the daily routine.

2.2 Clinical decision support systems

Wyatt and Spiegelhalter (1991) define a clinical decision system (CDSS) as "an active knowledge systems which use two or more items of patient data to generate case-specific advice." Clinical Decision Support Systems help a physician by suggesting a diagnosis based on findings and/or suggesting a treatment. Diagnostic support can be especially useful for rare and complex diseases, though planning support for therapies is an even more interesting application of CDSSs, since it supports evidence-based medicine (EBM) and best practices. Programs that support diagnostic decision making have been shown to improve a physician's diagnostic performance significantly, as shown by Berner et al. (1999). Programs can also support a clinican's therapy planning, improving the quality of care, as shown in a recent trial (Field et al., 2009).

The following subsections discuss a small selection of current decision support systems. DxPlain is a decision support system that helps physicians in the diagnostic decision making process. CARDSS has been implemented to improve physicians' adherence to cardiac rehabilitation guidelines and the screening of patients. TREAT is a system designed to improve the prescription of antibiotics.

DXplain has been developed at the Laboratory of Computer Science at the Massachusetts General Hospital. Development of DXplain started in 1984 with information on 500 diseases being available in the initial release in 1986. The article (Barnett et al., 1987) is the earliest paper describing the system. DXplain can be accessed through the web, and since 1996 it is the only method of distribution, replacing the stand-alone program that was in use until then. It operates in two modes: it can serve as an electronic medical textbook, and it is a medical reference system. The knowledge base of DXplain contains information on 2200 diseases and 4900 clinical findings. Clinical findings can be symptoms, signs, epidemiologic data and laboratory, endoscopic and radiological findings. Based on the findings observed by the physician, the system will determine a ranked list of diseases as well as a detailed description of the disease. The users and developers have been fine-tuning the knowledge base for more than 20 years, so it can be assumed that DXplain offers good sensitivity and specificity. DXplain does not offer decision support that goes beyond diagnostic decision making. However, simply by suggesting additional diagnoses and findings, it can help physicians detect rare diseases they would usually not have considered.

CARDSS stands for "Cardiac Rehabilitation Decision Support System" and is a computer-based guideline implementation system for cardiac rehabilitation screening (Goud et al., 2005). It was developed concurrently with recently released guidelines of the Netherlands

Heart Foundation. The decision support system has been developed in order to improve the assessment of a patient's need for cardiac rehabilitation. A major part, and in fact the main focus of CARDSS, is the screening procedure that can be described as flowchart containing 15 to 30 questions to be answered, covering the patient's clinical history as well as the current situation. The purpose of the screening procedure is to determine whether or not the patient should be considered for cardiac rehabilitation, and if so, what the patient's goal of the rehabilitation should be and what therapy should be chosen. A large factor that contributed to the success of CARDSS during its pilot study is the concurrent development of the new cardiac rehabilitation guidelines and CARDSS so that the paper-based guidelines and the decision making in the DSS mimic each other.

TREAT (Leibovici et al., 2007) is a decision support system for antibiotic treatment in inpatients with common bacterial infections and is based on a causal probabilistic network and uses a cost-benefit model for antibiotic treatment, including costs assigned to future resistance. The system has been tested in a cluster randomized trial (Paul et al. 2006). According to the study, the length of hospital stay, costs related to future resistance and total antibiotic costs were lower in intervention versus control wards, which leads to the conclusion that TREAT improves the rate of appropriate empirical antibiotic treatment while reducing antibiotic costs and the use of broad-spectrum antibiotic treatment.

2.3 Computer-interpretable practice guidelines

The systems discussed in the previous section are specifically tailored systems that are isolated from the information systems usually used in clinical practice. The process of transforming a paper-based guideline into a computer-interpretable format and adapting it to local workflows is time-consuming; that is why approaches that allow the sharing of computer-interpretable guidelines are being sought. For this purpose, various frameworks for computer-interpretable guidelines (CIGs) have been developed. However, Sonnenberg and Hagerty (2006) reported that "at this time, there is no dominant CIG framework and no system that is in widespread clinical use outside the institution in which it was developed", and this assessment still holds to date. Comparing all recently proposed and implemented frameworks would be beyond the scope of this section. Other articles describing and comparing current frameworks are the following: Peleg et al. (2003) compared six guideline models: Asbru, EON, GLIF, GUIDE, PRODIGY, and PROforma. Sonnenberg and Hagerty (2006) discuss the state of art and also compare Arden Syntax, GLIF, Asbru, PROforma, EON, GUIDE, PRODIGY and DILEMMA/PRESTIGE. Isern and Moreno (2008) compared Arezzo, DeGeL, GLARE, GLEE, HeCaSe2, NewGuide, SAGE and SpEM. Another comparison of five frameworks can be found in de Clercq et al. (2004), where the Arden Syntax, GLIF, PROforma, Asbru, and EON are discussed. This section will focus on a format called GLIF, the Guideline Interchange Format, since it is a typical framework.

The Guideline Interchange Format (GLIF) was developed by the InterMed Collaboratory and is a collaboration of Stanford Medical Informatics, Harvard University, McGill University and Columbia University. The first published version of GLIF was released in 1998 (Ohno-Machado et al., 1998). As the name suggests, the aspect of sharing guidelines between various medical institutions was one of the design goals of GLIF. This intended sharing is supposed to work for humans (who can read the guidelines) and for automatic parsing by computers and integration in a clinical decision support system. Guidelines in GLIF should be (1) human-readable, (2) computer-interpretable and (3) share-able and thus adaptable by different institutions. These aims are reflected by the three-layered approach of

GLIF. This layered approach of GLIF also helps facilitate the collaboration process required for the transformation of paper-based guidelines into a computer-readable format that is integrated into the clinic's electronic patient record. The conceptual layer is the layer experts from the medical domain are mostly involved with. On the conceptual level, a GLIF guideline consists of a sequence of steps that are linked in a directed graph that can be represented as flowchart. The flowchart representation of a small portion of a guideline is shown in Fig. 2.

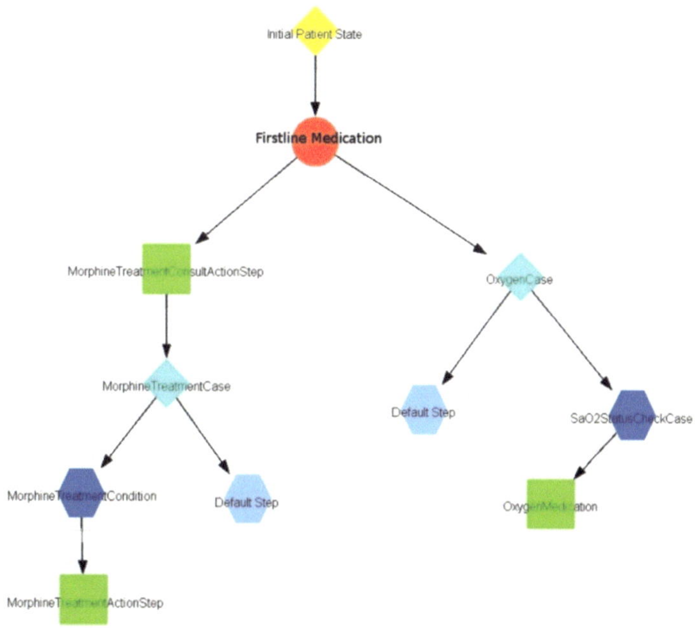

Fig. 2. Flowchart representation of a GLIF-encoded guideline

However, this sequence is not executable yet. The computational layer of GLIF is used to provide the necessary definitions and formalizations. The third layer, the implementation layer deals with the integration of the formalized guideline into the flow of clinical data. Here concepts from the guideline are mapped to clinical data that is retrieved from various clinical information systems. The elements in this layer may be non-sharable.

GLIF defines five steps: decision steps, patient state steps, branch steps, synchronization steps, and action steps. As the name suggests, decision steps are used at points in a guideline if there is more than one possible step to follow the currently active one. In Fig. 2, the step labeled 'OxygenCase' is such a step, where a decision is made whether the patient should receive oxygen or not. There are two kinds of decision steps, case steps and choice steps. 'OxygenCase' is a case step, which means that it contains at least one logical expression that determines the further flow of the guideline through the various alternatives following the case step. In the example, the further steps depend on the evaluation of the logical expression that compares the patient's oxygen saturation against a specified threshold. Choice steps are used to represent a situation where the further execution of the guideline depends on a choice being made by an external agent (for example a clinician using a user interface) based on preferences suggested by the guideline. Choice steps contain rules that support or oppose the various preferences.

Patient state steps can be seen as labels that are used to describe the current patient state as it is expected by the guideline after having executed the previous steps. A patient state step can also be used as an entry point in the guideline, depending on the current patient's state. The patient's state is described with attributes that are contained in the patient state step. If used as an entry point, the guideline is executed when criteria match the attributes.

Guidelines may require the concurrent execution of clinical tasks (i.e. running lab tests while waiting for the results of an X-Ray). Branch steps are used to model this concurrency and are used in conjunction with synchronization steps. Once the corresponding synchronization step is reached after a number of steps have been performed within a branch, a logical expression serving as continuation attribute specifies whether all, some, or one of the preceding steps must have been completed before control can move to the next step. Actions steps are used to represent medical tasks that have to (or should) be performed.

3. Decision support in a homecare scenario

Consider a treatment scenario that is aimed toward cardiac patients after successful treatment and rehabilitation. It takes place at a patient's home - which is why we shall refer to it as 'homecare scenario' - and is designed to facilitate a safe, medically supervised training. The rationale behind this scenario is a reduction of the length of the costly in-patient phase of the rehabilitation, and more importantly, the reduction of re-hospitalizations through better secondary prevention. A scenario like this is realized with a software-hardware system. Aside from device that captures the patient's electrocardiogram, the patient is also equipped with a pulse oximeter that measures the oxygen concentration in the patient's blood and a blood pressure sensor. As a training device, the patients use a modified ergometer bike that has been fitted with a Panel PC. This ergometer bike and the sensors can be seen in Fig. 3-a. The Panel PC with its touch screen not only serves as user interface for the patient but also as a gateway that gathers the data from the sensors, controls the ergometer load and connects the patient's home with the rehabilitation clinic so training plans can be updated and training sessions be monitored remotely.

a) 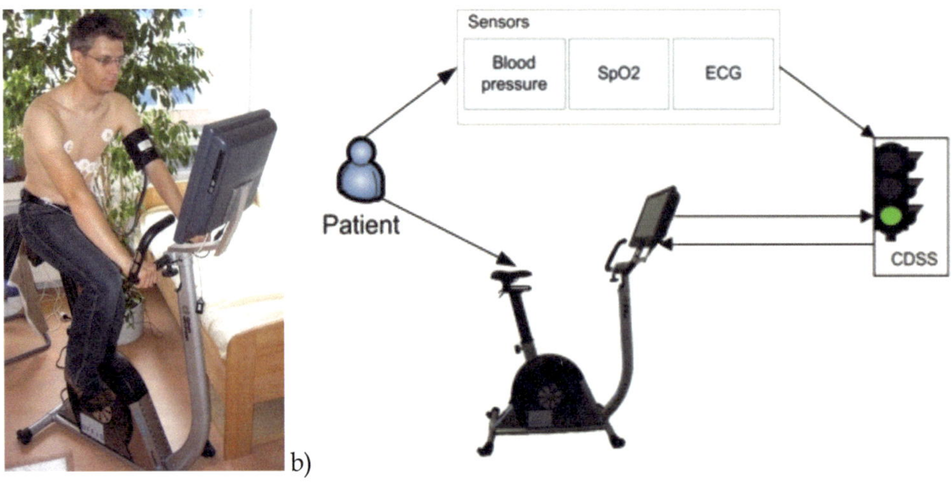 b)

Fig. 3. a) Modified ergometer bike and sensors used in the homecare scenario and b) Flow of sensor and actor data to CDSS

However, in order to ensure the patient's safety during the training sessions, the software needs to go beyond the simple streaming of sensor data to the rehabilitation clinic. The data needs to be analyzed locally, through a sensor flow shown in Fig. 3-b, allowing the system to adapt the training load or abort the training session if the patient's state is no longer stable.
The patient's state - and with it the status of the running training session, can be represented with a traffic light schema that is easily understood by patients and doctors alike. A green light means that the session can commence or continue because the patient's state is stable. Since the training program is tailored to the patient's treatment and rehabilitation progress, this is the expected state. The yellow light state is used if the patient's vital parameters exceed the expected thresholds but do not pose a danger to the patient. In that case, the training can continue, though the training load may be lowered to keep the patient in a stable state until the end of the training session. However, a red light signals the end of the training session because the patient's vital parameters exceed the set thresholds to such a degree that the patient may be in danger if the training session is continued. Adverse events like that are rare but need to be treated with care. The patient could be in danger and should see a doctor as soon as possible, and the treating physician should be notified of the alert and seek contact with the patient. The patient can also signal problems by pressing a corresponding red or yellow button on the graphical user interface. The mock-up of a typical interface in a homecare scenario is shown in Fig. 4. The interface was developed for the OSAMI-D project by C-LAB, a research institute of the University of Paderborn and Siemens SIS.

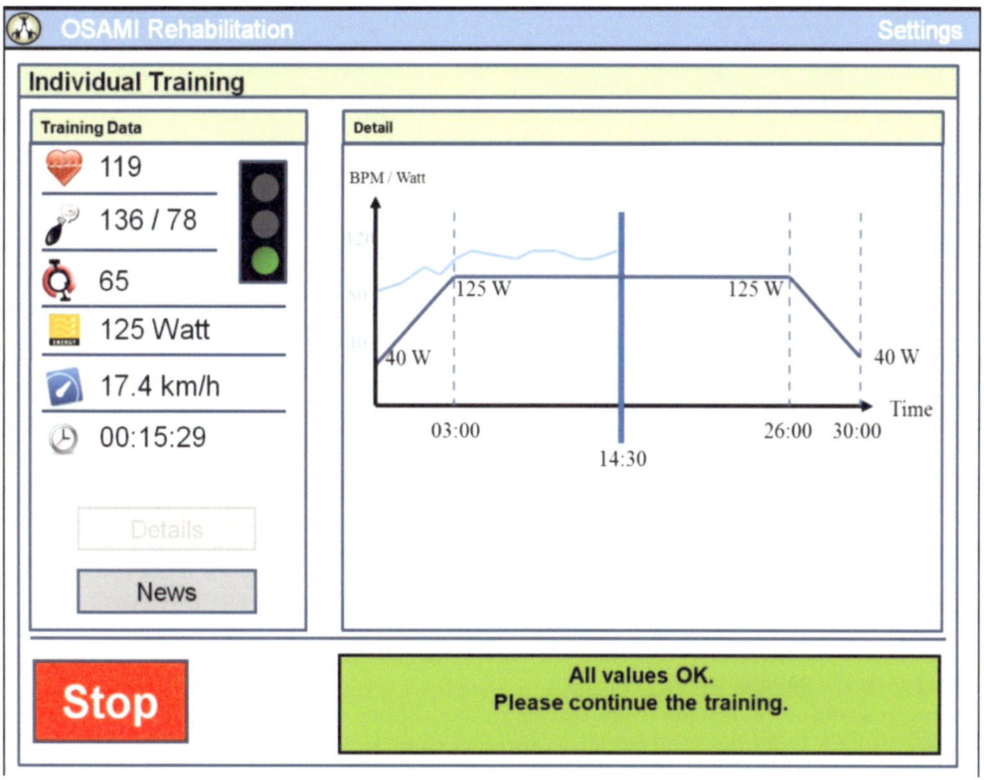

Fig. 4. User interface for a homecare application

The simplicity of the traffic light schema hides the fact that analyzing the sensor data is not a trivial task; dealing with simple data items such as the blood pressure, the blood oxygen saturation or the heart rate poses less of a challenge than the signal processing and analysis of ECG signals. The continuous analysis of ECG signals, however, is a vital step in ensuring the patient's safety.

A concept for decision support in a homecare scenario is shown in Fig. 5. The homecare system is a distributed approach between the clinic's side and the system deployed in the patient's home. In the clinic, an individual training program is created for the patient by adapting the generic exercise guideline for the patient, taking into account data gathered during the therapy, the inpatient rehabilitation, a number of reference training sessions and the results/reports of the last sessions performed at the patient's home. This adapted guideline is downloaded by the system in the patient's home at the start of the training session and is used to determine the parameters of the patient stabilization loop and for the generation of alerts. One possible implementation of the components realizing the stabilization loop and alert generation is described in the next section.

4. A rule-based approach

Nee et al. (2008) describe a system that realized a system like the one shown in Fig. 5. At the patient's home a CDSS is implemented that uses a rule-based approach for patient stabilization and alert generation. Before this actual implementation is discussed, the patient stabilization loop needs to be detailed further.

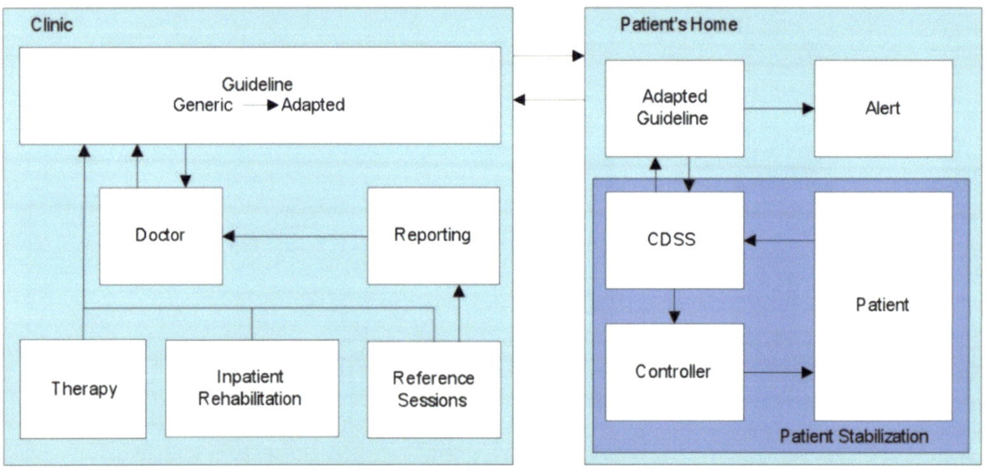

Fig. 5. Concept for decision support in a homecare scenario

4.1 Control loop for patient stabilization

The control loop for the patient stabilization during the training at home is shown in Fig. 6. It consists of the patient, the ergometer, a CDSS, and a controller. The patient is observed by the sampled sensor values $y_p(k)$, that consist of blood pressure (BP), heart rate (HR), oxygen saturation (SpO2), and the ECG signal acquired via 4 or 10 defined positions on the patient's body (3/6/12 channel-ECG). Depending on sensed values $y_p(k)$, the power $P_p(k)$ applied by the patient to the ergometer (measured and transmitted as $y_e(k)$) and initial parameters and thresholds the CDSS derives the patient state *x(k)* and the control difference *e(k)*. The control difference *e(k)* is used continuously by the controller to derive control output (increase or decrease of brake force) to the ergometer $u_e(k)$ and to the patient via visual display $u_p(k)$. In this way the training can be defined either as power/load over time (see Fig. 4) or HR over time. In addition, the discrete patient state *x(k)* derived from the CDSS accordingly to predefined rules is used to switch between different states of a training session, to initiate alerts and to report the training results to the clinic.

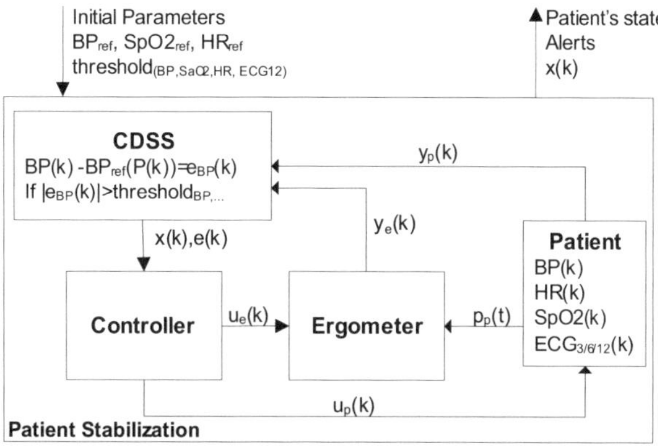

Fig. 6. Control loop for patient stabilization

The patient stabilization is defined to reach the following aims:

1. *Improvement of patient's compliance to the predefined training plan*: Because of safety reasons there is only a weak coupling between ergometer and patient. That means, that neither the training itself nor the power transmitted from the patient to the ergometer during the training can be controlled directly. Due to this, the parameter HR (an in principle also BP) can be used as input to the control loop and can be stabilized automatically by varying the ergometer's brake power.
2. *Determination of potentially critical states*: According to [Gi02] absolute, the differential and the relative thresholds can be used to derive the patient's state *x(k)* from the observed parameters $y_p(k)$ to control the training:
   - Absolute thresholds are defined independent on the training state of the patient. Example is the oxygen saturation that should not fall below a certain level, e.g. (SpO2) < 90%. These levels can differ from patient to patient and have to be defined based on the initial training in the clinic.
   - Differential and relative thresholds depend on one hand on the training state $y_e(k)$ of the patient (e.g. blood pressure (BP) before the training start should < 200/110 mmHg and during the training < 250/115 mmHg). On the other hand either the change of one parameter should not exceed a threshold (e.g. drop of BP by 10 mmHg despite increased workload) or the chronological sequence of one parameter should not be abnormal in respect to the reference curves recorded during the initial training in the clinic (e.g. respiration).

   Depending on the identified deviation *e(k)* and classified patient's state either the training is eased by opening the ergometer's brakes and informing the patient to slow down or the training will be interrupted and the clinic will be informed via alert channels.

3. *Identification of technical problems*: The detection of sensor failure or erroneous sensor placement is of special importance to avoid false alerts. Critical are problems during the placement of the sensors (especially ECG electrodes) and during recording and interpretation of ECG and blood pressure because these parameters are used as indicators for the termination of the training.

4.2 Implementation of the rule-based approach

The model discussed in section 4.1 was realized using the rule engine Jess and a number of rules that examine the vital parameters, generating alert events if they exceed thresholds. Jess has been chosen because of its execution speed and the easy integration in Java. A Jess rule has a left hand side (LHS) that determines when a rule is activated and a right hand side (RHS) that describes what actions will be executed if the conditions defined in the LHS are met. Consider the following rule for the detection of high systolic blood pressure:

```
(bpmeasurement {systolicP > 200})
(not (alarm {sensor == BP && severity > 1}))                                    (1)
```

```
(assert (alarm (patientID ?patID) (sensor BP) (alarmType bptoohigh) (date ?date)
(time ?time) (severity 2) (alarmMessage "BP > 200mmHg")))                       (2)
(alarm-to-db "BP > 200 mmHG" BP 2)
```

The conditions of the LHS are contained in (1), the RHS in (2). Every alarm has a severity, ranging from 0 ("green") to 2 ("red"). So the LHS says that the rule should be triggered if the systolic blood pressure is higher than 200 mmHg and if there hasn't been a previous red alert caused by high blood pressure. The RHS generates the actual alert messages, one that is sent to other components, such as the training controller that stops the training at a red alert, and one that is written to the database for reporting.

A simple rule like the one shown in (1) and (2) is too likely to be triggered by artefacts in signals that are susceptible. For data items that are generated every second (such as data coming from the pulse oximeter), a counter helps mitigate this problem. For the heart rate and oxygen saturation measured by the pulse oximeter, it takes three consecutive measurements to trigger an alert.

Since Doctors generally do not want to write rules using a rather complex syntax, the customization of the rules is performed through a graphical user interface that allows thresholds to be changed at any point during the training. In order to reflect the dynamic nature of a training session, at least three sets of thresholds need to be defined: the first set decides if the actual training can commence, and the other two sets are used during the warm-up phase and the cool-down phase.

4.3 Evaluation of the rule-based approach

While the rule-based approach appears to be the easiest and most natural one, it has displayed some shortcomings when the alarm generation system was tested with patients. The first shortcoming has already been mentioned in the last section: even simple comparisons require complex rules with functions that are not obvious, which makes it hard for medical doctors to validate the behavior of the system. Debugging these rules is not trivial. These weaknesses could be mitigated by using a simplified domain-specific language (DSL) that exposes only a subset of the Jess language.

However, the performance of the alert system was not satisfactory. Four patients - three men, one woman - (38.5 ± 18.5 years, 183.5 ± 7.8 cm, 77.5 ±7.8 kg, BMI 23.5 ± 1.3kg/m^2) agreed to participate and test the bicycle ergometer. The patients trained on 9.75 ± 1.71 days, and 42 training reports were generated. A training report was only generated if sensor data has been recorded. There may have been attempts to start training sessions that were aborted because of issues with the sensors or for other reasons. If difficulties occurred, they have been recorded. No serious events were caused by the heart disease, but a number of minor difficulties regarding sensor operability.

Despite the number of events recorded for each patient, the system worked as expected. However, the results of the patient are a good starting point for a discussion on the sensor data that needs to be dealt with in a realistic setting. Fig. 7 shows a 10 second segment of ECG data that is typical for ECG data with motion artefacts. Reliable automatic interpretation of such signals is very hard. The signal quality and the capabilities of the ECG analysis software that was used in the project allow for rhythm analysis at best, and quite often not even that.

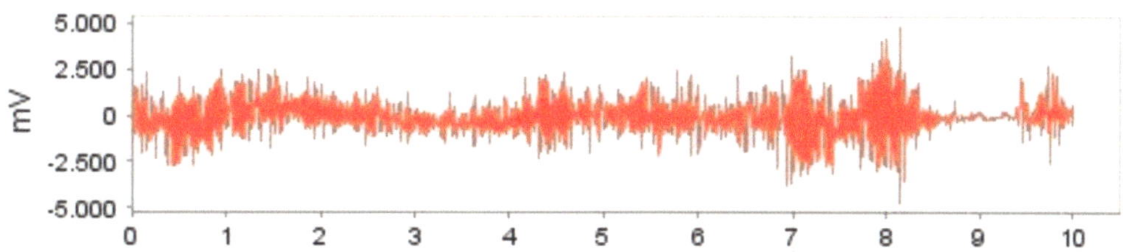

Fig. 7. ECG signal with motion artifacts

The vast majority (≥95%) of events documented in the reports are ECG-related. At this point it is important to remember that the physicians who supervised the training sessions did not find any major events, and the patients did not report any physical discomfort. Also, the training sessions were completed within two weeks, so no drastic changes in the ECG results are to be expected. This is why the high number of ECG-related alerts is most likely due to misinterpretations from the analysis software.

So while this approach allows for an easy specification of alarm conditions and can be mapped to the traffic light schema used in the homecare scenario, it is an agnostic one: the analysis of the vital parameters and signals at a given discrete time point k does not build on the results from $k-1$. For data gathered by the pulse oximeter, alarms are only triggered if the specified threshold is exceeded by three consecutive thresholds. While this method prevents a great number of false alarms, it treats each measurement result with the same degree of belief and thereby in fact amplifies the effect of motion artifacts on the generation of alarms. The strict Boolean approach of rules does not consider concepts like uncertainty and belief and cannot be used to capture the probabilistic nature of medical domain knowledge.

5. Clinical practice guidelines and Bayesian networks

One formalism that has been shown to be suitable for dealing with reasoning under certainty are probabilistic networks called Bayesian Networks (BN), which are also known as Bayesian Belief Networks or Bayes Nets. In the remainder of this chapter, either the term Bayesian Networks or its acronym will be used. Covering Bayesian networks and their construction in depth would be well beyond the scope of this work. A more thorough

treatment can be found in the seminal work of Pearl (1988) or the more accessible Neapolitan (2003).
A Bayesian network $B = (Pr, G)$ is a joint (or multivariate) probability distribution over a set of random variables with a graphical structure G and an associated probability distribution Pr. The graphical structure is a directed graph $G = (V(G),A(G))$ with nodes $V(G)=\{V_1,\ldots,V_n\}$, $n \geq 1$ and arcs $A(G)\subseteq V(G)\times V(G)$. Each node V_i represents a random variable having a finite set of mutually exclusive states. The graph is acyclic, which means that there is no directed path $V_1 \rightarrow V_n$ so that $V_1 = V_n$. The arcs are used to model the probabilistic influences between the variables. The parents of a variable V_i are denoted as $\Pi(V_i)$. The joint probability distribution Pr is given in a factorised form. For each variable V_i, there is a specified set of probability distributions $\Pr(V_i \mid \Pi(V_i))$ describing the joint effect of a specific combination of values for the parents $\Pi(V_i)$ of V_i on the probability distribution of V_i. The joint probability distribution of $V_1,\ldots,V_n$ is given in (3).

$$Pr(V_1,\ldots,V_n) = \prod_{i=1}^{n} Pr(V_1 | \Pi(V_i)) \quad (3)$$

Due to the Markov condition, the number of probabilities necessary for the joint probability distribution grows in a linear fashion $O(n)$ rather than exponentially $O(2^n)$, resulting in less effort for specification and computation. As long as they are acyclic, the graphs representing Bayesian networks can be arbitrarily complex and make use of nesting. Classification problems can usually be solved with a specific class of networks that have a limited topology.
Bayesian networks can be constructed manually or learned from data. Through learning, the topology of the Bayesian network and the joint probability distribution can be constructed, or the learning process can be used to generate the underlying probability distribution. Since the joint probability distribution grows in a linear fashion rather than an exponential one, allowing even complex causal interaction between many variables to be specified and interpreted with reasonable effort. The graphical representation makes it easy for domain experts to create and interpret a Bayesian network for a part of their domain.
Aside from its topology, a Bayesian network requires the specification of the joint probability distribution. This is usually done via a conditional probability table (CPT), which is defined for each variable, taking into account the probabilities of the parent variables. The CPTs can be specified by domain experts, or they can be learned from data. Learning the topology and the CPTs from data is also possible but is computationally expensive because of a huge search space. The flexibility of how a Bayesian network can be constructed and refined is one of the distinct advantages of this approach.

5.1 Bayesian networks in medical applications

Medicine has so far been the most popular field for the application of Bayesian networks. Given the complexity of the domain, the amount of knowledge (often implicitly) held by medical practitioners, there has long been a strong interest in expert systems that aid medical personnel. The ability to explicitly model causal dependencies and their simple and effective visualization through nodes and vertices are part of the appeal of Bayesian Networks. Lucas et al. (2004) identified four important types of problem solving where Bayesian network methods have been applied: diagnostic reasoning, prognostic reasoning and treatment selection, and the discovery of functional interactions.

When constructing a diagnostic hypothesis and during the elimination process, the inherent uncertainty of diagnostic testing needs to be taken into consideration in order to prevent a misdiagnosis. This type of reasoning with uncertainty can easily be modelled with Bayesian networks. PATHFINDER (Heckerman et al., 1992) is an expert system for the diagnosis of lymph node diseases. Another early example is the MUNIN network (Andreassen et al., 1987) for the interpretation of electromyographic findings. A more recent application is the BayPAD network (Luciani et al., 2003). The acronym 'BayPAD' stands for 'Bayesian network for Pulmonary embolism Assisted Diagnosis'. The network for the diagnosis of pulmonary embolism includes 72 random variables that represent both the risk factors and the pathophysiological consequences of the disease, which can be detected by diagnostic tests. Diagnostic reasoning performed with Bayesian networks can also be exploited for e-learning purposes, as presented with CardioBayes (Seebold et al., 2005). CardioBayes was designed as a learning environment for students and is based on a Bayesian network design by domain experts. One example for prognostic reasoning is NasoNet (Galan et al., 2002), which extends a Bayesian network model with temporal reasoning. TREAT, a system for treatment selection, has already been introduced in section 2.2. The selection of treatments requires a combination of diagnostic reasoning and prognostic reasoning. Decision support systems often use Bayesian networks as a basis when suggesting possible treatments. However, it is also possible to extend the Bayesian network model in order to capture concepts like preferences and costs that are necessary for decision support. Influence diagrams (Owens et al., 1997) can be used for this task.

5.2 Application in the homecare scenario

To address the shortcomings of a guideline modelling language like GLIF and in order to add robustness through reasoning under uncertainty to guidelines during their runtime, a combination of Bayesian network techniques and GLIF is being sought.

The core of a guideline-based training control implements an alarm system for a Homecare Scenario based on Bayesian networks, building on the results of the well known ALARM Bayesian network (Beinlich et al., 1989). The resulting system will be compared with the rule-based alarm system described in section 4.2, which uses a set of rules written for and executed by the Jess engine. Using thresholds defined by the clinician for each patient, the conditional probability tables (CPTs) of the Bayesian net will be refined and tested with data from actual training sessions.

Fig. 8 shows the basic outline of a guideline that can be used to control a training session in a homecare scenario. The decision step "Training OK?" and the action step "Training" use Bayesian networks to determine if the patient's state allows the training session to commence or to continue.

5.3 Implementation

The first step of the implementation is the extension of the Guideline Interchange Format to incorporate Bayesian networks. Fig. 9 shows the extended format, with the actual extensions being limited to the classes BayesNet_Node, BayesNet_Criterion and Meta_Patient_State.

The class BayesNet_Node captures the topology and probabilities of a Bayesian network, while the class BayesNet_Criterion makes it available for the decision making process in GLIF decision steps. The class Meta_Patient_State is used to store a Bayesian network that might be queried by more than one decision step. Although it would be possible to use these

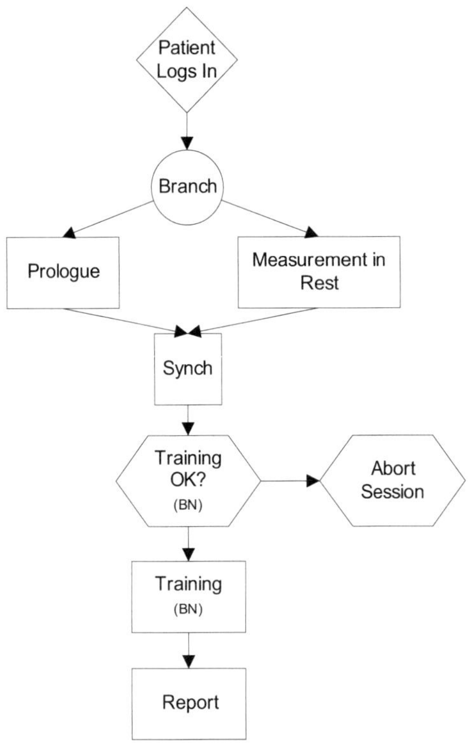

Fig. 8. Training control with a GLIF guideline

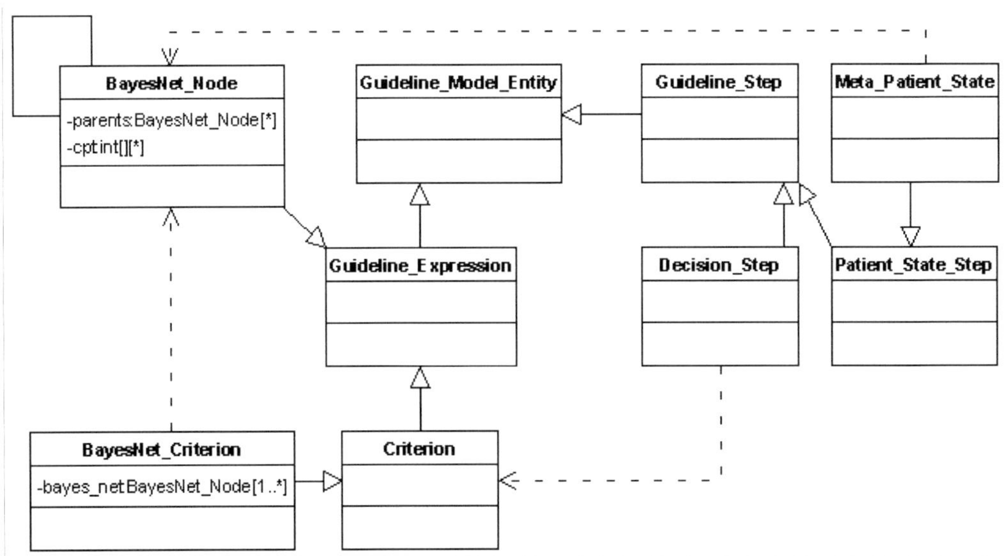

Fig. 9. Extended Guideline Interchange Format

extensions to specify a Bayesian network directly in GLIF using the Protégé editor, this is not the preferred method because of the poor support for tables in the underlying OWL model. This is why the Bayesian networks have been created using a third-party application, with the BaysianNetwork class merely pointing to the file created by the application. That application is also used to fine-tune the CPTs and to evaluate the Bayesian network based on the findings entered during the guideline execution process.

5.4 Evaluation

The approach was evaluated by constructing a Bayesian network that realizes the decision processes that take place in the step 'Training OK?' shown in Fig. 8. A slightly simplified version of that network is shown in Fig. 10.

The topology of the network is largely defined by the availability of data items. In order to compare this approach with the rule-based approach described in section 4.2, no additional data should be used for the decision making process. The node labelled 'Alert' is not a chance node but a deterministic node that yields 'true' when any of the sensor alert nodes is true. The sensor alert nodes are simple Boolean chance nodes. In order to map the results to the traffic light schema of the rule-based approach, the sensor data of the sensor that triggered the alert would need to be examined for risk stratification.

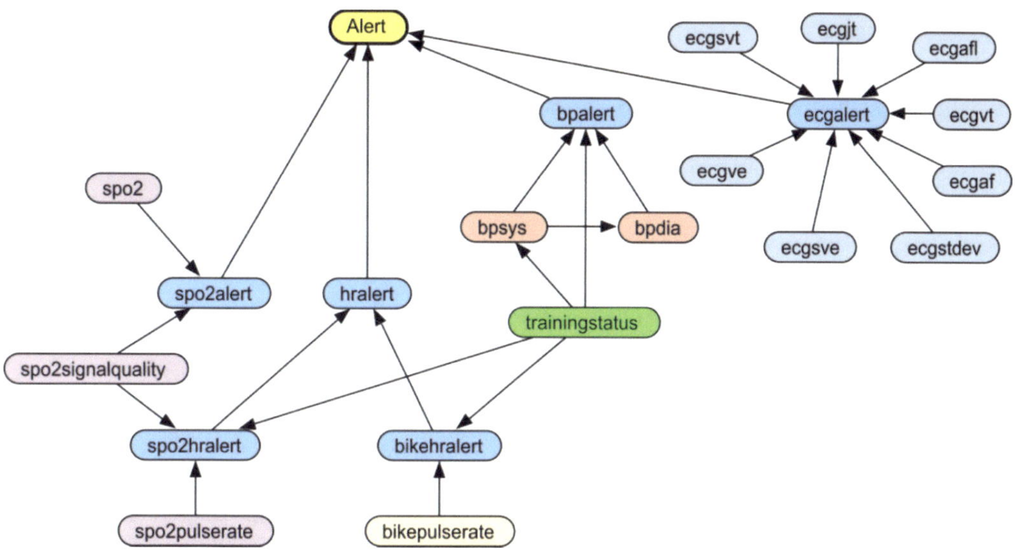

Fig. 10. Bayesian network for alert generation

The reason the alert system has been reduced to Boolean values lies in the number of states of the random variables and the conditional probability tables (CPTs) defined over these states. As mentioned in the introduction of section 5, CPTs can be specified by domain experts, be learned through data or derived through a combination of the two approaches. In the evaluation, we wanted to build the necessary CPTs by using a number of reference sessions, for which the sensor data and the results of the rule-based alarm system had been collected. In order to be tractable, the number of states of each random variable needs to be smaller than the range of sensor values. For example for the node representing the systolic blood pressure measured in mmHg has six states, sorting the measurements into 'buckets' representing values from smaller than 100 mmHg to values greater than 160 mmHg. The size of these 'buckets' has to be small enough to represent the medical meaning but big enough to gather enough experience for the learning process. For sensors like the blood pressure sensors that deliver only a few measurements during a training session, this process is harder than for sensors like the pulse oximeter which yield one measurement per second.

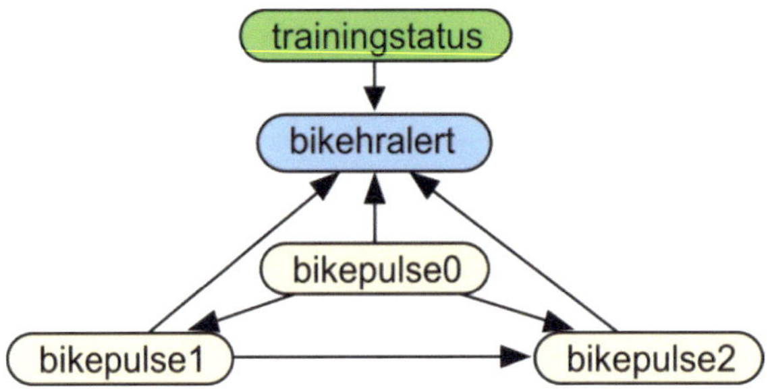

Fig. 11. Expanded portion of the alert net

As mentioned in section 4.2, alerts would be triggered too easily by motion artifacts if only the current measurement is used to decide whether or not a threshold has been exceeded. The rule-based approach of taking three measurements into consideration is used for the Bayes net version as well. This is shown in Fig. 11 for the portion that uses the pulse rate measured by the ergometer bike to determine if the patient's heart rate is too high depending on the phase (or status) of the training session. This is done for data from the pulse oximeter, the ergometer bike and for the results from the ECG analysis software. Although more than one measurement or analysis result is taken into consideration, this does not mean that no decision is made until all values are present. It merely means that the degree of belief increases with each measurement that is available.

The resulting network consists of 57 nodes, which are connected by 84 links and contain 10526 conditional probabilities. Rather than learning the CPTs for one big network, the network has been broken down into a branch dealing with ECG analysis results, a branch for the blood pressure measurements, one for the heart rate and one for the blood oxygen. In order to collect enough experience for the blood pressure nodes, 29 measurements taken during 10 completed sessions have been used. The remaining nodes were learned by using data from five typical sessions of that patient. So in addition to the blood pressure measurements, 5252 SpO2 measurements, 4395 ergometer measurements, and 364 ECG analysis results were used to build the CPTs.

Once the CPTs were learned, the network was tested using sessions that had not been used for the learning process. The result was a reduction of false-positive event reports by 78%. Further testing revealed that the initial error rate of the ECG alert network of 2.496% increases greatly for previously unobserved results. This is true to an even greater degree for the blood pressure network. However, this result is not surprising, considering how little data was available for the learning process. For example if no blood pressure of 160/100 mmHg has been observed, there is no experience that would define how the system should react. This shortcoming can easily be mitigated by entering such experience manually, allowing the network to learn and to fine-tune the CPTs accordingly. In a practical setting, the treating physician would usually validate the data and the analysis results by inspecting reports generated by the system. If the system's predictions are not as expected, the new data (including the physician's corrections) can be incorporated, automatically fine-tuning the conditional probability distributions further until the outcome meets the expectations.

6. Further applications

One of the advantages of the approach described in the previous section is the exploitation of the semantic layers of GLIF. Ordinarily, a Bayesian network would be agnostic about the semantic categories of the random variables and the states, making the deployment of a network in other environments a cumbersome task. However, with the extensions shown in Fig. 10 and the semantic mediation techniques demonstrated by Laleci et al. (2008), semi-automatic deployment of guidelines containing Bayesian networks is possible. This allows modifications and extensions of the scenario, adding new sensors (such as a glucose meter for diabetic patients, or a spirometer for patients suffering from lung problems). The alarm system discussed in section 5 is only one possible application of a Bayesian network. As mentioned in section 5.1, these networks can be used for other aspects of decision making as well. With influence diagrams, the utility of decisions can be considered when proposing alternative options. This would typically be exploited in the decision support system that helps the physician plan the patient's therapy. Embedding Bayesian networks in GLIF combines the strengths of GLIF on a macro level and the power of Bayesian networks for diagnostic and prognostic reasoning and for the discovery of functional interactions.
The scenario that motivated this work is from the medical field, but the applications of are not limited to it. After all, the problem of making decisions under uncertainty with incomplete and potentially unreliable data is not one that is unique. In this context, GLIF should be seen as framework for modelling workflows. To make this approach more suitable for other fields, GLIF could be replaced by other modelling workflow formalism, such as the XML Process Definition Language (XPDL).

7. Conclusion

In this chapter the state of the art of decision support in medicine along with clinical guidelines has been described. Especially in fields of medicine where workflows are highly standardized and do not depend in a great extend on intra-individual variations, clinical guidelines are well accepted. In these fields the clinician can benefit from computer assistance. The implementation of a CDSS requires on one hand the formalization of the clinical guidelines and mechanisms for reasoning. This chapter is focused on GLIF for the formalization and a rule-based approach for the execution of the guideline. As a potential application this approach has been used for the monitoring of a patient at home during his/her rehabilitation training. The patient benefit from the CDSS because a clinician cannot continuously monitor the training and in case of the breakdown of the connection to the clinic the systems has to act autonomously. A first evaluation has shown that the rule-based approach results in a great number of false alarms. Therefore, an extension of the CDSS by a Bayesian networks has been proposed. In this way, the state of the patient can be monitored and interpreted in a more reliable manner. Especially in the context of the advent of mobile, personal and continuous worn sensors for vital parameters (pulse, ECG, blood pressure, SpO2, etc.) Bayesian networks for the modelling of the patient's state seem to be a good approach to provide reliable and high-quality data at discrete time points where a diagnostic or therapeutic workflow and decision process requires these data.

8. References

Andreassen, S. et al. (1987). MUNIN - A causal probabilistic network for interpretation of electromyographic findings. *Proceedings of the 10th International Joint Conference on Artificial Intelligence*, pp. 366-372, Milan (Italy), August 1987, Morgan Kaufman, San Francisco

Barnett, O. et al. (1987). DXplain. An evolving diagnostic decision-support system. *Journal of the American Medical Association*, Vol. 258, No. 1, pp. 67-74,

Beinlich, I. et al. (1989). The ALARM monitoring system: A case study with two probabilistic inference techniques for belief networks. *Proceedings of the Second European Conf. on Artificial Intelligence in Medicine*, pp. 247-256, Springer, Berlin

Berner, E. et al. (1999). Effects of a Decision Support System on Physicians' Diagnostic Performance. *Journal* of the *American Medical Informatics Association*, Vol. 6, No. 5, pp. 420-427. ISSN 1067-5027

Bertrand, M. et al. (2004). Management of acute coronary syndromes in patients presenting without persistent ST-segment elevation. *European Heart Journal*, 2004, Vol. 23, No. 23, pp. 1809-1840, ISSN 0195-668x

de Clercq, P. et al. (2004). Approaches for creating computer-interpretable guidelines that facilitate decision support. Artificial Intelligence in Medicine, Vol. 31, No. 1, pp. 1-27, ISSN 0933-3657

Elstein, A. (2004). On the origins and development of evidence-based medicine and medical decision making. *Inflammation Research*, Vol. 52, Suppl.2 , pp. 184-189, ISSN 1023-3830

Field, M. & Lohr, K. (eds.). (1994). *Guidelines for Clinical Practice: From Development to Use*, National Academies Press, ISBN 0-30904589-4

Field, T. et al. (2009). Computerized Clinical Decision Support During Medication Ordering for Long-term Care Residents with Renal Insufficiency. *Journal* of the *American Medical* Informatics *Association*, Vol. 16, No. 4, ISSN 1067-5027

Galan, S. et al. (2002). NasoNet, modeling the spread of nasopharyngeal cancer with networks of probabilistic events in discrete time. *Artificial Intelligence in Medicine*, Vol. 25, No. 3, pp. 247-264, ISSN 0933-3657

Goud, R. et al. (2005). A computer-based guideline implementation system for cardiac rehabilitation screening. *Proceedings of Computers in Cardiology*, pp. 323-326, ISBN 0-78039337-6, Lyon, September 2005, IEEE Computer Society Press

Heckerman, D. E.; Horvitz, E.J. & Nathwani, B.N. (1992). Toward normative expert systems: Part I - The Pathfinder Project. *Methods of Information in Medicine,* Vol. 31, No. 2, pp. 90-105, ISSN 0026-1270

Isern, D. & Moreno, A. (2008). Computer-based execution of clinical guidelines: A review. *International Journal of Medical Informatics,* Vol. 77, No. 12, pp. 787-808, ISSN 1386-5056

Laleci, G.B. et al. (2008). SAPHIRE: A Multi-Agent System for Remote Healthcare Monitoring through Computerized Clinical Guidelines. In: *Agent Technology and e-Health,* Annicchiarico, R.; Cortés, U. & Urdiales, C. (eds.), pp. 25-44, Birkäuser Basel

Leibovici, L. et al. (2007). The TREAT project: decision support and prediction using causal probabilistic networks. *International Journal of Antimicrobial Agents,* Vol. 30, Suppl. 1, November 2007, pp. 93-102, ISSN 0924-8579

Lucas P. J. F.; van der Gaag, L. C. & Abu-Hanna, A. (2004). Bayesian networks in biomedicine and health-care. *Artificial Intelligence in Medicine,* Vol. 30, No. 3, pp. 201-214, ISSN 0933-3657

Luciani, D.; Marchesi, M. & Bertolini, G. (2003). The role of Bayesian Networks in the diagnosis of pulmonary embolism. *Journal of Thrombosis and Haemostasis,* Vol. 1, No. 4, pp. 698-707, ISSN 1538-7933

Owens, D. et al. (1997). Representation and Analysis of Medical Decision Problems with Influence Diagrams. *Medical Decision Making,* Vol. 17, No. 3, pp. 241-262, ISSN 0272-989X

Neapolitan, R. (2003). *Learning Bayesian Networks,* Prentice Hall, ISBN 0-13-012534-2, NJ

Nee, O. et al. (2008). SAPHIRE: Intelligent Healthcare Monitoring based on Semantic Interoperability Platform - Pilot Applications, *IEE Proceedings,* Vol. 2, No. 2, February 2008, pp. 192-201

Ohno-Machado, L. et al. (1998). The GuideLine Interchange Format: A Model for Representing Guidelines. *Journal of the American Medical Informatics Association,* Vol. 5, No. 5, pp. 357-372, ISSN 1067-5027

Paul, M. et al. (2006). Improving empirical antibiotic treatment using TREAT, a computerized decision support system: cluster randomized trial. *Journal of Antimicrobial Chemotherapy,* Vol. 58, No. 6, pp. 1238-1245, ISSN 0305-7453

Pearl, J. (1988). *Probabilistic Reasoning in Intelligent Systems: Networks of Plausible Inference,* Morgan Kaufman Publishing, ISBN 1-55860479-0

Peleg, M. et al. (2003). Comparing Computer-interpretable Guideline Models: A Case-study Approach. *Journal of the American Medical Informatics Association,* Vol. 10, No. 1, pp. 52-68, ISSN 1067-5027

Seebold, H.; Lüdtke A. & Möbus, C. (2005). Bayesian Belief Network based Diagnostics in a Problem-oriented Learning Environment for Cardiology. *Proceedings of Training, Education Simulation International,* Maastricht, March 2005, Nexus Media

Sonnenberg, F.A. & Hagerty, C.G. (2006). Computer-Interpretable Clinical Practice Guidelines: Where are We and where Are We Going? In: *IMIA Yearbook of Medical Informatics*, Haux, R. & Kulikowski, C. (eds.), pp. 72-80

Wyatt, J. & Spiegelhalter, D. (1991). Field trials of medical decision-aids: potential problems and solutions, *Proceedings of the 15th Symposium on Computer Applications in Medical Care*, pp. 3-8, Washington, 1991

10

Computerized Interpretation of Cardiovascular Physiological Signals[1]

Bing Nan LI[1,2], Mang I VAI[1] and Ming Chui DONG[1]
[1]*Department of Electrical & Electronics Engineering, University of Macau, Taipa,*
[2]*NUS Graduate School for Integrative Science & Engineering National University of Singapore, Kent Ridge,*
[1]*Macau*
[2]*Singapore*

1. Introduction

The conventional mode of health delivery can be profiled as follows: a patient, if he does not feel good, will visit his physician and report his symptoms (e.g., headache, bellyache, and nausea, etc); the physician strives to make a few empirical hypotheses based on the patient's complaints and medical history; in general, the physician has to further examine the patient's vital signs (e.g., body temperature, blood pressure, and pulse, etc.) so as to confirm or reject his initial hypotheses; if the physician is confident enough on his hypotheses, the final diagnosis decision can be made and the according treatments are hereby delivered; if not, the physician will resort to various medical instruments (e.g., electrocardiography, ultrasonography, and computed tomography, etc) and laboratory tests (e.g., blood test, urinalysis, and immunological analysis, etc); during this procedure, the initial hypotheses may be updated at any time; to those complicated diseases, the physicians will propose a few tentative treatments and modify them in accordance with clinical observations.

It is noteworthy that above procedure is triggered and driven by patients' symptoms. But most symptoms are subjective, and are late manifestations of a disease or a group of diseases. In other words, they often incur expensive and painful clinical treatments. Furthermore, once the patients perceive malign symptoms, they may have missed the best opportunity of medical treatments. Take cardiovascular diseases (CVDs) for an example. Nowadays it is possible to treat or relieve nearly all CVDs by medical interventions, such as controlling blood pressure and blood cholesterol. In the case of refractory or congenital CVDs, various sophisticated clinical instruments and operations, including pacemakers, prosthetic valves, coronary artery bypass and even whole heart transplantation, have been developed and practiced too. As a consequence, the World Health Organization (WHO) reports "… at least 80% of premature deaths from heart disease and stroke could be avoided

---

[1] Adapted from LI Bing Nan (2009) Wavelet Neural Networks: The Fusion of HC and SC for Computerized Physiological Signal Interpretation, PhD Dissertation, University of Macau, Taipa, Macau

through effective reduction of risk factors." Unfortunately, it is still reported over 861,826 American deaths due to CVDs (35.2% of all deaths) in 2005 (Rosamond et al., 2008), and over 4.35 million European deaths (49% of all deaths) each year (Petersen et al., 2005). Such paradoxical results may be attributed to that various cardiovascular risks, such as arteriosclerosis and other peripheral arterial diseases, are asymptomatic whereas they have been able to cause a deadly stroke or heart attack (Cohn et al., 2003).

For better healthcare, the individuals are hereby being expected to assume more responsibility for their own health, for example, having their blood pressure checked regularly (WHO, 1998). It is now one of the hottest topics in science and engineering to make such self-examination easier. For instance, IBM has declared their understandings on the future healthcare: "...the ability to securely capture sensitive medical data has the potential to allow healthcare to move from the traditional doctor's office to wherever the patient happens to be... in the future, technology will enable: millions of people with chronic diseases will be able to have their conditions monitored as they go about their daily life through sensors at home... a pill dispenser will help patients track their drug regimen and automatically transmit such data to caregivers... virtual doctors can check blood pressure, pulse and others remotely, and follow up if necessary..." (http://www-07.ibm.com/innovation/in/ideas/five_in_five/). As a matter of fact, there have been a few cost-effective instrumentations recommended and practiced for self-serviced healthcare at home (Korhonen et al., 2003), (Scalvini et al., 2005). In contrast to those subjective symptoms, the measured vital signs or physiological signals are generally more sensitive to various pathophysiological alterations. Then home subjects can take care of their own health condition better. However, till now their prevalence is not as optimistic as expected yet. The reason is multifold. We argue that the competence of computerized interpretation of cardiovascular physiological signals, such as electrocardiograms (ECG) and arterial blood pressure (ABP) waveforms from self-serviced cardiovascular health monitoring, should be paid special attention.

1.1 Cardiovascular system and diseases

Various nutrients and oxygen necessary for life maintenance are transported by the blood circulation in cardiovascular system (CVS). Meanwhile, circulatory system is responsible to discharge various metabolic wastes away. Hosting blood circulation, CVS is thus of vital importance for body health. In a broad sense, CVS is comprised of the subsystems for a complete blood circulation, namely pulmonary circulation, cardiac circulation and systemic circulation (Fig. 1). The subsystems in red, originated from the pulmonary capillaries, to left heart, arterial system and systemic capillaries, are responsible to transporting the oxygenic blood to various body organs and tissues. In contrast, those subsystems in blue, including systemic capillaries, venous system, right heart and pulmonary arteries, are in charge of collecting deoxygenated blood back to pulmonary circulation. The capillary circulations connect the venous circulation and the arterial one. But the heart is at the center of circulatory system. It coordinates and drives the overall procedure of blood circulation.

The heart, the lung, the vasculature and the blood are vital components for cardiovascular circulation. Any adverse alteration in them will evoke a series of deadly threatens to body health. Therefore it is not surprising that CVDs have been one of leading causes of death for years. In general, CVDs may result in arrhythmia. It disturbs the essential procedure of blood perfusion and nourishment. But the cardiovascular deterioration often commences with arteriosclerosis, a procedure of plaque deposit so that the vasculature turns to stiffened. The stiffened vasculature increases cardiac workload as well as blood pressure. High blood pressure not only impairs myocardium but also further exacerbates arteriosclerosis to stenosis. The late implications are often thrombosis and embolism, which may cause cerebral ischemia (stroke) or cardiac ischemia (heart attack). In a word, it is important to have cardiovascular rhythm and vascular elasticity checked frequently.

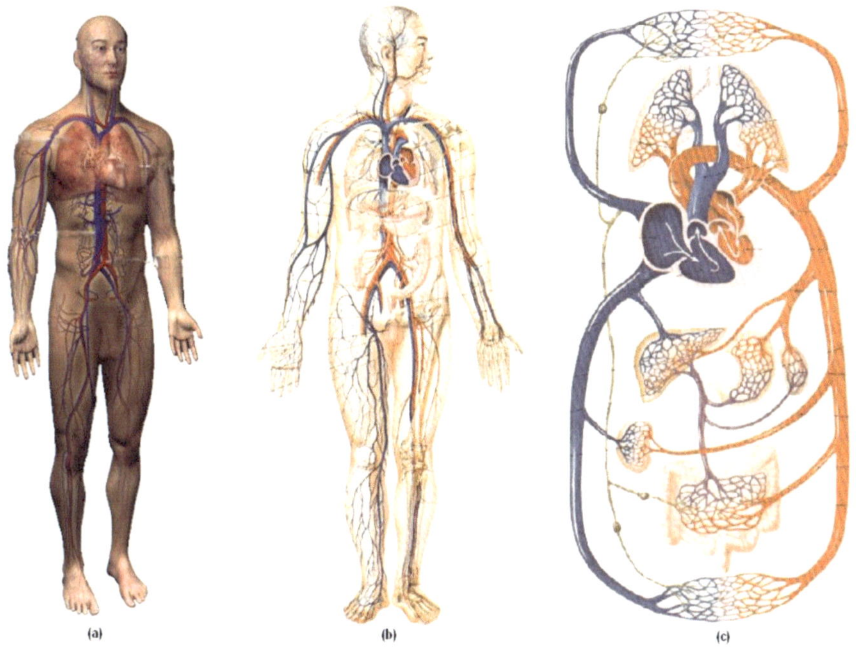

Fig. 1. The circulatory system
(a) Adapted from www.3dscience.com 2009; (b) and (c) Adapted from www.bbioo.com 2009

1.2 Non-invasive cardiovascular health monitoring

In respect to the importance of CVS on body health, the relevant investigations never cease in the past centuries; various methodological and technological breakthroughs keep advancing the development of cardiovascular health monitoring and treatments in clinical medicine (WHO and CDC 2004). Modern healthcare technologies make clinical physicians able to inspect CVS condition in depth. However, with respect to their complexity or costs, most of them are not suitable for routine cardiovascular health monitoring at home. Up to now, merely a few cost-effective technologies, such as electrocardiography and sphygmography, have been extensively investigated and practiced for that purpose (Welkowitz 1981).

1.2.1 Electrocardiography

Electrocardiography strives to manifest the cardiac electrical conduct system, which supervises the myocardial behaviours of systole and diastole. A normal cardiac rhythm commences with the electrical impulse by sinoatrial node (Fig. 2). It propagates to right and left atria and makes their myocardium contract. Then, the stimulus travels to atrioventricular node. After a delay, it conducts throughout ventricular myocardium in the line of HIS bundle, Left and Right Bundle Branches, and a dense network of Purkinje Fibers (Klabunde 2004). Following that electrical stimulus, four cardiac chambers contract and pump blood step by step. In other words, for efficient blood circulation, the electrical conduct system is of vital importance as it controls and coordinates the overall procedure of myocardial systole and diastole.

In essence, electrocardiography takes advantage of human body's homogeneous conduction, which projects the variation of myocardial potentials over time to body surface. To measure myocardial behaviours from different perspectives, electrocardiography has been evolved to 12-lead ECGs (Fig. 3). Among them, one to three of bipolar leads (i.e., Lead I, II, and III) or unipolar leads (i.e., Lead *a*VR, *a*VL, and *a*VF) are friendly for user manipulation, and hereby receive more attention for home health monitoring.

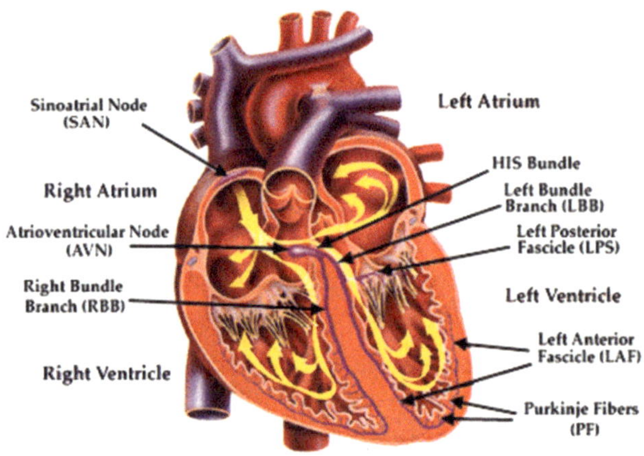

Fig. 2. Cardiac electrical conduction system (courtesy of Marquette Electronics 1996)

Electrocardiography is widely recommended in clinical medicine for the analysis of cardiac arrhythmia, conduction abnormality, electrolyte disturbances, and so on (Bacquer et al., 1998). But it is noteworthy that ECG is not able to reflect myocardial contractility directly, whereas they may give a rough indication of increased or decreased contractility. In contrast, arterial blood pressure and its waveforms have been long recommended as the quantitative indicators of myocardial contractility and the workloads (Rego and Souza 2002).

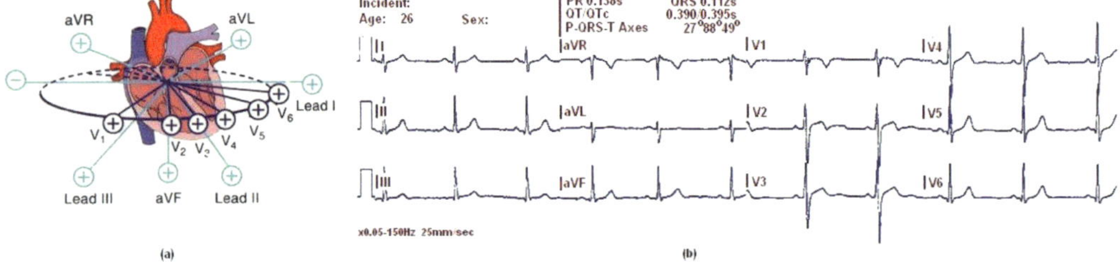

Fig. 3. 12-lead ECG monitoring (adapted from www.wikipedia.com 2009)
(a) Illustrative lead placement; (b) Exemplified ECG recordings

1.2.2 Sphygmography

The assessment of arterial blood pressure is an integral part of cardiovascular examination in clinical medicine. Various sphygmomanometers have been well developed for blood pressure measurement. But they merely report a few rough estimates of arterial blood pressure, including systolic pressure, diastolic pressure and mean pressure. They are obviously not enough to characterize the complicated procedure of blood circulation. Hence, other than blood pressure values, those experienced physicians are apt to master the variations of arterial blood pressure. In general, they palpate the variations by their fingers at accessible arteries and evaluate cardiovascular circulation comprehensively (Fig. 4a). Nowadays there have been many technologies developed for measuring sphygmograms, namely, recording the dynamical ABP waveforms precisely. It is definitely beneficial to the reproducible interpretation. As a matter of fact, the routine practice of non-invasive cardiovascular health monitoring prefers the techniques of applanation tonometry (Fig. 4b).

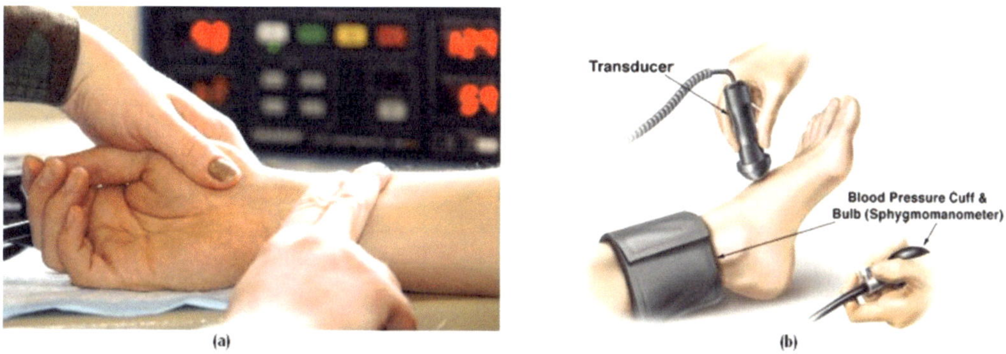

Fig. 4. Non-invasive monitoring of ABP waveforms (adapted from www.wikimedia.org 2009)

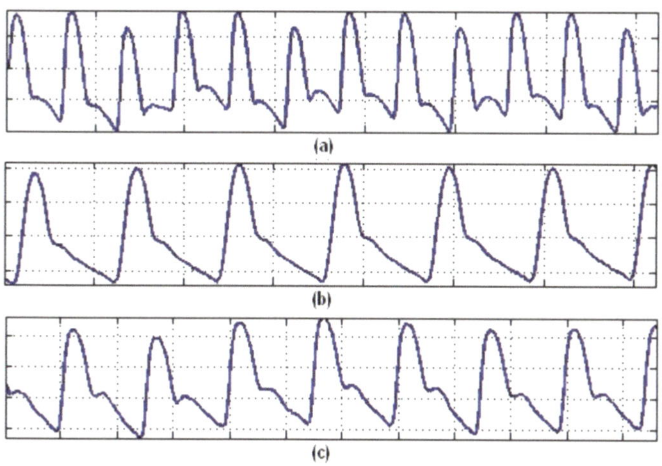

Fig. 5. Illustrative ABP waveforms
(a): Catheterization [MIMIC/03701: 0-5.8s];
(b): Photoplethysmography [FANTASIA/f2o01: 0-5.8s];
(c): Applanation tonometry [GXABP/05607080306: 0-5.8s]

In non-invasive applanation tonometry, a high-fidelity tonometer is placed on the accessible arteries with gentle pressure so as to occlude blood flow partially. It is hereby possible to capture the variation of arterial blood pressure through that site and convert it into other types of electrical signals (Fig. 5). It has been claimed by previous investigators that such non-invasive ABP waveforms are reliable and comparative to those obtained invasively by intra-arterial measurement (Sato et al., 1993).

2. Computerized physiological signal interpretation

Year	Regularization	Delineation	Quality Evaluation	Modeling	Recognition and Classification
1960	Spectral analyis				Spectral analysis
1961			Heuristic decision		Heuristic decision
1962	Linear regression	Derivative analysis			Adaptive filters
1968	Linear filters				Thresholding
1973					Template matching
1975		Syntactic method			
1978					Bayesian theory
1980					Decision table
1985	Filter banks				
1989					FL
1990				Spectrotemporal analysis	Hidden Markov models
1991					Multilayer perceptrons (MLP)
1995		GA		WT	ART
1996				HT	Fuzzy ARTMAP; WN
1997					Gaussian probability network
1998				PCA	RBF
1999					Complexity measurement
2000				Combined HT and SOM	
2001		Fuzzy NN			
2002	ICA				
2003					Inductive logic programming
2004					Competitive WN
2006					Data mining
2007					Geometric matching

Table 1. Advances of computerized ECG interpretation in chronicle

Disease diagnosis and health prognosis by arterial pulse waveforms came into being in the centuries B.C. in China, but till 1896 the Italian scientist Scipione Riva-Rocci invented the first quantitative sphygmomanometer to measure blood pressure (WHO and CDC 2004). The advances of applanation tonometers (Papaioannou et al., 2004) and photoplethysmographers (Allen 2007) make it possible to quantitatively observe the hemodynamical procedure of arterial blood pressure. The first contemporary electrocardiograph was invented by Willem Einthoven (Holland, 1860-1927) in 1901, and the first portable Holter Monitor was introduced in 1949 for obtaining ambulatory ECG. The introduction of computers into their interpretation can be gone back to 1960s (Warner 1965), but became commercially available in 1970s (Bailey et al., 1974). The readers may refer (Cox et al., 1972) and (Thomas et al., 1979) for a detailed review on the early-stage development of computerized physiological signal interpretation.

2.1 Overview

Year	Preprocessing and Modeling	Recognition and Classification	Cardiovascular System Modeling	
			Cardiac Function	Vascular Property
1967				LPM
1968	Thresholding			
1971	Polynomial			
1972	Heuristic decision			
1973			Diastolic waveform analysis	Linear LPM
1974		Linear curvature		
1976		Syntactic method		4-element LPM
1983			Spectral analysis	
1985	Filter banks			
1986				Area analysis
1988	PCA			
1992	NN			
1993			Transfer function	
1994			Template matching	
1995				Transit time
1997				Physical model
1998			8-element LPM	
1999				Windkessel model
2002	Refractory period		Linear regression	
2003				Systolic waveform analysis
2004	Fuzzy logics			
2005	WT	Adaptive filter banks		
2006			Modified Windkessel model	
2007				Support vector machine

Table 2. Advances of computerized ABP interpretation in chronicle

In general, a system oriented to ECG interpretation is comprised of the essential modules for (1) signal regularization to suppress various noises and artefacts; (2) adaptive delineation of critical points; (3) signal quality evaluation to find out those "dominant" and "ectopic" beats; (4) feature characterization for reliable and consistent classification; and (5) recognition and classification to assist medical diagnosis or health prognosis (Kligfield et al., 2007). Till now a plethora of computational methods and techniques have been proposed and validated for that purpose. A few representative ones were selected and listed in Table 1. Note that it is extremely difficult to figure out the progressive participation of different methods and techniques in computerized ECG interpretation. So Table 1 is absolutely not exhaustive. The situation is similar to Table 2, which illustrates the progressive development of computerized ABP interpretation. However, the major contributions of computers in this field are cardiovascular system modelling and risk factor derivation, but not pattern analysis and waveform classification.

2.2 Current state of the art

In essence, computerized interpretation is oriented to inferring the intrinsic health messages from non-invasive ECG and/or ABP. In the early stage of computerized ECG interpretation, the advances were mainly focused on modelling the practical expertise by heuristic decisions and syntactic methods. In addition, various well-developed methods, such as spectral analysis and linear regression, were programmed for automated signal processing and recognition. Later, to cope with ECG complexity as well as variability, more analytical methods, including Hilbert transform (HT), Hermite decomposition (HD), wavelet transform (WT), principal component analysis (PCA) and independent component analysis (ICA), were introduced step by step. It is deemed such alternative descriptions are more suitable for computerized interpretation.

To different signals and applications, above techniques keep invariant in terms of their analytical models and computing methods. It is totally different from the methods like neural networks (NN), fuzzy logics (FL), genetic algorithms (GA) and adaptive resonance theory (ART), whose models are dynamically adjustable in different cases. Consequently, they are particularly suitable for discovering the nonlinear relationships between physiological signals and health prognosis. Zadeh and other pioneer investigators defined the latter paradigms as soft computing (Zadeh 2007). In essence, soft computing is oriented to attacking the uncertainty and the imprecision in the real world by a consortium of NN, FL and other evolutionary computing techniques. As a comparison, it is appropriate to term the analytical methodologies like spectral analysis and WT as hard computing.

Since the models of hard computing have been formulated exactly, there are not so many stories reported on the integration of hard computing paradigms. On the contrary, soft computing is integrative in nature (Kecman 2001). As a consequence, many integrative paradigms, such as Fuzzy ARTMAP (Ham & Han 1996) and GreyART Network (Wen et al., 2007), were applied to computerized ECG interpretation soon after the introduction of soft computing. In addition, as stated in reference (Ovaska et al., 2002), (Tsoukalas & Uhrig 1997), (Thuillard 2001), (Iyengar 2002), the methodologies of hard computing and soft computing are not in a competitive position, but often complementarily implemented in various engineering applications. As to computerized ECG interpretation, the investigators are now more interested to fuse the paradigms of hard computing and soft computing for integrative advantages.

By observing the published investigations, the integration is generally achieved with two different kinds of paradigms. The first one is to extract patterns and features by hard computing but associate them to health prognosis adaptively by soft computing. This kind of paradigms is easily understandable, and not so challenging in terms of engineering implementation. Hence, a plethora of successful stories have been reported, including the combination of PCA and Multilayer Perceptrons (MLP) (Papaloukas et al., 2002), the combination of Hermite polynomials and neuro-fuzzy systems (Linh et al., 2003), and the combination of HD and Support Vector Machines (SVM) (Osowski et al., 2004). Another kind of paradigms is to fully integrate the analytical models and the computing methods of hard computing and soft computing. They are conceptually elegant but more challenging for engineering implementation. The pilot paradigms with applications in ECG interpretation include Wavelet Networks (Dickhaus & Heinrich 1996), Bayesian Probability Network (Long et al., 1997), and so forth.

Despite with a long history in clinical medicine, the advances of computerized ABP interpretation are not as optimistic as those of ECG interpretation (Table 2). It may be due to the intrinsically qualitative methodology in traditional Pulse Diagnostics (Fei 2003). On the contrary, the computers are good at digital and quantitative processing and analysis only. Thus it is necessary to introduce various quantitative indices for computerized ABP interpretation (Luo et al., 2005). The prevailing methods and techniques in this field are mainly focused on deriving quantitative risk factors, including cardiac output, arterial compliance and vascular resistance, by means of various analogous electrical models representing a CVS. Those models are possibly comprised of the capacitances analogous to arterial compliance, the resistances analogous to vascular resistance, the inductances analogous to blood inertia, and so on. However, no matter the low-order Windkessel models (Goldwyn & Watt 1967) or the high-order transmission line models (Heldt et al., 2002), their effectiveness and reliability are still arguing and pending for further investigation (Frank et al., 1973; Murray and Foster 1996).

Quite few paradigms were reported to recognize and classify non-invasive ABP waveforms by means of pattern recognition and computational intelligence, which on the contrary have been prevalent for computerized ECG interpretation. In this chapter, one of our ultimate goals is to investigate the applications of hard computing, soft computing and their fusion for computerized ABP interpretation. The attention will be particularly concentrated on the refractory variability of non-invasive physiological signals.

3. Physiological signal modelling

3.1 Conventional waveform analysis

In clinical medicine, the cardiologists are concerned with the rhythms, amplitudes and waveforms as a whole for physiological signal interpretation (Fei 2003; Yanowitz 2007). It is possible to formulate their expertise and experience into computer languages, and let the computers analyze those physiological signals automatically (Miyahara et al., 1968; Belforte et al., 1979; Degani & Bortolan 1989). The first step in advancing computerized physiological signal interpretation was to mimic the decision making procedure of clinical experts. In general, the clinical experts have been trained well to inspect various metrics of physiological signals, including their rhythms, amplitudes, waveforms and various derivative parameters (Fig. 6). From this point of view, the computers are even better to measure those parameters (Caceres et al., 1962). Nevertheless, such kind of information is susceptible to various instrumental and manual artefacts. In terms of non-invasive physiological measurements, it is particularly difficult to guarantee the accuracy of amplitude information. That is why morphological analysis and rhythm information turn to more and more popular in computerized physiological signal interpretation.

As early as in 1960s (Okajima et al., 1963), a few pioneer investigators have noticed the uniqueness of computer ECG interpretation. In order to disregard the effects of insignificant factors, such as pulse rate and age, they proposed to extract and normalize the QRS complex for pattern recognition. This idea, namely morphological analysis instead of metric measurement, was revisited more than once in the following years (Bemmel et al., 1973; Maitra & Zucker 1975; Suppappola et al., 1997; Laguna et al., 1999). In those systems, the ECG waveforms or their components (e.g., QRS complex, ST-T segmentation, etc) were regularized and normalized beat by beat for morphological analysis. Thus the beat-to-beat amplitude variations were diminished in those paradigms. It was deemed that various insignificant constituents in ECGs may be suppressed effectively. As a consequence, although the amplitudes bring important pathophysiological clues (Petrutiu et al., 2006), morphological analysis becomes more and more popular in computerized ECG interpretation (Weiben et al., 1999; Lagerholm et al., 2000; Linh et al., 2003; Chazal et al., 2004; Osowski et al., 2004; Christov et al., 2005).

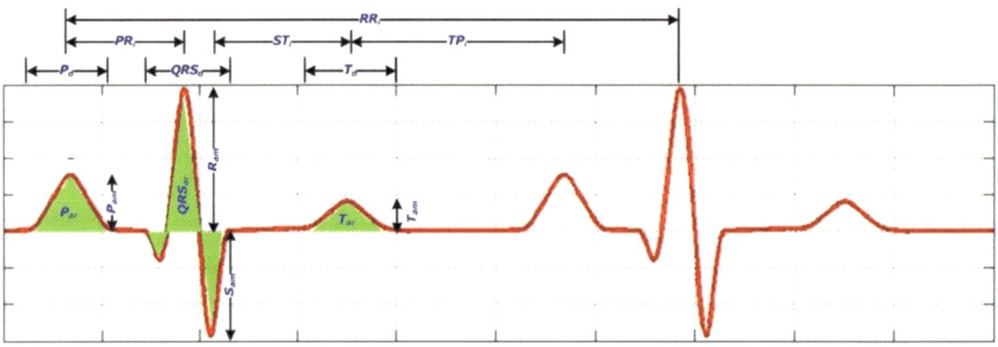

(a)

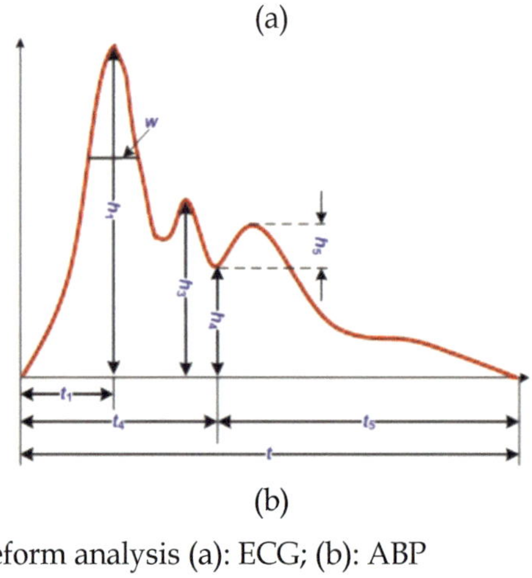

(b)

Fig. 6. Physiological waveform analysis (a): ECG; (b): ABP

The pioneer investigators were interested in pulse waveform analysis and pattern recognition in the beginning of computerized ABP interpretation (Fei 2003). However, unlike ECGs, there is a lack of authoritative ABP benchmark with beat-by-beat annotations. In addition, it is extremely difficult to convert the qualitative, ambiguous knowledge in traditional Pulse Diagnostics into computer languages. The investigators were hereby more interested to associate ABP waveforms with other quantitative risk factors for cardiovascular health prognosis (Table 2). However, by means of those techniques, the ABP waveforms had to be calibrated with ABP values that were recorded separately. Additional errors and biases would be introduced in above procedure (Li et al., 2008). Consequently, there were still a few, although not so many, investigators working on ABP morphological analysis (Martin et al., 1994; Li et al., 2008).

It is difficult to calibrate non-invasive physiological signals with regard to the accidental instrumental inaccuracy and human artefacts as well. Thus many investigators chose to normalize those physiological signals and concentrated on morphological analysis (Weiben et al., 1999; Lagerholm et al., 2000; Linh et al., 2003; Chazal et al., 2004; Osowski et al., 2004; Christov et al., 2005). Moreover, it has been reported that the morphological features from normalized ECGs are comparable to those from original ones in computerized interpretation (Chazal et al., 2004).

To normalize physiological signals, several common filters were firstly applied to remove baseline wandering, muscular tremor, electrical line interference, and other noises (Lagerholm et al., 2000; Chazal et al., 2004; Christov et al., 2005). After the basic filters, those physiological signals were then normalized, in a beat by beat manner, to the amplitudes within [-1, 1] and the intervals within [0, 1]. Then the same group of physiological signals, no matter ECGs or ABP waveforms, turned to more consistent and amenable to computational interpretation. Following the strategies in reference (Chazal et al., 2004), it is possible to derive the morphological features out by nonlinear sampling. As to ECG signals, the sampling was carried out within two windows (Fig. 7a). The first one (150ms) attempted to characterize the QRS complex while the other one (350ms) for the T wave. Within each window, 10 points of physiological signals were uniformly sampled. In terms of ABP waveforms, the unique sampling window (500ms) was oriented to the region between systolic and diastolic complexes (Fig. 7b). Similarly, there were totally 20 points sampled

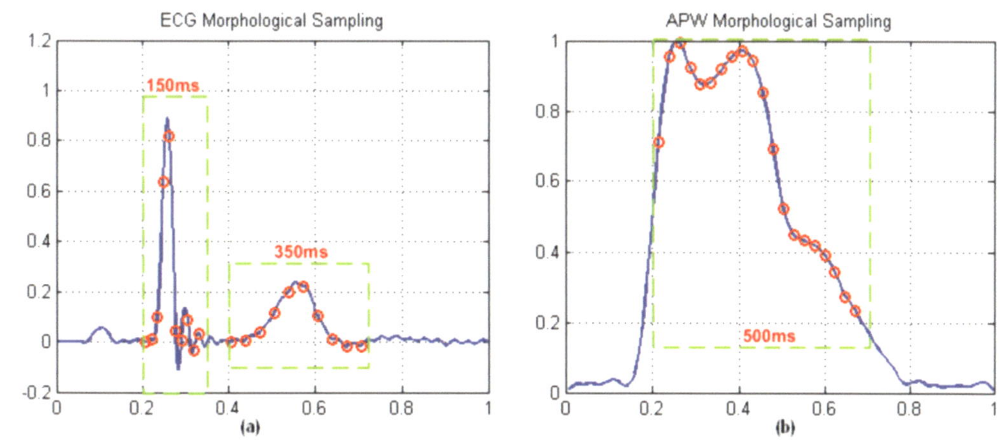

Fig. 7. Nonlinear sampling for morphological feature characterization (a): ECG; (b): ABP

from each beat of ABP waveforms. Those sampling points formed the morphological features for subsequent computerized recognition and classification.

3.2 Adaptive physiological signal modelling

The conventional strategies, including signal regularization and morphological analysis, are helpful to suppress physiological signal variability in some sense. It seems the results are amenable to computerized interpretation, too. However, it is meanwhile observed that morphological feature sets are not sparse and not robust enough. Actually, signal representation in time domain is legible but redundant, which may be evidenced by means of PCA (Geva 1998; Stamkopoulos et al., 1998). As a consequence, morphological analysis was generally combined with domain transformation, such as Hilbert transform (Bolton & Westphal 1981), HD (Rasiah et al., 1997; Lagerholm et al., 2000; Linh et al., 2003) and WT (Senhadii et al., 1995; AI-Farhoum & Howitt 1999; Saxena et al., 2002; Engin 2007), in those published paradigms of computerized physiological signal interpretation.

Domain transformation, unlike direct morphological analysis, attempts to characterize physiological signals in an alternative space, where the genuine signal components are more discernible from noises and artefacts. For instance, the well-known spectral analysis is exactly based on a classical domain transformation, namely Fourier transform. It is hereby possible to suppress baseline wandering by a high-pass filter, or remove electrical line interference with a notch filter.

In domain transformation, the recorded physiological signals are alternatively characterized by a set of singular basis functions. In general, those basis functions, either orthonormal or not, have no explicit physical meanings, which make them abstract for understanding. But lots of refractory problems may turn resolvable in those alternative function spaces. Take computerized ECG arrhythmia interpretation for an example. It has been confirmed that Hermite basis functions (HBFs) and wavelet energy descriptors are among those most competitive ones for feature characterization in discrimination analysis (Senhadii et al., 1995; Rasiah et al., 1997; AI-Farhoum & Howitt 1999; Lagerholm et al., 2000; Saxena et al., 2002; Linh et al., 2003; Engin 2007).

3.2.1 Hermite decomposition

It is possible to carry out domain transformation and signal modeling by orthonormal basis functions or not. But the orthonormal basis functions are usually preferred due to the fast implementation. It is hereby desired to find out a series of orthonormal basis functions for compact physiological signal modeling. Nevertheless, to be orthonormal, the basis functions have to meet a set of rigorous mathematical regularities. In other words, most orthonormal basis functions, such as cosine basis functions for Fourier Transform, are not efficient for physiological signal modeling. On the contrary, it has been found that HBFs share the resembling waveforms with electrocardiograms (ECGs). Thus they can be utilized to model ECG waveforms compactly (Rasiah et al., 1997; Lagerholm et al., 2000; Linh et al., 2003).

In mathematics, HBFs are derived from Hermite polynomials:

$$\mathbf{\Phi}_m = \frac{1}{\sqrt{2^m m! \sqrt{\pi}}} e^{-t^2/2} \mathbf{H}_m(t), \tag{1}$$

where $\mathbf{H}_m(t)$ is the mth Hermite polynomial:

$$\mathbf{H}_m(t) = 2t\mathbf{H}_{m-1}(t) - 2(k-1)\mathbf{H}_{m-2}(t)\,, \tag{2}$$

where $\mathbf{H}_0(t)$=1 and $\mathbf{H}_1(t)$=2t. Hermite polynomials are a classical orthogonal polynomial sequence, and with common usages in probabilistic analysis and physics.
To cope with physiological signal variability, two modulating parameters, σ and τ, were applied to the conventional HBF in this dissertation. So they turned to be:

$$\mathbf{\Phi}_m = \frac{1}{\sqrt{\sigma 2^m m!\sqrt{\pi}}} e^{-t^2/2} \mathbf{H}_m(t)\,, \tag{3}$$

where t was modulated as $(n\text{-}\tau)/\sigma$ (σ and τ are dilation and translation factors respectively). Then it is possible to approximate and model a physiological signal compactly as:

$$\mathbf{S}' = \sum_{m=1}^{M} c_m \mathbf{\Phi}_m(n)\,. \tag{4}$$

The object is to find out the appropriate model order M, the optimal modulating parameters σ and τ in HBFs, as well as the according weight c_m.

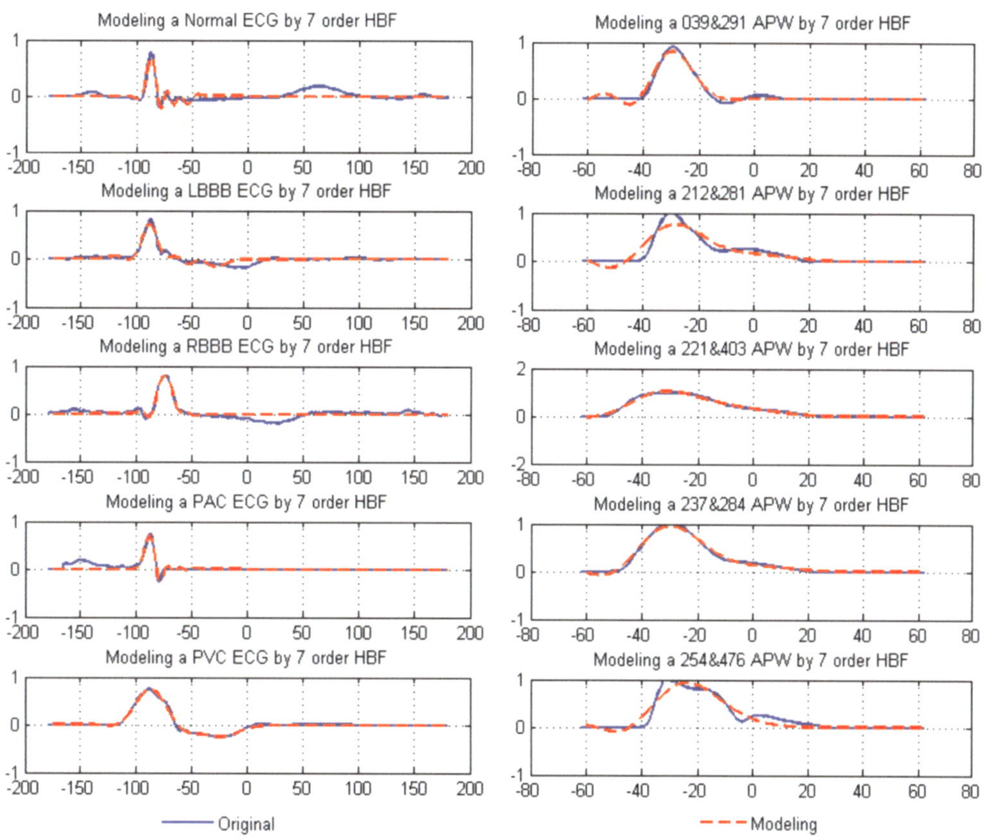

Fig. 8. Modelling physiological signals by 7 order HBFs (a): ECG; (b): ABP

However, in practice, it has been found that physiological signal modelling by the modulated HBFs often suffers from excessive computing. The heuristic gradient descent algorithms have been advocated for this problem (Rasiah et al., 1997). Here a special algorithm was adopted to achieve fast implementation. In summary, the algorithm strives to find an approximately optimal solution in the fixed transformation grids. Firstly, it adaptively estimates the spans of dilation and translation in accordance with the incoming physiological signal. In the second, that limited transformation space is segmented into M-by-M grids (M was designated in advance). Then, the algorithm generates an estimate in each transformation grid, and evaluates it against the original physiological signal. Such procedure iterates throughout the entire transformation grids (M^2). The final results are taken as those parameters leading to the minimum approximation error. As shown in Fig. 8, such fast algorithm performed fairly well, and a few low-order HBFs have been able to approximate those physiological signals.

3.2.2 Wavelet analysis

The advantages of wavelet transform over other techniques lie in its unified time-frequency analysis. In other words, by wavelet transform it is possible to characterize a physiological signal with its temporal and spectral features simultaneously. Thus a variety of successful applications have been reported on physiological signal processing and analysis, covering from adaptive denoising, compression, delineation to feature characterization, pattern recognition, and others. In terms of feature characterization, the investigators paid substantial attention on wavelet energy (Senhadii et al., 1995; AI-Farhoum & Howitt 1999), wavelet entropy (Rosso et al., 2001) and other energy-dense wavelet coefficients (Senhadii et al., 1995).

In essence, wavelet transform can be considered as a kind of multirate filter banks. The signal components within distinct spectra emerge at different scale levels of wavelet transform. The investigators in reference (Senhadii et al., 1995) hereby proposed to characterize ECG signals by a feature vector containing energies at different wavelet scales. The DWT with 10 levels was employed there. The authors in reference (AI-Farhoum & Howitt 1999) further investigated on the relative wavelet energy, which was concerned with both spectral and temporal aspects of wavelet transform. A 6-element feature vector was formed with the wavelet energies at scale 2, 3, 4 and before, within, after the QRS complex in each beat of ECG.

The results of wavelet transform manifest the resemblance of a physiological signal and the modulated wavelets at different scales and shifts, which is quite similar to spectral analysis by Fourier transform. Therefore, taking a signal's wavelet transform as $W_{a,b}$, it is possible to define the total wavelet energy as:

$$Er_{tot} = \sum_a \sum_b |\mathbf{W}_{a,b}|^2 = \sum_a Er_a , \tag{5}$$

where Er_a is the wavelet energy at scale a:

$$Er_a = \sum_b |\mathbf{W}_{a,b}|^2 . \tag{6}$$

The relative wavelet energy at each scale is then defined as:

$$REr_a = Er_a \,/\, Er_{tot} , \tag{7}$$

which reflects the probability distribution of energy scale by scale. Then, coming to wavelet entropy, it will be defined as in the reference (Blanco et al., 1998):

$$Ep = -\sum_{a} REr_a \cdot \ln(REr_a)\,. \tag{8}$$

Wavelet entropy may serve as a measure of order/disorder degree of a physiological signal. Thus it provides useful information about the underlying dynamical process associated with that signal.

Another kind of features comes from the energy-dense components of wavelet transform. Two different strategies have been proposed and validated to derive them (Senhadii et al., 1995; Christov et al., 2005). The first one was desired to find out them by matching pursuits from time-frequency dictionaries, which will be elucidated in next chapter. The second one was based on the fast DWT. Given the results of DWT as $\mathbf{W}_{AM}(n/2^M)$ and $\mathbf{W}_{Dm}(n/2^m)$ (m=1,2,...M), the feature sets were derived from the maximum coefficients at $\mathbf{W}_{AM}(n/2^M)$ and each scale band $\mathbf{W}_{Dm}(n/2^m)$. Hereafter those extrema at different scales will be termed as wavelet scale maxima.

In this chapter, the feature sets based on relative wavelet energies, regional wavelet entropies and wavelet scale maxima were evaluated for physiological signal variability. It is noteworthy that wavelet transform by different mother wavelets, owing to their distinct properties (e.g., support, regularity, and vanishing moments), generally lead to different analytical results. Here the 3-order Gaussian derivative was chose as the mother wavelet. The energy of ECG QRS complexes have been identified within 5~15Hz approximately (Pan & Tompkins 1985). Obviously, the energies of ECG P and T waves concentrate within a spectral band less than 5Hz. Meanwhile, it has been found in our practice that, no matter ABP systolic or diastolic complex, their spectral energies are in a region less than 5Hz. The spectral resolution of 3-order Gaussian wavelet is obviously appropriate for ECG and ABP analysis.

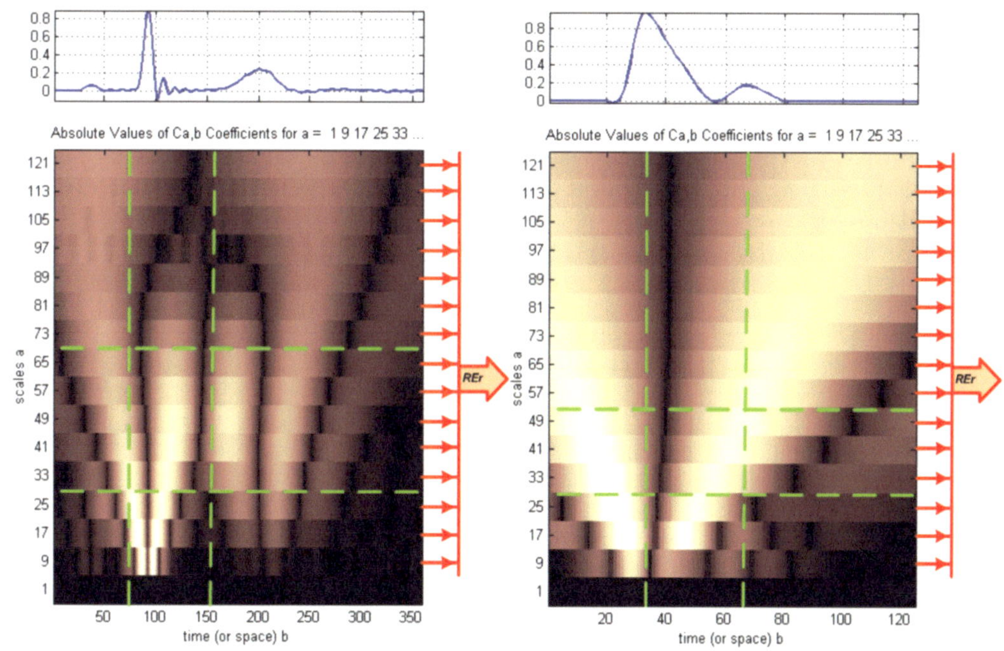

Fig. 9. Feature characterization by wavelet-based time-frequency analysis (a): ECG; (b): ABP

In terms of physiological signal characterization, the ratios of all wavelet scales, except the first one, were chosen for relative wavelet energy (Fig. 9). Then, the results of wavelet transform were partitioned into 9 segments based on wavelet spectral bands and temporal fiducial marks (Fig. 9). Coming to ECG signals, wavelet spectral bands were chosen as the scales {9; 17; 25}, the scales {33; 41; 49; 57; 65} and the left scales till 121. They were desired to characterize the spectral energies of QRS complex, P and T waves respectively. The temporal partition took advantage of a 200ms window (50ms before and 150ms after the R point). The entropy in each segment was computed and rated for regional wavelet entropies. With regard to APW signals, the spectral bands were chosen as {9; 17; 25}, {33; 41; 49} and the left scales. The temporal fiducial marks were based on the systolic peak and diastolic peak of ABP waveforms (Fig. 9).

3.2.3 Matching pursuits

In view of the advantages of fast implementation, it is attractive to screen the energy-dense wavelet coefficients and model physiological signals under the frameworks of fast DWT. As a matter of fact, the abovementioned paradigm of wavelet shrinkage was exactly by means of this idea. However, it is noteworthy that orthonormal wavelet basis functions (WBFs), due to their mathematical regularity, are not efficient for physiological signal modeling. The authors in reference (Mallat & Zhang 1993) hereby proposed a technique of matching pursuits based on WP analysis, by which it is possible to adaptively select the appropriate wavelet coefficients out from a large and redundant dictionary of time-frequency atoms.
In fast DWT, a signal is split into an approximation part and a detail one by a pair of quadrature mirror filters (QMF). Then the approximation part will be iteratively separated by that pair of QMF. Unlike DWT, WP analysis splits both parts of approximation and detail iteratively. Such paradigm preserves the advantages of fast implementation, but incurs the risk of redundancy in time-frequency representation. It rewards the extra flexibility for noise suppression and signal compression (Mallat 1998). There have been standard algorithms for WBF selection, based on information entropy minimization, from the redundant dictionary of time-frequency atoms (Coifman & Wickerhauser 1992). Nevertheless, they are not oriented to compact signal characterization. Under the framework of WP analysis, the technique of matching pursuits attempts to characterize a complicated signal concisely with several adaptive WBFs.
Physiological signal decomposition and modelling by matching pursuits is similar to the standard WT:

$$s(n) = \sum_{m=1}^{M} < R^m f, \psi_m > \psi_m + R^{M+1} f \, , \tag{9}$$

where ψ_m is the modulated orthonormal wavelet, and $R^m f$ is the decomposition residue at level m. However, unlike the common WBF, the ψ_m here is characterized as [4.3]:

$$\psi_m(n) = \frac{1}{\sqrt{2^j}} \psi\left(\frac{n}{2^j} - \left(p + \frac{1}{2}\right)\right) e^{i2\pi \cdot n \cdot 2^{-j}(k + 1/2)} \, , \tag{10}$$

where $0 \le j \le \log_2 N; 0 \le p \le 2^{-j} N; 0 \le k \le 2^j$. It was in essence a discrete mother wavelet dilated by 2^j, centred at $2^j (p+1/2)$ and modulated by a sinusoidal wave with frequency $2\pi 2^{-j} (k+1/2)$. By matching pursuits, those wavelets best matching the residue at each scale level would be chosen for physiological signal characterization. In other words, the technique of matching pursuits here is greedy and locally optimized in contrast to those globally-optimizing algorithms based on information entropy.

The authors in reference (Mallat & Zhang 1993) demonstrated the competence of matching pursuits for complicated signal modelling by means of Gabor wavelets as an example. Actually, matching pursuits is a general technique under the framework of WP analysis (Suppappola & Suppappola 2002). For instance, the symmlet wavelet with 8-order vanishing moments has been proved effective (Christov et al., 2005). In this chapter, the Daubechies wavelet with 8-order vanishing moments was evaluated for physiological signal modelling. The pending decisions include the desired number of wavelets, the tuning parameters of wavelets, and the level of WP decomposition.

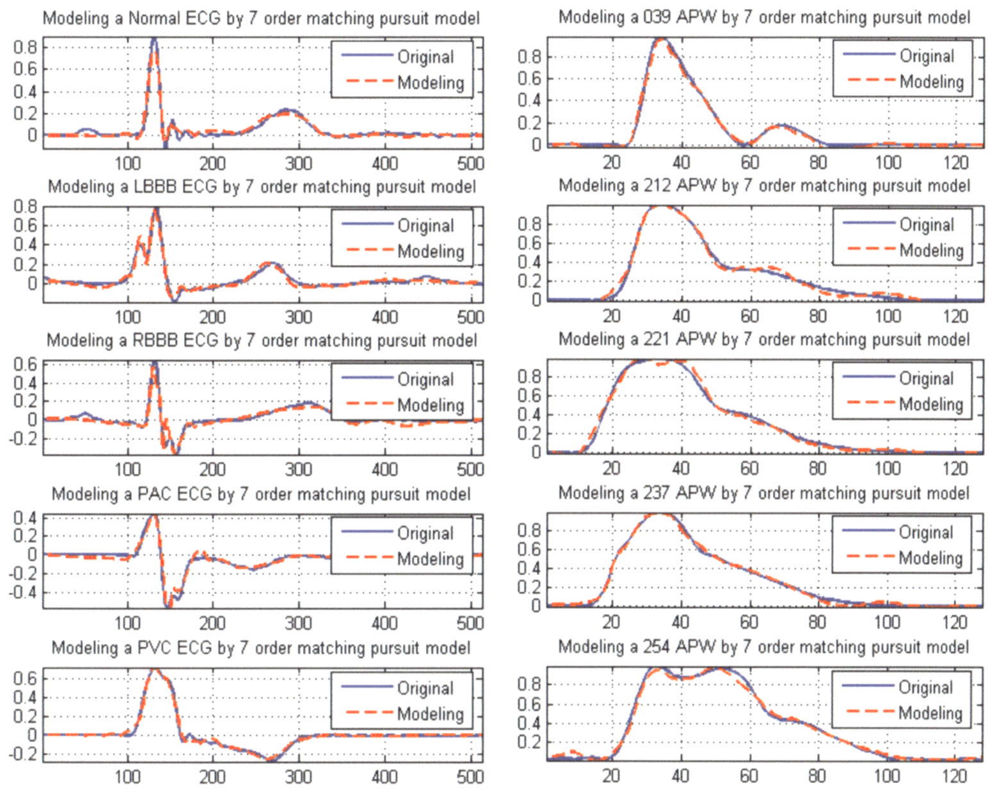

Fig. 10. Modelling physiological signals by 7 order matching pursuits (a): ECG; (b): ABP

We are interested in modelling physiological signals by adaptive wavelets. The first of all, to accomplish the dyadic WP analysis, the signal length should be equivalent to a power of two, such as 128 (2^7), 512 (2^9) and 1024 (2^{10}). In this chapter, all physiological signals were re-sampled or interpolated, instead of zero-padding, to approach those standard lengths. In the second aspect, the resultant models should be as compact as better. It has been reported in reference (Suppappola & Suppappola 2002) that, by matching pursuits, 10-order WBFs were generally enough to characterize the ECG signals in MIT/BIH Arrhythmia Database (Moody 1997). Nevertheless, 5 orders of them seem not enough. As a consequence, the order of WBFs is empirically chosen as 7 for compact physiological signal models with fair performance. In the third aspect, by referring to their octave spectral bands, 8 level of WP analysis seems appropriate to capture most of the essential components of cardiovascular physiological signals. Then, the WBFs are adaptively traced and tuned by matching pursuits. Compared with those HBF models, no matter for ECG signals or ABP waveforms, the WBF models (Fig. 10) are obviously better than them.

4. Adaptive clustering and classification

The underlying objective of non-invasive cardiovascular monitoring is to tell 'normal' or 'abnormal' health conditions. If possible, it is desired to further elucidate the causes of 'abnormal' health conditions, for example, left ventricular hypertrophy, aortic valve stenosis, arteriosclerosis, or others. The physiological signals, either ECGs or ABP waveforms, bring important messages of blood circulation within cardiovascular system. Thus it is a tradition of interest to observe their properties as well as variations from normal subjects and the patients with various symptoms. Recording effective physiological signals is not an easy task in respect to pathophysiological variability, instrumental inaccuracy and manual inconsistency. On the other hand, it is even more challenging to interpret those recorded physiological signals clearly. As a matter of fact, even clinical physicians have to take long-term career training in order to obtain and maintain their skills, let alone electronic computers.

The most intuitive ways for computerized physiological signal interpretation come into being as knowledge engineering and expert systems. By them, it is possible to formulate and convert medical experts' knowledge and experience into computer-compatible data and information (MN ECG Coding Center 2009). Nevertheless, it has been found that the abstract and qualitative medical knowledge is not so amenable to nonclinical computer engineers. For instance, most clinical physicians are good at coping with various physiological signal variations and artefacts, but they are generally not able to elucidate their extraordinary capability to nonclinical engineers in a quantitative manner. On the other hand, computer engineers are good at constructing knowledge base and inference machines, but lack of proper medical knowledge and diagnostic experience. Without their thorough cooperation, those computerized medical expert systems are not robust enough with regard to physiological signal variability.

As a consequence, nonclinical scientists and engineers attempted to resolve such challenge from another aspect. Suppose there are lots of recorded physiological signals with credible annotations by a group of medical experts. The investigators are concerned with the methods and techniques by which those physiological signals may be related to their annotations automatically. In this regard, a good many of computational methods, including template matching and statistical analysis in hard computing (Long et al., 1997; Gerencsér et al., 2002), Artificial Neural Networks (ANNs) and Fuzzy Logics (FL) in soft computing (Suzuki 1995; Tatara & Gnar 2002; Lei et al., 2008), have been proposed and validated for computerized physiological signal interpretation.

In general, those techniques do not simply resort to the empirical thresholds of amplitudes and rhythms any more. In stead, the advanced signal processing methods, such as wavelet analysis and HD, are utilized to find out the underlying properties of physiological signals. Whereas their results are not intuitive to visual inspection, it is deemed that the alternative features are more suitable than original physiological signals for computerized interpretation. In above sections, some of signal processing techniques, including morphological sampling, adaptive HBFs, relative wavelet energies, regional wavelet entropies, wavelet scale maxima and adaptive WBFs, have been investigated carefully to attack physiological signal variability.

It is noteworthy that, in those alternative feature spaces, the conventional medical knowledge accumulated in clinical medicine does not hold any more. The new rules and explanatory statements have to be established in order to recognize and classify physiological signals. We are concerned with the autonomous organization and clustering of physiological signals in this section. Actually, if those physiological signals could be organized together for similar groups but separately for different groups, it is not so difficult any more to classify them by computational methods. In addition, it is extremely difficult or expensive to request medical experts to carefully review and annotate so many physiological signals. Take the MIT/BIH Arrhythmia Database (MAD) at PhysioNet (Moody 1997) for an example. Whereas each recording lasts 30 minutes only, there have been over tens of thousands of beats with variant annotations in it.

As a consequence, the techniques of self-organizing and data clustering receive much attention in computational intelligence. A variety of them, including fuzzy c-means (FCM) (Lei et al., 2008) and self-organizing maps (SOM) (Lagerholm et al., 2000), have been extensively investigated for physiological signal analysis. By them it is possible to fuse the advantages of wavelet analysis and computational intelligence for self-organizing physiological signals.

4.1 Self-organizing physiological signals

As mentioned above, annotating physiological signals by hands is an extremely challenging task. Unfortunately, it is even more challenging at present to carry out fully-automated recognition and classification by computers. However, at least, it is possible to organize and cluster physiological signals by computers in an autonomous manner. The results may serve as a reference to medical experts in analyzing and annotating physiological signals. Unsupervised classification, also known as data clustering, is exactly the techniques designed to find out the intrinsic distributions of unknown signals or data (Jain et al., 2000). The metrics of similarity and the criterion function, but not human intervention, determine the final results of data clustering.

There have been a variety of clustering algorithms, most of which are based on either iterative error minimization or hierarchical clustering (Duda et al., 2001). Hierarchical techniques organize signals or data in a nested sequence of groups which can be displayed in a dendrogram. In contrast, the error minimizing algorithms desire to work out a systemic partition that minimizes the internal variances and maximizes the mutual discrepancies. The latter paradigms are more frequently utilized in computerized physiological signal interpretation.

4.1.1 Self-organization by error minimization

The issue of data clustering can be elucidated in a formal language: Given N feature vectors in a d-dimensional metric space, determine one of their distributions in K groups, so that the members in the same group are more similar to each other than to those in different groups. The value of K may or may not be specified, but a clustering criterion function must be designated for optimization. In essence, the error minimization is a kind of local criteria because it is sensitive to the initial clustering, the similarity metrics and the criterion function. The interested readers are advised to look through the reference (Jain & Dubes 1988) for details on algorithms and techniques in this field.

Take the classical algorithm of *k*-means for an example. It seeks to assign N patterns, based on their attributes and the designed metrics, into K groups $\{C_1, C_2, \ldots, C_K \mid K<<N\}$. Then, each cluster C_k has n_k members and each member is in exactly one cluster. The results are comprised of prototyping templates and the pattern affiliation to each group. In *k*-means, the prototyping template for each group is defined as its centroid:

$$C_k = \sum x_i^k \Big/ n_k \,, \tag{11}$$

where x_i^k is the *i*th pattern belonging to the group *k*. Error minimization seeks to reduce (12) as a criterion function:

$$J = \sum e_k^2 \,, \tag{12}$$

where e_k is the Euclidean norm or a similar metric within each group

$$e_k = \sqrt{\sum_{i=1}^{n_k} (x_i^k - C_k)^T (x_i^k - C_k)} \,. \tag{13}$$

The ideal results of a *k*-means algorithm will minimize the internal variance within each group but maximize the mutual discrepancies between different groups.

In the *k*-means algorithm, each pattern is limited to one and only one of K groups, which is often not true in computerized physiological signal interpretation. As a matter of fact, the physiological signals from cardiovascular health monitoring are subject to multifold effects of cardiac functions, vascular elasticity and even blood viscosity. In other words, it is usually not appropriate to simply assign a physiological signal to a single group. To this issue, two kinds of paradigms, namely FCM and SOM, have been proposed and practiced with success.

FCM applies a membership degree μ_{ij} to indicate the belongingness of the *j*th pattern to the *i*th group. The criterion function of FCM is similar to that of *k*-means:

$$J = \sum_{n=1}^{N} \sum_{k=1}^{K} \mu_{kn}^m \left\| x_n - C_k \right\|^2 \,, \tag{14}$$

where μ_{kn} represents the membership degree of feature vector x_n in the *k*th group, C_k is the *k*th group centroid, and *m* (m>1) is a constant controlling the resultant fuzziness.

There are constraints oriented to the normalization of probabilistic distribution. By that, it has been proved in reference (Duda et al., 2001) that data clustering in the light of maximum likelihood is equivalent to a centriod-based clustering by their averages. Then, in accordance with Equations (15) and (16), the membership degrees μ_{kn} and the centroids C_k are updated iteration by iteration respectively:

$$\mu_{kn} = \frac{\left\| x_n - C_k \right\|^{-2/(m-1)}}{\sum_{k=1}^{K} \left\| x_n - C_k \right\|^{-2/(m-1)}} \,; \tag{15}$$

$$C_k = \frac{\sum_{n=1}^{N} \mu_{kn}^m x_n}{\sum_{n=1}^{N} \mu_{kn}^m}. \tag{16}$$

The algorithm is optimized when the patterns close to their group centroids are assigned with high membership degrees, and those far away from their centroids are with low membership degrees.

4.2 Neural computation

SOM is another popular paradigm for adaptive data clustering. It follows the strategies of ANNs instead of that of FCM. ANNs are generally comprised of various computational models originated from biological neural networks. In neuroscience, a neural network describes a population of physically interconnected neurons whose inputs and outputs define a recognizable network (Figure 11a). Communication between different neurons often involves electrochemical processes abstracted as synapses. In general, a neuron will trigger an action potential and further transmit it to the associated neurons if it perceives the incoming stimulations over a certain threshold (Hebb 1949). Similarly, a computational ANN model takes an ensemble of simple processing elements as neurons, and linear connections between them as synapses (Figure 11b). Each neuron merely carries out a simple linear or nonlinear transform, but their aggregation with linear connection often exhibits complex global behaviours. In other words, the functional characterization of an ANN relies not only on its basic processing elements but also on the systematic connections.

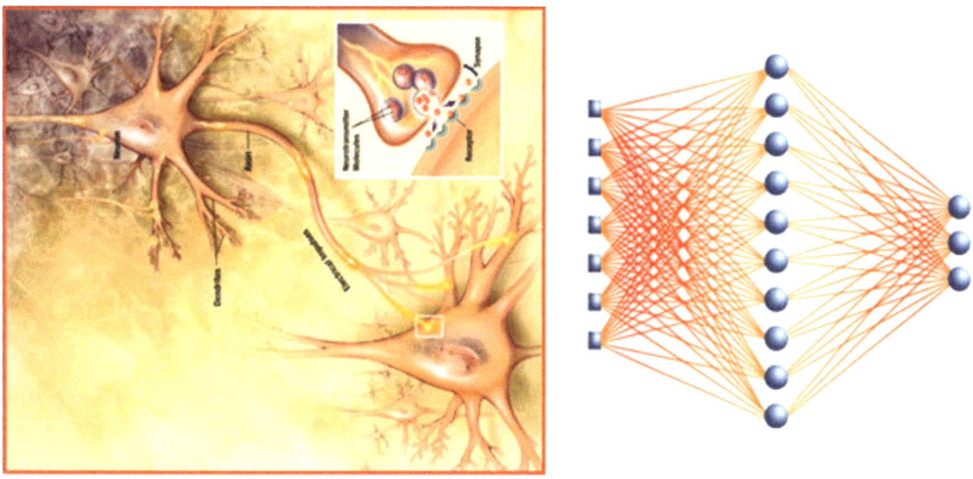

(a) (b)

Fig. 11. Biological vs. artificial neural networks (adapted from www.neurevoluion.net 2009)

ANNs are claimed for their competence in nonlinear mapping as well as self-adaptation. Suppose the ANNs input space is comprised of the N-dimension continuous or discrete feature vectors $\{\mathbf{X} \in d^N\}$, its output space consists of the M-dimension continuous or discrete responses, categories or decisions $\{\mathbf{Y} \in d^M\}$. It has been proved that an ANN, with appropriate infrastructure and controlling parameters, may establish a nonlinear map $f(\mathbf{X} \Rightarrow \mathbf{Y})$ approaching their genuine relationships arbitrarily well. Take computerized ECG interpretation for an example. The incoming feature vectors may be the 20-dimension morphological sampling, the 10-dimension HBFs, the 15-dimension relative wavelet energies, the 9-dimension regional wavelet entropies, or the 7-dimension WBFs. The output vectors may be "normal" and "abnormal" in one dimension, the 5-dimension AAMI heartbeat classes, the 15-dimension MIT/BIH arrhythmia types (Moody 1997) or even hundred-dimension cardiovascular diseases. Then the ANN may be configured and tuned by means of the annotated physiological signals. The popular paradigms include (Jain et al., 2000) multilayer perceptrons (MLPs), radial basis function (RBF) networks, probabilistic neural networks (PNNs), and so forth. In contrast, there are also many ANN paradigms specially designed for the cases of no prefixed responses. SOM and adaptive resonance theory (ART) are the typical examples of them. It is deemed that their outputs may reflect the intrinsic properties of physiological signals in some sense.

An ANN may be characterized by its basic processing elements and the connections between them. Different from conventional analytical models, the controlling parameters in an ANN are unknown in advance, and have to be identified by self-adaptive learning. The underlying discrepancies of abovementioned paradigms exactly lie in their learning mechanisms. Those supervised ANNs often rely on error minimization. Namely, the ANN parameters are tuned step by step in order to minimize mapping errors. On the contrary, the unsupervised ANNs generally adopt the strategies of competitive learning. Merely those most similar nodes to network inputs will be updated accordingly. In a nutshell, their underlying mechanisms of self-adaptation are utterly different:

- ***Error Minimization***: In supervised ANN learning, an input $\boldsymbol{X}$ is presented to that ANN with unknown parameters $\{\boldsymbol{\theta} \mid \Theta_i^k ; w_{ij}^k\}$, its actual output $\boldsymbol{Y}^*$ will be evaluated against the target output $\boldsymbol{Y}$. An artificial objective function J, usually as the square of the errors, is introduced to relate $\boldsymbol{\theta}$ and network performance $|\boldsymbol{Y} - \boldsymbol{Y}^*|$. As the ultimate target is to reduce $|\boldsymbol{Y} - \boldsymbol{Y}^*|$ to the minimum, it is a reasonable choice to update those parameters in the gradient descent direction. Of course, a prerequisite assumption is that J is smooth and differentiable everywhere. The topics worthy of investigation in this field include how to arrive at the global minimum but local minima, how to speed up evolution while avoiding oscillation, and so forth.
- ***Competition and Resonance***: Competitive learning is complementary to above supervised learning by means of error minimization. A central point of this kind of systems is pattern matching that searches and updates the internal memories of a network against an external input. The common SOM networks compete for an updating in a prefixed feature space. In other words, even the outliers may stimulate the internal behaviours of a SOM network. On the contrary, the ART networks lead either to a resonant state or to a parallel memory. If pattern matching ends at an established node, the prototyping template may either remain the same or incorporate information from matched portions of new input. Otherwise, if ends at a new status, the ART network learns the new input. Anyway, such match-based learning stands for a totally new style of network self-adaptation.

The rationale of supervised ANNs is built on an underlying assumption: any complex relationship or association can be modelled as a function, and meanwhile, that function can be approximated by a linear combination of simple linear or nonlinear basis functions. The essence of supervised learning means utilizing some form of quantitative algorithms to reduce the errors or costs on a set of known training data. At present, a good many of gradient descent or conjugate gradient algorithms, and their variants, have been well established to evolve ANNs for reducing the specific errors or costs. Suppose a function can be characterized by its unknown parameters $f(\Theta \mid \theta_k, k=1, \ldots, K)$. Then, on a training dataset, the incoming pattern $s_j(n)$ and the desired response y_j should have been confirmed. However, if the function response from f does not equal to the desired one, there is an empirical error $e_j = |f(s_j(n)) - y_j|$. The idea of ANN evolution is to minimize the error square by means of the gradient information.

In above paradigms of supervised learning, the optimization is oriented to minimize the apparent errors or costs. However, there is no any warranty that the final results are optimal and reside at the global optimum. Even after different enhancing strategies are incorporated, the optimum can be guaranteed with respect to the available training dataset only. If the training dataset is representative enough to cover the whole space of interest, it is safe to convey the optimality of ANNs to the unknown testing dataset. However, it is often not the case. The problem is, what we are really interested in is the optimality in testing but not training dataset. The relevant research is mainly focused on the generalization and expectation risk minimization. Based on the concept of margin, Vapnik proposed the optimum separation hyperplane for classification and recognition (Vapnik 1998). The margin can be modeled as the shortest distance of training data to a separation hyperplane. In a word, to a linear classification problem, the optimum separation hyperplane is the one with the maximal margin among all possible separation hyperplanes. Vapnik and his colleagues also proposed the technique of Support Vector Machines (SVMs) for hunting that optimum separation hyperplane. Nowadays SVMs are considered as one of the most promising techniques in computational intelligence.

After decades of years of development, there has been a variety of ANN models with successful applications to adaptive clustering, function learning, pattern classification and nonlinear prediction. SOM, multilayer perceptrons (MLPs), radial basis function (RBF) networks, recurrent (Hopfield) networks and adaptive resonance theory (ART) networks are all well-established and have been widely validated in various real-life applications [6.15]. MLPs originate from linear perceptrons, which is one of the earliest ANN models. The rationale of utilizing MLPs for classification is quite intuitive: it is possible to approximate any function by a linear combination of simple basis functions. Then, in MLPs, there are a layer of input neurons, one or several layers of hidden neurons and one layer of output neurons. If we take each output neuron as a target function, to a specific incoming pattern, the neuron with the biggest response in the output layer is then assumed as the one representing the expected result. To define the MLPs, it is necessary to decide the number of hidden layers and the number of neurons in each hidden layer. Generally speaking, one or two hidden layers have been powerful enough, provided enough neurons in each layer, to approximate a function with any complexity. The adaptation or optimization of MLPs mainly relies on the algorithm of error backpropagation. Its essence is similar to gradient descent algorithm. The rationale of RBF networks for classification is similar to that of MLPs. Furthermore, their architectures are quite similar, too. However, the localization of neuronal transfer functions determines many unique properties of RBF networks. Firstly, there is always a single layer of hidden neurons in RBF networks. In other words, it is comparatively manageable to develop RBF networks. Secondly, there are merely several hidden neurons covering a specific incoming pattern; hence merely those involved neurons will adapt themselves accordingly. Namely it is easier for RBF networks to arrive at their optima than MLPs if the target space is appropriately covered by initial RBF neurons. However, due to the localization of response, more hidden neurons are also necessary for RBF networks at the same time.

5. Simulations

The part of experiments in this chapter was built on a workbench dataset (Fig. 12)., which was excerpted from the recording 207 of the MAD workbench. The different types of arrhythmia ECGs often intertwine together. At the same time, the single group of arrhythmia ECGs often has diversified morphologies, too. The dataset consists of 2 leads of synchronous ECG recordings, namely MLII and V1. There are 6 types of arrhythmia patterns identified by medical experts. All data have been normalized before adaptive modelling in order to suppress physiological signal variability. The feature descriptors, including HBFs, relative wavelet energies, wavelet scale maxima and matching pursuits, were utilized for physiological signal modelling. Those descriptors were then transferred to a subsequent FCM or SOM for adaptive clustering. In addition, the supervised MLP and PNN were taken advantages for physiological signal classification. The performance of all paradigms were evaluated quantitatively.

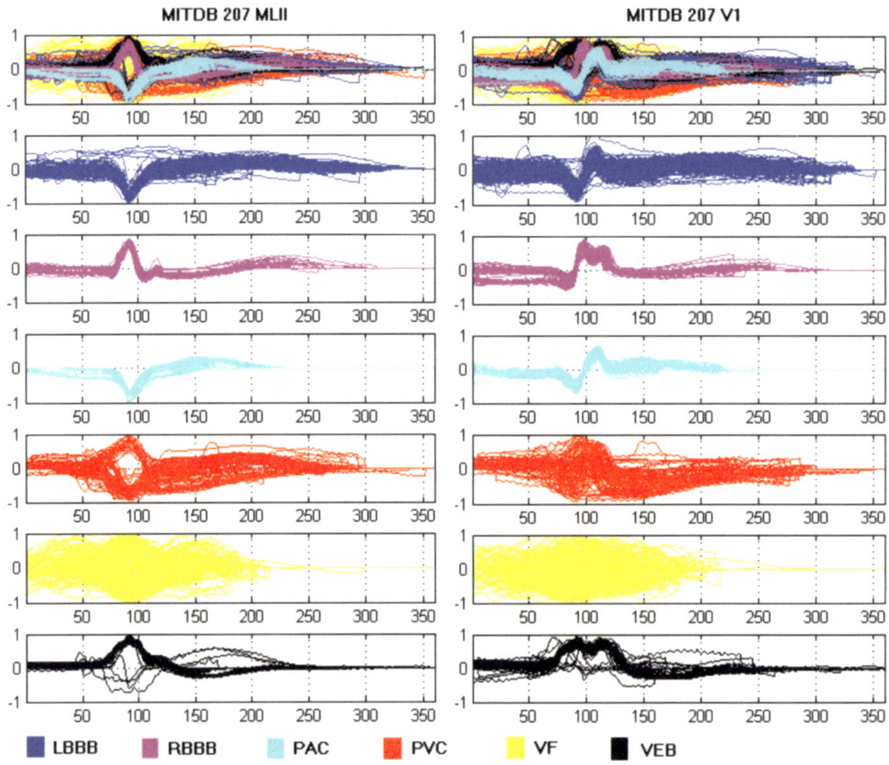

Fig. 12. Selected arrhythmia ECG beats from MAD

The orders of Hermite modeling, relative wavelet energies, wavelet scale maxima and matching pursuits were set as 7, 15, 16 and 7. The subsequent FCM or SOM adapted the input layer in accordance with the incoming patterns, while had a fixed output layer with 12 nodes. In other words, 12 clusters eventually came into being. Note that it is necessary to assign a larger cluster number than the genuine one. In most cases, patterns vary even within a same group. As shown in Fig. 13, the ECG beats are classified in accordance with their abstract model parameters but not the intuitive morphological features any more.

In Fig. 13, the ECG beats within each same cluster have been identified by their canonical annotations. For computerized interpretation, it is desirable to have those within-cluster ECG beats being the same group, for example, the LBBB beats. However, many of them are mixed together in most cases. It degrades the quality of computerized interpretation substantially. Without the priori knowledge on the incoming ECG beats, we have to take those in a cluster as a single type of arrhythmia. We hereby took a strategy of majority voting to evaluate the performance of adaptive clustering quantitatively. As shown in Fig. 13, the majority beat of the first and second clusters is VF (!) while the one of the forth cluster is PVC (V). In other words, the 339 beats of the first two clusters will be taken as VF while the 70 beats in the forth cluster are PVC. Then, based on the following confusion matrix, it is possible to calculate the quantitative accuracy of adaptive clustering.

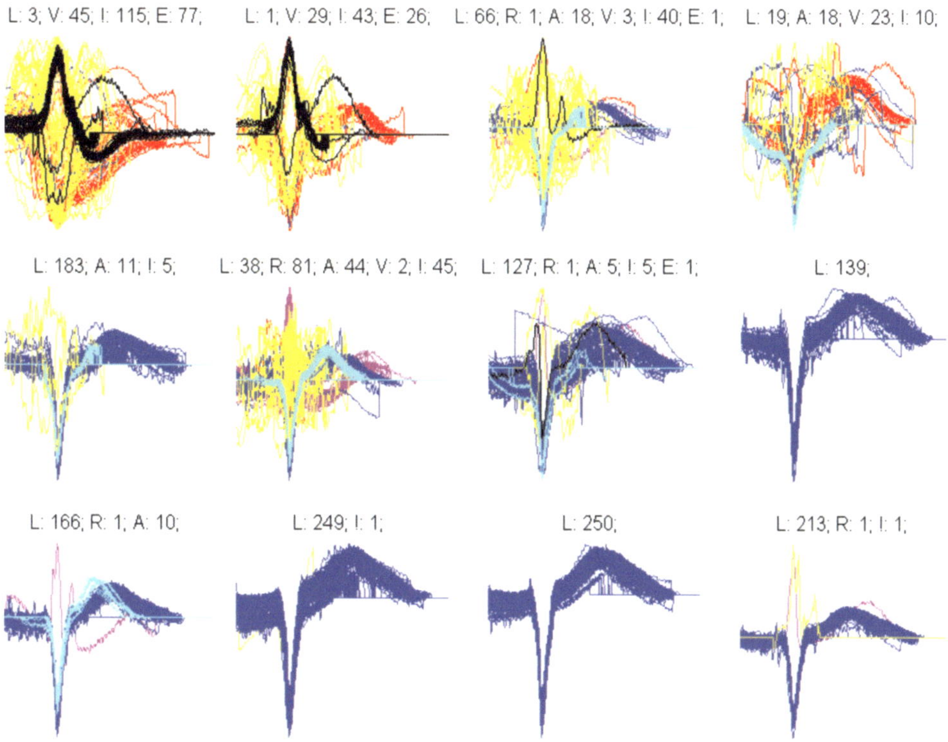

Fig. 13. Adaptive ECG arrhythmia clustering with WSM and SOM

	LBBB	RBBB	APC	PVC	VF	VEB	*total*
LBBB	1393	4	44	3	52	2	1498
RBBB	38	81	44	2	45	0	210
APC	0	0	0	0	0	0	0
PVC	19	0	18	23	10	0	70
VF	4	0	0	74	158	103	339
VEB	0	0	0	0	0	0	0
total	1454	85	106	102	265	105	2117

Table 3. The confusion matrix of adaptive clustering by the system in Fig. 13

The sensitivity *Se* may be defined as (Lagerholm et al., 2000):

$$Se = \frac{\mathrm{TP}}{\mathrm{TP} + \mathrm{FN}}, \tag{17}$$

and the accuracy is based on the quantitative error rate:

$$Error(\%) = \frac{\mathrm{FP} + \mathrm{FN}}{\mathrm{TP} + \mathrm{FP}}, \tag{18}$$

where TP stands for the amount of true positives, FN for false negatives, and FP means false positives. By means of above indices, the performance of various wavelet networks for clustering can be evaluated quantitatively, as listed in the following Table 4.

	TP	FP	FN	*Se*	*Error* (%)
HBF-SOM	1519	598	598	0.718	56.5
HBF-FCM	1560	557	557	0.737	52.6
RWE-SOM	1576	541	541	0.744	51.1
RWE-FCM	1605	512	512	0.758	48.4
WSM-SOM	1655	462	462	0.782	43.6
WSM-FCM	1695	422	422	0.801	39.9
MP-SOM	1574	543	543	0.744	51.3
MP-FCM	1564	553	553	0.739	52.2
PCA-SOM	1627	490	490	0.769	46.3
PCA-FCM	1666	451	451	0.787	42.6

Table 4. Clustering performance comparison of wavelet networks

There are several points worthy of noting in Table 4. The first of all, no any method achieved a good result as expected due to the intrinsic harshness of the selected ECG recording. Among various paradigms of computational intelligence for clustering, the one by WSM is most competitive. In the second aspect, the clustering results of FCM are better than those of SOM, although the improvement is not so much. In the third aspect, FP and FN are same in all cases. No matter FCM or SOM, it attempts to assign an incoming pattern to a specific cluster even though that pattern may be far away from all clusters. Therefore, any inaccurately assigned pattern is both false positive for other clusters and false negative for the right cluster. Finally, it seems that the energy-oriented models (e.g., relative wavelet energies (RWE) and WSM) are better for adaptive clustering than the morphology-oriented ones (e.g., HBFs and matching pursuits (MPs)).

There are six groups of ECG beats with known arrhythmia in Fig. 12, namely LBBB, right bundle branch block beat (RBBB), premature atrial contraction (PAC), premature ventricular contract (PVC), ventricular flutter (VF) wave and ventricular escape beat (VEB). Each group has different number of normalized ECG beats, namely 1454 LBBBs, 85 RBBBs, 106 PACs, 102 PVCs, 265 VFs and 105 VEBs.

In essence, each ECG beat after normalization could be characterized as a 360-dimensional multivariate vector. Obviously it is not a good idea to apply them directly for network interpretation due to the "curse-of-dimensionality" and the inter-dimensional crosstalk. As a consequence, the modelling parameters instead of the original signals were imported for training and evaluation. It is not only contributive to concise network architecture but also more robust against physiological signal variability (Li et al., 2009).

To train and test the computational paradigms for classification, each group of the dataset was randomly divided into two subgroups with the ratio 0.8:0.2. In other words, 80% ECG beats were utilized to train the classifiers, while the left 20% were reserved for network validation. Such procedure was repeated for five times, hence each computational paradigm was trained and evaluated five times independently. The final performance was based on the averaged recognition rate and classification accuracy. It is hereby possible to estimate the generalization capability of a computational paradigm by means of such "leave-one-out" strategy.

Three types of ANN were implemented and evaluated for supervised classification, that is, a MLP, a PNN and a kNN. Both MLPs and PNNs attempt to approximate the prototype of the specific group of physiological signals with the neurons and associated weights. The category of an incoming pattern is assigned according to the output neuron with maximal response (MLPs) or the winner neuron in competitive learning (PNNs). Their performance has been reported in the following Table 5.

		MLPs	PNNs	*k*NN
HBFs	mean (μ)	19.11	7.42	8.56
	std (σ)	2.29	1.59	1.49
RWE	mean (μ)	19.44	9.13	8.89
	std (σ)	1.58	1.18	0.98
WSM	mean (μ)	17.53	6.9	8.56
	std (σ)	1.23	1.24	1.09
MPs	mean (μ)	26.9	13.9	13.29
	std (σ)	3.21	0.91	1.05

Table 5. Performance evaluation of three types of supervised classifiers

Obviously the PNN classifier performed better than the MLP one in most cases. For instance, no matter by means of which kind of physiological signal modelling, the classification error rates of the MLP classifier range from 17.53% to 26.9%. On the contrary, the worst result of PNN classifier is 13.9% only. Furthermore, the results in Table 5 indicate that, although methodologically simple, kNNs achieved the competitive classification performance for uneven datasets. The classification error rates are comparable to those by PNNs in most cases. As a matter of fact, if with a narrow spread of Gaussian basis functions, a PNN classifier can be in essence considered as a kNN one. Nevertheless, the PNNs are generally with comparatively abstract neurons for category prototyping. In contrast, kNNs rely on the isolated training patterns only. Theoretically speaking, after supervised training, the PNN classifiers with appropriate configuration run faster than the kNN ones.

From the viewpoint of physiological signal modelling, the best performance of recognition and classification should be attributed to WSM. No matter by which kind of supervised classifier, the WSM models always lead to a minimal error rate in comparison with other kind of adaptive models. Note that the energy-oriented modelling strategies, including relative wavelet energies (RWE) and WSM, are inefficient for physiological signal representation. However, they performed well for adaptive clustering and supervised classification. It is exactly opposite to those morphology-oriented modelling schemes, for example, HBFs and MPs. In summary, the energy-oriented modelling schemes are better than those morphology-oriented ones for computerized recognition and classification.

6. Conclusion

The central idea of this chapter is focused on computerized interpretation of cardiovascular physiological signals, including ECG and ABP waveforms. Both of them are easily accessible by means of contemporary biosensors and transducers. However, their computerized interpretation has to confront the intrinsic variability due to pathophysiological artefacts, instrumental inaccuracy and inconsistent measurement. The techniques based on domain transformation and signal modelling, including RWE, WSM, HBFs and MPs, were elaborated and evaluated carefully in this chapter. In addition, the paradigms of adaptive clustering and supervised classification were introduced for computerized physiological signal interpretation. A few computerized paradigms were carried out by combining them and evaluated on a real-world workbench database. Although intriguing, the results indicate that there is no any prevailing paradigm for computerized interpretation of cardiovascular physiological signals yet. It hereby calls for more sophisticated paradigms, for example, wavelet networks, wavelet SVMs, wavelet ARTMAP, and so on.

7. Acknowledgement

This work was partially supported by Macau Science and Technology Development Fund, and in part by the University of Macau Research Committee. The technical contributions from Ms. Fu Binbin and Mr. Lei Waikei are particularly appreciated.

8. References

Rosamond, W.; Flegal, K. & Go, A., et al (2008). Heart disease and stroke statistics—2008 update: A report from the American Heart Association Statistics Committee and Stroke Statistics Subcommittee. *Circulation*, vol. 117, e25-e146

Petersen, S.; Peto, V. & Rayner, M., et al (2005). *European Cardiovascular Disease Statistics* (2005 Edition), European Heart Network and the British Heart Foundation, London

Cohn, J.N.; Hoke, L. & Whitwam, W., et al (2003). Screening for early detection of cardiovascular disease in asymptomatic individuals. *American Heart Journal*, vol. 146, 679-685

WHO (1998) *The WHO Health Report 1998: Life in the 21st Century*, WHO Press

Korhonen, I.; Parkka, J. & VanGils, M. (2003). Health monitoring in the home of the future. *IEEE Engineering in Medicine and Biology Magazine*, vol. 22, no. 3, 66-73

Scalvini, S.; Martinelli, G. & Baratti, D., et al (2005). Telecardiology: one-lead electrocardiogram monitoring and nurse triage in chronic heart failure. *Journal of Telemedicine and Telecare*, vol. 11, 18-20

Welkowitz, W. (1981). Indices of cardiac status. *IEEE Transactions on Biomedical Engineering*, vol. 28, no. 8, 553-567

Klabunde, R.E. (2004). *Cardiovascular Physiology Concepts*, Lippincott Williams & Wilkins.

Bacquer, D.D.; Backer, G.D. & Kornitzer, M., et al (1998). Prognostic value of ECG findings for total, cardiovascular disease, and coronary heart disease death in men and women. *Heart*, vol. 80, 570–577

Rego, L.C. & Souza, F.M.C. (2002) Improved estimation of left ventricular hypertrophy: Models based on data from ABPM-24h and on arterial compliance as alternatives to using electrocardiograms. *IEEE Engineering in Medicine and Biology Magazine*, vol. 21, no. 1, 66-73

Sato, T.; Nishinaga, M. & Kawamoto, A., et al (1993). Accuracy of a continuous blood pressure monitor based on arterial tonometry. *Hypertension*, vol. 21, 866-874

World Health Organization (WHO) & Center for Disease Control and Prevention (CDC) (2004) *The Atlas of Heart Disease and Stroke*, WHO Press

Papaioannou, T.G.; Stamatelopoulos, K.S. & Gialafos, E., et al (2004). Monitoring of arterial stiffness indices by applanation tonometry and pulse wave analysis. *Journal of Clinical Monitoring*, vol. 18, 137-144

Allen, J. (2007). Photoplethysmography and its application in clinical physiological measurement. *Physiological Measurement*, vol. 28, R1–R39

Warner, H.R. (1965). Some computer techniques of value for study of circulation. *Computers and Biomedical Research*, vol. 2, 239-268

Bailey, J.J.; Itscoitz, S.B. & Hirshfeld, J.W., et al (1974). A method for evaluating computer programs for electrocardiographic interpretation: I. Application to the experimental IBM program of 1971. *Circulation*, vol. 50, 73-79

Cox, J.R.; Nolle, F.M. & Martin, A.R. (1972). Digital analysis of the electroencephalogram, the blood pressure wave, and the electrocardiogram. *Proceedings of the IEEE*, vol. 60, no. 10, 1137-1164

Thomas, L.J.; Clark, K.W. & Mead, C.N., et al (1979). Automated cardiac dysrhythmia analysis. *Proceedings of the IEEE*, vol. 67, no. 9, 1322-1137

Kligfield, P.; Gettes, L.S. & Bailey, J.J., et al (2007). Recommendations for the standardization and interpretation of the electrocardiogram. Part I: The electrocardiogram and its technology. *Circulation*, vol. 115, 1306-1124

Zadeh, L.A. (2007). *A definition of soft computing in greater detail* (http://www.cs.berkeley.edu/~zadeh/, accessed in October 2007)

Kecman, V. (2001). *Learning and Soft Computing: Support Vector Machines, Neural Networks, and Fuzzy Logic Models*, Massachusetts Institute of Technology, Cambridge, MA.

Ham, F.M. & Han, S. (1996). Classification of cardiac arrhythmias using fuzzy ARTMAP. *IEEE Transactions on Biomedical Engineering*, vol. 43, no. 4, 425–430

Wen, C.; Yeh, M.F. & Chang, K.C. (2007). ECG beat classification using GreyART network. *IET Signal Processing*, vol. 1, no. 1, 19–28

Ovaska, S.J.; Van Landingham, H.F. & Kamiya, A. (2002). Fusion of soft computing and hard computing in industrial applications: an overview. *IEEE Transactions on Systems, Man, and Cybernetics – Part C: Applications and Reviews*, vol. 32, no. 2, 72-79

Tsoukalas, L.H. & Uhrig, R.E. (1997). *Fuzzy and Neural Approaches in Engineering*, John Wiley & Sons.

Thuillard, M. (2001). *Wavelets in Soft Computing*, World Scientific, Singapore.

Iyengar, S.S.; Cho, E.C. & Phoha, V.V. (2002). *Foundations of Wavelet Network and Applications*, Chapman & Hall/CRC.

Papaloukas, C.; Fotiadis, D.I. & Likas, A., et al (2002). An ischemia detection method based on artificial neural networks. *Artificial Intelligence in Medicine*, vol. 24, 167–178

Linh, T.H.; Osowski, S. & Stodolski, M. (2003) On-line heart beat recognition using Hermite Polynomials and Neuro-Fuzzy Network. *IEEE Transactions on Instrumentation and Measurement*, vol. 52, no. 4, 1224-1231

Osowski, S.; Linh, T.H. & Markiewicz, T. (2004). Support Vector Machine-based expert system for reliable heartbeat recognition. *IEEE Transactions on Biomedical Engineering*, vol. 51, no. 4, 582-589

Dickhaus, H. & Heinrich, H. (1996). Classifying biosignals with wavelet networks: a method for noninvasive diagnosis. *IEEE Engineering in Medicine and Biology Magazine*, vol. 15, no. 5, 103-111

Long, W.J.; Fraser, H. & Naimi, S. (1997). Reasoning requirements for diagnosis of heart disease. *Artificial Intelligence in Medicine*, vol. 10, 5-24

Fei, Z.X. (2003). *Contemporary Sphygmology in Chinese Medicine*, People's Health Publisher, Beijing, China.

Luo, Z.C.; Zhang, S. & Yang, Y. (2005). Pulse Wave Analysis and Its Clinical Applications, Science Publisher, Beijing, China.

Goldwyn, R.M. & Watt, T.B. (1967). Arterial pressure pulse contour analysis via a mathematical model for the clinical quantification of human vascular properties. *IEEE Transactions on Biomedical Engineering*, vol. 14, 11-17

Heldt, T.; Shim, E.B. & Kamm, R.D., et al (2002). Computational modeling of cardiovascular response to orthostatic stress. *Journal of Applied Physiology*, vol. 92, 1239–1254

Frank, S.C.; Mchale, P.A. & Cobb, F.R., et al (1973). Evaluation of several methods for computing stroke volume from central aortic pressure. *Circulation Research*, vol. 33, 139-148

Murray, W.B. & Foster, P.A. (1996). The peripheral pulse wave: Information overlooked? *Journal of Clinical Monitoring*, vol. 12, 365-377

Yanowitz, F.G. (2007). *The "ALAN E. LINDSAY ECG TUTORIAL"* (V6.0), University of Utah School of Medicine.

Miyahara, H.; Whipple, G.H. & Teager, H.M., et al (1968). Cardiac arrhythmia diagnosis by digital computer. *Computers and Biomedical Research*, vol. 1, 277-300

Belforte, G.; Mori, R.D. & Ferraris, F. (1979). A contribution to the automatic processing of electrocardiograms using syntactic methods. *IEEE Transactions on Biomedical Engineering*, vol. 26, no. 3, 125-136

Degani, R. & Bortolan, G. (1989). Fuzzy decision-making in electrocardiography. *Artificial Intelligence in Medicine*, vol. 1, no. 2, 87-91

Caceres, C.A.; Steinberg, C.A. & Abraham, S., et al (1962). Computer extraction of electrocardiographic parameters. *Circulation*, vol. 25, 356-362

Okajima, M.; Stark, L. & Whipple, G.H. (1963). Computer pattern recognition techniques: Some results with real electrocardiographic data. *IEEE Transactions on Biomedical Engineering*, vol. 10, no. 3, 106-114

Bemmel, J.H.V.; Talmon, J.L. & Duisterhout, J.S., et al (1973). Template waveform recognition applied to ECG-VCG analysis. *Computers and Biomedical Research*, vol. 6, no. 5, 430-441

Maitra, S. & Zucker, S. (1975). A concise parametric representation of electrocardiograms. *IEEE Transactions on Biomedical Engineering*, vol. 22, no. 4, 350-355

Suppappola, S.; Sun, Y. & Chiaramida, S.A. (1997). Gaussian pulse decomposition: An intuitive model of electrocardiogram waveforms. *Annals of Biomedical Engineering*, vol. 25, 252-260

Laguna, P.; Moody, G.B. & Garcio, J., et al (1999). Analysis of the ST-T complex of the electrocardiogram using the Karhunen-Loeve transform: adaptive monitoring and alternans detection. *Medical & Biological Engineering & Computing*, vol. 37, 175-189

Petrutiu, S.; Ng, J. & Nijm, G.M., et al (2006). Atrial fibrillation and waveform characterization. *IEEE Engineering in Biology and Medicine Magazine*, vol. 25, no. 6, 24-30

Lagerholm, M.; Peterson, G. & Braccini, G., et al (2000). Clustering ECG complex using Hermite functions and self-organizing maps. *IEEE Transactions on Biomedical Engineering*, vol. 47, no. 7, 838–848

Chazal, P.; O'Dwyer, M. & Reilly, R.B. (2004). Automatic classification of heartbeats using ECG morphology and heartbeat interval features. *IEEE Transactions on Biomedical Engineering*, vol. 51, no. 7, 1196-1206

Osowski, S; Linh, T.H. & Markiewicz, T. (2004). Support Vector Machine-based expert system for reliable heartbeat recognition. *IEEE Transactions on Biomedical Engineering*, vol. 51, no. 4, 582-589

Wei, B.; Afonso, V.X. & Tompkins, W.J. (1999). Classification of premature ventricular complexes using filter bank features, induction of decision trees and a fuzzy-based rule system. *Medical & Biological Engineering & Computing*, vol. 37, 560-565

Christov, I.; Gomaz-Herrero, G. & Krasteva, V., et al (2005). Comparative study of morphological and time-frequency ECG descriptors for heartbeat classification. *Medical Engineering & Physics*, vol. 28, 876-887

Li, B.N.; Fu, B.B. & Dong, M.C. (2008). Development of a mobile pulse waveform analyzer for cardiovascular health monitoring. *Computers in Biology and Medicine*, vol. 38, no. 4, 438-445

Martin, J.F.; Volfson, L.B. & Kirzon-Zolin, V.V., et al (1994). Application of pattern recognition and image classification techniques to determine continuous cardiac output from the arterial pressure waveform. *IEEE Transactions on Biomedical Engineering*, vol. 41, no. 10, 913-920

Geva, A.V. (1998) Feature extraction and state identification in biomedical signals using hierarchical fuzzy clustering. *Medical & Biological Engineering & Computing*, vol. 36, 608-614

Stamkopoulos, T.; Diamantaras, K. & Maglaveras, N., et al (1998). ECG analysis using nonlinear PCA neural networks for ischemia detection. *IEEE Transactions on Signal Processing*, vol. 46, no. 11, 3058-3067

Bolton, R. & Westphal, L.C. (1981). Preliminary results in display and abnormality recognition of Hilbert transformed ECGs. *Medical & Biological Engineering & Computing*, vol. 19, no. 3, 377-384

Rasiah, A.I.; Togneri, R. & Attikiouzel, Y. (1997). Modeling 1-D signals using Hermite basis functions. *IEE Proceedings on Vision, Image, and Signal Processing*, vol. 144, no. 6, 345-354

Saxena, S.C.; Kumar, V. & Hamde, S.T. (2002). Feature extraction from ECG signals using wavelet transforms for disease diagnostics. *International Journal of Systems Science*, vol. 33, no. 13, 1073-1085

Senhadii, L.; Carrault, G. & Bellanger, J.J., et al (1995). Comparing wavelet transforms for recognizing cardiac patterns. IEEE Engineering in Medicine and Biology Magazine, vol. 14, no. 2, 167-173

Al-Farhoum, A.S. & Howitt, I. (1999). Combined wavelet transformation and radial basis neural networks for classifying life-threatening cardiac arrhythmias. *Medical & Biological Engineering & Computing*, vol. 37, 566-573

Engin, M. (2007). Spectral and wavelet based assessment of congestive heart failure patients. *Computers in Biology and Medicine*, vol. 37, 820-828

Rosso, O.A.; Blanco, S. & Yordanova, J. (2001). Wavelet entropy: a new tool for analysis of short duration brain electrical signals. *Journal of Neuroscience Methods*, vol. 105, 65–75

Blanco, S.; Figliola, A. & Quian, Q.R., et al (1998). Time–frequency analysis of electroencephalogram series (III): wavelet packets and information cost function. *Physical Review – E*, vol. 57, 932–940

Pan, J. & Tompkins, W.J. (1985). A real-time QRS detection algorithm. *IEEE Transactions on Biomedical Engineering*, vol. 32, no. 3, 230-236

Mallat, S.G. & Zhang, Z.F. (1993). Matching pursuits with time-frequency dictionaries. *IEEE Transactions on Signal Processing*, vol. 41, no. 12, 3397-3415

Mallat, S. (1998). *A Wavelet Tour of Signal Processing*, Academic Press, Burlington, MA:

Coifman, R.R. & Wickerhauser, M.V. (1992). Entropy-based algorithms for best basis selection. *IEEE Transactions on Information Theory*, vol. 38, no. 2, 713-718

Suppappola, A.P. & Suppappola, S.B. (2002). Analysis and classification of time-varying signals with time-frequency structures. *IEEE Signal Processing Letters*, vol. 9, no. 3, 92-95

Christov, I.; Gomaz-Herrero, G. & Krasteva, V., et al (2005). Comparative study of morphological and time-frequency ECG descriptors for heartbeat classification. *Medical Engineering & Physics*, vol. 28, 876-887

Moody, G.B. (1997). *MIT-BIH Arrhythmia Database* (http://www.physionet.org/ physiobank/database/mitdb/, accessed in November 2007)

The Minnesota Code Classification System for Electrocardiographic Findings (http://www.epi.umn.edu/ecg/mncode.pdf, accessed in February 2009)

Long, W.J. & Fraser, H. & Naimi, S. (1997). Reasoning requirements for diagnosis of heart disease. *Artificial Intelligence in Medicine*, vol. 10, 5-24.

Gerencsér, L.; Kozmann, G. & Vágó, Z., et al (2002). The use of the SPSA method in ECG analysis. *IEEE Transactions on Biomedical Engineering*, vol. 49, no. 10, 1094-1101

Tatara, E. & Gnar, A. (2002). Interpreting ECG data by integrating statistical and artificial intelligence tools: Combining knowledge-based systems with statistical methods for more robust intelligent patient monitoring. *IEEE Engineering in Biology and Medicine Magazine*, vol. 21, no. 1, 36-41

Suzuki, Y. (1995). Self-organizing QRS-wave recognition in ECG using neural networks. *IEEE Transactions on Neural Networks*, vol. 6, no. 6, 1469-1477

Lei, W.K.; Li, B.N.; Dong, M.C. & Fu, B.B. (2008). An application of morphological feature extraction and Support Vector Machines in computerized ECG interpretation. *Proceedings of MICAI 2007*, pp. 82-90, Mexico, Oct 2007, IEEE CSP, New York

Jain, A.K.; Duin, R.P.W. & Mao, J.C. (2000). Statistical pattern recognition: A review. *IEEE Transactions on Pattern Recognition and Machine Intelligence*, vol. 22, no. 1, 4-37.

Duda, R.O.; Hart, P.E. & Stock, D.G. (2001). *Pattern Classification* (2nd ed.), John Wiley, New York

Jain, A.K. & Dubes, R.C. (1988). *Algorithms for Clustering Data*, Prentice Hall, Englewood Cliffs, NJ

Hebb, D.O. (1949). *The Organization of Behaviors*, Wiley & Sons, New York

Vapnik, V. (1998). *Statistical Learning Theory*, Wiley-Interscience, New York

Haykin, S. (1999). *Neural Networks: A Comprehensive Foundation*, Prentice Hall, Upper Saddle River, NJ

Li, B.N.; Dong, M.C. & Vai, M.I. (2009). Modelling cardiovascular physiological signals using adaptive Hermite and wavelet basis functions. *IET Signal Processing*, in press.

11

Decision Support System for Truck Route Modelling (D – TRM)

Devlin, Dr Ger
Biosystems Engineering, University College Dublin
Belfield, Dublin 4,
Ireland

1. Introduction

Since the 1970's Decision Support Systems (DSS) have become popular following the development in computer technology. A DSS aims to support in the solving of specific problems with both human and computer techniques. The purpose of this research was to design and develop a DSS for application involved with the cost calculations and revenue calculations of contracted timber haulage in Ireland. The DSS allows the costs and revenue of timber haulage to be calculated on a daily basis and a route specific basis. This implies that the user interface allows for certain criteria such as truck configuration, truck model, engine size, horsepower and design gross vehicle weight (d.g.v.w) to be selected. Both the revenue and running costs are directly related to the payload weight and the distance travelled. To generate the routes travelled and provide a sophisticated interface for spatial road map information a Geographic Information System (GIS) was used. ESRI's (Environmental Systems Research Institute) Arcview 8.3 was used which provides its own application programming in the form of Visual Basic for Applications (VBA). VBA was used to design and create the DSS while the GIS provides the spatial interface, database and route modelling component. A DSS by definition is a combination of databases, user interfaces and modelling components directed at solving a specific problem. For this *specific problem* a GIS alone is not a DSS. However, the GIS and DSS together combine to create a Spatial Decision Support System (SDSS) to extend the range of decision support through its ability to define route selection (using the Network Analyst tool (NAT) in Arcview 8.3) and also the display of spatial road vector data for the user interface can greatly enhance the decision making process.

The trend in routing systems in transport applications in general is to build and design the DSS around the geographical interface, where the user can interact with the problem and lead to better decision support. For this SDSS, interaction between the spatial road vector network of Ireland and other geographic data (cities, towns, X and Y co-ordinates of processing sawmill locations and timber harvesting sites, forest boundaries and internal forest road network) is needed. Use of the NAT to select the routes between the origin and destination is also required before the DSS can be implemented and interacted with. Human intervention in the actual routing process can substantially improve the route generated based on local knowledge. With this SDSS, the road network of scale 1: 50,000 forms part of a geometric network from which a "cost-weighting" can be applied when using the NAT to predict the most likely and most cost saving route to be taken by the haulier.

The growth of SDSS is made possible by the growing availability of spatial data for GIS software. In comparison to the United States, United Kingdom and continental Europe, Ireland's availability of spatial data (both vector and raster) has been expensive and of poor quality. However, several private sector companies are now producing their own digital maps from satellite photography, remote sensing and GPS surveys. It is estimated that up to 80% of data needed for the activities of business and government is spatially related (Franklin, 1992).

In its most basic form, a routing problem involves travelling from origin to destination with a minimum of distance travelled. Within the GIS "cost-weights" can be applied when using the NAT which attempts to simulate the route to be taken in terms of shortest distance, road class, speed limits and the most probable route the haulier would take (Devlin et al. 2007). Each route returns a total distance travelled and the DSS can then be used to determine the cost of travelling such a route and compare results for routes of varying cost-weights.

The potential production of roundwood from the forests of Ireland will reach 5 million m^3 per annum by the year 2015 (Coford, 2001). Road transport will remain the most important mode of timber transport in Ireland, forming a substantial part of the timber industry's raw material costs and having a major influence on the sector's overall economic performance and competitiveness (Coillte, 2003). Within the Irish forestry sector, however, (both private plantations and state owned) there is a necessity to incorporate Information Technology (I.T.) into the timber haulage sector (Optilog, 2003). Information technology in this situation implies the use of GPS for tracking of timber trucks from forest harvesting site to sawmill destination and incorporating this positional technology with Geographical Information Systems (GIS) to reference the timber truck on a map. The GIS map is used to determine if the truck is located at the harvesting site, travelling on a national route or unloading within a sawmill (Frisk et al. 2005). GPS and GIS technology have already been successfully implemented and utilised in many fleet management situations such as the effective management of ambulances (Derekenaris et al. 2001), hazardous material truck routing (Frank et al. 2000), milk collection (Butler et al. 2005) and real - time multi vehicle truckload pick-up and delivery problems (Yang et al. 2004). Thus the research is working towards a fully integrated pre-planning approach to timber haulage in an effort to optimise routes travelled in terms of, 1) haulage costs, 2) distance 3) time, 4) volume of timber transported and 5) savings from avoidance of empty return journeys and to create and develop flexible and cost effective haulage control system for the Irish timber haulage sector.

2. Development of a Spatial Decision Support System model (SDSS)

2.1 Decision support model designed with Visual Basic for Applications (VBA) within GIS

This involves designing and developing a Decision Support System (DSS) for route costing calculations. The DSS allows the cost of timber haulage to be calculated on a daily basis or route specific basis - cost per kilometre (CPK). Calculation of the CPK involves the use of the GIS in conjunction with the Network Analyst Tool (NAT), to generate and simulate the routes travelled and to provide a geographical user interface (GUI) for the spatial road network of Ireland (Devlin et al, 2007). The DSS is designed so that the user interface allows for certain criteria such as truck configuration, truck model, engine size, horsepower and design gross vehicle weight (d.g.v.w) to be selected. ArcMap 8.3 provides its own application programming in the form of Visual Basic for Application (VBA). The VBA was used to design and create the DSS, while the GIS provides the spatial interface, database and route modelling component. A DSS by definition is a combination of databases, user interfaces and modelling components directed at solving a specific problem. For this *specific problem* a GIS alone is not a DSS. However, the GIS and DSS together combine to create a Spatial Decision Support System (SDSS) for route costing calculations.

2.2 Customising the ArcMap interface - GIS + DSS = SDSS.

ArcMap comes pre-installed with Visual Basic for Applications. VBA is not a standalone program. VBA provides integration into the Visual Basic Editor (VBE) that allows code to be written in the visual basic programming language. ArcMap has a main menu and a standard toolbar that appear by default. Although the main menu contains only menus and the standard toolbar contains menus, tools, combo boxes and edit boxes, both are still referred to as *toolbars*. One of the principal methods of tailoring the ArcMap interface is through the Customise dialog box that adds new toolbars and menus through simple drag and drop techniques. Customisation must be saved if the ArcMap interface is to be re-opened with more than just the default toolbars. These changes can be saved in 3 ways - 1) The current map document with .mxd file extension. Changes will only be present when this particular map document is opened. 2) A base template document with .mxt file extension. Templates are used as a quick method to create new map documents. 3) The normal template document with file name Normal.mxt. This template stores changes that are available every time ArcMap is loaded.

The VBE can be opened from the Tools menu and scrolling down to the *macros* tab (Alt + F11). This opens the VBE from within ArcMap. The code for the DSS was written and saved in the Normal.mxt template in order to make it available for all ArcMap documents. A custom command to automate the opening of the VBE was created through a UIButtonControl and added to the ArcMap interface. The image and text of the new buttoncontrol can only be edited once the Customise dialog box is open. The code attached to the macro automates the initialising of the DSS and is written as:

```
Private Sub UIButtonControl1_Click()
    Login.Show
    Login.txtpassword.Text = "" 'Clear the password
End Sub
```

This avoids having to continuously open the VBE, open the code of the DSS and then run the visual basic program before being able to manually operate the DSS. Clicking this buttoncontrol activates the Login screen to the DSS that requires the correct username and password in order to access it (figure 1).

Within the VBA environment, as many forms, modules and class module can be added to complete the project. ArcMap has a default project that is listed in the Project Explorer as Project followed by the name of the open map document. Saving any work in this default project makes it accessible only to the associated map document. To make the project available with all ArcMap documents, the VBA work must be saved in the Normal.mxt project. A project is basically a collection of items to which code is added. A module is a set of declarations followed by procedures (instructions that the code performs). The user form is the container for designing the DSS user interface controls where command buttons, text

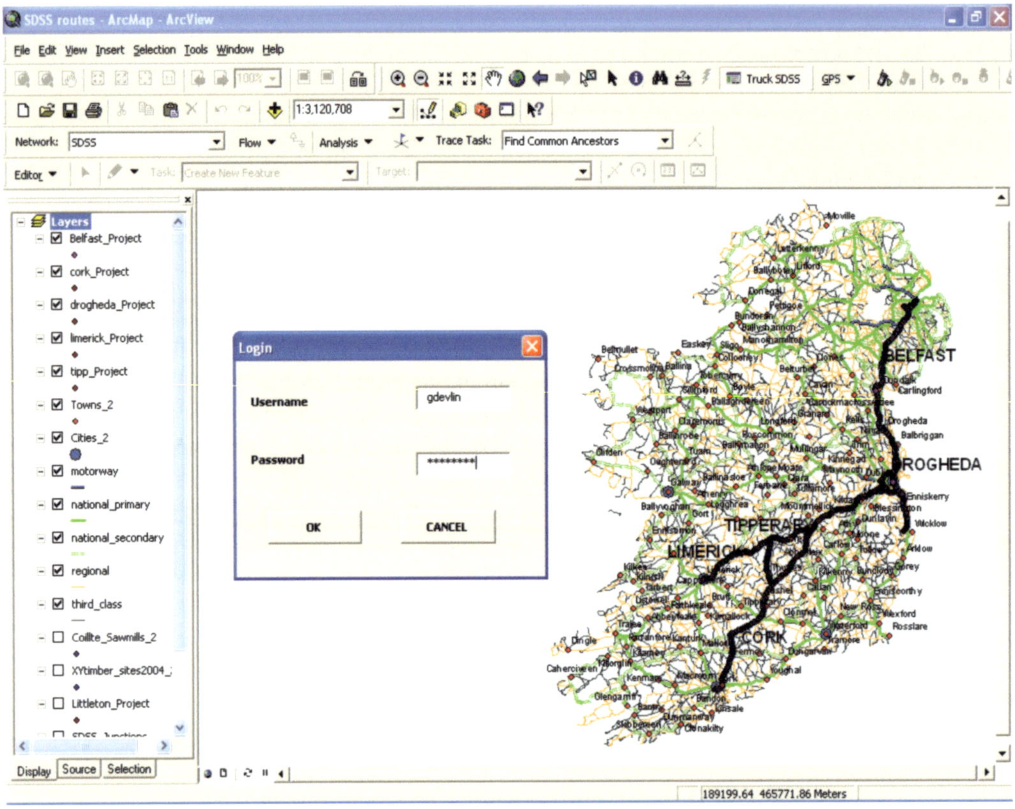

Fig. 1. Screenshot of ArcMap interface with Truck SDSS button control, DSS Login screen and GIS road map.

boxes, list boxes and combo boxes are added. The user forms are used because the user must be able to input information, display outputs and activate event procedures based on the context of each of the 5 user forms - Login, Truck Configuration, Route Calculations, Standing Variables and Costs and Results (figures 2 - 5). To insert a user form, firstly select the project where the form is to be saved – in this case the Normal.mxt, so that the DSS can be accessible from any opened map document. From the Insert menu, click UserForm. VBA inserts the user form and the Controls Toolbox for adding the controls to the user interface. Visual basic code can be added by simply double clicking each control and opening the code window. Once the code is written, it can be run within the VBA to test and debug the code for any errors. As mentioned earlier, the code is run automatically from clicking the *TruckDSS* buttoncontrol within the ArcMap interface, figure 1 above.

2.3 Determining the cost per kilometre (CPK)

It is essential for any transport company to know their vehicle operating costs, whether it is one or two vans, rigid trucks or articulated trucks. Operating costs should be available in some form or another, however, it is how the costs are formulated that allows a full understanding of the transport costs. Transport costs cannot be just a measure of time related costs and distance (kilometre) related costs. Vehicle operating costs (VOC) are a mixture of costs per day and cost per kilometre, simply because time related costs occur

Screenshots of the SDSS for Belfast GIS simulated route

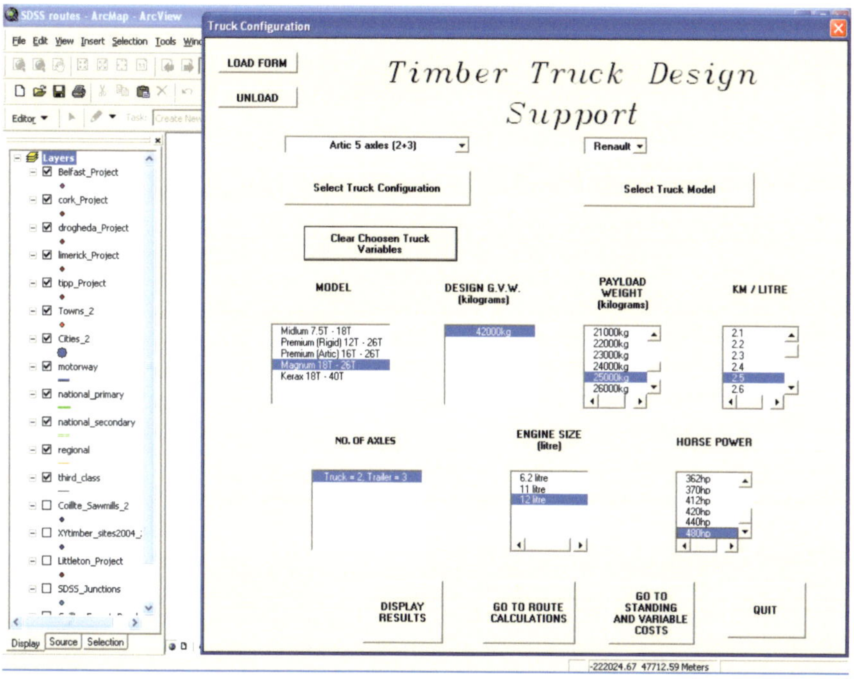

Fig. 2. Screenshot of the Truck Configuration userform.

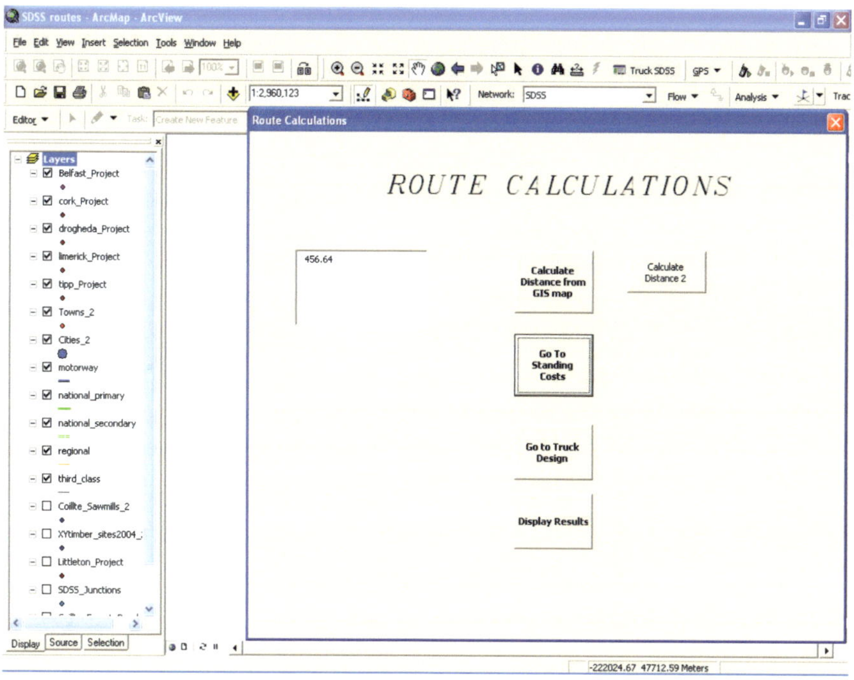

Fig. 3. Screenshot of the Route Calculation userform that reads the GIS distance of the simulated route.

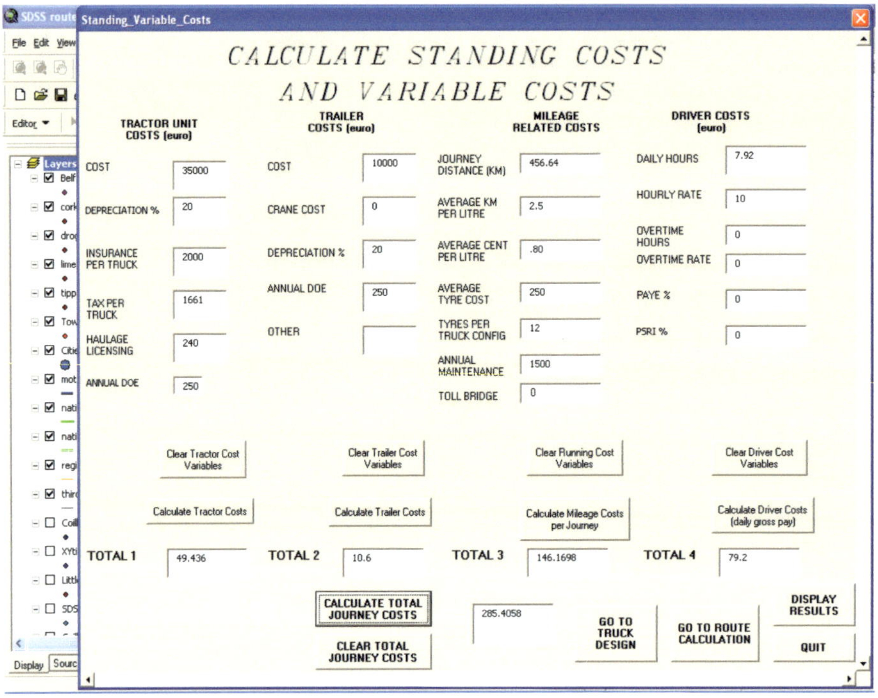

Fig. 4. Screenshot of the Standing Variables and Costs userform

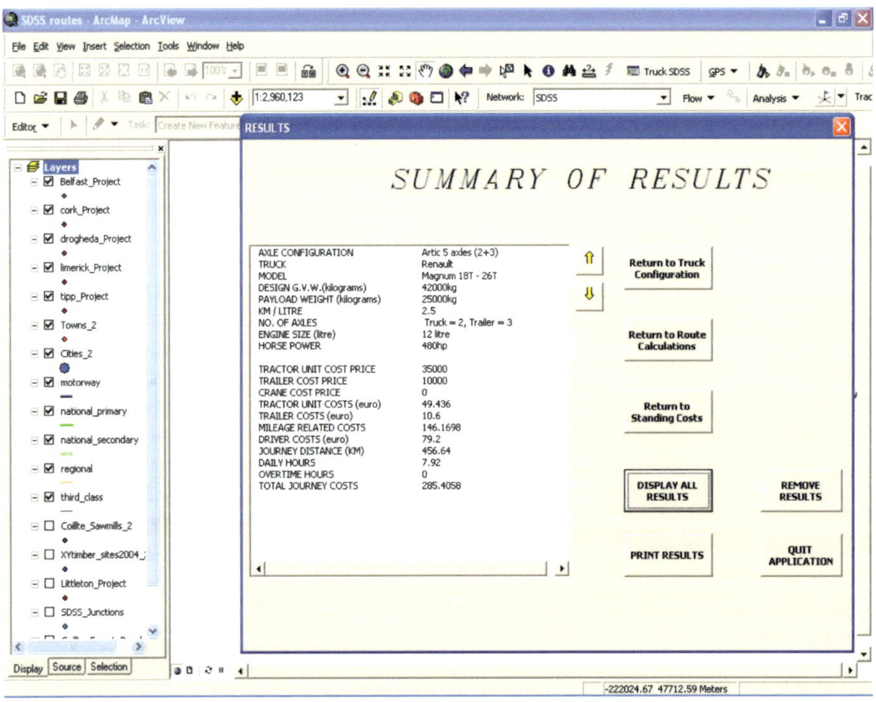

Fig. 5. Screenshot of the Summary of Results from all userforms.

even when the truck is not in use and distances will vary considerably depending on the eventual destination. A full understanding of transport costs will enable a company, family business or owner / truck driver to: 1) Identify operational changes such as route changes, being paid by the kilometre or being paid by the payload weight (kilograms); 2) Identify the most competitive route in terms of cost per kilometre versus revenue per kilometre; 3) Decide on the suitability of one truck configuration / truck model over another and 4) Compare costs to a 3rd party transport company - possibility of outsourcing the transport needs of a company.

The DSS was designed and the VB code written to formulate transport costs and calculate the CPK based on the explanation below:

- Capital costs (truck + trailer + crane)
- Time related costs (standing costs)
- Mileage related costs (running costs)

Capital costs;

- The initial cost of the truck and trailer purchased. The daily cost is calculated as 20% annual depreciation of the total initial cost over a 5 year period. The truck was second-hand at a value of €35,000. The trailer was also second-hand at a value of €10,000.

Time related costs include;

- Wages - Employee's gross daily pay based on the time taken for the particular journey - paid by the hour.
- Depreciation - Calculated as a percentage (20%) of the cost price over the depreciation period, normally 5 years.
- Insurance - Cost of insuring the vehicle and goods in transit insurance. Goods in transit insurance for hazardous chemicals are considerably higher.
- Tax - Goods vehicle road tax (based on the un-laden weight (u.l.w.) of the truck and trailer). Trailer tax is based on the u.l.w. also.
- Licence - National road freight carriers licence (renewed every five years). The cost per truck is higher if the haulage licence is International (for travel inside and outside of Ireland) as opposed to just National (only within Ireland).
- DOE - Trucks and trailers must pass an annual road-worthiness test. Without a road-worthiness certificate, no truck or trailer can be taxed. It is against road legislation to travel on public roads without appropriate road tax.

Mileage related costs include;

- Fuel - Calculate total kilometres for route driven (From GIS). Identify average km / gallon. This can be retrieved from the Infomax software.
- Tyres - Calculate by dividing the average cost per tyre by the total journey distance over a yearly period. The annual kilometres travelled for this truck is approximately between 100,000 - 120,000 kilometres. This implies a daily distance of between 400 and 500 kilometres per day, with approximately 250 working days per year. These figures comply with the readings of the digital tachometer on the truck.
- Maintenance - Calculate by dividing annual maintenance spend by total journey distance over a yearly period.
- Toll bridge - Some motorways in Ireland require a toll fee to be paid for travelling on it. The fee for a 5 axle truck configuration on the M50 toll bridge (most travelled) is €5.60.

For the purpose of this DSS there are 250 working days in the year. Therefore to calculate certain costs such as tyres and maintenance on a daily distance basis, the annual spend is divided by the average distance travelled by the truck which is approximately 100,000 kilometres.

2.4 Engine diagnostic recording of Renault truck with Infomax 4.0 software.

This section of the study involved another period of GPS tracking of the truck. The articulated truck used was a Renault Magnum 480 4 * 2 tractor unit - two wheels on front axle and four wheels on the back, road friendly air suspension (driving) axle (figure 6). This truck replaced the DAF XF from the previous GPS tracking studies because it was not possible to record any engine diagnostics from the DAF XF. Renault Commercial Vehicles sell an *off the shelf* software package known as Infomax, for engine diagnostic management for any Renault truck model. DAF truck manufacturers, on the other hand, do not sell such a software package, hence the reason for switching trucks for the study.

Fig. 6. Photo of the Renault Magnum 480 (to the right). DAF XF is to the left.

2.5 Extraction of data

The Infomax used was version 4.0. Infomax is basically an assistance tool designed to optimise vehicle use. The software must be installed through the CD- ROM on a portable laptop. The adaptor cable must be connected to the serial port of the laptop and also to the default communication port on the truck. Infomax extracts data recorded by the trucks Fleet Management System (FMS). Extraction is carried out at the end of each working day. It is not necessary and not possible to extract data in real-time. The truck must be switched off and in a stationary position. Once the laptop is connected to the truck FMS with the adaptor cable, the ignition must be switched on to proceed with the data extraction process. The extraction process consists of 4 stages:

- Preparation for communication - Infomax checks the connection to the vehicle and identifies itself to the vehicle.
- Identification of the vehicle - Infomax determines whether the vehicle has already been created in its database.
- If the vehicle is unknown in the database, then it must be first created in order to continue with the extraction.
- Infomax then reads the diagnostic data stored in the FMS and saves it to the database.

All modern trucks on continental Europe and Ireland are manufactured with an FMS as part of the design build. Infomax 4.0 provides detailed reports of the engine diagnostics on the truck's performance throughout each working day. It provides details such as distance travelled, diesel used, average consumption of diesel when moving and idling, average speed with engine running and the time with vehicle running as well as other information specific to the engine such as, cruise control, truck and trailer brakes, engine retarder and percentage of transported mass data.

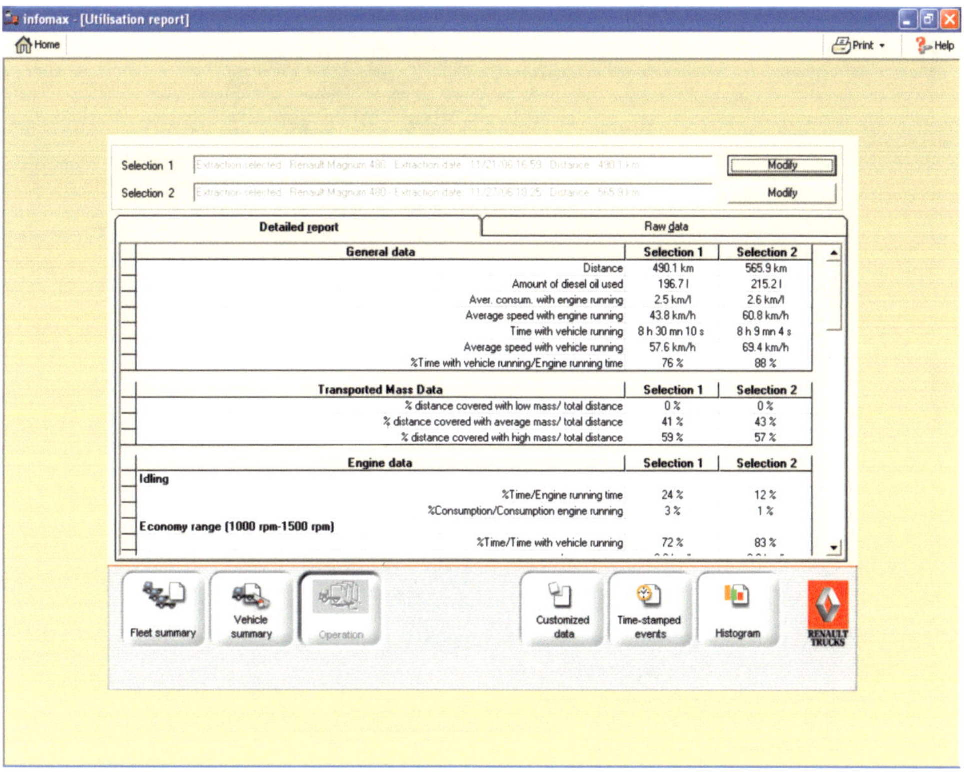

Fig. 7. Screenshot of the Infomax interface showing extracted data for the Belfast (selection 1) and Cork (selection 2) route

2.6 Combination of SDSS with Infomax 4.0 data to determine the CPK

The articulated Renault Magnum truck travelled 5 individual routes. Each route was also GPS tracked using the Trimble GeoXT. The GPS was set to record data every 20 seconds along each of the routes. Each route provided between 1200 and 1300 sample points, of which approximately between 700 and 900 points were dynamic. There was on average 7

Fig. 8a. Belfast GPS and GIS route.

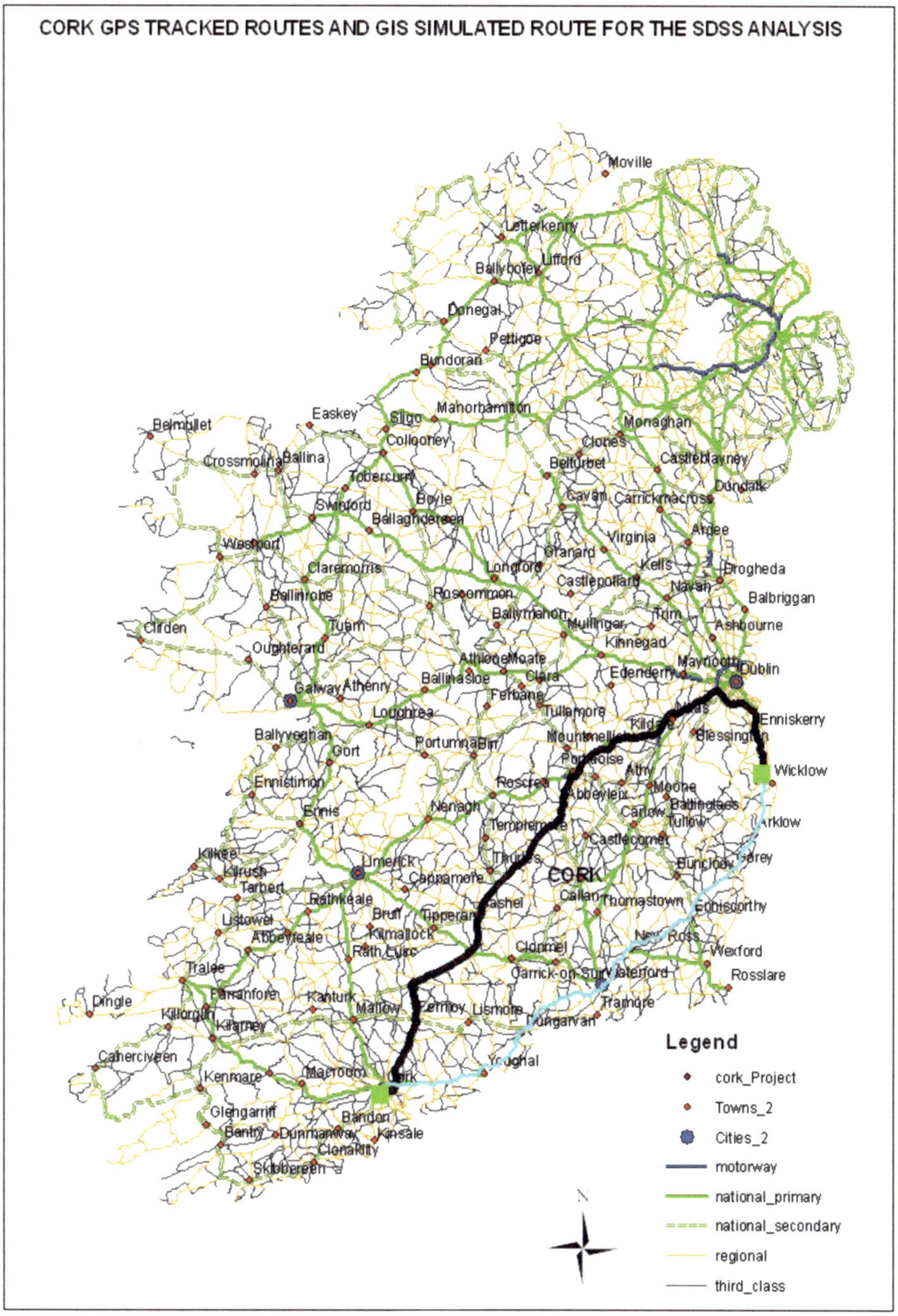

Fig. 8b. Cork GPS and GIS route.

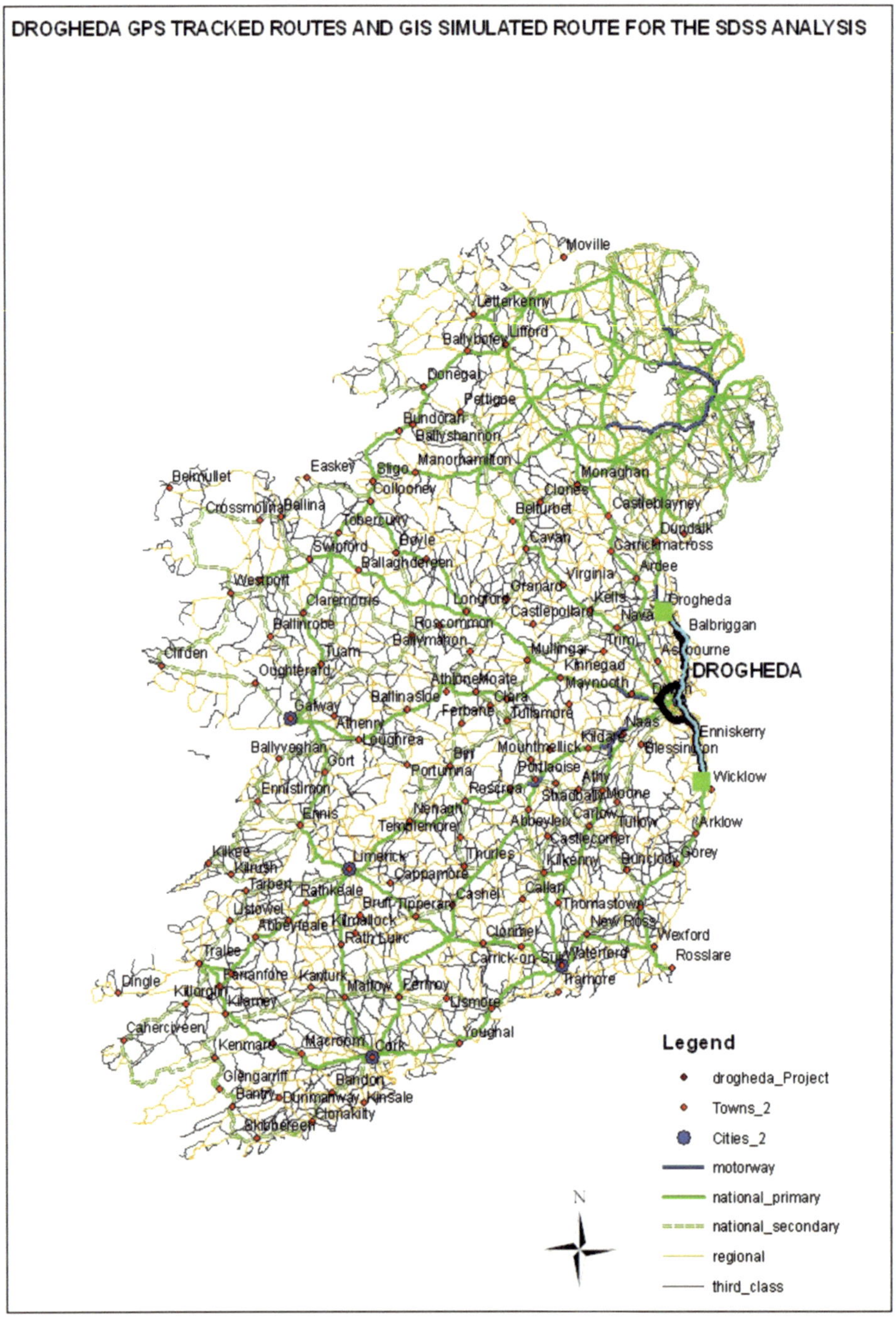

Fig. 8c. Drogheda GPS and GIS route.

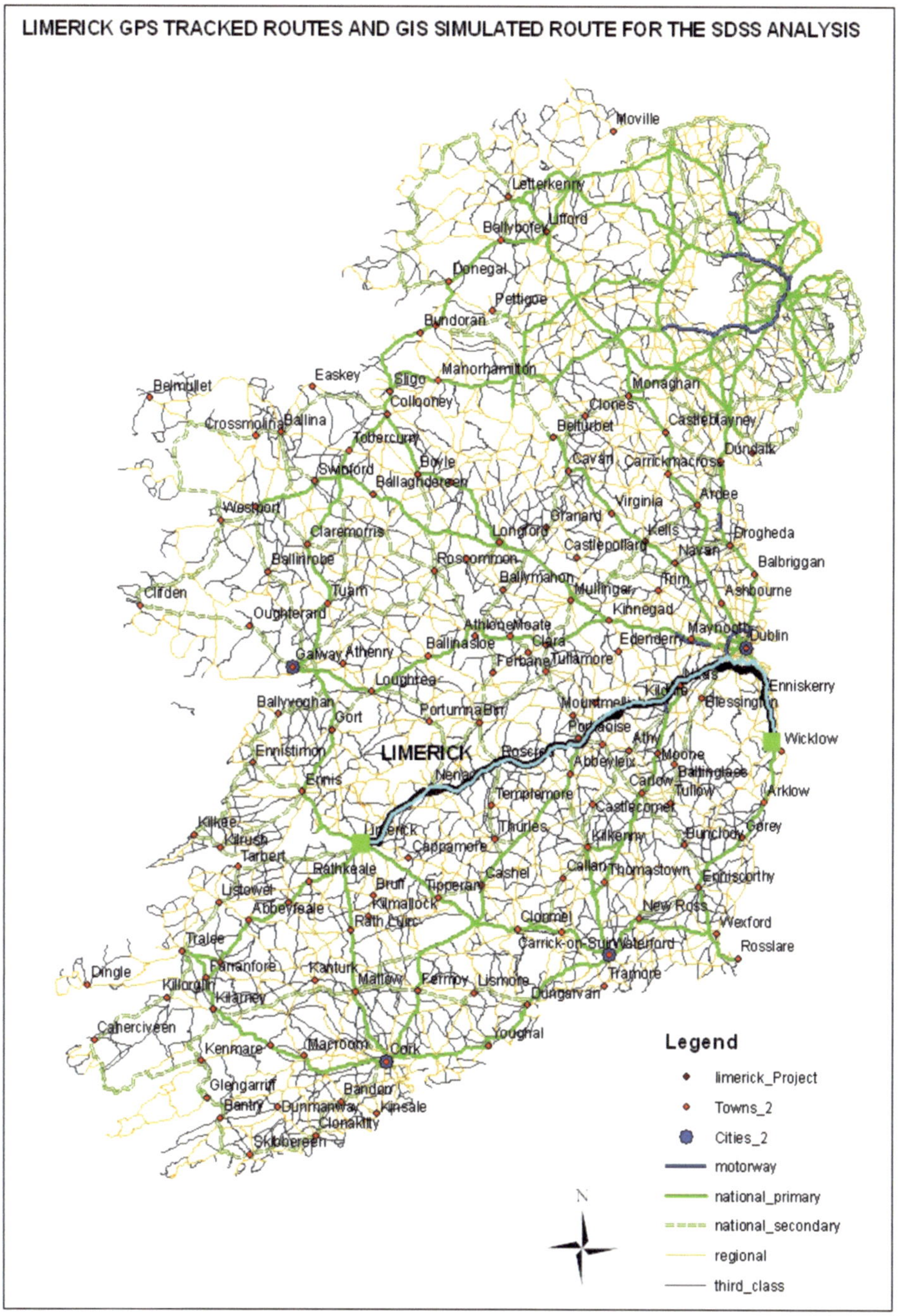

Fig. 8d. Limerick GPS and GIS route.

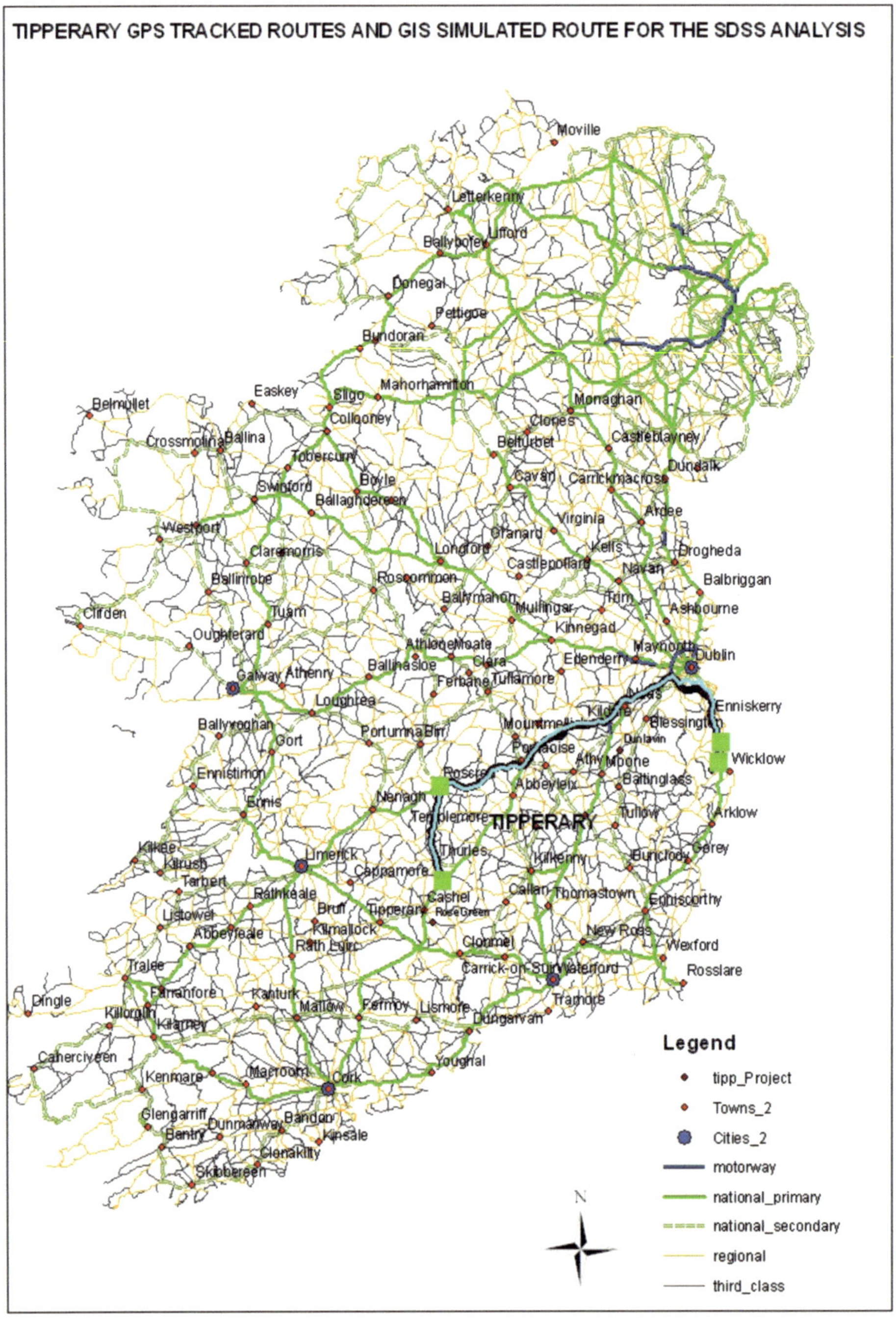

Fig. 8e. Tipperary GPS and GIS route.

Fig. 8. GIS map of each GPS and GIS route – Belfast, Cork, Drogheda, Limerick and Tipperary.

satellites acquired for each of the sample points recorded. In 3 out of the 5 routes the number of satellites acquired reached as high as 11. Data was assigned its geographic co-ordinate system (TM65) and its projected co-ordinate system (Irish National Grid) with the tools in ArcToolbox. The GPS routes could then be layered onto the GIS road vector map (figure 8). Each route is simulated within the GIS using the Network Analyst Tool (NAT) and assigned the same cost - weightings (Devlin et al, 2007). The SDSS is used to calculate the CPK for each of the GPS (Infomax) route versus the CPK for the simulated GIS route. The costs involved for each route were broken down into both variable and fixed costs. The fixed costs relate to the capital costs of the truck and trailer. These values remain the same for each route cost calculation. The variable costs include both the mileage costs and driver costs for the time taken for the journey. These values change for each of the 5 routes travelled. The time taken for each journey, the exact travelling distance and the kilometre per litre is data that must be extracted from the Infomax software to use in the DSS calculation of the CPK for each route - 5 GPS tracked routes and 5 GIS simulated routes (figure 8).

3. Results and discussions

This SDSS was used to calculate the costs of each of the 5 specific routes taken by the truck i.e. how much it costs to travel a certain distance. The costs involved for each route were broken down into both variable and fixed costs. The fixed costs relate to the capital costs of the truck and trailer. These values remain the same for each route cost calculation. The variable costs include both the mileage costs and driver costs for the time taken for the journey. These values change for each of the 5 routes travelled. The time taken for each journey, the exact travelling distance and the kilometre per litre are data that can be extracted using the Infomax software. This data is used to calculate the variable costs. Table 1 shows the related costs for each GPS route based on the distance extracted from the Infomax software.

INFOMAX ROUTE	*BELFAST*	*CORK*	*DROGHEDA*	*LIMERICK*	*TIPPERARY*
Infomax Distance (km)	490.10	565.90	235.40	545.30	406.00
kilometre / litre	2.50	2.60	2.50	2.30	2.30
Journey Time (hrs)	8.50	8.15	4.96	8.56	7.00
Journey Costs (€)	162.48	174.17	80.97	189.71	141.26
Driver Costs (€)	85.00	81.50	49.60	85.60	70.00
Tractor Unit Costs (€)	49.44	49.44	49.44	49.44	49.44
Trailer Costs (€)	10.60	10.60	10.60	10.60	10.60
TOTAL COSTS (€)	307.52	315.71	190.61	335.35	271.30
Infomax Cost per kilometre (€)	0.63	0.56	0.81	0.61	0.67

Table 1. Details of GPS route.

Table 2 shows the corresponding costs for the distance extracted from the GIS.

GIS ROUTE	BELFAST	CORK	DROGHEDA	LIMERICK	TIPPERARY
GIS Distance (km)	456.64	517.08	189.82	537.50	405.46
kilometre / litre	2.50	2.60	2.50	2.30	2.30
Average Speed (km/hr)	57.60	69.40	47.30	63.60	57.90
Journey Time (hrs)	7.92	7.45	4.01	8.45	7.00
Journey Costs (€)	146.17	159.15	60.79	187.00	141.07
Driver Costs (€)	79.20	74.50	40.10	84.50	70.00
Tractor Unit Costs (€)	49.44	49.44	49.44	49.44	49.44
Trailer Costs (€)	10.60	10.60	10.60	10.60	10.60
TOTAL COSTS (€)	285.41	293.69	160.93	331.54	271.11
GIS Cost per kilometre (€)	0.63	0.57	0.84	0.62	0.67

Table 2. Details of GIS route.

This distance reflects the most probable route that is defined within the geometric network. Graphically, the routes look very similar and indeed they are except for small differences in the actual distance. In an effort to reflect the actual time taken for the GIS routes to be travelled, the average kilometre per hour was extracted from the Infomax software. This value for each route was used to estimate the approximate travelling time based on the formula Speed = Distance / Time.

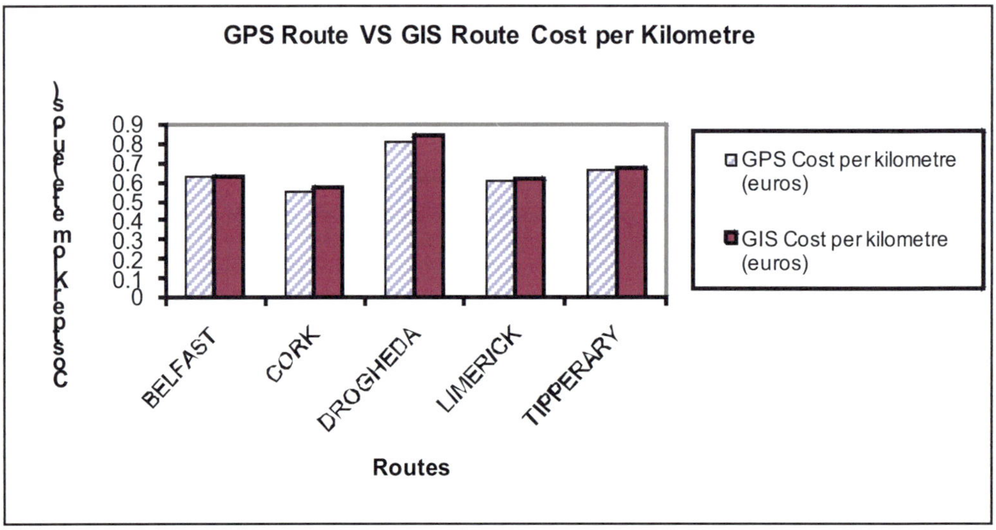

Fig. 9. Graph of CPK for GPS vs GIS routes.

From the Cork route (figure 8b) it can be seen that the GIS actually defined an entirely different route from the GPS route that was travelled, with a difference in distance of 48.82km. The actual difference in cost per kilometre (CPK) was in fact negligible at €0.57 and €0.56 respectively. An important point to note here is that the GPS actually tracked the truck on the return journey to be the same route defined by the GIS.

Another point to note is the route defined by the GIS for the Drogheda journey (figure 8c). This route travels through Dublin city and returns this route also. The truck travelled through the city early in the morning simply because of no traffic congestion at that period of the day. The GIS route is in fact shorter than the route travelled home through, but there is the added bonus of avoiding the toll charges for use of the ring road known as the M50 around Dublin city. Notice, however, that the GPS route returned through the toll bridge. The reason for this is the fact that the ring road does provide a faster journey than through the city in the afternoons. This is in fact the normal travelling procedure for the truck driver when travelling to the north of Ireland and leaving the depot early in the morning, usually around 4am. From table 1, the CPK for the GPS Drogheda route was €0.81 while the CPK for the GIS route through the city was in fact a higher value of €0.84. This actually proves that by avoiding the city on the return trip the CPK is decreased even with having the added charge of the toll bridge of €5.60 for 5 axle truck configurations. City driving can be full of stopping and starting, gear changing and braking, all of which can lead to an increase in CPK despite the actual shorter distance being travelled. The Belfast route (figure 8a) was a similar situation as regards the use of the toll bridge but the CPK remained consistent at €0.63.

New legislation from February 2007 in Ireland no longer permit heavy goods vehicles (HGV) to travel through Dublin City between the hours of 7am and 7pm. All trucks must use the outer ring road known as the M50 or the Dublin Port Tunnel. All HGV's that work in Dublin port must now use the Port Tunnel to avoid travelling in the city. The Tunnel is 4.5km long and takes approximately 6 minutes to travel through, joining Dublin Port with the M50 outer ring road that provides convenient access to all other major national routes. It is estimated that the Port Tunnel will remove approximately 6,000 trucks a day from Dublin City. This newly constructed tunnel under Dublin City is the longest urban tunnel in Europe. It is toll free for trucks and was opened on the 20th December 2006 at a cost of €751 million to the Irish economy (Department of Transport, 2006).

4. Conclusion

The introduction of Information Technology (IT) into the Irish Forestry sector is becoming ever increasing. During the Gudrun hurricane in Sweden in January 2005, thousands of cubic metres of timber were clearfelled by the ferocity of the storm. Irish timber harvesters and hauliers travelled to Sweden to aid in the recovery effort. The Irish workers experienced the impressive use of IT in the Swedish Forestry Industry at first hand for perhaps the first time. There is a strong belief now that the same technology can be implemented into the Irish forestry situation for an increase in efficiency in harvesting and haulage operations. This work is another step into the overall integration of IT into the timber sector in Ireland. The development of this Spatial Decision Support System can be used to calculate the costs per kilometre associated with timber haulage. It works in conjunction with a GIS road map and the Network Analyst tool. The NAT is used to define routes most probable for the timber haulier and the DSS can then analyse the CPK associated with these routes. Routes were verified through GPS tracking of the truck. The CPK were compared to the GPS route and the GIS simulated route. The results of the study certainly discovered some interesting facts. For example, the GIS Drogheda route that defined its route through Dublin City had a higher CPK of €0.84 as opposed to the GPS route. Even though the GPS route was longer and travelled the ring road around Dublin City at an extra cost of €5.60, the GPS route

returned a lower CPK of €0.81. All of the other GPS routes were longer in distance than the GIS routes but the difference in CPK was only approximately €0.01.
To take this study further, funding has just been secured to analyse the movements of the truck on the internal forest road network. The project aims to use the SDSS to define CPK on the forest roads and combine these values with the CPK of the public roads. The truck will also GPS tracked and its positional accuracy will be quantified within the more difficult terrain of the forest canopy. It is well documented that GPS performance becomes degraded under forest environments. For this reason, it is predicted that other GPS services such as Differential GPS and the European Geostationary Navigation Overlay Service (EGNOS) will be used to optimise the GPS performance while tracking the truck.

5. References

Butler, M., P. Herlihy and P. B. Keenan. 2005. Integrating information technology and operational research in the management of milk collection. Journal of Food Engineering 70 (3) 341 - 349.

Coford. 2001. Forecast of Roundwood Production from the Forests of Ireland 2001 - 2015.

Coillte. 2003. Annual Report. Department of Transport (DOT) 2006, www.transport.ie Accessed November 2006.

Derekenaris, G., J. Garofalakis, C. Makris, J. Prentzas, S. Sioutas and A. Tsakalidis. 2001. Integrating GIS, GPS and GSM technologies for the effective management of ambulances. Computers, Environment and Urban Systems. (25) 267 - 278.

Devlin, G. J., K. P. Donnell and S. M. Ward. 2007. Timber Haulage in Ireland: An Analysis using GIS and GPS. Journal of Transport Geography 16 (1) 63-72.

Frank, William C., Jean - Claude Thill and Rajan Batta. 2000. Spatial decision support for hazardous material truck routing. Transportation Research Part C 8 337 - 359.

Franklin, C. 1992. An introduction to Geographic Information Systems: Linking Maps to Databases. Database 15(2) 12 - 21.

Optilog, 2003. - An efficiency analysis of the sale, purchase, harvesting and haulage of timber in the Irish Forestry Sector. © *Irish Timber Council and Coillte.*

Yang, Jian., Patrick Jaillet and Hani Mahmassani. 2004. Real-time multivehicle truckload pick-up and delivery problems. Transportation Science Vol 38 (2) 135 - 148.

12

A Proposed Decision Support System for Location Selection using Fuzzy Quality Function Deployment

R. Tavakkoli-Moghaddam[1], S. Hassanzadeh Amin[2] and G. Zhang[2]
[1]Department of Industrial Engineering, College of Engineering, University of Tehran,
[2]Department of Industrial and Manufacturing Systems Eng., University of Windsor,
[1]Iran
[2]Canada

1. Introduction

Location selection is a multi-criteria decision making (MCDM) problem that includes both tangible and intangible factors (Kahraman et al., 2003). Location problems involve the determination of the location of one or more new facilities in one or several potential sites. Obviously, the number of sites should be at least equal to the number of new facilities being located (Heragu, 2006). The majority of research approaches for location selection focus on heuristics (Berman et al., 2001) and mathematical programming, such as integer programming (Melkote & Daskin, 2001), dynamic programming (Canel et al., 2001), and nonlinear programming (Nanthavanij & Yenradee, 1999). However, the mathematical programming cannot consider qualitative criteria. Moreover, the decision makers do not contribute in decision making process, and the roll of experience is ignored. Another problem is appeared when there are a lot of alternatives. In this condition, the decision makers prefer to select a group of alternatives, called pre-qualified alternatives. Then, decision makers will select the best alternative from the new group. A pre-qualification stage decreases time and costs of the decision making process. In addition, the characteristics of products affect on the location of factories. For instance, the location of a factory that manufactures heavy products should be different from ordinary factories. However in previous researches, the relationship between location criteria and product criteria is ignored.
In this chapter, we propose a new model for location selection consisting of two phases. In the first phase (i.e., pre-qualification stage), we propose a novel fuzzy based decision making model to take into account both qualitative and quantitative criteria. In the second phase (i.e., final selection), quality function deployment (QFD) is applied to select the best location to establish a factory. Not only QFD is a planning tool used in quality control, but also it is a useful tool in decision making. QFD enables us to consider the relationship between product criteria and location criteria to select the best location. This feature distinguishes QFD from other decision making tools. Moreover, the fuzzy sets theory, linguistic variables, and triangular fuzzy numbers are utilized. A major contribution of the fuzzy sets theory is its capability of representing vague data. In other words, it can

overcome the uncertainty in human's judgments. Finally, an illustrative example is conducted to show the phases of location selection. In this example, eight potential alternatives (locations) are assessed in the first phase in order to select three alternatives. Then, fuzzy QFD is applied to select the best location. The implementation of the proposed model is easy and does not need any optimization background.

This chapter is organized as follows. Section 2 gives a literature review. Section 3 presents a description for the fuzzy sets theory. Section 4 describes the problem. Then, the proposed model is presented in Section 5. Furthermore, an illustrative example is given in Section 6. Finally, conclusions are provided in Section 7.

2. Literature review

Location selection is a multi-criteria decision making (MCDM) problem that includes both qualitative and quantitative metrics. In this section, a literature review is presented in two sections, called location selection and quality function deployment (QFD).

2.1 Location selection

In this section, we imply on the papers of location selection using MCDM techniques. Tzeng & Chen (1999) proposed a location model based on a fuzzy multi-objective approach. This model helps in determining the optimal number and sites of fire stations at an international airport, and also determining the best location. Chen (2001) used triangular fuzzy numbers to select the best distribution location. Furthermore, he proposed a stepwise ranking procedure to rank fuzzy numbers. Kuo et al. (2002) proposed an algorithm for determining the location of a store. The model is based on fuzzy analytical hierarchy process (AHP). Kahraman et al. (2003) solved facility location problems using different solutions of fuzzy multi-attribute group decision-making. They compared four fuzzy models. Chou et al. (2008) presented a fuzzy multi-criteria decision making (FMCDM) model for location selection of the international tourist hotel based on triangular fuzzy numbers. Furthermore, they categorized hotels criteria as a hierarchy. Guneri et al. (2009) used the analytic network process (ANP) to select the best location. However, in all of these models the relationship between product characteristics and location criteria is ignored. QFD is a unique tool that can overcome this drawback.

2.2. QFD

Quality function deployment (QFD) has been widely used for numerous years. It was originated in Japan in 1970s and became increasingly popular in the western world in the 1980s (Houser & Clausing, 1988). In general, it is used by many companies because of three reasons: (1) it saves design and development time, (2) it focuses on the satisfaction of customer, and (3) it improves communication at all levels of the organization (Myint, 2003). Although QFD has a lot of advantages, it also has some drawbacks, such as the amount of time required to implement QFD, and the qualitative and subjective decision-making process (Cohen, 1995; Bouchereau & Rowlands, 2000). Because of the lack of precise information from customer requirements, QFD team members usually determine the relationships between customer requirements and engineering design requirements subjectively (Chen & Weng, 2003). Fig. 1 shows the number of articles on QFD from 1999 until 2008, which is obtained by Scopus on 21 June 2009. The increasing trend shows that this field of study has a lot of opportunity for future research. QFD basically consists of four matrixes: namely planning matrix, designing matrix, operating matrix, and control matrix as shown in Fig. 2.

The house of quality (HOQ) is an important tool for QFD activities, containing information on "what"(customer requirements), "how" (design requirements), relationship between "what" and "how", and the relationship between the "how" factors themselves (Chen & Ko, 2009). Fig. 3 illustrates a HOQ including customer requirements (CR), design requirements (DR), parts requirements (PR), process operations (PO), and production characteristics (PC).

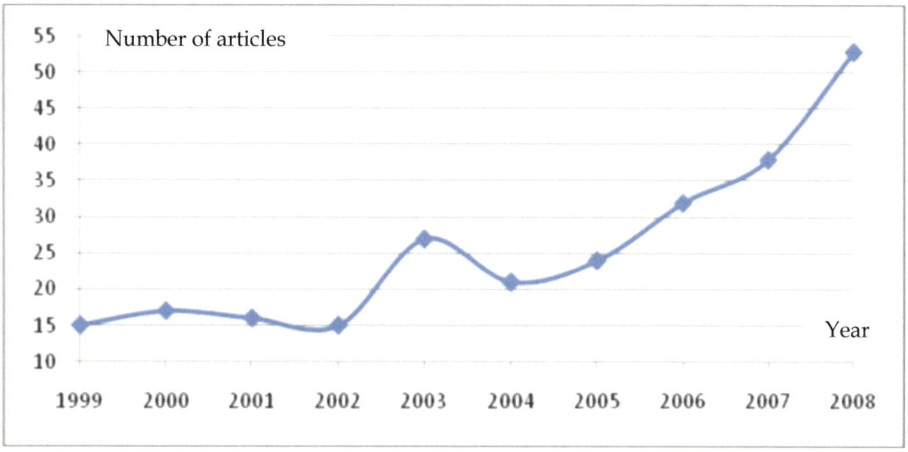

Fig. 1. Numbers of scientific articles in the HOQ or QFD

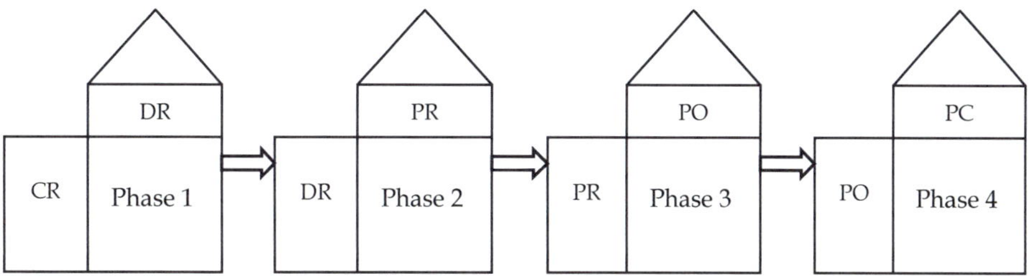

Fig. 2. QFD in four phases

Chan & Wu (2002) presented a literature review for QFD. They also reviewed historical development of QFD, especially in Japan and USA. They categorized functional fields of QFD as product development, quality management, customer needs analysis, design, planning, decision-making, engineering, management, teamwork, timing, and costing. Sharma et al. (2008) reviewed a literature on the topic and application of QFD. They implied that intelligent quantitative methods, such as artificial neural networks, analytical heirarchy process (AHP) and fuzzy logic, can be combined with the model to improve the reliability of decisions.

QFD has been applied in several fields from manufacturing to service environments. Some of researchers have combined fuzzy concepts or AHP to overcome the uncertainty in the assessment process. Halog et al. (2001) utilized the QFD model to determine the emissions that need to be analysed for environmental performance improvement. Partovi &

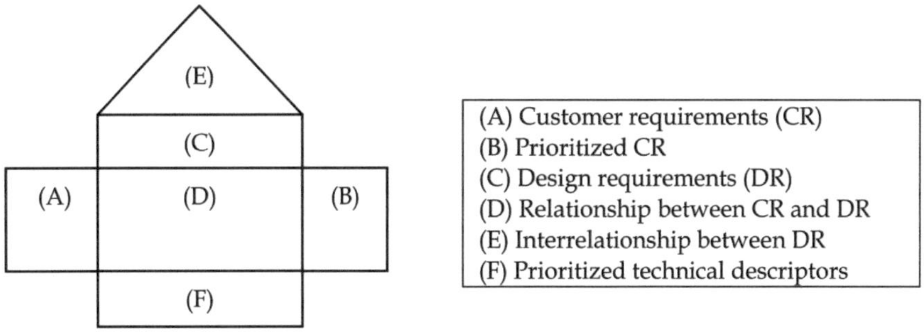

Fig. 3. House of quality

Corredoira (2002) presented a model for prioritizing and designing rule changes for the game of soccer. The model is designed based on QFD. In addition, the AHP and analytic network process (ANP) are used to determine the intensity of the relationship between the row and column variables of three matrices. Myint (2003) provided a methodology for the development of the intelligent quality function deployment (IQFD) application in the discrete parts and assembly environment. The method consists of four matrices. Yang et al. (2003) used the house of quality (HOQ) to meet the needs of buildable designs in the construction industry and to develop a fuzzy QFD system for buildable design evaluation. Chan & Wu (2005) used entropy method instead of using the quite subjective sales-point concept, and derived competitive priority ratings. Furthermore, they utilized triangular fuzzy numbers. Bevilacqua et al. (2006) suggested a new method that transfers the HOQ approach and typical of QFD problems to the supplier selection process. Buyukozkan et al. (2007) also used triangular fuzzy numbers in designing house of quality model. Li & Kuo (2007) adopted the genetic chaotic neural network (GCNN) technique to identify customer's needs and their priorities and proposed the enhanced QFD. Lee et al. (2008) utilized the fuzzy and Kano models simultaneously to determine the relationship between customer requirements and technical characteristics. Raharjo et al. (2008) applied the ANP in the QFD model to take into account uncertainty in human's judgments. Liu (2009) stated that previous researches have focused on the fuzzy HOQ; however, there are other matrices in the QFD model. They proposed a new model for product planning and part deployment. In addition, they used fuzzy clustering. Hassanzadeh Amin & Razmi (2009) proposed a general framework for supplier selection, evaluation, and development. They applied a fuzzy HOQ for selecting the best internet service provider (ISP). In addition, they integrated a quantitative model with QFD in order to consider quantitative and qualitative criteria, simultaneously. Utne (2009) applied the HOQ to improve the environmental performance of the fishing fleet. However, he ignored the subjective assessment problem of QFD and used crisp numbers.

In a few papers, QFD is utilized for location selection. Chuang (2002) presented approaches including a single QFD matrix for relating customer wants to facility location. They identified location requirements by sampling. Then, the location evaluating criteria are established from location requirements, and central relationship matrix is filled. Partovi (2006) presented a strategic solution to a facility location problem by using the AHP, ANP, and QFD, concurrently. He considered internal and external criteria. However, these models did not take into account the impression and vagueness of humans' judgments.

Some researchers have focused on the problem of subjective assessment in QFD. They usually use mathematical models to decrease the imprecision in human's judgements. Temponi et al. (1999) proposed a mathematical model to identify relationships between requirements and overcome the vague data. They utilized fuzzy logic. Kim et al. (2000) developed mathematical models by determining the major model components, such as objectives and constraints in a crisp or fuzzy way using multi attribute value theory combined with the fuzzy regression and fuzzy optimization theory. Tang et al. (2002) proposed two types of fuzzy optimisation models to cover the weaknesses of the QFD model. They utilized a genetic-based interactive approach. Karsak et al. (2002) employed the analytic network process (ANP) to fulfill the relationship between customer requirements (CR) and engineering design requirements (DR). Furthermore, they took into account the multi-objective nature of the problem by incorporating other goals, such as cost, extendibility and manufacturability of PTRs.

Chen & Weng (2003) developed QFD model by using fuzzy programming to represent the relationships between CR and DR. However, they did not provide a case study. Karsak (2004) presented a multi-objective programming approach that incorporates imprecise and subjective information inherent in the QFD planning process to determine the level of fulfillment of design requirements. In addition, they used triangular fuzzy numbers. According to the difficulties of prioritizing engineering characteristics, Han et al. (2004) suggested a linear partial ordering approach for assessing the knowledge from participants and prioritizing engineering characteristics. Fung et al. (2006) proposed a fuzzy linear regression approach to estimate the functional relationships for product planning based on QFD. In addition, they extended asymmetric triangular fuzzy coefficients to asymmetric trapezoidal fuzzy coefficients using the basic concept of the fuzzy regression. Chen & Ko (2008) extended the previous model. They presented a fuzzy nonlinear model to determine the performance level of each DR for maximizing customer satisfaction considering Kano's category of design requirements. Delice & Gungor proposed a new QFD optimization approach combining mixed-integer linear programming and Kano model to determine levels of design requirements. Chin et al. (2009) presented an evidential reasoning (ER) based methodology for synthesizing various types of assessment information provided by a group of customers and multiple QFD team members. They stated that they can overcome the uncertainty in QFD. Zhang & Chu (2009) proposed a group decision-making approach including two optimization models (i.e., logarithmic and weighted least squares models) to aggregate multi-format and multi-granularity linguistic judgments. They stated that this method can handle subjective assessments. Ramanathan & Yunfeng (2009) used the data envelopment analysis (DEA) for deriving the relative importance of DRs when several additional factors are considered. They applied the model for the design of security fasteners for a company. Chen & Ko (2009) proposed fuzzy nonlinear programming models based on Kano's concept to determine the fulfillment levels of part characteristics with the aim of achieving the determined contribution levels of design requirements. Moreover, they used fuzzy numbers.

3. Fuzzy sets theory

Nowadays, operations research is applied for solving decision making problems. Unfortunately, real world situations are not often deterministic. As a result, precise mathematical models are not enough to cover practical situations (Lai & Hwang, 1995). To deal with imprecision, the fuzzy set theory (FST) can be used. This concept was proposed by Zadeh (1965). The FST considers the situations involving the human factor with all its vagueness of perception, subjectively, attitudes, goals and conceptions. A membership function of fuzzy sets and operators play a crucial role in the fuzzy set theory. A membership function is a number between 0 and 1, which is denoted by μ (Zimmermann, 2001).

Triangular fuzzy numbers (TFN) are utilized in the decision making process. A triangular fuzzy number can be denoted by $E = (f, g, h)$ as shown in Fig. 4. In addition, the membership function is given by Eq. (1). The related results of applying fuzzy arithmetic on the fuzzy numbers, $A = (a, b, c)$ and $E = (f, g, h)$, are as follows (Lai & Hwang, 1995; Zimmermann, 2001).

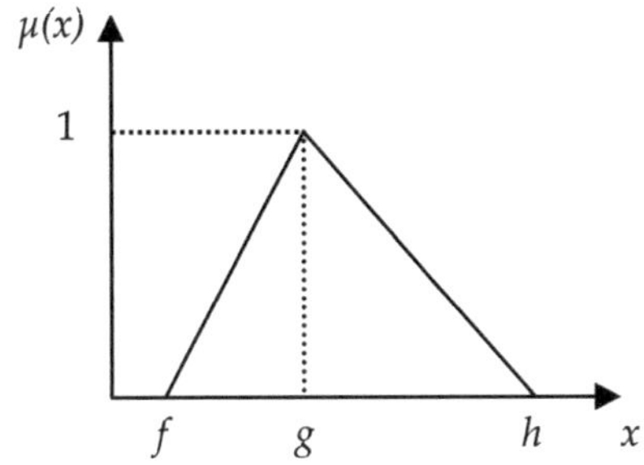

Fig. 4. A triangular fuzzy number

$$\mu(x) = \begin{cases} 0, & x < f \\ \dfrac{x-f}{g-f}, & f \le x \le g \\ \dfrac{h-x}{h-g}, & g \le x \le h \\ 0, & x > h \end{cases} \tag{1}$$

i. Addition of two fuzzy numbers

$$A \oplus E = (a+f, b+g, c+h) \tag{2}$$

ii. Multiplication of two fuzzy numbers

$$A \otimes E = (a \times f, b \times g, c \times h) \tag{3}$$

iii. Multiplication of any number k and a fuzzy number

$$k \otimes E = (k \times f, k \times g, k \times h) \tag{4}$$

4. Problem definition

A manufacturer wants to establish a new factory. One of the most important factors of this decision is to select the most suitable location. Each location can be considered as an alternative. In addition, the suitable location should be chosen based on several metrics, such as facilities and the cost of land. The related criteria consist of both qualitative and quantitative ones. Furthermore, it is important to take into account product characteristics as well as location criteria because product criteria have influence on location selection. For instance, the location of a factory producings heavy products should be close to customers in order to decrease transportation costs.

5. Proposed model

In this section, we propose an integrated model to select the best location. The model includes two phases. In the first phase, a collection of alternatives (i.e., locations) is selected based on a set of criteria. The new fuzzy method is applied to overcome the uncertainty. The pre-qualification stage can decrease the time and costs of assessment when a lot of alternatives exist. In the second phase, a fuzzy QFD method is proposed to select the best location. QFD is a unique tool considering the relationship between product and location criteria.

5.1 Phase 1

In this pahse, a new method based on linguistic variables and triangular fuzzy numbers (TFNs) is proposed. The output of this stage is a set of qualified locations. First, the members of a decision making group should be selected. Three or five managers can contribute in the decision making process. Suppose that there are N decision makers ($n = 1, 2, \ldots, N$), M criteria ($m = 1, 2, \ldots, M$), and K qualified locations ($k = 1, 2, \ldots, K$). The steps of the proposed algorithm are as follows:

Step 1: Define the proper criteria: the decision making group organizes meeting and determines the appropriate criteria consisting of qualitative and quantitative factors.

Step 2: Let U = {VL, L, M, H, VH} be the linguistic set used to express opinions on the group of criteria. The linguistic variables of U can be quantified using triangular fuzzy numbers (please refer to Fig. 5). Each decision maker establishes a level of importance for each criterion by using linguistic variables and TFNs. Then, they are combined by Eq. (5), and the weights of criteria are computed.

$$w_m = \frac{w_{m1} \oplus w_{m2} \oplus \ldots \oplus w_{mN}}{N} \tag{5}$$

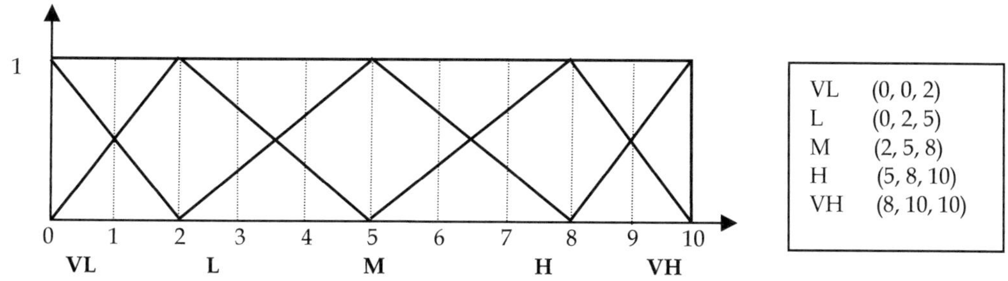

Fig. 5. A linguistic scale for triangular fuzzy numbers

Step 3: Location k (A_k) is assessed based on qualitative criteria. This process is carried out for all alternatives. In other words, decision makers establish the level of importance. Then results are combined by Eq. (6), and aggregated weights are computed that are TFNs.

$$A_{mk} = \frac{A_{mk1} \oplus A_{mk2} \oplus ... \oplus A_{mkN}}{N} \tag{6}$$

Step 4: In this step, the required data are collected for quantitative attributes, such as the cost of land. Then, the numbers are normalized by Eqs. (7) and (8). The purpose of normalization is to unify the scales of the key factors.
Benefit-criteria normalization:

$$A_{mk} = \frac{B_{mk}}{\max_k B_{mk}} \times 10 \qquad m = 1,2,...,M \qquad k = 1,2,...,K \tag{7}$$

Cost-criteria normalization:

$$A_{mk} = \frac{\min_k B_{mk}}{B_{mk}} \times 10 \qquad m = 1,2,...,M \qquad k = 1,2,...,K \tag{8}$$

Step 5: In this step, the weights of criteria are multiplied by the aggregated weights that are computed in Steps 3 and 4. Eq. (9) displays the formula. In this equation, a_k is a TFN. Now, the numbers should be defuzzified. In this chapter, a simple method is applied to defuzzify the numbers. A deffuzzified number of $a_k = (a, b, c)$ is calculated by Eq. (10). Now, the locations can be ranked. The result of this step is a collection of the best locations.

$$a_k = (w_1 \otimes A_{1k}) \oplus (w_2 \otimes A_{2k}) \oplus ... \oplus (w_M \otimes A_{Mk}) \tag{9}$$

$$be_k = \frac{a + 2b + c}{4} \tag{10}$$

5.2 Phase 2

In phase 2, the best location is selected. QFD enables us to consider relationship between product and location characteristics. The main steps of our proposed model are as follows:
Step 1: List customer requirements (CR or product criteria).
Step 2: List design requirements (DR or location criteria).
Step 3: Determine prioritized customer requirement. Each decision maker determines a weight for each CR. Triangular fuzzy numbers are used to quantify the linguistic variables.
Step 4: Determine a weight of each decision maker. Suppose the weight of DM_n is r_n. This parameter can be determined by a manager of company. These variables are designed according to authority, experience, and the responsibilities of different DMs. In addition, Eq. (11) should be satisfied where N is the number of decision makers (n = 1, 2,…, N).

$$\sum_{n=1}^{N} r_n = 1 \tag{11}$$

Step 5: Calculate the aggregated weight for CR: The assigned weights by the decision makers for customer requirement should be aggregated. The aggregated weight (w_p) is calculated by Eq. (12) where P is the number of CR (p = 1, 2,..., P).

$$w_p = (r_1 \otimes w_{p1}) \oplus (r_2 \otimes w_{p2}) \oplus ... \oplus (r_N \otimes w_{pN}) \tag{12}$$

Step 6: Determine the relationship between CR and DR. Each decision maker is asked to express opinion by using the linguistic variables on the impact of each DR on each CR. Here again, triangular fuzzy numbers are used to quantify the linguistic variables.
Step 7: Calculate the aggregated weight between CR and DR. The aggregated weight (a_{pm}) is calculated by the Eq. (13) where N is the number of decision makers ($n = 1, 2,\ldots, N$), P is the number of CR ($p = 1, 2,\ldots, P$), and M is the number of DR ($m = 1, 2,\ldots, M$).

$$a_{pm} = (r_1 \otimes a_{pm1}) \oplus (r_2 \otimes a_{pm2}) \oplus \ldots \oplus (r_N \otimes a_{pmN}) \tag{13}$$

Step 8: Determine prioritized technical descriptors. Now we can complete the matrix by calculating the weights of the DR (f_m), from the aggregated weight for CR (w_p), and the aggregated weight between CR and DR (a_{pm}) according to Eq. (14). These variables also are triangular fuzzy numbers.

$$f_m = (w_1 \otimes a_{1m}) \oplus \ldots \oplus (w_P \otimes a_{Pm}) \tag{14}$$

Step 9: Determine the impact of each location on the attributes: It is necessary to evaluate locations according to the attributes and combine said assessments with the weight of each attribute in order to establish a final ranking. In the same way as before, the linguistic variables are used to quantify triangular fuzzy numbers, then the location rating (LR) is calculated based on Eq. (15) where K is the number of locations ($k = 1, 2, \ldots, K$).

$$LR_{km} = (r_1 \otimes lr_{km1}) \oplus (r_2 \otimes lr_{km2}) \oplus \ldots \oplus (r_N \otimes lr_{kmN}) \tag{15}$$

Step 10: Calculate the fuzzy index (FI) that expresses the degree to which a location satisfies a given requirement. The FI is a triangular fuzzy number, which is obtained from the previous scores. Eq. (16) illustrates the formula.

$$FI_k = \frac{1}{M} \otimes [(LR_{k1} \otimes f_1) \oplus \ldots \oplus (LR_{kM} \otimes f_M)] \tag{16}$$

Step 11: Defuzzifiy the numbers and rank the alternatives. Eq. (10) is applied to defuzzify the numbers. Now, the locations can be ranked.

6. Illustrative example

In this section, an illustrative example is conducted to show the proposed model. A famous company that manufactures bicycle components, such as cranks, hubs, rims, and so forth wants to establish another factory to expand its supply chain. Therefore, this company should focus on product design during the location selection process. Preliminary investigation shows that eight sites are considered as the most desirable locations. The required data are collected by means of interviews with three experts. Fig. 6 shows the appropriate criteria selected by decision makers for the first phase.
In the first step, decision makers determine the importance of criteria. The results are illustrated in Table 1. Then the alternatives are assessed based on qualitative factors. Table 2 shows the output of assessment for Location 1. Other locations are assessed in the same way. Then, the required data for quantitative criteria are collected. Table 3 illustrates the assessment process. In the next step, final scores are calculated. The score of Location 1 is illustrated in Table 4. Then, the triangular fuzzy numbers are defuzzified, and finally the

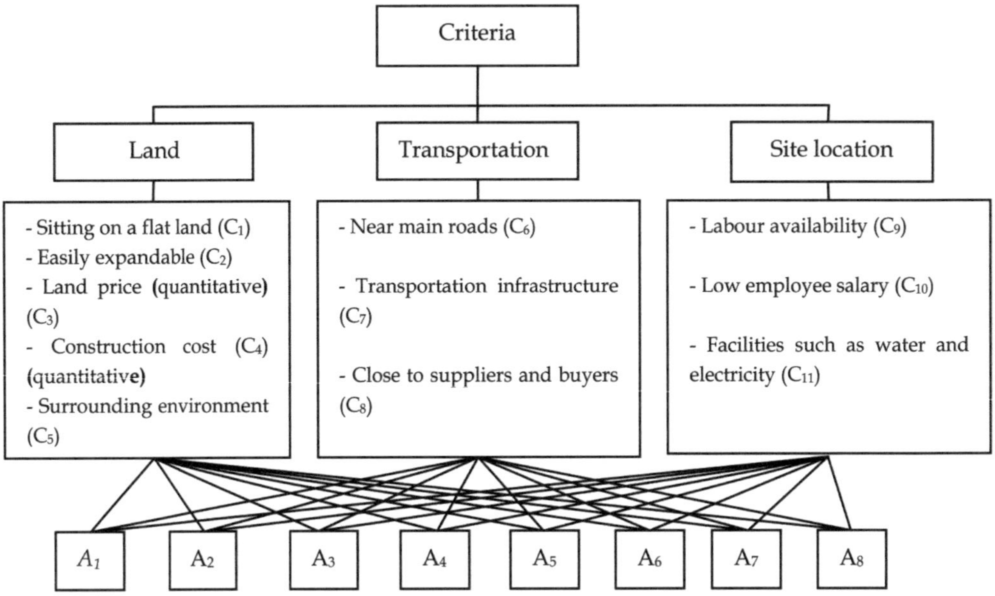

Fig. 6. Location criteria

Criteria	DM_1	DM_2	DM_3	Weights of criteria (w_m)
C_1	M	M	L	(1.3 ,4 ,7)
C_2	M	H	H	(4, 7, 9.3)
C_3	VH	VH	H	(7, 9.3, 10)
C_4	M	L	M	(1.3, 4, 7)
C_5	M	L	M	(1.3, 4, 7)
C_6	VH	H	H	(6, 8.7, 10)
C_7	H	H	H	(5, 8, 10)
C_8	H	M	M	(3, 6, 8.7)
C_9	H	H	H	(5, 8, 10)
C_{10}	M	M	M	(2, 5, 8)
C_{11}	H	VH	VH	(7, 9.3, 10)

Table 1. Importance of criteria

A_1	DM_1	DM_2	DM_3	Aggregated weights (A_{m1})
C_1	M	L	M	(1.3, 4, 7)
C_2	L	VL	M	(0.7, 2.3, 5)
C_5	H	H	M	(4, 7, 9.3)
C_6	VH	H	VH	(7, 9.3, 10)
C_7	L	L	VL	(0, 1.3, 4)
C_8	M	M	L	(1.3, 4, 7)
C_9	H	H	M	(4, 7, 9.3)
C_{10}	H	VH	H	(0, 8.7, 10)
C_{11}	L	VL	L	(0, 1.3, 4)

Table 2. Assessment of location 1

Data	A_1	A_2	A_3	A_4	A_5	A_6	A_7	A_8
C_3	26	30	31	30	40	25	30	28
C_4	12	15	12	14	10	15	13	13
Normalised	**data**							
C_3	9.6	8.3	8.1	8.3	6.3	10	8.3	8.9
C_4	8.3	6.7	8.3	7.1	10	6.7	7.7	7.7

Table 3. Assessment of all locations based on quantitative criteria

	C_1	C_2	C_3	C_4	C_5	C_6	C_7	C_8	C_9	C_{10}	C_{11}	**Score**	**Defuzzified score**
w_m	(1.3 ,4 ,7)	(4, 7, 9.3)	(7, 9.3, 10)	(1.3, 4, 7)	(1.3, 4, 7)	(6, 8.7, 10)	(5, 8, 10)	(3, 6, 8.7)	(5, 8, 10)	(2, 5, 8)	(7, 9.3, 10)		
A_1	(1.3, 4, 7)	(0.7, 2.3, 5)	(9.6, 9.6, 9.6)	(8.3, 8.3, 8.3)	(4, 7, 9.3)	(7, 9.3, 10)	(0, 1.3, 4)	(1.3, 4, 7)	(4, 7, 9.3)	(0, 8.7, 10)	(0, 1.3, 4)	(153.58, 409.48, 728.6)	425.29

Table 4. Score of Location 1

	A_1	A_2	A_3	A_4	A_5	A_6	A_7	A_8
Defuzzified score	425.29	423.50	432.47	454.22	431.45	459.73	442.07	455.66
Rank	7	8	5	3	6	1	4	2

Table 5. Final ranking for the first phase

locations are ranked. It can be inferred from Table 5 that the best three locations are A_6, A_8, and A_4. The decision makers evaluate these three alternatives in the second phase.

In the second phase, locations A_4, A_6, and A_8 are evaluated by the fuzzy QFD method to select the best alternative. Reasonable Cost, Nice Finish, Lightweight, Strength and Durable are chosen as customer requirements. Now, the decision makers should define suitable location criteria. The location criteria include Economic (EC), Technological (TE), Social (SO), Political (PO), and Environmental (EC) factors. The linguistic set is utilized to express the opinions of experts. Each of three decision makers established the level of importance or weight for customer requirements. The related results are shown in Table 6.

The manager of the company has determined a weight for each decision maker. In this example, there are three decision makers. However, one of them has more experience. Therefore, the manager has devoted the weights as r_1 = 0.4, r_2 = 0.3, and r_3 = 0.3. The aggregated weights are calculated in Table 7, where P = 5, M = 5, and K = 3. The opinions of three decision-makers, on the impact of each DR on each CR are shown in Table 8.

Customer requirements (CR)	DM$_1$	DM$_2$	DM$_3$
Reasonable Cost	H	L	M
Nice Finish	L	M	H
Lightweight	H	VH	H
Strength	H	M	H
Durable	M	L	L

Table 6. Importance of CR

CR	DM$_1$	DM$_2$	DM$_3$	
r_i	0.4	0.3	0.3	Aggregated weights
Reasonable Cost	(5, 8, 10)	(0, 2, 5)	(2, 5, 8)	(2.6, 5.3, 7.9)
Nice Finish	(0, 2, 5)	(2, 5, 8)	(5, 8, 10)	(2.1, 4.7, 7.4)
Lightweight	(5, 8, 10)	(8, 10, 10)	(5, 8, 10)	(5.9, 8.6, 10)
Strength	(5, 8, 10)	(2, 5, 8)	(5, 8, 10)	(4.1, 7.1, 9.4)
Durable	(2, 5, 8)	(0, 2, 5)	(0, 2, 5)	(0.8, 3.2, 6.2)

Table 7. Aggregated weight

DR	Economic (EC)			Technical (TE)			Social (SO)		
CR	DM$_1$	DM$_2$	DM$_3$	DM$_1$	DM$_2$	DM$_3$	DM$_1$	DM$_2$	DM$_3$
Reasonable Cost	VH	H	H	M	H	H	H	H	H
Nice Finish	M	H	M	H	L	M	L	M	L
Lightweight	M	H	L	VH	VH	H	VL	VL	M
Strength	M	H	H	M	M	H	L	M	L
Durable	L	M	M	H	H	H	L	M	M

DR	Political (PO)			Environmental (EN)		
CR	DM$_1$	DM$_2$	DM$_3$	DM$_1$	DM$_2$	DM$_3$
Reasonable Cost	L	M	M	H	M	H
Nice Finish	H	H	VH	L	VL	L
Lightweight	H	M	H	L	L	L
Strength	VH	H	H	VL	L	L
Durable	H	VH	H	L	M	L

Table 8. Impact of each design requirement (DR) on each customer requirement (CR)

The aggregated weights between CR and DR are calculated. Here again, the a_{mp} elements are triangular fuzzy numbers (Fig. 7). Besides, prioritized technical descriptors are obtained. The fuzzy values are shown in matrix F of Fig. 7. Then, the impact of each potential location on the attributes is considered. Table 9 shows each decision maker's opinions on the various locations in relation to each attribute. Then, location rating is calculated. The FI is calculated by using Eq. (16). The related results are written in Table 10. Furthermore, triangular fuzzy numbers have defuzzified by Eq. (10). Now, the alternatives can be ranked. Ultimate ranking and scores are given in Table 11. According to this table, the eighth alternative (i.e., A_8) is the best one to establish a new factory.

	Economic (EC)	Technical (TE)	Social (SO)	Political (PO)	Environmental (EN)	
Cost	(6.2, 8.8, 10)	(3.8, 6.8, 9.2)	(5, 8, 10)	(1.2, 3.8, 6.8)	(4.1, 7.1, 9.4)	(2.6, 5.3, 7.9)
Nice Finish	(2.9, 5.9, 8.6)	(2.6, 5.3, 7.9)	(0.6, 2.9, 5.9)	(5.9, 8.6, 10)	(0, 1.4, 4.1)	(2.1, 4.7, 7.4)
Lightweight	(2.3, 5, 7.7)	(7.1, 9.4, 10)	(0.6, 1.5, 3.8)	(4.1, 7.1, 9.4)	(0, 2, 5)	(5.9, 8.6, 10)
Strength	(3.8, 6.8, 9.2)	(2.9, 5.9, 8.6)	(0.6, 2.9, 5.9)	(6.2, 8.8, 10)	(0, 1.2, 3.8)	(4.1, 7.1, 9.4)
Durable	(1.2, 3.8, 6.8)	(5, 8, 10)	(1.2, 3.8, 6.8)	(5.9, 8.6, 10)	(0.6, 2.9, 5.9)	(0.8, 3.2, 6.2)
	f_1	f_2	f_3	f_4	f_5	
	(52.3, 177.8, 348.2)	(73.1, 209.2, 373.9)	(21.2, 101.6, 258.2)	(69.8, 211.6, 377.7)	(11.1, 79.2, 226.9)	

Fig. 7. Completed fuzzy HOQ

DR	Economic **(EC)**			Technical **(TE)**			Social **(SO)**		
CR	**DM$_1$**	**DM$_2$**	**DM$_3$**	**DM$_1$**	**DM$_2$**	**DM$_3$**	**DM$_1$**	**DM$_2$**	**DM$_3$**
A_4	L	VL	L	H	VH	H	H	M	H
A_6	L	L	M	L	M	H	M	L	M
A_8	M	H	M	H	H	VH	H	M	H

DR	Political **(PO)**			Environmental **(EN)**		
CR	**DM$_1$**	**DM$_2$**	**DM$_3$**	**DM$_1$**	**DM$_2$**	**DM$_3$**
A_4	H	H	H	M	H	M
A_6	M	M	L	H	H	H
A_8	H	H	H	VL	L	L

Table 9. Impact of each location on the attributes

FI	a	b	c
A_4	179	985	2664
A_6	73	683	2321
A_8	203	1071	2759

Table 10. Calculation of the FI index

	Score	Rank
A_4	1204	2
A_6	940	3
A_8	1276	1

Table 11. Defuzzification

7. Conclusions

Location selection is a multi-criteria decision making (MCDM) problem. In this chapter, this selection is performed in two phases. In the first phase (i.e., pre-qualification selection), a set of alternatives are selected by the proposed fuzzy method. This method can handle qualitative and quantitative criteria. In the second phase (i.e., final selection), quality function deployment (QFD) is utilized to select the best location. QFD is a unique tool considering the relationship between product and location criteria. In addition, linguistic variables and triangular fuzzy numbers are used to overcome the vagueness in human's thought.

In this study, the matrix of the house of quality (HOQ) is applied to select the best alternative. Future research can be performed based on two or more QFD matrices. For instance, the roll of process operations can also be taken into account. Besides, the fuzzy set theory can be replaced by some methods, such as robust and stochastic optimization for determining the relationship between product criteria and engineering design characteristics. It is worth to apply these methods in QFD and compare the efficiency of them.

8. References

Berman, O., Drezner, Z., & Wesolowsky, G. O. (2001). Location of facilities on a network with groups of demand points, *IIE Transactions*, 33(8), 637-648.

Bevilacqua, M., Ciarapica, F. E., & Giacchetta, G. (2006). A fuzzy QFD approach to supplier selection, *Journal Purchasing and Supply Management*, 12(1) 14-27.

Bouchereau, V., & Rowlands, H. (2000). Methods and techniques to help quality function deployment (QFD), *The International Journal of Quality and Reliability Management*, 7(1), 8-19.

Buyukozkan, G., Feyzioglu, O., & Ruan, D. (2007). Fuzzy group decision-making to multiple preference formats in quality function deployment, *Computers in Industry*, 58(5), 392-402.

Canel, C., Khumawala, B. M., Law, J., & Loh, A. (2001). Algorithm for the capacitated multi-commodity multi-period facility location problem, *Computers and Operations Research*, 28(5), 411-427.

Chan, L. K., & Wu, M. L. (2002). Quality function deployment: A literature review, *European Journal of Operational Research*, 143(3), 463-497.

Chan, L. K., & Wu, M. L. (2005). A systematic approach to quality function deployment with a full illustrative example, *Omega*, 33(2), 119-139.

Chen, C. T. (2001). A fuzzy approach to select the location of the distribution center, *Fuzzy Sets and Systems*, 118(1), 65-73.

Chen, L. H., & Weng, M. C. (2003). A fuzzy model for exploiting quality function deployment, *Mathematical and Computer Modelling*, 38(5-6), 559-570.

Chen, L. H., & Ko, W. C. (2008). A fuzzy nonlinear model for quality function deployment considering Kano's concept, *Mathematical and Computer Modelling*, 48(3-4), 581-593.

Chen, L. H., & Ko, W. C. (2009). Fuzzy approaches to quality function deployment for new product design, *Fuzzy sets and systems*, 160(18), 2620-2639.

Chin, K. S., Wang, Y. M., & Yang, J. B., & Poon, K. K. G. (2009). An evidential reasoning based approach for quality function deployment under uncertainty, *Expert Systems with Applications*, 36(3), 5684-5694.

Chou, T. Y., Hsu, C. L., & Chen, M. C. (2008). A fuzzy multi-criteria decision model for international tourist hotels location selection, *International Journal of Hospitality Management*, 27(2), 293-301.

Chuang, P. (2002). A QFD approach for distribution's location model, *International Journal of Quality & Reliability Management*, 19(8-9), 1037-1054.

Cohen, L. (1995). *Quality Function Deployment – How to Make QFD Work for You*, Addison-Wesley Publishing, Reading, MA, UK.

Delice, E. K., & Gungor, Z. (2009). A new mixed integer linear programming model for product development using quality function deployment, *Computers & Industrial Engineering*, 57(3), 906-912.

Fung, R. Y. K., Chena, Y., & Tang, J. (2006). Estimating the functional relationships for quality function deployment under uncertainties, *Fuzzy Sets and Systems*, 157(1), 98-120.

Guneri, A. F., Cengiz, M., & Seker, S. (2009). A fuzzy ANP approach to shipyard location selection, *Expert Systems with Applications*, 36(4), 7992-7999.

Halog, A., Schultmann, F., & Rentz, O. (2001). Using quality function deployment for technique selection for optimum environmental performance improvement, *Journal of Cleaner Production*, 9(5), 387-394.

Han, C. H., Kimb, J. K., & Choi, S. H. (2004). Prioritizing engineering characteristics in quality function deployment with incomplete information: A linear partial ordering approach, *International Journal of Production Economics*, 91(3), 235-249.

Hassanzadeh Amin, S., & Razmi, J. (2009). An integrated fuzzy model for supplier management: A case study of ISP selection and evaluation, *Expert Systems with Applications*, 36(4), 8639-8648.

Hauser, J. R., & Clausing, D. (1988). The house of quality, *Harvard Business Review*, (May/June), 63-73.

Heragu, S. S. (2006). *Facilities Design*, Second edition. iUniverse, Lincoln, NE.

Kahraman, C., Ruan, D., Dogan, I. (2003). Fuzzy group decision-making for facility location selection, *Information Sciences*, 157, 135-153.

Karsak, E. E., Sozer, S., & Alptekin, S. E. (2002). Product planning in quality function deployment using a combined analytic network process and goal programming approach, *Computers & Industrial Engineering*, 44(1), 171-190.

Karsak, E. E. (2004). Fuzzy multiple objective programming framework to prioritize design requirements in quality function deployment, *Computers & Industrial Engineering*, 47(2-3), 149-163.

Kim, K. J., Moskowitz, H., & Dhingra, A., & Evans, G. (2000). Fuzzy multi criteria models for quality function deployment, *European Journal of Operational Research*, 121(3), 504-518.

Kuo, R. J., Chi, S. C., & Kao, S. S. (2002). A decision support system for selecting convenience store location through integration of fuzzy AHP and artificial neural network, *Computers in Industry*, 47(2), 199-214.

Lai, Y. J., & Hwang, C. L. (1995). *Fuzzy Mathematical Programming: Methods and Applications*. Springer-Verlag New York, Inc.

Lee, Y. C., Sheu, L. C., Tsou, Y. G. (2008). Quality function deployment implementation based on Fuzzy Kano model: An application in PLM system, *Computers & Industrial Engineering*, 55(1), 48-63.

Li, S. G., & Kuo, X. (2007). The enhanced quality function deployment for developing virtual items in massive multiplayer online role playing games, *Computers & Industrial Engineering*, 53(4) 628-641.

Liu, H. T. (2009). The extension of fuzzy QFD: From product planning to part deployment, *Expert Systems with Applications*, 36(8), 11131–11144.

Melkote, S., & Daskin, M. S. (2001). Capacitated facility location/network design problems, *European Journal of Operational Research*, 129(3), 481-495.

Myint, S. (2003). A framework of an intelligent quality function deployment (IQFD) for discrete assembly environment, *Computers & Industrial Engineering*, 45(2) 269-283.

Nanthavanij, S.,Yenradee, P. (1999). Predicting the optimum number, location, and signal sound level of auditory warning devices for manufacturing facilities, *International Journal of Industrial Ergonomics*, 24(6), 569-578.

Partovi, F. Y., & Corredoira, R. A. (2002). Quality function deployment for the good of soccer, *European Journal of Operational Research*, 137(3), 642-656.

Partovi, F. Y. (2006). An analytic model for locating facilities strategically, *Omega*, 34(1) 41-55.

Raharjo, H., Brombacher, A. C., & Xie, M. (2008). Dealing with subjectivity in early product design phase: A systematic approach to exploit Quality Function Deployment potentials, *Computers & Industrial Engineering*, 55(1), 253-278.

Ramanathan, R., & Yunfeng, J. (2009). Incorporating cost and environmental factors in quality function deployment using data envelopment analysis, *Omega*, 37(3), 711-723.

Sharma, J. R., Rawani, A. M., & Barahate, M. (2008). Quality function deployment: a comprehensive literature review, *Int. J. Data Analysis Techniques and Strategies*, 1(1), 78-103.

Tang, J., Fung, R. Y. K., Xu, B., & Wang, D. (2002). A new approach to quality function deployment planning with financial consideration, *Computers & Operations Research*, 29(11), 1447-1463.

Temponi, C., Yen, J., & Tiao, W. A. (1999). House of quality: A fuzzy logic-based requirements analysis, *European Journal of Operational Research*, 117(2), 340-354.

Tzeng, G. H., & Chen, Y. W. (1999). Optimal location of airport fire stations: a fuzzy multi-objective programming and revised genetic algorithm approach, *Transportation Planning and Technology*, 23(1), 37-55.

Utne, I. B. (2009). Improving the environmental performance of the fishing fleet by use of Quality Function Deployment (QFD), *Journal of Cleaner Production*, 17(8), 724-731.

Yang, Y. O., Wang, S. O., Dulaimic, M., & Lowa, S. P. (2003). A fuzzy quality function deployment system for buildable design decision-makings, *Automation in Construction*, 12(4), 381-393.

Zadeh, L. A. (1965). Fuzzy sets, *Information and Control*, 8(1), 338-353.

Zhang, Z., & Chu, X. (2009). Fuzzy group decision-making for multi-format and multi-granularity linguistic judgments in quality function deployment, *Expert Systems with Applications*, 36(5), 9150-9158.

Zimmermann, H. (2001). *Fuzzy set theory and its applications*. Boston: Kluwer Academic Publishers.

13

Simultaneous Pick-up and Delivery Decision Support Systems

Cevriye Gencer[1], Emel Kızılkaya Aydoğan[2] and Suna Çetin[3]
[1]Department of Industrial Engineering, Faculty of Engineering and Architecture, Gazi University,
[2]Department of Industrial Engineering, Faculty of Engineering, Erciyes University,
[3]Department of Industrial Engineering, Faculty of Engineering, Kırıkkale University
Turkey

1. Introduction

The problems concerning the distribution of goods between depots and final users are known as Vehicle Routing Problems (VRP). Dantzig & Ramser (1959) introduced VRP. The authors described a real world application and proposed the first mathematical programming formulation and algorithmic approach for the solution of the problem.

Let G= (V, A) is a graph where $V=\{v_0,v_1,\cdots v_n\}$ is a vertex set and $A=\{(v_i,v_j):v_i,v_j\in V, i\neq j\}$ is an arc set. v_0 represents depot and v_i represents customers. Every customer has a nonnegative demand q_i.

VRP consist of finding a collection of vehicle routes with minimum cost such that (1) each route starts and end at the depot, (2) each customer is visited exactly once by one vehicle, (3) the total demand of each route does not exceed vehicle capacity, (4) the total duration of each route (including travel and service times) does not exceed a present limit, (5) the total routing cost is minimized. Typical applications of VRP are solid waste collection, street cleaning, school bus routing, transportation of handicapped persons etc.

Variants of VRP, which have some extensions on basic VRP, are given in Figure 1 (Toth & Vigo, 2002).

In vehicle routing problems with pick up and delivery (VRPPD) every customer has two demands as pick up demand (*pi*) and delivery demand (*di*). Delivery demand refers to amount of goods transporting from depot to customer, pickup demands refers to amount of goods transporting from customer to depot. VRPPD is classified into three groups due to servicing delivery and pick up demands as

- Delivery first- pickup second,
- Mixed pickups and deliveries,
- Simultaneous pickups and deliveries.

Delivery first- pickup second VRPPD: Customers are visited more than once. Goods are transported from depot to delivery customers then pick up customers are visited and goods are transported back to the depot. There is precedence between delivery and pick up customers.

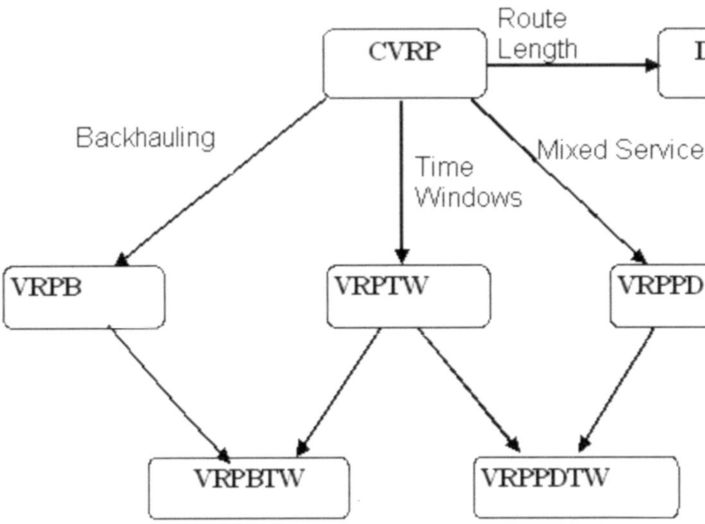

Fig. 1. The basic problems of the VRP

Mixed pickups and deliveries VRPPD: There is not precedence between delivery and pick up customers in. Delivery demand and pick up demands is serviced in a mixed sequence. Customers are visited more than once.

Simultaneous pickups and deliveries VRPPD: Delivery and pick up demand are serviced simultaneously (this problem is denoted as VRPSPD). Customers are visited only once.

VRPSPD is NP -hard combinatorial optimization problem as it is a version of VRP. VRPSPD consists of finding a set of routes such that,

- Each route starts and ends at the depot,
- Each customer is visited by one vehicle,
- Pick up and delivery demands are totally satisfied,
- Through the route load of vehicle does not exceed vehicle capacity,
- Total cost is minimized.

VRPSPD is encountered in real life. In the soft drink industry full bottles are transported from depot to markets, empty bottles are returned back to the depots in the grocery industry goods flow from depot to market while outdated products flow to depots are examples for VRPSPD.

VRP classified into two groups considering properties of vehicles as capacity, fixed and variable cost. If all vehicles have same capacity, variable and fixed cost values this problem is called as homogeneous VRP; otherwise, means one or more of these properties are different for a vehicle, problem is known as heterogeneous VRP (HVRP).

In the literature, three HVRP versions have been studied. The first one was introduced by Golden, in which variable costs are uniformly given over all vehicle types with the number of available vehicles assumed to be unlimited for each type. This version is also called the vehicle fleet mix (VFM), the fleet size and mix VRP or the fleet size and composition VRP.

The second version considers the variable costs, dependent on vehicle type, which is neglected in the first version. This version is the one dealt with in this paper, and referred to as the HVRP, the VFM with variable unit running costs or the mix fleet VRP. The third one, called the VRP with a heterogeneous fleet of vehicles or heterogeneous fixed fleet VRP, generalizes the second version by limiting the number of available vehicles of each type (Choi & Tcha, 2007).

2. Literature review of VRPSPD

VRPSPD was introduced by Min (1989). He proposed an algorithm for transportation of books between libraries, with one depot, two vehicles and 22 customers. His algorithm is based on cluster first-route second approach. Dethloff (2001) proposed mathematical formulation for the problem and also he develops an insertion-based heuristic to solve the problem. The insertion criterion takes into account three metrics: travel distance, residual capacity, and radial surcharge. Nagy & Salhi (2005) presented a number of heuristics for vehicle routing problem with picks up and deliveries, which are capable of solving both VRPSPD, and mixed VRPPD. Bianchess & Righini (2007) presented and compare performance of constructive algorithms, local search and tabu search algorithms. Tang Montane & Galvao (2006) proposed a mathematical formulation and a tabu search algorithm, which is intensified and diversified by the use of frequency penalization scheme for VRPSPD. Zachariadis et al. (2009a) proposed a hybrid metaheuristic approach based on tabu search and guided local search. Gajpal & Abad (2009) presented an ant colony system algorithm for VRPSPD. Ai & Kachitvchyanukul (2009) proposed mathematical formulation and a particle swarm optimization algorithm for VRPSPD. The formulation is generalizations of mathematical formulation of VRPSPD literatures Min, Dethloff, Tang and Galvao. Chen & Wu (2006) proposed a hybrid metaheuristic method based on record-to-record travel tabu list and route improvements routines. Zachariadis et al. (2009b) presented an adaptive memory programming methodology algorithm fort he VRPSPD.

3. Decision support systems

The limitations of OR algorithms alone to fully meet the needs of business decision-makers became obvious in a number of fields and this led to the development of the concept of a DSS. A Decision Support System (DSS) assists management decision making by combining data, sophisticated analytical models and tools, and user-friendly software into a single powerful system that can support semi structured or unstructured decision making. The main purpose of DSS is not to make a decision but to assist making a decision.

Power (2001) has presented an expanded decision support system framework containing the model driven DSS, data driven DSS, communications-driven DSS, document driven DSS and web-based DSS.

Model-driven DSS emphasizes access to and manipulation of financial, optimization and/or simulation models. Model-driven DSS use limited data and parameters provided by decision makers to aid decision makers in analyzing a situation (Power, 2002). Data-driven DSS emphasizes access to and manipulation of a time-series of internal company data and sometimes external and real-time data. Communications-driven DSS use network and communications technologies to facilitate decision-relevant collaboration and communication (Power, 2002). Document-driven DSS uses computer storage and processing

technologies to provide document retrieval and analysis. Knowledge-driven DSS can suggest or recommend actions to managers. These DSS are person-computer systems with specialized problem-solving expertise (Power, 2002). Power (1998) defined a Web-based decision support system as a computerized system that delivers decision support information or decision support tools to a manager or business analyst using a "thin-client" Web browser like Netscape Navigator or Internet Explorer.
In our chapter, we will use model-driven DSS and interfaces are written in Visual Basic 6.0, and computations are executed by a program coded in C++ 6.0. This DSS provides the user a simple data entry and result processing environment.

4. The illustrative applications for DSS

The applications related to the use of DDS with homogenous fleet VRPSPD and heterogeneous fleet VRPSPD are included in this chapter.

4.1. DSS for homogeneous fleet VRPSPD

Same or different vehicle characteristics in VRP define a new VRP. Homogeneous fleet VRP is the VRP adopted in case the vehicles have the same capacity, fixed and variable costs. Since NP-hard structure of VRP and variance of its vehicle characteristics make this structure more complex, generally homogeneous structure is studied in the literature.
Application 1: A decision support system application, which is based on simultaneous pickup and delivery vehicle routing models for transporting the domestic transfer demands reported to the Transportation Command (Gencer & Yaşa, 2007).
Within the Transportation Command, seven permanent shuttle routes are assigned in nationwide and, the weekly transportation service on these routes is organized. Assigned permanent shuttle routes are as follows:

1. Shuttle A (1860 km.)
2. Shuttle B (2030 km.)
3. Shuttle C (824 km)
4. Shuttle D (1920 km.)
5. Shuttle E (1570 km)
6. Shuttle F (1550 km.)
7. Shuttle G (983 km)

Present Condition

The route of shuttle and the number of routes are established in time considering the need. This number is not questioned scientifically. While assigning the routes, it is regarded to have a factory command on each of the routes; however, the amount of demand is not taken into evaluation. Routes to be followed are permanent; demands are variable. Consequently, routes should change according to the varying demands.

Suggested DSS

The aim of this application is to maintain the VRP 2.0 route program decision support system, which would minimize the distance travelled for shuttle tours and the number of vehicles to be used. The software is developed on the basis of the mathematical model of Dethloff (Dethloff, 2001). Dethloff's algorithm is an insertion basis heuristic algorithm. Transportation Command aims to ensure a safe transportation at a minimum cost.

Problem Assumptions

Demands are known beforehand (before the vehicles start their routes)
Demands are covered from one depot.
Depot is the starting and final point of every vehicle.
No transportation is made between the points on the route.
Pick-up and delivery demands of every customer are serviced simultaneously
Each customer should be visited for once.
There are enough vehicles for transportation.
DSS main components of VRP 2.0 Route program are shown in Figure 2.

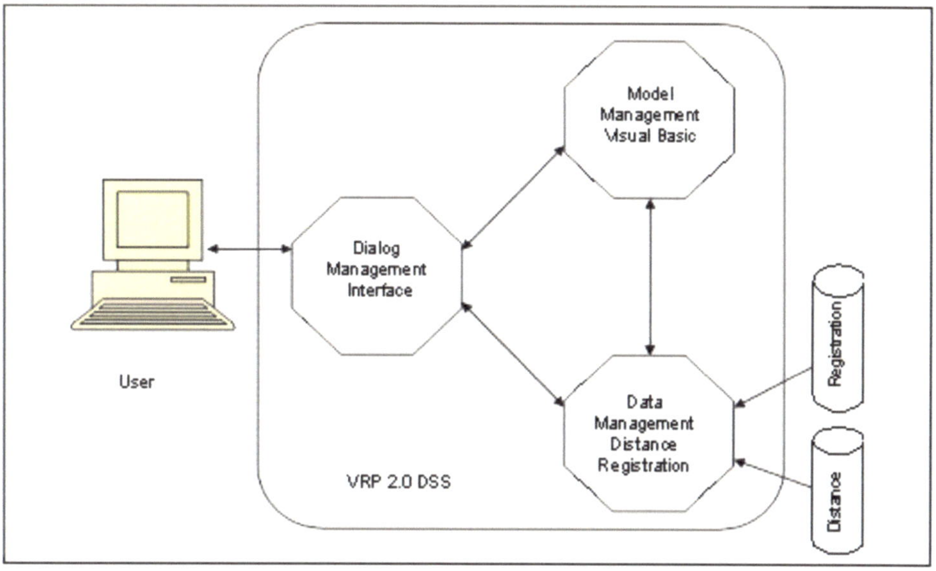

Fig. 2. DSS's Main Components of the VRP 2.0 Route Program

VRP2.0 program is composed of two interfaces, which enable to find the shortest routes and to computerize the routes. The first interface is the interface into which data and calculation criteria are entered. The amount of supply to be delivered to and picked-up from the provinces and capacity of vehicle to be used are entered into this interface. In the program, there are boxes for the vehicles with a capacity of 15m^3 , 30 m^3, 45 m^3, 60 m^3. While different capacities are defined for the vehicles, homogeneous fleet vehicles are used. Considering the possible use of different vehicles in future, the choice of "other" is added which enables manual entry into the system. During data entry, the program automatically collects delivery and pick-up amounts that have been entered till "load to be delivered" and "load to be picked-up" boxes. GAMA and LAMDA values, which show the penalty and bonus coefficients, are entered in the form of 0 and 1. After all data and calculation criteria are entered; calculation button is pushed and calculation process starts. The calculation interface of the program is given in Figure 3. When the calculation process is completed, the results are displayed in the final interface shown in Figure 4. This interface presents the number of routes and the provinces creating the route respectively, the length of that route and the information of the total amount of load to be delivered and picked-up on the route;

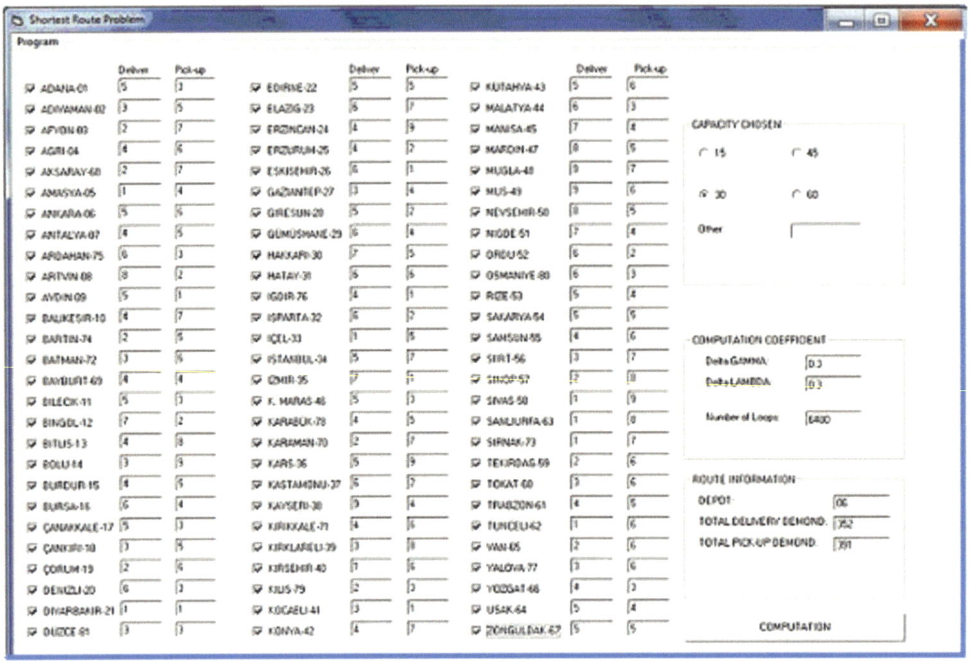

Fig. 3. Computation Interface of the VRP 2.0 Program

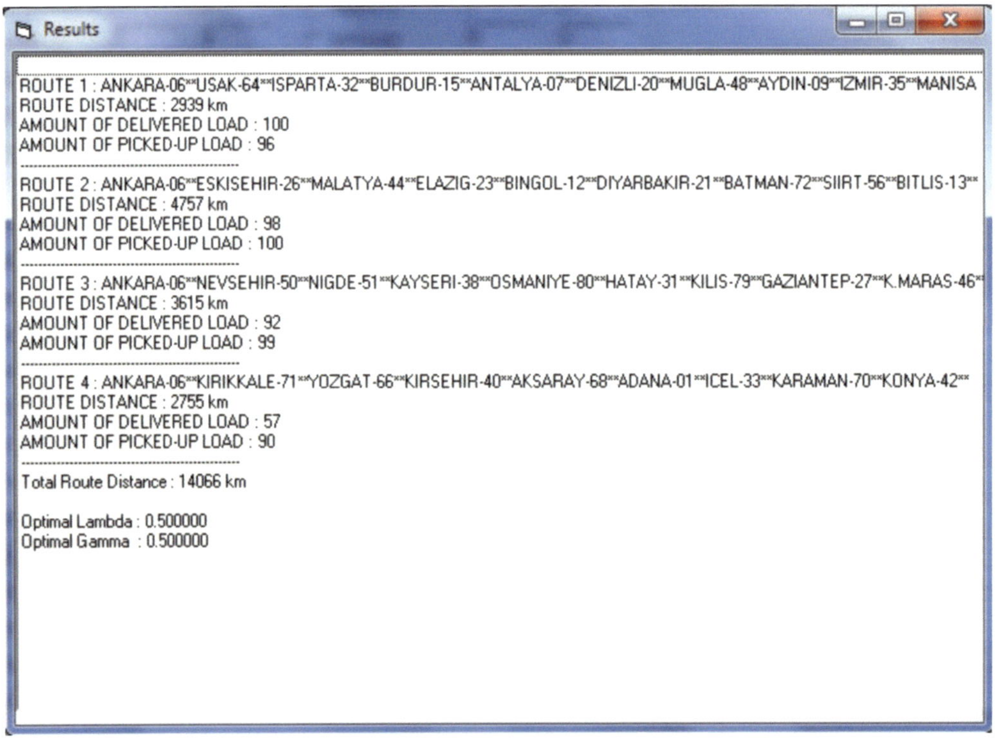

Fig. 4. Conclusion Interface of the VRP2.0 Program

moreover the total length of all routes and the penalty and bonus coefficients related to the routes. When double-clicked, any of the lines in the final interface is displayed in a message box format. Figure 5, for instance, shows which provinces are involved in the first route respectively. First route is: Ankara - Uşak - Isparta - Burdur - Antalya - Denizli -Muğla - Aydın - İzmir - Manisa -Balıkesir - Çanakkale - Edirne - Kırklareli - Tekirdağ- İstanbul - Bursa - Yalova - Kocaeli – Sakarya-Düzce - Bolu - Ankara.
In VRP2.0 software, interfaces are derived by visual basic 6.0 programming language; calculations are derived via a program that is coded in C++ 6.0 language.

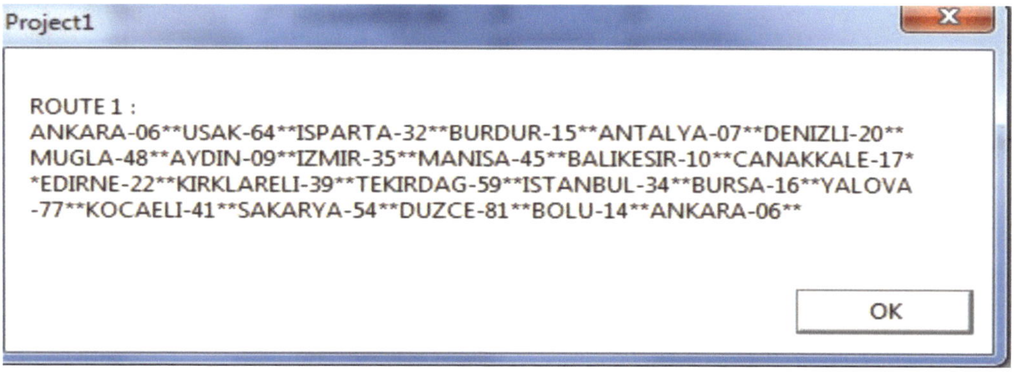

Fig. 5. Route Message Box of the VRP2.0 Program

4.2 DSS for heterogonous fleet VRPSPD

Although it is encountered frequently in theory, vehicle fleets of application are generally heterogeneous rather than homogeneous. In other words; vehicle fleets are composed of vehicles with different capacity, fixed and variable costs or specific containers. Consequently; in real life applications, heterogeneous fleet vehicle routing problems are encountered. However; since the resolution of heterogeneous fleet VRP is difficult, it is not regarded as an issue to be studied by the researchers. Therefore, only limited numbers of studies have been conducted on this issue to date.
Application 2: A decision support system application which is based on heterogeneous fleet vehicle routing problem with simultaneous pick up and delivery for transporting the domestic transfer demands reported to the Transportation Command (Özkütük, 2008).
In addition to the assumptions in Application 1, the assumptions below are defined.

- There is no heterogeneous vehicle fleet in depot
- Every type of vehicle in depot is restricted.
- Fixed and variable costs of every type of vehicle are variable and different from each other.

Flowchart diagram for Application 2 is shown in Figure 6.
"Calculate all combinations of the vehicles in each route" box in Figure 6 is a result of heterogeneous VRP of problem. The third type heterogeneous fleet VRP "the number of vehicles from every type is restricted and every type of vehicle has a different cost", which is identified in literature, was studied during the study. Determining the proposed algorithm vehicle fleet compound is developed on the basis of Taillard's (1996) algorithm and, comparison of costs method is applied.

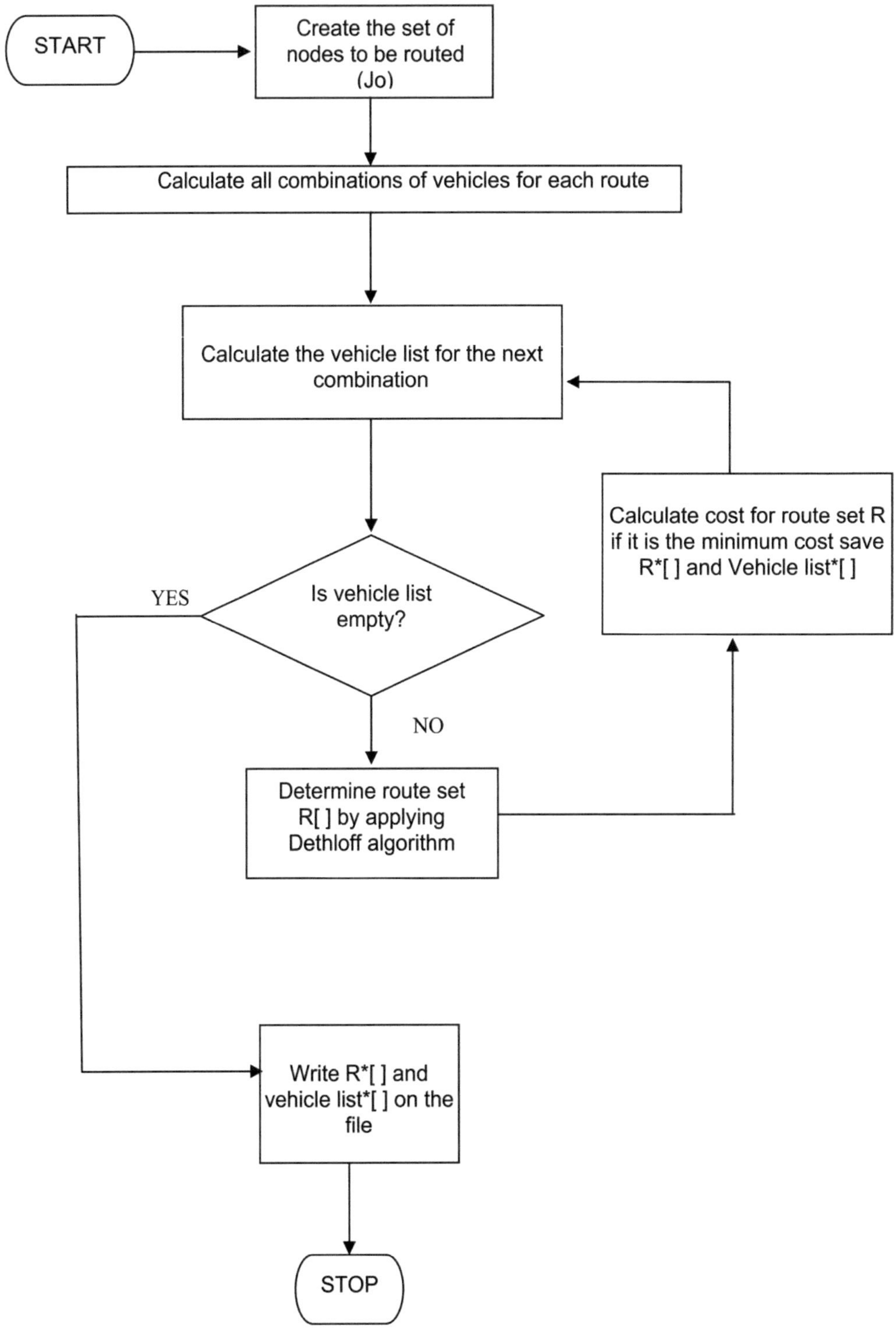

Fig. 6. Flowchart of proposed algorithm

The DSS interfaces related to the problem was prepared using Visual Basic 6.0 and the computation algorithm is coded using C++. The program has two main interfaces; the first one is where the data is entered and the second one is where results are presented. The input interface is where data and calculation criteria is entered by the user. Here, delivery and pick up nodes are determined preliminarily, and pick up and delivery demand of each customer is entered. Total delivery demand and total pick up demand are computed automatically as the data is entered. In capacity option, numbers of each vehicle type, capacity, fixed and variable cost of each vehicle are entered. If total delivered and total picked up load is more than vehicle capacity, a warning with red character as "total vehicle capacity is not enough" is written in Route Information option and program does not carry on calculation. After entering material and vehicle information, penalty and bonus coefficients gamma and lamda respectively, which are between 0 and 1 are entered in computation coefficient option. Clicking computation button starts the calculation. In order to avoid repetitive data entry by the user if repeating material transfers exist, two buttons namely "Save" and "Load" is located at the program menu. After entering the data using "Save" button all transfer information is registered and "Load" button may be used to call same data to the program. Input interface of the program is given in Figure 7.

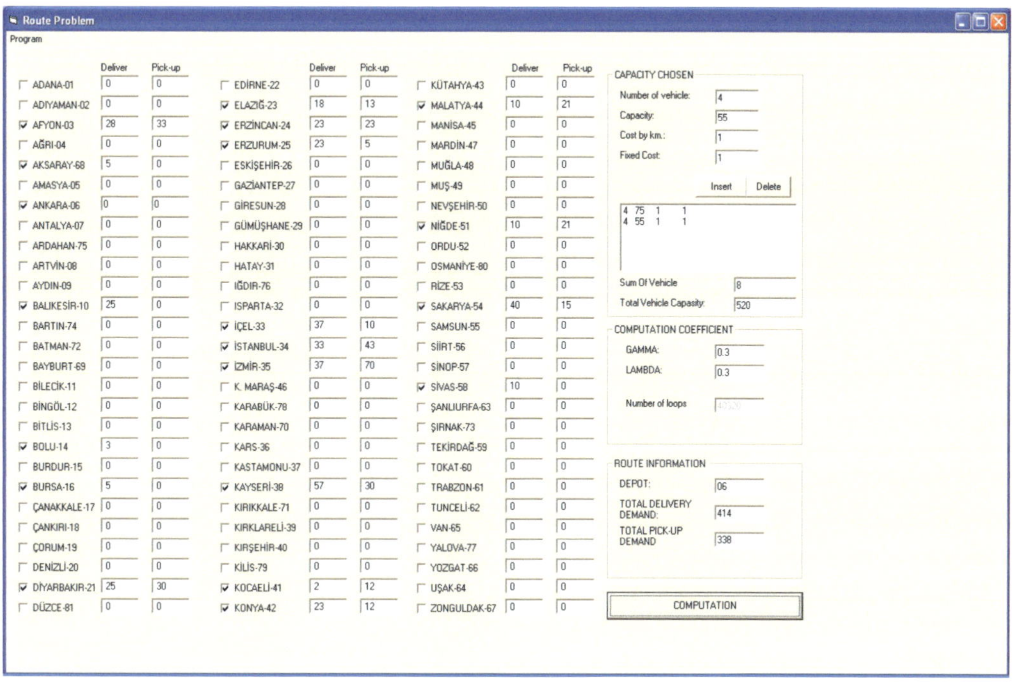

Fig. 7. Decision Support System Input Interface

While "computation" button is used, if the depot is not chosen a warning message as given in Figure 8.

When calculation is finished, an interface, where routes are shown on an output interface, where details of the route is given in Figure 9. Routes, vehicle types used in route, total distance, total cost and amount of picked up and delivered load are given in output interface.

Fig. 8. Warning when depot is not chosen

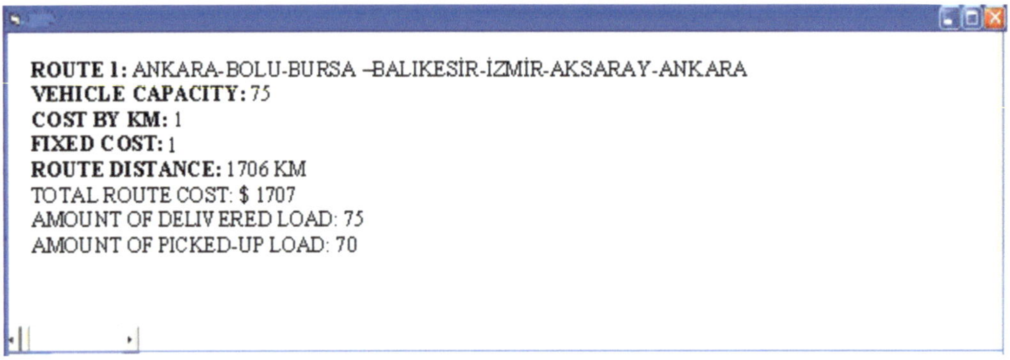

Fig. 9. Output Interface

5. Conclusion

Model-oriented DSS was proposed for the solution of homogeneous and heterogeneous fleet VRPSPD encountered in real life situations.

DSS is a system which enables better understanding of the data about the decision; gives support to decision-maker in establishing more effective decision options and determining the alternatives and; increases the possibility of making the right decision. Mainly DSS constitutes a scientific environment which the decision maker uses and analyzes as he wants and which gives the opportunity to make the decision in a more informed way about the conditions requiring decision making.

VRPSPD are the problems in which delivery and pick-up demands of customers are covered simultaneously along the route. So the customers are visited only for once. VRPSPD are applied in real life in cargo firms; delivery of milk/soda/coke/beer and the empty bottle pick up; delivery and pick up of the personnel to stations in the firms working on shift basis; domestic or local medication delivery and the expired medication pick up; goods delivery and defective or recycle supply pick up from factories to main dealer or from main dealer to small dealers;, and sending the required blood from blood centers to hospitals and transferring the donated blood to blood centers. As understood from the application fields, VRPSPD is used in both service and production systems.

The components need to be known are the order of the delivery and pick up points (by considering the extent of vehicle capacity), where delivery and pick up process is carried out; the number of the vehicle characteristics to be used; their intersected distance; and related costs. In the places where the identified duties are performed regularly, delivery and pick up activities might show repetition from the monthly-weekly-daily or within day aspect. A decision maker system would be required to perform these repetitive procedures in a fast, effective and a scientific way. DSS might be helpful to cover the requirement of a decision maker. Therefore; the solution of VRPSPD could be used for DSS.

6. References

Ai, T. & Kachitvichyanukul, V. (2009). A particle swarm optimization for the vehicle routing problem with simultaneous pickup and delivery. *Computers & Operations Research,* 36, 1693-1702

Bianchessi, N. & Righini, G. (2007). Heuristic algorithms for the vehicle routing problem with simultaneous pick-up and delivery. *Computers & Operations Research,* 34, 578-594

Chen, JF. & Wu, TH. (2006). Vehicle routing problem with simultaneous deliveries and pickups. *The Journal of the Operational Research Society*, 57, 5, 579-587

Choi, E. & Tcha, DW. (2007). A column generation approach to the heterogeneous fleet vehicle routing problem. *Computers & Operations Research,*34, 2080-2095

Dantzig, G.B. & Ramser, J.H. (1959). The truck dispatching problem, Management Science, 6-80

Dethloff, J. (2001). Vehicle routing and reverse logistics:the vehicle routing problem with simultaneous delivery and pick-up. *OR Spectrum*, 23, 79-96

Gajpal, Y. & Abad, P. (2009). An ant colony system (ACS) for vehicle routing problem with simultaneous delivery and pick up. *Computers & Operations Research,* 36, 3215-3223

Gencer, C. & Yaşa, Ö. (2007). Simultaneous pick-up and delivery decision support systems of transportation command shuttle tour's. Journal of the Faculty of Engineering an Architecture of *Gazi University*, 22(3), 437-450

Min, H. (1989). The multiple vehicle routing problem with simultaneous delivery and pick up points. *Transportation Research A*, 23,5, 377-386

Nagy, G. & Salhi, S. (2005). Heuristic algorithms for single and multiple depot vehicle routing problems with pickups and deliveries. European journal of operational research, 162, 1, 126-141

Özkütük E. (2008). A heuristic algorithm for solving the heterogeneous fleet vehicle routing problem with simultaneous delivery and pick up and decision support system with an application, Master Thesis, Turkish Military Academy Defence Science Institute

Power, D. J. (1998). Web-based Decision Support Systems. *DSstar, The On-Line Executive Journal for Data-Intensive Decision Support*, 2, 33-34.

Power, D. J. (2001) Supporting Decision-Makers: An Expanded Framework, In *Harriger, A. (Editor), e-Proceedings Informing Science Conference*, Krakow, Poland, June 19-22, 431-436.

Power, D. J. (2002) *Decision Support Systems: Concepts and Resources for Managers*, Westport, CT: Greenwood/Quorum

Taillard, E.D. (1996). A heuristic column generation methof for the heterogeneous fleet VRP, *Publication CRT*, 3, 1-13

Tang Montane F.A. & Galvao R.D. (2006). A tabu search algorithm for the vehicle routing problem with simultaneous pick up and delivery service, *Computers & Operations Research*, 33, 595-619

Toth, P. & Vigo, D. (2002). *The Vehicle Routing Problem.* SIAM

Zachariadis, E.E; Tarantilis, C.D. & Kiranoudis, C. T. (2009). An adaptive memory and methodology for the vehicle routing problem with simultaneous pick-ups and deliveries, *European Journal Of Operational Research*

Zachariadis, E.E.; Tarantilis, C.D. & Kiranoudis, C. T. (2009). A hybrid metaheuristic algorithm for the vehicle routing problem with simultaneous delivery and pick-up service, Expert System with Applications, 36, 1070-1081

14

Decision Mining and Modeling in a Virtual Collaborative Decision Environment

Razvan Petrusel
Babes-Bolyai University of Cluj-Napoca
Romania

1. Introduction

We aim to show in this chapter some meaningful insights regarding a Virtual Collaborative Decision Environment (VCDE) prototype. The main goal of VCDE is to provide an environment for enterprise collaborative decisions using a DSS-like approach. The simulation is DSS-like because it provides the user with all the necessary information and tools that ensure a documented decision regarding all major aspects of a virtual company. The characteristics of the multi-agent systems as autonomy, local views and decentralization are also present in the VCDE. Therefore, the user is provided with knowledge over the marketplace; his organization's business capabilities and business processes; and, at a certain extent, over the business knowledge. He is required to use that explicit knowledge in conjunction with his implicit knowledge in order to make decisions over his virtual enterprise. Then, considering the actions of the actors involved in the virtual environment we will automatically mine mainly for the business strategy view, the social networks and also, at a certain extent, for the implicit business knowledge.

This system is developed primarily in order to simulate decision situations as a part of the academic training of students. The second goal of the system is to provide us with user activity logs that will be used in the process of decision pattern mining and decision modeling. This is an important step in achieving our final goal of transforming implicit knowledge of decision makers in explicit knowledge that can be shared. In order to reach our two goals, we first need to model the decisions that will be made by the managers and then, by following every action of each user, mine the activity logs in order to gain insights into the decision making style of each participant.

In the second section of this chapter we will introduce the reader into the particularities of the problem domain to be presented and we will show how we intend to connect to previous research.

In the third part, the proposed architecture of the system will be introduced. After giving the reader the overview of the system we elaborate on several key aspects of the system like some of the decisions that need to be made, the decision models, the variables involved and the relations between them.

In the fourth section of this chapter, we provide evidence regarding the possibility of: mining decision models from user activity logs; comparing different decision making strategies of users; and building decision reference models. In this section we will also

discuss the methods we implemented for user activity logging, the format of the logs and the proposed mining methods.
In the last section we state our findings so far, as well as the future flow of the project. We also argue the strong points of our research and we show the aspects that still need to be improved.

2. The problem domain and previous research

As stated in the first section we are developing a Virtual Collaborative Decision Environment using a DSS-like approach. There has been done a lot of research in decision support systems, multi agent environments as well as in business simulations. Since it is out of scope to discuss decision support systems definitions and history we will resume ourselves to underlining the most important features of such a system that will be implemented in VCDE. A DSS must provide the decision maker, in an interactive user friendly interface, with all the necessary data and information that allows him to identify a decisional situation and choose one alternative, provide data analysis tools (such as what-if analyzes and simulations). The reason why we consider we have a DSS-like approach over VCDE is that in the software engineering process we mainly focus on decision model development. What we intend to build is a system that acts and looks like a DSS from the user point of view.
Multi agent systems have already been used for modeling and simulating organizational decision making (Sun & Naveh, 2004). We are aiming to create a virtual environment in which students will be represented as intelligent agents managing a company and will interact with each other through the environment. The characteristics of multi agent systems will be present since each company will be autonomous, each company will have access only to a limited view of the entire environment and there will be no super entity controlling the agents. Each agent will exercise free will by responding in its own time and manner to the changes in the environment. This means that behind the user interface the system needs to enable the interaction between the virtual companies.
One branch of computer based simulations is real business simulations employed for teaching company management. Students gain a lot of knowledge by applying theoretical knowledge in a simulated virtual company since students "rarely take economics as a free elective - especially beyond principles." (Allgood et al., 2004). Students involved in management simulations show great improvements in education and knowledge (Lean et al., 2006). We argue that in order to actually create a virtual business simulation the best approach can be DSS theory and practice since there are two activities implied: it allows student to theoretically model decisions and it also provides them with facts, data and information that require model implementation.
Because we are developing a simulation for academic training purposes we need to use existent knowledge in human-computer interaction science since the students will interact with the virtual environment using computers. The main concern in this direction must be a compromise between an interface easy to use and an appropriate amount of data and information needed for describing a decisional situation. The user must also be provided with an interface that will allow model building and a high degree of personalization. Each decision maker may consider some data to be relevant and some not. Therefore, the system should allow the user to add figures, tables, charts to a fully customizable decision making

workspace. By following and analyzing each customized workspace we will be able to compare the foundation of the decision making process for each decision maker.

The second goal is to develop means for logging the user's actions and, by mining those logs, automatically build an individual model of decision making. In achieving this goal we must rely on previous research regarding workflows as well as process mining. A workflow was defined as a depiction of the sequence of activities performed by an individual (van der Aalst & van Hee, 2002). There is also an extended research in process mining domain. Process mining aims to use event logs produced by different systems involved in the enterprise's operations in order to create a model of the processes and workflows that actually take place in the company (van der Aalst et al., 2004); (Ingvaldsen & Gulla, 2006). Another goal of process mining is to compare a prescribed model with the model obtained after mining (Dongen et al., 2005). Also, using process mining algorithms the analysis of decision points can be performed (Rozinat & van der Aalst, 2006a). A common and well known definition of a decision is that it is a cognitive process that starts with the discovery of the need for a decision and ends with the choice of one alternative (Holsapple & Whinston, 1996). Considering what we stated above we argue that "a decision workflow represents the depiction of the sequential activities performed by the decision maker starting with the discovery of the need for a decision and ending with the execution of the chosen alternative" (Petrusel, 2009). We also argue decision mining is the activity that, based on the activity and event logs obtained from a software tool (usually a DSS), extracts and creates a model of the decision making process depicted as a decision workflow (decision model).

The decision mining problem was approached before in (Rozinat & van der Aalst, 2006b). The mining algorithms are implemented in a plug-in called Decision Miner that is implemented in ProM Framework. This approach uses a derivation of C4.5 algorithm to build decision trees that allow analysis of choices in the decision points of a workflow. Rozinat proposes the use of Petri Nets in order to determine the points in which a choice was made and one or other of the branches were followed. After the decision point is identified the problem is turned into a classification problem that tries to determine if the cases with certain properties follow specific routes. However, this approach is different from our approach. We do not try to determine the points where one of the branches in a decision tree is selected and to determine the case data that influences the choice. We try to follow the actions of the decision maker and to identify the overall strategy employed in decision making. We try to determine what is the data and information used in the decision making process, how is this data used and what is the knowledge employed by the decision maker in choosing one alternative. The model that we create is very different from a decision tree because it is linear and basically does not have a decision point. The tree like structure can be obtained only if a large number of models are aggregated. The aggregation method is actually more similar to creating reference models. The approach proposed by Rozinat can be applied only to the reference model.

Once each individual decision model is mined and automatically created we aim to create reference models for each category of decisions implemented in VCDE. This requires us to rely on previous work regarding the creation of reference models (Fettke & Loos, 2006). A decision reference model aims to embody the necessary actions to be taken in order to make a certain kind of decision. We argue that the decision reference model can be depicted as a decision workflow improved with the data and information needed for decision making.

We also need to compare decision workflow models in order to determine the differences between them or between the reference model and one actual model. In achieving this aim we can rely on conformance checker which is a tool already developed for process model comparison and verification.

Regarding the methodologies, techniques and tools we must employ in developing our project we need to cover certain aspects. First we need to decide the representation of decision models. Another aspect that needs to be addressed is the means for decision model validation. Then, based on the conceptual architecture of the system, we need to decide the actual development environment that will suit our needs. Then we must decide over the tools and algorithms used for decision mining.

In our approach over the software architecture we consider the Business Architecture as presented by OMG (BAWG, 2008), also present in the Zachman framework and subsequent derivations. The key views of Zachman framework are: business strategies; business capabilities; business processes; business knowledge; and organizational overview. What is different from the usual approach is that we will fully specify the business capabilities; business processes and the organizational overview but we will determine the business strategies and the business knowledge once the software is implemented by mining the activity logs of the decision makers within the VCDE. This is why the software engineering process's goal is different than the one in the classical approaches. We do not try to specify the requirements of the user and then develop the software around those needs as in most of the other software processes. Instead, we aim to create software that will force the user to reason and decide on several pre-defined decisional situations. Our goal is not to fulfill the needs of a user but to use the software as a discovery tool. This needs to be done while logging all his actions and to force him to transform each mental activity in one explicit action within the software. What we do is very similar to modeling a business process and then creating the software that will support that process (Ouyang et al., 2009).

3. The virtual collaborative decision environment

In this section we will underline some of the most important aspects of VCDE. In the first sub-section we will give an overview of the general concepts and the architecture of the system. In the second sub-section we will show some of the most important decision models we included in the VCDE, the implementation and the means we used for model validation.

3.1 The architecture

The general concept is that of a multi-agent system. This means that the system is intended to be used by students that will act as intelligent agents in the environment. Each agent will act on its own free will and needs to compete with all other agents over limited resources.

We use the classic client-server architecture. All data regarding the environment is stored on the server while the users will connect to it using a client computer that has only the role of presenting data and information.

The VCDE will be populated by enterprises either in the same business field or in several related fields. The first alternative is more appropriate for the academic training since it allows us to compare and grade the evolution of each student. Each enterprise interacts with the other enterprises through the "marketplace". This consists in data and information that is available to all enterprises as well as the software modules that facilitate interaction (such as an auction system, news bulletins, a financial market and a loaning agent for credits and leasing).

Each enterprise is divided into six departments that interact with each other and require specific decisions from the managers. Besides the connection with other departments there will be a permanent data exchange with the marketplace. The composition of the enterprise and the internal and external relationships are depicted in Fig. 1.

Fig. 1. Internal and external relationships of a virtual enterprise's departments

There can be one or several decision makers. There can be different configurations of decision responsibilities within each enterprise. The common set-up is with one decision maker that will manage all departments. Alternative setups can include:

- several decision makers that are in charge with all the departments and a decision requires either consensus or 51% of the votes;
- several decision makers that are in charge with different departments;
- a hierarchy of decision makers in which the lower level reviews the decisional situation and presents to the higher level decision makers a condensed view and a couple of recommended decision alternatives.

The different possible decision setups of an enterprise are presented in Fig. 2.

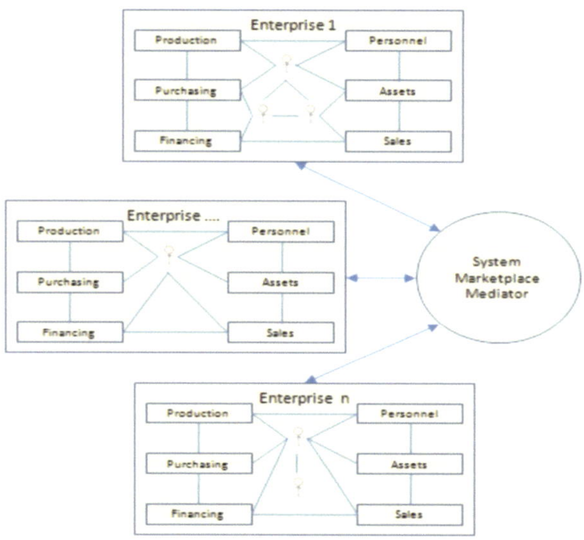

Fig. 2. Possible decision setups

The next important point in the enterprise is the actual activities performed by the decision maker which were depicted as the general use-case diagram of the system (Fig. 3.).

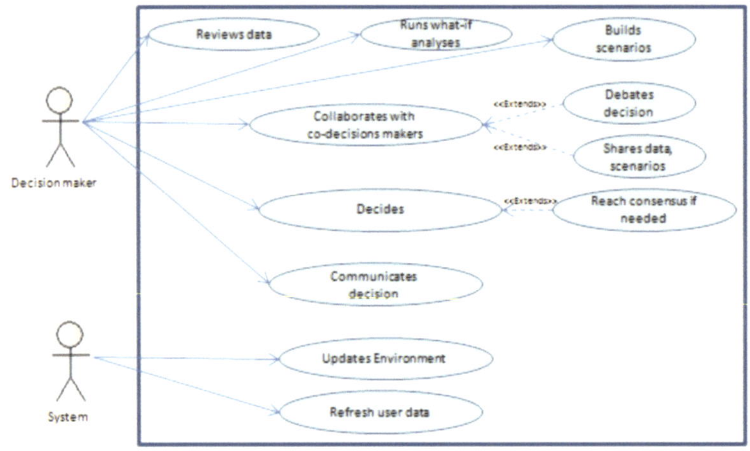

Fig. 3. General use-case diagram of VCDE

There are two main actors in the environment: the decision makers of each enterprise and the system/mediator of the environment. We aim to create an environment that will be entirely autonomous but in the early stages of deployment some of the actions that are intended for automatic processing will be conducted by the instructor which will thus asume the role of a mediator.

The first set of activities the decision maker performs regards information gathering for the next decision to be made. The manager first needs to review available data and information and then needs to develop some kind of strategy towards creating decision alternatives and selecting one of those alternatives as the final decision. This is the process that interests us the most. Therefore, besides providing the necessary figures, VCDE allows the user to start from existing data and build his own what-if analyses and scenarios using Excel-like tables, formulas and functions. Each action of the user will be logged for later usage.

The second set of activities that require the manager's involvement is the collaboration process in order to reach a decision. This is important because often a decision of one individual decision maker is different then the decision made by a group. We are also extremely interested in logging each action in the process of collaboration since it is the best source of information regarding what actually happens. The VCDE enables collaborative decision making through several tools as file sharing, instant messaging and voting.

The activity that ends the decision process is the choice of one alternative and the communication of that alternative to the system (the marketplace). This is done by sending updates to the server regarding the action that is implemented by the company. The instance of this action can be, for example, setting a figure for advertisment expenses, hiring a new employee, etc. This particular moment of the decision making process is extremely important for us because we consider that the decision process starts with the recognition of the need for a decision and ends with the choice of one alternative. Therefore, all the activities logged between the timestamp of the "start decision research" action and the timestamp of the "decision submit" action belong to that particular decision process. This is the base of the decision mining theory that we will introduce in the fourth section.

The system interacts with all the enterprises as the marketplace in the real economy. In VCDE this means that the system is accepting updates regarding the decisions of each enterprise, consolidates the actions of all enterprises and returns the new situation on the marketplace as updates for each enterprise. However, each particular enterprise will only have access to a pesonalized view of the marketplace for every department. This means, for example, that in the personnel department a company will have access to the labour fource only based on the advertising expenses for the available positions in the company. If the company invests in local advertising (small sums of money) it will be provided with a view containing less persons with low qualification available for hire, compared to the available emplyees generated by national advertising (larger sums of money required). If the company does not advertise open positions it will have no access to the labour market and will be able to hire only untrained new employees.

3.2 Decisions in VCDE

Each user of VCDE will be the manager (or one of the managers) of one virtual enterprise. The game takes place over a limited number of years divided into months. A decision once made will be effective starting next months and will continue its influence until another decision is made. Each company starts with the same fixed sum of money and must build the business from the beginning. The overall goal is to distribute the largest dividends to the owners over each fiscal period (a year starting January and ending December). The winner is the company that holds the lowest overall rank determined as the sum of ranks in each year.

The VCDE is modeled as an environment of virtual companies from several different related business domains. However, for the prototype, all companies will compete in the restaurant business because it is a business regarding to which all students should have some knowledge.

The decisions that managers need to make were divided into two major groups: decisions at the start of the company and decisions for each period.

Decisions that need to be made at the start of the company are:

- choice of the type of company to be established;
- choice of the location where the business will function;
- amounts invested in the restaurant's environment;
- choices over the staff to be hired,
- choices over the raw materials to be used
- choice over the advertising of the initial grand opening.

Since VCDE is designed to be a tool used in academic training, all those decisions will be first explored by students in a business plan developed before the actual simulation will start. Each decision will also be discussed in class and each student will be required to present motivation and a coherent strategy behind the selected alternative. In the next paragraphs we will discuss shortly the framework for each decision, as implemented in VCDE.

First decision will be to choose what kind of company the manager starts and is the most important decision since it affects the future of the enterprise. Alternatives are: gourmet, traditional and fast food. A gourmet restaurant aims an elite customer base. Some of the requirements that need to be considered by the decision maker are: location (not important), environment (critical), employee number (important), employee quality (critical), raw materials used (critical), customer satisfaction (critical), customer rate of return (critical - must be kept very high), meal quality (critical), meal innovation (important), meal price (very high), return per meal (very high). A traditional restaurant aims an average customer base. The requirements are: location (important), environment (medium), employee number (medium), employee quality (medium), raw materials (medium), customer satisfaction (critical), customer rate of return (important - must be kept high), meal quality (very important), meal innovation (unimportant), meal price (average), return per meal (average). A fast-food restaurant aims an extended customer base. The requirements are: location (very important), environment (not important), employee number (important), employee quality (medium), raw materials (medium), customer satisfaction (critical), customer rate of return (important - must be kept average), meal quality (important), meal innovation (unimportant), meal price (low), return per meal (low). Overall value of the business is calculated as %location + %environment + %employee quality + %customer satisfaction + %profit + %dividends paid. Variation of overall value influences the growth percentage of the future incomes.

The second decision will be to bid for one of the available commercial spaces (location) using the VCDE auction system. The general environment is similar to a mall's food court: there are central spaces, medium spaces and peripheral spaces. The commercial space is characterized by variables as: the quality, number of new visitors, rent and purchase price. It influences variables as the overall value of the business and the number of new visitors.

Third decision will be to invest in interior design of the restaurant. Depending on the type of restaurant the investment needs to be bigger or lower. Investment is a value set by the decision maker.

Fourth decision will be to find raw materials suppliers. The raw materials are important for the overall quality of food. There are five alternatives for food quality: low, poor, average, good and excellent, each with a different price tag.

Fifth decision will be to hire employees. The marketplace will supply only a limited number of specialists (like cooks, waiters) and an unlimited number of untrained employees. According to the advertising expenses the manager will have a complete or partial view of available resources. If several managers have access to the same view and decide to hire more persons than the maximum allowed an auction will start. Every year a new set of specialists will become available. Over specific periods of time each type of employee will automatically gain training levels if they are used in the same specialty. The managers can decide to invest in employee training in order to speed level gaining. This will be done at a cost that increases with each training level. The training levels vary from 1 (untrained) to 10 (expert). If the company lacks employees in one specialty and has excess employees in other specialties, employees will be shifted automatically and the needed positions will be filled at training level 1.

Sixth decision will be to advertise the grand opening. There are three levels of advertising: local, regional and national. There are four means of advertising: flyers, newspapers, radio and TV. Advertising can be done for: location, food or hiring. Each kind of advertising will have different impact on the new customers or available staff.

Some of the decisions of the managers will result in a competition over limited resources (for example several companies want to hire cooks but on the market there is only one highly qualified person). In such a situation there is an auction system which is available to all users. There can be closed auctions and open auctions. Closed auctions are visible only to the bidding enterprises. Open auctions are visible to all the companies on the market. For example bidding for hiring a level 10 chef is visible only to the companies that invested enough in advertising to discover the employee while bidding for shares on the stock exchange is visible to all companies. Auctions allow multiple bids, each bid must be higher than the previous (in fixed increments). All participants are informed of each bid and the winner is the last bidder. When using the auction system it is also very important to log all the actions of the manager in order to create a personalized decision model and to determine what are the key figures used by the decision maker and what is the strategy employed during the auction.

The decisions for each period are divided according to the time frame affected and to the frequency a new similar decision needs to be made into three categories: operational, tactical and strategic decisions.

Some of the operational decisions are:

- Decide on monthly expenses. This means reviewing all the previous financial data, analyzing data, building personal decision model then setting the necessary decision variables to the selected figures. The main data sources are: cash-flow (CF), profit and loss (P&L) and several key indicators calculated within VCDE. Each decision maker is able personalize the decision workspace by extracting and analyzing only the desired data (by building charts, what-if analyzes and scenarios). In order to mine for a personalized decision pattern each action performed by the decision maker is logged. The alternative source of information for the managers that provides external data will be reports from commissioned work like market research, head hunting companies, etc. For example, by employing a marketing company the decision maker will receive a customer satisfaction survey report that will show the food quality, service quality, environment, crowding, service time, and menu suggestions. If a larger amount of money is invested, the survey will also show some data regarding the competing companies. Another source of information will be the monthly news report from the marketplace. This will state extraordinary events, will show yearly hierarchies of company values, etc.
- Decide on employee policy. This includes decisions regarding wages, new hires, advertising available jobs.
- Decide on investments to be made like amounts spent on current repairs, improvements to the location.
- Decide amounts invested in advertising the company's business.

Some of the tactical decisions are:

- Training employees. Can be done by investing money in one or several employees in order to improve scores for overall employee quality.
- Insuring the company's location. At a certain point in time each of the companies will suffer one disaster (like fire, earthquake). Logging this moment is very important because we can show the manager's attitude and strategies while dealing with crisis situations.
- Selling own shares. Each company is present on the stock exchange and starts by owning 80% of its own shares. One way of getting cash is to sell own shares on the stock market. This is done in packages of 10%. Each package price is calculated according to the company's overall value. Selling is done by using the auction system each time one company sells shares. Each competitor can buy shares from any other

company. Each shareholder is entitled to a percentage of the dividends distributed at the end of each year by the company. The sums distributed as dividends are the major criteria for victory.

- Paying dividends to the shareholders. Since the sums distributed as dividends are the major criteria for victory, each company should consider paying large dividends to the shareholders. The sum is distributed among the shareholders. The money will be withdrawn from the accounts when decided by the manager but no later than end of June of the following year. If there is not enough money available, an overdraft on the bank account will be automatically established for a limited period at a high interest rate. If the overdraw is not paid, shares of the company will be automatically sold in order to cover the debt. If one company owns shares from another company it will get the dividends amount as a cashing in the bank account.
- Getting a loan or a leasing. In order to cover current expenses each company will get a small overdraft on the bank account for which it will have to pay interest each month. However, larger loans can be granted by the marketplace if the company has enough fixed assets to be mortgaged. In order to finance some major improvements of the company or to buy out a competitor the loan is the only source of extra cash. The company can purchase equipment (e.g. kitchen equipment) by leasing if enough cash is not available. This way the equipment is already mortgaged and becomes the property of the company only when paid in full.

One of the most important strategic decisions is to expand the business. In VCDE this can be done by buying out a competitor by using the stock exchange. This means adding: a new location to the company, new employees, new type of business, etc.

One of the goals of VCDE is to provide the students with a structured, rational approach over decision making. The first step is to avoid poorly documented decisions based on instincts. The decision modeling is done using the Criterium Decision Plus (CDP) software tool created by InfoHarvest. This tool offers support from the early stages of modeling (like the initial brainstorming) to the last stages (like validation of the model). The reason for which we selected this particular tool is that the modeling effort is well supported and is easy to understand for students. The easiness of use is also aided by the fact that the modeling can be done using ratings instead of complex mathematical equations. This also improves understanding of the model and keeps the focus of the students on the model itself instead of the formalism used. Before VCDE simulation starts, the students are presented with some details of the decisional situations in which they will be later involved and are required to model them using CDP. After the VCDE simulation is ended, the students are again required to model the same decisional situations, this time with the benefit of the experience gained while using VCDE. The initial and the final models can be compared and this way we can evaluate and grade the progress done by each student. The students are also graded after the second VCDE simulation run. The winner is graded with top marks. All other students are graded with decreasing marks (according to the results of their virtual companies) up to the student that manages the worst company who gets a failing grade.

The main activities performed when creating a decision model are:

- define the goal of the problem,
- define the decision group,
- identify factors or criteria important to achieving the goal,

- expand each criteria further until a criteria that can be easily evaluated is found,
- assign weights to each criteria,

evaluate decision alternatives against each criteria,

- check and validate the model using sensitivity analyzes and decision simulations.

There are three main phases in creating a model using CDP: the brainstorming when alternatives and criteria are defined; the creation of the hierarchy, weight assignment and rules; and the fine tuning of the model and final validation.

Before the VCDE simulation will start, the students are required to decide the type of virtual restaurant to be opened. Each student is required to use CDP in order to build a decisional model based on the previous class discussions that underline the criteria most relevant for the decision. One possible initial brainstorming model is presented in Fig. 4:

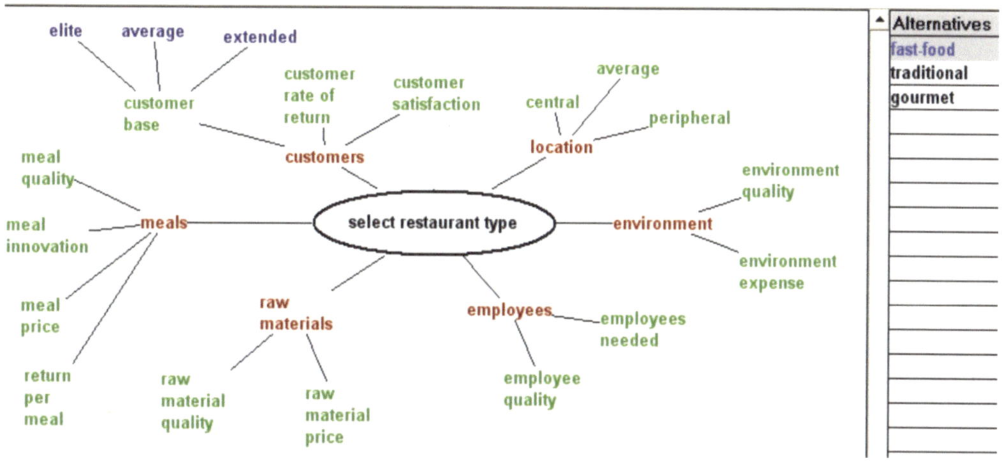

Fig. 4. Decision model for selecting the restaurant type

The goal is to select the restaurant type by choosing one of the three available alternatives: fast-food, traditional and gourmet. There are six primary criterions each with several sub-criterions.

The second phase is weighting each criterion and sub-criterion and then creating a hierarchy. CDP implements analytical hierarchy process (AHP) that was also associated with strategic decision making by (Bhushan & Rai, 2004) and Simple Multiattribute Utility Technique (SMART). AHP divides the weight of each criterion to the sum of all weights for the same level of criterions. This way each criterion gets a score between 0 and 1. SMART uses a function (linear, exponential or user-defined) to convert a weight for one criterion to an internal score of the criterion also in the 0 to 1 range. The weighting for each criterion can be done by direct comparison or by pair-wise comparison. Direct comparison means that a weight is set by the decision maker by comparing the criterion with other criterions on the same level, according to previous experience or by using third party information. Pair-wise comparison means comparing every possible pair of criterions and assigning the weights for each pair at a time. Rules can also be defined at this moment. There can be created either simple rules (e.g. expenses cannot be greater than 1000) or if/then rules (e.g. if raw material price is 100 then meal price must be greater than 100). Each student must create weights and rules for his own model. Since each person assigns different weights to criterions and sub-criterions the alternative ranking produced by each model will be different. The model can

be further enhanced by taking into account uncertainty. Each criterion may be assigned with different degrees of uncertainty for the values of the weights.
After successfully creating the model the fine tuning and validation of the model will be performed. This means making sure that weights are correctly distributed and that there is no criterion that will fully decide the best alternative. One of the important analyzes is the contribution of each criteria to the final score of each alternative. The validation is done in CDP also by sensitivity analysis of the preferred alternative to changes in weights or rating values.
Each model created by the students, besides the validation of weights and rules needs to be mapped to the "reality" in VCDE. For example, in the model presented in Fig. 4. the weights and rules are set so that CDP determines the best alternative is a traditional restaurant. But if a rule limits the monthly rent to a certain amount, and in the auction that amount is surpassed CDP could determine that the new best alternative is a gourmet restaurant. In this case, the whole model needs to be changed in order to include the new situation.
Since we created also a numerical business simulation many of the business models are implemented in VCDE using variables and constants. There are three categories of variables: decisional, environment and calculated. Decisional variables (DV) are set by the decision maker. Some examples are: dividends to be paid, number of employees, employee salary, product price, etc. Environment variables (EV) are set within the system and cannot be changed or influenced by the actions of the companies. Some examples are: maximum number of customers, minimum number of employees needed, employee minimum salary/specialty, employee training cost/level, etc. Calculated variables (CV) can be based on any of the previous two and, therefore, can only be influenced by the decision maker but not altered directly. Some examples are: overall value of company, number of returning visitors, company's yearly rank, overall employee quality, etc. A constant is a fixed value that does not change over time. Some examples are: the score of location, the interest for credits, the interest for deposits, etc.
The variables and constants are used to create business models for VCDE. One example of a variable calculation is:

Fig. 5. The dependencies of the variable customers next month

In Fig. 5. we show the last four steps involved in the calculation of the number of customers the company will have next month. The customers next month variable is numeric and is obtained by adding the numerical variables: returning customers and new customers. Returning customers are calculated as the number of customers in the previous month multiplied with the variable customer rate of return which is expressed as a percentage. The customer rate of return depends on the variables: environment of the restaurant, employee quality and customer satisfaction with the meals served. Each variable is expressed as a percentage and customer rate of return is calculated as an average rate of the three. The last three variables are also calculated based on others but, in order to keep the example short, the dependencies were not depicted.

The mathematical equation that summarizes the model and is implemented in VCDE for the partial model depicted above is:

$$cust\_next\_month = \left(\frac{envir + emp\_qual + cust\_satisf}{3}\right) * cust\_curr + \frac{\frac{loc}{100} + \frac{adv\_\exp * adv\_lvl / 10}{adv\_\min\_\exp}}{2} * cust\_all \quad (1)$$

For each calculated variable in VCDE we created a similar model. The models are then validated using scenarios in order to balance each variable in the model and the influence on others.

We create decision models in order to determine the alternatives that will be available to the decision maker and to determine how choosing one alternative regarding a variable affects the other variables in VCDE.

Is obvious that the models created for one calculated variable are related to other models implemented in VCDE. There are a lot of cases in which the same variable (decision, calculated or environment) is present in several models. In order to show a partial model of interaction between the variables we created the following diagram:

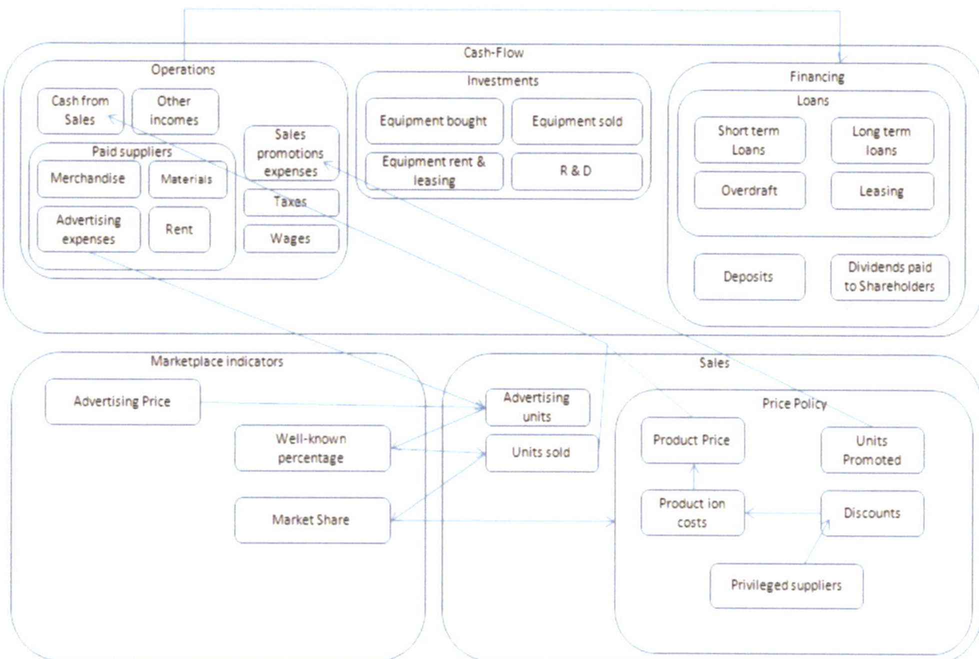

Fig. 6. Partial model of interaction between variables in VCDE

In this model advertising expenses is a decisional variable set by the manager for each month. Corroborated with the advertising price (environment variable) it influences the advertising units for the company which, in turn, will further influence the product units sold. The sales of the each company will be added up so that the total market is calculated. Each company will therefore hold a market share of the total market. This is an extremely important indicator for the decision making process regarding the price strategy of the company. But the sold units also influence the revenues of the company. Based on the cash revenues from sales and all the expenses, the financing need variable is calculated. It will influence the decision making process regarding the loaning strategy (if sales are not big enough) or the dividends distributed to the shareholders (which is the major criteria for winning).

4. Decision mining and decision models

As we argued in the second section of the paper, a decision process consists of a series of cognitive actions undertaken by the decision maker from the moment the need for a decision arises until the choice of one alternative. This is why the decision process actually resembles a workflow. The challenge is to create means of transposing cognitive processes to physical actions. Since Business Process Modeling Notation (BPMN) is the de facto standard in depicting workflows we chose this notation to model the prescribed collaborative decision process that is implemented in VCDE:

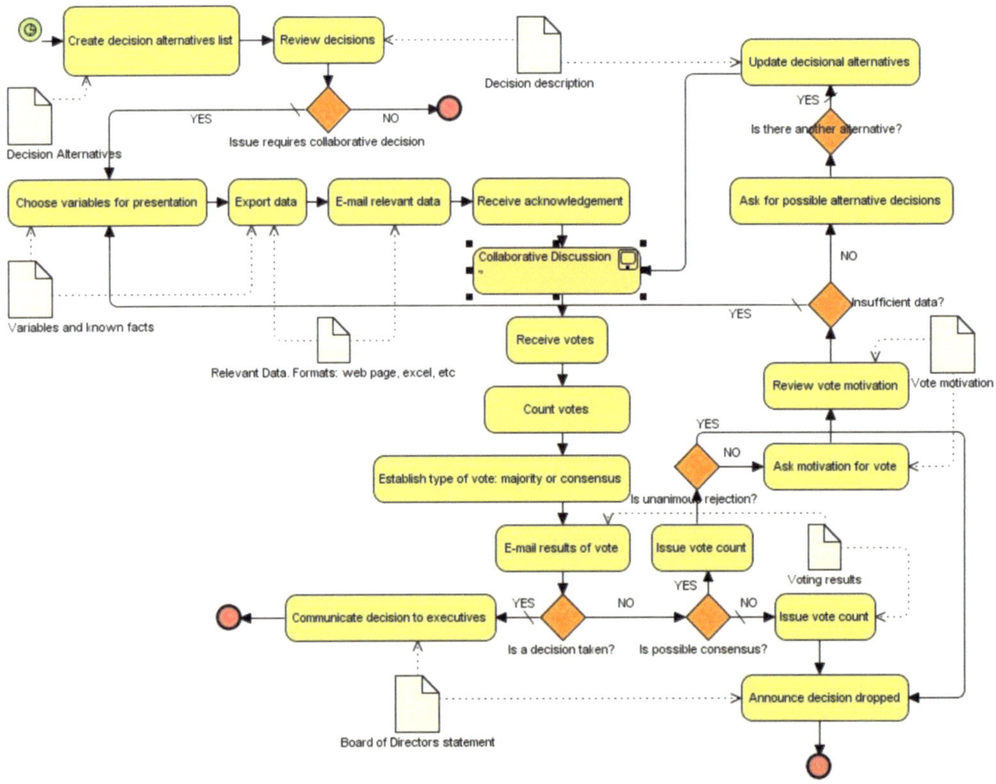

Fig. 7. The collaborative decision process in VCDE

The process starts when a decision situation requires the intervention of the managers of the virtual enterprises. The focus in this model is the capture of the activities performed and also the enactment of implicit knowledge of the decision makers. Each activity in the model is mapped within the system to several objects. Each artifact of the model is created in order to facilitate the mining of the decision workflow. VCDE is designed so that the decision makers use the software for all communication and no face to face meetings are permitted. This is why in VCDE there is a sub-system designed for voting (Fig. 8.) seen as the only mean of deciding over one alternative or another. The only choice available to the users is whether the vote requires majority or consensus in order to choose one alternative.

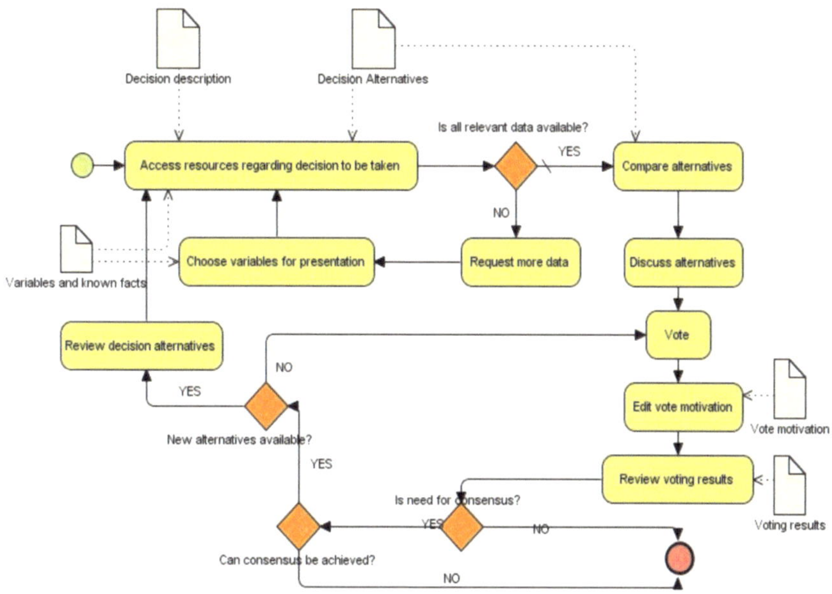

Fig. 8. The collaborative discussion implemented in VCDE

Since VCDE will only be used in class starting the spring semester of 2010, in the next part we will show the results we already obtained by using a DSS designed for enterprise financial decision making (Petrusel, 2008). Those preliminary results are very similar to those that will be available after the VCDE simulation. What we try to do is provide a view of our completed first experiment (Petrusel, 2009) as an example of what we expect to accomplish by using VCDE. This experiment aimed to prove a priori that decision mining is feasible and that the decision models created this way can improve our understanding over the whole decision process (Petrusel, 2009). The principles that we already used and the ones employed in VCDE are the same; the only difference will be that the logs available for mining will be considerably larger.

When mining for the decision model there are several goals we try to accomplish. First goal is to determine the control-flow perspective over the decision process. This mainly means to establish dependencies among tasks. In order to do that we have to answer several questions: which activity precedes which, are there any activities that imply others, are there concurrent activities (we observed that in decision processes concurrent activities usually means reviewing information from two or more sources) and if there are any loops (in decision processes we observed that loops appear mainly when what-if analyses and scenarios are reviewed). Another important piece of information is whether a path is more frequent than the others. If there is not a high frequency for one path it means that the user does not have a routine but searches for information in random places. This was found mainly in unstructured decisions that appear rarely (like strategic decisions and sometimes tactical ones). In operational decisions, the path is almost always the same. Another goal is to mine for the social networks when the decision is collaborative. This means answering to one critical question "how are the communications between actors performed and what are the dependencies between the decision makers?". Another important question is whether a decision maker influences the others.

Once the model is created, ProM Framework allows the validation of the model by using conformance checker. It allows us to see how much the model matches existing execution data and to highlight discrepancies. Conformance checker is also useful when a prescriptive model exists and we need to check if the real execution data follows the model. ProM Framework allows decision point analysis that aims to detect data dependencies that affect the routing of a case (Rozinat & van der Aalst, 2006a). By analyzing decision points we can determine the probability for a certain action to follow another action, thus providing us with the possibility of also mining for business rules.

As we already suggested, each action of the user within the system is logged for further analysis by decision mining algorithms. The entity-relationship diagram for the tables implemented in VCDE for logging purposes is similar to the one recommended by ProM Import Tool and is presented in Fig. 9.

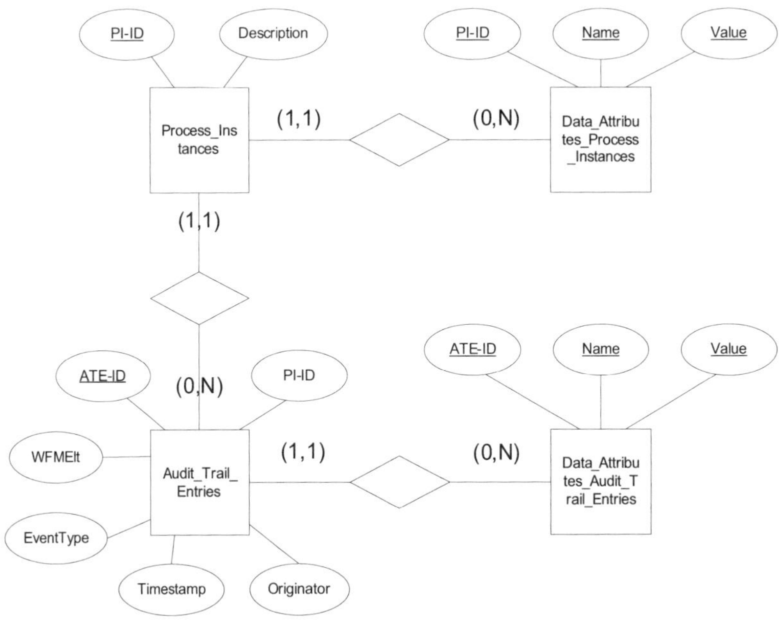

Fig. 9. ERD of tables required for user activity logging in VCDE

Data is added in the four tables at every action of every user. The result we obtained for our financial DSS are presented in Fig. 10. The four tables were converted by using ProM Import Tool to the MXML format required by ProM Framework. Cleaning the logs is required once the import is finished. Cleaning the logs aims to remove incomplete processes that can affect the quality of the model and is mainly done manually. Incomplete processes are the ones that either do not start with "decision start" activity or do not end with "communicate decision" or "drop decision" events. Incomplete processes usually show up when the decision maker starts researching one decisional situation and then aborts the process without choosing one alternative. After the cleaning is finished the decisional model needs to be created. This involves several activities: ordering the activities, assigning activities to the correct processes (there can be the case when several decisions are researched or made at the same time by the same decision makers) and building several views of the process model in order to ensure a better analyze. We created decision models by using three logically different process mining algorithms: alpha++, heuristic miner and fuzzy miner. Because in this first experiment the decision situation and environment was simulated, the logs were almost noiseless and all three algorithms produced about the same results. However, we expect to obtain much noisier logs after the VCDE simulation is run. This is why we plan to evaluate the performance of each algorithm on longer, noisier logs at a later time.

In the preliminary experiment we created only three companies and nine decisional situations. Starting from the logging tables (on the left side of Fig. 10.) we mined the following models (on the right side of Fig. 10.):

Audit_Trail_Entries

ATE-ID	PI-ID	WFMElt	EventType	Timestamp	Originator
87	18	decision needed	start	10/24/2008 3:01:51 PM	D1
88	18	decision needed	start	10/24/2008 3:01:54 PM	D2
89	18	historic c-f	start	10/24/2008 3:02:14 PM	D1
90	18	c-f simulation	start	10/24/2008 3:06:26 PM	D1
91	18	historic c-f	start	10/24/2008 3:02:16 PM	D2
92	18	c-f simulation	start	10/24/2008 3:07:09 PM	D2
93	18	input data	start	10/24/2008 3:08:56 PM	D1
94	18	c-f simulation	start	10/24/2008 3:09:17 PM	D1
95	18	revenues and expenses	start	10/24/2008 3:10:24 PM	D1
96	18	indicators: debt%	start	10/24/2008 3:10:33 PM	D1
97	18	input data	start	10/24/2008 3:11:28 PM	D1
98	18	c-f simulation	start	10/24/2008 3:10:43 PM	D2
99	18	revenues and expenses	start	10/24/2008 3:13:31 PM	D2
100	18	c-f simulation	start	10/24/2008 3:11:59 PM	D1
101	18	indicators: share eq	start	10/24/2008 3:13:44 PM	D1
102	18	conference: write	start	10/24/2008 3:15:36 PM	D1
103	18	conference: re	start	10/24/2008 3:15:57 PM	D2
104	18	conference: send xls	start	10/24/2008 3:19:42 PM	D1
105	18	conference: rcv xls	start	10/24/2008 3:19:43 PM	D2
106	18	conference: re	start	10/24/2008 3:22:48 PM	D2
107	18	vote decision	start	10/24/2008 3:24:05 PM	D1
108	18	vote decision	start	10/24/2008 3:25:15 PM	D2
109	18	vote result	start	10/24/2008 3:25:16 PM	system
110	18	vote review	start	10/24/2008 3:25:17 PM	D1
111	18	vote review	start	10/24/2008 3:25:17 PM	D2
112	18	decision taken	stop	10/24/2008 3:25:18 PM	system

Data_Attributes_Audit_Trail_Entries

ATE-ID	Name	Value
87	type test code	c3s6
88	type test code	c3s6
89	choose period: begins	january
89	choose period: ends	october
90	choose period: begins	nov/08
90	choose period: ends	oct/09
91	choose period: begins	june
91	choose period: ends	october
92	choose period: begins	nov/08
92	choose period: ends	mar/09
94	choose period: begins	nov/08
94	choose period: ends	oct/09
98	choose period: begins	mar/09
98	choose period: begins	nov/09
100	choose period: begins	nov/08
100	choose period: ends	oct/09
107	vote	financial leasing
108	vote	financial leasing
109	consensus	yes
112	decision: D1	execute
112	decision: D2	execute
112	decision: result	financial leasing
112	decision: send	e-mail

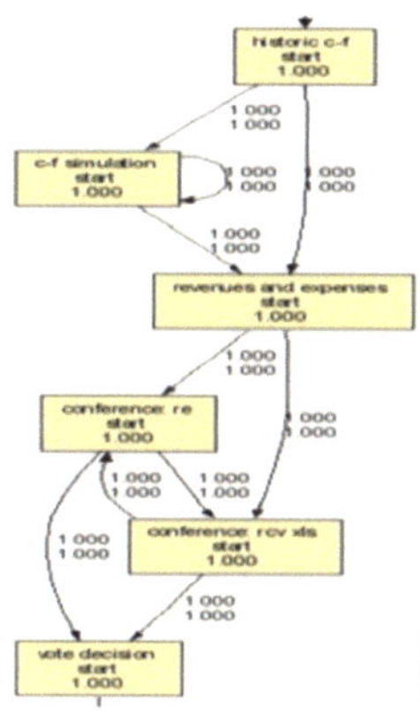

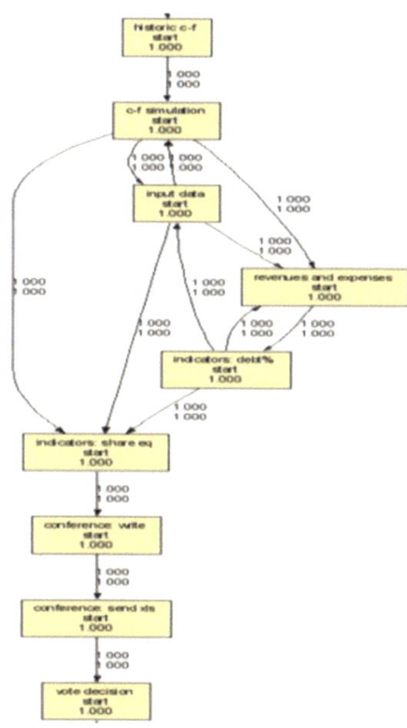

Fig. 10. Log tables and the mined models

In the mined company there are two decision makers (D1 and D2). In the scenario presented in Fig. 10. the decision makers had to decide over the financing sources to be used when buying a car. It can be seen that D1 is more analytical and relies on more simulations and what-if analyses then D2. By feeding new data into the system he changes the initial values and tries to broaden his perspective over the decisional situation. D2 relies only on simulations based on accounting data and jumps to the decision without careful consideration. It also can be seen that D1 initiates the debate over the right decision and sends an Excel file to support his option. By following the two decision workflows we can argue that D1 has carefully considered all the alternatives and his choice is based on an analysis. Meanwhile, D2 briefly reviewed available data and jumped to the decision (possibly relying on experience). Even though the decision needs consensus, it can be argued that D1 influenced the final decision since he initiated a debate and sent a file to D2 in order to back up his choice. Because there is no significant difference between the two decision makers from the point of view of former experience and studies (both have worked around eight years in similar positions and have graduated an economics faculty) it can be said that D1 is more involved in decision making and usually influences the other decision maker. When we disclosed our findings regarding their decision profiles, both decision makers agreed that, in the majority of cases, the alternative suggested by D1 is the one chosen. This is why we can argue that our decisional patterns are close to reality. However, if we take into consideration the prescribed decisional model presented in Fig. 7. we can state that it is not followed entirely. Since VCDE simulation will be run twice for the students in one semester, we plan to use conformance checker in order to compare the models mined after each simulation. We expect to see better decision models by observing less noise (less incomplete processes) and by observing less random activities (the decision makers should be using the first experience in developing some decision strategies regarding specific decisions).

5. Conclusion and future work

We focus our research on two main objectives. The first one is creating an academic DSS-like virtual enterprise simulation. The second one is creating decision models by mining user activity logs obtained after the simulation. In order to reach each objective we must rely on previous research from various fields like simulations, multi-agent environments, decision theory, and process mining.

In the third section of the paper we introduced the general setup of the virtual environment, the possible internal setups of enterprises and the user interaction with the system. In order to present the VCDE we shortly described some of decisions that the managers of the virtual enterprises must face. Because the interaction with the system is DSS-like the decision maker will be able to document the decisional situations, build decision strategies and analyze data in a fully customizable decision workspace by using what-if analyzes and scenarios. Moreover, in order to reach our second goal, the software is developed so that all communication between the users takes place only through the specific tools of the system (as file sharing, instant messaging, etc). All the actions of the decision makers while using the systems will be logged, thus creating a very important source of knowledge that can be exploited in order to better understand the decision processes. This section is intended to argue the point that in the Decision Support Systems course the usage of a system as VCDE can be invaluable. The students will be able to learn how to research a decisional situation, how to structure the decision making process, how to build decision models that will help them evaluate alternatives, how to actually implement the chosen alternative and how to follow up the results of the decision and make necessary adjustments if the results are not the ones predicted.

In the fourth section of the paper we show the interaction model implemented in VCDE for reaching a collaborative decision. Then we show how logging is actually implemented and an initial experiment that presents a partial log and the resulting decision model. The aim of this section is to show that logging the actions of the users in a DSS is possible and should be done. Such a log can be mined by using either existent or new algorithms in order to create decision models and patterns. New insights are available on the decision making process as the control flow perspective, the organizational perspective and the social networks of collaborative decisions. Those models show how the decision is made, how the decision maker researches a situation, what are the strategies employed, how is the collaboration between decision makers, how is one of the alternatives actually chosen. Creating a model for the decision workflow also offers the possibility of comparing either different decision makers or the actual decision pattern with a prescribed model. The advantages are great, considering that this way we can indicate the process that provided a good alternative and compare it with a decision workflow that led to the choice of the wrong alternative. This way we expect to discover enacted implicit knowledge of the decision maker.

While keeping in mind that the system will first function in the spring semester of 2010 we can identify some shortcomings that still need to be improved. The most important one is that we still have not developed a specific decision mining algorithm and are still using process mining algorithms. On our initial experiment we concluded that process algorithms build fair decision models but based on noiseless, short logs. However, since we expect long logs with multiple incomplete processes we plan to build a specific decision mining algorithm. It is also necessary to develop either an algorithm that will not require log cleaning or a separate script for log cleaning.

The main point we want to argue is our new approach over decision mining. This is a new research direction that aims to explain the decision process based on what the decision maker is actually doing when using the DSS software. What we want to achieve is a large number of logged decision behaviors in the simulated environment that can be exploited by mining for decision patterns and models. If enough models are mined and if the patterns are similar, then we can create reference models for that decisional situation. The models can later be used in conjunction with an evaluation of decision effectiveness.

One other higher purpose of this research is to promote our beliefs that using decision mining and a carefully designed system we can turn decision maker's implicit knowledge into explicit knowledge that can be captured, reviewed, explained and compared.

6. Acknowledgements

This research was founded through Grant type PN2 no. 91-049 / 2007 "Intelligent Systems for Business Decision Support (SIDE)".

7. References

Allgood, S.; Bosshardt, W.; Van der Klaauw, W. & Watts, M. (2004). What Students Remember and Say about College Economics Years Later, *American Economic Review* Vol. 94, No. 2/2004, pp. 259-265, ISSN 0002-8282

Bhushan, N. & Rai, K. (2004). *Strategic Decision Making: Applying the Analytic Hierarchy Process*, Springer-Verlag, ISBN 1-8523375-6-7, London

BAWG (2009) OMG Business Architecture Overview, available online (04/09/2009) at: http://bawg.omg.org/business_architecture_overview.htm

Dongen, B.; Medeiros, A.; Verbeek, H.; Weijters, A. & van der Aalst, W. M. P. (2005). The ProM framework: A New Era in Process Mining Tool Support, *Lecture Notes in Computer Science: Application and Theory of Petri Nets,* Vol. 3536, pp. 444-454, ISSN 1611-3349

Fettke, P. & Loos, P. (2006). *Reference Modeling for Business Systems Analysis,* Idea Group Inc ISBN 1599040549, Hershey USA

Holsapple, C. W. & Whinston, A. B. (1996). *Decision support systems: a knowledge-based approach,* Course Technology, ISBN 0-324-03578-0, Cambridge

Ingvaldsen, J. E. & Gulla, J. A. (2006). Model Based Business Process Mining, *Journal of Information Systems Management*, Vol. 23, No. 1/2006, pp. 19-31, ISSN 0739-9014

Lean, J.; Moizer, M. & Towler, C. A. (2006). Active Learning in Higher Education, *Journal of Simulation and games,* Vol. 7, No. 3/2006, pp. 227–242, ISSN 1046-8781

Ouyang, C.; Dumas, M.; van der Aalst, W. M. P.; ter Hofstede, A. H. M. & Mendling, J. (2009). From Business Process Models to Process-oriented Software Systems, *ACM Transactions on Software Engineering and Methodology,* Volume 19, No. 1/2009, pp. 18 - 31, ISSN:1049-331X

Petrusel, R. (2008). A Decision Support System Taylored for Romanian Small and Medium Enterprises, *Proceedings of ICEIS Information Systems Analysis and Specification*, pp. 208-211, ISBN 978-989-8111-38-8, Barcelona Spain, June 2008, INSTICC Press, Portugal

Petrusel, R. (2009). Mining and modeling decision workflows from DSS user activity logs, *Proceedings of ICEIS Information Systems Analysis and Specification*, pp 144-149, ISBN 978-989-8111-86-9, Milano Italy, May 2009, INSTICC Press, Portugal.

Rozinat, A. & van der Aalst, W. M. P. (2006a) Decision Mining in ProM, *Lecture Notes in Computer Science,* Vol. 4102, pp. 420-425, ISSN 1611-3349

Rozinat, A. & van der Aalst, W. M. P. (2006b) Decision Mining in Business Processes, *BPM Center Report* BPM-06-10, BPMcenter.org.

Sun, R. & Naveh, I. (2004). Simulating Organizational Decision-Making Using a Cognitively Realistic Agent Model, *Journal of Artificial Societies and Social Simulation*, Vol. 7, No. 3/2004, pp. 45-68, ISSN 1460-7425

Van der Aalst, W. M. P. & van Hee, K. (2002). *Workflow management: models, methods, and systems*, MIT Press, ISBN 978-0-262-01189-1, Cambridge

Van der Aalst, W. M. P.; van der Weijters, A. & Maruster, L. (2004). Workflow Mining: Discovering Process Models from Event Logs, *IEEE Transactions on Knowledge and Data Engineering*, Vol. 16, No. 9/2004, pp. 1128-1142, ISSN 1041-4347

15

Decision Support Using Simulation for Customer-Driven Manufacturing System Design and Operations Planning

Juhani Heilala, Jari Montonen, Paula Järvinen and Sauli Kivikunnas
VTT Technical Research Centre of Finland
Finland

1. Introduction

Agile, fast and flexible production networks are a must in today's global competition. The interrelations between manufacturing systems and processes are becoming more complex and the amount of data for decision making is growing. Manufacturing, engineering and production management decisions involve the consideration of multiple parameters. These often complex, interdependent factors and variables are too many for the human mind to cope with at one time. Agile production needs a management and evaluation tool for production changes, manufacturing system development, configuration and operations planning. A decision support system based on manufacturing simulation is one suitable solution.

Discrete Event Simulation (DES) has mainly been used as a production system analysis tool to evaluate new production system concepts, layout and control logic. Recent development has enhanced DES models for use in the day-to-day operational production planning of manufacturing facilities. These "as built" models provide manufacturers with the ability to evaluate the capacity of the system for new orders, unforeseen events such as equipment downtime, and changes in operations. After a simulation model has been built, experiments are performed by changing the input parameters and predicting the response. Experimentation is normally carried out by asking "what-if" questions and using the model to predict the likely outcome.

A simulation-based Decision Support System (DSS) can be used to augment the tasks of planners and schedulers to run production more efficiently (Figure 1). Some of the benefits of implementing an operational simulation scheduling system include: less effort required to plan day-to-day scheduling, customer order due date conformance, synchronisation of flow through the plant, minimisation of set-ups/changeovers, early warnings of potential problems, checks of critical resources and materials, and, naturally, "what-if" scenario analysis for capacity planning.

Although dedicated software packages are currently available, there are limited examples of the use of simulation tools in the operational planning of manufacturing. This chapter also sheds light on development challenges and current development efforts to solve these challenges for this data and model-driven DSS. The major challenges are: 1) data integration, 2) automated simulation model creation and updates, and 3) visualisation of results for interactive and effective decision making.

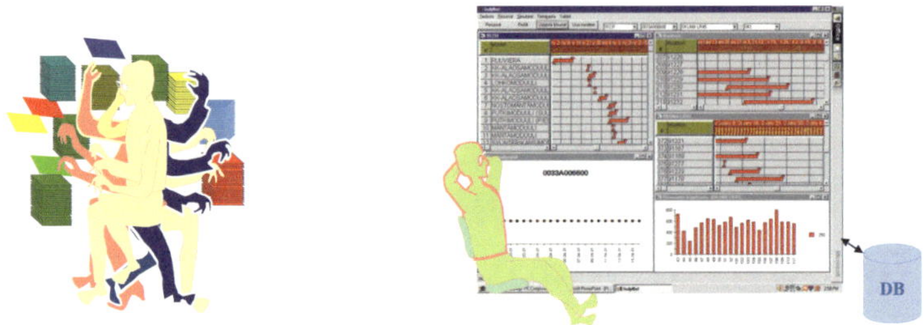

Fig. 1. Simulation and modelling-based system helps operators in daily operations planning.

The costs of integrating simulation systems with other manufacturing applications are high; there is always a need to transfer and share data between the simulation and other manufacturing software applications. Custom-built proprietary interfaces require extensive customisation and the current standardisation landscape for system integration is challenging. Development efforts to solve this problem are ongoing. Naturally, if managers are using a simulation model to plan operations, the model must be precise enough and kept up to date. There is a need for permanent, always on, synchronised factory models that can be created automatically on-demand from ERP and other data sources. Users need fast analysis and methods to perform "what-if" scenarios. Simulation results can provide suggestions for feasible and optimised finite scheduling, but the human in the loop will make the final decision. The users also need a visually effective user interface. Visual analytics provides visual and interactive tools for analytical reasoning and decision making from data. The basic idea is to combine the strengths of automatic data analysis with the visual perception and analysis capabilities of the human user. The use of simulation with an easy-to-use graphical user interface provides tools and methods for manufacturing scenario evaluation, scheduling optimisation, and production planning even for simulation non-experts. Some of the past case studies are described to illustrate the system solution. The benefits of simulation-based DSS in the customer-driven manufacturing domain and the suitable user groups are discussed.

1.1 Manufacturing system complexity

A manufacturing system is made up of entities (input and outputs), activities, resources and controls. It encompasses processes but also includes the resources and controls for carrying them out, as shown in Figure 2. Manufacturing system design involves a number of interrelated subjects, including tooling strategy, material handling systems, system size, process flow configuration, flexibility needed for future engineering changes or capacity adjustments, and space strategy.

There are many challenging factors: the need to boost system performance due to global competition and the growing complexity of both the manufacturing systems and products to be manufactured. The operations planning and capacity management of these complex manufacturing systems are indeed challenging. Productivity enhancement is also a major objective for manufacturing enterprises. Manufacturers are experiencing fluctuating market demand for their products, with ever shorter lead times and smaller but more frequent order quantities, accompanied by increasingly frequent changes in product specifications - even during manufacture. Product life cycles are shorter and it is becoming more difficult to forecast demand. All this requires agility and flexibility on the part of the factory, which runs counter to the built-in inertia and the gravitational force to 'conduct business as usual', combined with the limited ability of management to reconsider decisions almost 'in real time'.

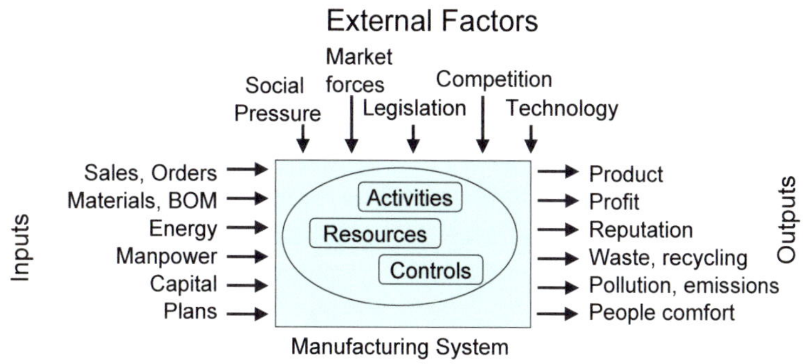

Fig. 2. Manufacturing system (modified from Harrel and Tumay, 1995).

1.2 Customer-driven manufacturing

Customers define the business. They want high-quality personalised products. Time-to-customer, punctuality and throughput time are important competitive factors in customer-driven manufacturing. The products are usually complex systems consisting of components that are manufactured in different factories, sometimes in different countries. The whole production network - including both component manufacturing and assembly - has to be flexible and able to react to changes in production capacity requirements.

Manufacturing is performed on the basis of customer orders. Each order can be unique, consisting of different components, and batch sizes vary. Naturally, the throughput times of the products may differ from one another. A new order is a 'disturbance' to the current situation in production. All this makes the design and management of production networks a complex task. One of the risks is the occurrence of dynamic bottlenecks, in which the demand for capacity in one particular operation suddenly turns out to be excessive and the resulting delays reverberate throughout the rest of the production system. The changing location of bottlenecks depends on the status of production resources, equipment, materials, human operators and orders in production.

Features of customer-driven manufacturing:

- Promises to the customer must be kept (always); Time, Quality and Cost
- Need for speed and flexibility due to dynamic global competition
- Order book shrinks while delivery times shorten
- Outsourcing, supply and value networks
- Productivity improvements from supply chain management and coordination.

The order entry point defines the customers' influence on the features of the product:

- Make-to-Stock (MTS): the customer selects a product from stock and the product is shipped to the customer. No customisation.
- Assemble-to-Order (ATO): the customer order initiates the assembly from components and modules in stock. Customisation is based on customer requirements in assembly before delivery.
- Make-to-Order (MTO): the customer order initiates material purchases, component and module manufacturing and assembly of the product.
- Engineer-to-Order (ETO): customer specifications initiate the engineering process before material purchases are made and component manufacturing and assembly are started.

The deeper the order entry point is into the manufacturing process, the more challenging and complex the production planning. The case studies of operations planning provided in this chapter have features of ATO, MTO and ETO. In current global competition and in lean and agile manufacturing, material stocks are kept as small as possible, while expensive resource utilisation should be kept as high as possible. Production personnel must seek a balance between customer orders and limited resources. Every new order disturbs the current balance (Figure 3). The resources are equipment, machinery, human operators as well the material needed for the manufacturing operations.

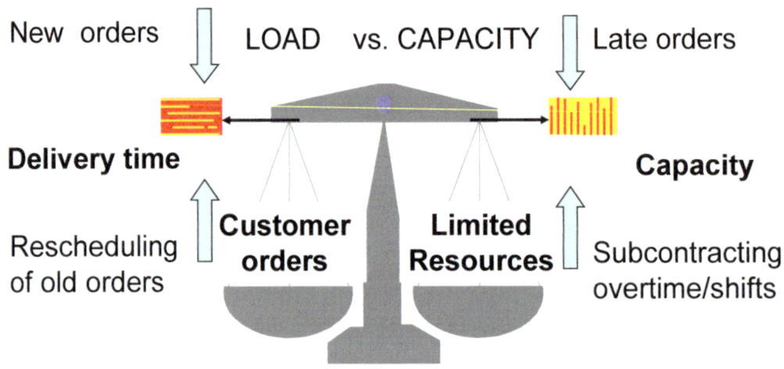

Fig. 3. Production balancing between orders and limited resources.

The accuracy of order date delivery promises is a key element in customer satisfaction. One of the important decisions in production planning is the scheduling and synchronisation of activities, resources and material flow. Old static production planning methods are not adequate; production planners need accurate and dynamic models of production, i.e. a simulation model using production network and real shop floor data in near real time.

In this complex world, the development of decision support for human operators and information management is a key asset in managing "better-faster-cheaper" competition. Simulation analysis with real data provides forecasts on the basis of the given input values. This gives production managers the time to react to potential problems and evaluate alternatives. A better balance between multiple parallel customer orders and finite resources can be found.

2. Decision support systems

A Decision Support System (DSS) is an interactive computer-based system or subsystem intended to help decision makers use communications technologies, data, documents, knowledge and/or models to identify and solve problems, complete decision process tasks, and make decisions. Decision Support System is a general term for any computer application that enhances a person or group's ability to make decisions. In general, Decision Support Systems are a class of computerised information systems that support decision-making activities. Five more specific DSS types include (Power 2009)

- Communications-Driven DSS,
- Data-Driven DSS,
- Document-Driven DSS,
- Knowledge-Driven DSS and
- Model-Driven DSS.

2.1 Decision making in production engineering and management

There are multiple decision-making aims in the manufacturing system domain. Strategic and tactical aims focus on the design or selection of a new manufacturing system or the improvement of the existing manufacturing system, and the planning time horizon is years or months (Figure 4). Operational aims, which involve the running of the existing system, have a much shorter time frame - days, hours or minutes to solve problems in manufacturing.

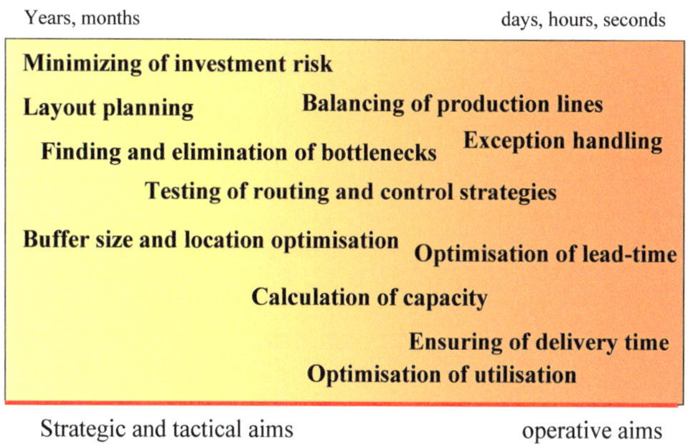

Fig. 4. The planning horizon and aims in production engineering and management.

The production engineering and management decision is typically based on the data and information available at the moment of the decision. Operators and managers can use all the quantitative data at their disposal, but they still have to distrust it and use their own intelligence and judgement. Production managers, sales and customer service engineers have traditionally made their decisions based on the following data, information and factors:

- Own intuition, long experience and asking the "experts"
- Use of tables and handbooks, given static information, order books, legacy systems, ERP
- Use of own calculations, spreadsheets and other static calculation methods
- Use of simulation and optimisation methods

There is a need for a quick response tool to evaluate alternatives and scenarios before strategic, tactical or operational decisions are made (see Figure 1). Optimisation and simulation modelling could be used to provide information for decision makers.

2.2 Visual analytics

Visual analytics provides visual and interactive tools for analytical reasoning and decision making from data. The basic idea is to combine the strengths of automatic data analysis with the visual perception and analysis capabilities of the human user. It is especially focused on situations where the huge amount of data and the complexity of the problem make automatic reasoning impossible without human interaction. It combines different data sources containing complex and heterogeneous data of various types and qualities. (Järvinen et al. 2009).

Visual analytics is a new and active research field that has its origins in U.S. national security. It is a multi-disciplinary research area, combining information visualisation science, data mining, mathematical and statistical methods, data management, user interface techniques as well as human perception and cognition research. It can be applied in all areas where decisions need to be made on the basis of accumulated data. The manufacturing industry is one promising application area. All phases of the manufacturing process generate data, which is often stored in separate and heterogeneous data stores, and quick decision making on the basis of data is required to keep the production process effective.

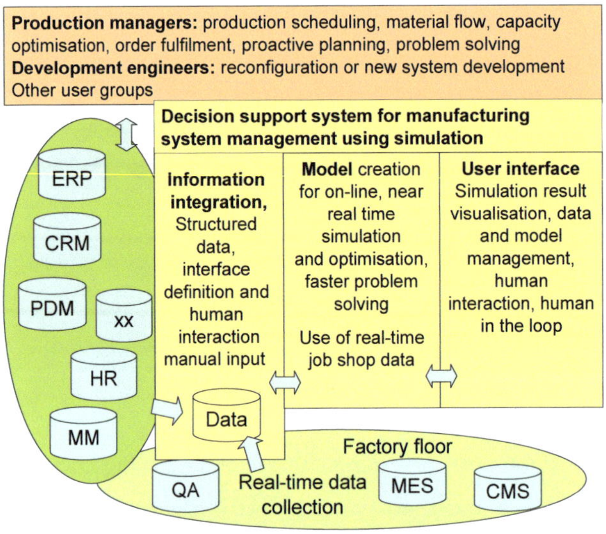

Fig. 5. Heterogeneous information systems (business, product and facility) as well as factory-floor software parallel to a simulation-based decision support system.

Manufacturing system operations planning is usually performed in a heterogeneous information system environment (see Figure 5). There are business-oriented systems like Enterprise Resource Planning (ERP) - or Manufacturing Resource Planning (MPRII) or Material Requirements Planning (MRP) - Customer Relationship Management (CRM), facility-related systems like Enterprise Asset Management (EAM) or Maintenance Management System (MMS) and Product Data Management systems (PDM). Systems potentially used on the factory floor include a Manufacturing Execution System (MES), job shop data acquisition systems, quality control system, individual machine control systems and so on. A dedicated decision support system for manufacturing operations planning does not replace those existing systems; they remain in place as parallel systems, serving as sources of information for decision making. Depending on the role of the decision support system user, he or she also has access to these other systems.

2.3 Use of discrete event simulation in the manufacturing life cycle

"Simulation is the imitation of the operation of the real-world process or system over time. Simulation involves the generation of an artificial history of the system and the observation of that artificial history to draw inferences concerning the operating characteristics of the real system that is represented". (Banks et al. 1996)

Manufacturing simulation focuses on modelling the behaviour of manufacturing organisations, processes and systems. Traditionally simulation tools have been used in system planning and design. Simulation models live as long as there is a need for strategic planning. Once the system has been implemented, the model loses its value and is set aside until other strategic decisions have to be made. Today, simulation models are used in all the different system levels and phases of the manufacturing system life cycle (see Figure 6). The more accurate the model, with detailed process elements, the more complex it is to build, and the more data is needed. The following steps are found: concept creation, layout planning, production simulation, software development and operator training (Heilala et al. 2001, 2007). Naturally, there are a wide variety of simulation tools in the manufacturing domain.

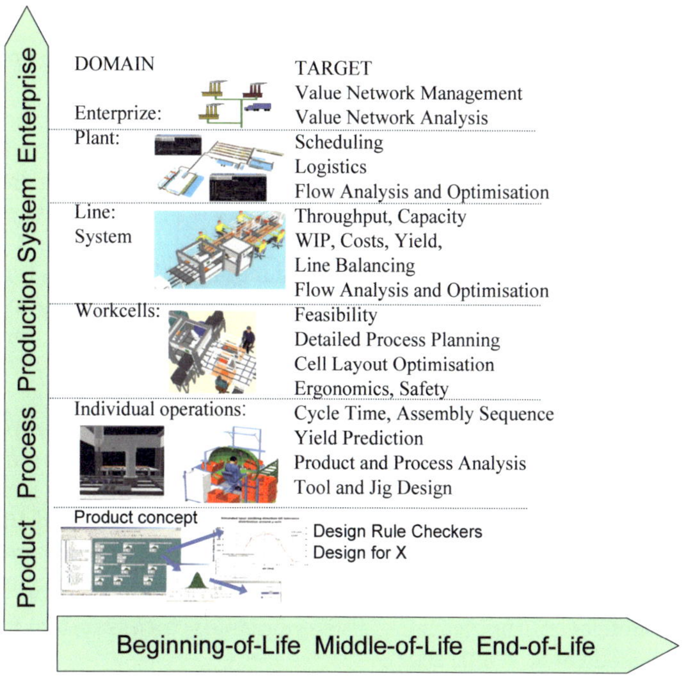

Fig. 6. Manufacturing systems modelling and simulation has many hierarchical levels and development aims, and can be used in different life cycle phases.

The use of discrete event simulation (DES) can be enhanced to also cover production operations planning as a decision support tool, as suggested by Thomson (1993). Table 1 summarises the use of discrete event simulation in manufacturing life cycle phases. The design and analysis of the system concept provide input for strategic decisions. Production planning with simulation provides input for operational decisions.

Discrete event simulation methods are feasible for analysis of all types of discrete manufacturing systems, from project shops to automated production and assembly lines, and even all the way to the supply chain. A review on simulation-based real-time decision making for manufacturing automation systems is presented by Yoon and Shen (2006). Kádár et al. (2006) present how to use discrete event simulation for supporting production planning and scheduling decisions. In general, the annual Winter Simulation conference (http://www.wintersim.org/) is a good source for finding ongoing research and development results.

System life-cycle phase	What and how	Why
Concept creation, layout planning of cells, lines and factories.	2D and 3D visualisation, communication, animation, easy and fast modelling are needed.	Selling and developing ideas and concepts. Fast elimination of those that are unsuitable.
Production simulation, detailed development of the system, design optimisation.	Analysis of control principles, routing, buffer sizes, capacity, utilisation, throughput time, bottlenecks, etc. Data analysis, reports, multiple runs, stochastic values.	Investment insurance, strategic decision support and detailed evaluation of alternatives. Simulation model is an intelligent document of the system.
Control software development, debugging and validation.	Control software debugging and validation against virtual system, emulation. Real-time integration with validated simulation model and control software.	Debugging and testing the control system, shortening the development time, faster system installation, off-line control system development.
Training of operators, ramp-up and installation of system.	Training with virtual model and control software. Emulation, integration of validated simulation model and control software.	Experience for operators, normal use and exceptions, faster ramp-up.
Operational use, problem solving in exceptions, validation of production plans.	Simulation tools for production managers. Data integration, easy to use graphical user interface, fast analysis, embedded simulation.	Decision support for operations planning, short-term scheduling, operational and tactical capacity planning, order-book validation.

Table 1. Use of discrete event simulation in different manufacturing system life-cycle phases, based on Heilala et al. (2001, 2007).

2.4 Operational use

While some DES models are used for planning and design, other models are used in the day-to-day operational production planning of manufacturing facilities. These "as built"' models provide manufacturers with the ability to evaluate the capacity of the system for new orders, unforeseen events such as equipment downtime, effects of missing materials, and changes in operations. Having built a simulation and calculations model, experiments are then performed by changing the input parameters and predicting the response. Experimentation is normally carried out by asking 'what-if' questions and using the model to predict the likely outcome. Some operations models also provide schedules that manufacturers can use to run their facilities. Simulation can complement other planning and scheduling systems to validate plans and confirm schedules. Before taking a new order from a customer, a simulation model can show when the order will be completed and how taking the new order will affect other orders in the facility. Simulation can be used to support planners and schedulers and thereby boost production efficiency (Figure 1).

It is important to recognise that normally simulation primarily serves as a decision support and evaluation tool for feasible scheduling and does not directly seek optimal solutions. Optimisation algorithms or scheduling rules can be embedded into the simulation model or the system could combine optimisation and simulation as presented by Appelqvist and Lehtonen (2005) and Vasudevan et al. (2008).
Potential uses of simulation-aided decision support for production planning are shown in Figure 7. In operations planning, a validated and tested simulation model is a must, as is having reliable data for analysis. The challenges of manufacturing system simulation and modelling are discussed later in the text.

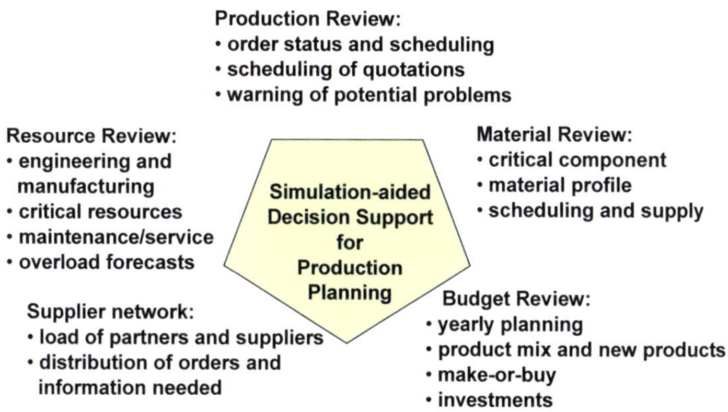

Fig. 7. Potential use of simulation-aided decision support for production planning.

2.5 Current status of simulation-aided operations planning

Simulation-based scheduling and planning tools are actively being developed. Commercial solutions exist; some of the latest examples have been presented by Hindle and Duffin (2006) and Vasudevan et al. (2008). The semiconductor and process industries have been leading the way. Clear reasons for this include expensive equipment, the need to keep equipment utilisation high and customer service. In the mechanical industry, there are limited examples of the use of simulation or optimisation tools in operational planning, the finite scheduling of manufacturing, despite the availability of dedicated software packages like Preactor (www.preactor.com), Asprova (www.asprova.com), and others made by simulation engineering offices, like Simul8-Planner (www.simul8-planner.com) and Delfoi Planner (www.delfoi.com/web/en_GB/). Commercial simulation software can potentially be used as a development platform.
The cheapest packages have fixed data structures and menus. This kind of Gantt chart scheduling software is targeted at users with simple production scheduling problems typical of small job shops. Open source softwares from a research institutes are available. Such software is usually targeted at simpler production scheduling problems or educational use. More information is available at the Production Scheduling Portal (www.productionscheduling.com).
The more advanced, customised solutions are expensive and their costs are not limited to the price of the software. The costs of integrating simulation systems with other manufacturing applications are high; there is always a need to transfer and share data between the simulation and other manufacturing software applications. Custom-built proprietary

interfaces are too costly, making it prohibitive for users to use simulation technology. Thus applications need to be customised extensively; due to the lack of standardisation, system integration is challenging. Naturally, if managers are using a simulation model to plan operations, the model must be precise enough and use accurate data.
Some of the benefits of implementing an operational simulation scheduling system include: less effort required to plan day-to-day scheduling, customer order due date conformance, synchronisation of the flow through the plant; minimisation of set-ups/changeovers, early warnings of potential problems, checks of critical resources and materials, and, of course, "what-if" scenario analysis for capacity planning.

2.6 User groups

An operational decision support system has many potential users (Table 2), from the operator on the production line to the plant manager. Present Factory Information System (FIS) capability is geared towards supporting operators and engineers, not planners, financial analysts, and upper management. Manufacturers have begun the transition from passive data monitoring to converting data to information, and they have not attempted proactive, operational and strategic decision making.
Different users require, or are allowed access to, different types of information, or the same information is presented differently. Users should be given enough information to enable them to make the decisions necessary to optimise the performance of their job function. One of the challenges is to provide the appropriate granularity of information needed by each class of user.

Organisational and operational level	**User**	**Time frame**	**Data and information**	**Decision**
Manufacturing Cell/Line	Supervisor Process Engineer Production Planners	Minutes/Hours/ Shifts	Production line data, e.g. process data, equipment utilisation, material availability	Assignment of order to each line/machine, scheduling of orders.
Business Unit/Plant	Plant Manager Production Teams Customer service	Shifts/Days/ Weeks	Summarised data from Cell/Line level e.g. production, subcontracting, materials	Determination of an order list, workload, scheduling of order book and forecasts
Enterprise	Upper Management	Days/Weeks/ Months	Summarised data from Business Unit/Plant level	Make or buy, production mix, budget planning, game plans
Suppliers	OEMs Partners	Days/Weeks/ Months	Supply data such as production numbers, due dates.	Production planning

Table 2. Decision and planning data at different organisational levels.

3. Developing a model-driven decision support system

3.1 Challenges and research needs

Manufacturing systems, processes and data are growing and becoming more complex. Manufacturing engineering and production management decisions involve the consideration of many interdependent factors and variables. These often complex, interdependent factors and variables are probably too many for the human mind to cope with at one time (McLean & Leong 2001a; 2001b). Simulation modelling and analysis could help. Discrete event/material flow/factory simulation is used commonly in the manufacturing system design phase to evaluate the concept and optimise system solutions, sometimes also for training operators or selling ideas to potential customers, using a "virtual factory" as shown in this chapter.

The IMTI Modelling and Simulation for Affordable Manufacturing Roadmap (IMTI 2003) defines 75 top-level goals and 250 supporting requirements for research, development, and implementation of modelling and simulation technologies and capabilities. Subsequent processing has distilled these needs into four focused, high-level goals:

1. **Automated Model Generation** - Develop techniques to enable automated generation and management of models at various levels of abstraction for multiple domains.
2. **Automated Model-Based Process Planning** - Provide the capability to automatically generate manufacturing process plans based on product, process, and enterprise models, with integrated tools to evaluate the producibility of features, resources, and repeatability.
3. **Interoperable Unit Process Models** - Develop a shared base of robust, validated models for all materials and manufacturing processes to enable fast, accurate modelling simulation of any combination of processing steps.
4. **Scalable Life-Cycle Models** - Provide the capability to create and apply scalable product life-cycle models in every phase of the life cycle and across all tiers of the supply chain.

Another list of challenges (Fowler and Rose, 2004) identifies the following:

5. **Grandest Challenge 1: An order-of-magnitude reduction in problem solving cycles.** The simulation process for manufacturing systems analysis, model design, model development and deployment.
6. **Emerging Grand Challenge 2: Development of real-time simulation based problem solving capability.** Permanent, always on, synchronised factory models, on-demand, automatically built factory models.
7. **Emerging Grand Challenge 3: True plug-and-play interoperability of simulations and supporting software within a specific application domain.**
8. **Big Challenge 4: Greater acceptance** of modelling and simulation within industry.

These challenges partially overlap. One other common challenge is input data collection and management as presented by Skoogh (2009). The following sections addresses these challenges and discusses selected public case studies carried out at VTT.

4. VTT system development

The VTT solution concept presented here is a hybrid decision support system solution. The industrial cases presented in this chapter use complex multi-criteria models, i.e. discrete manufacturing system simulation, to provide decision support. The solutions use data from existing manufacturing information systems and parameters provided by decision makers to aid decision makers in analysing current and future production situations. Visualisation of the current and future factory-floor status is essential in decision making as well as interactive user-system communication for "what-if" scenario analysis. The system can be called a model-oriented or model-based decision support system (see Figure 1).

4.1 Past development

The earlier development of some applied research projects has been discussed elsewhere (Heilala et al., 1999; 2001). Both then and now, similar aims have been set for development: to increase customer order delivery accuracy, capacity planning and synchronisation of manufacturing tasks in customer-driven manufacturing. The developed functional prototype tools increased the agility of the production network in fast-changing environments; performance was evaluated by users, but actual research into the benefits of using the systems was not carried out. Past industrial pilot cases were from the mechanical, heavy mechanical and electronic industries.

The basic concept is still the same. Although similarities can be found in the user interface, each of the pilots is unique. The past generic system environment is shown in Figures 8 and 9. Integration into other enterprise applications, like ERP or MRP, was done using formatted ASCII text files or CSV files. ASCII text transfer is a robust traditional method. SQL query has also been used. The number of input and parameter files depended on the enterprise IT system structure. The parameter file could be created and updated using spreadsheets or a simple text editor. The user interface also incorporated tools for data management.

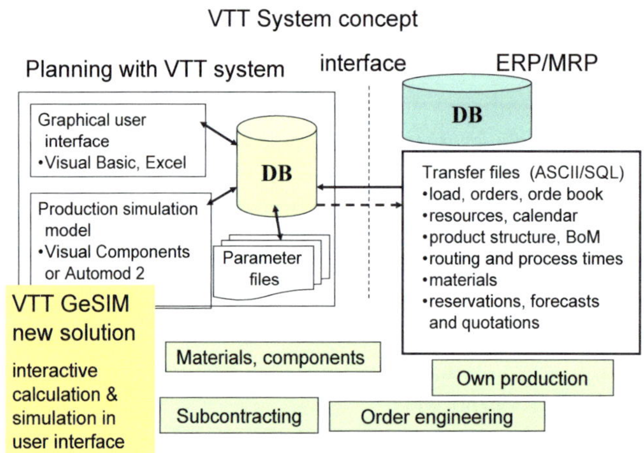

Fig. 8. Current VTT system concept for manufacturing operations planning

The analysis run in these pilot applications was a batch process (Figure 9). The target was to create a daily work list, short-term scheduling, capacity planning, order book creation and validation, and "what-if" scenarios in general. The length of a simulation run ranged from a single shift to a few weeks, months, or even years of simulated production time. It is important to note that there is a human in the loop; the user accepts or modifies the solution provided by the system.

The user interface consisted of graphics, bar and Gantt charts, and custom reports pointing out potential problem areas in production, such as resource overload, unnecessary waiting times or missing components and orders that would be late in the future. The status of work centres and customer orders could even be seen at the component level.

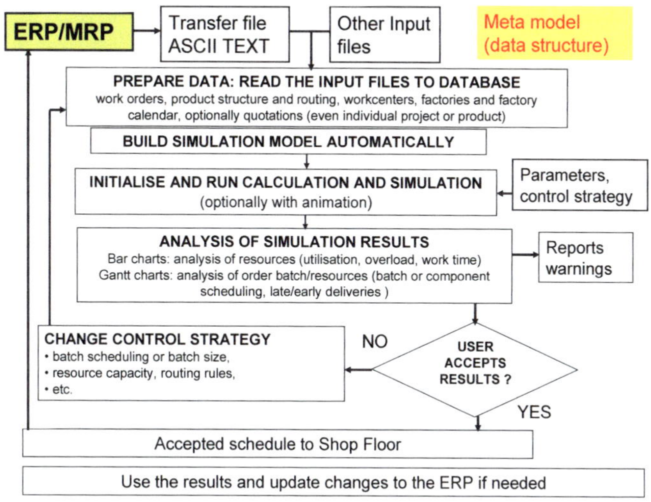

Fig. 9. Analysis workflow.

The graphical user interface (GUI) can have several windows. Scheduling changes could be done interactively, e.g. with a mouse and simple drag and drop. The first GUIs were based on MS Office tools, MS Excel and MS Project as reported by Heilala et al. (1999), but there were limitations. In later cases the user interfaces were programmed using Visual Basic and some OCX libraries (Heilala et al., 2001; 2007).

The two first case studies, carried out in 1997-1999 (Heilala et al. 1999), a commercial simulation software Automod was used (www.automod.com). The run-time features were enhanced with C programming language algorithms. One of the main results was a generic and parametric model, which was automatically initialised and configured based on input data files.

Analysis of the process flow is shown in Figure 9. Optionally, a simple 3D animation of the simulation could have been used, but since more computer capacity would have been required for this, it was normally not used in daily operations planning. Production managers were satisfied with bar and Gantt chart type visualisation. It is important to note that the user approved all the changes and he or she had control of the decision. The user could initiate an optional what-if analysis, such as of machine breakdowns, by editing the input files or using the user-interface functionality. Later case studies, carried out in 1999-2001 (Heilala et al. 2001), studied also the potential to do simulation calculations directly in the graphical user interface and to also add new features for analysis. In addition, those early cases included the order engineering phase, and partly subcontracting of selected critical components.

4.2 Recent case studies

The latest public case studies have been presented at the Winter Simulation conference by Heilala et al. (2007). The industrial partners in the pilot cases were Sandvik Mining and Construction Oy (www.sandvik.com), a producer of rock drilling equipment, single and multi-boom mining and tunnelling jumbos and long-hole production drill rigs, and Raute Corporation (www.raute.com), a supplier of a complete range of machinery, systems and technology for the production of plywood and veneer, including log handling, peeling, drying, veneer handling, plywood layup and pressing, panel handling and automation and control.

The industrial pilots had different aims and development platforms. The heavy machinery case, Sandvik, which involves the customer-driven manufacturing of mining equipment, is purely an operational simulation case with tools for production managers. It is based on an embedded simulation platform, VTT's proprietary GESIM (Generic Simulation). The Raute case involves plywood factory design and operational manufacturing simulation with simulation software based on the Visual Components 3DCreate®. Simulation development and modelling support the system sales process, equipment development, factory planning and later also operational planning at the real plywood factory.

In the use of simulation methods for operations planning and scheduling, the key issue is getting the correct analysis data to make simulation as easy as possible. In both cases, generic development yielded improvements to the integration of manufacturing-related data from existing legacy systems, like ERP. Also, methods for automated model building were developed and advanced methods for simulation model management using a graphical user interface were studied. Simulation results must be presented in a visually effective way and some new ideas were evaluated in case studies. The development of tools and methods seeks to create easy-to-use, user-friendly solutions.

4.3 Heavy mechanical industry – Sandvik

An initial implementation of the Sandvik case study includes a graphical user interface (GUI) with simulation capabilities for production managers (Figure 10). Data integration is partially generic using custom-built proprietary interfaces. Simulation data is fed from the ERP as text files in CSV format; this is a robust integration into the ERP system. Current ERP systems usually have output to Excel or text files and thus the VTT system concept can be adapted to a new ERP system if needed. A simulation engine and calculations are embedded in the user interface and there is no 3D factory model. Simulation results are shown with a windows-style graphical user interface, bar and Gantt charts. The simulation system is parametric; adding resource data to the ERP also adds resources automatically to the simulation model when data is read into the system.

The current GESIM-Sandvik solution has a wide range of functionalities. A wealth of information is readily available through pop-up windows with mouse interaction as well as functions for planning production operations. It is easy to re-schedule orders as well as forecasts, and to add and delete orders. The user interface shows the factory status: all orders are displayed in the upper window, while the workload on a selected resource is in the middle window, including estimates of the selected subcontractor's workload and orders in the selected resource. Potential critical material shortages are displayed along with certain other warnings.

Final assembly production is configured as flow line and products are moved to the next workplace at predefined time intervals. Since each order can have a different configuration, the workload on the workplaces varies. The solution here is to adjust the number of human operators in the workplaces. Simulation analysis shows the need for workers, or actually the work time needed in each process phase.

There are several potential user groups in the company, but the principal planned users are production managers and production line foremen. Information flow is from the ERP system to the simulation. The evaluated and selected scenario must be entered manually into the ERP system, so the user is in control. The simulation tool helps in the planning of dynamic operations by enabling production managers to make better decisions.

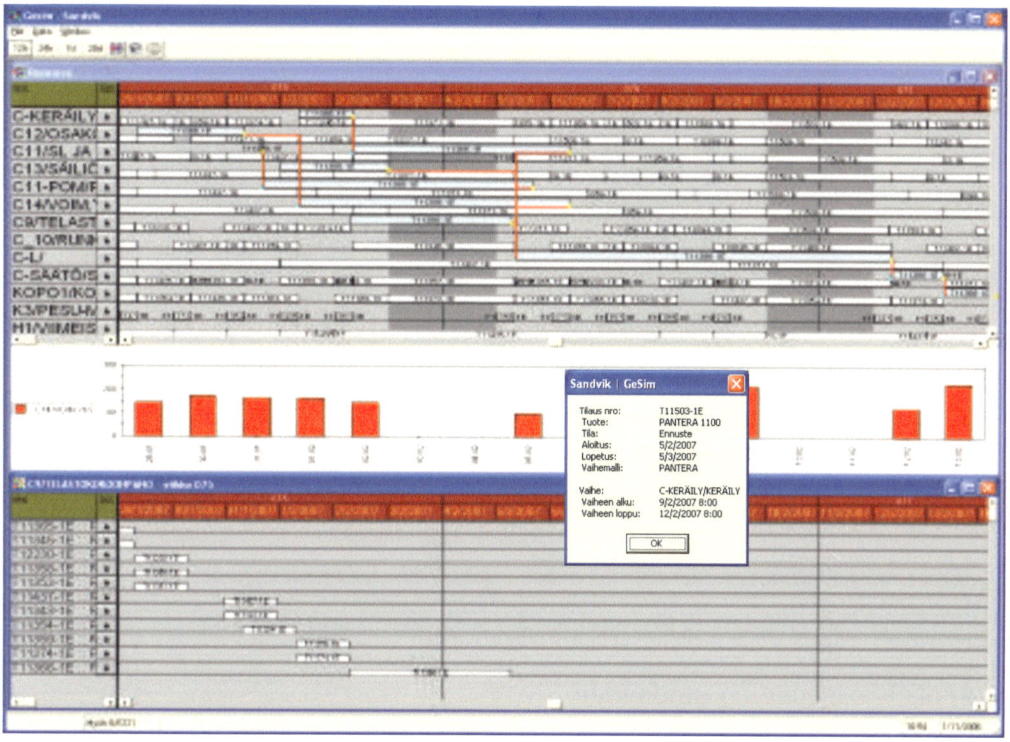

Fig. 10. User interface, case Sandvik. Upper windows shows all orders and the critical path of the selected order, middle windows shows manual working hour in the selected resource and lower windows shows orders in the same selected resource or process phase.

4.4 Plywood manufacturing - Raute

The Raute case study – implementation of a simulation tool for plywood factory planning using Raute equipment models and later for scheduling plywood mill operations. An initial implementation is available, shown in Figure 11.

The 3D factory simulation provides information on equipment and storage status. Some additional information can be shown using a Gantt chart type window. Depending on which windows are made active through the software user interface, other interactive menus will be opened.

The first development focus was the creation of methods for simulation model building. Means of transferring simulation data from the database to the actual simulation model and controlling the simulation with an easy-to-use interface were developed. The automated model building functionality was developed with Visual Component software as well.

The developed methods have many potential uses. For instance, they can serve as a tool for sales engineering or factory design. Later the methods can be used for the planning and optimisation of day-to-day factory operations. The current version evaluates the work schedules of the ERP systems and compares them with simulation run results. The user interface has many functions that are not presented here. The tool that was developed is an add-on for Visual Components 3DCreate®.

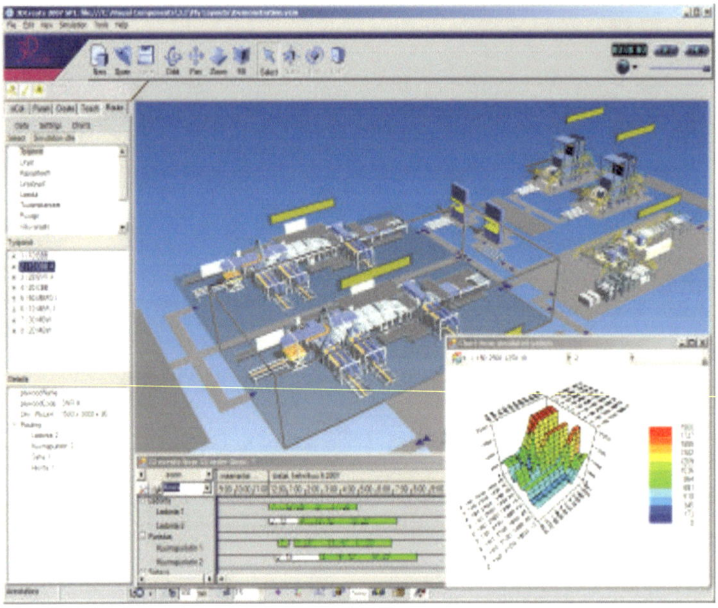

Fig. 11. Raute case simulation, plywood factory with Raute equipments.

5. Application building guidelines

The tool concept created during the development projects can be adapted for different companies as described previously. The building of each application is still a project: that requires a resource commitment from both the developers and the end-user. Application set-up is simple within an enterprise if all its manufacturing information systems are the same; it is just a configuration task. This has been evaluated and tested in the past cases.

A typical simulation project is described in many simulation textbooks, for example Banks et al. (1996). Now the aim is to create an integrated or embedded simulation application for manufacturing personnel. This project is more challenging. The application needs data from various other manufacturing information systems. Furthermore, the human aspect - user interaction with the planned system - must be carefully developed.

Based on earlier development tasks at VTT, the guidelines from enterprise application integration (Linthicum, 2000), simulation project steps (Banks et al., 1996; Banks, 1998) and the user-centred design principle (Vilpola & Terho, 2008; ISO 13407 standard; Sears & Jacko, 2009), the following procedure for application building has been identified. These activities should be considered when approaching the development and implementation of operational simulation applications.

The 10 steps in application building are (this is not a comprehensive list):

1. Defining the needs with the end-users
2. Defining the business processes and way of working
3. Specifying data and file structures, making sense of the data,
4. Collecting and creating data, interfacing
5. Specifying the graphical user interface, visualisation, user-centric design
6. Programming the graphical user interface
7. Implementing changes to the simulation and calculation model

8. Testing and validating the model and system
9. Integrating the application into the ERP or MRP system and other legacy systems
10. User training and documentation

The first steps are critical for successful implementation. These steps are required for requirements gathering. The input of the final end-user is necessary. Final end-user resources are also required in testing and system validation. This is an iterative and parallel development process.

Understanding the enterprise and problem domain, steps 1 and 2: This is one of the most complex and time-consuming parts of the process. Understanding the problem domain requires working with many organisation and department heads in order to get a handle on the structure and content of the various information systems, as well as to determine the business requirements of each organisation. This process is a basic requirements-gathering problem. It requires interfacing with paper, people, and systems to determine the information that will allow the problem to be defined correctly so that it can be analysed, modelled and refined.

Making sense of the data, steps 3 and 4: The data-level implementation comes down to understanding where the data exists, gathering information about the data, and applying business principles to determine which data flows where, and why. There are basic sub-steps that must be followed:

1. Identifying the data
2. Cataloguing the data
3. Building the enterprise manufacturing metadata models
4. Definition of interfaces between systems

User-centric development, step 5: The specification of the graphical user interface, simulation data management, effective visualisation and reporting as well user interaction with the system are challenging. The development team should apply user-centric design methodology (Vilpola & Terho, 2008; ISO 13407:1999 standard; Sears & Jacko, 2009). This means keeping the planned end-users in the development loop. User feedback is essential during development. The success of the system depends on how easy it is to use.

The other steps: The steps can be done parallel to simulation modelling and graphical user interface development. The development of the graphical user interface and adapting the simulation and calculation model is demanding as well and is based on the requirements collected in steps 1-5. The value of validation and testing must never be underestimated, as it usually takes a significant amount of time. The users must be able to rely on the data and information provided by the system.

6. Faster model building and rebuilding

6.1 Component-based simulation model creation

For the system sales process, the use of component-based simulation brings clear speed advantages to model building. But pre-engineered simulation components must be available. Model building centres on configuring a layout by selecting the right components to fulfil the process flow and setting the right parameters. In some VTT cases, Visual Components software is used as the development platform (www.visualcomponents.com). The selected software supports system modularity and reuse of existing simulation library elements. Similar development can be done with other object-oriented simulation software.

The use of a simulation model can shorten the sales cycle of the production system – especially if the model can be created during the sales meeting and it creates additional information during the meeting, such as key performance indicators, capacity analyses and other decision-making parameters, for example system life cycle and other cost analyses. This is also the aim in one of the other industrial pilots of the recent development project, presented elsewhere Heilala et al. (2007b).

6.2 Database-driven model building

Automated model building from ERP data is also being developed and tested in the industrial pilot cases with different simulation software. Depending on the 3D visualisation needs, manual input from a simulation engineer might be required. In general, the model and simulation load can be initiated based on information such as:

- work orders (order book from ERP database), optional quotation book (from CRM or sales offices), production scheduling
- product structure and routing, standard phase times
- work centres and component factories, layout, equipment capability
- stock items, buffers, material supply
- factory calendar, holidays, absences, planned maintenance, etc.
- equipment availability, efficiency
- simulation parameters: depth of product structure, work order release rules
- optional what-if analysis (machine breakdowns) and new orders, others.

The other generic development point has been simulation data management. Simulation data is exported in both pilot cases from ERP and potentially some other manufacturing information system as formatted ASCII text and CSV files. The user interface incorporates tools to map the data fields of different source files to the simulation database data fields. Means of controlling the simulation with an easy-to-use interface and presenting the simulation results were also developed.

7. Potential in standardised neutral interfaces

The use of standardised structured manufacturing data in a neutral format (like XML) could clearly increase interoperability between the manufacturing information system and the simulation, and also speed up modelling and problem solving cycles.

The Core Manufacturing Simulation Data (CMSD) specification (SISO 2009) is intended to define a neutral format for the exchange of data between simulations and other manufacturing applications. The CMSD specification is being developed by NIST under the auspices of the Simulation Interoperability Standards Organisation (SISO). Over the last few years, several projects involving researchers from different industries have been undertaken where the draft CMSD specification (SISO 2006) is used to integrate manufacturing applications. Examples of these projects can be found in Kibira and McLean (2007), Johansson et al. (2007), McLean et al. (2007), Riddick and Lee (2008).

The CMSD specification was developed to address interoperability issues related to information definition and exchange as it provides a neutral framework for modelling manufacturing information, with an emphasis on the information needed for manufacturing simulations. Information coding and representation problems increase the time and effort required to construct simulations and limit the application of simulation technology in manufacturing. Usually manufacturing simulation data is difficult to exchange between different simulation applications and other manufacturing applications. The Core Manufacturing Simulation Data specification is intended to be a neutral data format for addressing interoperability problems such as these. CMSD is defined as an information model using the Unified Modelling Language (UML) with a mapping to an exchangeable eXtensible Markup Language (XML) format.

The CMSD information model describes essential entities in the manufacturing domain and relationships between those entities needed to create manufacturing-oriented simulations. This specification facilitates the exchange of information between manufacturing-oriented simulations and other manufacturing applications such as process planning, scheduling, inventory management, production management, and plant layout. Six UML packages define manufacturing information (SISO 2009). These packages are:

- Layout
- Part Information
- Support
- Resource Information
- Production Operations
- Production Planning.

Leong et al. (2006) give a detailed description of these packages. The draft specification (SISO 2009) provides the complete specification of CMSD. The formal balloting process for this specification is slated to begin in late 2009.

Other standardisation activities also might be useful in the future. For instance, ISA-95 (www.isa.org or www.isa-95.com) is focusing on MES/ERP integration. MIMOSA (ww.mimosa.org) is developing and encouraging the adoption of open information standards for operations and maintenance in manufacturing and facility environments. The MIMOSA open standard enables collaborative asset lifecycle management. The MTConnect Institute (www.mtconnect.org) is designing an open communication standard for interconnectability in the manufacturing arena. The MTConnect standard allows devices and systems to send out understandable information. Similarly, AutomationML (www.automationml.org) developed Automation Markup Language (AutomationML™) as an intermediate standardised format for the digital factory. All these standardisation efforts could help in getting real-time status information on manufacturing equipment.

8. Simulation result visualisation

Simulation analysis produces a great deal of numerical information consisting of tables, listings, and reports. It is difficult for a human decision maker to locate the relevant pieces of information. That is why normal operational users and production managers need tools for data mining. In addition, the simulation results have to be presented in a visually effective way to speed up and improve the way the results will be understood.

Different users require, or are allowed access to, different types of information or the same information is presented differently. For instance, a line supervisor and plant manager rely on different levels of data to base their business decisions – too little or too much data and its utility is diminished, if not lost. Time is an important factor in defining how much and what kind of data should be aggregated for the upper levels of the organisation; a manager cannot afford to be "swimming in data" when making a quick decision. (Heilala et al., 2001; 2007)

The system gives, for example, a proposal for rescheduling production orders by showing late or early orders and overloaded components or resources. The user can change control and routing strategies and add resources to overloaded workplaces, either by adding more human operators, increasing working hours or using subcontracting. The user can reschedule orders, change batch sizes and so on with the visual interface and has the option of re-running the simulation to check the results.

9. Summary of VTT system constraints and benefits

The development of the method is still ongoing at VTT, as shown in Figure 12.

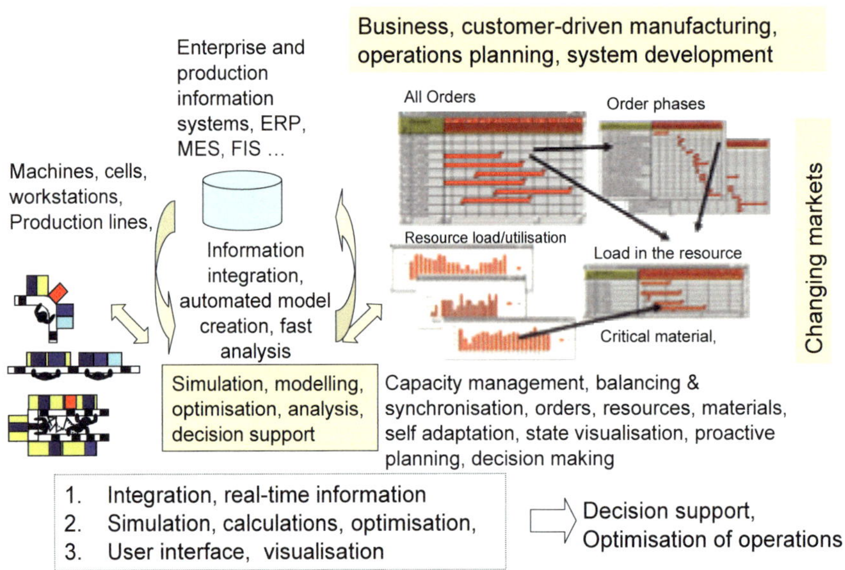

Fig. 12. Ongoing development efforts at VTT 2009-2010, improvements to use near real-time information, simulation and user interface development

The following list describes the features of the VTT solution:

- Independent system, analysis is done offline from the ERP/MRP database
- Batch process, no real-time integration to the ERP or MRP system, new iterations will use near real time factory status data
- Traditional information transfer, earlier ASCII text, CSV files or SQL query; XML-based methods are now also being studied
- Sensitive to quality of data, garbage in - garbage out, in the manner of all simulation and modelling
- Deterministic simulation model for speed, using standard operation times, no stochastic values used
- Visualisation of the order book, resource status, material availability
- Window to future events with given input, scenario, evaluation of alternatives, proactive planning

- Generic manufacturing system model, model updates and reconfiguration based on database information (some limitations)
- Decisions are made by the user

9.1 Real-time issues and data latency

The VTT solution presented here is not a real-time solution, as there is some data latency. Data latency is the characteristic of the data that defines how current the information needs to be (Linthicum, 2000).

- Real time: data is current, up-to-the second.
- Near time: data refers to information that is updated in set intervals rather than instantaneously.
- One time: data is typically updated only once or very rarely.

Some of the input files are "one time": only the modifications to the parameters are updated. Some other input files are "near time": analysis can either be started by the user or is performed automatically at selected intervals. The latest version seeks to use the following near real-time data from other manufacturing information systems: maintenance management data, machine utilisation data and real-time work flow management data. In some earlier iterations, reliable data was several days old, and the current situation was simulated.

9.2 Modelling issues

The simulation and calculation model used in the cases could either have capacity constraints or unlimited capacity depending on the objectives of the user. In the first case, capacity constraints, the analysis shows when the order will be ready and how late it will be; it can also pinpoint the reason for late completion, such as a shortage of material, overload in manufacturing resources, and so on. In the latter case, unlimited capacity, the analysis shows the amount of resources needed in order to keep the customer promise, and the managers have the option to add, for example, human operators to critical manufacturing phases. Typically manual labour -intensive final assembly can be analysed with unlimited capacity if it is easy to add human operators when and where necessary. The model also checks the critical materials, i.e. stock values and ordered components, and indicates whether materials might run out at a certain time in the future (see also Figure 7). Scheduling control strategies can be embedded directly into the simulation model or can be kept as a separate file, enabling users to adjust the parameters as necessary.

10. Summary and conclusion

The authors have developed several simulation-based decision support systems (DSS) for customer-driven manufacturing. Selected cases are presented here: DSS for sales engineers (Raute) and operations planning (Sandvik and Raute). Both presented cases use complex multi-criteria models to provide decision support. The solutions use data and parameters provided by decision makers to help analyse future production situations.

An operational decision support system has many potential users, from the operator on the production line to the plant manager and even upper management. Present Factory

Information System (FIS) capability is geared towards supporting operators and engineers, not planners, financial analysts, and upper management. ERP or MRP systems have other limitations; they are usually based on static resource models with unlimited capacity. At present, manufacturing scenarios cannot be studied efficiently with the ERP system. Manufacturers have begun the transition from passive data monitoring to converting data to information, and must seek to engage in proactive, operational and strategic decision making in the future.

The developed tool is useful in customer-driven manufacturing because it adds features for production planners and capacity managers that were not provided by standard tools in the past. By integrating discrete event simulation and traditional production planning methods, it is possible to forecast the required workloads with given input values. The simulation model and the developed graphical user interface make it possible to visualise the occurrence of potential bottlenecks or other production problems and to take corrective actions. The load data for simulation, indicating the product, its parameters as well as required quantities and delivery dates, will be obtained from marketing offices and ERP systems, so both orders and quotations can be used. Simulation gives the users a window to the future and information for decision making. It becomes possible to adjust work queues and orders, and to achieve a balanced rate of resource utilisation. Delivery days can be confirmed on the basis of the simulation model. Overload situations and unnecessary waiting time can be eliminated. The use of the tool is not limited only to operational planning; it is useful for strategic planning as well. The effects of additional equipment can be analysed.

Many other similar tools are available. One limiting factor for the wider use of the technology is the cost of data integration, the integration of the simulation model and other manufacturing information systems; in other words, the customisation cost is high. There is no commonly accepted data model standard. Neutral standardised interfaces are needed and efforts are ongoing to aid the integration and development of reusable simulation models and objects. These interfaces would make modelling easier and reduce the costs associated with both model construction and data exchange between simulations and other manufacturing software applications. This would make simulation technology more affordable and accessible to a wide range of industrial users. The authors used ASCII text files in the presented case studies, but perhaps in the future XML will provide a better solution.

The developed simulation tools can be adapted for new industrial fields and implemented for other enterprises. The developers must have a deep understanding of the processes of the field in question in order to be able to model the specific features of the industry. Naturally, modifications to the user interface and data interface are required. Both the end-user and system developer must commit development resources to the implementation project.

Simulation software has evolved and most of the current software is object oriented with a graphical windows-style user interface. At the same time, however, the complexity of manufacturing systems and products has increased. There are development needs in manufacturing system modelling and simulation: e.g. integration of different simulation and modelling methods - use of multi-disciplinary simulation with different abstraction levels. A simulation model and a manufacturing system life cycle should be combined, and the

model should be a virtual, concurrently evolving digital image of the real system. Thus there is a need for real-time data coupling from the factory floor.
Another future aim could be hybrid methods – simulation, optimisation and other manufacturing information systems in an integrated application. These could be used by non-simulation experts, even online and in real-time on the factory floor (plug and simulate), enabling science-based system management.
Future development includes evaluation of the use of new optimisation parameters, such as energy consumption and other environmental aspects. The development of using environmental aspects in the system design phase has been presented by Heilala et al. (2008), Lind et al. (2009). The next step would be to use these parameters for production scheduling decisions as well.

11. Acknowledgements

The chapter is a summary of following national public research projects: "Integrated dynamic simulation model of enterprise for planning of operations", (1997-1999); "Integrated dynamic customer driven production network management using operative simulation" (2000-2001) and "Integrated dynamic electronic production and suppliers control and planning of resources" (2000-2001). Development work was later carried out in the projects "Modelling and simulation of manufacturing systems for value networks" (2005-2007) and "Optimisation of autonomous production cell - real time production intelligence", (2009-2010). The industrial partners, VTT and TEKES (the Finnish Funding Agency for Technology and Innovation) have funded the work carried out by VTT.

12. References

Appelqvist, P. & Lehtonen, J.-M. (2005). Combining optimisation and simulation for steel production scheduling. *Journal of Manufacturing Technology Management*, Vol. 16, No. 2, pp. 197-210, ISSN: 1741-038X

Banks, J.; Carson J.S. & Nelson B.L. (1996). *Discrete-Event System Simulation* (2nd ed.), Prentice Hall, ISBN 0132174499, Upper Saddle River, N.J.

Banks, J. (ed) (1998). *Handbook of Simulation. Principles, Methodology, Advances, Applications, and Practice.* John Wiley & Sons, ISBN 978-0-471-13403-9, New York.

Fowler, J. W. & Rose, O. (2004). Grand Challenges in Modelling and Simulation of Complex Manufacturing Systems. *SIMULATION*, Vol. 80, No. 9, pp. 469-476

Harrell, C. R. & Tumay, K. (1995). *Simulation made easy. A manager's guide*, Industrial Engineering and Management Press. Institute of Industrial Engineers. ISBN 0-89806-136-9,

Heilala, J.; Montonen, J.; Salonen, T.; Sorvali, E. & Suuronen, J. (1999). Simulation Based Operations Planning In Make-To-Order Manufacturing. 15th International Conference on Production Research (ICPR-15) "Manufacturing for a Global Market". Limerick, IR, 9 - 12 August 1999. University of Limerick, pp. 1467 – 1470.

Heilala, J.; Hentula, M.; Montonen, J.; Alhainen, J.; Voho, P.; Salo, J.; Kuokkanen, K.; Leivo, K. & Ali-Raatikainen, J. (2001) Simulation aided decision support for customer driven manufacturing. *16th International Conference on Production Research* (ICPR-16). Prague, Czech Republic, 29 July - 3 August 2001

Heilala, J.; Montonen J.; Salmela A. & Järvenpää P. (2007). Modelling and Simulation for Customer Driven Manufacturing System Design and Operations Planning. *Proceedings of the 2007 Winter Simulation Conference.* S. G. Henderson, B. Biller, M.-H. Hsieh, J. Shortle, J. D. Tew, and R. R. Barton, eds. Washington D.C. 9-12 December, 2007.

Heilala, J.; Väätäinen, O.; Montonen, J.; Kulmala, H. & Laaksonen, T. (2007). Decision Support and Simulation Methods For Assembly System Sales Engineers. *6th EUROSIM Congress on Modelling and Simulation.* September 9-13, 2007 Ljubljana, Slovenia.

Heilala, J; Vatanen, S; Montonen, J; Tonteri, H; Johansson, B, Stahre, J. & Lind, S. (2008). Simulation-Based Sustainable Manufacturing System Design. *Proceedings of the 2008 Winter Simulation Conference.* S. J. Mason, R. R. Hill, L. Mönch, O. Rose, T. Jefferson, J. W. Fowler (eds.). IEEE, ss. 1922 - 1930,

Hindle, K. & Duffin, M. (2006). Simul8-planner for Composites Manufacturing. *Proceedings of the 2006 Winter Simulation Conference.*

IMTI 2003. Roadmap Modelling and Simulation for Af-fordable Manufacturing", January 2003, (http://www.imti21.org/resources/roadmaps.html)

ISO 13407:1999. Human-centred design processes for interactive systems. International Organization for standardization

Johansson, M., Leong, S.; Lee, Y. T.; Riddick, F.; Shao, G.; Johansson, B.; Skoogh, A. & Klingstam, P. (2007). Generic Simulation of Automotive Assembly for Interoperability Testing, In *Proceedings of the 2007 Winter Simulation Conference*, eds. S. G. Henderson, B. Biller, M.-H. Hsieh, J. Shortle, J. D. Tew, and R. R. Barton, 1035-1043, IEEE.

Järvinen, P.; Puolamäki, K.; Siltanen, P. & Ylikerälä, M. (2009). Visual Analytics.Final report. Espoo, VTT. 45 p. + app. 3 p. VTT Working Papers; 117. ISBN 978-951-38-7178-9. http://www.vtt.fi/inf/pdf/workingpapers/2009/W117 .pdf

Kádár, B.; Pfeiffer, A. & Monostori, L. (2004). Discrete event simulation for supporting production planning and scheduling decisions in digital factories. *Proceedings of the 37th CIRP International Seminar on Manufacturing Systems; Digital enterprises, production networks*, Budapest, Hungary, 444-448.

Kibira, D., & McLean, C. (2007). Generic Simulation of Automotive Assembly for Interoperability Testing, In *Proceedings of the 2007 Winter Simulation Conference*, eds. S. G. Henderson, B. Biller, M.-H. Hsieh, J. Shortle, J. D. Tew, and R. R. Barton, 1035-1043. IEEE .

Leong, S.; Lee, Y. T.; & Riddick, F. (2006). A Core Manufacturing Simulation Data Information Model for Manufacturing Applications. Simulation Interoperability Workshop, Simulation Interoperability and Standards Organization, September 10-15, 2006, Orlando.

Lind, S.; Johansson, B.; Stahre, J.; Berlin, C.; Fasth, Å.; Heilala, J.; Helin, K.; Kiviranta, S.; Krassi, B.; Montonen, J.; Tonteri, H.; Vatanen, S. & Viitaniemi, J. (2009). SIMTER - A Joint Simulation Tool for Production Development. Espoo, VTT. 49 p. VTT Working

Papers; 125. ISBN 978-951-38-7185-7. http://www.vtt.fi/inf/pdf/workingpapers/2009/W125.pdf

Linthicum, D. S. (2000). *Enterprise application integration.* Addison-Wesley Longman Inc. ISBN 0-201-61583-5, Reading, MA.

McLean, C. & Leong, S. (2001a). The Expanding Role Of Simulation In Future Manufacturing. *Proceedings of the 2001 Winter Simulation Conference.*

McLean, C. & Leong, S. (2001b). The Role of Simulation in Strategic Manufacturing. Working Group on Inte-grated Production, 2001. Available at www.nist.gov/msidlibrary/doc/ifip5.pdf

McLean, C.; Jain, S.; Riddick, F. & Lee, Y. T. (2007). A simulation Architecture for Manufacturing Interoperability Testing In *Proceedings of the 2007 Winter Simulation Conference*, eds. S. G. Henderson, B. Biller, M.-H. Hsieh, J. Shortle, J. D. Tew, and R. R. Barton. IEEE

Power, D. J., DSSResources.COM, URL http://DSSResources.COM, accessed 7 August, 2009.

Riddick, F.; & Lee, Y. T. (2008). Representing Layout Information in the CMSD Specification, In *Proceedings of the 2008 Winter Simulation Conference,* eds. S. J. Mason, R. R. Hill, L. Mönch, O. Rose, T. Jefferson, and J. W. Fowler, Piscataway, IEEE.

Sears, A. & Jacko, J. A. (eds) (2009). *Human-Computer Interaction: Development Process.* CRC Press 2009. ISBN: 9781420088908, Boca Raton, FL

SISO (2006). Core Manufacturing Simulation Data Information Model, (CMSDIM), PART 1: UML Model. CMSD Product Development Group. Simulation In-teroperability Standards Organization. Revision Date: September 13, 2006. www.sisostds.org.

SISO (2009). Pending standard: Core Manufacturing Simulation Data: UML model, SISO-STD-008-2009. CMSD Product Development Group, Simulation Interoperability Standards Organization. Available at http://discussions.sisostds.org/file.asp?file=CMSDBallotingDraft%2DReviewVersion%2Epdf [accessed July 28, 2009]

Skoogh, A. (2009). Methods for Input Data Management - Reducing the Time-Consumption in Discrete Event Simulation. Research series from Chalmers University of Technology, Department of Product and Production Development: report, ISSN 1652-9243; nr 44.

Thompson, M. B. (1993). The Marriage between Simulation & Real-time Control. APICS - The performance advantage. 8:43-46.

Vasudevan, K. K.; Lote, R.; Williams, E. J. & Ulgen, O. (2008). Iterative Use Of Simulation And Scheduling Methodologies To Improve Productivity. *Proceedings of the 2008 Winter Simulation Conference.* eds S. J. Mason, R. R. Hill, L. Mönch, O. Rose, T. Jefferson, J. W. Fowler IEEE.

Vilpola, I. & Terho, K. (2008). Efficiency to manufacturing information systems – end-user involvement in the specification. In Finnish: Tehokkuutta tuotannon tietojärjestelmiin - loppukäyttäjät mukaan määrittelyyn. Teknologiateollisuuden julkaisu 5/2008. ISBN 978-951-817-992-7.

Yoon, H. J. & Shen, W. (2006). Simulation-based real-time decision making for manufacturing automation systems: a review. *Int. J. Manufacturing Technology and Management*, Vol. 8, No. 1/2/3, pp.188–202

16

Intelligent Techniques for Decision Support System in Human Resource Management

Hamidah Jantan[1], Abdul Razak Hamdan[2] and Zulaiha Ali Othman[2]
[1]Faculty of Computer and Mathematical Sciences
UiTM, Terengganu, 23000 Dungun, Terengganu,
[2]Faculty of Information Science and Technology
UKM, 43600 Bangi, Selangor,
Malaysia

1. Introduction

Nowadays, the evolution of information technology applications makes it an absolute obligation on behalf of the decision makers to continuously make the best decisions in the shortest possible time. Decision Support System (DSS) is a technology and application that assists managerial decision makers utilizing data and models to solve semi-structured and unstructured problems (Qian et al., 2004). This chapter discusses general issues on DSS technologies and an idea to apply DSS technologies into Human Resources Management (HRM) field. Recently, the collaboration between DSS technologies and Artificial Intelligent techniques has produced another type of DSS technology known as Active DSS, it is a technology that will take place in the new millennium era (Shim et al., 2002). Active DSS is an outcome of new DSS technologies and also known as a part of Intelligent System applications. Active DSS applications such as Expert System, Knowledge-based System, Adaptive DSS and Intelligent Decision Support System (IDSS) are categorized as part of Intelligent System studies. Expert systems technology, which was a crucial area for enterprise capital in 1985-1990, is now being replaced by the intelligent system applications (Faye et al., 1998). Intelligent systems are developed to fulfill the two main functions. Firstly, to screening, shifting and filtering the increasing overflow of data, information and knowledge. Secondly, as a supporter of an effective and productive decision making that is suitable to the user needs. Intelligent systems can be developed for these purposes; range from self-organizing maps to smart add-on modules to make the use of applications more effective and useful for the users (Shim et al., 2002).

Human is important and a very valuable asset for an organization and managed by Human Resource professional. HRM system is an important element in the success of an organization, known as an integrated and interrelated approaches to managing human resources (DeNisi & Griffin, 2005). Activities in HRM involve a lot of unstructured processes such as staffing, training, motivation and maintenance (DeCenZo & Robbins, 2005). Besides that, decision making for unstructured processes in HRM usually depends on human judgment and preference. However, human decisions are subject to the limitation because sometimes people forget the crucial details of the problem, and besides, fairness and consistency are very important in any types of decisions. Computer applications as decision support tool can be used to provide fair and consistent decisions, and at the same time it can improve the effectiveness of decision making process (Palma-dos-Reis & Zahedi, 1999). In general, the traditional functions of DSS is used to support managerial decision makers in semi-structured and unstructured decision situations, a part from being assistant to the decision makers to extend their capabilities but not to replace their judgment(Turban et al., 2007). In the enhancement to DSS traditional approach, advance intelligent techniques are available in designing an intelligent system application. DSS applications which are embedded with intelligent components can improve the traditional DSS such as for reasoning and learning capabilities, and also known as IDSS. In order to improve human resource decisions, the high-quality HRM applications are required to produce precise and reliable decisions. Due to these reasons, this study presents an idea to apply IDSS approach in human resources decision making activities by using some of the potential intelligent techniques.

2. Artificial intelligent in decision support system

2.1 Intelligent ability and behaviors

In general, intelligence is the ability to think and understand instead of doing things by instinct or automatically (Negnevitsky, 2005). The basic ideas of intelligence are the studying thought processes of humans, dealing with representing and duplicating those processes via machines (e.g., computer, robots), and exploring the behavior by a machine but performed by human being. Artificial Intelligence (AI) study is how to make computers do things at which, at the moment people are better, some of intelligent behaviors in a computer system are:

- Learn and understand from experience
- Conclude in situation where exist fuzziness and uncertainty
- Use knowledge and experience to manipulate the environment
- Think and reasoning
- Understand and infer in ordinary, rational ways.
- Respond quickly and successfully to new situations.
- Recognize the relative importance of different elements in a situation
- Make sense out of ambiguous or contradictory messages (Turban et al., 2007)

Intelligent abilities and behaviors integrate with computer system will produce an intelligent machine. The machine should help humans to make decision, to search for information, to control complex objects, and finally to understand the meaning of words. In order to develop intelligent computer system, we have to capture, organize and use human expert knowledge in some narrow areas of expertise; upgrade the computational power of the system's brain with the sophistication of algorithms using sensory processing, world modeling, behavior generation, value judgment and global communication; the amount of information and values the system has stored in its memory; and the sophistication of the process of the system functioning (Negnevitsky, 2005). Besides that, intelligent system is defined as the ability of a system to act appropriately in an uncertain environment to increase the probability of success, and the success is the achievement of behavioral sub goals that support the system's ultimate goal (Meystel & Albus, 2002). In system development, some AI features that can be used to develop an intelligent system are:

- Symbolic processing which is non algorithmic methods of problem solving
- Heuristics which is intuitive knowledge or rules of thumb, learned from experience.
- Inference that includes reasoning capabilities that can build higher-level knowledge from existing heuristics (from facts and rules using heuristics or other search approaches)
- Machine learning that allows system to adjust their behavior and react to changes in the outside environment (e.g: Inductive learning, Artificial Neural Networks and Genetics Algorithms and etc.) (Turban et al., 2007)

2.2 The families of DSS

An application uses to support decision making is usually known as DSS and can be categorized into three categories which are passive DSS, active DSS and proactive DSS (Kwon et al., 2005). Passive DSS is a traditional DSS with functionalities to react as a personalized decision support built-in knowledge, no content and only for static user preference. Besides that, the components of passive DSS are Data warehouse, OLAP and rule-based. The second category of DSS is active DSS which is known as a personalized decision support with learning capability, no content and for static user preference. Expert system, adaptive DSS, knowledge-based system (KBS) are categorized as part of Intelligent DSS (IDSS). In this category, agent and machine learning are the main component of active DSS. Finally, the third category is proactive DSS, which known as Ubiquitous Computing Technology-based DSS (ubiDSS) which contains decision making and context aware functionalities. This type of DSS has mobility, portability and pro-activeness capabilities. Pull-based proactive, push-based proactive and push-based automated are the proactive DSS applications. In this study, we focus on active DSS, which known as Intelligent DSS (IDSS) using machine learning approach.

3. Intelligent Decision Support System (IDSS)

3.1 IDSS application

An Intelligent Decision Support System (IDSS) is developed to help decision makers during different phases of decision making by integrating modeling tools and human knowledge. IDSSs are tools to help decision making process where uncertainty or incomplete information exists and where decisions involving risk must be made using human judgment and preferences. IDSS as its name implied, is used to support decision making and not intended to replace the decision maker's task. In addition, IDSS works under an assumption that the decision maker is familiar with the problem to be solved. In that case, IDSS gives full control to the user regarding information acquisition, evaluation and making the final decision. IDSS is an interactive system, flexible, adaptable and specifically developed to support the solution of a non-structured management problem for improved decision-making (Quintero et al., 2005).

Besides that, an IDSS is also known as a possible theoretical model of incorporation by adapting an existing DSS system to execute in an Expert System style, such adapted systems are considered by many DSS researchers to be IDSS with the focus on the functioning of 'man and machine' together. An IDSS is more cognitive rather than a technological system, the fundamental difference is that even basic characteristics of intelligence cannot be captured in mechanistic(Malhotra et al., 2003). Most researchers agree that the purpose of

IDSS is to support the solution of a non-structured management and enable knowledge processing with communication capabilities (Qian et al., 2004; Quintero et al., 2005). IDSS can incorporate specific domain knowledge and perform some types of intelligent behaviors, such as learning and reasoning, in order to support decision-making processes (Qian et al., 2004; Viademonte & Burstein, 2006). IDSS applications are developed in various areas such as in product development and planning; management decisions; enterprise and manufacturing industries; services and etc (Table 1). In this study, we categorize the application areas into seven areas i.e medical, management, development, planning, business, manufacturing and web services. Most of the applications are specific to problem domain in that area. For example, in business industries, IDSS is used for sales prediction (Baba & Suto, 2000), stock trading forecasting (Kuo et al., 2001), financial investment (Palma-dos-Reis & Zahedi, 1999) and etc. From the literature, we list the application areas for the specific problem domains in Table 1. Most of IDSS applications that are listed in Table 1 use IDSS conventional name and of course they are different in purpose, implementation, design and intelligent techniques applied. In this study we found that, there are many

Application Area	*Problem Domain*
Medical	Veterinary medicine (Gorzalczany & Piasta, 1999) Breast Cancer (Malhotra et al., 2003)
Management	Organizational Memory System (Linger & Burstein, 1998) Irrigation System (Faye et al., 1998) Environment (Seder et al., 2000) Petroleum-contaminated (Liqiang et al., 2001) Air pollution Control (Qian et al., 2004) Urban infrastructure (Quintero et al., 2005) Flood (Sajjad & Slobodan, 2006) Boiler breakdown (Adla & Zarate, 2006)
Development	Product development (Matsatsinis & Siskos, 1999) Urban development (Shan & Lida, 1999) Weather forecasting (Viademonte & Burstein, 2006) Information visualization (Tong et al., 2001) Digital preservation (Ferreira et al., 2007)
Planning	Aerial Combat Identification (Brain, 1999) Service network planning (Waiman et al., 2005) Budget planning (Wen et al., 2005) IT outsourcing planning (Buyukozkan & Feyzioglu, 2006)
Business	Financial-Investment (Palma-dos-Reis & Zahedi, 1999) Stock trading (Kuo et al., 2001) Sales prediction (Baba & Suto, 2000) Evaluating state-owned enterprises (Wei-Kang et al., 2007)
Manufacturing	Dairy Industry (Hussein et al., 1998) Manufacturing system (Delen & Pratt, 2006)
Web services	Personalized E-services (Yu, 2004) UbiDSS - Proactive services (Kwon et al., 2005)

Table 1. IDSS Application Area

areas and problem domains that can be explored by the intelligent system researchers or system developers. This can help to increase the IDSS products in market place as alternative tools to support and improve decision making processes for the specific problem domains.

3.2 Intelligent techniques in IDSS

Recently, there are quite a number of computer applications that have applied intelligent techniques and used DSS concepts and components. However, some researchers claim it as an essential of DSS which uses the conventional name known as IDSS and others classified it as a member of intelligent system. In this case, the application's name is given based on the intelligent techniques that they use, such as expert system which uses rules based system, knowledge based system (KBS), fuzzy sets, Neural Network for reasoning and learning capabilities. In this study, we focus our discussion on IDSS applications, which are embedded with the related intelligent techniques. In fact, there are various types of Artificial Intelligent technologies that are used for reasoning, machine learning, automatic programming, artificial life, data mining and data visualization. For example, the reasoning process can use specific rules, categorization, past experience, heuristics and expectations approaches. Computer can do the reasoning through frames (e.g.: Semantic Network), rule-based, case-based and pattern recognition. In addition, the examples of machine learning approaches are Artificial Neural Network (ANN), genetic algorithms and fuzzy logic [7]. IDSS is expected to incorporate specific domain knowledge and perform certain types of intelligent behavior such as learning and reasoning, in order to support decision making process. The need to incorporate domain knowledge and intelligent capabilities in decision support system has been identified in various forms and models by many researchers [6]. IDSS incorporating knowledge component (through case base, rule base, knowledge acquisition subsystem or domain models) and intelligent component (through an intelligent advisory system, intelligent supervisor or model solver) can produce the intelligent applications.

Intelligent behaviors presented by an intelligent system are related to the abilities of gathering and incorporating domain knowledge, learning from the acquired knowledge, reasoning about such knowledge and when enquired, being able to issue recommendations and justify outcomes. These intelligent behaviors are potential intelligent techniques that can be corporated with intelligent component in IDSS. IDSS has consolidated the intelligent behaviors in its inference engine component. In this case, with the intelligent behaviors, IDSS applications can have abilities to do learning and reasoning. These abilities are used to support the decision making processes. There are various types of intelligent techniques that are applied in IDSS applications such as knowledge base system(Quintero et al., 2005),(Adla & Zarate, 2006), (Waiman et al., 2005),(Malhotra et al., 2003),(Palma-dos-Reis & Zahedi, 1999),(Matsatsinis & Siskos, 1999),(Linger & Burstein, 1998) and (Seder et al., 2000), data warehouse(Yu, 2004), fuzzy set theory(Liqiang et al., 2001), ANN(Sajjad & Slobodan, 2006), rough set classifier (Gorzalczany & Piasta, 1999), multi agent (Kwon et al., 2005) and etc. From the literature study, we found that most applications use Knowledge Based System, especially for rules based approach in their methodology and system implementation. In fact, most researchers agree with the advantage of using this technique. Not only it is easier to understand and implement, but the KBS using rule-based also supports the basic reasoning capabilities. However, intelligent system and soft computing technologies are new technological platforms, whereby intelligent logic is now usually inherent in the processing of all decision support tools [2].

3.3 Research trends in IDSS

Research and system developments in this field increase year by year with new ideas and approaches. In that case, there are some IDSS applications using hybrid techniques to develop IDSS applications. They integrate more than one intelligent technique in their application system development. This approach makes IDSS applications more capable to do learning and reasoning processes. Table 2 lists some of IDSS applications that use hybrid approach. From the literature, we found that IDSS applications used hybrid approach by integrating the intelligent techniques such as Data Mining, Artificial Neural Network, Fuzzy logic, Knowledge-based system, Agent and Genetic Algorithm. Most researchers agree that these intelligent techniques are more suitable for learning and reasoning activities. In that case, the integration between DSS and hybrid intelligent techniques will advance the capabilities of IDSS applications. However, some studies are needed to validate the abilities of IDSS applications with hybrid techniques, because in some cases may be single technique can produce the same result as hybrid techniques, and it also depend on the nature of the problems that to be solved.

Hybrid Intelligent Techniques	***Task***
Data Mining and ANN	Weather forecasting (Viademonte & Burstein, 2001), Selection and allocation of sires and dams (Hussein et al., 1998)
Artificial Neural Network (ANN) and TD Learning method	Sales prediction (Baba & Suto, 2000)
Genetic Algorithm based Fuzzy Neural Network	Measure the qualitative effect on the stock market (Kuo et al., 2001)
Fuzzy set and Gaussian dispersion model	Air pollution control at coal-fired power plants (Qian et al., 2004)
Case-based, mobile agent and multi-agent	Strategic choices in term of technical interventions on municipal infrastructure (Quintero et al., 2005)
Model based and Rule based	Measure enterprise performance (Wen et al., 2007)
Knowledge-based system and ANN	Evaluation of urban development (Shan & Lida, 1999)
Knowledge-based system and Fuzzy theory	Effective IT outsourcing management (Buyukozkan & Feyzioglu, 2006)

Table 2. Hybrid Intelligent Techniques in IDSS

4. IDSS for Human Resource (HR IDSS)

4.1 Application and techniques

Today's HR has been linked to increased productivity, good customer service, greater profitability and overall organizational survival. To reach such link, management must not only face current issues of human resource management but also deal with future challenges to HRM effectively (Stavrou-Costea, 2005). Recently, among the challenges of HRM professionals are development and technology (Okpara & Wynn, 2008). On the other hand, the major potential prospect for HRM is technology selection and implementation. The benefits of technology applications in HRM are easily to deliver information from the top to bottom workers in an organization, convenient to communicate with employees and it is easier for HR professionals to formulate managerial decisions. For these reasons, HR decision application can be used to achieve the HR goals in any types of decision making tasks. The potentials of HR decision applications are increased productivity, consistent performance and institutionalized expertise which are among the system capabilities embedded into specific programs (Hooper et al., 1998). However, HRM involves a lot of managerial decisions, where according to DeCenzo (DeCenZo & Robbins, 2005), HR professionals need to focus the goal for each of HR activities as follows:

- Staffing is to locate and secure competent employees,
- Training and development - to adapt competent workers to the organization and help them obtain up-to date skill, knowledge and abilities
- Motivation is to provide competent and adaptable employees who have up-to date skill, knowledge and abilities with an environment that encourages them to exert high energy level
- Maintenance is to help competent and adaptable employees who have up-to date skill, knowledge and abilities and exerting high level energy level to maintain their commitment and loyalty to the organization.

Research in HR IDSS can be classified into four categories according to HRM main activities; staffing, training and development, motivation and administration. There are some studies on HR IDSS applications and the intelligent techniques used are shown in Table 3. HR IDSS is used for the specific HRM domains and most of them use expert system or Knowledge-based system (KBS) approaches. The commercial emergence of Knowledge-based information technology systems (KBS) is representing a tremendous opportunity to enhance the practice of human resource management (Martinsons, 1995). The KBS benefits are more permanent, easier to duplicate, less expensive and automatically documented. Besides that, the limitations of KBS systems are difficult to capture informal knowledge; knowledge has not been documented and difficult to verbalize. The techniques used to verify and validate conventional systems are considered to be inadequate and KBS-specific methods are still immature. For these reasons, most of the new HR decision system research use other intelligent approaches such as in personnel selection, they use Data Mining and Neural Network approaches. From this study, we found that not many research have been done in HR decision systems area. Besides, the problem domains that they try to solve are also limited to specific domains. In this study, we found that most of the human resource DSS applications use expert system approach. Expert system in HRM activities has its limitations such as incorrect knowledge because of the difficulty in obtaining knowledge from appropriate experts, difficulty in representing that knowledge in a computer model and not being able to handle complex cognitive tasks (inability of the system to learn)(Hooper et al., 1998). Due to these reasons, to solve problems in expert system approach, other intelligent techniques such as hybrid intelligent techniques can be most effective when they are embedded with the HR IDSS. In HRM, there are several tasks that can be solved using this approach, for examples, selecting new employees, matching people to jobs, planning career paths, planning tanning needs for new and old employee, predicting current employee performance, predicting future employee and etc. Those problems can be solved using some machine learning approaches especially for prediction task. Recently, researches show some interest on applying machine learning approach in HRM field.

Category	*Intelligent Techniques*
Staffing Personnel Selection	Expert system/ Knowledge-based system (Hooper et al., 1998) and (Mehrabad & Brojeny, 2007) Data Mining (M. J. Huang et al., 2006) and (Chien & Chen, 2008) Artificial Neural Network (L. C. Huang et al., 2004)and (M. J. Huang et al., 2006)
Training and Development Training Development	Knowledge-based system (Liao, 2007) Expert System (Chen et al., 2007) Rough Set Theory (Chien & Chen, 2007)
Motivation Job Attitudes Performance appraisal	Artificial Neural Network (Tung et al., 2005) Fuzzy logic (Ruskova, 2002)
Administration Meeting scheduling	Software agent (Glenzer, 2003)

Table 3. Intelligent Techniques in HR IDSS

4.2 Knowledge Discovery in Database (KDD) for HR application

Knowledge Discovery in Database (KDD) or Data mining is an approach that is now receiving great attention and is being recognized as a newly emerging analysis tool (Tso & Yau, 2007). Data mining has given a great deal of concern and attention in the information industry and in society as a whole recently. This is due to the wide accessibility of enormous amounts of data and the important need for turning such data into useful information and knowledge (Han & Kamber, 2006). Computer application such as DSS that interfaces with Data mining tool can help executives to make more informed and objective decisions and help managers retrieve, summarize and analyze decision related data to make wiser and more informed decisions.

Data mining problems are generally categorized as clustering, association, classification and prediction (Chien & Chen, 2008; Ranjan, 2008). Over the years, Data mining has used various techniques including statistics, neural network, decision tree, genetic algorithm, and visualization techniques. Besides that, Data mining has been applied in many fields such as finance, marketing, manufacturing, health care, customer relationship and etc. Nevertheless, its application in HRM is rare (Chien & Chen, 2008). Prediction applications that use Data mining in HRM are infrequent, such as to predict the length of service, sales premiums, to persistence indices of insurance agents and analyze mis-operation behaviors of operators (Chien & Chen, 2008). The research to date has listed researches in HRM problems domain uses Data mining approach. Table 4 lists some of the HR applications that use Data mining, and it shows that there are few discussions about prediction tasks that use Data mining technique in human resource domain.

Data Mining method used	*Activity in HRM*
Fuzzy Data Mining and Fuzzy Artificial Neural Network	Employee development - Project Assignment (M. J. Huang et al., 2006)
Decision tree	Personnel selection (Chien & Chen, 2008) Job attitudes (Tung et al., 2005)
Association rule mining	Employee Development - Training (Chen et al., 2007)
Rough Set Theory	Personnel Selection - Recruit and Retain Talents (Chien & Chen, 2007)
Fuzzy Data Mining	Personnel Selection (Tai & Hsu, 2005)

Table 4. HR Applications using Data mining Techniques

Data mining is among the best approach to analyze records in databases. The analyzed results can be used for future planning. From the literature that we have discussed before, Data mining method had been also implemented in HR problem domains but focusing on personnel selection task and not many apply in other activities such as planning, training, managing talent and etc. Recently, the new demands and the increased visibility of HRM to seeks a strategic role by revolving to Data mining methods (Ranjan, 2008). This can be implemented by identifying generated patterns from the existing data in HR databases as useful knowledge. The patterns can be generated by using some of the major Data mining techniques i.e. clustering, association, prediction and classification. There are many human resources tasks that can be solved by using Data mining techniques such as employee performance evaluation, counseling techniques and performance management for effective and efficient decisions (Ranjan, 2008). In order to produce relevant Data mining results that are suitable to human resource tasks, several processes in Data mining process should be followed. The first step of data mining process is getting the main data sets for data set selection. These may be collected from human resource operational databases or where the human resource data warehouse is selected. The selected data then goes through cleaning and preprocessing for removing discrepancies and inconsistencies of data set and at the same time to improve quality of data set. Next, the data set is analyzed to identify patterns that represent relationship among data by applying algorithms, such as Neural nets, Decision Tree, Rough Set Theory and so on. Then patterns are validated with new human resource data sets. In addition, it should be possible to transform the generated patterns into actionable plans that are likely to help human resource people to achieve their goals. The steps in the mining process are repeated until meaningful knowledge is extracted. A pattern that satisfies these conditions becomes organizational knowledge and can be used in any related HR applications for human resource tasks. Fig 1 gives us an overview of fundamental Data mining process.

4.3 HR IDSS framework using KDD

The proposed HR IDSS framework employs the traditional DSS components (i.e. model management system, data management system and user interface) along with a knowledge-

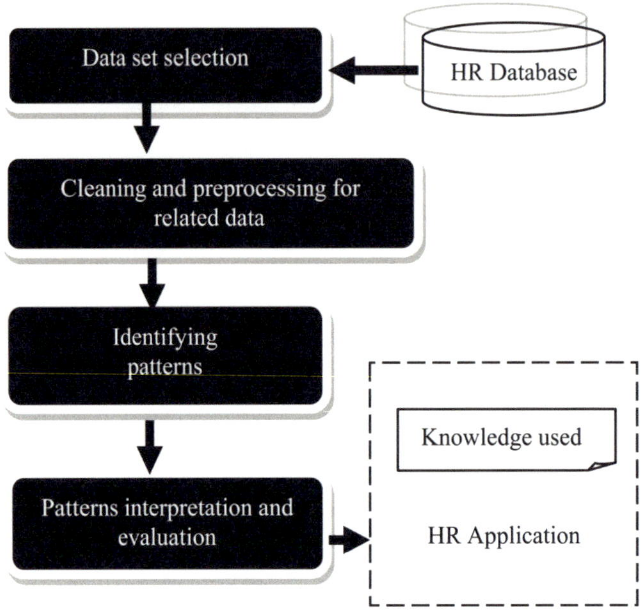

Fig. 1. Fundamental Data Mining Process

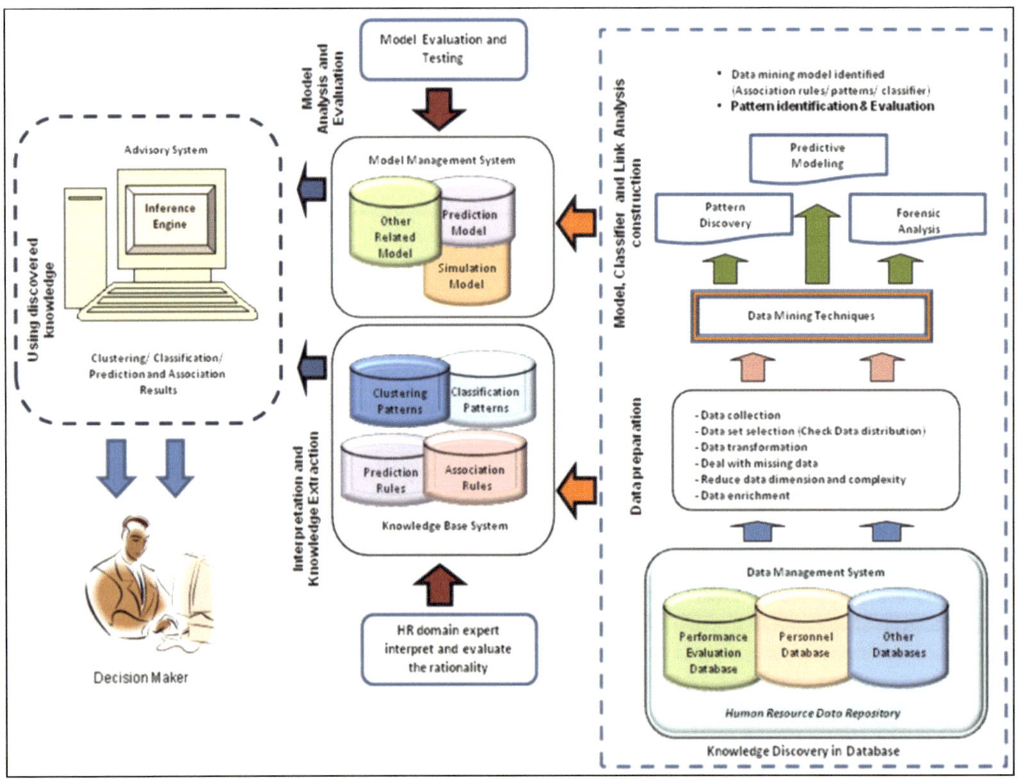

Fig. 2. Suggested HR IDSS Framework

based system component) (Delen & Pratt, 2006; Marakas, 1999; Shim et al., 2002). However, a typical IDSS consists of five main components, database system, model base system, knowledge-based System, user interface and kernel/inference engine (Delen & Pratt, 2006; Hussein et al., 1998; Matsatsinis & Siskos, 1999). In this study, we use Data mining techniques as inference component to solved HR problems. Fig.2 illustrates the proposed HR IDSS framework for HR problems. The proposed HR IDSS framework contains four main components:

a. *Knowledge Discovery in Database (KDD)* approach is used to develop predictive model and to find out the possible pattern and rules from existing database system. HR databases that is related to problems such as for employee performance prediction we can use personnel information, performance evaluation data and other related databases. The relevant data will be transformed into useful knowledge as predictive model through predictive modeling, generated rules by pattern discovery and extracted patterns to find unusual data elements by forensic analysis. All these discovery knowledge are useful for some of HR task.
b. *Model Management System is* a model based system, which store constructed model, existing simulation model and related models that can be used in appropriate decision making process. In fact, before using predictive model, the model must be evaluated and tested in model analysis and evaluation process.
c. *Knowledge Base System (KBS)* contains a set of facts and rules. In the suggested framework, KBS will contain information about patterns, association rules and any related facts and rules. The rules and patterns will be evaluated and interpreted by the HR domain experts.
d. *Advisory System* is as inference engine in HR DSS application that supervises the interactions among the various parts of HR application. Basically, this component will react as interface between user and the system itself, especially to display the prediction results, justify and explain the decision and sometimes if needed can instruct KBS to update the existing knowledge. In this study, the advisory system will display the results with some reasons, and suggest possible solutions.

On the other hand, this HR IDSS framework embedded Data mining techniques with other DSS components such as knowledge-based and model-based. On the other hand, this framework not only for prediction but also applied to other Data mining tasks such as association, classification and clustering.

5. Discussion and suggestion

HR IDSS as a part of Intelligent System applications play the same roles to assist decision making process. Applications and intelligent techniques of HR IDSS need a lot of attention and efforts, from both academicians and practitioners. In this study, we can see the potential of HR IDSS applications for future works. Firstly, there are many problem domains in HRM that can be explored by intelligent system researchers. In this case, the researchers should have teffort to identify problem domains where tools are needed to transform uncertain and incomplete data into useful knowledge. For that reason, we are trying to explore HR IDSS applications for human resource problems using machine learning approach. Secondly, researchers agree that hybrid intelligent techniques are the best approach to support decision making especially in reasoning and learning. In that case, we embedded HR IDSS framework using hybrid techniques i.e., Knowledge-based system and machine learning approaches. Thirdly, the academicians and practitioners should continuously improve the core knowledge on effective HR IDSS. This process can be enhanced through continuous development in web-enable tools, wireless protocol and group decision support system, which can expand the inter-activities and perverseness decision support technologies. For system development, we plan to use this technology to expand the capabilities of the application. Most researches were discussed from different categories. However, we would like to see more HR IDSS application and intelligent techniques applied to different problem domains in HRM field published in order to broaden our horizon of academic and practice work on HR IDSS. For that reason, we recommend the proposed HR IDSS framework as part of IDSS research in HRM problem domains.

6. Conclusion

This chapter has described the IDSS concepts, applications, related research in HRM, potential intelligent techniques and the suggested HR IDSS framework using machine learning approach. There are many areas, problem domains and intelligent techniques to be explored by academicians and practitioners. We conclude that IDSS applications and intelligent techniques applied are developed towards the expertise orientation and IDSS application development is a problem-oriented domain. Finally, the ability to continually change and obtain new understanding is the power of IDSS, and will be the IDSS applications for future work.

7. References

Adla, A., & Zarate, P. (2006). *A Cooperative Intelligent Decision Support System*. Paper presented at the International Conference on Service Systems and Service Management.

Baba, N., & Suto, H. (2000). Utilization of artificial neural networks and the TD-learning method for constructing intelligent decision support system. *European Journal of Operational Research, 122*(2), 501-508.

Brain, G. (1999). Aerial Combat Manoeuvre Identification - A Feasibility Study of an Intelligent Decision Support System. Unpublished MSc in Industrial Mathematic research. Loughborough University.

Buyukozkan, G., & Feyzioglu, O. (2006). *Fuzzy Systems and Knowledge Discovery - An Intelligent Decision Support System* (Vol. 4223). Berlin: Springer-Verlag Berlin Heidelberg.

Chen, K. K., Chen, M. Y., Wu, H. J., & Lee, Y. L. (2007). *Constructing a Web-based Employee Training Expert System with Data Mining Approach*. Paper presented at the Paper in The 9th IEEE International Conference on E-Commerce Technology and The 4th IEEE International Conference on Enterprise Computing, E-Commerce and E-Services (CEC-EEE 2007).

Chien, C. F., & Chen, L. F. (2007). Using Rough Set Theory to Recruit and Retain High-Potential Talents for Semiconductor Manufacturing. *IEEE Transactions on Semiconductor Manufacturing, 20*(4), 528-541.

Chien, C. F., & Chen, L. F. (2008). Data mining to improve personnel selection and enhance human capital: A case study in high-technology industry. *Expert Systems and Applications, 34*(1), 380-290.

DeCenZo, D. A., & Robbins, S. P. (2005). *Fundamentals of Human Resource Management* (8th Ed. ed.). New York: John Wiley & Son.Inc. .

Delen, D., & Pratt, D. B. (2006). An integerated and intelligent DSS for manufacturing systems. *Expert System with Applications, 30*(2), 325-336.

DeNisi, A. S., & Griffin, R. W. (2005). *Human Resource Management*. New York: Houghton Mifflin Company.

Faye, R. M., Mora-Camino, F., Sawadogo, S., & Niang, A. (1998). *An Intelligent Decision Support System for Irrigation System Management*. Paper presented at the IEEE International Conference

Ferreira, M., Baptista, A. A., & Ramalho, J. C. (2007). An intelligent decision support system for digital preservation. *International Journal Digital Library 6*(4), 295-304.

Glenzer, C. (2003). A conceptual model of an interorganizational intelligent meeting-scheduler (IIMS). *Strategic Information Systems, 12*(1), 47-70.

Gorzalczany, M. B., & Piasta, Z. (1999). Neuro-fuzzy approach versus rough-set inspired methodology for intelligent decision support. *Information Sciences, 120*(1-4), 45-68.

Han, J., & Kamber, M. (2006). *Data Mining : Concepts and Techniques*. San Francisco: Morgan Kaufmann Publisher.

Hooper, R. S., Galvin, T. P., Kilmer, R. A., & Liebowitz, J. (1998). Use of an Expert System in a personnel selection process. *Expert Systems and Applications, 14*(4), 425-432.

Huang, L. C., Huang, K. S., Huang, H. P., & Jaw, B. S. (2004). *Applying fuzzy neural network in human resource selection system*. Paper presented at the Proceeding NAFIPS '04. IEEE Annual Meeting of the Fuzzy information 2004.

Huang, M. J., Tsou, Y. L., & Lee, S. C. (2006). Integrating fuzzy data mining and fuzzy artificial neural networks for discovering implicit knowledge. *Knowledge-Based Systems, 19*(6), 396-403.

Hussein, A., Finn, G., & Towsey, M. (1998). *OR and Data Mining for Intelligent Decision Support in Australian Dairy Industry's Breeding Program*. Paper presented at the Proceedings of New Research in Operational Research.

Kuo, R. J., Chen, C. H., & Hwang, Y. C. (2001). An intelligent stock trading decision support system through integration of genetic algorithm based fuzzy neural network and artificial neural network. *Fuzzy Sets and Systems, 118*(2), 21-45.

Kwon, O., Yoo, K., & Suh, E. (2005). UbiDSS : A proactive intelligent decision support system as an expert system deploying ubiquitous computing technologies. *Expert System with Applications, 28*(1), 149-161.

Liao, S.-H. (2007). A knowledge-based architecture for implementing collaborative problem-solving methods in military e-training. *Expert Systems and Applications, In Press*(Corrected Proof).

Linger, H., & Burstein, F. (1998). *Learning in Organisational memory Systems : An Intelligent Decision Support Perspective.* Paper presented at the Proceedings of the Thirty-First Hawaii International Conference on System Sciences.

Liqiang, G., Zhi, C., Chan, C. W., & Huang, G. H. (2001). An intelligent decision support system for management of petroleum-contaminated sites. *Expert System with Applications, 20*(3), 251-260.

Malhotra, P., Burstein, F., Fisher, J., McKemmish, S., Anderson, J., & Manaszewicz, R. (2003). *Brest Cancer Knowledge On-Line Portal : An Intelligent Decision Support System Perspective.* Paper presented at the 14th Australasian Conference on Information System, Perth.

Marakas, G. M. (1999). *Decision Support System in the 21st Century*. New Jersey: Prentice Hall, Inc. .

Martinsons, M. G. (1995). Knowledge-based systems leverage human resource management expertise. *International Journal of Manpower, 16*(2), 17-34.

Matsatsinis, N. F., & Siskos, Y. (1999). MARKEX: An intelligent decision support system for product development decisions. *European Journal of Operational Research, 113*(2), 336-354.

Mehrabad, M. S., & Brojeny, M. F. (2007). The development of an expert system for effective selection and appointment of the jobs applicants in human resource management. *Computers & Industrial Engineering, 53*(2), 306-312.

Meystel, A. M., & Albus, J. S. (2002). *Intelligent System: Architecture, Design and Control.* New York: John Wiley & Son.Inc.

Negnevitsky, M. (2005). *Artificial Intelligence: A guide to Intelligent Systems*: Addison Wesley, England.

Okpara, J. O., & Wynn, P. (2008). Human resource management practices in a transition economy: Challenges and prospects. *Management Research News, 31*(1), 57-76.

Palma-dos-Reis, A., & Zahedi, F. M. (1999). Designing personalized intelligent financial support systems. *Decision Support System, 26*(1), 31-47.

Qian, Z., Huang, G. H., & Chan, C. W. (2004). Development of an intelligent decision support system for air pollution control at coal-fired power plants. *Expert System with Applications, 26*(3), 335-356.

Quintero, A., Konare, D., & Pierre, S. (2005). Prototyping an Intelligent Decision Support System for improving urban infrastructures management. *European Journal of Operational Research, 162*(3), 654-672.

Ranjan, J. (2008). Data Mining Techniques for better decisions in Human Resource Management Systems. *International Journal of Business Information Systems, 3*(5), 464-481.

Ruskova, N. A. (2002). *Decision Support System for Human Resource Appraisal and Selection.* Paper presented at the Paper in First International IEEE Symposium "Intelligent Systems".

Sajjad, A., & Slobodan, P. S. (2006). An Intelligent Decision Support System for Management of Floods. *Water Resources Management, 20*, 391-410.

Seder, I., Weinkauf, R., & Neumann, T. (2000). Knowledge-based databases and intelligent decision support for environment management in urban systems. *Computers, Environment and Urban Systems, 24*(3), 233-250.

Shan, F., & Lida, X. (1999). An intelligent decision support system for fuzzy comprehensive evaluation of urban development. *Expert System with Applications, 16*(1), 21-32.

Shim, J. P., Warkentin, M., Counrtney, J. F., Power, D. J., Sharda, R., & Carlsson, C. (2002). Past, present, and future of decision support technology. *Decision Support System, 33*(2), 111-126.

Stavrou-Costea, E. (2005). The challenges of human resource management towards organizational effectiveness A comparative study in Southern EU. *Journal of European Industrial, 29*(2), 112-134.

Tai, W. S., & Hsu, C. C. (2005). A Realistic Personnel Selection Tool Based on Fuzzy Data Mining Method. Retrieved from www.atlantis-press.com/php/ download_papaer?id=46 9/1/2008.

Tong, L., Shan, F., & Ling, X. L. (2001). Information visualization for intelligent decision support systems. *Knowledge-Based Systems, 14*(5-6), 259-262.

Tso, G. K. F., & Yau, K. K. W. (2007). Predicting electricity energy comsumption : A comparison of regression analysis, decision tree and nerural networks. *Energy, 32*, 1761 - 1768.

Tung, K. Y., Huang, I. C., Chen, S. L., & Shih, C. T. (2005). Mining the Generation Xer's job attitudes by artificial neural network and decision tree - empirical evidence in Taiwan. *Expert Systems and Applications, 29*(4), 783-794.

Turban, E., Aronson, J. E., Liang, T.-P., & Sharda, R. (2007). *Decision Support and Business Intelligence Systems* (Eighth ed.). New Jersey: Pearson Education International

Viademonte, S., & Burstein, F. (2001). *Intelligent Data Analysis - An Intelligent Decision Support Model for Aviation Weather Forecasting* (Vol. 2189). Berlin: Springer-Verlag Berlin Heidelberg.

Viademonte, S., & Burstein, F. (2006). *From Knowledge Discovery to computational Intelligent : A Framework for Intelligent Decision Support System*. London: Springer London.

Waiman, C., Leung, L. C., & Tam, P. C. F. (2005). An intelligent decision support system for service network planning. *Decision Support System, 39*(3), 415-428.

Wei-Kang, W., Hao-Chen, H., & Mei-Chi, L. (2007). Design of a knowledge-based performance evaluation system : A case of high-tech state-owned enterprises in an emerging economy. *Expert System with Applications, 34*(3), 1795-1803.

Wen, W., Chan, Y. H., & Chen, I. C. (2007). A knowledge-based decision support system for measuring enterprise performance. *Knowledge-Based Systems, In Press*(Corrected Proof).

Wen, W., Wang, W. K., & Wang, C. H. (2005). A knowledge-based intelligent decision support system for national defense budget planning. *Expert System with Applications, 28*(1), 55-66.

Yu, C. C. (2004). *A web-based consumer-oriented Intelligent Decision Support System for personalized E-Services.* Paper presented at the Sixth International Conference on Electronic Commerce.

17

Flexible Dialogues in Decision Support Systems

Flávio R. S. Oliveira and Fernando B. Lima Neto
University of Pernambuco
Brazil

1. Introduction

In addition to its obvious operational use, data contained in Information Systems can be also used to derive analytical models which may help decision makers to comprehend and better tackle semi-structured problems (Laudon & Laudon, 2004). This kind of problem is frequently characterized by having: (i) a large number of options to analyze, (ii) a reasonable level of uncertainty associated to available information about the problem and also, (iii) a high impact concerning the decision outcome (Turban, 1995). The most usual approach to solve semi-structured problems is to combine the expertise of a decision maker and analytical capabilities of Decision Support Systems (DSS), empowered by a model database.
Despite the potential aid DSS can offer, the empirical study performed by Moreau (Moreau, 2006) suggests that when the supportive tool is not considered enriching to decision processes it will probably be abandoned. This is because decision processes are in most cases so complex and consuming that it is not viable to add extra cognitive effort - for example, a decision tool not aligned to decision maker's preferences and restrictions.
In most cases, design and construction of analytical models to be used in a DSS focuses only on providing the best possible accuracy. Other cases encompass more than one objective, but they are frequently related to attributes associated to model-data relation. The user is sometimes left out and this not very smart approach often leads to a very accurate tool but not user friendly.
Some research results suggest that it is of high importance to take into consideration the user goals, needs, preferences and restrictions. Johnson (Johnson, 2008) suggests that the concept of cognitive exhaustion can have multiple interpretations and that it is useful to model some of its characteristics to provide better suited supportive environments. According to Chakraborty, the cognitive stile of decision maker influences the perception of utility and ease information systems usage (Chakraborty et al., 2008). Djamasbi shown through an experiment that the positive mood of decision makers causes a positive impact in the acceptance of new decision support tools (Djamasbi, 2008).
Based on these research findings the strategy devised here is to avoid DSS abandonment and to improve user satisfaction by providing flexible decision dialogues, incorporating information of the user cognitive profile. The cognitive profile information was employed to allow DSS to provide a kind of support more closely adapted to each user, thus reducing unexpected behaviors.
In order to provide DSS with flexibility to various problem characteristics, a new intelligent approach was proposed (iDSS). In which, three elements deserve special attention: (i)

creation of analytical models based on optimization of its attributes, (ii) hybrid system architecture and (iii) customized intelligent training method.
The validity and viability of ideas put forward here were tested in two proofs of concept. The first, concerns the adaptation of iDSS to its user. The second, regards the evolution of iDSS after initial training conclusion. In both (complementary) cases, attributes such as accuracy, decision tree height and cognitive appropriateness were noted down. Results suggest that the proposed approach would be viable for use in real world problems.
The remainder of this chapter is organized as follows:

- Section 2 includes relevant topics about DSS and Intelligent Computing techniques;
- Section 3 explains the proposed approach to provide flexible dialogues in DSS;
- Section 4 presents the two proofs of concept and includes discussion about obtained results;
- Section 5 includes the conclusion and final remarks.

2. Background

The following subsections present relevant information for comprehending details of this chapter. Subsection 2.1 recaps basic theoretical foundation about Decision Support Systems (DSS). Subsection 2.2 delves on DSS which employ Computational Intelligence Techniques as analytical models. Subsection 2.3 comments on Decision Trees which are used in the proofs of concept as means to parameterize decision dialogues. Finally, subsection 2.4 brings in important concepts of Genetic Algorithms and explains the customized version used here to generate Decision Trees.

2.1 Decision Support Systems (DSS)

The complexity and uncertainty involved in semi-structured problems prevent their complete specification in terms of information systems. Thus, the synergistic approach is used to tackle this kind of problem (which rely heavily on users expertise). A Decision Support System (DSS) is an interactive tool employed to improve analytical capabilities of a decision maker, in order to improve quality of decisions taken in semi-structured problems (Turban, 1995). Figure 1 shows an overview of a typical DSS, comprising five key elements: (i) access to external databases, (ii) a Database Manager, (iii) a Model Database Manager, (iv) a Dialogue Manager and (v) the Decision Maker.
The access to External Databases is used to obtain data from other information systems. Raw data can be processed to be converted in information, which in turn can be stored in the Internal Database for later use. This data can also be used to derive analytical models which will be stored in the Model Database.
The Database Manager is responsible for acquiring external data and mediating the access to Internal Database. The Model Database Manager stores meta-data about analytical models contained in Model Database and is used to manipulate these models during decision making processes.
The Dialogue Manager is the interface layer that combines the expertise of Decision Makers and system analytical capabilities comprised both in Model and Internal Databases, providing the greatly needed interactivity to DSS. A common problem with DSS is related to designing the Dialogue Manager that can obfuscate system usefulness encouraging it to be sub-utilized or even abandoned.

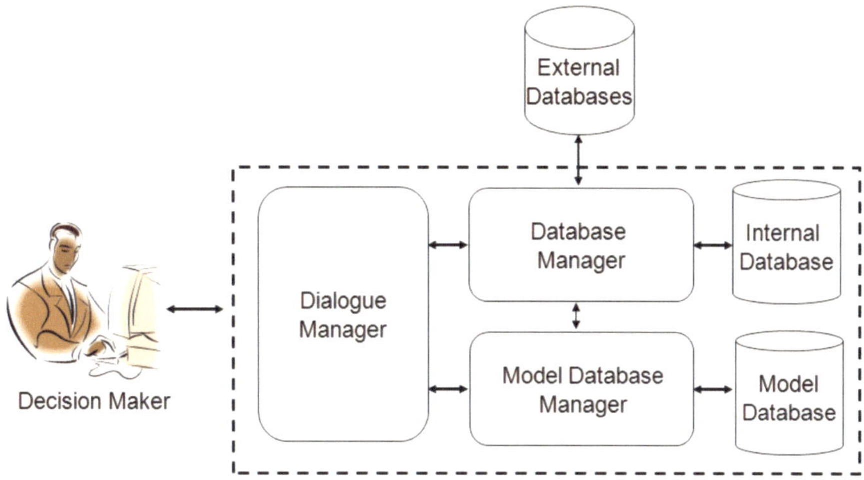

Fig. 1. Overview of a Decision Support System; adapted from (Laudon & Laudon, 2004).

A properly configured DSS can maximize the analytical capacity of a Decision Maker and, over time, is capable of improving the quality of decisions taken. The next subsection presents previous efforts to overcome some known limitations of DSS by employing Computational Intelligence Techniques.

2.2 Intelligent Decision Support Systems (iDSS)

Computational Intelligence Techniques are characterized by some distinguishing features such as capacities of learning, generalization and adaptation, all of them extremely useful in the domain of DSS.

Capacity of learning means that intelligent analytical models can be created based on examples, either input and output, related to phenomena involved in decision problems. This feature is important because real world problems sometimes cannot be easily formalized mathematically or statistically.

Capacity of generalization means that properly trained intelligent analytical models present coherent behaviors even when subject to patterns (*e.g.* decision problems) previously unseen.

Capacity of adaption means that intelligent analytical models are able to dynamically change its behavior to better deal with environmental circumstances. For example, some decision problems require fast response while others require a high accuracy. We stress that it is highly desirable that the DSS can switch its internal configuration to deal with both.

Oliveira, Pacheco and Lima Neto dealt with Database and Model Database Managers, in Hybrid Intelligent Decision Suite (HIDS) (Oliveira & Lima Neto, 2008) and Multi-Objective Hybrid Intelligent Decision Suite (MO-HIDS) (Pacheco et al., 2008). Both suites combined different computational intelligent techniques to solve decision problems related to general purpose benchmark databases (Newman, 1998) and real world decision problem such as sugarcane harvest (Pacheco et al., 2008).

The contribution of this chapter encompasses the dialogue manager and employs a new architecture to provide iDSS with (i) adaption to user and (ii) flexibility when dealing with different problem characteristics, all not seen in both decision suites previously mentioned.

2.3 Decision trees

The graphical view of information in most cases can improve comprehension of relations of cause and effect in problems. Decision Trees are Intelligent Computing technique (Russel & Norvig, 2002) extensively employed in Data Mining tasks (Rud, 2001) and widely accepted for use in Decision Support Systems. This favourable acceptance can be related to inherent facts about Decision Trees: (i) their training algorithms are usually fast, (ii) their level of accuracy is satisfactory in a wide range of problems and (iii) it is possible to obtain explanations about how a DT gets to the conclusion by inspecting its structure. Figure 2 shows a DT which could be used to parameterize decisions D1-D4, by means of dialogical questions Q1-Q3.

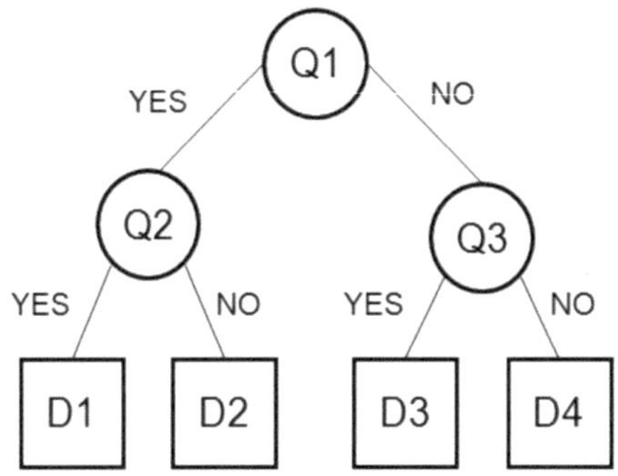

Fig. 2. Decision Tree used to parameterize a decision dialogue.

Below there is a hypothetical example of one decision dialogue parameterized by the decision tree presented in Figure 2:

1. DSS asks Question 1:
2. User answers NO:
3. DSS asks Question 3;
4. User answers YES;
5. DSS informs that the outcome is Decision 3.

In order to help in solving decision problems, the most common approach is to use problem related data to perform DT training. Some training algorithms always reach the same DT configuration for a given database; they often use metrics such as information gain and entropy (Quinlan, 1993)(Breiman et al., 1984).

In this work, Genetic Algorithms -GA (Haupt & Haupt, 2004) were employed as the training algorithm of DT. GA main contribution in this case is the possibility to create diverse models, and easily incorporating new metrics concerning DT and user cognitive profile.

2.4 Genetic algorithms

Decision processes (Chiavenato, 2004) presuppose a cycle in which candidate solutions are proposed, evaluated and selected. Genetic Algorithms (Haupt & Haupt, 2004) is a computational intelligence technique used primarily for optimization tasks. Figure 3 shows a typical GA cycle which is similar to a decision process cycle.

An initial population composed by candidate solutions is created and just after, according to problem specific criteria, it is evaluated. The fittest solutions are selected and combined in the crossover phase, aiming at new better solutions. A mutation phase occurs to provide an extra level of variability and also to avoid premature convergence. An evolved population

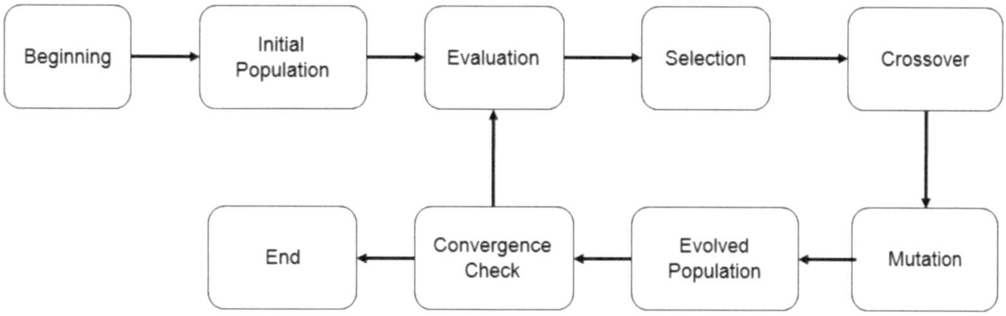

Fig. 3. Evolutive cycle of a basic Genetic Algorithm.

emerges from the mutation phase and it will be checked for convergence, concluding the evolutionary cycle or starting a new one. Figure 4 shows a special kind of GA specially designed to create DT. Input variables *db* stands for a database of patterns for training, *p* stands for a list of parameters and the output variable *dt* is the resulting decision tree.

The Aitkenhead algorithm (Aitkenhead, 2008) is composed of a main loop repeated until the stop criterion is met (line 2). A candidate decision tree *dt* is evaluated, suffers mutations to its original predictions (line 4) and questions (line 7). When these mutations lead to evolution (i.e. improvements in fitness) the decision tree must be stored. When the iterations are over, the best decision tree *dt* will be available for use.

This presented algorithm can automatically select the most relevant attributes and also, was customized to employ specific metrics in the fitness evaluation. More details can be seen in section 4.

```
1.  GenerateDecisionTree( db, p ): dt
2.    While stop criterion is not met
3.      Evaluate fitness of dt e atribute it to F1
4.      Performe x mutations to Question Nodes
5.      Store F1 into F2
6.      While j < number of mutations to Prediction Nodes
7.        Select and mutate a node
8.        Evaluate fitness F3 of mutated tree
9.        If F3 > F2
10.         Accept mutated tree
11.         Atribute F3 to F2
12.       End-If
13.     End-While
14.     If F2 > F1
15.       Atribute resulting tree to dt
16.       Atribute F2 to F1
17.     End-If
18.   End-While
19. Return dt
```

Fig. 4. Decision Tree training algorithm; adapted from (Aitkenhead, 2008).

3. An approach to provide flexible dialogues in decision support systems

The following subsections present our proposal to employ user cognitive profile information into analytical model creation, the system architecture and also the training method.

3.1 Intelligent model creation using cognitive profile information

The use of cognitive profile information was included in this approach to better bridge the gap between what the user expects and what the iDSS can offer. Also, by incorporating cognitive profile information it is easier to create an identification effect, making the user to perceive his own characteristics in the system, improving his confidence in the supportive tool.

User cognitive profile (CP) for purposes of this approach can be determined as shown in Equation 1 as a combination of Preferences (P) and Restrictions (R).

$$CP = (P, R) \tag{1}$$

In order to achieve flexible dialogues in an iDSS, it will be necessary to put forward specific metrics, and design a method to create intelligent models considering more than just accuracy. For this purpose, two classes of metrics were determined: model centric metrics (MCM) and user centric metrics (UCM).

Model centric metrics are those which can be determined by inspection of a model and are independent of user. Examples of MCM are accuracy or height of a Decision Tree.

User centric metrics are those which must be derived by user-model interaction and are thus subjective. Example of UCM is the satisfaction of a user with a given model when solving a decision problem.

Considering that an analytical model can be evaluated in terms of both classes of metrics, it is possible to think of model training as an optimization process such as Equation 2.

$$\text{Trained Model} = Max(\text{MCM}, \text{UCM}) \tag{2}$$

When dealing with multiple objectives, it is important to observe at least two situations: (i) when there is no conflict among objectives and (ii) when there is conflict among objectives.

When there are not conflicting objectives, they can be combined by an aggregative function and dealt with a single objective optimization technique such as Genetic Algorithms (Haupt & Haupt, 2004) or Particle Swarm Optimization (Eberhart & Kennedy, 1995).

When there are conflicting objectives, they must be optimized separately and literature suggests employing Multi-Objective Evolutionary Algorithms. SPEA2 (Zitzler et al., 2001) and NSGAII (Deb et al., 2000) have been widely used with success to generate Pareto fronts in conflicting multi-objective problems.

3.2 Proposed architecture

The architecture put forward here is composed of four main components: (i) a User Interface Module which concentrates on receiving inputs end emitting outputs, (ii) a Dialogue Manager responsible for selecting an appropriate analytical model and also responsible for exchanging information with decision maker, (iii) a System Memory where all relevant information about user and interactions are stored and (iv) a Model Manager, used to store and create new analytical models. Figure 5 shows the architecture employed to provide iDSS with flexibility to different problems and adaption to different user cognitive profiles.

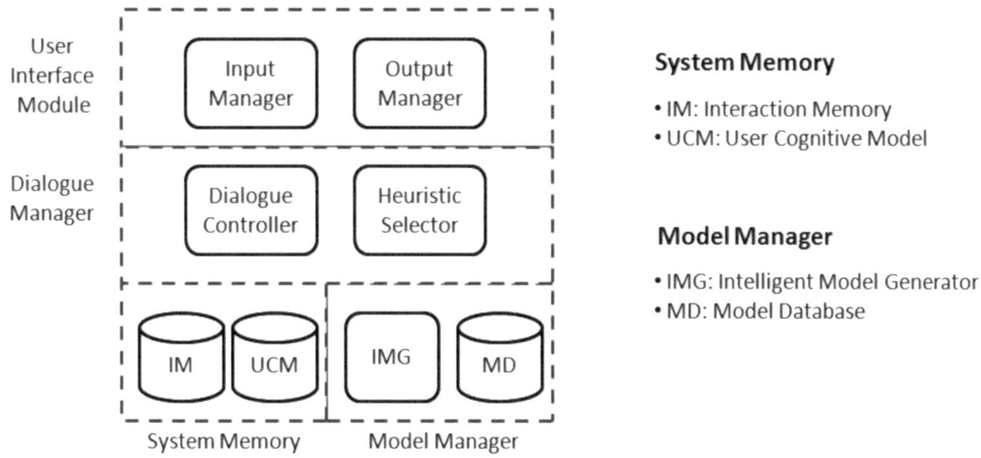

Fig. 5. Proposed Intelligent Decision Support System Architecture

Next we provide bottom-up explanations about architectural functioning:

1. Interaction Memory (IM) stores statistics about user interaction and feedbacks. Its content is useful for improving system performance over time;
2. User Cognitive Model (UCM) stores information about user, such as his preferences and restrictions. Its content is useful for creating analytical models which are appropriate according to user cognitive profile;
3. Intelligent Model Generator (IMG) is an active entity responsible for creating by demand models, employing information about each problem and the User Cognitive Model. The Decision Tree training algorithm presented in section 2.4 could be employed in this generator;
4. Model Database (MD) is a repository that contains all intelligent analytical models created;
5. Heuristic Selector is responsible for selecting an appropriate model according to problem specificities and according to User Cognitive Model and Interaction Manager. If a suitable model cannot be found, Intelligent Model Generator will be requested to create a new one;
6. Dialogue Controller, according to the selected model, requests and sends information to User Interface Module;
7. Input Manager is used to deal with user inputs, converting them to a suitable format for use by the adjacent Dialogue Controller. For example, Input Manager could receive inputs through checklists, plain text or even voice, converting them to a specific format required by Dialogue Controller;
8. Output Manager is used to put decision results into the best format according to each user. A decision to harvest some plots in a sugarcane harvest problem, for example, could be shown as textual lists, by abstract maps, or as geo-referenced map.

3.3 System training method

As an Intelligent System, iDSS must be subject to an effective training in order to work properly. Figure 6 shows five phases involved in training a iDSS created according to the architecture proposed in subsection 3.2.

Fig. 6. Bird-eye view of phases of the new iDSS training.

Next we provide further explanations regarding training phases:

1. The first step is to store the user cognitive model, comprising preferences and restrictions. This can be done explicitly, requesting the user to inform his preferences and restrictions directly, or implicitly, by asking some questions and deriving preferences and restrictions according to user answers;
2. Using Intelligent Model Generator and User Cognitive Model, a Model Database must be created, employing the approach informed in section 3.1;
3. After defining the model centric metrics relevant to iDSS operation, it is important to evaluate Model Database to extract statistics for each model, storing them into the System Memory;
4. At this point, iDSS could be put into work. However its user centric metrics would not be calibrated, since it wasn't yet used by real decision makers. Instead of overburdening decision makers with iDSS training, it is better to employ the User Cognitive Model to simulate various user-system interactions. Feedback offered by the simulated decision maker must be stored in Interaction Memory;
5. Continuous Improvement phase was included to accommodate the dynamism of users and environment. Since both tend to change at least slightly over time, the four previous phases should be performed again over specific (desirably, large) periods of time, or according to reductions in the system performance.

4. Experiments and results

Two proofs of concept were implemented in order to test the validity and viability of ideas presented in section 3 into a controlled environment. Their details and results are presented in subsections 4.1 and 4.2. Table 1 shows information about each database employed in both proofs of concept. These databases were obtained from a benchmark repository used in Data Mining tasks (Rud, 2001). Each one has different attributes, presenting various levels of difficulty for iDSS, in this case used to help in solving classification problems.

Database	# of Patterns	# of Attributes	# of Classes
Breast	569	30	2
Contraceptive	1682	9	3
Glass	214	9	5
Heart	297	13	2
Wine	178	13	3

Table 1. Databases employed in proofs of concept.

Two model centric metrics were evaluated: (i) accuracy and (ii) tree height. Also, two user centric measures were evaluated: (i) cognitive appropriateness and (ii) satisfaction.

The cognitive appropriateness is proportional to how many preferences were respected in decision tree. In this experiment, the preferences were modeled as problem attributes considered important by a user and should be used whenever possible. The only restriction considered was the maximum tree size.

In order to evaluate user satisfaction, three kinds of cognitive profiles were created: (i) accuracy oriented, (ii) similarity oriented and (iii) speed oriented. Each cognitive profile has a Primary Satisfaction Criteria (PSC) and a Secondary Satisfaction Criteria(SSC). In order of importance, these criteria were:

1. Accuracy oriented: Accuracy and Cognitive Appropriateness;
2. Similarity oriented: Cognitive Appropriateness and Accuracy;
3. Speed oriented: Speed and Accuracy;

The level of satisfaction related to each measure, was as follows:

1. Satisfaction with Cognitive Appropriateness (CA):
   a. If CA is bigger than 70%, then satisfaction is high;
   b. If CA is smaller than 40%, then satisfaction is low;
   c. Otherwise, then satisfaction is medium.
2. Satisfaction with Speed:
   a. If tree height is smaller than 5, then satisfaction is high;
   b. If tree height is bigger than 8, then satisfaction is low;
   c. Otherwise, then satisfaction is medium.
3. Satisfaction with Accuracy: according to Table 2. For example, if Accuracy in *Breast* Database is bigger than 80%, the satisfaction is high; if it is smaller than 50%, it is low; otherwise it is medium.

The global satisfaction was calculated according to Equation 3:

$$\text{Satisfaction} = Min(\text{ PSC, SSC}) \tag{3}$$

Database	High	Low
Breast	> 80 %	< 50%
Contraceptive	> 50%	< 30%
Glass	> 50%	< 30%
Heart	> 70%	< 50%
Wine	> 80%	< 50%

Table 2. Satisfaction criteria concerning Accuracy.

At each user-system interaction, a pattern would be selected from the database used. Some attributes (75%) were randomly sorted and used as a decision problem. Heuristic Selector was used to check if there was at least one analytical model according to available attributes. If there was a model, the decision process continues, and after extracting the four measures, the global satisfaction was calculated and recorded. In cases which there was not a suitable model, a new one had to be created under demand by Intelligent Model Generator, employing the algorithm shown in Figure 4.

4.1 Proof of concept 1

This experiment aims at verifying if the proposed architecture of iDSS could present good levels of adaption to user and flexibility to problem characteristics. Table 3 presents the experimental setup employed.

After 500 interactions using each of the five databases shown in Table 1, some results were extracted and presented in Tables 4 to 8.

Variable	Value
Number of Generations	1000
Mutations to Question Nodes	150
Mutations to Prediction Nodes	150
Maximum Tree Height	10
Available Information	75%
Number of Interactions	500

Table 3. Experimental setup for Proof of Concept 1.

A global analysis of satisfaction levels suggests that this proof of concept was concluded successfully. In all cases, more than 84% of interactions ended with a High or Medium satisfaction. The number of models is smaller than the number of interactions because in some cases, the same model could be employed in more than one decision problem.

Observed Variables		Accuracy Oriented	Similarity Oriented	Speed Oriented
Number of Models		151	151	169
Accuracy		81.5719 %	80.6971 %	80.8097 %
Cognitive Appropriateness		61.8377 %	60.9271 %	62.7958 %
Tree Height		6.0132	6.2119	6.0946
Satisfaction	High	81.8 %	36.8 %	34.2 %
	Medium	18.2 %	61.4 %	65.8 %
	Low	0	1.8%	0

Table 4. Observed results in *Breast* Database.

Observed Variables		Accuracy Oriented	Similarity Oriented	Speed Oriented
Number of Models		27	26	23
Accuracy		43.5822 %	43.7402 %	43.2494 %
Cognitive Appropriateness		53.7037 %	56.7307 %	53.2608 %
Tree Height		4.2222	5.0384	3.6956
Satisfaction	High	1.4 %	43 %	82.2 %
	Medium	92.2 %	50.4 %	15 %
	Low	6.4 %	6.6 %	2.8 %

Table 5. Observed results in *Contraceptive* Database.

Observed Variables		Accuracy Oriented	Similarity Oriented	Speed Oriented
Number of Models		56	51	57
Accuracy		44.1398 %	41.6459 %	40.9439 %
Cognitive Appropriateness		62.4999 %	61.1111 %	62.2807 %
Tree Height		5.7321	6.7450	6.0175
Satisfaction	High	36.8 %	7.6 %	29.2 %
	Medium	63.2 %	92.4 %	69.6 %
	Low	0	0	1.2 %

Table 6. Observed results in *Glass* Database.

Tree height was respected in all cases, but it varied according to complexity of each database. For example, decision trees created in *Contraceptive* database were the smallest while those created in *Wine* database were the biggest.
Accuracy values ranged from 40.9439% in *Glass* database to 80.8097% in *Breast* Database. This wide range of values was obtained because of inherent difficulties contained in each database. Also, the availability of 75% of information may have avoided the algorithm to employ important attributes to reach better accuracies, making the proof of concept harder but more realistic.

Observed Variables		**Accuracy Oriented**	**Similarity Oriented**	**Speed Oriented**
Number of Models		197	187	200
Accuracy		72.6554 %	73.5321 %	72.9747 %
Cognitive Appropriateness		65.4258 %	65.4783 %	65.6111 %
Tree Height		6.6446	6.7967	6.5600
Satisfaction	High	78.0 %	24.6 %	14.4 %
	Medium	22.0 %	75.4 %	85.4 %
	Low	0	0	0.2 %

Table 7. Observed results in *Heart* Database.

Cognitive appropriateness values were also influenced by this restriction of available attributes, because not all attributes considered important by the decision maker, could be used in all decisions.
Based on results and levels of high and medium satisfaction in all three cognitive profiles, it is reasonable to expect that the architecture proposed would be viable to use in real problems.

Observed Variables		**Accuracy Oriented**	**Similarity Oriented**	**Speed Oriented**
Number of Models		196	196	194
Accuracy		77.5942 %	75.2507 %	77.6777 %
Cognitive Appropriateness		64.6683 %	64.7959 %	64.6907 %
Tree Height		7.5000	7.9081	7.5979 %
Satisfaction	High	50.4 %	31.8 %	1.4 %
	Medium	44.2 %	68.2 %	83.0 %
	Low	5.4 %	0	15.6 %

Table 8. Observed results in *Wine* Database.

4.2 Proof of concept 2

In order to verify iDSS ability to evolve and further adapt to user cognitive profile, this second proof of concept was implemented. Its execution was similar to Proof of Concept 1, but after the first 100 interactions, the iDSS was re-trained and re-evaluated. Its experimental setup is shown in Table 9. After 10 re-trainings, final results of satisfaction were registered and plotted in graphs contained in Figure 7.
Figure 7 (a) and (e) show expressive improvements in high satisfaction level, respectively presenting improvements of approximately 30% and 15% respectively. Figure 7 (c) and (d)

presented modest improvements of approximately 5%. Figure 7 (b) presented a decrease in performance of approximately 5%.

Variable	Value
Number of Generations	1000
Mutations to Question Nodes	150
Mutations to Prediction Nodes	150
Maximum Tree Height	10
Available Information	75%
Number of Interactions	100
Number of Re-trainings	10

Table 9. Experimental setup for Proof of Concept 2

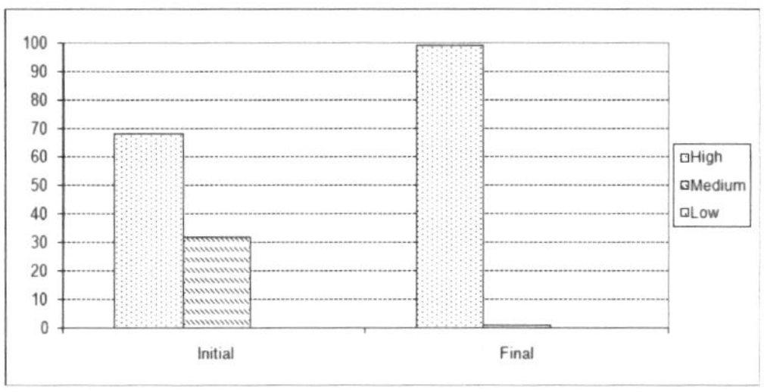

(a) *Breast* Database, Accuracy Oriented Profile

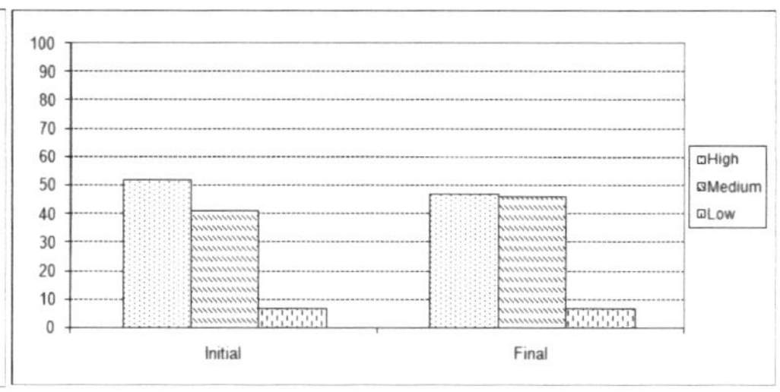

(b) *Contraceptive* Database, Speed Oriented Profile

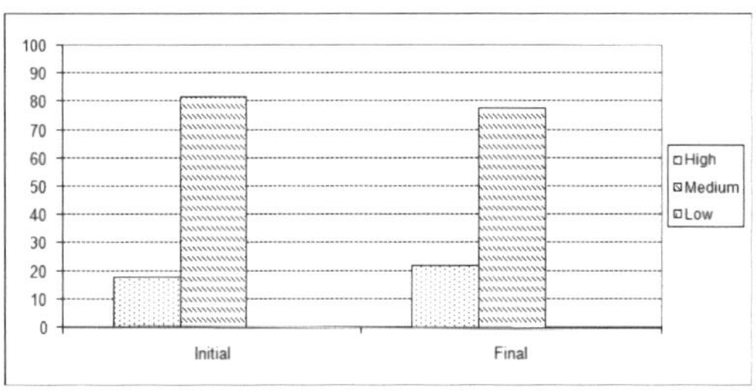

(c) *Glass* Database, Cognitive Appropriateness Profile

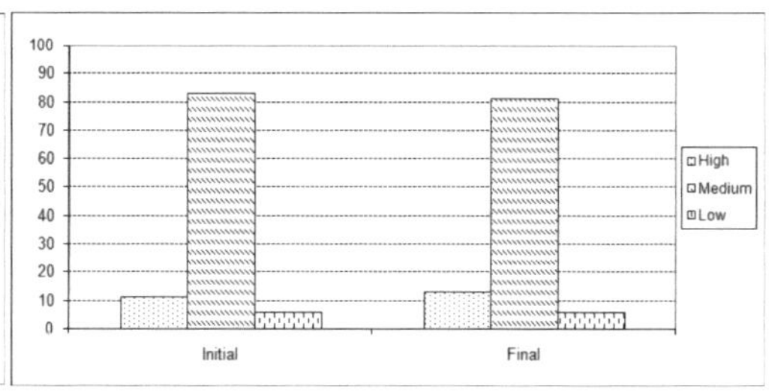

(d) *Heart* Database, Speed Oriented Profile

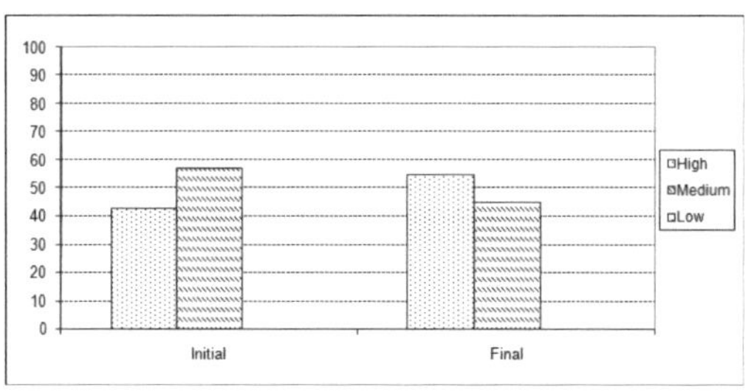

(e) *Wine* Database, Accuracy Oriented Profile

Fig. 7. Some results observed in Proof of Concept 2

These results suggest that the continuous improvement phase is important and useful to further guarantee adaption to user and problem flexibility, especially in real world problems. Satisfaction reduction, observed in Figure 7 (e), is related to training algorithm non-monotonic behavior. In some cases, model database it is already in the best possible configuration for a given problem database. Despite being relevant, it is important to create criteria to acknowledge the insertion of new models, preserving statistics about previous interactions and avoiding unwanted decreases in performance.

5. Conclusion

This chapter has presented an approach to provide DSS with flexibility to problem characteristics and adaption to user cognitive profile. This approach was comprised by: (i) a method that employs user cognitive profile information for decision models creation, (ii) a system architecture and (iii) a training method that enables the iDSS to interact with its user. Two proofs of concept were implemented and their results suggested that the proposed approach is valid and would be viable to tackle in real world decision problems.

The current version of the iDSS employed only Decision Trees to solve classification databases. It is important to highlight that the proposed approach is abstract and thus independent of technique and class of problem. Results shown could be further improved by fine tuning algorithmic parameters Also, other classification techniques could be employed to further improve system accuracy and capability to deal with different problems. For example, even though not eloquent regarding explanations about classifications performed by Artificial Neural Networks (Haykin, 1994) they could be used to double check if a classification is correct.

As for future works we foresee including three aspects: (i) use of new computational intelligence techniques, (ii) integration of current results with HIDS (Oliveira & Lima Neto 2008) and MO-HIDS (Pacheco et al., 2008), and (iii) study and solution of real world problems.

Classification and Regression problems may be dealt with different Intelligent Computing techniques. According to problem characteristics and user preferences (*e.g.* need for explanation), the more suitable technique could be selected. Another avenue that this research can take is to extend the range of IC techniques also for usage in Model Database.

The previously mentioned papers of authors have dealt with simulation of decision scenarios, optimization and suggestion of lines of action. However, they used a one-fits-all approach which gave room for almost no flexibility in iDSS, hence an improvement point.

We strongly encourage more real world case studies. A good starting point would be to tackle decision problems in the medical area, which require good levels of accuracy, reliability in the system-user interaction and also, the mandatory need for explanations.

6. References

Aitkenhead, M. (2008). *A Co-evolving Decision Tree Classification Method*, Expert Systems with Applications, n. 34, 2008, p. 18-25.

Breiman, L.; Friedman, J.; Olshen, R. & Stone, C. (1984). *Classification and regression trees*, Wadsworth, 1984.

Chacrkaborty,I; Hub, J. & Cuid, D. (2008). *Examining the effects of cognitive style in individuals' technology use decision making*, Decision Support Systems, Vol. 45, 2008, pp. 228-241.

Chiavenato, I. (2004). *Administração nos novos tempos*, 2nd Ed., Elsevier, Rio de Janeiro, 2004.

Deb, K.; Pratap, A.; Agarwal, S. & Meyarivan, T. (2000). *A fast and elist multi-objective Genetic algorithm: NSGA-II*, KanGAL technical report, Indian Institute of Technology, Kanpur, India, 2000.

Djamasbi, S. & Stronga, D. (2008). *The effect of positive mood on intention to use computerized decision aids*, Information & Management,Vol. 45, 2008, pp. 43-51.

Eberhart, R. & Kennedy, J. (1995). *A new optimizer using particle swarm theory*, Proceedings of the Sixth International Symposium on Micromachine and Human Science, Nagoya, Japan. p. 39-43, 1995.

Haykin, S. (1994). *Neural Networks - A Comprehensive Foundation*. Prentice-Hall International Editions, NJ, USA, 1994.

Haupt, R. & Haupt, S. (2004). *Practical Genetic Algorithms*, 2nd Ed., Wiley Interscience, 2004.

Jonhson, J. (2008). *Man, my brain is tired: Linking depletion and cognitive effort in choice*, Journal of Consumer Psychology, Vol. 18, 2008, pp. 14-16.

Laudon, K. & Laudon, J. (2004). *Sistemas de informação gerenciais: administrando a empresa digital*, 5ª Ed., Pearson Prentice Hall, 2004.

Moreau, E. (2006). *The impact of intelligent decision support systems on intellectual task success: An empirical investigation*, Decision Support Systems, n. 42, p. 593-607, 2006.

Newman, D.; Hettich, S.; Blake, C. & Merz, C. (1998). *UCI Repository of machine learning databases*, University of California, Irvine, Dept. of Information and Computer Sciences. USA, 1998.

Oliveira, F. & Lima Neto, F. (2008). *An Evolutionary Approach to Provide Flexible Decision Dialogues in Intelligent Decision Support Systems*, Proceedings of the 8th International Conference on Hybrid Intelligent Systems (HIS 2008), Barcelona, Spain, 2008.

Pacheco, D.; Oliveira, F. & Lima Neto, F. (2008). *Including Multi-objective Abilities in the Hybrid Intelligent Suite for Decision Support*, Proceedings of International Joint Conference on Neural Networks-IJCNN, 2008, Hong Kong, China.

Quinlan, R. (1993). *C4.5: Programs for Machine Learning*, Morgan Kaufmann Publishers, San Mateo, CA.

Rud, O. (2001). *Data Mining CookBook. Modeling Data for Marketing, Risk and Customer Relationship Management*, Wiley Computer Publishing, 2001.

Russel, S. & Norvig, P. (2002). *Artificial Intelligence, A modern Approach*, Prentice Hall, 2002.

Zitzler, E.; Laumanns, M & Thiele, L. (2008). *SPEA2: Improving the strength pareto evolutionary algorithm*, Technical Report 103, Computer Engineering and Networks Laboratory (TIK), Swiss Federal Institute of Technology (ETH), 2001.

18

iWDSS-Tender: Intelligent Web-based Decision Support System for Tender Evaluation

Noor Maizura Mohamad Noor and Mustafa Man
Universiti Malaysia Terengganu
Malaysia

1. Introduction

Tender evaluation for tendering process is crucial and critical because the tender selection is not only benefits both client and contractor, but also affecting their reputations in the future. In current practice, tender evaluation is performed by human or decision makers (DMs). We are using tender process standard from Jabatan Kerja Raya Malaysia (JKRM) as guidance since this standard is widely used by organizations in the country.

However, there are few constraints of the DMs and the current practice that can affect the accuracy and transparency of the decisions. Tender process usually takes a long time to finish since it involves a lot of steps and procedures. DMs might make mistakes or misjudge alternatives in making decisions. Besides, some other issues such as corruption and resource misuses can possibly happen. As a solution, the development of a computerized system to assist the tender evaluation process is a brilliant idea.

This paper introduces Intelligent Web-based Decision Support System (DSS) as a perfect solution for tender evaluation process. DSSs are computer program that aids DMs in problem solving or decision-making environment. An important performance objective of DSS is to support all phases of the decision-making process (Sprague R. H. Jr., 1982). DSS should not replace the functions of the DMs but gives a recommendation based on input by DMs.

DSS also can be described as computer-based interactive human-computer decision-making system that (Eom, 2001) support decision makers rather than replaces them, utilizes data and models, solves problems with ranging degree of structure (unstructured or ill-structured, semi-structured, semi-structured and unstructured) and focuses on effectiveness rather than efficiency in decision processes (facilitating decision process).

Intelligent DSS (iDSS) or also referred as Knowledge based DSS (KBDSS) is a comprehensive computer program which solves problems within a limited and specific field, using data on the problem, knowledge related to the problem, and intelligent decision-making capabilities (Fakhreddine O. Karray, 2004). iDSS is a DSS that integrates knowledge from experts. It is actually enhance the capabilities of decision support by supplying tool that directly support DMs and enhancing various computerized DSS (Turban et al., 2005).

World Wide Web (WWW) which offers universal information availability and user-friendliness become the best platform for the delivery of iDSS. This Intelligent Web-based DSS for Tender Evaluation (iWDSS-Tender) enables users to access the system from different locations and perform decision-making in just a few clicks.

The intelligence element is added in the DSS because intelligent systems have the capabilities of perception, reasoning, learning and making decisions from incomplete information (Fakhreddine O. Karray, 2004). DSS is expected to assist DMs to select among available alternatives, while intelligent is seen as an element that helps the system to make more accurate decisions. The study aims to achieve the following objectives:

i. To design and develop a framework for an iDSS,
ii. To develop an efficient Web-based iDSS for tender evaluation system,
iii. To test and analyze by demonstrating the applicability of the approach using a real world scenario.

This paper is divided into eight sections. Section 1 discussed the Introduction. Section 2 briefs the current electronic tendering process systems. Section 3 states the purposes of the research. Section 4 explains the approach of the research. Two major phases in tender evaluation process are explained in Section 5. Section 6 describes the research framework of the research. Then followed by the expected result in Section 7 and conclusions in Section 8.

2. Related work

a) Current electronic tendering applications

There are a few electronic applications in the market now such as e-Perolehan, TenderDirect and TenderSystem. e-Perolehan is an electronic procurement application system developed by Malaysian Government to help procurement activities and to increase the quality of services provided by the government. e-Perolehan has a tender module that enables suppliers or contractors to send quotations, download tender document and upload tender offer. TenderDirect is a system which is using a one-stop centre approach. This system will collect and gather all tenders information in Tender Collection Centre. TenderDirect involves downloading, payment and printing of tender documents. It serves contractors as a notice board system that will send alert messages via email, fax, telephone or pager. These alert messages contain latest tenders' updates and they need to check the website for further details.

TenderSystem also provides suppliers or contractors with downloading, uploading, quoting and alert system. Some of the systems allow contractors to buy the tender documents. But all current electronic procurement or Web-based tendering systems only provide the same process such as download, upload, quote and alert system, and also serve as a notice board to display tenders' information. To overcome the limitations of current electronic tendering applications, we propose to employ artificial intelligence technique as an improved element for the system.

b) Artificial intelligence

The term Artificial Intelligence (AI) was first used by John McCarthy who used it to mean "the science and engineering of making intelligent machines" (McCarthy, 2004). Artificial Neural Network (Haykin, 1994) is a massive parallel distributed processor that has a natural propensity for storing experiential knowledge and making it available for use. It resembles the brain in two respects. The first is knowledge acquired by the network through a learning process and the second is inter-neuron connection strengths known as synaptic weights are used to store the knowledge. Tender evaluation requires few criteria to be considered before any decision is made; therefore we propose multicriteria decision analysis methods.

c) Multicriteria Decision analysis Methods (MCDM)

In tender evaluation phase for tendering process, few criteria such as financial background, experiences, reputation and so on are taking into account. We need to rank the criteria based on their priority before we calculate points for each tender. Since it involves ranking different and conflicting criteria, we conclude that it is a multicriteria decision-making problem. Multicriteria Decision Analysis Methods are proposed to overcome the problem of multicriteria decision-making. There are three broad categories of Multicriteria Decision Analysis Methods:

a. Value measurement models is s numerical score (or value) is assigned to the alternative, using this approach, various criteria are given weight, *w* that represent their partial contribution to the overall score, based on how important this criteria is for decision maker. Most commonly used is an additive value function (AVF).
   i. MAVT (multi attribute value theory)
      MAVT is a simple and user-friendly approach where the DMs in the cooperation with the analyst, only need to specify value functions and define weights for the criteria (Figueira et al., 2004).
   ii. MAUT (multi attribute utility theory)
      This is an extension to MAVT, more rigorous methodology for how to incorporate risk preferences and uncertainty into multicriteria decision support methods (Keeney & Raiffa, 1976).
   iii. AHP (analytical hierarchy process)
      Similar to MAVT which use pair-wise comparisons- used both to compare the alternatives with respect to the various criteria and to estimate criteria weights (Saaty, 1980).

b. Goal, aspiration and reference level models. Examples of models;
   i. Goal Programming
      Is a try to determine the alternatives that in some sense are the closest to achieve a determined goal or aspiration level and often used as a first phase of a multicriteria process where there are many alternatives (Charnes et al., 1955).
   ii. STEM (step method)
      The ideal solution used as a goal for each criteria, the weights for the criteria are not specified by the decision maker, but are calculated by the relative range of values available on each criteria (Figueira et al., 2004).

c. Outranking models
   The alternatives are compared pair-wise to check which of them is preferred regarding each criteria. When aggregating the preference information for all the relevant criteria, the model determines to what extent one of the alternatives can be said to outrank another. For example, alternative an outrank *b* if there is enough evidence to conclude that *a* is at least as good as *b* when taking all criteria into account.
   i. ELECTRE
      Developed as an alternative to utility function and value function methods, the main idea is to choose alternative that are preferred for most of the criteria (Figueira et al., 2004).
   ii. PROMETHEE
      A pair-wise comparison of alternatives is performed to make up a preference function for each criterion (Brans and Vincke, 1985).

3. Motivation

Current Web-based systems have limitations to assist DMs in decision-making especially in tendering processes. Those systems only serve as an interface between the clients and contractors. They receive tenders' information (input) from the clients and display tenders' information (output) for the contractors. After the tender documents are collected, clients will take that information and do the evaluation manually.
There are no exact tender evaluation system has been developed to assist DMs in decision-making as we planned to achieved in this research. As stated in previous section, we introduce iWDSS-Tender as a perfect solution with a wide range of abilities of intelligent systems, Web-based and DSS. iWDSS-Tender is going to be a big help for the DMs to assist them in decision-making process during the tender evaluation phase.

4. Research approach

The approach we use in this research is as per Figure 1. The development of iWDSS-Tender involves 4 main phases of approach. There are:

a) Feasibility study

The research starts with a complete study on the research problem of the current practices for tender evaluation process. We refer guidelines and standards of tender conventional work flow from JKRM to get better understanding of the process. In this phase we define iWDSS-Tender as the best solution and we do the further study on other underlying disciplines such as intelligence, Web-based and DSS. The best decision-making model and intelligent DSS model are then determined.

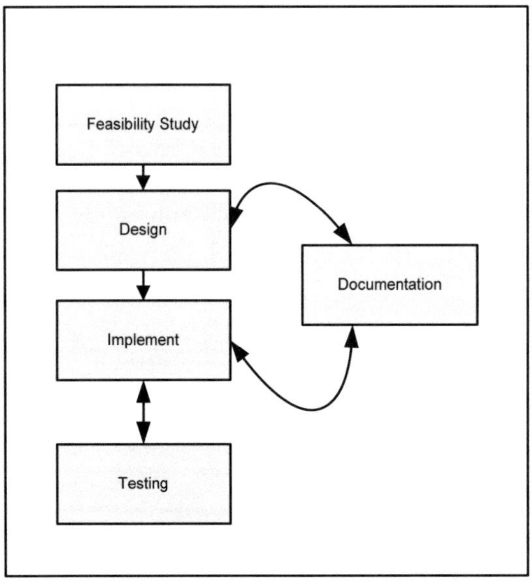

Fig. 1. iWDSS-Tender Research Approach

b) Design

In design phase, we design the framework which depicts the iWDSS-Tender as a whole. We also specified where to apply the intelligence element in the evaluation phase. User interface, requirements, specifications and constraints of the iWDSS-Tender are also emphasized during the design phase.

c) Implement

Implement phase is where all the designs previously created are implemented into real system by following the requirements, specifications and constraints defined. For example, implementation of the iWDSS-Tender database(s) and forms design.

d) Testing

We perform all modules, subsystems and system testing concurrent with the implementation. The testing must be done concurrently with the implementation therefore we can determine the errors at the early stages. For each iWDSS-Tender evaluation sub-module, testing will be conducted once the sub-module program is ready.

e) Documentation

Documentations of iWDSS-Tender is prepared after each phases or actions taken, which means that the documentation phase is also must be done concurrently with other phases. Documentation phase is important as records of the iWDSS-Tender development.

5. Phases of tender evaluation

Figure 2 shows the conventional work flow of the tender evaluation process. The tender evaluation process takes place after the system list down all qualified tenders. The list of qualified tenders will be forwarded to the tender evaluation module for more detailed evaluation. Tender evaluation consists of two evaluation phases:

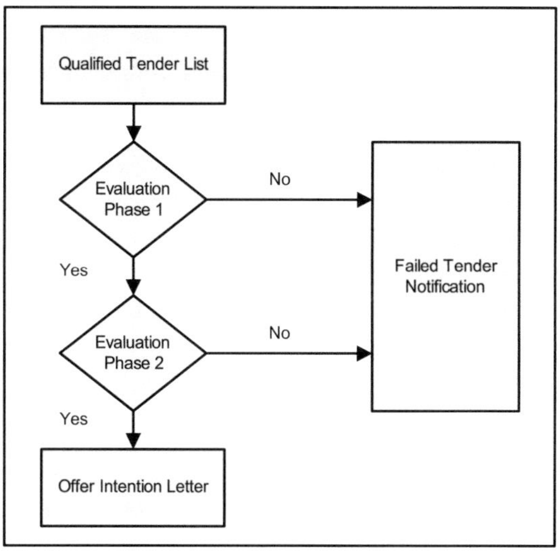

Fig. 2. Tender Evaluation Workflow

a) First Evaluation Phase

In first tender evaluation phase, all qualified tenders will be going through basic completeness document, financial and capital analysis. Tender documents that fail to fulfill all this basic analysis will then be discarded for second evaluation phase and system will send them a failure notification. The successful tenders will then be listed for the next evaluation phase. The first evaluation phase is as per Figure 3.

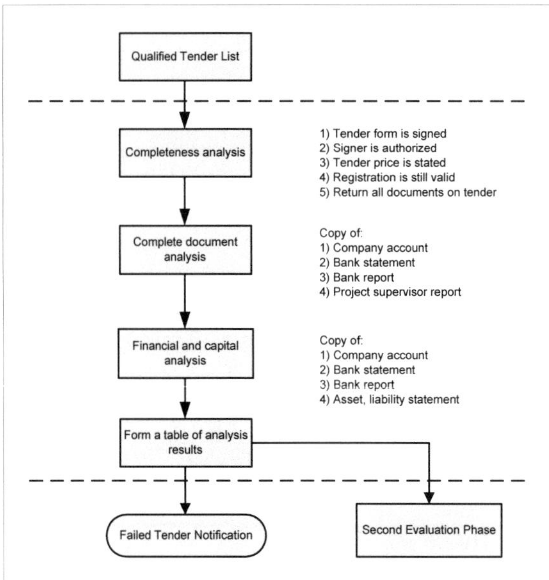

Fig. 3. First Evaluation Phase

b) Second Evaluation Phase

Figure 4 depicts the second evaluation phase. In this phase, tenders will be reexamined for calculating financial capability, experiences, technical staff and tools ownership. Each criterion will be given points for each item DMs scales. As an example for experience criterion, Tender A has three years of experiences and Tender B has 4 years of experiences. DMs decided that the years of experiences will be used as the scale for the item. Therefore, Tender A gets 3 points and Tender B gets 4 points. We expect a list of successful tenders with their overall points. The total points will be compared to the Minimum Evaluation Marks (MEM).

Those tenders that failed to reach the MEM are considered failed. Those success tenders are listed down based on the number of alternatives that the DMs want. The DMs will use this list to help them decide which tender to be selected. In the phase we will implement the intelligent model of MCDM analysis.

6. Research framework

The framework for this research is shown in Figure 5. iWDSS-Tender consists of 4 major modules; User Interface (UI), Database (DB), Knowledge-base (KB) and Model-base (MB).

i. User Interface

   User interface acts as a medium between user and the iWDSS-Tender. In this research, there are 2 types of user (i.e. contractors and clients). Clients are the DMs. At the initial process, contractors provide iWDSS-Tender with tender information such as the tender details and contractor details.

ii. Database(s)

   All tender information provided by users will be stored in the DB. This information might be retrieved by KB or MB to generate decision alternatives. Clients also might use DB for basic report analysis.

iii. Knowledge-base
KB is necessary for understanding, formulating and solving problems. KB might contain facts of problem situation and theory of the problem area.

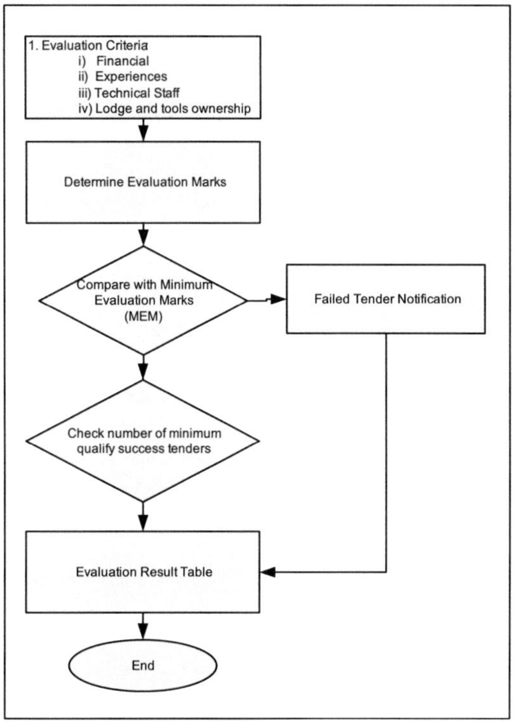

Fig. 4. Second Evaluation Phase

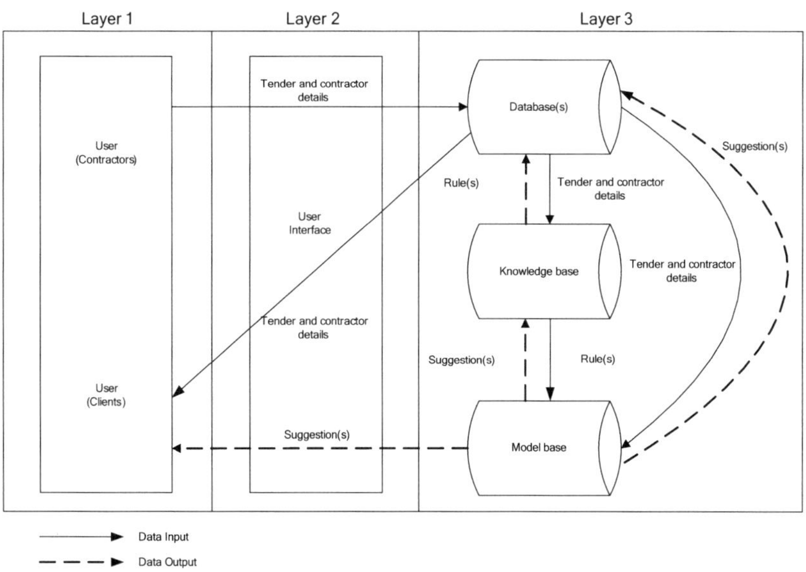

Fig. 5. iWDSS-Tender Detailed Framework

iv. Model-base
Model used to perform multi criteria decision-making analysis resides in MB, as well as the intelligent disciplines applied.

7. Expected result

iWDSS-Tender is expected to produce a complete electronic tendering systems. It helps users to do tender evaluation in a fast, efficient and accurate way. iWDSS-Tender provides a precise and transparent evaluation for DMs which may reduce the mistakes and increase the efficiency of the decisions.

8. Conclusion

Tendering is a crucial process, and it should implement a precise and transparent tender evaluation. This research introduces iWDSS-Tender as the best solution for tender evaluation. iWDSS-Tender allows DMs to take part in the decision-making process. At the final stage, DMs can select the best tender they prefer based on the points calculated by the MCDM analysis model. iWDSS-Tender also has the intelligent system capabilities such as learning ability, quickly and successfully response to new situations and applying knowledge to manipulate the environment. These capabilities give flexibility to the DMs and the decision-making process itself.

9. References

Brans, J. P. & Vincke, P. (1985) A Preference Ranking Organization Method. *Management Science,* 31, 647-656.

Charnes, A., Cooper, W. & Ferguson, R. (1955) Optimal Estimation Of Executive Compensation By Linear Programming. *Management Science*, 138-151.

Eom, S. B. (2001) *Decision Support Systems, International Encyclopedia Of Business And Management,* London, International Thomson Business Publishing Co.

Fakhreddine O. Karray, C. D. S. (2004) *Soft Computing And Intelligent Systems Design Theory, Tools And Applications*, Addison Wesley.

Figueira, J. E., Greco, S. & Ehrgott, M. (2004) *Multiple Criteria Decision Analysis: State Of The Art Surveys,* New York, Springer.

Haykin, S. (1994) *Neural Network: A Comprehensive Foundation*, Macmillan.

Keeney, R. & Raiffa, H. (1976) *Decisions With Multiple Objectives: Preferences And Value Tradeoffs*, Wiley.

Mccarthy, J. (2004) What Is Artificial Intelligence?

"MSC e-Government Flagship Applications," vol. 2007. [Online]. Available: http://www.eperolehan.com.my

Saaty, T. L. (1980) *The Analytic Hierarchy Process*, Mcgraw Hill.

Sprague R. H. Jr., C. E. D. (1982) *Building Effective Decision Support System*, Prentice Hall.

"Tender Direct". [Online]. Available: http://www. tenderdirect.com.my

"Tendersystem". [Online]. Available: http://www. tenderdirect.com.my

Turban, E., Aronson, J. E. & Liang, T. P. (2005) *Decision Support Systems And Intelligent Systems,* United States Of America, Pearson Education Ltd.

19

Towards an Optimal Decision Support System

Witold Kosiński[1], Grzegorz Dziczkowski[2],
Bruno Golénia[3] and Katarzyna Węgrzyn-Wolska[4]
[1]*Polish-Japanese Institute of Information Technology,*
[2]*Univ Lille Nord de France, Ecole des Mines de Douai, IA,*
[3]*University of Bristol,*
[4] *Ecole Superieur d'Ingenieurs en Informatique et Genie des Telecommunicatiom,*
[1]*Poland*
[2,4]*France*
[3]*United Kingdom*

1. Introduction

Nowadays the internet is an essential tool for the exchange of information on a personal and professional level. The web offers us a world of prodigious information and has evolved from simple sets of static information to services which are more and more complex. These services cover making purchases, reading ones favorite newspaper, meeting the love of ones life, the possibility of discussion in many different forums and through a blog.

The internet contains a huge amount of information and for most of us it is the first place we look for information, book a plane or a hotel, to buy products or to consult the opinion of other consumers on the products we wish to buy, to read commentaries before choosing a film or going to the cinema, to see other peoples propositions before choosing wedding gifts etc. The principal problem is no longer knowing whether there is information on the web or not but finding it for the information flow is excessively abundant. Another problem which is not specifically linked to the internet but rather to society is the global invasion. We have access to more products than we can comprehend.

A human makes a decision every day; often he/she needs the intervention of a domain expert. Decision support system is concerned at making a decision, in purpose to replace the need of an expert. Traditionally, decision support systems are represented as a set of rules (Boolean of fuzzy) which fire to provide the decision. Currently, such systems are developed under heuristics.

Prediction engines are often developed to offer the user alternative products. People like to see other peoples opinions before forming there own. On line predictions are very useful for customers. Prediction engines algorithms are based on the experience and opinion of other users. The algorithms give very useful results if they can find users with similar results. In order to do this prediction engines need to have an extremely large user profile base.

The general objective of our research is to generate user profiles so that they can be used by predictive algorithms. The profiles concern cinema films and the general objective is to create an autonomous system which will serve as a support for prediction engines. The role of such a system is to find critics, to mark their sentiments automatically and to create final profiles. The research activity concerns the notation of the opinions which is an ambiguous task. We propose approaches based on a deep linguistic treatment so as to improve the attribution of each mark to the intensity of an opinion.

In the first part of the chapter we describe the study and development of a system designed for the evaluation of sentiments within cinema reviews. In order to improve the application results of predictive algorithms the objective of this system is to supply a support system for the prediction engines analyzing users profiles. The system evaluates and automatically attributes a mark to the opinion expressed in the cinema reviews. Presented work in this part is in the realm of Opinion Mining. Our system uses three different methods for the classification of opinions. We present two new methods; one founded on pure linguistic knowledge and the other on a combination of statistic and linguistic analysis. We wish to show the advantages of deep linguistic analysis which is less commonly used than statistical analysis in the domain of sentiment analysis.

In the second part we show how the construction of a decision support system can be turned into the construction of an approximator of a function. We are using artificial neural networks and fuzzy inference system. To do so, we assume multidimensional data represented by attributes with their associated decision. Then, we gather them into a set TRE, called at other occasions the training set. Then different grouping procedures are applied to the set of data. With each element of three families of clusters membership functions are attached to. The creation of our reasoning system is performed in two stages. In the first stage feed-forward neural networks are constructed and trained on each cluster. After, learning the parameters of the feed-forward neural networks, we design a fuzzy inference system of Takagi-Sugeno-Kang type. Our fuzzy rules are built on each triple of clusters from those three families of clusters. Finally, the final decision of our system is an aggregation of outputs of the networks as the consequences of three-conditional fuzzy rules. We present results on a test set TES according to a standard benchmark. Our results show the benefits of parallel computation and comparison between different membership functions: polynomials of third and second degree, and generalized Gaussian functions. We also show the issues resting in our approach which should be solved to get an optimal decision support system.

2. Knowledge base for decision support system

Decision Support Systems (DSS) is a specialized information system including knowledge-based systems that support decision-making functions. Three fundamental components of DSS architecture are: the database (or knowledge base), the model (i.e., the decision context and user criteria), and the user interface. In this section we presented an input module of decision support system responsible of collecting and preparing the knowledge base for DSS.

2.1 Knowledge collecting system

System presented in this section carries out the automatic collection, evaluation and rating of the textual opinion written in natural language due to the preparation of the huge knowledge base for the DSS. First, the system searches and retrieves texts of opinions from the Internet. Subsequently, the system carries out an evaluation and rating of those texts. Finally, the system automatically creates users profile database. Our system uses linguistics and statistic methods for classifying opinions. All retrieved relevant information used by a second module responsible of opinion marking it means that after collecting the text, we will assign notes by using the classifiers. The classifiers provide ratings from users' feelings. The classifier uses three different methods for assigning a mark to the text. Those methods are based on different approaches of corpus classification.

2.2 Data needs

An efficient Decision Support Systems requires a lot of effective information to analyze. The need to have an extremely large database is crucial for the DSS algorithms. Processes like collecting, analyzing, tracking and retrieving any piece of information, which may hold value for DSS is very important. The source of information also varies, information can comes from centrally maintained data systems, from organized file systems or remote storage, from networked systems and more and more frequently at present from external open web sources. We are interested in this last source, web that offers us a lot of prodigious information and which has evolved from simple sets of static information to services which are more and more complex.

2.3 Opinion detection

One of the kinds of the data that we are interested in is the profile of the human, it means all of the information which describes one person, like the taste, custom and habits. We can find and extract a lot of such information from the Web. The objective is to extract maximum of data concerning each person. While the internet becomes an essential tool for search and the exchange of information on a personal and professional level, we can find and extract from it a lot of information which describe the human custom and taste. In the goal of understanding the human opinions and sentiments written in natural language, Opinion Mining knowledge was necessary to implement. For this reason, we presented in this section our new approaches to automatically detect opinion from the text. We have proposed two kinds of classifications: first based on the group conduct and second linguistic. Then, we have compared our two approaches with the approach generally used in this field, it means, the statistical classification based on Naive Bayes classifiers.

3. Related works

Techniques used for sentimental analysis Das & Chen (2001), are known as Opinion Mining Dave et al. (2003). The research in this field covers different subjects, in particular the learning of words' or expressions' semantic orientation, the sentimental analysis of documents and opinions and attitudes analysis regarding some subjects or products Lewis & Haues (1994), Joachims & Sebastiani (2002).

3.1 Opinion mining and sentiments analysis

In order to determine the complexity of opinion marking, we are going to take an example of a review. The example is:

> "It's A Wonderful Life. I've only met 2 people in real life and 1 person on the IMDB who hates this one. My favorite film ever!"

As we have noticed, the review is composed of three phrases, which have opposite polarity. Even though, we can easily deduct that the first sentence is the movie title, *Wonderful life,* we will have two subjective phrases but hard to mark correctly. The last phrase is rather easy to

mark: *"My favorite film ever!"*. However, there is a problem for the marking of the phrase: *I've only met... who hates this this one*, because a statistical study shows us that the polarity is negative for this phrase but in fact the polarity is positive and with high intensity.
Sentiments can often be expressed in a subtle manner, which creates a difficulty in the identification of the document units when considering them separately. If we consider a phrase, which indicates a strong opinion, it is hard to associate this opinion with keywords or expressions in this phrase. In general, sentiments and subjectivity are highly sensitive to the context and dependent of the field.
Moreover, on the Internet, everyone is using its own vocabulary, which adds difficulties to the task; even though it is in the same field. Furthermore, it is very hard to correctly allocate the weight of phrases in the review.
It is not yet possible to find out an ideal case of sentiment marking in a text written by different users because it does not follow a rule and it is impossible to schedule every possible case. Moreover, frequently the same phrase can be considered as positive for one person and negative for another one.

3.2 Different approaches for the sentiment analysis

The semantic orientation of words has been elaborated first of all for the adjectives Hatzivassiloglou (1997), Whitelaw et al. (2005). The works on the subjectivity detection have revealed a high correlation between the adjective presence and the subjectivity of phrases Hatzivassiloglou & Wiebe (2000). This observation has often been considered as the proof that some adjectives are good sentiment indicators. A certain number of approaches based on the adjectives presence or polarity have been created in order to deduct the text subjectivity or polarity.

Turney's approach

One of the first approaches has been proposed by Turney (2002) and can be presented in four stages:

- First of all, there is a need to make phrase segmentation (part-of-speech)
- Then, we are putting together adjectives and adverbs in series of two words
- We apply afterwards SO-PMI (Semantic Orientation Using Pointwise Mutual Information) in order to calculate the semantic orientation of each detected series,
- Finally, we carry out a text classification as positive or negative by calculating the average of all orientations.

Results obtained by this approach are different compared to the field: for cars= 84%, for banking documents= 80% and for cinematographic reviews= 65%. The fact that adjectives are good opinion preachers is not diminishing the other words signification. Pang et al. (2002), in the polarity study of cinematographic criteria, have demonstrated that using only adjectives as characteristics gives result less relevant than using the same number of unigrams.

Pang's approach

Pang & Lee (2004) are proposing another approach for the polarity classification of cinematographic reviews. The approach is composed of two stages (first the detection of subjectivity is performed, then the detection of polarity is performed only on subjective sentences) Figure 1. The first goal is to detect the document's parts, which are subjective. Then, they are using the same statistical classifier to detect the polarity only on subjective fragments detected previously. Instead of doing the subjectivity classification for each phrase separately, they admit that they can see a certain degree of continuity in the phrases subjectivity - a writer generally is not changing often between the fact to be subjective or objective. They give preferences in order to have proximity phrases, which have the same level of subjectivity. Every phrase in the document is then labeled as subjective or objective in the process of collective classification.

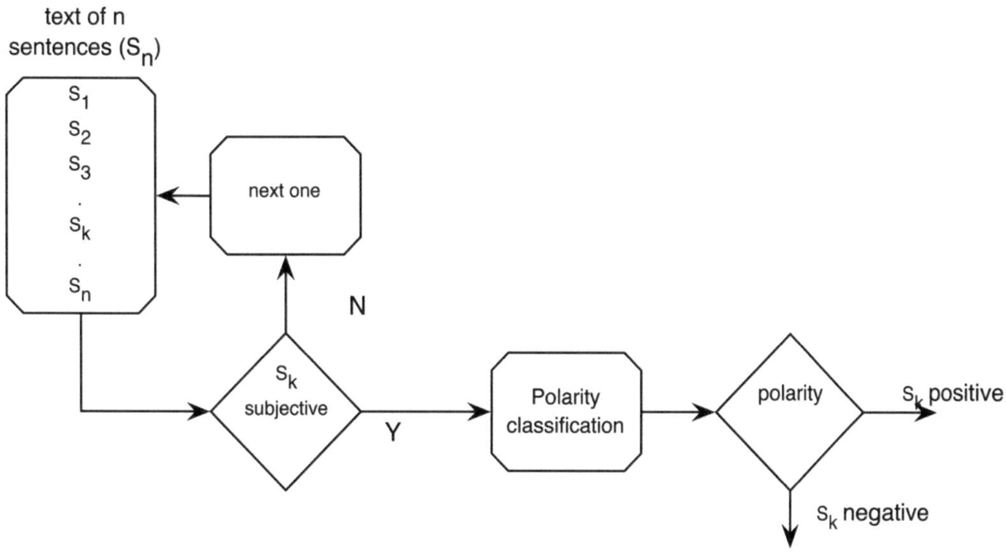

Fig. 1. Pang's approach - Utilization of the same classification technique for the detection of subjectivity and afterwards of phrases polarity labeled as subjective.

4. General system architecture

Our goal is to create the huge database of profiles which interacts with the taste of users. Principal modules of our architecture are [Figure 2]: research and collect of texts on the internet (Web Spider), text analyze, opinion detection, attribution of a mark for each text and storage of all the interesting information in database.

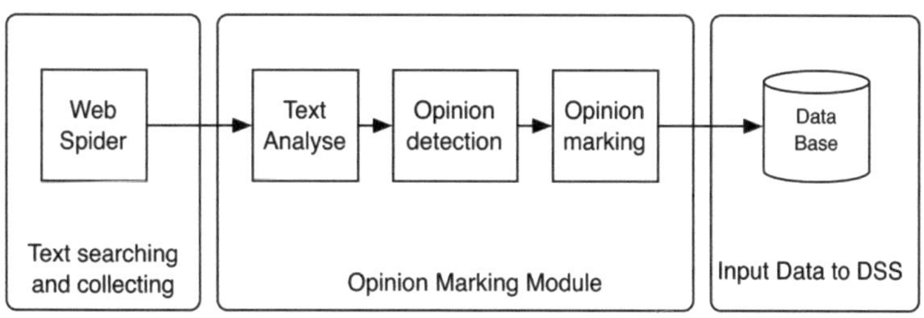

Fig. 2. Input Data architecture.

The first module collects information on the internet. In fact, we use spider retrieved the web pages for subsequent search purposes. Than all of these pages are analyze in the *Opinion marking module* described in [section 4.1]. The results of this analyze with all the appropriated information is stored in knowledge base.

4.1 Opinion marking module

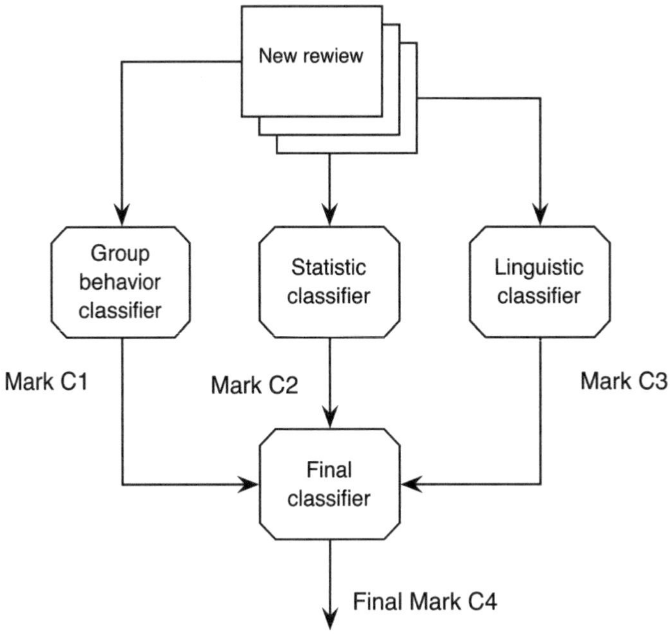

Fig. 3. The three principal marking modules

The Opinion Marking module [Figure 3] proceeds three different methods for the attribution of a mark:

- The group behavior classifier [section 4.2]
- The statistical classifier [section 4.3]
- The linguistic classifier [section 4.4]

Those measures are based on different approaches of document classification. Secondly, we have developed, for each method, a classifier, which assign separately the mark Dziczkowski & Wegrzyn-Wolska (2008b), Dziczkowski &Wegrzyn-Wolska (2007). We have obtained, therefore, three marks for each text, which can be different. We have used, finally, another classifier, which assign the final mark, based only on the three marks attributed previously in the classification process Dziczkowski &Wegrzyn-Wolska (2008a). For the calculation of the final mark, we have used the values of the three marks previously attributed and their probabilities.

On a research point of view, the most important part of the system conceived is the opinion marking module.

4.2 Group behavior classifier

In this section, we present the classifier used for the opinion marking. The general approach is based on the verification that opinions, having the same associated mark, have common characteristics. Then, we determine a behavior, for those having the same mark. We determine therefore, the general behavior of each group (5 groups corresponding to five different opinion marks, 5 groups correspond to the users' notation of our learning base). We have a data set composed of 300 opinions already marked (828 sentences for a group number 5, 588 sentences for group 4, 657 sentences for 3, 431 for 2, and 1130 for the group number 1). We have gathered together all the opinions according to their mark. We obtain, then, five different groups. Afterwards, we have tried to determine typical characteristics of each group. We have defined all parameters, which can characterize the group behavior such as:

- Characteristic words,
- Characteristic expressions,
- The phrase length,
- The opinion size,
- The frequency of several words repetition,
- The negation,
- The number of punctuation signs (!, ;), ?)

The choice of criteria that we have kept for the analysis of the group behavior has been done in an empirical way. First of all, by analyzing the texts corpus, we have defined criteria that seems interesting and that could determine group behaviour. Then, we have tested those criteria on a training base containing a thousand of opinions. If results showed differences between groups, we considered those criteria as valid criteria for our research work. In this approach, we present the statistical study on linguistic data. The training base has been used for the opinion analysis, of those having the same mark, in order to find characteristics, which determine the behavior of each group. Each approach used in our research is based on different characteristics, in order not to repeat them in the classification process. However, we have borrowed semantic classes from the linguistic approach for the creation of the words list characteristics. The utilization of those data is different in those two groups. After having select criteria that characterize mark groups, we have analyzed the corpus in order to obtain statistical results. Results show huge differences between the characteristics of those groups. The creation of the global behavior of each groups, enable to determine the group in which a new opinion is. We have calculated for new opinions, the distance between its characteristics and those of the groups.

4.3 Statistical classifier

In this section, we propose a general approach used in the sentiment analysis. We use this method to compare results of our approaches with the same training base. The way to carry out a classification is to find a characteristic of each category and to associate a belonging function. Among known methods, we can mention Bayes classifiers and the SVM method. We have obtained better results for the classifier of Naive Bayes, we are going therefore to based ourselves on this classifier. In our research work, we have used this classifier first of all to determine the subjectivity or objectivity of phrases, then in order to attribute a mark to subjective phrases of the opinion. The general process needs the preparation of training base for two classifiers to attribute a mark. The intermediate stages are the followings:

- Preprocessing and lemmatization,
- Vectorization and calculation of complete index,
- Constitution of training base for each classifier,
- Reduction of the index dedicate to the classifier,
- Addition of synonyms,
- Classification of texts

We are using, for the attribution of a mark to the sentiment via a statistical approach, two classifiers: a first one to filter the objective and the subjective phrases and a second one to

mark the opinion. The marking is done only on subjective phrases. Those classifiers rely on a vectorial representation of the text of the training base. This vectorial representation needs in a first time a linguistic preprocessing for the segmentation of the phrase, for the lemmatization and for the suppression of all words, which has no impact on the sense of the document. This preprocessing has been carried out for the linguistic classifier.
We carry out the preprocessing thanks to the application Unitex. We are already disposing of linguistic resources prepared for this task as, for example, the grammar of the phrase segmentation or dictionaries. Then, we take off term with no sense, such as defined or undefined articles or prepositions. We can conduct this task because those grammatical elements have a low impact on the text sense as, for example, on the opinion, contrary to adverbs, which give a high contribution to value judgment. Afterwards, on a training corpus, we calculate the dimension of the vectorial space of the text representation in order to carry out all lemma enumeration - the entire index. Each document is then represented by a vector, which contains the number of occurrences of each lemma present in the document. Every document of the training base is represented by a vector, which dimension corresponds to the whole index and components are occurrences frequencies of the index units in the document. Therefore, at this stage of the process, texts are seen as a set of phrases. Now, each phrase is labeled according to the construction of classifiers (the subjective classifier and the marking classifier). Labels correspond to subjective phrases (PS) or objective ones (PO) and the estimating mark attributed to those phrases (N from 1 to 5). A phrase j of the document i is marked as follows:

$$\vec{V}_{D_iP_j} = (f_{D_iP_j1}, \ldots f_{D_iP_jk}, \ldots f_{D_iP_j|D|}, PS / PO, N) \tag{1}$$

where $f_{D_iP_jk}$ represents the occurrences number of the lemma k in the phrase j of the document i. The stage of the labeling was based on the opinions' marks of the training base and subjective phrases have been labeled manually. This is how we have built the set of training necessary to the determination of classifiers of subjectivity and of sentiment marking.
The last stage of the vectorial representation of the document corpus is the reduction of the entire index dedicate to the classifier. The reduction of the complete index consists in eliminating from the vectorial space of the training base, vectors, which have many components always null. This task enables us to eliminate the noise in the classifier calculation Cover & Thomas (1991). We have used the method of mutual information associated to each vectorial space dimension.
In our works, we have used two classifiers: the classification based on Bayes model and the classification using SVM. The two methods have been tested and the best results (F-score) have been obtained by the Bayes classifiers. It is, as a result, Bayes classifier who was used in the system. In the process of the statistical classification, we have at first classified subjective phrases and then we have attributed a mark.
Interesting phrases to carry out the opinion marking are subjective phrases because there are the only ones which contain the author point of view. For this reason, we have first of all carried out the filtration of subjective phrases. The diagram, which represents those tasks, is shown in the Figure 4.
The process presented enables to filter only subjective phrases, those expressing an opinion. The different stages are as follow:

- The preprocessing consists in carrying out the phrase segmentation, the lemmatization and the elimination in our research of words without sense.

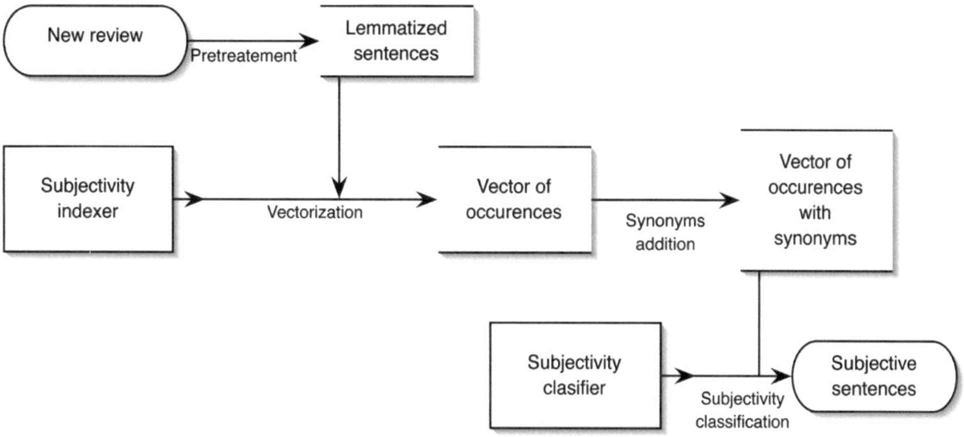

Fig. 4. Subjectivity classification - the classification steps

- The vectorization consists in putting all phrases in the form of vector of occurrences and to reduce the complete index.
- The addition of synonym consists to add terms (synonyms) in the vector of occurrences thanks to the linguistic analysis.
- The subjectivity classification consists in gathering together phrases in subjective or objective phrases. The classification is based on Bayes theorem. For the rest of the classification (marking), we keep only subjective phrases.

After carrying out the subjectivity classification, we only keep subjective phrases. We conduct a classification in order to be able to attribute a mark to those phrases of each analyzed opinion. The diagram representing those tasks is presented in Figure 5. The process presented enables to attribute a mark to phrases classified in the subjective phrases. The marking varies between 1 and 5. The stages are the following ones:

- The vectorization and the reduction of the complete index dedicated to the classification of the marking
- The addition of synonyms
- The marking classification, which consists in putting together phrases according to the sentiment intensity. Marks are between 1 and 5.

At this stage of the process, we obtain marks associated to every subjective phrase. The global mark of an opinion of the statistical classification is the arithmetical average of all the phrases of this opinion.

4.4 Linguistic classifier

We carry out marking on a scale going from 1 to 5. We have created for the linguistic approach a grammar rule for each of those groups. This grammar is based on texts' analysis of the training base, which contains approximately 2000 phrases for each mark (the same database than for the other classifiers). The principal goal of the linguistic classifier is the attribution of a mark according to sentiment. The marking is done phrase by phrase. The texts' study of the training base has been carried out in the aim of creating grammar rules for each mark (in this case, the mark is between 1 and 5). Five grammars have been created, one for each mark. Each grammar contains a huge number of rules taken from local grammar. For each grammar, more than thirty local grammars have been created. The

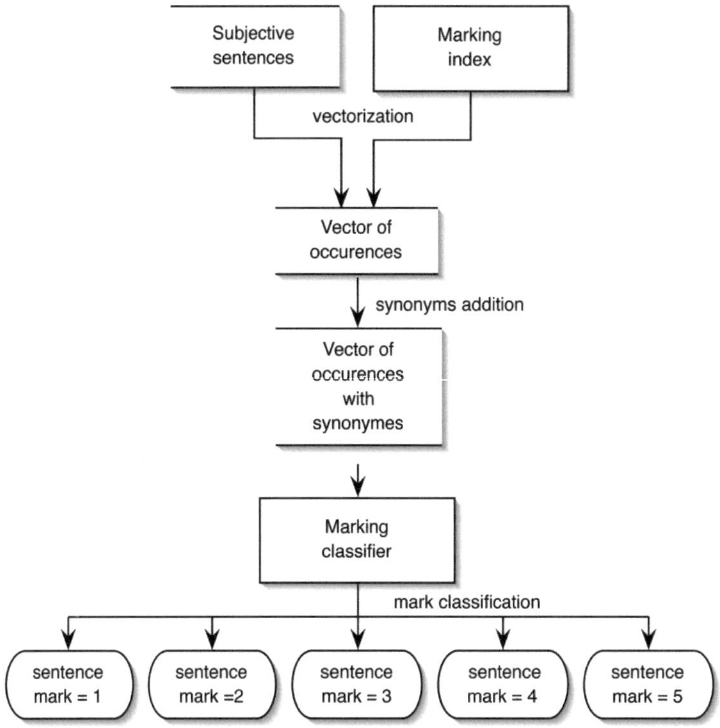

Fig. 5. Subjectivity classification - the classification steps

analysis is done phrase by phrase to attribute a mark to a new text in order to find a rule (from our rules base) corresponding to the studied phrase. At the end of this processing, we obtain phase of the new studied text with matching grammar rules. The final mark of this classification is the average of marks corresponding to general grammars.

The construction of local grammar has been carried out manually via phrases analysis of the texts having the same associated mark. Local grammar can not be too general because this tends to add ambiguity to results. However, if the grammar is too specific and complex, the use of this grammar is indeterminate because silence grows in a significant way. Grammars have been created to detect the opinion polarity and intensity in a phrase thanks to the local grammars form, which constitute a general grammar for each marking group. Research works are based only on local grammars form. Other characteristics purely statistical like words or characteristic expressions, phrase size, words frequency, words repetition, the number of punctuation signs and so on, are not taken into account. Of course, characteristic words are in dictionaries with semantic categories and in local grammar, but this approach is a linguistic processing (grammar is necessary) not a statistical one (like the two other classifiers).

The creation of local grammar is a tiresome task. Grammars used in our system have been created in an empirical way. We have carried out in the following way: first of all, we have constructed general grammars, then we added a complexity level to the linguistic analysis and we have made tests. After those tests, we have repeated the process (addition of a complexity level). For each level, we have conducted tests and calculated the F-score. The final result of grammars rules forms have been chose in order to obtain the best result of F-score. Unfortunately, we can not be sure of the fact that our choice is the most coherent one. We have taken into account the fact that each classifier presented in our system should have its own criteria and characteristics. It is important to mention that the linguistic classifier provide the best results. We can observe, in particular, that the precision parameter is better than the one obtained by using other approaches.

5. Final classifier

Until now, we have presented three different methods to attribute a mark. Thus, we obtain three different estimations (one for each classifier). The marking is carried out each time in a different way. Marks are therefore not always the same. As we are obtaining three different marks, another problem consists in conducting the final marking in order to attribute only one mark to the text. We need a final classification to obtain the final mark.

5.1 Neural network classifier

We have observed that, if we are calculating the final average obtained by the three classifiers, results are less efficient than those obtained by the linguistic classifier.
We have also observed that often a classifier in specific situations gives best results, whereas in other circumstances, it would be another one. For example [Figure 6], we have observed that often when the first classifier gives a mark equal to 2 and the last two ones give a mark of 1, the correct results is 2. As a consequence, the first classifier is determinant in this case. By implementation of neural networks for this stage and by taking into consideration each probability for each score for each classifier we improved our results for 3 to 7% depending on the class.
We are using, for this reason, a final classifier. For this classification we are applying a neural network. The choice of this classifier is justified by the presence of a data base, already annotated, which will be useful for the training base. Moreover, it is easy to implement those data, for it to be used in the training base. The classifier takes into account only the probability of the mark of each classifier. No other characteristics are taken in consideration. This choice is acceptable because we think that we have used all other possible characteristics in the marking process (by using the three classifiers mentioned previously) and we do not wish to repeat those characteristics in the classifications. Furthermore, the utilization of a characteristic of an opinion marking classifier in the final classification can influence the choice of this classifier.
For the entries of the final classifier, we have used marks of the previous classifiers. The marks of each classifier represented by the belonging probability of one of the five marks categories. For example, the linguistic classifier attributes the mark in the following way: the probability that the mark is:

- equal to 5 is p_5=0,6
- equal to 4 is p_4=0,2
- equal to 3 is p_3=0,1
- equal to 2 is p_2=0,1
- equal to 1 is p_1=0

We have used a neural network to determine the correlation between marks obtained by the three classifiers. We are using the neural network of multilayer perceptron with the algorithm of back propagation with 3 layers. The set of TRE is composed of 1000 reviews

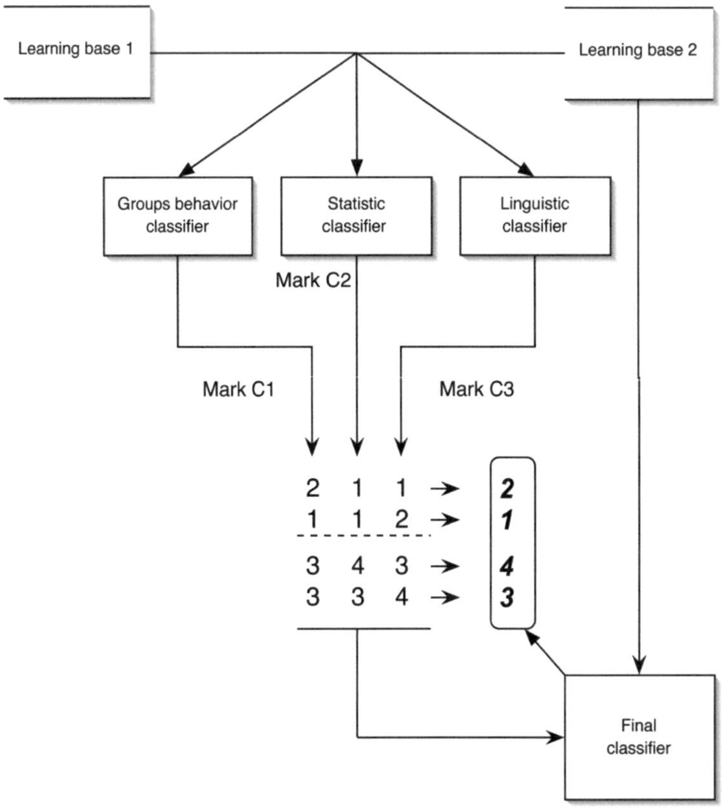

Fig. 6. Final classification- the marks behavior shows the presence of a determinant classifier in some situations

already annotated by the authors (200 reviews for each mark). We have one output (final mark) and 15 inputs (3 marks, each mark is composed by the probabilities of each mark p_1 – p_5). The meaning of theses probabilities are different for each classifier because the calculation of theses probabilities change depending of classifier. For linguistic classifier the mark probabilities are calculated like the sum of the sentences finding by the local grammars annotated like grammars of this mark, taking into account the complexity of linguistic analysis (the local grammars the most complexes so those with higher precision and less recall have the weight more important than the generals local grammars - low precision, high recall). For the group behavior classifier the mark probabilities are calculated according to distance of characteristic of a new review to the characteristics of each group. For statistic classifier the probabilities are calculated like the frequencies of the words for each mark.

We use another training set for learning 3 classifiers and another training set for training our neural network [Fig. 6]. We cannot use the same training set for entire system because the results of each classifier are based on this set. For example the form of local grammars is based on the reviews sentences from training set. In the case of using the same training set the results of classifiers would be incorrectly good, even ideal. And the neural network would learn on wrong examples.

Our system has a parallel architecture and the neural network is the final stage to combine three marks of each classifier. We notice that we can't implement a sequential architecture because the classifiers are based on different characteristic and for this reason it is not possible to approve or improve the results of one classifier by another one.

Temporary results

After carrying out tests, we can observe that we have succeeded to implement an innovative method based on a linguistic classifier. The results obtained after this classification give the better results. We can, therefore, conclude that the deeper linguistic analysis is an important issue in the field of Sentiment Analysis.
We have observed that the best results find for the three approaches were those expressing extreme opinions. Knowing the principle that it is an obligation to dispose of grammars more complex, we have demonstrate that the linguistic classifier gives better results than the statistical or the group behavior ones [Table 1]. The corpus of movie reviews in presented test used by three classifiers contains 2264 sentences for a mark equal to 5, 1957 sentences for 4, 1308 sentences for 3, 1925 sentences for 2 and 1835 sentences for 1. We present in our results the percent value of F-score.

	mark 5	mark 4	mark 3	mark 2	mark 1
Linguistic classifier	85 %	77.6 %	72.9 %	69.6 %	77.8 %
Group behavior classifier	73.8 %	71 %	70.8 %	66.1 %	68.3 %
Statistic classifier	70 %	70.7 %	66.1 %	63.3 %	73 %
Final classifier	83.1 %	81.2 %	74.5 %	72.2 %	81.4 %

Table 1. Classifiers results

Despite the fact that the linguistic classifier enables to obtain the best results, its utilization cannot be universal. Its application to a new field requires the creation of a new linguistic resource base and it is necessary to carry out the deep linguistic analysis again. Those processing are unavoidable because the language is highly dependent of the field.

5.2 Fuzzy inference classifier

In data-driven DSS the main module deals with data, from which knowledge and then rules are constructed. In this part of our chapter we are concerned with the presentation of stages necessary to construct a decision making engine driven by mutidimensional numerical data base.

General idea

At the final stage the engine takes a form of an approximator. For its construction methods developed by the authors and their coworkers are used Weigl & Kosiński (1996), Kosiński et al. (1997), Kosiński, Weigl & Michalewicz (1998), Kowalczyk (1999), Kosiński & Weigl (2000), Kosiński & Kowalczyk (2007), Kosiński et al. (2007), Kosiński & Golénia (2008), Golénia et al. (2009)). In the construction process an unknown function relationship is looked for when a set of training data TRE relevant for the wanted relationship is given.
In the first part of our Chapter we have constructed the classifiers of opinions, having the same associated mark, i.e. common characteristics. We determine therefore, the general behavior of each group (5 groups corresponding to five different opinion marks). We have gathered together all the opinions according to their mark. We obtain, then, five different

groups. We have, for example, defined in subsection 4.2 all parameters, which can characterize the group behavior. However, we have applied three different methods for the attribution of a mark: the group behavior classifier, the statistical one and the linguistic classifier. Those three different methods correspond to some extend to three methods of grouping of the whole data set. Attributed mark can be compared with what will be called here a specified decision of expert. Then the final classifier has been constructed with the use of neural networks in which all three classifiers have their contribution. Notice that in the first part of our chapter different groups of data correspond to different marks attached to each opinion. Grouping procedures proposed here can be applied when output values are continuous even, not necessarily discrete.

In this part we are going to propose a construction of a little more complex module of the finial classifier in which not only neural networks will be present but also a module of multiconditional If–Then fuzzy rules. Those rules will be fuzzy in their premise parts, while their consequent parts will be of functional type. In this way the final classifier will be of a generalized Takagai-Sugeno-Kang type (Jang (1993),Jang & Sun (1993), Weigl & Kosiński (1996), Kosiński & Weigl (2000)). Three grouping procedures applied to the same data set will play the role of three classifiers, which have been described in the first part of our chapter.

The fuzzy sets which appear in each rule are constructed based on characteristic features of each group of data (previously, each was characterized by the same marks). Three different procedures will lead to three families of fuzzy sets which encompass groups of data of common characteristics of output values. Hence the fuzzy rules will be three-conditional. The level of belonging (membership) of individual data to each triple sets will results in the contribution of their output values, as the consequence of the rule, in the overall, final value of the system.

For our purpose and thinking on the construction of decision support information system, we assume that an expert has supplied us with a number, say P, of examples which form TRE, called at other occasions the *training set*. Each element of TRE is an ordered pair: given data vector and given by an expert a specified decision related to it. Each data vector has been encoded in an n-dimensional vector from $\mathbf{R}^n$ while the decision - in a number, so we deal with pairs (x,y) that form the database TRE which is a subset $\mathcal{Z}$ of $\mathcal{X} \times \mathcal{Y}$, n-dimensional input space, say $\mathcal{X}$, and 1D output one, say $\mathcal{Y}$.

Together with that partitioning of the data base we perform the projection on the space $\mathcal{X}$ to get a splitting of the input domain into subdomains called groups of clusters.

The partitioning is the first stage of construction procedure then the next one appears in which on each cluster a feed-forward neural network (FNN) is designed and trained. Moreover, to each cluster a fuzzy set is attached with corresponding membership function in the form of a generalized Gaussian function or polynominal one. Each function depends on scalar variable that measures the distance of the running point from each centroid of the cluster, and possesses in its definition two characteristic features of the cluster: its covariance matrix S and the centroid a. Then a module of three-conditional rules It–Then for a fuzzy inference system is constructed, consequent parts of which are convex combinations of outputs of artificial feed-forward neural networks already constructed. In each premise part of the rules a triple of fuzzy sets attached to the triple of clusters from three partitions (cluster coverings) appear. In general the number of rules is equal to the product of the numbers of clusters of those three coverings. However, one can try to prune some rules during the learning process.

The proposed type of procedure of triple covering can greatly reduce the discrepancy and noise contained in the numerical data of TRE. Then the overall output of the information system is defined as a convex combination of all outputs given by consequent parts of all rules, where the coefficients of the combination are (normalized) levels of activity of individual rules calculated from weighted, aggregated values of their membership functions.

Two parameters characterize each Gaussian membership function. In the case of polynomial functions one parameter is free only. To fix parameters on which membership functions depend the next learning process is performed on the whole set TRE. In this way the membership functions involved in the fuzzy sets of the fuzzy rules can be tuned. The constructed information system has grounded rather well the term a fuzzy–neural system.

Grouping of data

The set TRE is composed of so-called training pairs:

$$\text{TRE} = \{\, p^q = (\, x^q, y^q) \in \mathbf{R}^{n+1} : q = 1,2,\ldots P\} \tag{2}$$

that represent a discrete number of points. Each value x can be regarded as an input value (or independent variable) to which a desired valued y, regarded as an output value, is given. If the data are given as numerical vectors (points) from a subset Z of n + 1-dimensional Euclidean space, then the concept of the similarity can be defined in terms of Euclidean distance function (Euclidean metric) – a very popular and commonly used metric. There are other possible distance functions, like l^p, with p = 1, 2, .., sup-norm and Mahalanobis metrics. The latter one is defined for any two individuals (vectors) u,w form Z as follows:

$$d_W(\, u,\, w) := \{(\, u - w) \cdot W^{-1}(\, u - w)\}^{\frac{1}{2}}, \tag{3}$$

where W is a symmetric, positive define matrix and the dot denotes a scalar product between the vectors $u - w$ and $W^{-1}(u - w)$. Note that if $W = I$, where I is the identity matrix, we get the classical Euclidean metric. However, if W is the so-called scatter matrix[1] Duran & Odell (1974), then the Mahalanobis metric is invariant under any non-singular affine point transformation of the set Z. Notice that any normalization procedure made on the numerical data can be represented by a non-singular affine point transformation. However, in the case of training pairs a more complex distance function should be used than Euclidean one, to balance the influence of the independent (x) and dependent (y) variables in the grouping procedure. In our previous publications (Koleśnik et al., 1999; Kosiński, Weigl & Michalewicz, 1998), Kosiński et al. (1997) we have described seed growing approach and

---

[1] If a discrete set of points Z is given, then its scatter matrix W_Z is defined by

$$W_Z = L^{-1}\sum_{p=1}^{L}(z_p - z^h) \otimes (z_p - z^h),$$

where z_h is the mean point (centriod) of Z and L is the number of points in Z.

evolutionary method of clustering of elements from the set TRE. Here, we omit those descriptions and assume that they have been already done.

Coverings

Hence, we assume that we have for our disposal three groupings (coverings[2]) of TRE by groups (clusters), i.e. three families of clusters $\{\mathcal{K}_{a1},\mathcal{K}_{a2}, \ldots,\mathcal{K}_{aM_a}\}$, a = 1, 2,3 such that

$$\mathsf{TRE} = \bigcup_{h=1}^{M_a} \mathcal{K}_{ah} \text{ for each } a = 1,2,3. \tag{4}$$

For each cluster $\mathcal{K}_{ah} \subset \mathbf{R}^{n+1}$ its centroid $p^{ah} = (a^{ah}, d^{ah}) \in \mathcal{Z}$ is defined

$$p^{ah} = \frac{1}{N_{ah}} \sum_{j=1}^{N_{ah}} p_j^{ah}, \ p_j^{ah} \in \mathcal{K}_{ah}, \text{ for each } j = 1,\ldots,N_{ah}, \tag{5}$$

with N_{ah} as the size of $\mathcal{K}_{ah}$.

Now for each a = 1, 2,3 the projection of each $\mathcal{K}_{ah} \subset \mathbf{R}^{n+1}$ on the input space $\mathcal{X} \subset \mathbf{R}^n$ forms three families $\{\mathcal{X}_{a1},\mathcal{X}_{a2}, \ldots,\mathcal{X}_{aM_a}\}$, a = 1, 2,3 of subdomains (input clusters, groups) that forms three coverings of the input data x's from $\mathcal{X}$. To each cluster $\mathcal{X}_{ah}$ we relate its scatter (variance-covariance) matrix S_{ah} of dimension $n \times n$ calculated according to the formula Anderberg (1973):

$$S_{ah} = \frac{1}{N_{ah}} \sum_{j=1}^{N_{ah}} (x^{aj} - a^{ah}) \otimes (x^{aj} - a^{ah}), \forall\, x^{aj} \in \mathcal{X}_{ah} \tag{6}$$

where $\otimes$ denotes the tensor product of two vectors. The scatter matrix can be used to measure the efficiency of the grouping in the definition of the fitness function Kosiński, Weigl & Michalewicz (1998).

Let us notice that the matrices S_{ah} are symmetric and positive semi-definite. The eigenvectors corresponding to the vanishing eigenvalues determine the directions of the vanishing „thickness" of the cluster. These observations can be used in reducing the data.

In the previous publications Kosiński & Weigl (1998); Kosiński, Weigl & Michalewicz (1998); Kosiński & Kowalczyk (2007); Kosiński & Golénia (2008) we assumed for simplicity that matrices S_{ah} are nonsingular. Here, we are not going to adapt this assumption. We assume, that in general, the number of positive eigenvalues of particular scatter matrix S_{ah} is less or equal to the dimension n.

Let us take one of those matrices, say S_α corresponding to the cluster $\mathcal{X}_\alpha$, where $\alpha = ah$. If the number m_α of its positive eigenvalues $\lambda_{\alpha i}$ is equal to n, then the standard inverse matrix exits S_α^{-1}, and satisfies the identity

$$S_\alpha S_\alpha^{-1} = S_\alpha^{-1} S_\alpha = I. \tag{7}$$

[2] Coverings may differ by the number of groups (clusters) M_a. More coverings may be constructed and then multi-conditional fuzzy rules can be used later on, instead of (17).

On the other hand, if $\lambda_{\alpha 1}, \ldots \lambda_{\alpha m_\alpha}$, with $m_\alpha < n$, are only positive eigenvalues of S_α, with the corresponding orthonormal eigenvectors $e_{\alpha i}$, $i = 1 \ldots m_\alpha$, then we may define its pseudo-inverse $\tilde{S}_\alpha^{-1}$ by the formula

$$\tilde{S}_\alpha^{-1} = \sum_{i=1}^{m_\alpha} \lambda_{\alpha i}^{-1}\, e_{\alpha i} \otimes e_{\alpha i}. \tag{8}$$

Later on we will use one symbol S_α^{-1} only, to denote each of them: the standard inverse (7) and the pseudo-inverse (8) of the scatter matrix S_α.

To measure the distance between the placement of a point x from the centroid a^α of the cluster, $\mathcal{X}_\alpha$ we use the Mahalanobis metric (3) based on the scatter matrix

$$d_{S_\alpha}(x, a^\alpha) = \{(x - a^\alpha) \cdot S_\alpha^{-1}(x - a^\alpha)\}^{\frac{1}{2}} =: d_\alpha(x). \tag{9}$$

It is obvious that for each $x \in \mathcal{X}$ we have

$$d_\alpha(a^\alpha) = 0 \text{ and } (d_\alpha(x))^2 = \sum_i \lambda_{\alpha i}^{-1}[(x - a^\alpha) \cdot e_{\alpha i}]^2. \tag{10}$$

It is possible to estimate the maximal value of each d_α on $\mathcal{X}_\alpha$ due to the definition (6), by the inequality, for each $x \in \mathcal{X}_\alpha$

$$d_\alpha(x) = \{\sum_i \lambda_{\alpha i}^{-1}[(x - a^\alpha) \cdot e_{\alpha i}]^2\}^{1/2} \le \{\frac{\max_j \lambda_{\alpha j}}{\min_i \lambda_{\alpha i}}\}^{1/2} =: d_{\alpha 0}, \tag{11}$$

where N_α denotes the number of elements (points) in the cluster $\mathcal{X}_\alpha$, while m_α is the number of positive (non vanishing) eigenvalues of the scatter matrix S_α and $i, j = 1, \ldots, m_\alpha$; of course we have $m_\alpha \le n$, in general. This inequality will be used in defining the membership functions of fuzzy sets.

Neural networks

On each cluster from families: $\{\mathcal{X}_{a1}, \mathcal{X}_{a2}, \ldots \mathcal{X}_{aM_a}\}$, $a = 1, 2, 3$, we construct a single mapping neural network which is *Feed-forward Neural Network* (FNN). The α-th FNN is composed of one hidden layer. The number of neurons in the input layer is n, while the number of neurons in the hidden layer is l_α. We restrict ourself to a perceptron type neural network, which is a universal approximator Cybenko (1989); Hornik (1991). Hence, in the α-th FNN each neuron of hidden layer is equipped with an activation function, say σ_α, which is not a polynomial. The activation function can be taken from the family of two-parameter generalized sigmoidal functions, implemented by the present authors in a number of publications (cf. Kosiński, Weigl & Michalewicz (1998); Kosiński et al., (1998); Kowalczyk (1999); Weigl & Kosiński (1996)):

$$\sigma_\alpha(z) = \frac{r_\alpha}{1 + \exp(-\delta_\alpha z)}. \tag{12}$$

The family of parameters r_α and δ_α give more flexibility in the adaptation process. Moreover, their appearance has given a possibility to design a corrected adaptation algorithm for neural network weight vector Gołąbek et al. (1999). Another type of activation functions was proposed in Duch & Jankowski (1997).
More complex neuron networks are also possible. However, in the present paper output layer nodes (neurons) have the identity activation function, and hence neurons can be characterized by constants, only. Hence the output from the α-th network, denoted by y_α, can be written as

$$y_\alpha = f_\alpha(x,\Omega_\alpha) = \sum_{j=0}^{l} \omega^{II}_{\alpha j} \sigma_\alpha (\sum_{i=0}^{n} \omega^{I}_{\alpha ji} x_i), \tag{13}$$

where $\omega^{II}_{\alpha j}$ and $\omega^{I}_{\alpha ji}$ wIaji, j =1, ..., l_α, are constant components of the weight vectors ω^{II}_{α}, $\omega^{I}_{\alpha j}$. Here the zero component x_0 of the input variable x is equal to 1 and was introduced to incorporate the bias $\omega^{I}_{\alpha j0}$ under one summation sign. The vector Ω_α incorporate all above components of weight vector together with parameters r_α and δ_α of the activation function.
Each FNN is trained on the data from TRE belonging to the corresponding cluster, i.e. each f_α is trained on the cluster $\mathcal{K}_\alpha$.

5.3 Fuzzy inference system of Takagi-Sugeno-Kang

The next stage of construction of the our information system is to define three families of fuzzy sets: A_{1h} B_{2k} and C_{3l} corresponding to the family of clusters $\mathcal{X}_{1h}$, $\mathcal{X}_{2k}$ and $\mathcal{X}_{3l}$, respectively, in the input domain.

Membership functions

Previously Koleśnik et al. (1999); Kosiński et al. (1997); Kosiński, Weigl & Michalewicz (1998); Kosiński et al., (1998); Kosiński & Kowalczyk (2007) we have used generalized Gaussian functions

$$\mu_\alpha(x) = d^\alpha \exp(-0.5((x - a^\alpha) \cdot S_\alpha^{-1}(x - a^\alpha))^{b^\alpha}), \tag{14}$$

with some parameters d^α and b^α. In our publications (Kosiński & Weigl (1998)) Weigl & Kosiński (1996)) it was shown that by introducing two additional adaptable parameters d^α and b^α one makes the system more flexible. The parameter d^α has to be non-negative and such that the maximum value of the membership function does not exceed 1. A crucial adaptive features is contained in exponent b^α. Depending on its value (i.e. whether it is smaller or bigger than 1, or even non-negative) we can reach for a particular membership function practically a constant value or a singleton. The negative exponent b^α is also possible. In the last paper Golénia et al. (2009) the membership functions are assumed as polynomial of third degree of the form

$$\mu_\alpha(x) = a_\alpha d_\alpha(x)^3 + 1 \tag{15}$$

with an appropriate constant a_α. Now we can suggest the next family of polynomial functions, namely

$$\mu_\alpha(x) = 1 - 2(\frac{d_\alpha(x)}{d_{\alpha 0}})^2, \quad \text{for } 0 \le d_\alpha(x) \le \frac{d_{\alpha 0}}{2},$$

$$\mu_\alpha(x) = 2\left(\frac{(1-2\delta)d_\alpha(x) - (1-\delta)d_{\alpha 0}}{d_{\alpha 0}}\right)^2, \quad \text{for } \frac{d_{\alpha 0}}{2} \le d_\alpha(x) \le \frac{1-\delta}{1-2\delta} d_{\alpha 0}, \tag{16}$$

$$\mu_\alpha(x) = 0 \text{ for } \frac{1-\delta}{1-2\delta} d_{\alpha 0} \le d_\alpha(x),$$

where $\delta = \sqrt{\frac{\epsilon}{2}}$. For the center (centroid) of each cluster we assume the highest level of membership, i.e. $\mu_\alpha(a^\alpha) = 1$. However, if we move out of the center the membership level should diminish, and outside of the cluster $\mathcal{X}_\alpha$, the membership level should be zero.

It is acceptable to make the main, universal assumption[3] about the decay of the membership level, and take a small number $\epsilon << 1$, which gives the membership level of points at the boundary of each cluster. Due to our estimation (11) of the maximal distance d_α of points of each cluster, we put

$$a_\alpha d_{0\alpha}^3 + 1 = \epsilon.$$

From here we derive for the family of membership functions (15) the expression $a_\alpha = (\epsilon - 1)/ d_{0\alpha}^3$. Similar assumption is made for the quadratic case (16). Membership functions from the last family (16) have the value ϵ at $d_{\alpha 0}$ and 1/2 at $d_{\alpha 0}/2$. Notice, that all parameters of membership polynomial functions (15,16) are determined in terms of one parameter ϵ and the characteristic features of cluster contained in the scatter matrix S_α and $d_{\alpha 0}$.

Fuzzy rules

Constructing the fuzzy inference system for our problem we consider a family $\{\mathcal{R}_m : m = 1, 2, ..., Q\}$ of three-conditional rules of the form

$$\textbf{if } x \text{ is } A_{1h} \textbf{ and } x \text{ is } B_{2k} \textbf{ and } x \text{ is } C_{2l} \text{ then } y \text{ is } C_{hkl}(x), \tag{17}$$

with $Q = M_1 \cdot M_2 \cdot M_3$, since all possible triple (h, k, l) are admitted, in which the consequent part C_{hkl} is not a fuzzy set but a weighted combination of three functions f_{ah} with $a = 1, 2, 3$, namely

$$C_{hkl}(x,\Omega,\epsilon) = \{\mu_{1h}(x)f_{1h}(x,\Omega_{1h}) + \mu_{2k}(x)f_{2k}(x,\Omega_{2k}) + \mu_{3l}(x)f_{3l}(x,\Omega_{3l})\}\gamma_{hkl}(x), \tag{18}$$

where

$$\gamma_{hkl}(x) = \{\mu_{1h}(x) + \mu_{2k}(x) + \mu_{3l}(x)\}^{-1}.$$

We can see that the consequence of each rule is a weighted (convex) combination of individual outputs of the neural networks. This type of generalized Takagi-Sugeno-Kang's fuzzy rule will appear in the final construction stage.

---

[3] In order to diminish the number of parameters to be tuned later on.

Aggregation

We define the aggregation of all $Q = M_1 \cdot M_2 \cdot M_3$ rules. Now we calculate the activation level of each three-conditional fuzzy rule using the multiplication method (cf. Weigl & Kosiński (1996); Kosiński et al. (1997)). Activation level, denoted by v_{hkl} of the typical rule (17), will be

$$v_{hkl}(x) = \mu_{1h}(x) \cdot \mu_{2k}(x) \cdot \mu_{3l}(x). \tag{19}$$

Then we normalized all activation levels in such way, that their sum up to 1, i.e. the normalized level of activation of the rule (17) will be

$$\overline{v}_{hkl}(x) = \frac{v_{hkl}(x)}{S(x)}, \text{ where } S(x) = \sum_{h'=1}^{M_1} \sum_{k'=1}^{M_2} \sum_{l'=1}^{M_3} v_{h'k'l'}(x). \tag{20}$$

Hence the overall output of the FUZZy-Neural Inference System (FUZZNIS) will be

$$z = f(x,\Omega,\epsilon) = \sum_{h=1}^{M_1} \sum_{k=1}^{M_2} \sum_{l=1}^{M_3} \overline{v}_{hkl}(x) C_{hkl}(x,\Omega_{1h},\Omega_{2k},\Omega_{3l},\epsilon). \tag{21}$$

Here Ω is a collection of all individual vectors $\Omega_{1h},\Omega_{2k},\Omega_{3l}$. When the generalized Gaussian functions appear additional to Ω the extra weight vector Θ appears, which is a collections of all parameters of Gaussian membership functions (14), namely (d^{α}, b^{α}) with α as a multi-indices $1h$, $2k$, $3l$. In the case of both polynomial functions (15, 16) only one parameter ϵ needs adaptation.

It is worthwhile to mention that when more different fuzzy domain coverings are constructed, one can assume multi-conditional rules in the module Kosiński et al. (1997); Kowalczyk (1999).

Final adaptation

Constructed in the last sections the information system presented in the form of (21) needs the last stage of adaptation of the parameter ϵ influencing all polynomial membership functions or parameters (d^{α}, b^{α}) in the case of Gaussian functions, and then the convex combination (21). To end this we have to define a new error function

$$E(\epsilon,\mathsf{TRE}) := \frac{1}{Q} \sum_{x,y \in \mathsf{TRE}} | f(x,\Omega,\epsilon) - y_{dis} |^2, \tag{22}$$

where y_{dis} is desired output value (i.e. decision) to the input value x. Now the terminal stage of the construction follows in which the error function (22) will be minimized over all points (x,y) taken from TRE. The gradient descent method or a genetic algorithm can be implemented for this purpose, since the error function is non-quadratic in the variables ϵ. As initial values some small, comparing to 1 positive value for ϵ could be taken, e.g. 10^{-2}.

The presented algorithm has been implemented in C++ and is in a testing stage for 4-D input data. We have adapted our system using 216 elements of training data in TRE and other 125 elements as testing data TES. The training and testing pairs were chosen randomly from the graph of the real-valued function of 3 variables

$$y = F(x_1, x_2, x_3) = (1 + x_1^{0.5} + x_2^{-1} + x_3^{-1.5})^2 \tag{23}$$

where x_1, x_2, x_3 were randomly taken from the interval [1,6]. Output values y were in the interval [5.101, 22.049].

First we make a comparison of computational results when the membership functions (14,15,16) are taken, on a distributed memory architecture of a supercomputer with 8 processors at the University of Bristol. Each covering was discovered (formed) in the grouping phase which evolved during 2000 iterations. Each neural network f_α was adapted over 10000 iterations with a test set corresponding to half of the size of $\mathcal{K}_\alpha$. The test set for f_α was formed with the maximum of its associated membership function on TES set.

	APE			RMSE		
Level	Min	Avg	Max	Min	Avg	Max
Low-level: Neural networks						
Neural network	2.7046 2.5328	4.0375 25.6537	5.8498 67.4742	0.3801 0.2680	0.8084 3.0134	2.2332 6.3280
Medium-level: Fuzzy rules						
Polynomial	2.7046 12.9252	14.6289 23.3371	26.1748 38.4051	0.3801 1.9672	1.9577 3.2252	3.8075 4.5419
Quadratic	2.7046 6.1638	9.5942 18.9901	15.1276 38.4051	0.3801 0.9787	1.4735 2.7037	2.7539 4.5419
Gaussian	2.7046 13.4063	17.3242 25.8251	40.7523 38.4051	0.3801 2.5151	2.2424 3.5423	5.0633 4.5419
Top-level: Overall output						
Polynomial		17.6714 18.5190			2.56067 2.67368	
Quadratic		11.0716 12.4913			1.81720 1.90090	
Gaussian		22.8443 23.3547			3.18962 3.31610	

Table 2. Error analysis of FUZZNIS

The absolute error function (AE) was defined as follows, on each cluster $\mathcal{X}_\alpha$ on TRE:

$$AbsoluteError(X_\alpha, \mathsf{TRE}) = \frac{1}{size(\mathsf{TRE})} \sum_{(x,y)\in \mathsf{TRE}} | f_\alpha(x) - y_{des} |, \tag{24}$$

and similarly on TES.

In Table 2, we observe the errors inside the FUZZNIS for different levels of granularity: Low level (the first stage of construction of the system of FNN's): neural networks, Medium level

(the second stage of construction of the system): fuzzy rules, and Top level (the final stage of construction - aggregation): overall output. That has been done with different membership functions (Polynomial of 3ed degree, Quadratic and Gaussian). The errors are given in Absolute Percent Error (APE) and Root Mean Square Error (RMSE) with eq.(25) and eq.(26) for each level using a local TRE and TES. In Table for each level and each membership function, the errors in the first row corresponds to the set TRE whereas in the second row to TST. In both equations below the word TREST refers to either the set TRE or to TES, while $net(x)$ refers to the real output of the network, and y_{des} denotes the desired output. We have used $f_\alpha(x, \Omega_\alpha)$ from(13) for the low-level, $C_\alpha(x)$ from(18) for the medium-level and $f(x, \Omega, \epsilon)$ from(21) for the top-level.
In the low-level, for each neural network, the set TRE was taken as a common part of the whole set TRE and the corresponding cluster. For this level, the accuracy was relatively good for a small TRE with 4% (± 1.8%). However, a high value of error was noticed for TES. In the medium-level, the fuzzy rules were evaluated by pair of clusters. In the top-level, the overall output of the FUZZNIS, the TRE and TES were taken completely.
Independently of the membership functions the following trend was remarked:
For the medium-level, we established for the TRE that the error is increasing whilst decreasing for the TES in average compared to the low level.
For the overall output at the top-level, the error was higher for the TRE and lower for the TES than for the medium-level up to the point to be regularly closed.
Among the membership functions the results clearly showed that the Quadratic function was the best membership function, followed by the Polynomial and finally by the Gaussian.

$$\text{APE}(x,y,\text{TREST}) = \frac{1}{size(\text{TREST})} \sum_{k=1}^{size(\text{TREST})} \left| \frac{net(x^k) - y_{des}^k}{net(x^k)} \right| \cdot 100\% \tag{25}$$

$$\text{RMSE}(x,y,\text{TREST}) = \sqrt{\frac{1}{size(\text{TREST})} \sum_{k=1}^{size(\text{TREST})} (net(x^k) - y_{des}^k)^2} \tag{26}$$

In Table 2 for each case of membership functions the double lines contain errors on TRE in the upper line, and similarly on TES in the lower line.
In Table 3 we show for each case of membership functions the minimal absolute error on individual clusters on TRE and TES, respectively.

Membership function	AE on TRE	AE on TES
Polynomial 3ed degree	0.153063	0.200833
Quadratic	0.070613	0.0765449
Gaussian	0.222665	0.235378

Table 3. Absolute error (AE) on individual clusters for the membership functions

We can see that our quadratic membership function makes pretty well. The results for the Gaussian function obtained with new overall output function are better than in the previous case Golénia et al. (2009) when different overall output function appeared.
Moreover, we found out that the utilization of the supercomputer is really useful for working with an information decision systems in comparison to several hours in the previous case Kosiński & Golénia (2008).
It can be mentioned that our membership functions (14,15,16) of fuzzy sets can be generalized to include ordered fuzzy numbers, recently invented by the first author W.K. and his coworkers, cf. Kosiński (2006); Kosiński et al. (2003).

6. Conclusions

In the goal of understanding the opinions written in natural language, an Opinion Mining knowledge was necessary to implement. For this reason, we presented in this chapter new approaches to automatically detect opinion from the text. The two classifications (group conduct and linguistic) have been proposed by us. Then, we have compared our approaches with the approach generally used in this field (the statistical classification, which is based on Naive Bayes classifiers). After carrying out tests, we can observe that we have succeeded to implement a first innovative method based on a linguistic classifier. The results obtained after this classification give us satisfaction. We can, therefore, conclude that the linguistic analysis, which is deeper, is an important research path in the field of Sentiment Analysis.
The final classifier can be constructed as a FUZZy-Neural Inference System (FUZZNIS) by copying the method known in approximation of multivariant functions. The designing procedure of FUZZNIS has been presented in Section 5.2. The results concerning its application to an approximation of a benchmark function of 3 variables (23) allow us to say that by applying FUZZNIS as the final classifier an optimal decision support system can be obtained.

7. Acknowledgement

A part of this work was done when the second author B. G. stayed at PJIIT supported by the scholarship of the Polish Ministry of Science and Higher Education. Calculation of the approximation problem was carried out using the computational facilities of the Advanced Computing Research Centre, University of Bristol - http://www.bris.ac.uk/acrc/.

8. References

Anderberg, M. (1973). Cluster analysis for applications, Probability and Mathematical Statistics. Mathematical Statistics. New York.

Cover, T.M., & Thomas, J.A. 1991. Elements of Information Theory. John Wiley.

Cybenko, G. (1989). Approximation by superpositions of sigmoidal function., *Mathematics of Control, Signals, and Systems* 2: 303–314.

Das, S. & Chen, M. (2001). Yahoo! for amazon: Extracting market sentiment from stock message boards., *the 8th Asia Pacific Finance Association Annual Conference (APFA)*.

Dave, K., Lawrence, S., & M., Pennock D. 2003. Mining the Peanut Gallery: Opinion Extraction and Semantic Classification of Product Reviews. Pages 519–528 of: Proceedings of WWW.

Duch, W. & Jankowski, N. (1997). New neural transfer functions, *Int. J. Appl. Math. Comput. Sci.* 7: 639–658.

Duran, B. S. & Odell, P. (1974). Cluster analysis - a survey, Lecture Notes in Economics and Mathematical Systems, Vol. 100, Springer-Verlag, Berlin.

Dziczkowski, G. & Wegrzyn-Wolska, K. (2007). Rcss - rating critics support system purpose built for movies recommendation., *Advances in Intelligent Web Mastering.*

Dziczkowski, G. & Wegrzyn-Wolska, K. (2008a). An autonomous system designed for automatic detection and rating of film. extraction and linguistic analysis of sentiments., *In Proceedings of IEEE/WIC/ACM inter. conference on Web intelligence and intelligent agent technology* WI: 847–850.

Dziczkowski, G. & Wegrzyn-Wolska, K. (2008b). Tool of the intelligence economic: Recognition function of reviews critics., *In ICSOFT 2008 Proceedings.*

Gołąbek, B., Kosiński, W. & Weigl, M. (1999). Adaptation of learning rate via adaptation of weight vector in modified m-delta networks., *Computational Intelligence and Appli cations* P.S. Szczepaniak (Ed.), Studies in Fuzziness and Soft Computing, Vol. 23, Physica-Verlag, c/o Springer-Verlag,: 156–163.

Golénia, B., Kosiński, W. & Weigl, M. (2009). *Recent Advances in Intelligent Information Systems*, EXIT, Warsaw, ISBN 978-83-60434-59-8, chapter An Evolutionary Method for Designing Decision Support, pp. 275–288.

Hatzivassiloglou, V., & McKeown, K. 1997. Predicting the semantic orientation of adjectives., *In Proc. of the Joint ACL/EACL Conference.*

Hatzivassiloglou, V. & Wiebe, J. (2000). Effects of adjective orientation and gradability on sentence subjectivity., *In Proceedings of the International Conference on Computational Linguistics (COLING).*

Hornik, K. (1991). Approximation capabilities of multilayer feedforward, *Neural Networks4 251–257.*

Jang, J.-S. (1993). Anfis: adaptive-network-based fuzzy inference system, *Systems, Man and Cybernetics* 23: 665–685.

Jang, J. & Sun, T. C. (1993). Functional equivalence between radial basis function networks and fuzzy inference system., *IEEE Transaction on Neural Networks 156–159.*

Joachims, T. & Sebastiani, F. (2002). Guest editors introduction to the special issue on automated text categorization., *Intell. Inform. Syst.*

Koleśnik, R., Koleśnik, L. & Kosiński, W. (1999). Genetic operators for clustering analysis, *Intelligent Information Systems VIII* Proc. of theWorkshop held in Ustroń, Poland: 203- 208.

Kosiński, W. (2006). On fuzzy number calculus., *Int. J. Appl. Math. Comput. Sci.* 16: 51 57.

Kosiński, W. & Golénia, B. (2008). Double covering of data for multivariate approximation, *Development in Fuzzy Sets, Intuitionistic Fuzzy Sets, Generalized Sets and Related Topics. Foundations* K. Atanasov et al. (Eds.), EXIT, Warsaw: 97–111.

Kosiński, W. & Kowalczyk, D. (2007). Adaptive decision support system using web-users profile data,, *Advances in Intelligent Web Mastering* K. M. Węgrzyn-Wolska and P.S.

Szczepaniak (Eds.), Proc. of 5th AWIV'2007, Fontainebleau, France, ASC, vol. 43, Springer-Verlag, Berlin Heidelberg: 180–185.

Kosiński, W., Kowalczyk, D. & Weigl, M. (2007). Multivariate data approximation with preprocessing of data, *Computer Assisted Mechanics and Engineering Sciences* 14: 651–656.

Kosiński, W., Prokopowicz, P. & Ślęzak, D. (2003). Ordered fuzzy numbers, *Bulletin of the Polish Academy of Sciences, Sér Sci Math* 51: 327–338.

Kosiński, W. &Weigl, M. (1998). General mapping approximation problems solving by neural networks and fuzzy inference systems., *Systems Analysis Modelling Simulation* 30: 11- 28.

Kosiński, W. & Weigl, M. (2000). Adaptive information systems for data approximation problems., *Fuzzy Control Theory and Practice* Hampel R., Wagenknecht M., Chaker N.(Eds); Physica-Verlag, Springer, Heidelberg New York,: 109–120.

Kosiński, W., Weigl, M. & Kieś, P. (1997). Fuzzy domain covering of an inference system, *Proceedings of the Third National Conference on Neural Networks and Their Applications* Kule n. Częstochowa, PNNS, Częstochowa: 310–321.

Kosiński, W., Weigl, M. & Michalewicz, Z. (1998). Evolutionary domain covering of an inference system for function approximation., *Evolutionary Programming VII; V.M. Port, N. Saravanam, D. Waagen and A. E. Eiben (Eds.)* Proceedings of the 7th International Conference, EP'98, San Diego California, NCS, vol. 1447, New York: 167–180.

Kosiński, W., Weigl, M., Michalewicz., Z. & Koleśnik, W. (1998). Genetic algorithms for preprocessing of data for universal approximators., *Intelligent Information Systems VII* Proceedings of the Workshop held in Malbork, Poland, Instytut Podstaw Informatyki, PAN,Warszawa: 320–331.

Kowalczyk, D. (1999). *An adaptive fuzzy inference system as a fuzzy controller. rozmyty adaptacyjny system wnioskujący jako sterownik rozmyty*, Master's thesis, WSP w Bydgoszczy, Wydział Matematyki, Techniki i Nauk Przyrodniczych, Specjalność: Technika Komputerowa, Bydgoszcz.

Lewis, D. & Haues, P. J. (1994). Guest editorial for the special issue on text categorization., *ACM Trans. Inform. Syst.*

Pang, B. & Lee, L. (2004). A sentimental education: Sentiment analysis using subjectivity summarization based on minimum cuts., *In Proceedings of the Association for Computational Linguistics (ACL).*

Pang, B., Lee, L. & Vaithyanathan, S. (2002). Thumbs up? sentiment classification using machine learning techniques., *In Proceedings of the Conference on Empirical Methods in Natural Language Processing (EMNLP).*

Turney, P. (2002). Thumbs up or thumbs down? semantic orientation applied to unsupervised classification of reviews., *In Proceedings of the Association for Computational Linguistics (ACL).*

Weigl, M. & Kosiński, W. (1996). Approximation of multivariate functions by generalized adaptive fuzzy inference network., *Proceedings of the 9-th International Symposium on Methodologies for Intelligent Systems* ISMIS'96, Zakopane, IPI PAN, Warszawa,: 120–133.

Whitelaw, C., Garg, N & Argamon, S. (2005). Using appraisal groups for sentiment analysis., *In Proceedings of the ACM SIGIR Conference on Information and Knowledge Management (CIKM).*

20

A Silvicultural Decision Support System to Compare Forest Management Scenarios for Larch Stands on a Multicriteria Basis.

Jacques Rondeux, Jacques Hebert, Hugues Claessens and Philippe Lejeune
Gembloux Agricultural University, Unit of Forest and Nature Management
Belgium

1. Introduction

In forest resource planning choosing a silvicultural scenario is becoming a complex problem especially due to the multiplicity of goals and wide-ranging criteria that forest managers have to consider in any decision making process (Diaz-Balteiro & Romero, 2008; Kangas & Kangas, 2005; Maness & Farrell, 2004). For a long time, research focussed on growth modelling aimed at describing stand evolution through the construction of growth models for even or uneven-aged stands. These tools are useful for predicting and analysing stand evolution over time but they are not designed to compare and help to select appropriate silvicultural scenarios.

With reference to that, DSS (Decision Support System) is a computer application typically designed to address the multi-faceted nature of management questions. Every decision can affect criteria of various kinds like: environmental issues (e.g., biodiversity conservation, carbon sequestration,..), economic issues (e.g., timber, wood quality, source of energy, ..) or social issues (e.g,. recreation, employment,..). Considering the increasing complexity of new challenges in forestry such systems are very useful in a wide range of fields, especially in sustainable natural resource management, business planning, transportation, timber harvest scheduling, … (Gordon et al., 2004 ; Reynolds, 2005).

In this paper we propose a silvicultural decision support system (SDSS) which is an extension of this concept. It consists in the selection of a silvicultural treatment that fits the best to the objectives assigned to pure even-aged stands which are, in this case, larch plantations.

This SDSS has been developed to predict the influence of silvicultural alternatives on larch stand evolution and help forest managers choose scenarios according to preset goals. It is made of three interconnected modules designed for (i) growth prediction based on initial stand density, thinning regime and site index (scenario building), (ii) assessment of a set of indicators defining scenarios, and (iii) comparison of scenarios according to appropriate indicators using a Multi-Criteria Decision-Making - MCDM approach (Pauwels et al., 2007).

Financial, technico-economic and ecological or environmental indicators are calculated in order to characterize wood production both qualitatively and quantitatively at the stand level. The SDSS is integrated into a user-friendly software package called "MGC_Larch (Make Good Choice for Larch)". It has been developed for pure and even-aged larch stands

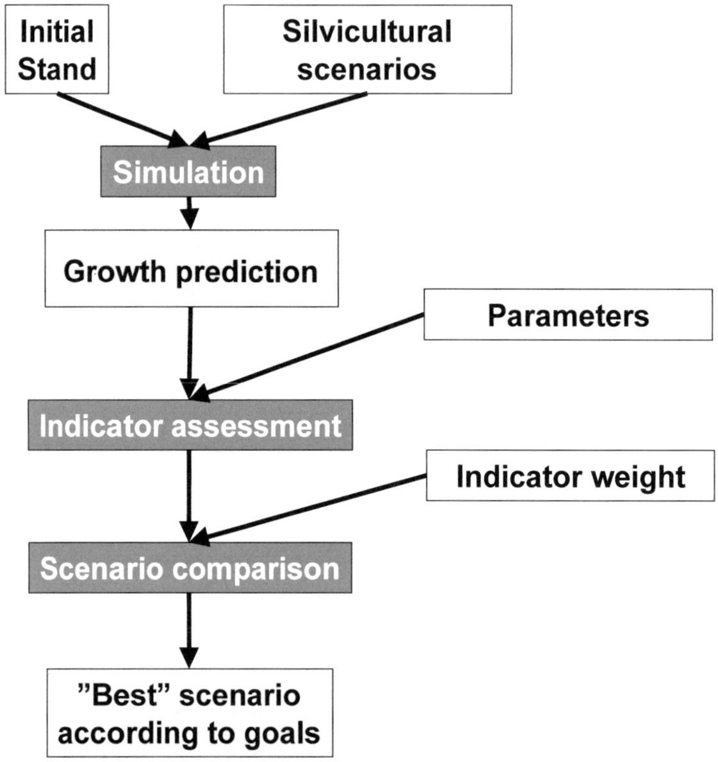

Fig. 1. General architecture of the silvicultural decision support system "MGC_larch".

[European larch (Larix decidua Mill.), Japanese larch (Larix kaempferi (Lamb.) Carr.) and hybrid larch (Larix eurolepis Henry)] growing in lowland areas where site conditions are similar to those in Southern Belgium.

The larch stand dynamics have been carefully designed to enhance this system, with several generalized silvicultural alternatives being either intuitive or already applied to other conifers such as spruce or Douglas fir. Furthermore, larch offers a wide range of marked or nonmarked-priced goods and ecological and financial potential in a multi-functional management context (Pauwels & Rondeux, 2000). This study can be used both for research purposes and for practical forest planning especially for use at the scale of an individual property. It is based on a very large database and a knowledge-based system from which indicators have been calculated.

2. Materials and methods

2.1 General decision system approach

The SDSS is based on a structure made of two main components. The first one consists in the building of a growth model used to simulate the development of a stand in response to different silvicultural treatments or "scenarios". The resulting data describing the evolution of the trees are recorded in a database which the second component uses to assess several indicators expressing different goals to be achieved by the applied silvicultural system. These indicators are then used to carry out a multi-criteria analysis of the user-defined scenarios. These two components are completed by an interface that enables the keyboard input of data as well as managing successively growth simulations, indicator assessment, scenarios comparison and results display (Figure 1).

The main body of the data required was obtained from permanent growth plots and trees measured at different occasions. The data sets consisted of selected stands and trees for whom numbers and types of collected data vary according to the modelling objectives, growth modelling being clearly at the heart of the SDSS.

2.2 Growth modelling

Several regression equations have been built to fit the observations collected in larch stands located at low elevations (< 625 m) in Southern Belgium. Goodness-of-fit was tested by the squared correlation coefficient (R^2) and the root mean square error (RMSE). Four integrated sub-models predict the change over time of the principal stand variables: average height of dominant trees, number of trees, girth and stem volume over bark. The materials and methods used to build these models are described in detail in Pauwels (2003), Pauwels et al. (1999), Pauwels et al. (2002b). Only the main results are however presented in this paper.

Multiple least-square estimation was used to construct the models. A stepwise regression was first used with various combinations of variables (either plain or transformed) to expand the information on explanatory variables.

A selection based on different aspects was then considered about the variables: easily available, high biological expression, consistent signs of the estimates.

The four sub-models organized consistently were dealing with dominant height and age (site curves), self-thinning, girth growth and volume estimation (Figure 2).

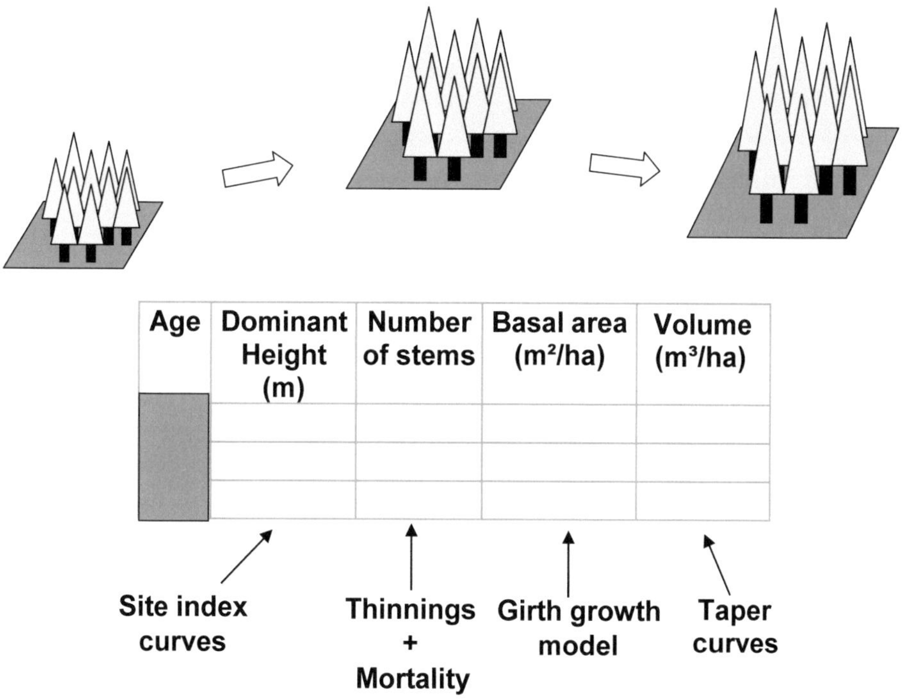

Fig. 2. Organization overview of the prediction models dealing with the stand growth

Site Index curves

The first sub-model concerns site index curves which express the relationship between dominant height, conventionally the average total height of the 100 biggest trees/ha (Rondeux, 1999), and age were constructed from stem analysis data (102 dominant trees cut from inside 55 stands). We used the model IV of Duplat and Tran-Ha (Duplat & Tran-Ha, 1986) based on polymorphic techniques, which has the following formula:

$$Hdom = (a.\ln(Age+1)+b_i).\left[1-e^{\left(-\left(\frac{Age}{c}\right)^d\right)}\right]+p.Age \tag{1}$$

where Hdom is the dominant height, Age is the total age (from seeds, in years) of the stand, a, c, d and p are the fixed parameters of the model, and b_i is a variable parameter related to the stand site index (dominant height reached at 50 years) specific to each site curve. The 4 parameters of the models built for the three larch species are presented in Table 1.

Self-thinning model

The second sub-model was developed to quantify reduction in the number of stems per hectare, especially due to the so-called self-thinning process (Puettmann et al., 1993) occuring in the event of excessive stock growth. This model, which is used to simulate the natural mortality of trees, predicts the maximum number of potential living stems (Rondeux, 1999). A curve of the quadratic mean stand diameters for maximum number of trees per hectare fitted with a log linear regression yields the following function:

$$\log \bar{d}q = 2.81549 - 0.47277 \,.\, \log Nha \tag{2}$$

with $R^2 = 0.985$ and RMSE = 1.67 cm ,
where $\bar{d}q$ is the quadratic mean stand diameter and Nha is the number of living trees per ha

Japanese larch	European larch	Hybrid larch
a = 7.500786 c = 23.238596 d = 1.0001 p = -0.016670	a = 6.418427 c = 12.889385 d = 1.0001 p = 0.090711	a = 4.817541 c = 10.544177 d = 1.0001 p = 0.275817
R^2 = 99.4% RMSE = 0.70m	R^2 = 99.6% RMSE = 0.51m	R^2 = 99.6% RMSE = 0.53m

Table 1. Parameters of the Duplat and Tran-Ha model IV used to describe the dominant height of larch.

This equation is based on data derived from 10 fully stocked stands, and was "validated" on a sample of 268 stands (the line corresponding to the equation is located in the upper part of the scatter of points showing the relationship between $\bar{d}q$ and Nha which were calculated for all the sampled stands). Expressed in terms of stand density index, the equation has been rewritten as:

$$Nha = 10.e^{\left(\frac{\log \bar{d}q - 2.81549}{-0.47277}\right)} \quad (3)$$

Girth growth model

The third sub-model is a distance-independent individual tree model that was developed to predict girth increment based on tree girth itself, dominant height, stand age, site index and stand basal area. The corresponding equation is written as:

$$MPGI = 6.1048 + \frac{33.325}{Gha} - 1.92103 . \ln\left(\frac{Hdom}{c} . 100\right) + 0.00046251 . H50^2 + \frac{6.9526}{Age} \quad (4)$$

where MPGI is the mean periodic girth increment in cm yr^{-1} (girth being considered at a reference height of 1.3 m above ground level), Gha is the stand basal area (in m^2 ha^{-1}), Hdom is the dominant height of the stand (in m), *c* is the individual girth at 1.3 m, H50 is the site index of the stand (in m), and Age is the age of the stand (in years).

This tree model was built from data collected in 99 stands (sample of 2,578 trees) and was validated on a sample of 48 other stands (sample of 1,283 trees). The R^2 of this model is 0.605 and the RMSE equals 0.64 cm yr^{-1}. It is based upon explanatory variables easy to collect and results from a comparative analysis of more than 15 models using various distance independent competition indices (Adreassen & Tomter, 2003; Pauwels et al., 2002b).

Volume estimation

The fourth sub-model was developed on the basis of taper functions predicting stem profile (Husch et al., 2003) which can also give volume estimates as well as detailed information on merchantable log sizes that can be potentially produced from a tree. It is based on Biging's model (Biging, 1984) using three independent variables: tree diameter, tree total height and age.

$$\hat{d}(h) = d . \left[b_1 + b_2 . \ln\left[1 - \left(1 - e^{\left(-\frac{b_1}{b_2}\right)} \right) . \left(\frac{h}{htot} \right)^{1/3} \right] \right] \quad (5)$$

with:

$$b_1 = 1.64041 - 0.17938 . \ln(htot) - 0.02569 . \ln(Age) + 0.07317 . \ln(d)$$

$$b_2 = 0.50322 + \frac{1.6526}{Age} + 0.19668 . \ln(d) - 0.25565 . \ln(htot)$$

where $\hat{d}(h)$ is the predicted stem diameter (cm) at the height h (m), d is the diameter measured at 1.3 m above the ground level, htot is the total height (m) of the tree, and Age is the stand age, b_1 can be interpreted as a position parameter, while b_2 is a parameter of curvature. In order to make the model usable in connexion with field data, these two parameters have been linked to tree diameter, stand age and total height. The model was

developed using sets of data measured on 1,134 trees. It fits the data very acceptably (R^2=0.988 and RMSE=1.53 cm).
All these 4 sub-models are then integrated into a simulation framework that can be used to assess the main characteristics of the stand at each cutting cycle, provided the thinning parameters are known. This estimated information is displayed in a form very similar to a yield table.
All other conditions being known, stand evolution obviously depends on the manipulation of stand density values, which are affected by thinning parameters. The user defines these either by their types (high crown thinning, neutral thinning, or low thinning) and weights (intensity of removals) or by the basal area remaining after cutting, or by a specified mean annual girth increment of dominant trees. Specific algorithms have been designed to select the trees to be removed so as to meet the thinning parameters defined at stand level. These algorithms are described in Pauwels (2003).

2.3 Indicator assessment

The indicators are defined at stand level and are assessed based on simulated stand-level or tree-level variables. The choice of indicators is subject to limiting factors such as reproducibility, clear understanding, simulation potentialities and the knowledge necessary to describe the evolution of certain stand or tree characteristics. Nine indicators, which are presented in Table 2, are used to factor in the six following objectives for which sets of data were available: wood production, economics, technico-economics, ecology, stability facing windstorm damages and wood quality properties.

Wood production indicator

The production objective only takes into account wood quantity, regardless of its quality. It can be set to meet the requirements of wood pulp industries, or simply for wood as a source of energy or a tool for carbon sequestration. The corresponding indicator is the mean annual volume increment (MAVI) in $m^3\ ha^{-1}\ yr^{-1}$, formulated as:

$$MAVI=\frac{Vf+\sum_{j=1}^{n} Vth_j}{r} \qquad (6)$$

where Vf is the stand volume (in m^3) estimated at the end of the rotation age (in years), Vth_j is the volume of living trees (in m^3) removed at thinning cycle j, n is the number of thinning cycles and r is the rotation age (in years). The MAVI is calculated at the end of the rotation, since a silvicultural scenario is assumed to be repeated indefinitely.

Economics indicator

Concerning the economics objective, the forest investment decision indicator which has been adopted to match the management objectives, is the land expectation value, LEV, which corresponds to the well-known Faustmann formula (Brazee, 2001). It is a special case of PNW (present net worth or net discounted value) which maximises the capitalized land value, factoring in all costs and revenues except land cost which is specifically excluded (Leuschner, 1984). It is currently used for optimizing rotation age (Brazee, 2001) and comparing various management objectives (Buongiorno, 2001).
Since PNW is given by:

$$\sum_{i=1}^{r}\left(R_i - C_i\right) / \left(1 + \text{rate}\right)^i \tag{7}$$

then:

$$\text{LEV} = \text{PNW} \,.\, \frac{(1+\text{rate})^r}{(1+\text{rate})^r - 1} \tag{8}$$

where R_i and C_i are the revenues and costs per hectare, i is the year in which the cash flows occur, r is the rotation (number of years in the planning period) and rate is the guideline discount rate. This can be chosen in the range 1 to 5% (the default value is set at 3%). In addition to discount rate, the user has to set the stumpage prices and the costs of successive silvicultural operations (plantation, cleaning, pruning, etc.).

Goals	**Indicators**	**Unit**	**Target**
Production	Mean annual volume increment	$m^3\ ha^{-1}\ yr^{-1}$	Maximisation
Economics	Land expectation value	€/ha	Maximisation
Technico-economics	Value of stems after bucking optimisation	€/ha	Maximisation
Ecology: Plant biodiversity	Biodiversity under the canopy	%	Maximisation
Plant "bioquantity"	Plant cover under the canopy	%	Maximisation
Stability	Stand stability index	%	Maximisation
Wood quality	Proportion of mature wood	%	Maximisation
	Ring width variation	%	Minimisation
	Modulus of elasticity	MPa	Maximisation

Table 2. Indicators used to compare silvicultural scenarios according to different predefined goals (objectives).

Technico-economic indicator

The technico-economic objective deals with the evaluation of a silvicultural scenario capability to produce logs of high economic value. The corresponding indicator is derived from a bucking optimization algorithm that uses the abovementioned taper function in a dynamic programming approach (Pauwels, 2003). The input parameters of this process are the characteristics and expected prices of the different potential stem sections which can be produced according to the uses (pulp wood, saw logs, veneer, etc.).

Ecological indicators

Two indicators are taken into account to define the general objective "ecology". The first concerns the *potential biodiversity* (diversity of ground vegetation) that might grow under the canopy, while the second describes its cover and is conventionally named *bioquantity* indicator. Both are based on predicted relative irradiance (IR, expressed as a percentage). This parameter represents the ratio between irradiance under the canopy and measured daylight irradiance.

The prediction equation for the relative irradiance is derived from Balandier et al.(2002b):

$$IR\left(\%\right) = e^{\left(-0.114.Gha+0.021.Age\right)} . 100 \tag{9}$$

with R^2=0.932 and RMSE=6.4% ,
where Gha is the stand basal area per hectare (in m^2) and Age is the stand age (in years). This model was developed using data from 40 plots (13 stands) for which relative irradiance has been calculated.

The *biodiversity* indicator is defined as the proportion of rotation time (%) during which relative irradiance is within a range that can be considered as optimal for maximal species development. This range is set as 12% to 18% based on studies conducted in France and Belgium on the plant composition of larch plots presenting different densities under the same site conditions (Balandier et al., 2002a).

The so-called *bioquantity* indicator (plant biomass) is based on the composition and the extent of growth of lesser vegetation. It represents the mean value (%) during the rotation of the cover, and is estimated indirectly from irradiance (Balandier et al; 2002a) as follows:

$$Cover = [-0.63 + 0.82 . \ln(IR)] . 100 \tag{10}$$

with R^2 = 0.720, RMSE = 40.5%.

Cover ranges from 0 (bare soils) to 300%, and expresses the proportion of soil covered by the vertical projection of the leaf area of understory species.

Stand stability indicator

The "stability" objective deals with the risk of potential windstorm damage. It is quantified as the proportion of time during which the stand can be considered as wind-stable according to its stability index as defined by Riou-Nivert (Riou-Nivert, 2001), and is calculated based on dominant height and mean stand diameter. Three zones have been defined (Figure 3): stable, risky and unstable. The index also takes into account thinning intensity when the stand is located in the risky zone (Pauwels, 2003).

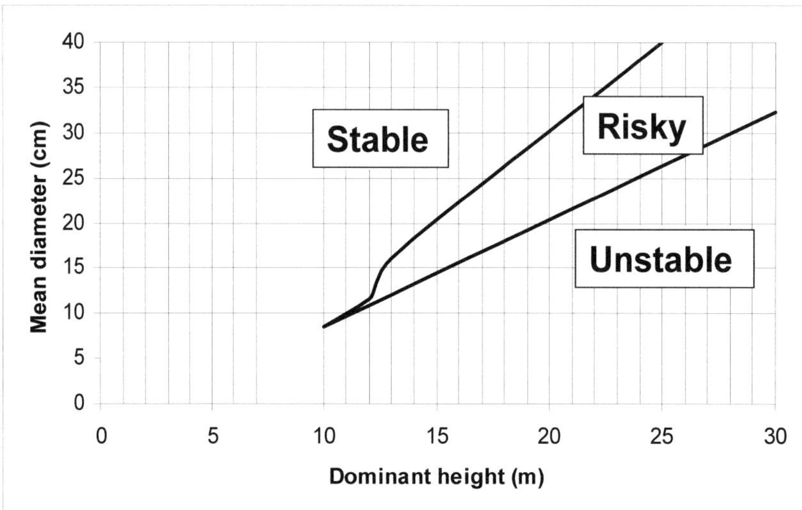

Fig. 3. Wind stability zones for even-aged coniferous stands based upon the dominant height and the mean stand diameter (Riou-Nivert, 2001).

Wood quality indicator

Three indicators have been proposed to characterize the wood quality objective: *proportion of mature wood, ring width variation* and *modulus of elasticity*. The straightness of the tree and the knots have not been considered because there is currently no model able to predict the impact of silvicultural treatment on these characteristics, which indeed appear to be more influenced by genetic quality.

Proportion of mature wood (%) is the difference between heartwood rate and juvenile wood rate which are calculated for the mean tree girth of the final stand and expressed in percentage of basal area at 1.3m. Heartwood rate (*Hw*) is predicted from age, diameter at breast height (1.3 m) and species (Pauwels et al. 2002a):

$$Hw\% = -51.011 + 19.513 \,.\, \ln(Age) + 10.637 \,.\, \ln(d) - 3.8548 \,.\, ME \quad (11)$$

with R^2=0.859, RMSE=7.02% ,

where Age is the tree age (in years), d is the diameter at breast height (1.3 m), and ME is a dummy variable that takes the value of 1 for European larches and 0 for the other two species (Japanese and hybrid). This model was fitted with data derived from 382 trees. Juvenile wood is defined by the 15 rings close to the pith, with ring width being estimated using the girth growth model.

The *ring width variation* (RWV %) is defined for the "average tree" (tree of quadratic mean diameter) of the final stand as the ratio of the standard deviation to the weighted mean of the ring width. So each ring has an importance proportional to its surface in the log section. Unlike the other indicators, this indicator has to be minimized because the target is to produce rings that are as regular as possible.

It can be written as:

$$RWV = \frac{wrstd}{wmrw} \,.\, 100 \quad (12)$$

$$wrstd = \sqrt{\frac{\sum_{i=1}^{n} \left(rw_i - wmrw\right)^2}{n}} \quad (13)$$

$$wmrw = \frac{\sum_{i=1}^{n} rw_i \,.\, rarea_i}{\sum_{i=1}^{n} rarea_i} \quad (14)$$

where RWV is the coefficient of variation of the ring width (%), wrstd is the standard deviation of weighted mean of the ring width, wmrw is the weighted mean ring width, rw_i is the width of the ring i, $rarea_i$ is the ring i area and n is the total number of rings.

The *modulus of elasticity* (MOE) is estimated for the average tree of the final stand, and is derived from the MOE_i calculated for each ring according to Leban & Haines (1999):

$$MOE_i = (1467 / rw_i + 7541) . \left[1 - e^{\left(-0.330.rage_i \right)} \right]^{12,1} \quad (15)$$

with R^2=0.63, RMSE=2205MPa ,
where rw_i is the width of ring *i* (in mm) and $rage_i$ is the age of ring *i* (in years).
This model was based on 492 wood samples extracted from 18 trees. The mean *MOE* is calculated by weighting MOE_i on the basis of ring area (Pauwels, 2003). The abovementioned indicators are calculated for each scenario and the evaluations are stored in a payoff matrix.

3. Scenario comparison

All the scenarios are compared according to indicator evaluations. The multi-criteria decision-making approach, Electre III (Bousson, 2001; Maystre et al., 1994) is used. It ranks scenarios from best to worst. This outranking method is aimed at enabling the user to estimate the order of priority of the alternatives with the minimum of assumptions, ELECTRE as POMETHEE come in a variety of versions, suitable for different situations. Its main advantage is that it doesn't require as complete preference data as is required by AHP ("Analytic Hierarchy Process") (Saaty, 1980), however from the viewpoint of participatory planning (which was not the objective of this study) the method is hard to interpret (Kangas & Kangas, 2005). Electre III starts the comparison from the payoff matrix and uses three thresholds (Figure 4) to take into account inaccuracy in the indicator evaluations.

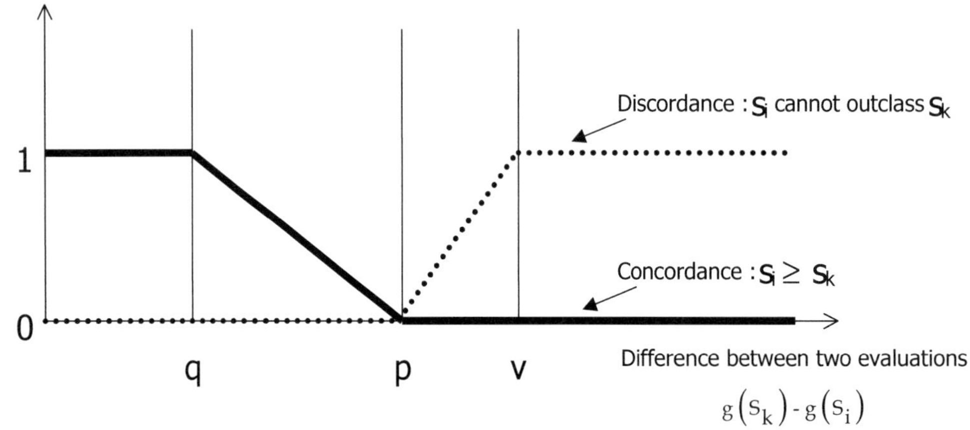

Fig. 4. Thresholds used to compare scenarios according to the Electre III multi-criteria method (thresholds : q = indifference threshold, p = strict preference, v = veto treshold, S_k and S_i = scenarios k and i)

The first threshold is the *indifference* threshold q. When the difference between two evaluations, $g(s_k)$-$g(s_i)$, is less than q, then the scenarios s_i and s_k are considered equivalent for the indicator (concordance index = 1).
The second threshold is the *strict preference* threshold p. If the difference between two evaluations $g(s_k)$-$g(s_i)$ is greater than p, then one scenario s_k is preferred to the other s_i

(concordance index = 0). If this difference is between q and p, a slight preference is given to the scenario s_k (0 < concordance index < 1).
The third threshold is the *veto* threshold v. It corresponds to the limit of the difference between two evaluations beyond which the scenario has to be rejected, even if this scenario comes out best for all the other indicators. This rejection is called discordance. If the difference between two evaluations, $g(s_k)-g(s_i)$, is greater than v, then discordance (s_i cannot outclass s_k) equals 1. Between p and v, the discordance is represented by a value comprised between 0 and 1. If the difference is less than p, then there is no discordance.
The method also factors in weightings assigned to each indicator according to the importance the user lends them.
Electre III compares the scenarios two-by-two. For each indicator j, a concordance index $c_j(s_i,s_k)$ is determined which compares evaluations according to the indifference and preference thresholds. Ranging between 0 and 1, it measures whether scenario s_i is at least as good as scenario s_k for the indicator.
Based on the concordance indices and the weight W_j associated to each indicator, a global concordance index, C_{ik}, is calculated:

$$C_{ik} = \frac{\sum_{j=1}^{n} W_j \cdot c_j(s_i,s_k)}{\sum_{j=1}^{n} W_j} \tag{16}$$

where n is the number of objectives assigned (9 in this study).
This global concordance index quantifies the preference for scenario s_i over scenario s_k.
The next step calculates discordance indices per indicator $d_j(s_i, s_k)$ according to preference and veto thresholds. Ranging between 0 and 1, these discordance indices measure, for each evaluation, to what extent they conflict with the global preference.
Using the global concordance index C_{ik} and the discordance indices $d_j(s_i, s_k)$, this method determines a degree of credibility δ_{ik} measured by:

$$\delta_{ik} = C_{ik} \cdot \prod_{j \in \bar{F}} \frac{1 - d_j(s_i, s_k)}{1 - C_{ik}} \tag{17}$$

where:

$$\bar{F} = \left\{ j \mid j \in F, d_j(s_i, s_j) > C_{ik} \right\} \quad \text{and} \quad F \supset \bar{F} \tag{18}$$

If the discordance index is higher than the concordance index, concordance will be weakened. Ranging between 0 and 1, the degree of credibility measures the validity of the assertion "scenario s_i outclasses scenario s_k".
A ranking algorithm specific to Electre III uses the degrees of credibility to rank the scenarios from best to worst. Two distillations are performed. The first one, called "downward" distillation, extracts the best scenario compared to all the others, and so on, step by step, while the second one, called "upward" distillation, extracts scenarios going from the worst to the best. Analysis of the two distillations gives a final rank to each

scenario, with the tested scenario of order 1 being considered the most appropriate for the goals to be achieved. This classification also indicates scenarios that outclass others, that are equivalent to others, or that cannot be readily compared with others. This latter case which corresponds to "incomparability" occurs between scenarios a and b when there is no clear evidence in favour of either a or b (Buchanán et al., 1999).

4. Results: examples of simulation and scenario comparison

As concerns the implementation of scenarios (scenarios building and comparison, definition of indicator parameters, ...), it is performed through user-friendly interfaces, data being stored in a Microsoft Access database. In the same way, the different expected results (values of indicators associated to scenarios, scenarios comparisons, ...) are presented in the form of charts and tables, these latter being exportable to Microsoft Excel environment.
The parameters of the different models are stored in another Microsoft Access database, which enables to extend the use of this application to other species as far as the corresponding models are available for these species.
"MGC_Larch" is designed to generate and compare numerous silvicultural scenarios.
In order to illustrate the use of MGC-Larch, we present the comparison of 6 silvicultural scenarios (Table 3), all being based on a 12-year-old Japanese larch stand with an initial

Scenario No.	Building mode	Cutting cycle (years)	1st thinning (years)	Rotation (years)	Final No. of stems/ha	Final mean girth c and diameter (d) (cm)
1	Moderate thinnings (Proportion of thinned stems at each cycle = 25%)	12	12	84	170	187 (59.5)
2	Heavy thinnings (Proportion of thinned stems at each cycle = 35-40%)	6	12	54	109	181 (57.6)
3	Residual basal area (after thinning) = 15 m^2 ha^{-1}	6	15	45	122	159 (50.6)
4	Residual basal area (after thinning) chosen to improve the biodiversity indicator	6	12	60	107	184 (58.6)
5	Increment of dominant trees = 2.5 cm yr^{-1} (0.80 cm in diameter)	3	18	60	103	165 (52.5)
6	Increment of dominant trees = 3.1 cm yr^{-1} (1 cm in diameter)	3	15	45	94	151 (48.1)

Table 3. Characteristics of the 6 silvicultural scenarios compared.

density of 1,333 stems/ha (spacing: 2.5 x 3 m) and belonging to an average site index class (dominant height reached at 50 years: H50 = 28 m). Scenario 1 is characterized by moderate thinnings (25% of stems removal at each cutting cycle), the longest rotation (84 years), and the production of a mature stand with an important growing stock (680 m^3 ha^{-1}) and big trees (mean girth = 187 cm). Scenario 2 is based upon thinnings that are more heavy that in scenario 1 (35-40% of stems removal at each cutting cycle), a relatively short rotation (54 years) leading to a mature stand with a less important stock (140 m^3 ha^{-1}). Scenario 3 is characterized by the shortest rotation (45 years) and thinnings that are designed so as to maintain a constant and relatively low basal area after each cutting cycle (15m^2 ha^{-1}). The rotation of scenario 4 is fixed to 60 years. As for scenario 3, the thinnings are designed to lead to a fixed remaining stand basal area which in this case is variable from cycle to cycle and is calculated to optimize the biodiversity indicator. The particularity of scenario 5, whose rotation is fixed to 60 years, is that thinnings are calibrated so as to obtain dominant trees with a more or less a constant ring width fixed to 0.4 cm. The scenario 6 is only a variant of scenario 5, where the target ring width is fixed to 0.5 cm and the rotation is reduced from 60 to 45 years.

The indicators are calculated for each scenario according to user-defined parameters and are arranged in the payoff matrix (Table 4). In the first step, all indicators are weighted equally. It can be shown that, when modifying the weights allocated to each indicator and/or the parameters used to calculate the indicators, the results and the position of the silvicultural scenarios are varying very little. The thresholds are set according to the observed evaluations and the estimated inaccuracy of each indicator.

Scenario No.	INDICATORS								
	MAVI (m^3/ha /year)	**LEV (€/ha)**	**Techn-eco. (€/ha)**	**Biodiv. (%)**	**Bioqu. (%)**	**Stab. (%)**	**Mature wood (%)**	**Ring variation (%)**	**MOE (MPa)**
1	**16.9**	**93**	**101058**	4	47	86	**63**	67	**11867**
2	13.1	-407	48405	31	183	**100**	51	45	9746
3	12.8	-907	39044	22	190	**100**	41	**41**	9289
4	14.3	-53	59214	**55**	158	**100**	55	51	10174
5	14.4	-14	56621	8	161	90	49	53	10203
6	12.7	-1248	35704	9	**196**	**100**	38	43	9244
Weights	1	1	1	1	1	1	1	1	1
Threshold q	1	200	10000	5	20	5	3	5	1000
Threshold p	2	400	20000	10	40	10	6	10	2000
Threshold v	5	1000	50000	25	100	25	15	25	5000

MAVI is the mean annual volume increment, LEV is the land expectation value, MOE is the modulus of elasticity

Table 4. Payoff matrix characterizing the six compared scenarios

The scenarios analysed by the Electre III procedure are ranked from best to worst (Figure 5). The arrows point from better scenarios towards worse scenarios ("outclass" relation). Scenarios that are not connected by an arrow cannot be compared ("incomparability" relation). For example, that means that Scenario 1 cannot be compared with Scenario 2. Scenario 1 is relevant for wood production, and financial and technico-economic objectives but less adequate for ecological goals. It can also be seen that Scenario 2 leads to opposite results. Scenario 4, defined by residual basal areas that can improve the biodiversity indicator, comes out best, while Scenario 6, which refers to a girth increment of the dominant trees of 3.1 cm yr^{-1}, comes out worst.

Goal	Indicator weight	"Best" Scenario	"Worst" Scenario
Multiple	Same weights for all indicators	4	6
Economic	Same weights for production, economic and technico-economic indicators, null weights for the others.	1	6
Ecological	Same weights for the 2 biological and the stand stability indicators, null weights for the others.	4	1
Wood quality	Same weights for the 3 wood quality indicators, null weights for the others.	2	5

Table 5. Best scenario according to the main goals to be achieved.

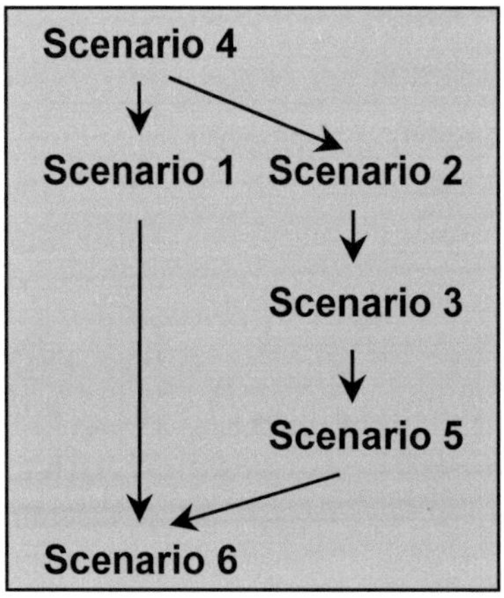

Fig. 5. Scenario classification resulting from the Electre III method with all indicators weighted equally (the arrows point from better towards worse scenarios, scenarios that are not connected are considered as incomparable).

5. Discussion

5.1 Growth simulation

Several models have been developed to describe the growth and development of larch stands in Southern Belgium following different silvicultural scenarios. It can be reasonably assumed that these models could be applied to larch planted elsewhere in Western Europe at low elevation (< 600 m) as far as it would be calibrated. The "MGC_Larch" software application helps the user to interactively generate numerous alternative silvicultural scenarios within a defined range of site conditions and thinning regimes especially.

5.2 Indicator assessment

The number of indicators used to compare scenarios is obviously limited by the amount and quality of the knowledge available on larch. Knots and basal sweep, for example, have not been taken into account, even though these two factors became increasingly important in larch silviculture. Nevertheless, the 9 objectives that have been defined offer a good overview of the many possible interactions between the silviculture of larch stands and how these stands achieve the goals initially defined.

6. Scenario comparison

Scenario classification can be modified by weighting each indicator according to the relative importance assigned to the expected goals. Examples are illustrated in Table 5. Scenario 1, characterized by a moderate silviculture, has reached the best scores for 4 out of 7 non ecological indicators and the worst scores for the 2 ecological ones. It is thus not surprising that this scenario is placed first choice when referring to an economic goal, and the worst in the case of an ecological goal. Scenario 4 appears to be the best one for both "multiple" and "ecological" goals. This is mainly due to a more dynamic silviculture (based on weight of thinnings and age of 1st thinning) which maximizes biodiversity (abundance and nature of understory vegetation) and reduces rotation length which is favourable to financial performance (LEV) and, to a certain extent, to volume production.

On the other side, scenario 6 which emphasizes dominant trees increment and a very short rotation (45 years) leads to the worst or nearly the worst scores for 7 out the 9 indicators, and is placed last for both multiple and economic goals.

The user can modify the parameters used to calculate the financial and technico-economic indicators (discount rate, stumpage prices, list of silvicultural operations, characteristics and prices of potential stem sections or log lengths) and then test their influence in a kind of sensitivity analysis. The usefulness of pruning carefully selected trees at a higher height (e.g. 6 m) can also be evaluated. Classifications based on Electre III become increasingly useful as the number of scenarios to be evaluated increases. However, the user must keep in mind that the final classification is still quite relative. It can thus be modified according to the scenarios compared. It is also possible to identify a non-tested scenario that could meet the predefined goals even better.

7. Conclusions

A silvicultural decision support system (SDSS) has been developed to predict larch stand growth according to different kinds of thinning with different weightings. This tool can also be used to rank the silvicultural scenarios generated according to the importance assigned to a range of indicators expressing the following objectives: wood production, economics, technico-economics, ecology, tree stability facing windstorm and wood quality. A weakness of this system, due to a lack of information, is that some factors that ought to be taken into accounts in larch silviculture (e.g., knottiness and basal sweep) are not included among the suggested indicators. However, the user-friendly "MGC_Larch" software application remains a useful tool to help forest managers choose the scenarios that will best meet their priority goals. More generally the method used seems to be promising to measure forest sustainability and to evaluate its multifunctionality especially when negotiations have to be started upon.

8. Acknowledgements

This research was funded by the European Union as part of the "Towards a European larch wood chain" contract (FAIR-CT98-3354).

9. References

Adreassen, K. & Tomter, S.M. (2003). Basal area growth models for individual trees of Norway spruce, Scots pine, birch and other broadleaves in Norway. *For. Ecol. Manage.* 180, 11-24.

Balandier, P.; Landre, F. ; Lampin, N. & Ruchaud, F. (2002a). Understorey vegetation diversity, composition and cover according to light level under canopies of larch stands thinned with different intensities. In: *Poplar summaries of the Fourth International Conference on Forest Vegetation Management*, Frochot, H.; Collet, C. & Balandier, P. (Eds.), Nancy, France, 17-21 juin 2002, INRA, 157-159.

Balandier, P. ; Ruchaud, F. ; Pauwels, D. & Jouvie, R. (2002b). Predicting light transmission through canopies of larch stands (Larix sp.) in France and Belgium. In: *Improvement of larch (Larix sp.) for better growth, stem form and wood quality, Symposium proceedings*, Gap, Auvergne et Limousin, France, 16-21/09/2002, 340-349.

Biging, G.S. (1984). Taper equations for second growth mixed conifers of northern California. *Forest Sci.* 30, 1103-1117.

Bousson, E. (2001). Gestion forestière intégrée. Approche basée sur l'analyse multicritère. *Les Presses agronomiques de Gembloux*, Gembloux, 303 p., 86 ill., 52 tab.

Brazee, R.J. (2001). The Faustmann Formula: Fundamental to Forest Economics 150 years after publication. *For. Sci.* 47(4), 441-442.

Buchanan, J.; Sheppard, P. & Vanderpoorten, D. (1999). Ranking Projects Using the ELECTRE Method, *http://www.esc.auckland.ac.nz/organizations/ORSNZ/conf33/papers/p58.pd.*

Buongiorno, J. (2001). Generalization of Faustmann's formula for stochastic forest growth and prices with Markov decision process models. *For. Sci.* 47 (4), 466-474.

Diaz-Balteiro, L. & Romero, C. (2008). Making forestry decisions with multiple criteria : A review and an assessment. *For. Ecol. Manage.* 255, 3222-3241.

Duplat, P. & Tran-Ha, M. (1986). Modèles de croissance en hauteur dominante pour le hêtre, le sapin pectiné, le pin sylvestre dans le massif de l'Aigoual. *Office National des Forêts*, Section technique 86/1, Paris.

Gordon, S.N.; Johnson, K.N.; Reynolds, K.M.; Crist, P. & Brown, N. (2004). Decision Support Systems for Forest Biodiversity: Evaluation of Current Systems and Future Needs. Final Report - Project A10, *National Commission on Science and Sustainable Forestry*, 37 p.

Husch, B.; Beers, T.W. & Kershaw, J.A Jr. (2003). *Forest mensuration*. John Wiley & Sons, Inc., Hoboken, New Jersey, 443p.

Kangas, J. & Kangas, A. (2005). Multiple criteria decision support in forest management - the approach, methods applied, and experiences gained. *For. Ecol. Manage.* 207, 133-143.

Leban, J.-M. & Haines, D.W. (1999). The modulus of elasticity of hybrid larch predicted by density, rings per centimetre, and age. *Wood Fiber Sci.* 31, 394-402.

Leuschner, W. (1984). *Introduction to forest resource management*. John Wiley & Sons New York, 298 p.

Maness, T. & Farrell, R. (2004). A multi-objective scenario evaluation model for sustainable forest management using criteria and indicators. *Can. J. For. Res.* 34, 2004-2017 [IV,E].

Maystre, L.Y. ; Pictet, J. & Simos, J. (1994). Méthodes multicritères ELECTRE. Description, conseils pratiques et cas d'application à la gestion environnementale. *Presses polytechniques et universitaires romandes*, Lausanne.

Pauwels, D. (2003). Conception d'un système d'aide à la décision permettant d'orienter le choix d'un scénario sylvicole : Application aux peuplements de mélèze en Région wallonne. Faculté universitaire des Sciences agronomiques. Gembloux, *Thèse de Doctorat*, 236 p. + annexes (available at www.fsagx.ac.be/gf).

Pauwels, D. & Rondeux, J. (2000). Le mélèze, une essence à haut potentiel de production. *Silva Belgica* 107, 6-10.

Pauwels, D. ; Lejeune, P.; Pâques, L.E. & Rondeux, J. (2002a). Développement d'un modèle prédictif de la proportion de duramen et d'écorce des espèces de mélèzes cultivées en zones de basse altitude en Europe de l'ouest (Larix leptolepis Gord., Larix decidua Miller, Larix eurolepis Henry). *Ann. For. Sci.* 60, 227-235.

Pauwels, D. ; Lejeune, P. & Rondeux, J. (2002b). Modèle de croissance pour les plantations de mélèzes. Biotechnol. *Agron. Soc. Environ.* 7, 87-97.

Pauwels, D. ; Thibaut, A. ; Lejeune, P. & Rondeux, J. (1999). Elaboration de courbes de croissance en hauteur dominante pour les mélèzes (Larix decidua Mill. et Larix kaempferi (Lamb.) Carr.) en Belgique méridionale. *Ann. For. Sci.* 56, 27-34.

Pauwels, D. ; Lejeune P. & Rondeux, J. (2007). A decision support system to simulate and compare silvicultural scenarios for pure even-aged larch stands. *Ann. For. Sci..* 64, 345-353.

Puettmann, K.J.; Hann, D.W. & Hibbs, D.E. (1993). Evaluation of size-density relationships for pure red alder and Douglas-fir stands. *Forest Sci.* 39, 7-27.

Reynolds, K.M. (2005). Integrated decision support for sustainable forest management in the United States: Fact or fiction?. *Computers and electronics in Agriculture* 49, 6-23.

Riou-Nivert, P. (2001). Facteurs de stabilité des peuplements et gestion de l'équilibre. *Forêt Entreprise* 139, 17-25.

Rondeux, J. (1999). La mesure des arbres et des peuplements forestiers. *Les Presses agronomiques de Gembloux*, 521 p.

Saaty, T.L. (1980). *The Analytic Hierarchy Process.* McGraw-Hill, New York.